HANDBOOK OF
CORPORATE FINANCE

FT Prentice Hall
FINANCIAL TIMES

In an increasingly competitive world, we believe it's quality of thinking that will give you the edge – an idea that opens new doors, a technique that solves a problem, or an insight that simply makes sense of it all. The more you know, the smarter and faster you can go.

That's why we work with the best minds in business and finance to bring cutting-edge thinking and best learning practice to a global market.

Under a range of leading imprints, including *Financial Times Prentice Hall*, we create world-class print publications and electronic products bringing our readers knowledge, skills and understanding which can be applied whether studying or at work.

To find out more about Pearson Education publications, or tell us about the books you'd like to find, you can visit us at
www.pearsoned.co.uk

HANDBOOK OF CORPORATE FINANCE

A business companion to financial markets, decisions & techniques

2nd edition

Glen Arnold

Financial Times
Prentice Hall
is an imprint of

Harlow, England • London • New York • Boston • San Francisco • Toronto • Sydney • Singapore • Hong Kong
Tokyo • Seoul • Taipei • New Delhi • Cape Town • Madrid • Mexico City • Amsterdam • Munich • Paris • Milan

PEARSON EDUCATION LIMITED

Edinburgh Gate
Harlow CM20 2JE
Tel: +44 (0)1279 623623
Fax: +44 (0)1279 431059
Website: www.pearsoned.co.uk

First published in Great Britain in 2005

© Pearson Education Limited 2005, 2010

The right of Glen Arnold to be identified as author of this work has been asserted
by him in accordance with the Copyright, Designs and Patents Act 1988.

Pearson Education is not responsible for the content of third party internet sites.

ISBN 978-0-273-72656-2

British Library Cataloguing-in-Publication Data
A catalogue record for this book is available from the British Library

Library of Congress Cataloging-in-Publication Data
Arnold, Glen.
  Financial Times handbook of corporate finance : a business companion to financial
markets, decisions & techniques / Glen Arnold. -- 2nd ed.
     p. cm.
  ISBN 978-0-273-72656-2 (pbk.)
  1. Corporations--Finance--Handbooks, manuals, etc. 2. Industrial management--
Handbooks, manuals, etc. I. Title. II. Title: Handbook of corporate finance.
   HG4027.3.A76 2010
   658.15--dc22

                                          2010021365

ARP Impression 98
Printed in Great Britain by Clays Ltd, St Ives plc

Typeset in 10/13 pt CentITC by 30

CONTENTS

To Ben, Sam, Poppy and George

ABOUT THE AUTHOR

Glen Arnold, Ph.D., investor, businessman is also a professor of finance (part time) at the University of Salford. He heads a research team focused on stock market mispricing of shares and the exploitation of that mispricing. His university textbook *Corporate Financial Management* has quickly established its place as the leading UK-based textbook for undergraduates and post-graduates. He also wrote *The Financial Times Guide to Investing*, which provides a comprehensive introduction to investment and the financial markets – it, too, is the best seller in its field. The book *The Financial Times Guide to Value Investing* describes the approaches of the great investors and synthesizes their insights into a disciplined form of investing.

ACKNOWLEDGMENTS

We are grateful to the following for permission to reproduce copyright material:

Case studies
Case study 10.1 from http://www.henkel.com/SID-0AC8330A-30F020C3/about-henkel/performance-measurement-11917.htm; Case study 7.1 from 'Lessons from practice: VBN at Lloyds TSB' in *Value-Based Management*, Arnold & Davies. 2000. © John Wiley & Sons Limited. Reproduced with permission.

Exhibits
Exhibit I.1 from 'Madame Tussauds set for public stage as Merlin tries to sprinkle IPO magic', *Financial Times*, 24th October 2009, p1 (Johnson, M., Arnold, M., and Blitz, R.) © The Financial Times Ltd; Exhibit 1.1 from Wendelin Wiedeking in 'Porsche's disdainful capitalist' by Richard Milne, *Financial Times*, p16, 14th May 2007, © The Financial Times Ltd; Exhibit 1.2 from 'United Airlines: the experiment that fell to earth', *Financial Times*, 18th March 2003 (Daniel, C., London, S.,) © The Financial Times Ltd; Exhibit 1.3 from 'GSK caps patent drug prices in poorest 50 countries', *Financial Times*, 14th February 2009, p14 (Jack, A.) © The Financial Times Ltd; Exhibit 1.4 from 'Which set of company rules are OK? US-style or UK?', *Financial Times*, 18th June 2009, p1 (Chapelle, T.,) © The Financial Times Ltd; Exhibit 1.5 from 'Investors up in arms over poor governance', *Financial Times*, 3rd March 2009, p19 (Burgess, K.,); Exhibit 1.7 from 'We need more responsible corporate ownership', *Financial Times*, 12th October 2009, p13 (Myners, P.) © The Financial Times Ltd; Exhibit 1.7 from 'We need more responsible corporate ownership' in *Financial Times* by Lord Paul Myners, 12th October 2009, p.13. Reprinted with the kind permission of Lord Paul Myners; Exhibit 1.8 from 'How to encourage managers to act more like owners', *Financial Times*, 7th July 2009, p12 (Stern, S.,) © The Financial Times Ltd; Exhibit 1.9 from 'Dividends to reap', *Financial Times*, 3rd July 2008, p13 (Nakamoto, M., Burgess, K.,) © The Financial Times Ltd; Exhibit 2.1 from 'Panama plan – a bigger canal can bring east and west closer', *Financial Times*, 20th October 2006, p15 (Wright, R.,) © The Financial Times Ltd; Exhibit 2.2 from 'Egdon egged on by positive gas storage tests', *Financial Times*, 29th June 2006 (Hume, N., Orr, R.,) © The Financial Times Ltd; Exhibit 2.3 from 'Bullish Ronson defies slump to carry on building apace', *Financial Times*, 4th June 2009, p23 (Ronson, G.,) © The Financial Times Ltd; Exhibit 4.1 from 'Entrepreneur fires broad attack on manufacturers', *Financial Times*, 17th January 2006, p5 (Marsh, P.,) © The Financial Times Ltd; Exhibit 4.2 from 'Tyranny of time', *Financial Times*, 1st June 1999, p18 (Martin, P.,) © The Financial Times Ltd; Exhibit 4.3 from 'New lines needed to justify

second high-speed rail route', *Financial Times*, 15th June 2009, p2 (Rowlands, D.,) © The Financial Times Ltd; Exhibit 4.4 from 'A healthy attitude to risk-taking', *Financial Times*, 14th August 2008, p14 (Schwan, S.) © The Financial Times Ltd; Exhibit 6.2 and 6.5 from 'Complacency will be pension funds' biggest killer', *Financial Times*, 27th March 2009, p16 (Hill, A.,) © The Financial Times Ltd; Exhibit 6.3 from 'A wake-up call for bean counters', *Financial Times*, 13th September 2003 (Plender. J.,) © The Financial Times Ltd; Exhibit 7.1 from 'When some of the parts don't add up', *Financial Times*, 7th September 2008, p10 (Baer, J., Guerrera, F.,) © The Financial Times Ltd; Exhibit 7.2 from 'Sir Stelios spells out fears for EasyJet', *Financial Times*, 24th November 2008, p21 (Done, K.,) © The Financial Times Ltd; Figure 9.1 from 'European conglomerates with below average value creation', *Financial Times*, © The Financial Times Ltd; Exhibit 10.1 from 'Water bill cuts put customers first', *Financial Times*, 24th July 2009, p3 (Fickling, D.,) © The Financial Times Ltd; Exhibit 11.1 from *Kraft/Cadbury* in 'The Lex Column' *Financial Times*, 8th September 2009, p16, © The Financial Times Ltd; Exhibit 11.2 from 'A winner's curse that haunts the banking behemoths', *Financial Times*, 13th July 2009, p16 (Plender, J.,) © The Financial Times Ltd; Exhibit 11.3 from 'GE to face call for Gecas separation', *Financial Times*, 6th June 2001 (Hargreaves, D.,) © The Financial Times Ltd; Exhibit 11.4 from 'Pharma spending spree could swallow biotech', *Financial Times*, 6th Janaury 2009, p22 (Saigol, L., Jack, A.,) © The Financial Times Ltd; Exhibit 11.5 from Warren Buffett, Berkshire Hathaway, Annual Report, 1981. Reprinted by kind permission of Warren Buffett. © Warren Buffett; Exhibit 11.6 from 'Banking fees are facing backlash', *Financial Times*, 8th June 2009, p20 (Saigol, L.,) © The Financial Times Ltd; Exhibit 11.7 from 'A match made in recession', *Financial Times*, 16th December 2008, p14 (MacIntosh, J.,) © The Financial Times Ltd; Exhibit 11.8 from Warren Buffett, Berkshire Hathaway, Annual Report, 1995. Reprinted by kind permission of Warren Buffett. © Warren Buffett; Exhibit 12.1 from 'Friends site sale hits obstacle', *Financial Times*, 3rd November 2009, p17 (Bradshaw, T., Fenton, B.,) © The Financial Times Ltd; Exhibit 12.2 from 'FSA clarifies position on activist investors', *Financial Times*, 20th August 2009, p17 (Masters, B., and Burgess, K.,) © The Financial Times Ltd; Exhibit 12.3 from 'Takeover Panel to force more disclosure over shareholdings', *Financial Times*, 9th May 2009, p14 (Cox, A., Saigol, L.,) © The Financial Times Ltd; Exhibit 12.4 from 'Kraft given deadline for Cadbury bid', *Financial Times*, 1st October 2009, p19 (Wiggins, J., Birchall, J.,) © The Financial Times Ltd; Exhibit 12.5 from Warren Buffett, Berkshire Hathaway, Annual Report, 1982. Reprinted by kind permission of Warren Buffett. © Warren Buffett; Exhibit 13.1 from 'Valuations complicated by lack of functioning market', *Financial Times*, 24th February 2009, p20 (Thomas, D.,) © The Financial Times Ltd; Exhibit 13.3 from 'New valuation method for ships triggers inflation fears', *Financial Times*, 26th October 2009, p25 (Wright, R.,) © The Financial Times Ltd; Exhibit 13.3 from 'Standard change risks rocking the boat', *Financial Times*, 24th February 2009, p20 (Wright, R.,) © The Financial Times Ltd; Exhibit 13.4 from 'Double-digit growth for BrightHouse', *Financial Times*, 9th November 2009, p23 (Bintliff, E.,)

cost-cutting move', *Financial Times*, 15th September 2007, p20 (Blackwell, D.,) © The Financial Times Ltd; Exhibit 17.4 from 'FSA grants 'light touch' to British LSE listing', *Financial Times*, 28th September 2009, p20 (Kwan Yuk, P.,) © The Financial Times Ltd; Exhibit 17.5 from 'Success expected for Lloyds right issue', *Financial Times*, 25th November 2009, p19 (Goff, S.,) © The Financial Times Ltd; Exhibit 17.6 from 'Moves to cut cost of equity underwriting', *Financial Times*, 26th October 2009, p23 (Burgess, K.,) © The Financial Times Ltd; Exhibit 17.7 from 'Housebuilder succumbs to risk factor', *Financial Times*, 3rd July 2008, p21 (Masters, B., Burgess, K.,) © The Financial Times Ltd; Exhibit 17.8 from 'Urgent call for more 'lead' angles', *Financial Times*, 30th May 2009, p32 (Moules, J.,) © The Financial Times Ltd; Exhibit 18.1 from *Fingers crossed* in 'Bouncers with biscuits presage a nerve-wracking game', *Financial Times*, 25th July 2009, p15 (Davies, P. J.,) © The Financial Times Ltd; Exhibit 18.2 from 'Debt woes rise for top 350', *Financial Times*, 15th January 2009, p17 (Sakoui, A.,) © The Financial Times Ltd; Exhibit 18.3 from 'Financing problems increase as crunch spreads', *Financial Times*, 18th September 2008 (Willman, J., Guthrie, J.,) © The Financial Times Ltd; Exhibit 18.4 from 'Debt for equity is the latest restructuring fashion', *Financial Times*, 23rd October 2009, p23 (Sakoui, A.,) © The Financial Times Ltd; Exhibit 18.5 from 'A good time to think again about capital structures', *Financial Times*, 28th October 2009, p34 (Plender, J.,) © The Financial Times Ltd; Exhibit 19.2 from 'GM pays Fiat 1.55bn Euros to end joint ventures', *Financial Times*, 14th February 2005, p1 (Michaels, A., Simon, B.,) © The Financial Times Ltd; Exhibit 20.2 from 'Hedging new second nature for food groups', *Financial Times*, 18th August 2008, p19 (Wiggins, J.,) © The Financial Times Ltd; Exhibit 20.5 from 'Betting on interest rates', *Financial Times*, 1st November 1995, © The Financial Times Ltd; Exhibit 20.6 from 'Northern Foods passes price rises to customers', *Financial Times*, 10th October 2007, p25 (Warwick-Ching, L., Crooks, E.,) © The Financial Times Ltd; Exhibit 20.7 from *Rate rise is music to the ears of 'swappers'* in *Money Section*, *Financial Times*, 30th June 2007, p2; Exhibit 20.8 from 'TVA, EIB find winning formula', *Financial Times*, 12th September 1996, © The Financial Times Ltd; Exhibit 20.9 from 'Clearing up the system', *Financial Times*, 2nd November 2009, p11, © The Financial Times Ltd; Exhibit 21.1 from 'Sterling's plunge adds to debt burden at Sage', *Financial Times*, 5th February 2009, p18 (Killgren, L.,) © The Financial Times Ltd; Exhibit 21.4 from 'Exchange rate woes hit GSK', *Financial Times*, 26th April 2007, p22 (Jack, A.,) © The Financial Times Ltd; Exhibit 21.5 from 'Small fry flounder in wake of surge', *Financial Times*, 10th October 2007, p15 (Minder, R.,) © The Financial Times Ltd; Exhibit 21.6 from 'EADS to insist on paying its suppliers in dollars', *Financial Times*, 12th March 2008, p27 (Done, K., Hollinger, P.,) © The Financial Times Ltd; Exhibit 21.7 from 'Extensive hedging mitigates exchange-rate windfalls for jet engine maker', *Financial Times*, 5th September 2008, p21 (Pfeifer, S.,) © The Financial Times Ltd; Exhibit 21.10 from 'Choose the correct path for viable deal', *Financial Times*, 25/01/2007, 2 (Politi, J.,) © The Financial Times Ltd.

Figures

Figure 11.5 from Crown Copyright material is reproduced with the permission of the Controller, Office of Public Sector Information (OPSI); Figure 21.1 from Thomson Reuters Datastream; Figure 21.2 from Thomson Reuters Datastream; Figure 6, page 144 from Thomson Reuters Datastream; Figure 9.1 from *Financial Times*, 13th July 2008, p.21.

Quotes

Quote on page 17 from *The Combined Code on Corporate Governance*, Financial Reporting Council (Financial Reporting Council 2003), p.4, © Financial Reporting Council (FRC). Adapted and reproduced with the kind permission of the Financial Reporting Council. All rights reserved. For further information please visit www.frc.org.uk or call +44 (0)20 7492 2300; Quote on page 143 from Sir Roy Gardner in 'Problems kept coming out of the woodwork' by Salamander Davoudi, *Financial Times*, p.19, 19th January 2007; Quote on page 144 from Richard Cousins in Compass 2008 Annual Group's Report, 26th November 2008; Quote on page 171 from Warren Buffett, Berkshire Hathaway, Annual Report, 1984. Reprinted by kind permission of Warren Buffett. © Warren Buffett; Quote on page 209 Anne Mulcahy in *Financial Times*, 23rd September 2005, p. 13, © The Financial Times Ltd; Quote on page 215 from David Turner in *Financial Times*, 27th December 2005, p.13, © The Financial Times Ltd; Quote on page 368 from Warren Buffett, Berkshire Hathaway, Annual Report, 2000. Reprinted by kind permission of Warren Buffett. © Warren Buffett; Quote on page 492 from Will Adderley in 'Dunelm founders in £120m windfall' by Philip Stafford, *Financial Times*, 22nd September 2006, © The Financial Times Ltd; Quote on page 559 from David Finch in '02 review could return more cash to investors' by Mark Odell, *Financial Times*, 21st July 2005, p.21, © The Financial Times Ltd; Quote on page 559 from Moger Wooley in 'Bristol Water plans to deliver a £30m payback' by Rebecca Bream, *Financial Times*, 21st/22nd May 2005, © The Financial Times Ltd; Quote on page 559 from John Murray in 'Bristol Water plans to return £50m cash' by Rebecca Bream, *Financial Times*, 22nd July 2003, © The Financial Times Ltd; Quote on page 559 from 'Porsche's disdainful capitalist' by Richard Milne, *Financial Times*, p.16, 5th May 2007, © The Financial Times Ltd; Quote on page 559 from Alan Parker in 'Whitbread looks to extend debt' by Matthew Garrahan, *Financial Times*, 15th June 2005, © The Financial Times Ltd.

Tables

Table 16.1 from www.fitchratings.com/creditdesk/reports/report_frame. cfm?rpt_id=428182; Tables 16.5 and 16.6 from Thomson Reuters, 02 December 2009; Table 19.1 from *Financial Times*, 7th December 2009. Reprinted with permission, © The Financial Times Ltd; Table 20.3 from *Financial Times*, www.ft.com, 22 October 2009 (no longer shown in the paper version of *FT*) © The Financial Times Ltd; Table 21.9 from Currency options US$/UK£ on the Chicago Mercantile Exchange. From CME Group.

In some instances we have been unable to trace the owners of copyright material, and we would appreciate any information that would enable us to do so.

AUTHOR'S ACKNOWLEDGMENTS

This book draws on the talents, knowledge and contributions of a great many people. I would especially like to thank the following:

Warren Buffett who kindly assisted the illustration of key points by allowing the use of his elegant, insightful and witty prose. Dr Mike Staunton and Professors Elroy Dimson and Paul Marsh of the London Business School who granted permission to present some important data.

The *Financial Times* writers who provided so many useful illustrative articles, and who, on a day-to-day basis, deepen my understanding of finance.

The team at Pearson Education who, at various stages, contributed to the production of the book: Christopher Cudmore, Melanie Carter, Colette Holden, Aisha Badmuss, Jennifer Mair, Martina O'Sullivan and Richard Stagg.

My personal assistants, Susan Henton and Rebecca Devlin, for their thoughtful help.

The financial crisis has highlighted the importance of making intelligent decisions on matters such as which investments within the firm to accept, what type of finance to raise, how to increase shareholder value and how to manage risk. These decisions must be informed by sound principles. The underlying principles have not altered since the publication of the first edition, but a lot of the detail, such as the workings of some financial markets, tools and techniques have been enhanced. Here are some of the ways in which this book improves on the old one:

Corporate governance. The section on how a business is governed (that is, the interaction, relative power and responsibilities of executive directors, non-executive directors and shareholders) is expanded to reflect the modern thinking and guidelines.

Taxation. A discussion of the impact of tax is incorporated into the sections on appraising whether to invest in a project; and in the section on the calculation of the discount rate to be used in financial decisions

Real options. Real options, that is managerial ability to undertake a range of alternative decisions as the future unfolds rather than be stuck with a commitment to an investment project, are given a much more detailed discussion.

EBITDA. A cautionary discussion of EBITDA (and EBITDA used with Enterprise value) is used to warn of the dangers of falling into the erroneous use of this measure.

Excess return. This new value metric, which overcomes some of the drawbacks of other value metrics, is described.

Sources of finance. Introduced are the Enterprise Finance Guarantee and Revolving credit facilities.

Equity risk premium. The latest evidence on the additional annual return equity investors have received above the return on government bonds is provided. This is a very important number, greatly impacting the discount rate used throughout the corporate and financial world.

Risk management. A wider discussion of the range of risks facing a firm.

Jargon-busting. There is now an 80 page glossary so that you can look up a wide range of words, phrases and concepts.

Financial Times articles. New FT articles are incorporated to illustrate and extend the points made in the text. They demonstrate the direct relevance of the material discussed in the book to the everyday lives of business people.

Up-to-date statistics. Throughout the book the latest statistics are used, whether that be returns on shares and bonds or merger activity.

INTRODUCTION

Managers climbing the corporate ladder find the further they go the more they need to understand the concepts and jargon of finance, both for internal decision making and external interaction with investors, bankers and the City.

It is normally the case that managers have not received any formal training in finance. Furthermore, they are not in a position to take time out from the business to dedicate themselves to study. So what they need is a guide that will allow them to absorb and apply the essential tools of finance while they continue with their executive responsibilities. This book is that guide.

It is designed to be comprehensive, crystal-clear and directed at real world problem solving. It is rigorous without over-burdening the reader. It is not academic in the sense of laboriously expounding theory, but it nevertheless presents state-of-the-art techniques and frameworks, with a focus on managerial action.

The imperatives of day-to-day management mean that all middle and senior executives must have a firm grasp of the fundamental financial issues. These will touch every aspect of the business, ranging from deciding which capital expenditure projects are worthy of backing to managing business units for shareholder value.

> The imperatives of day-to-day management mean that all middle and senior executives must have a firm grasp of the fundamental financial issues.

Discussion at boardroom level – which inevitably percolates down – is mostly couched in financial terms: what rate of return are we achieving? should we merge? how do we value a company? how do we control foreign exchange rate losses? etc. Because the language of business is largely financial, managers need to understand that language if they want to know what is going on, and to advance. They also need to read the financial pages of broadsheet newspapers to comprehend the wider environment in which the business operates. How can they expect to make senior level decisions without understanding the world around them? Newspapers such as the *Financial Times* assume knowledge of key financial concepts and jargon. This book will help with intelligent reading of these publications.

Some of the financial issues covered

- Value-based management is increasingly spoken of, but little understood. This book provides a thorough grounding.
- Mergers and the problem of merger failure (i.e. acquiring shareholders losing out) is discussed along with remedies.

- The proper use of derivatives as tools helping the business control risk, rather than increasing it, is explained in easy-to-follow and practically-oriented fashion.

- Modern investment appraisal techniques are contrasted with the traditional rules of thumb employed by many companies.

- There is an overview of modern financial markets and instruments with insight into the benefits brought by effective exploitation of the markets and perils of ignoring the demands of the finance providers.

The scope of corporate finance

To bring the book alive for readers, and to show the mutual reinforcement of practical management and finance theory, there are numerous examples of major UK companies employing the concepts and techniques discussed in each chapter. Much of the 'real-world' material is drawn from articles in the *Financial Times*. A typical case is shown in Exhibit I.1 which is used here to highlight the scope of the subject of corporate finance.

There are four key financial issues facing management:

In what projects are we going to invest our shareholders' money?

The directors of Merlin Entertainments believe that they have a fantastic investment opportunity in creating new outdoor attractions. Sound financial techniques are needed to make a judgment on whether it is worth committing the large sums required to build a theme park or city-centre tourist attraction. Furthermore, financial tools will be essential in choosing between the alternative projects of say (a) building another Alton Towers in Europe or (b) building another Madame Tussauds in the USA. Connected with the new strategy there will be dozens of smaller investment choices to be made, e.g. is it better to outsource particular operations or undertake the activity in-house? The first section of the book describes proven approaches adopted by all leading corporations in deciding where to concentrate the firm's financial resources. This class of decisions are sometimes referred to as capital expenditure or 'capex'.

How do we create and measure shareholder value creation?

> Value creation by a corporation or by individual business units is about much more than deciding whether to invest in specific projects.

Value creation by a corporation or by individual business units is about much more than deciding whether to invest in specific projects. Merlin will need to consider a number of strategic implications of its actions, such as: what is the current and likely future return on capital in the industry it is choosing

Madame Tussauds set for public stage as Merlin tries to sprinkle IPO magic

Miles Johnson, Martin Arnold and Roger Blitz

Merlin Entertainments, the Blackstone-owned theme park group whose assets include the Madame Tussauds, Legoland, and the London Eye, is preparing a stock market flotation, setting the stage for a flurry of UK listings in the new year.

The planned share offer, which would be the first big listing on the London Stock Exchange since the onset of the financial crisis, would value Merlin at about £2bn and is expected in early 2010.

Citigroup, Goldman Sachs, Deutsche Bank, UBS and Nomura are the investment banks lined up to advise on the listing, according to people familar with the situation.

Blackstone, the world's largest buy-out group, will remain Merlin's majority shareholder, although the proportion of the company listed will depend on the level of investor demand. Dubai International Capital, an investment vehicle for the Gulf emirate's ruling royal family, owns 20 per cent of Merlin.

While Blackstone is in advanced talks with banks, nothing has yet been signed.

Blackstone bought Merlin for £102m in 2005 and has turned it into the second-biggest theme park operator after Disney with a string of acquisitions.

Blackstone is expected to sell some shares in the planned IPO, but people familar with the plans said that, while the company has £1bn of debt, much of the issue would be of new shares to finance the construction of outdoor attractions.

Nick Varney, Merlin's chief executive, told the Financial Times in July there were opportunities for expanding 'midway' attractions – catering for city centre and short-stay visitors – in the US.

EXHIBIT I.1

Source: *Financial Times* 24/25 October 2009.

to enter? Will Merlin have a competitive edge over its rivals in that industry? Value-based management brings together a number of disciplines, such as strategy and resource management, and draws on the measures developed in the finance field to help judge the extent of value creation from current operations or from new strategic and tactical moves (covered in Chapters 6 to 9). At the centre of value-based management is recognition of the need to produce a return on capital devoted to an activity commensurate with the risk. Establishing the minimum required return is the 'cost of capital' issue – the logic behind this calculation is discussed in Chapter 10.

As Merlin grows it may ponder the possibility of merger with other companies. This is a seductive and potentially treacherous path. To succeed, managerial thought and planning must extend beyond the narrow task of deal making. Chapters 11 and 12 consider the major issues here.

Being able to value business units, companies and shares is a very useful skill. It can help avoid over-paying for an established business. It can also give an insight into how stock market investors value the manager's company. Merlin is preparing for a stock market flotation – managerial knowledge of how to value its shares could be crucial. Chapter 13 covers the main valuation approaches used today. A further key value decision is how much of the annual profit to keep in the business to support investment and how much to pay out to shareholders. Is a 50:50 split about right? Or, how about keeping just 30 percent in the company and paying the other 70 percent in dividends? This is not an easy decision, but someone has to make it. Chapter 14 outlines the key considerations.

What type of finance should we raise?

Blackstone and Dubai International Capital have pumped millions of pounds into Merlin. Private equity (e.g. buyout fund) capital is a very important source of finance for many firms. Others do not have access to money from large institutional funds to become established and grow. Fortunately for them the modern financial world presents a wide range of options from selling shares to issuing corporate bonds. The array of choices can be dizzying so the third part of the book provides some order, describing the characteristics of the main forms of finance and their relative advantages and drawbacks. Chapter 15 guides the reader through the benefits and dangers of using bank loans and overdrafts, hire purchase, leasing, trade credit and factoring. Then, we move to the forms of debt finance available to larger firms on the financial markets, from high-yield bonds to convertibles and Eurobonds. Jargon is explained and the reader is guided to the selection of the most suitable mixture of finance given the company's circumstances. The final chapter in this section deals with the process of gaining a stock market quotation for a company's shares – a particularly apposite chapter for Merlin's managers. It also describes alternative ways of raising money by selling shares, for example, a rights issue, venture capital or business angel capital.

How do we manage risk?

Merlin is faced with many operational risks. Perhaps it will fail to achieve the visitor numbers it projects. Perhaps its new attractions will be superseded by new destination resorts set up by competitors a couple of years down the line. There are some risks that firms have to accept, including these operational risks. However, there are many others that can be reduced by taking a few simple steps. For example, the risk of a rise in interest rates wiping out profits can be reduced/eliminated in various ways, ranging from choosing a less risky capital structure (proportion of finance from debt and share capital) to the use of interest rate futures on financial markets. Options, forwards and futures can be used to avoid the risk that comes from changes in foreign exchange rates. The final section of the book considers the various financial risks managers have to confront and describes how they can be reduced by some simple tactical moves as well as the use of derivatives.

> The final section of the book considers the various financial risks managers have to confront and describes how they can be reduced by some simple tactical moves as well as the use of derivatives.

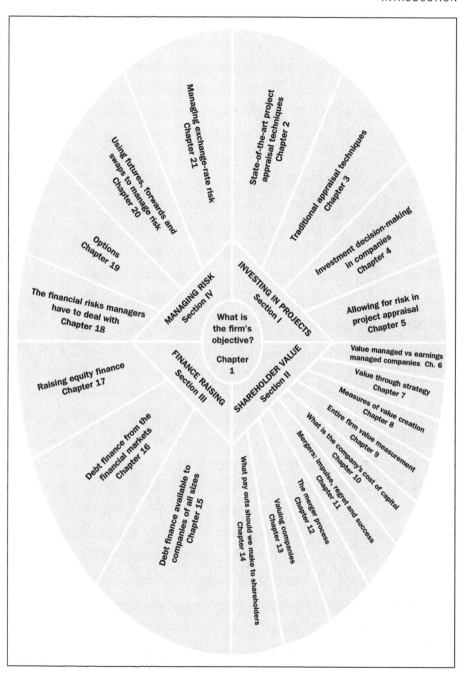

1

WHAT IS THE FIRM'S OBJECTIVE?

Introduction

This chapter considers the most fundamental question facing anyone trying to make decisions within an organization – what is the objective of the business? Without clarity on this point it is very difficult to run a business in a purposeful and effective manner. Unless we know what our objective is we cannot make sensible financial decisions, so it is essential we tackle what at first seems a fairly trivial question early in the book. As you will see the answers to this question are far from easy or trivial. They can be uncomfortable for many managers. They are also vital for the success of the business.

A common purpose

Cadbury, widely regarded as one of the best-managed companies in the world until its takeover by Kraft, had a clear statement of its objective – *see* Case study 1.1. Notice that Cadbury does not confuse the objective with the strategy to be employed to attain the objective. It first states the aim and then states the means to achieve the end. Many firms seem to believe that their *objective* is to operate in a particular market or take particular actions. They seem unable to distinguish market positions or actions from the ultimate purpose of the existence of the organization. This will not only lead to poor strategic decisions but frequently makes intelligent financial decisions impossible.

Case study 1.1

Cadbury plc

Our governing objective is to deliver superior shareowner returns by realising our vision to be the world's biggest and best confectionery company.

Introduced in June 2007, our Vision into Action (VIA) business plans sets out a bold agenda with the clear vision of becoming the world's biggest and best confectionery company. This aspiration, built around developing a strong total confectionery model, is supported by clear objectives, priorities and a financial performance scorecard. The strategy is underpinned by a strong focus on sustainability, culture and purpose that unifies the actions and objectives of the 45,000 people who work in Cadbury.

We believe that a balanced delivery of strong growth in revenue and margins, coupled with an increased focus on disciplined capital allocation will allow us to deliver superior returns for our shareholders.

Source: company website and annual report and accounts 2008.

This book is about practical decision-making in the real world. When people need to make choices in the harsh environment in which modern businesses have to operate, it is necessary to be clear about the purpose of the organization; to be clear about what objective is set for management to achieve. A multitude of small decisions are made every day; more importantly, every now and then major strategic commitments of resources are made. It is imperative that the management teams are aware of, respect and contribute to the fundamental objective of the firm in all these large and small decisions. Imagine the chaos and confusion that could result from the opposite situation where there is no clear, accepted objective. The outcome of each decision will frequently conflict with others and the direction of the firm will become random and rudderless. One manager on one occasion will decide to grant long holidays and a shorter working week, believing that the purpose of the institution's existence is to benefit employees; while on another occasion a different manager sacks 'surplus' staff and

> Before we can make decisions in the field of finance we need to establish what it is we are trying to achieve.

imposes lower wages, seeing the need to look after the owner's interests as a first priority. So, before we can make decisions in the field of finance we need to establish what it is we are trying to achieve.

You have probably encountered elsewhere the question, 'In whose interests is the firm run?' This is largely a political and philosophical question and many books have been written on the subject. Here we will provide a brief overview of the debate because of its central importance to making choices in finance. The list of interested parties in Figure 1.1 could be extended, but no doubt you can accept the point from this shortened version that there are a number of claimants on a firm.

Who gets any surplus?

Sound financial management is necessary for the survival of the firm and for its growth. Therefore all of these stakeholders, to some extent, have an interest in seeing sensible financial decisions being taken. Many business decisions do not involve a conflict between the objectives of each of the stakeholders. However, there are occasions when someone has to decide which claimants are to have their objectives maximized, and which are merely to be satisfied – that is, given just enough of a return to make their contributions. There are some strong views held on this subject:

FIGURE 1.1

A company has responsibilities to a number of interested parties

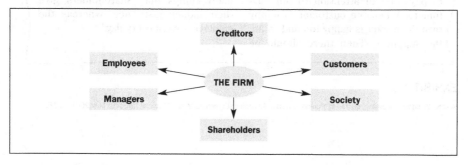

- **Shareholder supremacy** The pro-capitalist economists, such as Friedrich Hayek and Milton Friedman, believe that making shareholders' interests the paramount objective will benefit both the firm and society at large. This approach is not quite as extreme as it sounds because these thinkers generally accept that unbridled pursuit of shareholder returns, to the point of widespread pollution, murder and extortion, will not be in society's best interest and so add the proviso that maximizing shareholder wealth is the desired objective provided that firms remain within 'the rules of the game'. This includes obeying the laws and conventions of society, and behaving ethically and honestly. Without this form of enlightened self-interest, the market-based system will slow to a halt and shareholders, together with everyone else, will be worse off.

- **Workers' supremacy** At the opposite end of the political or philosophical spectrum are the left-wing advocates of the primacy of workers' rights and rewards. The belief here is that labour should have its rewards maximized. The employees should have all that is left over, after the other parties have been satisfied. Shareholders are given just enough of a return to provide capital, suppliers are given just enough to supply raw materials and so on. Exhibit 1.1 quotes Porsche's chief executive, Wendelin Wiedeking, advocating the placing of customers, workers and suppliers above shareholders.

- **Stakeholder approach** Standing somewhere in the middle are those keen on a balanced stakeholder approach. Here the (often conflicting) interests of each of the claimants are somehow maximized but within the constraints set by the necessity to compromise to provide a fair return to the other stakeholders.

Porsche

Wendelin Wiedeking

'We should not always look at getting the maximum return but we must look at people and make sure that they are taking part ... Our business model is only financed by customers. So we have to pay a lot of attention to our customers. When the customer is happy then the worker is happy too and so are the suppliers. Then there should be enough left for the shareholder. But that is the order of importance ...

... How can society allow capital to make all the rules? I have never understood shareholder value as it leaves so many things out. Shareholders give their money just once, whereas the employees work every day.'

EXHIBIT 1.1

Source: Wendelin Wiedeking, quoted in 'Porsche's disdainful capitalist', Richard Milne, *Financial Times* 14 May 2007, p. 16.

Variety of objectives: those admitted to (and those kept quiet)

A firm can choose from an infinitely long list of possible objectives. Some of these will appear noble and easily justified, others remain hidden, implicit, embarrassing, even subconscious. The following represent some of the most frequently encountered.

Achieving a target market share

In some industrial sectors to achieve a high share of the market gives high rewards. These may be in the form of improved profitability, survival chances or status. Quite often the winning of a particular market share is set as an objective because it acts as a proxy for other, more profound objectives, such as generating the maximum returns to shareholders. On other occasions matters can get out of hand and there is an obsessive pursuit of market share with only a thin veneer of shareholder wealth espousement. This attitude is particularly strong in the airline industry which collectively usually makes an annual loss.

Keeping employee agitation to a minimum

Here, return to the organization's owners is kept to the minimum level necessary. All surplus resources are directed to mollifying employees. Managers would be very reluctant to admit publicly that they place a high priority on reducing workplace tension, encouraging peace by appeasement and thereby, it is hoped, reducing their own stress levels, but actions tend to speak louder than words. An example of this kind of prioritization was evident in a number of state-owned UK industries in the 1960s and 1970s. Unemployment levels were low, workers were in a strong bargaining position and there were, generally, state funds available to bail out a loss-making firm. In these circumstances it was easier to buy peace by acquiescing to union demands than to fight on the picket lines. Some companies have tried to reduce workplace tension by giving workers a large proportion of the shares, i.e. making them part-owners. But, as the example of United Airlines shows, 'differences in expectations' can destroy the business. UA ended up with ever more extreme demands from the unions, followed by bankruptcy – see Exhibit 1.2.

Survival

There are circumstances where the overriding objective becomes the survival of the firm. Severe economic or market shock may force managers to focus purely on short-term issues to ensure the continuance of the business. In fire fighting they pay little attention to long-term growth and return to owners. However this focus is clearly inadequate in the long run – there must be other goals. If survival were the only objective then putting all the firm's cash reserves into a bank savings account might be the best option. When managers say that their objective

United Airlines: the experiment that fell to earth

Caroline Daniel and Simon London

Three months ago the world's second largest airline filed for bankruptcy amid spiralling losses. Last week, after nine years of 55 percent employee ownership, workers at last dumped enough stock to push their stake below 20 percent, triggering so-called 'sunset clauses'. The experiment was finally declared dead.

Differences in expectations emerged quickly, says one former employee. 'The silliest of all was when John Edwardson, [then number two] had a meeting with the pilots' union early on and the union said: "Now we are owners, we have the right to fire one officer every year" and John just looked at him and understood it wasn't a joke. It was a tense moment. And he replied: "I suppose then that officers can fire one pilots' union leader every year." Then the light went on.'

Moreover, it was hard to get employees to think like owners. Middle managers in particular were uneasy about giving up precious power. 'We started to say: "We are all owners now, instead of just bosses and employees, so bosses needed to learn quickly how to supervise as coaches, cajolers, advisers – but not with a whip." But some supervisors didn't get it and said: "If I criticise one of my people, and they write to the chief executive, I'll be in trouble."' ...

Along with restrictions over which aircraft would fly certain routes, the absurdity of some of the arcane work rules was underscored by the fact that the pilots' contract included a promise that the company would pick up the tab if a pilot moved city and his piano needed re-tuning, ... employees were given just three out of 12 board seats. But they were also granted the ability to veto chief executives and strategic decisions, such as acquisitions.

Wielding that power required enlightened union leaders. Instead, unions exploited it, denying Mr Edwardson the chief executive's post and later ousting Jim Goodwin, their own appointee, when he warned United would perish without wage cuts.

... Pilots' wages soared an immediate 29 percent, with 4.5 percent rises scheduled to follow.

Mr Dubinsky, then head of United's pilots' union, gloated that he intended to choke the golden goose 'by its neck until it gives us every last egg'.

A senior pilot recalls: '... From 2000 to 2002, labour costs rose $1.4bn (£886m) but at the same time revenues fell $5.5bn.'

The pilot continues: 'The problem was that United was employee-owned but union-controlled. Union leaders needed to satisfy their members who were concerned about work rules and wages, rather than valuation issues. There was a corrupting influence of politics on decision-making ... the equity culture never caught on.'

... the implications of union control over time led to the bleeding of management talent.

EXHIBIT 1.2

Source: *Financial Times* 18 March 2003.

is survival what they generally mean is the avoidance of large risks that endanger the firm's future. This may lead to a greater aversion to risk, and a rejection of activities that shareholders might wish the firm to undertake. Shareholders are in a position to diversify their investments: if one firm goes bankrupt they may be disappointed but they have other companies' shares to fall back on. However the managers of that one firm may have the majority of their income, prestige and security linked to the continuing existence of that firm. These managers may deliberately avoid high-risk/high-return investments and so deprive the owners of the possibility of large gains.

Creating an ever-expanding empire

This is an objective that is rarely openly discussed, but it seems reasonable to propose that some managers drive a firm forward, via organic growth or mergers, because of a desire to run an ever-larger enterprise. Often these motives become clearer with hindsight; when, for instance, a firm meets a calamitous end the *post mortem* often reveals that profit and efficiency were given second place to growth. The volume of sales, number of employees or overall stock market value of the firm have a much closer correlation with senior executive salaries, perks and status than do returns to shareholder funds. This may motivate some individuals to promote growth.

Maximization of profit

This is a much more acceptable objective, although not everyone would agree that maximization of profit should be the firm's purpose.

Maximization of long-term shareholder wealth

While many commentators concentrate on profit maximization, finance experts are aware of a number of drawbacks of profit. The maximization of the returns to shareholders in the long term is considered to be a superior goal. We look at the differences between profit maximization and wealth maximization later.

This list of possible objectives can easily be extended but it is not possible within the scope of this book to examine each of them. Suffice it to say, there can be an enormous variety of objectives and a large potential for conflict and confusion. Some sort of order must be introduced.

The assumed objective for finance

The company should make investment and financing decisions with the aim of maximizing long-term shareholder wealth.

Throughout the remainder of this book it is assumed that the firm gives primacy of purpose to the wealth of shareholders. This assumption is made mainly on practical grounds, but there are respectable theoretical justifications too.

The practical reasons

If one may assume that the decision-making agents of the firm (managers) are acting in the best interests of shareholders then decisions on such matters as which investment projects to undertake, or which method of financing to use, can be made much more simply. If the firm has a multiplicity of objectives, imagine the difficulty in deciding whether to introduce a new, more efficient machine to produce the firm's widgets, where the new machine both will be more labour efficient (thereby creating redundancies), and will eliminate the need to buy from one-half of the firm's suppliers. If one focuses solely on the benefits to shareholders a clear decision can be made. This entire book is about decision-making tools to aid those choices. These range from whether to produce a component in-house, to whether to buy another company. If for each decision scenario we have to contemplate a number of different objectives or some vague balance of stakeholder interests, the task is going to be much more complex. Once the basic decision-making frameworks are understood within the tight confines of shareholder wealth maximization, we can allow for complications caused by the modification of this assumption. For instance, shareholder wealth maximization is clearly not the only consideration motivating actions of organi-

GSK caps patent drug prices in poorest 50 countries

Andrew Jack in Boston

GlaxoSmithKline, the pharamaceuticals group, will cap the prices at which it sells its patented drugs in the poorest 50 countries at a quarter of the levels charged in the developed world.

It will also reinvest a fifth of any residual profits made in these countries in improving local healthcare, and share with other researchers the intellectual property on any of its experimental chemical compounds that could treat 'neglected' developing world diseases.

The initiatives are part of a broader range of efforts to improve patient access in the rich and poor worlds alike, announced yesterday by Andrew Witty, the company's chief executive.

Speaking about the need to redouble efforts to ensure patients could get the medicines they need, he said: 'Society expects us to do more ... To be frank, I agree. We have the capacity to do more and we can do more.'

Mr Witty, who, like other top pharmaceuticals company executives, has been holding talks in Washington on likely healthcare reform under Barack Obama, US president, stressed that his commitment included better access to medicines for poor Americans ...

He put total sales in least developed countries at about £30m a year and said that the price cap could cost GSK £5m, but stressed it would serve as a 'catalyst' for greater experimentation for GSK and other companies.

EXHIBIT 1.3

Source: *Financial Times* 14 February 2009.

zations such as building societies or the Co-operative Bank, with publicly stated ethical principles. Drugs companies are coming under pressure from shareholders to be more generous to the poor of the world – *see* Exhibit 1.3. Just how generous should they be and still be shareholder wealth maximizers? Real-world decision-making can be agonizingly hard.

The theoretical reasons

The risk bearers take the prize

The 'contractual theory' views the firm as a network of contracts, actual and implicit, which specify the roles to be played by various participants in the organization. For instance, the workers make both an explicit (employment contract) and an implicit (show initiative, reliability, etc.) deal with the firm to provide their services in return for salary and other benefits, and suppliers deliver necessary inputs in return for a known payment. Each party has well-defined rights and pay-offs. Most of the participants bargain for a limited risk and a fixed pay-off. Banks, for example, when they lend to a firm, often strenuously try to reduce risk by making sure that the firm is generating sufficient cash flow to repay, that there are assets that can be seized if the loan is not repaid and so on. The bankers' bargain, like that of many of the parties, is a low-risk one and so, the argument goes, they should be rewarded with just the bare minimum for them to provide their service to the firm. Shareholders, on the other hand, are asked to put money into the business at high risk. The deal here is: 'You give us your £10,000 nest egg that you need for your retirement and we, the directors of the firm, do not promise that you will receive a dividend or even see your capital again. We will try our hardest to produce a return on your money but we cannot give any guarantees. Sorry.' Thus the firm's owners are exposed to the possibilities that the firm may go bankrupt and all will be lost. Because of this unfair balance of risk between the different potential claimants on a firm's resources it seems only reasonable that the owners should be entitled to any surplus returns which result after all the other parties have been satisfied.

Alternatives can be bad for all stakeholders (in the long run)

Another theoretical reason hinges on the practicalities of operating in a free market system. In such a capitalist system, it is argued, if a firm chooses to reduce returns to shareholders because, say, it wishes to direct more of the firm's surplus to the workers, then this firm will find it difficult to survive. Some shareholders will sell their shares and invest in other firms more oriented towards their benefit (illustrated by United Airlines, where even the workers sold their shares). In the long run those individuals who do retain their shares may be amenable to a takeover bid from a firm that does concentrate on shareholder wealth creation. The acquirer will anticipate being able to cut costs, not least by lowering the returns to labour. In the absence of a takeover the company would be unable to raise more finance from shareholders and this might result in slow growth and liquidity problems and possibly corporate death, throwing all employees out of work. For over 200 years it has been argued that society is best served by businesses focusing on returns to the owner. Adam Smith (1776) expressed the argument very effectively:

> The businessman by directing ... industry in such a manner as its produce may be of the greatest value, intends only his own gain, and he is in this, as in many other cases, led by an invisible hand to promote an end which was no part of his intention. Nor is it always the worse for society that it was no part of it. By pursuing his own interest he frequently promotes that of the society more effectually than when he really intends to promote it. I have never known much good done by those who affected to trade for the public good. It is an affectation, indeed, not very common among merchants.
>
> Source: Adam Smith, *The Wealth of Nations*, 1776, p. 400.

In an interview in 2003, Milton Friedman focused on the main benefit of encouraging businesses to pursue high returns for owners. He said that this results in the best allocation of investment capital among competing industries and product lines. 'The self-interest of employees in retaining their jobs will often conflict with this overriding objective.' He went on:

> the best system of corporate governance is one that provides the best incentives to use capital efficiently ... You want control ... in the hands of those who are residual recipients [i.e. shareholders bear the residual risk when a company fails] because they are the ones with the direct interest in using the capital of the firm efficiently.
>
> Source: Simon London, *Financial Times Magazine*, 7 June 2003.

Thus, in striving to satisfy customers, businesses promote their own wellbeing and also benefit society. In trying to obtain high returns for owners they help to allocate society's scarce resources among the different forms of output across industries. In other words, consumers get the range of goods and services produced which are, in total, of most benefit to them. Scarce money is directed to the best use.

Consider an alternative system in which capital is directed by those whose aim is to maximize returns to labour. This leads to a misallocation and lower output – e.g. old industries would suck up large amounts of capital – 'To preserve jobs, you understand' – while new cutting-edge industry is starved of funds. Then there are those who would use society's investment capital to 'build a great nation'. Here you find scarce funds being directed towards pet projects of politicians, grand symbols of national pride, rather than into what the people truly need and want. For example, many chief executives are keen on medical research or environmental protection and believe that society would benefit from a large company gift to medical research or the saving of Amazonian rainforest. This is a form of theft of someone else's money (or at least a misappropriation) in the eyes of many thinkers.

Directors should be accountable for their stewardship of the firm's resources entrusted to them by the shareholders. By taking the line that they are balancing the needs of society or other stakeholders together with the claims of shareholders, they neatly leave themselves space to be unaccountable – if returns to shareholders are down, that's alright, we have boosted returns to some of the other claimants on the firm's resources. It gives a free hand for managers to promote their favourite causes with outsiders being unable to judge how effective they are. It is argued that the business of business is business, and it is for government to allocate funds raised through taxes to social projects.

There is a further argument when you consider who actual owns companies. These days shares are held by all of us through our pension, insurance and other savings schemes. We all rely on corporate managers to achieve good returns to fund retirement, etc. So ordinary people need managers to be shareholder wealth maximizers rather than general social maximizers.

Rights of ownership

One final, and powerful reason for advancing shareholders' interests above all others (subject to the rules of the game) is very simple: they own the firm, and therefore deserve any surplus it produces.

The Companies Act 2006 reinforces this by stating that directors' primary duty is to promote the success of the company for the benefit of its members; that is, the shareholders. Yet in the fulfilment of that duty, directors should have regard to the interests of employees, suppliers, customers, the environment and corporate reputation. Thus, in closing a factory, say, the interests of shareholders trump those of employees, but the latter's concerns should not be completely ignored.

This is not the place to advocate one philosophical approach or another which is applicable to all organizations at all times. Many organizations are clearly not shareholder wealth maximizers and are quite comfortable with that. Charities, government departments and other non-profit organizations are fully justified in emphasizing a different set of values to those espoused by the commercial firm. The reader is asked to be prepared for two levels of thought when using this book. While it

> Many organizations are clearly not shareholder wealth maximizers and are quite comfortable with that.

focuses on corporate shareholder wealth decision-making, it may be necessary to make small or large modifications to be able to apply the same frameworks and theories to organizations with different goals.

Football clubs are organizations that often have different objectives from commercial organizations. Many fans believe that the objectives of their club changed for the worse when it became a company quoted on the London Stock Exchange. A confusion of objectives can make decision-making complex and suspect.

Corporate social responsibility

The notion of corporate social responsibility, CSR, has grown in the conscious-ness of managers in recent years. CSR means different things to different people. For some it means a balancing of stakeholder interests to fulfil the firm's greater social role. In this view of the world shareholders are one amongst many claimants. Others view CSR as complementary to shareholder weath-maximiza-tion. Being kind to the environment, having good labour conditions and acting ethically first makes life better for those stakeholders, and second increases shareholder returns. Thus, shareholders benefit from doing good for others – but only so long as the benefits to the other stakeholders are not taken too far.

As we saw in the GSK example (Exhibit 1.3), many of the institutional investors (e.g. pension funds, insurance companies) now positively encourage this second form of CSR. Companies are asked to disclose their social, ethical and environmental risks and take action to alleviate these risks. They are often acutely aware of reputational risk, the potential backlash against 'heartless capitalists' and litigation (take BP following the Gulf oil spill in 2010), but there are more pos-itive reasons for the shift: people working within organizations are more committed if they feel that the firm is 'a force for good in the world'. This is a way to attract and retain good staff, leading to improved business performance. A simi-lar positive opinion about the firm's activities can be generated in the minds of the customers, which encourages sales.

Motivation and obliquity

Directors, even those who believe that the objective of the firm is to maximize shareholder wealth, frequently admit that such a goal is a bit of a turn-off when it comes to motivating employees. It may appear mean-spirited and selfish and to lack excitement. They therefore encourage (and are often motivated them-selves by) something bigger; for example, the ambition to put a PC on every desk; to organize the world's information and make it universally accessible and useful; to find a vaccine to treat malaria.

Many of the world's most successful generators of shareholder wealth actually focus first on an inspiring vision and excellence, and in an oblique way become shareholder value maximizers.[1] Take Boeing and the development of the Jumbo Jet in the 1960s. The engineers and managers were aiming to create the world's best passenger aircraft. Their focus was on technical brilliance and serving their customers well. They reasoned that if they got these right then shareholder wealth would follow. They thoroughly enjoyed the cutting edge, meeting daily technological challenges. They thrived on the ideas of breaking new ground in terms of brand new markets. It would have been stifling if the financial team had insisted that every new innovative step be demonstrated to enhance shareholder wealth before going ahead. Similarly, Microsoft's and Google's early challenges and triumphs in technology motivated the growth in the businesses.

What is shareholder value?

Maximizing wealth can be defined as maximizing purchasing power. The way in which an enterprise enables its owners to indulge in the pleasures of purchasing and consumption is by paying them a dividend. The promise of a flow of cash in the form of dividends is what prompts investors to sacrifice immediate consumption and hand over their savings to a management team through the purchase of shares. Shareholders are interested in a flow of dividends over a long time horizon and not necessarily in a quick payback. Take the electronics giant Siemens: it could release vast sums for short-term dividend payouts by ceasing all research and development (R&D) and selling off surplus sites. But this would not maximize shareholder wealth because, by retaining funds within the business, it is believed that new products and ideas, springing from the R&D programme, will produce much higher dividends in the future. Maximizing shareholder wealth means maximizing the flow of dividends to shareholders *through time* – there is a long-term perspective.

Profit maximization is not the same as shareholder wealth-maximization

Profit is a concept developed by accountants to aid decision-making, one decision being to judge the quality of stewardship shown over the owner's funds. The accountant has to take what is a continuous process, a business activity stretching over many years, and split this into accounting periods of say, a year, or six months. To some extent this exercise is bound to be artificial and fraught with problems. There are many reasons why accounting profit may not be a good proxy for shareholder wealth. Here are five:

■ **Prospects** Imagine that there are two firms that have reported identical profits but one firm is more highly valued by its shareholders than the other. One possible reason for this is that recent profit figures fail to reflect the relative potential of the two firms. The stock market will give a higher share value to the company that shows the greater future growth outlook. Perhaps one set of managers chose a short-term approach and raised their profits in the near term but have sacrificed long-term prospects. One way of achieving this is to raise prices and slash marketing spend – over the subsequent year profits might be boosted as customers are unable to switch suppliers immediately. Over the long term, however, competitors will respond and profits will fall.

■ **Risk** Again two firms could report identical average historic profit figures and have future prospects which indicate that they will produce the same average annual returns. However, one firm's returns are subject to much greater variability and so there will be years of losses and, in a particularly bad year, the possibility of bankruptcy. Figure 1.2 shows two firms with

FIGURE 1.2

Two firms with identical average profits but different risk levels

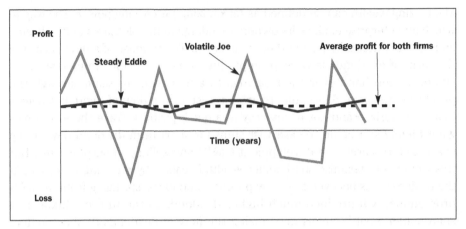

identical average profit, but Volatile Joe's profit is subject to much greater risk than that of Steady Eddie. Shareholders are likely to value the firm with stable income flows more highly than one with high risk.

- **Accounting problems** Drawing up a set of accounts is not as scientific and objective as some people try to make out. There is plenty of scope for judgment, guesswork or even cynical manipulation. Imagine the difficulty facing the company accountant and auditors of a clothes retailer when trying to value a dress which has been on sale for six months. Let us suppose the dress cost the firm £50. Perhaps this should go into the balance sheet and then the profit and loss account will not be affected. But what if the store manager says that he can only sell that dress if it is reduced to £30, and contradicting him the managing director says that if a little more effort was made £40 could be achieved? Which figure is the person who drafts the financial accounts going to take? Profits can vary significantly depending on a multitude of small judgments like this.

- **Communication** Investors realize and accept that buying a share is risky. However they like to reduce their uncertainty and nervousness by finding out as much as they can about the firm. If the firm is reluctant to tell shareholders about such matters as the origin of reported profits, then investors generally will tend to avoid those shares. Fears are likely to arise in the minds of poorly informed investors: did the profits come from the most risky activities and might they therefore disappear next year? Is the company being used to run guns to unsavoury regimes abroad? The senior executives of large quoted firms spend a great deal of time explaining their strategies, sources of income and future investment plans to the large institutional shareholders to make sure that these investors are aware of the quality of the firm and its prospects. Firms that ignore the importance of communication and image in the investment community may be doing their shareholders a disservice as the share price might fall.

■ **Additional capital** Profits can be increased simply by making use of more shareholders' money. If shareholders inject more money into the company or the firm merely retains profits (which belong to shareholders) their future profits can rise, but the return on shareholders' money may fall to less than that which is available elsewhere for the same level of risk. This is shareholder wealth destructive.

Corporate governance

In theory the shareholders, being the owners of the firm, control its activities. In practice, the large modern corporation often has a very diffuse and fragmented set of shareholders and control often lies in the hands of directors. It is extremely difficult to marshal thousands of shareholders, each with a small stake in the business, to push for change. Thus in many firms we have what is called a separation, or a divorce, of ownership and control. In times past the directors would usually be the same individuals as the owners. Today, however, less than 1 percent of the shares of most of the largest quoted firms are owned by the directors.

The separation of ownership and control raises worries that the management team may pursue objectives attractive to them but which are not necessarily beneficial to the shareholders – this is termed 'managerialism' or 'managementism'; for example, raising their own pay perks, expanding their empire, avoiding risky projects or boosting short-term results at the expense of long-term performance. This conflict is an example of the principal–agent problem. The principals (the shareholders) have to find ways of ensuring that their agents (the managers) act in their interests. This means incurring costs, 'agency costs', to (a) monitor managers' behaviour and (b) create incentive schemes and controls for managers to encourage the pursuit of shareholders' wealth maximization. These costs arise in addition to the agency cost of the loss of wealth caused by the extent to which prevention measures do not work and managers continue to pursue non-shareholder wealth goals.

Corporate governance means the system by which companies are managed and controlled. Its main focus is on the responsibilities and obligations placed on the executive directors and the non-executive directors, and on the relationships between the firm's owners, the board of directors and the top tier of managers. The interaction between these groups leads to the defining of the corporate objective, the placing of constraints on managerial behaviour, and the setting of targets and incentive payments based on achievement.

The board of directors has the responsibility of overseeing the company, acting as a check on managerialism, so that shareholders' best interests are appropriately prioritized. The board sets company-wide policy and strategic direction, leaving the executive directors to manage day-to-day activities. It also decides who will be an executive director (subject to shareholder vote) and sets their pay. In addition the board oversees the reporting of accounting results to shareholders. The board should also take a keen interest in the ethical behaviour of senior managers.

Annual general meeting

The board is expected to organize an annual general meeting (AGM) at which shareholders can vote to change the board of directors if they are dissatisfied (proxy votes may be assigned if a shareholder cannot attend). In theory the shareholders can strongly influence the strategic and operational decisions. However, this power is usually weakened:

- The cost of attending a meeting (or even sending in a proxy form) outweighs the benefit for many shareholders, leading to many (most) votes being unused.

- Many fund managers do not take their 'ownership' of stakes in a corporation seriously, and given that most shares quoted on public stock markets are now owned by institutional investors (e.g. pension finds, insurance funds) we find that when faced with the issue of what to do with a poor board of directors and senior management, rather than acting to remove them, most fund managers find it easier simply to sell the shares and move on.

Corporate governance regulations

There is a considerable range of legislation and other regulatory pressures designed to encourage directors to act in shareholders' interests. In the UK the Companies Acts require certain minimum standards of behaviour, as does the London Stock Exchange (LSE). For example, directors are forbidden to use their position to profit at the expense of shareholders, e.g. they cannot buy shares in their own company just before announcing unexpectly high profits. There is the back-up of the financial industry regulator, the Financial Services Authority (FSA) and the Financial Reporting Council (FRC) (an accounting body).

Following a number of financial scandals, guidelines of best practice in corporate governance were issued by the Cadbury, Greenbury, Hampel, Higgs and Smith committees, now consolidated in the UK Corporate Governance Code, which is backed by the FSA, LSE and FRC.

Under the code directors of companies listed[2] on the Main Market of the LSE are required to state in the accounts how the principles of the code have been applied. If the principles have not been followed they have to state why. The principles include:

- The board should include a balance of executive and non-executive directors (and in particular independent[3] non-executive directors) such that no individual or small group of individuals can dominate the board's decision taking. For large companies (the largest 350 on the LSE), at least half the board, excluding the chair, should comprise non-executive directors determined by the board to be independent. The independent non-executive directors can act as a powerful counterweight to the executive directors. These directors are not full time and not concerned with day-to-day management. They may be able to take a broader view than executive directors, who may become excessively focused on detail. The experienced individuals who become non-executive directors are not expected to be dependent on the director's fee for income and can therefore afford to be independently minded. They are expected to 'constructively challenge and help develop proposals on strategy ... scrutinize the performance of management in meeting agreed goals and objectives and monitor the reporting of performance' (Financial Services Authority, FSA, 2003, *The Combined Code on Corporate Governance*,[4] p. 4).

- There should be a balance of power on the board such that no one individual can dominate and impose their will. The running of the board of directors (by a chairperson) should be a separate responsibility conducted by a person who is not responsible for running the business, i.e. the chief executive officer (CEO) or managing director (MD) (this is frequently ignored in practice, which is permitted, if a written justification is presented to shareholders).

- There should be transparency on directors' renumeration requiring a remuneration committee consisting exclusively of non-executive directors, independent of management. No director should be involved in deciding his or her renumeration. A significant proportion of renumeration should be linked to corporate and individual performance.

- The procedure for the appointment of board directors should be formal (nomination committee), objective (based on merit) and transparent (information on the terms and conditions made available). Directors are to retire by rotation at least every three years (or every one year for the largest 350 companies) – they may be re-elected.

- The audit committee (responsible for validating financial figures, e.g. by appointing effective external auditors) should consist exclusively of independent non-executive directors, otherwise the committee would not be able to act as a check and balance to the executive directors.

- Directors are required to communicate with shareholders, e.g. to use the annual general meeting to explain the company's performance and encourage discussion.

The 'comply or explain' approach is in contrast to many other systems of regulation of corporate governance around the world – these are often strict rule-based systems with lawyers to the fore (e.g. Sarbanes–Oxley regulations in the USA, which have frightened companies away from listing on a US stock market). 'The flexibility it offers [the "comply or explain" approach] has been widely welcomed both by company boards and by investors. It is for shareholders and others to evaluate the company's statement. While it is expected that companies will comply with the Code's provisions most of the time, it is recognized that departure from the provisions of the Code may be justified in particular circumstances' (FSA, 2003, pp. 1–2). Furthermore, some of the provisions do not apply to companies smaller than the largest 350 listed on the London Stock Exchange. However, failure to comply or explain properly will result in suspension from the stock exchange. There is a brief discussion of the UK versus the US system of corporate governance in Exhibit 1.4. The article in Exhibit 1.5 highlights some room for improvement in the UK system.

Which set of company rules are OK? US-style or UK?

Tony Chapelle

While the debate rages as to whether the worst of the global recession is over, lawmakers in the US and regulators in Britain are engaged in another debate: over the rules that govern public companies.

Most experts say – when comparing their effectiveness – that the Combined Code in the UK fares better than the Sarbanes-Oxley Act of the US.

Indeed, many observers would like to see the US move to a model similar to Britain's.

'I think that the Combined Code is the preferred way to proceed, because it depends on voluntary action by the private sector,' says Ira Millstein, who is a renowned corporate board adviser and a partner at Weil, Gotschal & Manges, a law firm in New York.

Mr Millstein thinks that the requirements to comply with the Combined Code or explain why they have a good reason not to is 'more genteel – which is sort of the British way'.

The Combined Code, written to codify board director conduct, executive compensation and auditing issues, dates back to the 1990s and was most recently revised in 2006. It is currently under review.

The Financial Reporting Council (FRC), the UK's corporate governance regulator, asked British stakeholders for consultation on how well the Code is working. Those findings are expected to be published some time this year. Changes to the Code could follow.

The principle of comply or explain only works in countries where shareholders have meaningful rights in law, such as being able to vote individual directors on or off the board, says Chris Hodge, the head of the corporate governance unit at the FRC.

Without those rights, Mr Hodge explains, regulators have to play a more active role to protect investors.

Conversely, shareholders feel that a principles-based approach such as that of the Combined Code produces fewer obstacles to running businesses, says Leo Martin, a corporate ethics consultant at Good Corporation.

He cites as evidence the drop in listings on US exchanges since the passage of the Sarbanes-Oxley Act.

'Companies have voted with their feet. UK businesses are less encumbered,' Mr Martin comments.

In both countries, a host of financial institutions, including Lehman Brothers and Northern Rock, failed badly at overseeing systemic risk.

Yet that was not the problem the governance laws in either country was constructed to manage.

The Sarbanes-Oxley Act, for instance, was created to assure accuracy in financial reporting.

'We don't know how much fraud did not occur because of Sarbanes-Oxley, but by and large, it's been beneficial,' says Eliot Spitzer, who prosecuted some of his country's largest securities fraud cases when he was attorney general of New York State.

So Sox, as it is called, is likely to stay intact.

Yet it almost certainly will be superseded by new corporate governance provisions such as a shareholders' bill of rights that was introduced in Congress last month. For one thing, Sox clearly did not solve the underlying problem of excessive financial leverage that later sank many banks.

'More cynical voices would say that Sarbanes-Oxley was akin to building the Maginot Line,' Mr Spitzer quips.

Americans claim that creating norms of corporate behaviour is easier in Britain because of the smaller community of regulators, stock exchanges, and investors such as shareholder insurance companies.

'You can call a meeting of most of the institutional owners of a big FTSE company within the City of London with, perhaps, a conference link to Edinburgh,' says Jon Lukomnik, a founding member of the International Corporate Governance Network.

That familiarity encourages what Mr Lukomnik calls 'quiet, constructive engagement'.

Thus, UK stakeholders have agreed on governance topics such as shareholders' right to vote on executive renumeration, required separation of the role of chief executive and chairman, and the point at which directors are 'overboarded' or sit on too many boards to be effective.

Some US companies voluntarily govern themselves by these practices but they remain the minority. That is likely to change, however, under the shareholder-friendly Obama adminstration.

Most observers agree on Sox's benefits, yet point to its imposing drawbacks.

Erroll Davis says that when he was chief executive of Alliant Energy, a $3bn public utility in the Midwest, he was put off by the 'prescriptiveness of Sox'.

He later came to appreciate it, because it forced his corporate managers to gain a deeper understanding of company internal controls and financials.

Today, says Mr Davis, who is an audit committee board member on both sides of the Atlantic, at General Motors and at BP, US regulators and accounting firms are now more receptive to using materiality and common sense in assessing companies' compliance with Sox.

One of the harshest critics of Sox is Harvey Pitt, a former chairman of the SEC. He calls Sarbanes-Oxley 'relatively ineffective' and 'hastily and badly drafted.' Mr Pitt says that Sox has fostered a tick-the-box mentality in corporate managers rather than an understanding of why risks exist.

'The approach of the Combined Code is superior. The most significant thing is to get businesses to be an active participant in the regulation of their own conduct,' Mr Pitt says.

Exhibit 1.4

Source: *Financial Times*, special section 'Corporate Governance', 18 June 2009, p. 1.

Investors up in arms over poor governance

Kate Burgess

After most periods of excess, comes the crash, the anger, the blame and then reform.

The last big UK overhaul of corporate governance came in 2003 in the wake of the dotcom crash and a series of financial scandals such as Enron in the US.

The Combined Code laid out a blueprint for boards, focusing on the balance between executives and non-executives and particularly on the role and responsibilities of the latter.

There are early signs that corporate governance in the UK is about to go through another bout of reform, triggered by the near-collapse of Britain's banking sector over the past year.

As the crisis has deepened, the spotlight has turned from the executives who ran the banks, to the non-executives and investors who owned them and appeared to let it all happen.

Lord Myners, now City minister but previously an influential figure in the fund management world, told the Financial Times: 'I do believe that when we ask about the state of the banks [we need to ask] what owners were doing and whether they should have done more for example about risk and leverage. Institutions should have been more challenging.'

He is pushing for what he calls a 'more informed and high-quality dialogue, a deeper form of engagement' between shareholders and boards which would define corporate governance less narrowly around compliance with the Combined Code.

A week ago, in response to MPs asking if there had been a breakdown in the UK's corporate governance, leading UK investment institutions conceded shareholders had not done enough to check the management of banks.

They admitted they had failed to curb companies' worst excesses or to call directors to account. Their preferred method of effecting change via behind-the-scenes consultation had failed.

'It is clear we haven't been as effective as we could have been,' said Peter Montagnon, investment affairs director at the Association of British Insurers, Britain's main investment body.

At that Treasury select committee hearing last week, Sir Peter Viggers, MP for Gosport, went further: had the current crisis shown shareholders, as owners of companies, were 'pretty toothless', he wanted to know.

Peter Chambers, chief executive of Legal & General Investment Management, replied that LGIM had met banking boards on average once a fortnight last year and had grilled banks about their capital needs early in 2008 after the Northern Rock failure.

'Did we engage enough? I think we did. The question is why we weren't listened to and I don't know the answer to that,' Mr Chambers said.

Too often, non-executive directors had failed to challenge executives and had then blocked investors who asked for checks and balances to be imposed on executives, Mr Chambers added. He highlighted in particular the Royal Bank of Scotland board.

His comments exposed a wider tension in relations between shareholders and boards that has been escalating as the recession has taken hold.

That tension has largely centred around the banks but has been manifest in a series of clashes between shareholders and companies.

Last year Marks and Spencer outraged its biggest shareholders with the sudden promotion of Stuart Rose, chief executive, to the post of executive chairman. In doing so, the retailer ran roughshod over one of the tenets of the Combined Code by vesting too much unchecked power in the hands of one individual. Shareholders said the move put at risk the long-term health and stability of the company.

In spite of investors' efforts – in public and private – to squeeze a compromise out of M&S, the retailer's board barely budged. Even threats to vote against directors up for re-election in the summer failed to work.

The episode – which Mr Chambers described as 'incredibly frustrating' – revealed the flaws in shareholders' fondness for behind-the-scenes negotiation and showed just how easily boards could ignore their biggest investors.

'The boards of big companies can run rings round us', said one leading UK shareholder. 'They divide and rule.'

'The shareholder base of big companies tends to be extremely diverse. No shareholder group owns enough that directors have to listen. It means that boards can tell us "you all want different things. You can't make up your minds. So we'll go on doing what we want".'

The failure of some banks' capital raisings and the nationalisation or near-nationalisation of UK banks only widened the cracks in the relationship between companies and shareholders as the economy headed into recession ...

As Lord Myners says: 'Voting is a rather blunt [tool]. Investors can only vote on things on the agenda. It is not a substitute for active and informed engagement.'

Now, though, as the recriminations fly over the causes of the banking crisis, investors are warning they will become more militant. They are threatening to scrutinise the performance of all directors more carefully, and say they will target the heads of the audit and remuneration committees in a bid to bring boards to account.

'We must be willing if necessary to vote them down', says Keith Skeoch, chairman of the ABI investment committee.

Mr Skeoch is initiating a series of high-level discussions with senior non-executives to determine where the breakdown in relations has occurred and how companies are able to 'to turn a deaf ear' to their owners.

The role of the senior independent director as a channel between investors and companies will be closely examined.

For now, at least, shareholders insist there is no need for regulatory change or a radical overhaul of the Combined Code.

'In the UK, the [corporate governance] framework is a good one', says Mr Montagnon. 'But we need to apply it better.'

EXHIBIT 1.5

Source: *Financial Times* 3 February 2009, p. 19.

There are various other (complementary) methods used to try to align the actions of senior management with the interests of shareholders, that is, to achieve 'goal congruence':

- **Linking rewards to shareholders wealth improvement** A technique widely employed in industry is to grant directors and other senior managers share options. These permit managers to purchase shares at some date in the future at a price that is fixed now. If the share price rises significantly between the date when the option was granted and the date when the shares can be brought, the manager can make a fortune by buying at the pre-arranged price and then selling in the marketplace. For example in 2012 managers might be granted the right to buy shares in 2017 at a price of £1.50. If the market price moves to say £2.30 in 2017, then the managers can buy and then sell the shares, making a gain of 80p. The managers under such a scheme have a clear interest in achieving a rise in share price and thus congruence comes about to some extent. An alternative method is to allot shares to managers if they achieve certain performance targets, for example growth in earnings per share or return on assets. Many companies have long-term incentive plans (LTIPs) for senior executives which at the end of three years or more pay bonuses if certain targets are surpassed, e.g. share price rise or high profit achieved. Exhibit 1.6 discusses share option schemes and other ways of encouraging managers to promote the interests of shareholders.

How to encourage managers to act more like owners

Stefan Stern

What would your customer say if they could see your expenses claim? The abstemious can rest easy. But extravagant restaurant receipts, first-class travel and accommodation, huge taxi fares – such things might not endear you to the people you are supposed to be serving. You should expect a tough conversation about the prices you charge if customers get the impression you are enjoying the high life with their money.

That is why smart business leaders advise their colleagues to imagine they are spending their own money when they are out on company business. Act like an owner, the adage goes. Be responsible. Think before you splash the company's cash about.

This is a micro-level example of what has been called the 'principal-agent problem'. Even the most senior managers are not, usually, the owners of the business they are working for. It may not be easy for them to think and act like an owner. At the same time, can owners be confident that managers are working in the company's best interests and not simply pursuing their own selfish agenda?

This question was explored by two academics, Michael Jensen and William Meckling, in a famous 1976 paper ('Theory of the firm: managerial behaviour, agency costs and ownership structure'), which popularised so-called agency theory. Their answer to the problem? Among other things, try to align the interests of managers and shareholders. Use share options to give managers 'skin in the game', a personal interest in the success – or failure – of the company. Incentives work: they should be deployed to get people working towards the same end.

There have been, to put it at its gentlest, regrettable unintended consequences to the spread of this theory. It turns out that the simple solution of share options does not solve the complicated problem of how to encourage and reward effective, responsible management.

For one thing, senior managers may not have the same time horizons as owners. A chief executive might reasonably calculate that he or she will be given no more than three or four years to run the business before their time is up. You would understand it if that CEO worked pretty hard to get the share price up fast in order to make those share options more valuable. And the longer-term consequences for the business in engineering such a rapid share prise rise?

Not necessarily the CEO's problem.

The shareholder base will, in any case, reflect a wide range of characters with varying priorities. There will be long-term institutional investors and hedge funds working in their own unique way. You can't easily be aligned with all of these people at the same time.

Prof Jensen conceded in 2002, in the wake of the dotom crash, that the incentives he regarded as crucial could do terrible harm. 'In the bubble, the carrots (options) became managerial heroin, encouraging a focus on short-term prices with destructive long-term consequences,' he said. 'It also encouraged behaviour that actually reduced the value of some firms to their shareholders.'

Stewardship – steady, long-term leadership that may not be reflected in rapid rises in the share price – is harder to reward with remuneration schemes based on stock markets.

In an important critique published in 2004 ('Bad management theories are destroying good management practices'), Sumantra Ghoshal condemned agency theory as an example of all that was wrong with modern management. Amoral theories taught in business schools, he said, had 'actively freed their students from any sense of moral responsibility'. Agency theory served to convert 'collective pessimism about managers into realised pathologies in management behaviours'.

According to this critique, the theory seems to launch a cycle of distrust. Managers are knaves, out for themselves, who have to be tied in with share options. But managers who feel regarded in this way can become unmotivated and in the end untrustworthy. Why has executive pay exploded over the past 20 years? Partly, Prof Ghoshal suggested, because managers have sunk to reach the low expectations people have for them.

So is the idea of managers acting like owners a futile dream? Not necessarily. Drawing on pointers given to him by a former boss, Phil Gerbyshak, a management blogger, has posted some apparently humdrum but, in fact, sensible thoughts on how managers could live up to that goal (my paraphrasing):

- Always act professionally. You never know who is going to hear what you're saying or see what you're doing.
- Treat everyone you talk to with respect, regardless of their position. Nothing and nobody is beneath you.
- A little overtime won't hurt. Work until the job is done.
- If you're the last one in the room, turn out the light.
- Be on time for meetings. Time is money. Why would you waste time?

Less exciting, perhaps, than holding plenty of in-the-money options. But more likely to do long-term good to a business.

EXHIBIT 1.6

Source: *Financial Times* 7 July 2009, pp. 12–13.

- **Sackings** The threat of being sacked with the accompanying humiliation and financial loss may encourage managers not to diverge too far from the shareholders' wealth path. However, this method is employed in extreme circumstances only. It is sometimes difficult to implement because of difficulties of making a coordinated shareholder effort. It is made easier if the majority of directors are independent of the executives.

■ **Selling shares and the takeover threat** Over 70 percent of the shares of the typical company quoted on the London stock market are owned by financial institutions such as pension and insurance funds. These organizations generally are not prepared to put large resources into monitoring and controlling all the hundreds of firms of which they own a part. Quite often their first response, if they observe that management is not acting in what they regard as their best interest, is to sell the share rather than intervene. This will result in a lower share price, making the raising of funds more difficult. It may also lower rewards to managers whose remuneration depends partly on the share price level. If this process continues the firm may become vulnerable to a merger bid by another group of managers, resulting in a loss of top management posts. Fear of being taken over can establish some sort of backstop position to prevent shareholder wealth considerations being totally ignored. Exhibit 1.7 discusses the problems caused by an extra layer of agents (fund managers) standing between the ultimate owners of the business and the directors.

■

We need more responsible corporate ownership

Paul Myners

Property right are supposed to be at the centre of capitalist economies. Ownership encourages responsibility and initiative. But many of the most important capitalist entities, listed corporations, are bordering on the ownerless.

Of course, companies have legal owners: shareholders, whose interest are represented by boards of directors. But in practice, shareholders do not act like owners in terms of exercising control consistent with the maximum long-term benefit of companies.

Ownership has become divorced from control. The problems this generates have been realised since Adam Smith wrote in 1776: 'Directors ... being the managers rather of other peoples' money than of their own, it cannot well be expected that they would watch over it with the same anxious vigilance.'

In more recent times, the growth of institutional investors means that ownership and control have become one step further removed. It is these fund managers who are the dominant shareholders. Adolph Berle described this as removing 'the one remaining power by which the recipient of corporate profits might have direct relation to corporate ownership'.

As Smith hinted, the incentives of executives may not be in line with the best interests of the companies they manage. Neither are the incentives of fund managers necessarily in synch with their investors' best interests. This disconnect might explain why many banks took on more risk than they could manage. Some fund managers tried to engage and challenge, but failed. Others did not try. It would be unfair to blame fund managers for this. They are responding rationally to the expectations placed on them by their clients. Investors use return over a fairly short period as the barometer of fund manager ability.

Investors' emphasis on short-term return communicates itself to business leaders who feel obliged to think and act short-term; take on more risk, which the fund manager reduces through diversification – an option not open to employees. Fund managers are expected to run a marathon in a series of 100 metre sprints, probably to provide clients with a false sense of being in control. However, I have yet to meet an active fund manager who did not believe that longer-term horizons would produces both superior results and better companies.

Clients of professional investors also need to question the relevance of expressing performance goals in terms of short-term returns relative to benchmark indices. Financial economics assumes that efficient valuation and capital allocation arises from self-interested selection among competing opportunities. Behaviours driven by seeking to second-guess the actions of others lose this efficiency in delivering good outcomes. They lead to herd-like behaviour; extremes of valuation, as it is too risky to be contrarian; portfolios that show low conviction through high diversification; and a nonsensical situation where some fund managers hold investments that they believe are overvalued or poorly managed because they fear being wrong and underperforming. We saw some of this during the dotcom boom.

The approach does not apply to all fund managers but it is common. For this to change, institutional investors, such as pension funds, need to show a capacity for thought independent from that of their agents. I am struck by the absence of a body in the UK that speaks on behalf of institutional investors without a commercial or trade association interest. Creating an independent Council for Institutional Investors would be a step forward.

Another barrier to responsible ownership is that active governance takes time, effort and expertise. It is a public good – if one investor expends the time to act as a responsible owner, all investors benefit. It is too easy for other investors to free-ride on the efforts of the few. This is why I strongly support the announcement from the Financial Services Authority that collective action by shareholders will not be considered market abuse.

Active, responsible ownership requires investors to demand that fund managers make use of the levers available to them and do more to engage with companies. Investors must demand that fund managers develop the skills needed to engage as owners and improve companies.

Governance cannot be solved by government alone, but it can help. Sir David Walker's interim report into the governance of UK banks has recommended changes to strengthen board challenges and shareholder oversight, and improve risk management. Beneficial investors, pensions funds and insurers need to support him. In parallel, the Financial Reporting Council is reviewing the Combined Code on Corporate Governance and considering which of Sir David's recommendations could be applied beyond the banking sector. The FSA is implementing remuneration principles that will ensure banking pay can never again lead to excessive and unmanaged risk. Government will ensure shareholders have the information necessary to fulfil their duties in challenging boards about risk and remuneration. Regulators can limit risky activities by making them less profitable, by requiring increased capital or, in extreme cases, varying a bank's ability to engage in certain activities. But owners, or their agent fund managers, must play their role, including ensuring remuneration is reasonable.

It is vital to the economy that corporations generate long-term value. To achieve it, we need a new enlightenment in governance. Investors must now rise to this challenge and take up the mantle of responsible ownership.

Exhibit 1.7

Source: *Financial Times* 12 October 2009, p. 13.

Information flow The accounting profession, the stock exchange and the investing institutions have conducted a continuous battle to encourage or force firms to release more accurate, timely and detailed information concerning their operations. The quality of corporate accounts and annual reports has generally improved, as has the availability of other forms of information flowing to investors and analysts, such as company briefings and company announcements (which are available from financial websites, e.g. www.advfn.com). All this helps to monitor firms, and identify any wealth-destroying actions by wayward managers early, but, as a number of recent scandals have shown, matters are still far from perfect.

What happens if control over directors is weak?

In some countries the interests of shareholders are often placed far below those of the controlling managers and other stakeholders. The absence of good corporate governance leads to many problems for a society – look at the trouble Japanese companies are having (Exhibit 1.8).

Dividends to reap

Michiyo Nakamoto and Kate Burgess

On a drizzly day in Tokyo last week, an anxious but determined Australian fund manager joined nearly 700 other shareholders at the annual meeting of J-Power, John Ho, Asia director of The Children's Investment Fund, was there on behalf of his UK-based employer, which owns a 9.9 percent stake in the Japanese electricity wholesaler.

In an impassioned speech, he entreated his fellow shareholders to stand up for their rights, Citing J-Power's falling profits and depressed share price, Mr Ho urged his audience to support the activist hedge fund's proposals for higher dividends, the appointment of outside directors and other measures to improve shareholder returns. 'We as shareholders deserve better respect and management needs to be accountable,' he said.

For the first time, Japanese companies are having to face up to the demands of long-neglected shareholders. Foreign activist funds such as TCI and Steel Partners are being joined by traditionally publicity-shy long-term investors such as Brandes and Calpers of the US in their quest for better returns on their investments in the country. Crucially, within Japan itself some domestic investors are starting to add their voice to the calls.

The confrontation pits traditionalists, who disparage assertive shareholders as short-term opportunists, against those who warn that unless companies improve their corporate governance, investors will turn their backs on Japan. The outcome will have far-reaching implications not just for foreign investment in the country but also for the well-being of its ageing society and the competitiveness of corporate Japan.

The fight between TCI and J-Power comes at a time when many international fund managers are considering raising their allocations to Japan, as one of the few economies that will benefit from higher global inflation and one in which banks appear to have avoided the effects of the credit crunch. If Japanese companies go even a small way towards adopting a more shareholder-friendly governance model and thereby boost investor returns, they say, there is a huge store of value that could be unlocked.

Over decades, Japan's approach to governance has encouraged executives to rank shareholders alongside – if not below – other stakeholders such as employees, customers, suppliers and the community at large. Management was accountable mainly to the company's primary lender, and usually only when things grew bad enough to threaten bankruptcy.

As a result, the idea that managements are agents of the shareholders and, as such, need to be monitored and held accountable for the company's performance is not accepted by the majority of Japanese boards. Those are new concepts in Japan, says Toshiaki Oguchi, representative director of Governance for Owners Japan, a fund manager and investor advisory group. He recalls explaining the importance of corporate governance to a group of Japanese managers to be asked: 'Why do you need such a thing?'

Institutional investors such as life assurance companies and banks have traditionally been silent owners, in many cases due to the wide-ranging business relationships they have with the companies in which they invest. Only about 40 percent of listed companies have outside directors, and even many of those come from group or affiliated companies.

But the Japanese management system, which worked well while the economy was growing, companies were thriving and the stock market was booming, is now under siege as globalisation and the greying of Japanese society change the investment landscape. As domestic investors, burnt during the stock market plunge in the 1990s' flocked overseas in search of higher returns and Japanese banks sold down their holdings to repair their battered balance sheets, foreigners have come in to fill the gap. Foreign shareholders now account for as much as 70 percent of trading on the Tokyo Stock Exchange and own nearly 30 percent of publicly traded shares.

With the Japanese stock market down by 60 percent in the past eight years, foreign investors have grown vocal as they struggle to meet their targets. Meanwhile, domestic investors are also feeling the need to achieve better returns, as a result of a dismal performance by Japan's pension funds. Corporate pension schemes have suffered enormous damage owing to the sharp fall in the stock market.

'In five years, 400 schemes have been dismantled and in four years, 900 have cut pensioners' benefits. That means more than 2m people have lost benefits, all because of the poor performance of Japanese companies,' says Tomomi Yano, executive managing director of the Pension Fund Association, one of Japan's largest pension fund groups.

About half the country's listed companies are trading below book value and many are sitting on cash piles for which managements have found no efficient use. Not surprisingly, 'there is a high level of frustration among foreign and domestic investors regarding corporate governance', says Mike Connors, senior adviser to Hermes, the UK fund.

The frustration is evident in the growing willingness of investors to press companies for higher dividends, share buy-backs, changes in strategy and even top-level resignations.

Of the 20 or so shareholder proposals put to companies in the current season of annual meetings, the majority were merely seeking a dividend boost. Yet most of the outside motions before

AGMs this year have been rejected – including TCI's demands at J-Power. Japanese companies are fighting back.

Among measures many have adopted in recent years are 'poison pill' defences against hostile takeover attempts, forming cross-shareholdings with friendly business partners and, in some cases, issuing highly dilutive third-party share allotments ...

Defenders of the status quo also point to Toyota and Fuji Photo Film, two of Japan's most successful companies, which have very Japanese systems of management – including a propensity to hoard cash rather than return it to shareholders.

Those who decry the arrival of activist shareholders point, moreover, to failings in Anglo-Saxon corporate governance, most recently in the sub-prime mortgage scandals.

But Atsushi Saito, head of the TSE, last month spoke in apocalyptic terms of Japan being forced to sell its national assets at rock-bottom prices to rival economies to fund its debt – now at 170 percent of gross domestic product – unless companies became more efficient.

Those opposed to bringing Japanese corporate governance into line with international standards would 'eventually dampen the future price of Japan'.

Frustrated shareholders argue that Japan's system of governance not only fails to protect shareholders' rights but is not 'meeting the needs of stakeholders or the nation at large', as the Asian Corporate Governance Association put it recently in a white paper on Japan. By returning some of their excess cash to shareholders, companies could at least raise their returns to international standards. The average return on equity in Japan of 8.71 percent is the lowest among developed economies, notes Nikko Citigroup in a report ....

'Companies are no longer as certain of the loyalty of their shareholders as they have been,' says Mr Nakanishi [chairman of Japan Shareholder Services, which provides shareholder relation services to companies]. 'The really positive thing that has come out of these developments is that the companies have become aware that they need to explain [their strategy] to shareholders.'

Exhibit 1.8

Source: *Financial Times* 3 July 2008, p. 13.

Conclusion

Readers will agree that all organizations need clarity of purpose. A multiplicity of objectives leads to confusion and contradictory decisions. While the single objective 'shareholder wealth-maximization' is controversial and subject to much debate, for the purpose of the decision-making frameworks and techniques discussed in the rest of the book we will take it as *the* objective at all times. This allows much simpler and clearer decisions to be made. At the very least, this has the benefit of allowing easy understanding of financial concepts.

The reader is then free, once the basics of finance are absorbed, to modify the objective to suit the organizational context. However, for most commercial organizations in competitive market environments, you are unlikely to be justified in straying too far from the straight and narrow path of shareholder wealth- maximization. Football clubs, building societies, co-ops, charities and government agencies however are a different story.

Notes

1 John Kay, economist and *Financial Times* columnist, developed the idea of obliquity.

2 Overseas companies listed on the Main Market are required to disclose the significant ways in which their corporate governance practices differ from those set out in the Code.

3 The board should determine whether the director is independent in character and judgment and whether there are relationships or circumstances which are likely to affect, or could appear to affect, the director's judgment. To be independent the non-executive directors generally should not, for example, be a customer, ex-employee, supplier, or friend of the founding family or the chief executive.

4 The latest version is available at www.frc.org.uk/corporate/ukcgcode.cfm.

Section I:

INVESTING IN PROJECTS

2

STATE-OF-THE-ART PROJECT APPRAISAL TECHNIQUES

Introduction

Shareholders supply funds to a firm for a reason. That reason, generally, is to receive a return on their precious resources. The return is generated by management using the finance provided to invest in real assets. It is vital for the health of the firm and the economic welfare of the finance providers that management employ the best techniques available when analyzing which of all the possible investment opportunities will give the best return.

Someone (or a group) within the organization may have to take the bold decision as to whether:

- it is better to build a new factory or extend the old;
- it is wiser to use an empty piece of land for a multi-storey car park or to invest a larger sum and build a shopping centre;
- whether shareholders would be better off if the firm returned their money in the form of dividends because shareholders can obtain a better return elsewhere; or
- the firm should pursue its expansion plan and invest in that new chain of hotels, or that large car showroom, or the new football stand.

These sorts of decisions require not only brave people, but informed people; individuals of the required calibre need to be informed about a range of issues: for example, the market environment and level of demand for the proposed activity, the internal environment, culture and capabilities of the firm, the types and levels of cost elements in the proposed area of activity, and, of course, an understanding of the risk and uncertainty appertaining to the project.

The Panama Canal Authority presumably considered all these factors before making its £2.81bn investment (Exhibit 2.1).

Bravery, information, knowledge and a sense of proportion are all essential ingredients when undertaking the onerous task of investing other people's money, but there is another element which is also crucial: that is, the employment of an investment appraisal technique which leads to the 'correct' decision; a technique which takes into account the fundamental considerations.

This chapter examines two approaches to evaluating investments within the firm. Both emphasize the central importance of the concept of the time value of money and are thus described as discounted cash flow (DCF) techniques. Net present value (NPV) and internal rate of return (IRR) are in common usage in most large commercial organizations and are regarded as more complete than the traditional techniques of payback and accounting rate of return (e.g. return on capital employed – ROCE). The relative merits and demerits of these alternative methods are discussed in Chapter 3. This chapter concentrates on gaining an understanding of how net present value and internal rate of return are calculated, as well as their theoretical under-pinnings.

Panama plan – a bigger canal can bring east and west closer

Robert Wright

While all the container ships in service before 1990 could fit through the canal's locks, nearly half those on order now are too large. And the canal is clogged with vessels: those that have not booked long in advance must often wait four days to get through.

But in 2014, a century after the opening, Panama should have a chance to celebrate properly. If a referendum on Sunday passes, which looks likely, an expansion to the canal should be completed around that year.

For the first time, it would accommodate a vessel more than 295 metres long and 33 metres wide – its current maximum.

... Panamax container carriers, as the largest ships that can use the present canal are known, carry at most 5,000 twenty-foot equivalent units (TEUs) of containers. On other routes some container ships now have more than twice that capacity ...

The canal authority wants to build a lane of locks, each 427m long by 55m wide. Three would lift ships up to the summit level while another three would lower them again at the other side. Some approach channels would be dredged deeper, while the water level in the summit would be raised, to increase the depth of the Culebra Cut. It says the programme will cost $5.25bn (£2.81bn, €4.18bn), to be funded by higher tolls for canal users.

EXHIBIT 2.1

Source: *Financial Times* 20 October 2006, p. 15.

How do you know whether an investment generates value for shareholders?

If we accept that the objective of investment within the firm is to create value for its owners then the purpose of allocating money to a particular division or project is to generate a cash inflow in the future, significantly greater than the amount invested. Put most simply, the project appraisal decision is one involving the comparison of the amount of cash put into an investment with the amount of cash returned. The key phrase and the tricky issue is 'significantly greater than'. For instance, would you, as part-owner of a firm, be content if that firm asked you to swap £10,000 of your hard-earned money for some new shares so that the management team could invest it only to hand back to you, in five years, the £10,000 plus £1,000? Is this a significant return? Would you feel that your wealth had been enhanced if you were aware that by investing the £10,000 yourself, by, for instance, lending to the government, you could have received a 5 percent return per year? Or that you could obtain a return of 15 percent per annum by investing in

> The project appraisal decision is one involving the comparison of the amount of cash put into an investment with the amount of cash returned.

other shares on the stock market? Naturally, you would feel let down by a management team that offered a return of less than 2 percent per year when you had alternative courses of action that would have produced much more.

This line of thought is leading us to a central concept in finance and, indeed, in business generally – the time value of money. Investors have alternative uses for their funds and they therefore have an opportunity cost if money is invested in a corporate project. The *investor's opportunity cost* is the sacrifice of the return available on the best forgone alternative.

> The investor's opportunity cost is the sacrifice of the return available on the best forgone alternative.

Investments must generate at least enough cash for all investors to obtain their required returns. If they produce less than the investor's opportunity cost then the wealth of shareholders will decline.

Figure 2.1 summarizes the process of good investment appraisal. The achievement of value or wealth creation is determined not only by the future cash flows to be derived from a project but also by the timing of those cash flows and by making an allowance for the fact that time has value.

Time is money

When people undertake to set aside money for investment something has to be given up now. For instance, if someone buys shares in a firm or lends to a business there is a sacrifice of consumption. One of the incentives to save is the possibility of gaining a higher level of future consumption by sacrificing some present consumption. So, some compensation is required to induce people to make a consumption sacrifice. Compensation will be required for at least three things:

- **Impatience to consume** That is, individuals generally prefer to have £1.00 today than £1.00 in five years' time. To put this formally: the utility of £1.00 now is greater than £1.00 received five years hence. Individuals are predisposed towards *impatience to consume* – they need an appropriate reward to begin the saving process. The rate of exchange between certain future consumption and certain current consumption is the *pure rate of interest* –

FIGURE 2.1

Investment appraisal: objective, inputs and process

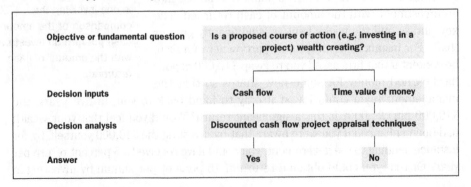

this occurs even in a world of no inflation and no risk. If you lived in such a world you might be willing to sacrifice £100 of consumption now if you were compensated with say £102.30 to be received in one year. This would mean that your *pure rate of interest* is 2.3 percent.

■ **Inflation** The price of time (or the interest rate needed to compensate for impatience to consume) exists even when there is no inflation, simply because people generally prefer consumption now to consumption later. If there is inflation then the providers of finance will have to be compensated for that loss in purchasing power as well as for time.

■ **Risk** The promise of the receipt of a sum of money some years hence generally carries with it an element of risk; the pay-out may not take place or the amount may be less than expected. Risk simply means that the future return has a variety of possible values. The issuer of a security, whether it be a share, a bond or a bank account, must be prepared to compensate the investor for impatience to consume, inflation and risk involved, otherwise no one will be willing to buy the security.

Take the case of Mrs Ann Investor who is considering a £1,000 one-year investment and requires compensation for three elements of time value. First, a return of 2.3 percent is required for the pure time value of money. Second, inflation is anticipated to be 3 percent over the year. Thus, at time zero (t_0) £1,000 buys one basket of goods and services. To buy the same basket of goods and services at time t_1 (one year later) £1,030 is needed. To compensate the investor for impatience to consume and inflation the investment needs to generate a return of 5.37 percent, that is:

$$(1 + 0.023)(1 + 0.03) - 1 = 0.0537$$

The figure of 5.37 percent may be regarded here as the risk-free return (RFR), the interest rate that is sufficient to induce investment assuming no uncertainty about the future cash flows.

Investors tend to view lending to reputable governments through the purchase of bonds or bills as the nearest they are going to get to risk-free investing, because these institutions have unlimited ability to raise income from taxes or to create money. The RFR forms the bedrock for time value of money calculations as the pure time value and the expected inflation rate affect all investments equally. Whether the investment is in property, bonds, shares or a factory, if expected inflation rises from 3 to 5 percent, then the investor's required return on all investments will increase by 2 percent.

However, different investment categories carry different degrees of uncertainty about the outcome of the investment. For instance, an investment on the Russian stock market, with its high volatility, may be regarded as more risky than the purchase of a share in AstraZeneca with its steady growth prospects. Investors require different risk premiums on top of the RFR to reflect the perceived level of extra risk. Thus:

$$\text{Required return} \quad = \quad \underset{\text{(Time value of money)}}{\text{RFR}} \quad + \quad \text{Risk premium}$$

In the case of Mrs Ann Investor, the risk premium pushes up the total return required to, say, 9 percent giving full compensation for all three elements of the time value of money.

Discounted cash flow

The net present value and internal rate of return techniques discussed in the rest of the chapter, both being discounted cash flow methods, take into account the time value of money. Table 2.1, which presents Project Alpha, suggests that on a straightforward analysis, Project Alpha generates more cash inflows than outflows. An outlay of £2,000 produces £2,400.

TABLE 2.1
Project Alpha, simple cash flow

Points in time (yearly intervals)	Cash flows (£)
0 Now	–2,000
1 (1 year from now)	+600
2	+600
3	+600
4	+600

However, we may be foolish to accept Project Alpha on the basis of this crude methodology. The £600 cash flows occur at different times, so are worth different amounts to a person standing at time zero. Quite naturally, such an individual would value the £600 received in one year more highly than the £600 received after four years. In other words, the present value of the pounds (at time zero) depends on when they are received.

It would be useful to convert all these different 'qualities' of pounds to a common currency, to some sort of common denominator. The conversion process is achieved by discounting all future cash flows by the time value of money, thereby expressing them as an equivalent amount received at time zero. The process of discounting relies on a variant of the compounding formula:

$$F = P(1+i)^n$$

where F = future value

           P = present value

           i = interest rate

           n = number of years over which compounding takes place

Note: It will be most important for many readers to turn to Appendix 2.1 at this point to get to grips with the key mathematical tools that will be used in this chapter and throughout the rest of the book.

If a saver deposited £100 in a bank account paying interest at 8 percent per annum, after three years the account will contain £125.97:

$$F = 100 (1 + 0.08)^3 = £125.97$$

This formula can be changed so that we can answer the following question: 'How much must I deposit in the bank now to receive £125.97 in three years?'

$$P = \frac{F}{(1 + i)^n} \quad \text{or} \quad F \times \frac{1}{(1 + i)^n}$$

$$P = \frac{125.97}{(1 + 0.08)^3} = 100$$

In this second case we have *discounted* the £125.97 back to a present value of £100. If this technique is now applied to Project Alpha to convert all the money cash flows of future years into their present value equivalents the result is as in Table 2.2 (assuming that the time value of money is 19 percent).

TABLE 2.2
Project Alpha, discounted cash flow

Points in time (yearly intervals)	Cash flows (£)	Discounted cash flows (£)
0	−2,000	−2,000.00
1	+600	$\frac{600}{1 + 0.19} = +504.20$
2	+600	$\frac{600}{(1 + 0.19)^2} = +423.70$
3	+600	$\frac{600}{(1 + 0.19)^3} = +356.05$
4	+600	$\frac{600}{(1 + 0.19)^4} = +299.20$

When these future pounds are converted to a common denominator, this investment involves a larger outflow (£2,000) than inflow (£1,583.15). In other words the return on the £2,000 is less than 19 percent.

Technical aside

If your calculator has a 'powers' function (usually represented by x^y or y^x) then compounding and discounting can be accomplished relatively quickly. Alternatively, you may obtain discount factors from the table in Appendix II at the end of the book. If we take the discounting of the fourth year's cash flow for Alpha as an illustration:

Calculator:

$$\frac{1}{(1 + 0.19)^4} \times 600$$

Input 1.19

Press y^x (or x^y) or ^

Input 4

Press =

Display 2.0053

Press $1/_x$

Display 0.4987

Multiply by 600

Answer 299.20.

Using Appendix II, look down the column 19% and along the row 4 years to find discount factor of 0.4987:

0.4987 × 600 = 299.20

State-of-the-art technique 1: net present value

The conceptual justification for, and the mathematics of, the net present value method of project appraisal will be illustrated through an imaginary but realistic decision-making process at the firm of Hard Decisions plc. This example, in addition to describing the technique, demonstrates the centrality of some key concepts such as opportunity cost and time value of money and shows the wealth-destroying effect of ignoring these issues.

Imagine you are the finance director of a large publicly quoted company called Hard Decisions plc. The board of directors agreed that the objective of the firm should be shareholder weath-maximization. Recently, the board appointed a new director, Mr Brightspark, as an 'ideas' man. He has a reputation as someone who can see opportunities where others see only problems. He has been hired especially to seek out new avenues for expansion and make better use of existing assets. In the past few weeks Mr Brightspark has been looking at some land that the company owns near the centre of Birmingham. This is a ten-acre site on which the flagship factory of the firm once stood; but that was 30 years ago and the site is now derelict. Mr Brightspark announces to a board meeting that he has three alternative proposals concerning the ten-acre site.

Mr Brightspark stands up to speak: Proposal 1 is to spend £5m clearing the site, cleaning it up, and decontaminating it. [The factory that stood on the site was used for chemical production.] It would then be possible to sell the ten acres to property developers for a sum of £12m in one year's time. Thus, we will make a profit of £7m over a one-year period.

Proposal 1: Clean up and sell – Mr Brightspark's figures

Clearing the site plus decontamination payable, t_0	–£5m
Sell the site in one year, t_1	£12m
Profit	£7m

The chairman of the board stops Mr Brightspark at that point and turns to you, in your capacity as the financial expert on the board, to ask what you think of the first proposal. Because you have studied your *Handbook of Corporate Finance* assiduously you are able to make the following observations:

- **Point 1** This company is valued by the stock market at £100m because our investors are content that the rate of return they receive from us is consistent with the going rate for our risk class of shares; that is, 15 percent per annum. In other words, the opportunity cost for our shareholders of buying shares in this firm is 15 percent. (Hard Decisions is an all-equity firm, no debt capital has been raised.) The alternative to investing their money with us is to invest it in another firm with similar risk characteristics yielding 15 percent per annum. Thus, we may take this *opportunity cost of capital* as our minimum required return from any project we undertake. This idea of opportunity cost can perhaps be better explained by the use of a diagram (*see* Figure 2.2).

FIGURE 2.2

The investment decision: alternative uses of firm's funds

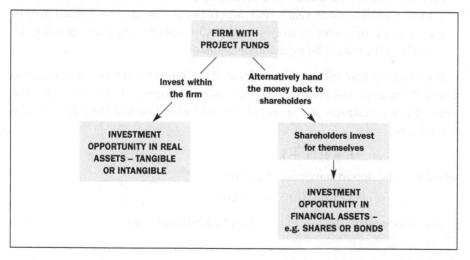

If we give a return of less than 15 percent then shareholders will lose out because they can obtain 15 percent elsewhere, so will suffer an opportunity cost.

We, as managers of shareholders' money, need to use a discount rate of 15 percent for any project of the same risk class that we analyze. The discount rate is the opportunity cost of investing in the project rather than the capital markets, for example, buying shares in other firms giving a 15 percent return. Instead of accepting this project the firm can always give the cash to the shareholders and let them invest it in financial assets.

■ **Point 2** I believe I am right in saying that we have received numerous offers for the ten-acre site over the past year. A reasonable estimate of its immediate sale value would be £6m. That is, I could call up one of the firms keen to get its hands on the site and squeeze out a price of about £6m. This £6m is an opportunity cost of the project, in that it is the value of the best alternative course of action. Thus, we should add to Mr Brightspark's £5m of clean-up costs, the £6m of opportunity cost because we are truly sacrificing £11m to put this proposal into operation. If we did not go ahead with Mr Brightspark's plan, but sold the site as it is, we could raise our bank balance by £6m, plus the £5m saved by not paying clean-up costs.

Proposal 1: Clean up and sell – Time t_0 cash flows

Immediate sale value (opportunity cost)	£6m
Clean up, etc.	£5m
Total sacrifice at t_0	£11m

■ **Point 3** I can accept Mr Brightspark's final sale price of £12m as being valid in the sense that he has, I know, employed some high quality experts to do the sum, but I do have a problem with comparing the initial outlay *directly* with the final cash flow on a simple *nominal* sum basis. The £12m is to be received in one year's time, whereas the £5m is to be handed over to the clean-up firm immediately, and the £6m opportunity cost sacrifice, by not selling the site, is being made immediately.

If we were to take the £11m initial cost of the project and invest it in financial assets of the same risk class as this firm, giving a return of 15 percent, then the value of that investment at the end of one year would be £12.65m. The calculation for this:

$$F = P(1 + k)$$

where k = the opportunity cost of capital:

$$11(1 + 0.15) = £12.65m$$

This is more than the return promised by Mr Brightspark.

Another way of looking at this problem is to calculate the net present value of the project. We start with the classic formula for net present value:

$$NPV = CF_0 + \frac{CF_1}{(1 + k)^n}$$

where CF_0 = cash flow at time zero (t_0), and

CF_1 = cash flow at time one (t_1), one year after time zero

n = number of years from the present for that cash flow – in this case, one:

$$NPV = -11 + \frac{12}{1 + 0.15} = -11 + 10.43 = -\pounds0.565m$$

All cash flows are expressed in the common currency of pounds at time zero. Everything is in present value terms. When the positives and negatives are netted out we have the *net* present value. The decision rules for net present value are:

$NPV \geqslant 0$	Accept
$NPV < 0$	Reject

Project proposal 1's negative NPV indicates that a return of less than 15 percent per annum will be achieved.

An investment proposal's net present value is derived by discounting the future net cash receipts at a rate which reflects the value of the alternative use of the funds, summing them over the life of the proposal and deducting the initial outlay.

In conclusion, ladies and gentlemen, given the choice between:

(a) selling the site immediately raising £6m and saving £5m of expenditure – a total of £11m, or

(b) developing the site along the lines of Mr Brightspark's proposal,

I would choose to sell it immediately because £11m would get a better return elsewhere.

The chairman thanks you and asks Mr Brightspark to explain Project Proposal 2. Proposal 2 consists of paying £5m immediately for a clean-up. Then, over the next two years, spending another £14m building an office complex. Tenants would not be found immediately on completion of the building. The office units would be let gradually over the following three years. Finally, when the office complex is fully let, in six years' time, it would be sold to an institution, such as a pension fund, for the sum of £40m (*see* Table 2.3).

Mr Brightspark claims an almost doubling of the money invested (£25m invested over the first two years leads to an inflow of £47m). The chairman turns to you and asks: Is this project really so beneficial to our shareholders?

TABLE 2.3
Proposal 2: Office complex – Mr Brightspark's figures

Points in time (yearly intervals)	Cash flows (£m)	Event
0 (now)	−5	Clean-up costs
0 (now)	−6	Opportunity cost
1	−4	Building cost
2	−10	Building cost
3	+1	Net rental income, $\frac{1}{4}$ of offices let
4	+2	Net rental income, $\frac{1}{2}$ of offices let
5	+4	Net rental income, all offices let
6	+40	Office complex sold
TOTAL	+22	Inflow £47m
		Outflow £25m
PROFIT	£22m	

Note: Mr Brightspark has accepted the validity of your argument about the opportunity cost of the alternative 'project' of selling the land immediately and has quickly added this −£6m to the figures.

You reply: The message rammed home to me by my finance book was that the best method of assessing whether a project is shareholder wealth enhancing is to discount all its cash flows at the opportunity cost of capital. This will enable a calculation of the net present value of those cash flows.

$$NPV = CF_0 + \frac{CF_1}{1 + k} + \frac{CF_2}{(1 + k)^2} + \frac{CF_3}{(1 + k)^3} \cdots + \frac{CF_n}{(1 + k)^n}$$

So, given that Mr Brightspark's figures are true cash flows, I can calculate the NPV of Proposal 2 – *see* Table 2.4.

Because the NPV is less than 0, we would serve our shareholders better by selling the site and saving the money spent on clearing and building and putting that money into financial assets yielding 15 percent per annum. Shareholders would end up with more in Year 6.

The chairman thanks you and asks Mr Brightspark for his third proposal. Proposal 3 involves the use of the site for a factory to manufacture the product 'Worldbeater'. Mr Brightspark says we have been producing 'Worldbeater' from our Liverpool factory for the past ten years. Despite its name, we have confined the selling of it to the UK market. I propose the setting up of a second 'Worldbeater' factory which will serve the European market. The figures are as follows (*see* Table 2.5).

TABLE 2.4

Proposal 2: Net present value

Points in time (yearly intervals)	Cash flows (£m)		Discounted cash flows (£m)
0	−5		−5
0	−6		−6
1	−4	$\dfrac{-4}{(1 + 0.15)}$	−3.48
2	−10	$\dfrac{-10}{(1 + 0.15)^2}$	−7.56
3	1	$\dfrac{1}{(1 + 0.15)^3}$	0.66
4	2	$\dfrac{2}{(1 + 0.15)^4}$	1.14
5	4	$\dfrac{4}{(1 + 0.15)^5}$	1.99
6	40	$\dfrac{40}{(1 + 0.15)^6}$	17.29
Net present value			**−0.96**

TABLE 2.5

Proposal 3: Manufacture of 'Worldbeater' – Mr Brightspark's figures

Points in time (yearly intervals)	Cash flows (£m)	Event
0	−5	Clean-up
0	−6	Opportunity cost
1	−10	Factory building
2	0	Net cash flows from operating
3 to infinity	+5	Net cash flows from additional sales of 'Worldbeater'

Note: Revenue is gained in Year 2 from sales but this is exactly offset by the cash flows created by the costs of production and distribution. The figures for Year 3 and all subsequent years are net cash flows, that is, cash outflows are subtracted from cash inflows generated by sales.

The chairman turns to you and asks your advice.

You reply: Worldbeater is a well-established product and has been very successful. I am happy to take the cash flow figures given by Mr Brightspark as the basis for my calculations, which are as follows (*see* Table 2.6).

TABLE 2.6

Proposal 3: Worldbeater Net Present Value

Points in time (yearly intervals)	Cash flows (£m)		Discounted cash flows (£m)
0	−11		−11
1	−10	$\dfrac{-10}{(1 + 0.15)}$	−8.7
2	0		
3 to infinity	5	Value of perpetuity at time t_2: $$P = \frac{F}{k} = \frac{5}{0.15} = 33.33.$$ This 33.33 has to be discounted back two years: $$\frac{33.33}{(1 + 0.15)^2}$$	= 25.20
Net present value			+ 5.5

Note: The perpetuity formula can be used on the assumption that the first payment arises one year from the time at which we are valuing. So, if the first inflow arises at time 3 we are valuing the perpetuity as though we are standing at time 2. The objective of this exercise is not to convert all cash flows to time 2 values, but rather to time 0 value. Therefore, it is necessary to discount the perpetuity value by two years. (If these calculations are confusing you are advised to read the mathematical Appendix 2.1 at the end of this chapter.)

This project gives an NPV that is positive, so is shareholder wealth enhancing because it gives a rate of return that is greater than 15 percent per annum. It provides a return of 15 percent plus a present value of £5.5m. Based on these figures I would recommend that the board examine Proposal 3 in more detail.

The chairman thanks you and suggests that this proposal be put to the vote.

Mr Brightspark (interrupts): Just a minute, are we not taking a lot on trust here? Our finance expert has stated that the way to evaluate these proposals is by using the NPV method, but in the firms where I have worked in the past, the internal rate of return (IRR) method of investment appraisal was used. I would like to see how these three proposals shape up when the IRR calculations are done.

The chairman turns to you and asks you to explain the IRR method, and to apply it to the figures provided by Mr Brightspark ...

Before continuing this boardroom drama it might be useful at this point to broaden the understanding of NPV by considering two worked examples.

Worked example 2.1
CAMRAT PLC

Camrat plc requires a return on investment of at least 10% per annum over the life of a project to meet the opportunity cost of its shareholders (Camrat is financed entirely by equity). The dynamic and thrusting strategic development team have been examining the possibility of entering the new market area of mosaic floor tiles. This will require an immediate outlay of £1m for factory purchase and tooling-up which will be followed by *net* (i.e. after all cash outflows (wages, variable costs, etc.)) cash inflows of £0.2m in one year, and £0.3m in two years' time. Thereafter, annual net cash inflows will be £180,000.

Required

Given these cash flows, will this investment provide a 10% return (per annum) over the life of the project? Assume for simplicity that all cash flows arise on anniversary dates.

Answer

First, lay out the cash flows with precise timing. (Note: the assumption that all cash flows arise on anniversary dates allows us to do this very simply.)

Points in time (yearly intervals)	0	1	2	3 to infinity
Cash flows (£)	−1m	0.2m	0.3m	0.18m

Second, discount these cash flows to their present value equivalents.

Points in time	0	1	2	3 to infinity
	CF_0	$\dfrac{CF_1}{1+k}$	$\dfrac{CF_2}{(1+k)^n}$	$\dfrac{CF_3}{k} \times \dfrac{1}{(1+k)^2}$
	−1m	$\dfrac{0.2}{1+0.1}$	$\dfrac{0.3}{(1+0.1)^2}$	$\dfrac{0.18}{0.1}$

This discounts back two years:

$$\frac{0.18/0.1}{(1+0.1)^2}$$

| | −1m | 0.1818 | 0.2479 | $\dfrac{1.8}{(1.1)^2} = 1.4876$ |

Third, net out the discounted cash flows to give the net present value.

$$-1.0000$$
$$+0.1818$$
$$+0.2479$$
$$+1.4876$$

Net present value $+0.9173$

Conclusion

The positive NPV result demonstrates that this project gives not only a return of 10% per annum but a large surplus above and beyond a 10% per annum return. This is an extremely attractive project: on a £1m investment the surplus generated beyond the opportunity cost of the shareholders (their time value of money) is £917,300; by accepting this project we would increase shareholder wealth by this amount.

Worked example 2.2
ACTARM PLC

Actarm plc is examining two projects, A and B. The cash flows are as follows:

	A £	B £
Initial outflow, t_0	240,000	240,000
Cash inflows:		
Time 1 (one year after t_0)	200,000	20,000
Time 2	100,000	120,000
Time 3	20,000	220,000

Using discount rates of 8%, and then 16%, calculate the NPVs and state which project is superior. Why do you get a different preference depending on the discount rate used?

Answer

Using 8% as the discount rate:

$$NPV = CF_0 + \frac{CF_1}{1+k} + \frac{CF_2}{(1+k)^2} + \frac{CF_3}{(1+k)^3}$$

Project A

$$-240,000 + \frac{200,000}{1+0.08} + \frac{100,000}{(1+0.08)^2} + \frac{20,000}{(1+0.08)^3}$$

$$-240,000 + 185,185 + 85,734 + 15,877 = +£46,796$$

Project B

$$-240,000 + \frac{20,000}{1 + 0.08} + \frac{120,000}{(1 + 0.08)^2} + \frac{220,000}{(1 + 0.08)^3}$$

–240,000 + 18,519 + 102,881 + 174,643 = +£56,043

Using an 8% discount rate, both projects produce positive NPVs so would enhance shareholder wealth. However, Project B is superior because it creates more value than Project A. If accepting one project excludes the possibility of accepting the other, then B is preferred.

Using 16% as the discount rate:

Project A

$$-240,000 + \frac{200,000}{1.16} + \frac{100,000}{(1.16)^2} + \frac{20,000}{(1.16)^3}$$

–240,000 + 172,414 + 74,316 + 12,813 = +£19,543

Project B

$$-240,000 + \frac{20,000}{1.16} + \frac{120,000}{(1.16)^2} + \frac{220,000}{(1.16)^3}$$

–240,000 + 17,241 + 89,180 + 140,945 = +£7,366

With a 16% discount rate Project A generates more shareholder value and so would be preferred to Project B. This is despite the fact that Project B, in pure undiscounted cash flow terms, produces an additional £40,000.

The different ranking (order of superiority) occurs because Project B has the bulk of its cash flows occurring towards the end of the project's life. These large distant cash flows, when discounted at a high discount rate, become relatively small compared with those of Project A, which has its high cash flows discounted by only one year. Obtaining the appropriate discount rate to use in calculations of this kind is discussed in Chapter 10.

Exhibit 2.2 shows that NPV is used by many people besides corporate finance teams.

Egdon egged on by positive gas storage tests

Neil Hume and Robert Orr

Egdon Resources jumped 36 percent to $134\frac{1}{2}$p as tests showed its site on the Isle of Portland in Dorset could be used as a giant underground gas storage facility ... house broker Seymour Pierce said the facility had a net present value equivalent to 341p a share and said it had 'no hesitation' in reiterating a 'buy' rating.

EXHIBIT 2.2

Source: *Financial Times* 29 June 2006.

State-of-the-art technique 2: internal rate of return

We now return to Hard Decisions plc. The chairman has asked you to explain internal rate of return (IRR).

You respond: The internal rate of return is a very popular method of project appraisal and it has much to commend it. In particular it takes into account the time value of money. I am not surprised to find that Mr Brightspark has encountered this appraisal technique in his previous employment. Basically, what the IRR tells you is the rate of interest you will receive by putting your money into a project. It describes by how much the cash inflows exceed the cash outflows on an annualized percentage basis, taking account of the timing of those cash flows.

The internal rate of return is the rate of return, r, that equates the present value of future cash flows with the outlay (or, for some projects, it equates discounted future cash outflows with initial inflow):

Outlay = Future cash flows discounted at rate r

Thus:

$$CF_0 = \frac{CF_1}{1+r} + \frac{CF_2}{(1+r)^2} + \frac{CF_3}{(1+r)^3} \cdots \frac{CF_n}{(1+r)^n}$$

IRR is also referred to as the 'yield' of a project.

Alternatively, the internal rate of return, r, is the discount rate at which the net present value is zero. It is the value for r that makes the following equation hold:

$$CF_0 + \frac{CF_1}{1+r} + \frac{CF_2}{(1+r)^2} + \frac{CF_3}{(1+r)^3} \cdots \frac{CF_n}{(1+r)^n} = 0$$

(*Note*: in the first formula CF_0 is expressed as a positive number, whereas in the second it is usually a negative.)

These two equations amount to the same thing. They both require knowledge of the cash flows and their precise timing. The element that is unknown is the rate of return that will make the time-adjusted outflows and inflows equal to each other.

I apologize, ladies and gentlemen, if this all sounds like too much jargon. Perhaps it would be helpful if you could see the IRR calculation in action. Let's apply the formula to Mr Brightspark's Proposal 1.

Proposal 1: Internal rate of return

Using the second version of the formula, our objective is to find an r that makes the discounted inflow at time 1 of £12m plus the initial £11m outflow equal to zero:

$$CF_0 + \frac{CF_1}{1+r} = 0$$

$$-11 + \frac{12}{1+r} = 0$$

The method I would recommend for establishing r is trial and error (assuming we do not have the relevant computer program available). So, to start with, simply pick an interest rate and plug it into the formula. Let's try 5 percent:

$$-11 + \frac{12}{1 + 0.05} = £0.42857m \text{ or } £428,571$$

A 5 percent rate is not correct because the discounted cash flows do not total to zero. The surplus of approximately £0.43m suggests that a higher interest rate will be more suitable. This will reduce the present value of the future cash inflow. Let's try 10 percent:

$$-11 + \frac{12}{1 + 0.1} = -£0.0909 \text{ or } -£90,909$$

Again, we have not hit on the correct discount rate. Let's try 9 percent:

$$-11 + \frac{12}{1 + 0.09} = +£0.009174 \text{ or } +£9,174$$

The last two calculations tell us that the interest rate that equates to the present value of the cash flows lies somewhere between 9 and 10 percent. The precise rate can be found through interpolation.

First, display all the facts so far established:

Discount rate, r	9%	?	10%
Net present value	+£9,174	0	−£90,909
Point	A	B	C

There is a yield rate (r) that lies between 9 and 10 percent that will produce an NPV of zero. The way to find that interest rate is to first find the distance between points A and B, as a proportion of the entire distance between points A and C.

$$\frac{A \to B}{A \to C} = \frac{9,174 - 0}{9,174 + 90,909} = 0.0917$$

The ? lies at a distance of 0.0917 away from the 9 percent point. IRR:

$$= 9 + \left(\frac{9,174}{100,083}\right) \times (10 - 9) = 9.0917 \text{ percent}$$

To check our result:

$$-11 + \frac{12}{1 + 0.090917}$$

$$-11 + 11 = 0$$

The IRR decision rules

The rule for internal rate of return decisions is:

- **If $k > r$ reject** If the opportunity cost of capital (k) is greater than the internal rate of return (r) on a project then the investor is better served by not going ahead with the project and applying the money to the best alternative use.

- **If $k \leq r$ accept** Here, the project under consideration produces the same or a higher yield than investment elsewhere for a similar risk level.

The IRR of Proposal 1 is 9.091 percent, which is below the 15 percent opportunity cost of capital used by Hard Decisions plc. Using the IRR method as well as the NPV method, this project should be rejected.

It might be enlightening to consider the relationship between NPV and IRR. Table 2.7 shows what happens to NPV as the discount rate is varied between zero and 10 percent for Proposal 1. At a zero discount rate the £12m received in one year is not discounted at all, so the NPV of £1m is simply the difference between the two cash flows. When the discount rate is raised to 10 percent the present value of the Year 1 cash flow becomes less than the current outlay. Where the initial outflow equals the *discounted* future inflows, i.e. when NPV is zero, we can read off the internal rate of return.

TABLE 2.7

The relationship between NPV and the discount rate (using Proposal 1's figures)

Discount rate (%)	NPV
10	–90,909
9.0917	0
9	9,174
8	111,111
7	214,953
6	320,755
5	428,571
4	538,461
3	650,485
2	764,706
1	881,188
0	1,000,000

Proposal 2: IRR

To calculate the IRR for Proposal 2 we first lay out the cash flows in the discount formula:

$$-11 + \frac{-4}{(1+r)} + \frac{-10}{(1+r)^2} + \frac{1}{(1+r)^3} + \frac{2}{(1+r)^4} + \frac{4}{(1+r)^5} + \frac{40}{(1+r)^6} = 0$$

Then we try alternative discount rates to find a rate, r, that gives a zero NPV:

Try 14 percent:

NPV (approx.) = –£0.043 or –£43,000

At 13 percent:

NPV = £932,000

Interpolation is required to find an internal rate of return accurate to at least one decimal place:

Discount rate r	13%	?	14%
NPV	+932,000	0	–43,000

$$13 + \frac{932,000}{975,000} \times (14 - 13) = 13.96\%$$

This project produces an IRR (13.96%), which is less than the opportunity cost of shareholders' funds (15%); so it should be rejected under the IRR method.

FIGURE 2.3

Graph of NPV for Proposal 2 when different discount rates are used

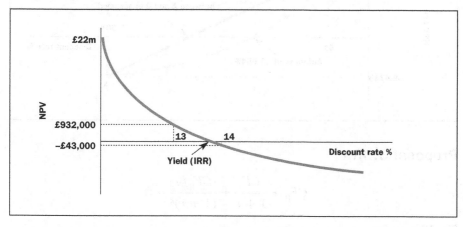

Because the line in Figure 2.3 is curved, it is important to have only a fairly small gap in trial and error interest rates prior to interpolation. The interpolation formula assumes a straight line between the two discount rates chosen. The effect of taking a wide range of interest rates can be illustrated if we calculate on the basis of 5 and 30 percent.

At 5%, NPV of Project 2 = £11.6121m.

At 30%, NPV of Project 2 = –£9.4743m.

Linear interpolation

Discount rate

r	5%	?	30%
NPV	+11.6121	0	–9.4743

$$5 + \left(\frac{11.6121}{11.6121 + 9.4743} \right) (30 - 5) = 18.77\%$$

The non-linearity of the relationship between NPV and the discount rate has created an IRR almost 5 percent removed from the true IRR – *see* Figure 2.4. This could lead to an erroneous acceptance of this project given the company's hurdle rate of 15 percent. In reality this project yields less than the company could earn by placing its money elsewhere for the same risk level.

FIGURE 2.4

Proposal 2: Graph of NPV using two extreme discount rates and interpolation between them

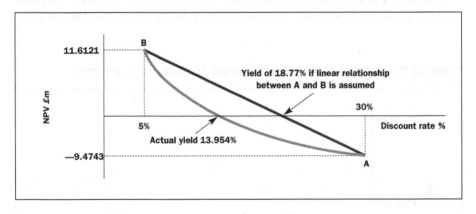

Proposal 3: IRR

$$CF_0 + \frac{CF_1}{1 + r} + \frac{CF_3/r}{(1 + r)^2} = 0$$

Try 19 percent:

$$-11 + \frac{-10}{1 + 0.19} + \frac{5/0.19}{(1 + 0.19)^2} = -\pounds0.82m$$

Try 18 percent:

$$-11 + \frac{-10}{1 + 0.18} + \frac{5/0.18}{(1 + 0.18)^2} = +\pounds0.475m$$

Linear interpolation

r	18%	?	19%
NPV	+475,000	0	–820,000

$$18 + \frac{475,000}{1,295,000} \times (19 - 18) = 18.37\%$$

Project 3 produces an internal rate of return of 18.37 percent which is higher than the opportunity cost of capital and therefore is to be commended.

IRR is a commonly used metric in business. Gerald Ronson, one of the richest people in the property development business, uses it to make decisions – *see* Exhibit 2.3.

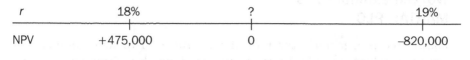

Bullish Ronson defies slump to carry on building apace

Daniel Thomas

Gerald Ronson strolls out of his Mercedes – the 'workhorse' he uses to cover 40,000 miles a year visiting his various projects in the UK – in front of his office building in Marylebone looking every inch the fighter that his reputation makes out.

He's in characteristically bullish mood. Heron, the property company he started with his father in 1965, is in robust health considering the extent of the property slump, which has wiped out the value of some properties by half over the past two years.

Heron, partly because it sold its UK investments and partly because European markets have performed relatively well, has held its net asset value almost static, and is looking for opportunities.

Mr Ronson says that most deals cross his large mahogany desk early on, but so far there have been few of interest. He has almost £140m to spend when the time is right.

'There will be interesting opportunities over the next 18–24 months but I have yet to see a deal that I consider we want to do. This is not the time to overpay, and you need to see a respectable return. We [want] to see a return over 20 percent on an IRR basis with low gearing,' he adds.

EXHIBIT 2.3

Source: *Financial Times* 4 June 2009, p. 23.

We temporarily leave the saga of Mr Brightspark and his proposals to reinforce understanding of NPV and IRR through the worked example of Martac plc.

Worked example 2.3
MARTAC PLC

Martac plc is a manufacturer of *Martac-aphro*. Two new automated process machines used in the production of Martac have been introduced to the market, the CAM and the ATR. Both will give cost savings over existing processes:

	CAM £000s	ATR £000s
Initial cost (machine purchase and installation, etc.)	120	250
Cash flow savings:		
At Time 1 (one year after the initial cash outflow)	48	90
At Time 2	48	90
At Time 3	48	90
At Time 4	48	90

All other factors remain constant and the firm has access to large amounts of capital. The required return on projects is 8%. Production ceases after four years and the machines will then have a zero scrap value.

Required:

(a) Calculate the IRR for CAM.
(b) Calculate the IRR for ATR.
(c) Based on IRR which machine would you purchase?
(d) Calculate the NPV for each machine.
(e) Based on NPV which machine would you buy?
(f) Is IRR or NPV the better decision tool?

Answers

In this problem the total cash flows associated with the alternative projects are not given. Instead the incremental cash flows are provided, for example, the additional savings available over the existing costs of production. This, however, is sufficient for a decision to be made about which machine to purchase.

(a) IRR for CAM

$$CF_0 + \frac{CF_1}{1 + r} + \frac{CF_2}{(1 + r)^2} + \frac{CF_3}{(1 + r)^3} + \frac{CF_4}{(1 + r)^4} = 0$$

Try 22%:

$-120,000 + 48,000 \times$ annuity factor (af) for 4 years @ 22%

(*See* Appendix 2.1 (p. 66) for annuity calculations and Appendix III (p. 671) for an annuity table.)

The annuity factor tells us the present value of four lots of £1 received at four annual intervals. This is 2.4936, meaning that the £4 in present value terms is worth just over £2.49.

$$-120,000 + 48,000 \times 2.4936 = -£307$$

Try 21%:

$$-120,000 + 48,000 \times \text{annuity factor (af) for 4 years @ 21\%}$$

$$-120,000 + 48,000 \times 2.5404 = +£1,939$$

Interpolation

Discount rate

	21%	?	22%
NPV	1,939	0	−307

$$21 + \left(\frac{1939}{1939 + 307} \right)(22 - 21) = 21.86\%$$

(b) IRR for ATR

Try 16%:

$$-250,000 + 90,000 \times 2.7982 = +£1,838$$

Try 17%:

$$-250,000 + 90,000 \times 2.7432 = -£3,112$$

Discount rate, r

	16%	?	17%
NPV	+1,838	0	−3,112

$$16 + \left(\frac{1,838}{1,838 + 3,112} \right) \times (17-16) = 16.37\%$$

(c) Choice of machine on basis of IRR

If IRR is the only decision tool available then as long as the IRRs exceed the discount rate (or cost of capital) the project with the higher IRR might appear to be the preferred choice. In this case CAM ranks higher than ATR.

(d) NPV for machines: CAM

$$-120,000 + 48,000 \times 3.3121 = +£38,981$$

NPV for ATR

$$-250,000 + 90,000 \times 3.3121 = +£48,089$$

(e) Choice of machine on basis of NPV

ATR generates a return which has a present value of £48,089 in addition to the minimum return on capital required. This is larger than for CAM and therefore ATR ranks higher than CAM if NPV is used as the decision tool.

(f) Choice of decision tool

This problem has produced conflicting decision outcomes, which depend on the project appraisal method employed. NPV is the better decision-making technique because it measures in absolute amounts of money. That is, it gives the increase in shareholder wealth available by accepting a project. In contrast, IRR expresses its return as a percentage which may result in an inferior low-scale project being preferred to a higher-scale project. So, if you cannot undertake both projects the one that returns most to shareholders is the one with the highest NPV rather than the highest IRR.

Choosing between NPV and IRR

We now return to Hard Decisions plc.

Mr Brightspark: I have noticed your tendency to prefer NPV to any other method. Yet, in the three projects we have been discussing, NPV and IRR give the same decision recommendation. That is, reject Projects 1 and 2, and accept Project 3. So, why not use IRR more often?

You reply: It is true that the NPV and IRR methods of capital investment appraisal are closely related. Both are 'time-adjusted' measures of profitability. The NPV and IRR methods gave the same result in the cases we have considered today because the problems associated with the IRR method are not present in the figures we have been working with. In the appraisal of other projects we may encounter the severe limitations of the IRR method and therefore I prefer to stick to the theoretically superior NPV technique.

I will illustrate two of the most important problems, multiple solutions and ranking.

Multiple solutions

There may be a number of possible IRRs. This can be explained by examining the problems Mr Flummoxed is having (*see* Worked example 2.4).

Worked example 2.4
MR FLUMMOXED

Mr Flummoxed of Deadhead plc has always used the IRR method of project appraisal. He has started to have doubts about its usefulness after examining the proposal for 'Project Oscillation'.

Project oscillation

Points in time (yearly intervals)	0	1	2
Cash flow	–3,000	+15,000	–13,000

Internal rates of return are found at 11.56% and 288.4%.

    Given that Deadhead plc has a required rate of return of 20%, it is impossible to decide whether to implement Project Oscillation using an unadjusted IRR methodology.

The cause of multiple solutions is unconventional cash flows. Conventional cash flows occur when an outflow is followed by a series of inflows or a cash inflow is followed by a series of cash outflows. Unconventional cash flows are a series of cash flows with more than one change in sign. In the case of Project Oscillation the sign changes from negative to positive once, and from positive to negative once. Multiple yields can be adjusted for while still using the IRR method, but the simplest approach is to switch to the NPV method.

Ranking

The IRR decision rule does not always rank projects in the same way as NPV. Sometimes it is important to find out, not only which project gives a positive return, but which one gives the greater positive return. For instance, projects may be mutually exclusive, that is, only one may be undertaken and a choice has to be made. The use of IRR alone sometimes leads to a poor choice (*see* Table 2.7).

    It is clear that the ranking of the projects by their IRRs is constant at 75 and 100 percent, regardless of the opportunity cost of capital (discount rate). Project A is always better. On the other hand, ranking the projects by the NPV method is not fixed. The NPV ranking depends on the discount rate. If the discount rate used in the NPV calculation is higher than 50 percent, the ranking under both IRR and NPV would be the same, i.e. Project A is superior. If the discount rate falls below 50 percent, Project B is the better choice. One of the major elements leading to the theoretical dominance of NPV is that it takes into account the scale of investment; the shareholders are made better off by £20.87m by undertaking Project B because the initial size of the project is larger. NPVs are measured in absolute amounts.

TABLE 2.7

Illustration of the IRR ranking problem

Project	Cash flows £m		IRR%	NPV (at 15%)
	Time 0	One year later		
A	−20	+40	100%	+14.78m
B	−40	+70	75%	+20.87m

NPV at different discount rates

Discount rate (%)	Project A	Project B
0	20	30
20	13.33	18.33
50	6.67	6.67
75	2.86	0
100	0	−5
125	−2.22	−8.89

Conclusion

This chapter has provided insight into the key factors to consider when an organization is contemplating using financial (or other) resources for investment. The analysis has been based on the assumption that the objective of any such investment is to maximize economic benefits to the owners of the enterprise. To achieve such an objective requires allowance for the opportunity cost of capital or time value of money as well as robust analysis of relevant cash flows. Given that time has a value, the precise timing of cash flows is important for project analysis. The net present value (NPV) and internal rate of return (IRR) methods of project appraisal are both discounted cash flow techniques so allow for the time value of money. However, the IRR method does present problems in a few special circumstances and so the theoretically preferred method is NPV.

NPV requires diligent studying and thought to be fully understood, and therefore it is not surprising to find in the workplace a bias in favour of communicating a project's viability in terms of percentages. In fact, most large organizations use three or four methods of project appraisal, rather than rely on only one for both rigorous analysis and communication – *see* Chapter 3 for more detail. The fundamental conclusion of this chapter is that the best method to maximize shareholder wealth in assessing investment projects is net present value.

APPENDIX 2.1

Mathematical tools for finance

The purpose of this Appendix is to explain essential mathematical skills that are needed for the rest of the book. The author has no love of mathematics for its own sake so only those techniques of direct relevance to the subject matter of this textbook are covered in this section.

Simple and compound interest

When there are time delays between receipt and payment of financial sums we need to make use of the concepts of simple and compound interest.

Simple interest

Interest is paid only on the original principal. No interest is paid on the accumulated interest payments.

Example 1

Suppose that a sum of £10 is deposited in a bank account that pays 12 percent per annum. At the end of year 1 the investor has £11.20 in the account. That is:

$$F = P(1 + i)$$

$$11.20 = 10(1 + 0.12)$$

where F = Future value, P = Present value, i = Interest rate.
The initial sum, called the principal, is multiplied by the interest rate to give the annual return.
At the end of five years:

$$F = P(1 + in)$$

where n = number of years. Thus:

$$16 = 10(1 + 0.12 \times 5)$$

Note from the example that the 12 percent return is a constant amount each year. Interest is not earned on the interest already accumulated from previous years.

Compound interest

The more usual situation in the real world is for interest to be paid on the sum that accumulates – whether or not that sum comes from the principal or from the interest received in previous periods. Interest is paid on the accumulated interest and principal.

Example 2

An investment of £10 is made at an interest rate of 12 percent with the interest being compounded. In one year the capital will grow by 12 percent to £11.20. In the second year the capital will grow by 12 percent, but this time the growth will be on the accumulated value of £11.20 so will amount to an extra £1.34. At the end of two years:

$$F = P(1 + i)(1 + i)$$

$$F = 11.20(1 + i)$$

$$F = 12.54$$

Alternatively,

$$F = P(1 + i)^2$$

Table 2.8 displays the future value of £1 invested at a number of different interest rates and for alternative numbers of years. (This is an extract from Appendix I at the end of the book.)

From the second row of the table we can read that £1 invested for two years at 12 percent amounts to £1.2544. The investment of £10 provides a future capital sum 1.2544 times the original amount:

$$£10 \times 1.2544 = £12.544$$

TABLE 2.8

The future value of £1

	Interest rate (percent per annum)				
Year	1	2	5	12	15
1	1.0100	1.0200	1.0500	1.1200	1.1500
2	1.0201	1.0404	1.1025	1.2544	1.3225
3	1.0303	1.0612	1.1576	1.4049	1.5209
4	1.0406	1.0824	1.2155	1.5735	1.7490
5	1.0510	1.1041	1.2763	1.7623	2.0114

Over five years the result is:

$$F = P(1 + i)^n$$

$$17.62 = 10(1 + 0.12)^5$$

The interest on the accumulated interest is the difference between the total arising from simple interest and that from compound interest:

$$£17.62 - £16.00 = £1.62$$

Almost all investments pay compound interest and so we will be using this throughout the book.

Present values

There are many occasions in financial management when you are given the future sums and need to find out what they are worth in present value terms today. For example, you wish to know how much you would have to put aside today which will accumulate, with compounded interest, to a defined sum in the future; or you are given the choice between receiving £200 in five years or £100 now and wish to know which is the better option, given anticipated interest rates; or a project gives a return of £1m in three years for an outlay of £800,000 now and you need to establish if this is the best use of the £800,000. By the process of discounting a sum of money to be received in the future is given a monetary value today.

Example 3

If we anticipate the receipt of £17.62 in five years' time we can determine its present value. Rearrangement of the compound formula, and assuming a discount rate of 12 percent, gives:

$$P = \frac{F}{(1 + i)^n} \text{ or } P = F \times \frac{1}{(1 + i)^n}$$

$$10 = \frac{17.62}{(1 + 0.12)^5}$$

Alternatively, discount factors may be used, as shown in Table 2.9. (This is an extract from Appendix II at the end of the book.) The factor needed to discount £1 receivable in five years when the discount rate is 12 percent is 0.5674, so the present value of £17.62 is:

$$0.5674 \times £17.62 = £10$$

TABLE 2.9
The present value of £1

	Interest rate (percent per annum)				
Year	*1*	*5*	*10*	*12*	*15*
1	0.9901	0.9524	0.9091	0.8929	0.8696
2	0.9803	0.9070	0.8264	0.7972	0.7561
3	0.9706	0.8638	0.7513	0.7118	0.6575
4	0.9610	0.8227	0.6830	0.6355	0.5718
5	0.9515	0.7835	0.6209	0.5674	0.4972

Examining the present value table in Appendix II you can see that as the discount rate increases the present value goes down. Also the further into the future the money is to be received, the less valuable it is in today's terms. Distant cash flows discounted at a high rate have a small present value; for instance, £1,000 receivable in 20 years when the discount rate is 17 percent has a present value of £43.30. Viewed from another angle, if you invested £43.30 for 20 years it would accumulate to £1,000 if interest compounds at 17 percent.

Determining the rate of interest

Sometimes you want to calculate the rate of return that a project is earning. For instance, a savings company may offer to pay you £10,000 in five years if you deposit £8,000 now, when interest rates on accounts elsewhere are offering 6 percent per annum. To make a comparison you need to know the annual rate being offered by the savings company. We need to find i in the discounting equation.

To be able to calculate i it is necessary to rearrange the compounding formula. Since:

$$F = P(1 + i)^n$$

First, divide both sides by P:

$$F/P = (1 + i)^n$$

(The P on the right side cancels out.)

Second, take the root to the power n of both sides and subtract 1 from each side:

$$i = \sqrt[n]{[F/P]} - 1 \text{ or } i = [F/P]^{1/n} - 1$$

$$i = \sqrt[5]{£10,000 / £8,000} - 1 = 0.046 \text{ or } 4.6\%.$$

Not a good deal compared with other accounts offering 6%.

Example 4

In the case of a five-year investment requiring an outlay of £10 and having a future value of £17.62 the rate of return is:

$$i = \sqrt[5]{\frac{17.62}{10}} - 1 = 12\%$$

or

$$i = [17.62 / 10]^{\frac{1}{5}} - 1 = 12\%$$

Technical aside

You can use the $\sqrt[x]{y}$, the $\sqrt[y]{x}$ button, or a combination of y^x and $\frac{1}{x}$, depending on the calculator.

Alternatively, use the future value table, an extract of which is shown in Table 2.8. In our example, the return on £1 worth of investment over five years is:

$$\frac{17.62}{10} = 1.762$$

In the body of the future value table look at the Year 5 row for a future value of 1.762. Read off the interest rate of 12 percent.

An interesting application of this technique outside finance is to use it to put into perspective the pronouncements of politicians. For example in 1994, John Major made a speech to the Conservative Party conference promising to double national income (the total quantity of goods and services produced) within 25 years. This sounds impressive, but let us see how ambitious this is in terms of an annual percentage increase.

$$i = \sqrt[25]{\frac{F}{P}} - 1$$

F, future income, is double P, the present income.

$$i = \sqrt[25]{\frac{2}{1}} - 1 = 0.0281 \text{ or } 2.81\%$$

The result is not too bad compared with the previous 20 years. However, performance in the 1950s and 1960s was better and Asian country growth rates are generally between 5 and 10 percent.

The investment period

Rearranging the standard equation so that we can find n (the number of years of the investment), we create the following equation:

$$F = P(1 + i)^n$$

$$F/P = (1 + i)^n$$

$$\log(F/P) = \log(1 + i)n$$

$$n = \frac{\log(F/P)}{\log(1 + i)}$$

Example 5

How many years does it take for £10 to grow to £17.62 when the interest rate is 12 percent?

$$n = \frac{\log(17.62/10)}{\log(1 + 0.12)}$$

Therefore $n = 5$ years.

An application outside finance

How many years will it take for China to double its real national income if growth rates continue at 10 percent per annum?

Answer:

$$n = \frac{\log(2/1)}{\log(1 + 0.1)} = 7.3 \text{ years (quadrupling in less than 15 years)}$$

Consider the geopolitical implications of this!

Annuities

Quite often there is not just one payment at the end of a certain number of years. There can be a series of identical payments made over a period of years. For instance:

- bonds usually pay a regular rate of interest;
- individuals can buy, from saving plan companies, the right to receive a number of identical payments over a number of years;
- a business might invest in a project which, it is estimated, will give regular cash inflows over a period of years;
- a typical house mortgage is an annuity.

An annuity is a series of payments or receipts of equal amounts. We are able to calculate the present value of this set of payments.

Example 6

For a regular payment of £10 per year for five years, when the interest rate is 12 percent, we can calculate the present value of the annuity by three methods.

Method 1

$$P_{an} = \frac{A}{(1 + i)} + \frac{A}{(1 + i)^2} + \frac{A}{(1 + i)^3} + \frac{A}{(1 + i)^4} + \frac{A}{(1+i)^5}$$

where A = the periodic receipt.

$$P_{10,5} = \frac{10}{(1.12)} + \frac{10}{(1.12)^2} + \frac{10}{(1.12)^3} + \frac{10}{(1.12)^4} + \frac{10}{(1.12)^5} = \text{£}36.05$$

Method 2

Using the derived formula:

$$P_{an} = \frac{1 - 1/(1+ i)^n}{i} \times A$$

$$P_{10,5} = \frac{1 - 1/(1 + 0.12)^5}{0.12} \times 10 = \text{£}36.05$$

Method 3

Use the 'Present Value of an Annuity' table. (*See* Table 2.10, an extract from the more complete annuity table in Appendix III.) Here we simply look along the year 5 row and 12 percent column to find the figure of 3.6048. This refers to the present value of five annual receipts of £1. Therefore we multiply by £10:

$$3.605 \times £10 = £36.05$$

TABLE 2.10
The present value of an annuity of £1 per annum

Year	Interest rate (percent per annum)				
	1	5	10	12	15
1	0.9901	0.9524	0.9091	0.8929	0.8696
2	1.9704	1.8594	1.7355	1.6901	1.6257
3	2.9410	2.7232	2.4869	2.4018	2.2832
4	3.9020	3.5460	3.1699	3.0373	2.8550
5	4.8534	4.3295	3.7908	3.6048	3.3522

The reader is strongly advised against using Method 1. This was presented for conceptual understanding only. For any but the simplest cases, this method can be very time consuming.

Perpetuities

Some contracts run indefinitely and there is no end to the payments. Perpetuities are rare in the private sector, but certain government securities do not have an end date; that is, the capital value of the bond will never be paid to the lender, only interest payments are made. For example, the UK government has issued Consolidated Stocks or War Loans that will never be redeemed. Also, in a number of project appraisals or share valuations it is useful to assume that regular annual payments go on forever. Perpetuities are annuities that continue indefinitely. The value of a perpetuity is simply the annual amount received divided by the interest rate when the latter is expressed as a decimal.

$$P = \frac{A}{i}$$

If £10 is to be received as an indefinite annual payment then the present value, at a discount rate of 12 percent, is:

$$P = \frac{10}{0.12} = £83.33$$

It is very important to note that to use this formula we are assuming that the first payment arises 365 days after the time at which we are standing (the present time or time zero).

Discounting semi-annually, monthly and daily

Sometimes financial transactions take place on the basis that interest will be calculated more frequently than once a year. For instance, if a bank account paid 12 percent nominal return per year, but credited 6 percent after half a year, in the second half of the year interest could be earned on the interest credited after the first six months. This will mean that the true annual rate of interest will be greater than 12 percent.

The greater the frequency with which interest is earned, the higher the future value of the deposit.

Example 7

If you put £10 in a bank account earning 12 percent per annum then your return after one year is:

$$10(1 + 0.12) = £11.20$$

If the interest is compounded semi-annually (at a nominal annual rate of 12 percent):

$$10(1 + [0.12/2])(1 + [0.12/2]) = 10(1 + [0.12/2])^2 = £11.236$$

The difference between annual compounding and semi-annual compounding is an extra 3.6p. After six months the bank credits the account with 60p in interest so that in the following six months the investor earns 6 percent on the £10.60.

If the interest is compounded quarterly:

$$10(1 + [0.12/4])^4 = £11.255$$

Daily compounding:

$$10(1 + [0.12/365])^{365} = £11.2747$$

Example 8

If £10 is deposited in a bank account that compounds interest quarterly and the nominal return per year is 12 percent, how much will be in the account after eight years?

$$10(1 + [0.12/4])^{4 \times 8} = £25.75$$

Converting monthly and daily rates to annual rates

Sometimes you are presented with a monthly or daily rate of interest and wish to know what that is equivalent to in terms of Annual Percentage Rates (APR) (Annual Equivalent Rate (AER) or Effective Annual Rate (EAR)).

If m is the monthly interest or discount rate, then over 12 months:

$$(1 + m)^{12} = 1 + i$$

where i is the annual compound rate.

$$i = (1 + m)^{12} - 1$$

If a credit card company charges 1.5 percent per month, the annual percentage rate (APR) is:

$$i = (1 + 0.015)^{12} - 1 = 19.56\%$$

If you want to find the monthly rate when you are given the APR:

$$m = (1 + i)^{1/12} - 1 \text{ or } m = \sqrt[12]{(1+i)} - 1$$

$$m = (1 + 0.1956)^{1/12} - 1 = 0.015 = 1.5\%$$

Daily rate:

$$(1 + d)^{365} = 1 + i$$

where d is the daily discount rate.

3

TRADITIONAL APPRAISAL TECHNIQUES

Introduction

The payback and accounting rate of return (ARR) methods of evaluating capital investment proposals have historically been, and continue to be, very popular approaches, despite the best efforts of a number of writers to denigrate them. It is important to understand the disadvantages of these methods, but it is also useful to be aware of why practical business people still see a great deal of merit in observing the outcome of these calculations.

What appraisal techniques do businesses use?

A number of surveys enquiring into the appraisal methods used in practice have been conducted over the past 20 years. The results from surveys conducted by Pike, by the author jointly with Panos Hatzopoulos, and by Alkaraan and Northcott are displayed in Table 3.1. Some striking features emerge from these and other studies. Payback remains in wide use, despite the increasing application of discounted cash flow techniques. Internal rate of return is at least as popular as net present value. Accounting rate of return continues to be the laggard, but is still used in over 50 percent of large firms. One observation that is emphasized in many studies is the tendency for decision-makers to use more than one method. In the 1997 study, 67 percent of firms use three or four of these techniques. These methods are regarded as being complementary rather than competitors.

> These methods are regarded as being complementary rather than competitors.

There is an indication in the literature that while some methods have superior theoretical justification, other, simpler, methods are used for purposes such as communicating project viability and gaining commitment throughout an organization. It is also suggested that those who sponsor and advance projects within organizations like to have the option of presenting their case in an alternative form which shows the proposal in the best light.

Another clear observation from the literature is that small and medium-sized firms use the sophisticated formal procedures less than their larger brethren.

Payback

The payback period for a capital investment is the length of time before the cumulated stream of forecasted cash flows equals the initial investment.

The decision rule is that if a project's payback period is less than or equal to a predetermined threshold figure it is acceptable. Consider the case of Tradfirm's three mutually exclusive proposed investments (see Table 3.2).

TABLE 3.1

Appraisal techniques used

	Proportion of companies using technique								
	Pike surveys[a]				Arnold and Hatzopoulos survey[b]				Alkaraan and Northcott[c]
	1975	1980	1986	1992	1997				2002
	%	%	%	%	Small %	Medium %	Large %	Total %	Large %
Payback	73	81	92	94	71	75	66	70	96
Accounting rate of return	51	49	56	50	62	50	55	56	60
Internal rate of return	44	57	75	81	76	83	84	81	89
Net present value	32	39	68	74	62	79	97	80	99

Capital budget (per year) for companies in Arnold and Hatzopoulos study approx: Small: £1–50m. Medium: £1–100m. Large: £100m+

Notes

(a) Pike's studies focus on 100 large UK firms.

(b) In the Arnold and Hatzopoulos study (2000), 300 finance directors of UK companies taken from *The Times* 1000 (London: Times Books), ranked according to capital employed (excluding investment trusts), were asked dozens of questions about project appraisal techniques, sources of finance and performance measurement. The first 100 (large size) of the sample are the top 100; another 100 are in the rankings at 250–400 (medium size); the final 100 are ranked 820–1,000 (small size). The capital employed ranges between £1.3bn and £24bn for the large firms, £207m and £400m for the medium-sized firms, and £40m and £60m for the small companies. Ninety-six usable replies were received: 38 large, 24 medium and 34 small.

(c) Alkaraan and Northcott focus on UK manufacturing companies each with at least a turnover of £100m, 1,000 employees and assets of £50m. A total of 83 companies returned questionnaires.

Sources: R.H. Pike (1988) 'An empirical study of the adoption of sophisticated capital budgeting practices and decision making effectiveness', *Accounting and Business Research*, 18 (72), Autumn, pp. 341–51. R.H.Pike (1996) 'A longitudinal survey of capital budgeting practices', *Journal of Business Finance and Accounting*, 23(1), pp.79–92. Arnold and Hatzopoulos (2000) 'The theory practice gap in capital budgeting: evidence from the United Kingdom', *Journal of Business Finance and Accounting*, 27(5) and (6), June/July, pp. 603–26. F. Alkaraan and D. Northcott (2006) 'Strategic capital investment decision-making: a role for emergent analysis tools? A study of practice in large UK manufacturing companies', *British Accounting Review*, 38, pp. 149–73.

TABLE 3.2

Tradfirm

	Cash flows (£m)						
Points in time (yearly intervals)	0	1	2	3	4	5	6
Project A	−10	6	2	1	1	2	2
Project B	−10	1	1	2	6	2	2
Project C	−10	3	2	2	2	15	10

Note: Production ceases after six years, and all cash flows occur on anniversary dates.

There is a boardroom battle in Tradfirm, with older members preferring the payback rule. They set four years as the decision benchmark. For both A and B the £10m initial outflow is recouped after four years. In the case of C it takes five years for the cash inflows to cumulate to £10m. Thus payback for the three projects is as follows:

Project A:	4 years
Project B:	4 years
Project C:	5 years

If the payback rule is rigidly applied, the older members of the board will reject the third project, and they are left with a degree of indecisiveness over whether to accept A or B. The younger members prefer the NPV rule and are thus able to offer a clear decision.

Tradfirm: Net Present Values (£m)

$$\text{Project A} \quad -10 + \frac{6}{1.1} + \frac{2}{(1.1)^2} + \frac{1}{(1.1)^3} + \frac{1}{(1.1)^4} + \frac{2}{(1.1)^5} + \frac{2}{(1.1)^6} = £0.913m$$

$$\text{Project B} \quad -10 + \frac{1}{1.1} + \frac{1}{(1.1)^2} + \frac{2}{(1.1)^3} + \frac{6}{(1.1)^4} + \frac{2}{(1.1)^5} + \frac{2}{(1.1)^6} = -£0.293m$$

$$\text{Project C} \quad -10 + \frac{3}{1.1} + \frac{2}{(1.1)^2} + \frac{2}{(1.1)^3} + \frac{2}{(1.1)^4} + \frac{15}{(1.1)^5} + \frac{10}{(1.1)^6} = £12.207m$$

Note: The discount rate is 10 percent.

Project A has a positive NPV and is shareholder wealth-enhancing. Project B has a negative NPV; the firm would be better served by investing the £10m in the alternative that offers a 10 percent return. Project C has the largest positive NPV so it creates most shareholder wealth.

Drawbacks of payback

- It makes no allowance for the time value of money. It ignores the need to compare future cash flows with the initial investment after they have been discounted to their present values.

- Receipts beyond the payback period are ignored. This problem is particularly obvious in the case of Project C.

- The arbitrary selection of the cut-off point. There is no theoretical basis for setting the appropriate time period and so guesswork, whim and manipulation take over.

Discounted payback

With discounted payback the future cash flows are discounted prior to calculating the payback period. This is an improvement on the simple payback method in that it takes into account the time value of money. In Table 3.3 the *discounted* cash inflows are added together to calculate payback. In the case of Project B the discounted cash inflows never reach the level of the cash outflow.

This modification tackles the first drawback of the simple payback method but it is still necessary to make an arbitrary decision about the cut-off date and it ignores cash flows beyond that date.

TABLE 3.3
Discounted payback: Tradfirm plc (£m)

Points in time (yearly intervals)	0	1	2	3	4	5	6	Discounted payback
Project A								
Undiscounted cash flow	−10	6	2	1	1	2	2	
Discounted cash flow	−10	5.45	1.65	0.75	0.68	1.24	1.13	Year 6
Project B								
Undiscounted cash flow	−10	1	1	2	6	2	2	Outflow −10m
Discounted cash flow	−10	0.909	0.826	1.5	4.1	1.24	1.13	Inflow +£9.7m
Project C								
Undiscounted cash flow	−10	3	2	2	2	15	10	
Discounted cash flow	−10	2.73	1.65	1.5	1.37	9.3	5.64	Year 5

Note: The discount rate is 10 percent.

Reasons for the continuing popularity of payback

Payback remains a widely used project appraisal method despite its drawbacks. This requires some explanation.

- The first fact to note is that payback is rarely used as the primary investment technique, but rather as a secondary method which supplements the more sophisticated methods. Although it appears irrational to employ payback when the issue is examined in isolation, we may begin to see the logic behind its use if we take into account the organizational context and the complementary nature of alternative techniques. For example, payback may be used at an early stage to filter out projects that have clearly unacceptable risk and return characteristics. Identifying those projects at a preliminary stage avoids the need for more detailed evaluation through a discounted cash flow method, thus increasing the efficiency of the appraisal process. This early sifting has to be carefully implemented to avoid premature rejection.

■ Payback also has one extraordinarily endearing quality to busy managers: it is simple and easy to use. Executives often admit that the payback rule, used indiscriminately, does not always give the best decisions, but it is the simplest way to communicate an idea of project profitability. NPV is difficult to understand, so it is useful to have an alternative measure which all managers can follow. In the workplace a project's success often relies on the gaining of widespread employee commitment. Discussion, negotiation and communication of ideas often need to be carried out in a simple form so that non-quantitative managers can make their contribution and, eventually, give their commitment. Communication in terms of the sophisticated models may lead to alienation and exclusion and, ultimately, project failure.

> Payback is simple and easy to use.

■ Another argument advanced by practitioners is that projects that return their outlay quickly reduce the exposure of the firm to risk. In the world beyond the simplifications needed in academic exercises there is a great deal of uncertainty about future cash flows. Managers often distrust forecasts for more distant years. Payback has an implicit assumption that the risk of cash flows is directly related to the time distance from project implementation date. By focusing on near-term returns this approach uses only those data in which management have greatest faith. Take the case of the web-based music download industry. Here, competitive forces and technology are changing so rapidly that it is difficult to forecast for eight months ahead, let alone for eight years, so managers may choose to ignore cash flow projections beyond a certain number of years. Those who advocate NPV counter this approach by saying that risk is accounted for in a better way in the NPV model than is done by simply excluding data – it certainly does not ignore cash flows beyond the payback period. Adjusting for risk in NPV calculations is considered in Chapter 5.

■ A further advantage of payback, as perceived by many managers, is its use in situations of capital shortage. If funds are limited, there is an advantage in receiving a return on projects earlier rather than later, as this permits investment in other profitable opportunities. But, as we have seen with Project C, relying solely on payback because of the speedy return of capital can result in the sacrifice of massive cash flows just after the cut off.

This section is not meant to promote the use of payback. It remains a theoretically inferior method to the discounted cash flow approaches. Payback has a number of valuable attributes, but the primary method of project appraisal in most organizations should take into account all of the relevant cash flows and then discount them.

Accounting rate of return

The accounting rate of return (ARR) method may be known to readers by other names such as the return on capital employed (ROCE) or return on investment (ROI). The ARR is a ratio of the accounting profit to the investment in the project, expressed as a percentage.

The *decision rule* is that if the ARR is greater than, or equal to, a hurdle rate then accept the project.

This ratio can be calculated in a number of ways, but the most popular approach is to take profit after deduction of depreciation. For the investment figure we regard any increases in working capital as adding to the investment required. Three alternative versions of ARR are calculated for Timewarp plc which give markedly different results (*see* Worked example 3.1). These are just three of all the possible ways of calculating ARR – there are many more. The fact that there are many ways of calculating a measure of project valuation and performance should be ringing alarm bells – 'choose your result by choosing your method of calculation' is not a sound basis for decision-making.

Worked example 3.1
TIMEWARP PLC

Timewarp is to invest £30,000 in machinery for a project which has a life of three years. The machinery will have a zero scrap value and will be depreciated on a straight-line basis.

Accounting rate of return, version 1 (annual basis)

$$ARR = \frac{\text{Profit for the year}}{\text{Asset book value at start of year}} \times 100$$

Time (year)	1	2	3
	£	£	£
Profit before depreciation	15,000	15,000	15,000
Less depreciation	10,000	10,000	10,000
Profit after depreciation	5,000	5,000	5,000
Value of asset (book value)			
Start of year	30,000	20,000	10,000
End of year	20,000	10,000	0

Accounting rate of return $\dfrac{5,000}{30,000} = 16.67\%$ $\dfrac{5,000}{20,000} = 25\%$ $\dfrac{5,000}{10,000} = 50\%$

On average the ARR is: $1/3 \times (16.67 + 25 + 50)\% = 30.56\%$.

Note the illusion of an annual rise in profitability despite the profits remaining constant.

Accounting rate of return, version 2 (total investment basis)

$$\text{ARR} = \frac{\text{Average annual profit}}{\text{Initial capital invested}} \times 100$$

$$\text{ARR} = \frac{(5{,}000 + 5{,}000 + 5{,}000)/3}{30{,}000} \times 100 = 16.67\%$$

Accounting rate of return, version 3 (average investment basis)

$$\text{ARR} = \frac{\text{Average annual profit}}{\text{Average capital invested}} \times 100$$

$$\text{Average capital invested:} \; \frac{30{,}000}{2} = 15{,}000$$

(at time 0 the machinery has a value of £30,000, three years later it has a value of zero. If we assume constant devaluation then the average value of the machinery is £15,000).

$$\text{ARR} = \frac{(5{,}000 + 5{,}000 + 5{,}000)/3}{15{,}000} \times 100 = 33.33\%$$

Drawbacks of accounting rate of return

■ The number of alternative ARR calculations can be continued beyond the three possibilities described in Worked example 3.1. Each alternative would be a legitimate variant and would find favour with some managers and accountants. The almost wide-open field for selecting profit and asset definitions is a major weakness of ARR. This flexibility may tempt decision-makers to abuse the technique to suit their purposes.

■ The inflow and outflow of cash should be the focus of investment analysis appraisals. Profit figures are very poor substitutes for cash flow because they frequently fail to show when cash is received and when it flows out. For example, a £10m machine purchase this year is a cash outflow of £10m, but may result in a depreciation entry for the profit and loss account of only £1m. The £9m difference is merely one of hundreds of accounting entries that make profit figures inappropriate for project evaluation. Another area of concern is working capital. For example, a project requiring an increase in inventory (e.g. raw material) will see an outflow of cash for this purpose, but the accountant's profit calculations for the project do not change just because one current asset, i.e. cash, has been used up, because it has been replaced by an equal amount of another asset, i.e. inventory, such as raw materials. There is no effect on profit but there could be a large effect on cash flow. Shareholders' wealth depends on when cash goes in and when it comes out. The same issue exists for cash used to increase the level of trade debtors or the release of cash by using supplier cash to finance the business (by increasing trade credit).

■ The most important criticism of accounting rate of return is that it fails to take account of the time value of money. There is no allowance for the fact that cash received in Year 1 is more valuable than an identical sum received in Year 3.

■ There is a high degree of arbitrariness in defining the cut-off or hurdle rate. There is no sound logical reason for selecting 10, 15 or 20 percent as the acceptable ARR. It is a case of picking a number from the air. However, NPV has a firm logical base to the discount rate used by the company for a project. It is the opportunity cost of the suppliers of capital. We examine its calculation in Chapter 10.

■ Accounting rate of return can lead to some perverse decisions. For example, suppose that Timewarp use the second version, the total investment ARR, with a hurdle rate of 15 percent, and the appraisal team discover that the machinery will in fact generate an additional profit of £1,000 in a fourth year. Common sense suggests that if all other factors remain constant this new situation is better than the old one, and yet the ARR declines to below the threshold level (15 percent) because the profits are averaged over four years rather than three and the project is therefore rejected.

The original situation is:

$$\text{ARR} = \frac{(5,000 + 5,000 + 5,000)/3}{30,000} \times 100 = 16.67\% \qquad \textbf{Accepted}$$

The new situation is:

$$\text{ARR} = \frac{(5,000 + 5,000 + 5,000 + 1,000)/4}{30,000} \times 100 = 13.33\% \qquad \textbf{Rejected}$$

An alternative way of viewing this problem is to think of two projects that are identical except that one offers the additional £1,000. If only one project can be accepted which will the managers go for? If they are motivated by ARR (e.g. by bonuses related to ARR achieved) they may be inclined to accept the project that offers the highest ARR even if this means sacrificing £1,000 of shareholders' money.

Reasons for the continued use of accounting rate of returns

Table 3.1 shows that over one-half of large firms calculate ARR when appraising projects, so the conclusion must be that in the practical world of business, some merit is seen in this technique. One possible explanation is that managers are familiar with this ancient and extensively used profitability measure. The financial press regularly report accounting rates of return. Divisional performance is often judged on a profit-to-assets-employed ratio. Indeed, the entire firm is often analyzed and management evaluated on this ratio. Because performance is measured in this way, managers have a natural bias towards using it in appraising future projects. Conflicting signals are sometimes sent to managers controlling a division. They are expected to use a discounted cash flow approach for investment decisions, but find that their performance is being monitored on a profit-to-investment ratio basis. This dichotomy may produce a resistance to proposed projects that produce low returns in the early years and thus report a low ARR to head office. This may result in excellent long-term opportunities being missed.

Internal rate of return: reasons for continued popularity

Table 3.1 shows that firms use IRR as much as the theoretically superior NPV. Given the problems associated with IRR described in Chapter 2, this may seem strange. It is all the more perplexing if one considers that IRR is often more difficult to calculate manually than NPV (although, with modern computer programs, the computational difficulties virtually disappear). Some possible explanations follow.

■ **Psychological** Managers are familiar with expressing financial data in the form of a percentage. It is intuitively easier to grasp what is meant by an IRR of 15 percent than, say, an NPV of £2,000.

■ **IRR can be calculated without knowledge of the required rate of return** Making a decision using the IRR involves two separate stages. Stage 1 involves gathering data and then computing the IRR. Stage 2 involves comparing this with the cut-off rate. By contrast, it is not possible to calculate NPV without knowing the required rate of return. The proposal has to be analyzed in one stage only. In a large company it is possible for senior managers to request that profit centres and divisions appraise projects on the basis of their IRRs, while refusing to communicate in advance the rate of return required. This has at least two potential advantages. First, the required rate may change over time and it becomes a simple matter of changing the cut-off comparison rate at head office once the IRR computations are received from lower down the organization. With NPV, each project's cash flows would need to be calculated again at the new discount rate. Secondly, managers are only human and there is a tendency to bias information passed upwards so as to achieve their personal goals. For instance, it has been known for ambitious managers to be excessively optimistic concerning the prospects for projects that would lead to an expansion of their domain. If they are provided with a cut-off rate prior to evaluating projects you can be sure that all projects they sponsor will have cash flows 'forecasted' to produce a return greater than the target. If the head office team choose not to communicate a cut-off rate, this leaves them free to adjust the required return to allow for factors such as over-optimisim. They may also adjust the minimum rate of return for perceived risk associated with particular projects or divisions.

■ **Ranking** Some managers are not familiar with the drawbacks of IRR and believe that ranking projects to select between them is most accurately and most easily carried out using the percentage-based IRR method. This was, in Chapter 2, shown not to be the case.

Conclusion

We can see why most firms use three or four measures when evaluating the return on a project. Payback, ARR and IRR provide alternative perspectives, and are useful for communicating project viability to a wide range of team members. However, the preferred method for the final decision must be NPV in a rationally managed, shareholder wealth-oriented company.

4

INVESTMENT DECISION-MAKING
IN COMPANIES

Introduction

An organization may be viewed simply as a collection of projects, some of which were started a long time ago, some only recently begun, many are major 'strategic' projects and others minor operating-unit-level schemes. It is in the nature of business for change to occur, and through change old activities, profit centres and methods die, to be replaced by the new. Without a continuous process of regeneration firms will cease to progress and be unable to compete in a dynamic environment. It is vital that the processes and systems that lead to the development of new production methods, new markets and products, and so on, are efficient. That is, both the project appraisal techniques and the entire process of proposal creation and selection lead to the achievement of the objective of the organization. Poor appraisal technique, set within the framework of an investment process that does not ask the right questions and which provides erroneous conclusions, will destroy the wealth of shareholders.

The employment of project appraisal techniques must be seen as merely one of the stages in the process of the allocation of resources within a firm. The appraisal stage can be reached only after ideas for the use of capital resources have been generated and those ideas have been filtered through a consideration of the strategic, budgetary and business resource capabilities of the firm. The appraisal stage is followed by the approval, implementation and post-completion auditing.

Any capital allocation system has to be viewed in the light of the complexity of organizational life. This aspect was ignored in Chapter 2, where mechanical analysis is applied. The balance is corrected in this chapter. It considers the process of project development, appraisal and post-investment monitoring.

No doubt the project to build the Airbus 380 (see Case study 4.1) has been through many of the stages of project development and implementation discussed in this chapter: from the generation of the idea, its screening for budgetary and strategic constraints, to a thorough analysis in quantitative terms. Now that the aircraft are being produced, there will be a capital expenditure control system designed to monitor progress against targets. And, over the next few years, there will be an audit of the entire project.

Case study 4.1

Will it fly?

Airbus's Superjumbo

Surely one of the biggest investment appraisal decisions ever made was when Airbus decided to go ahead and produce the A380 superjumbo. This is one of those 'bet the company' type investments. A massive $10,700m was needed to create this monster aircraft.

It was touch and go all through 2000 as to whether Airbus would dare to invest so much money. Before they said 'yes let's do it' they had to have firm orders for at least 50 aircraft. Finally, just before Christmas the sixth major buyer signed up to take the order book to 50 'definites' and 42 on option (the airlines have the right to buy, but not the obligation).

The A380 is significantly larger than Boeing's highly successful 747. It carries 555 passengers (compared with 416). It also cuts direct operating costs for the airlines by 15–20% compared with Boeing's 747–400 and is able to fly 10% further (8,150 nautical miles).

So, where is all the money on development and build going? This is a project at the cutting edge of technology. The remarkable innovations cost a tremendous amount in terms of up-front cost, but the benefit will be spread out over many decades. Here are some of the innovations:

- New, weight-saving materials
- Better aerodynamics
- Carbon-fibre reinforced plastic central wingbox. Forty percent of the structure and components is made from new carbon components and metal alloys.
- Upper fuselage shell is not aluminium but glare, a laminate with alternative layers of aluminium and glass-fibre reinforced adhesive
- Innovative hydraulic systems and air conditioning.

Airbus reckoned they needed to sell at least 250 aircraft to break even in cash flow terms. (Presumably meaning that nominal cumulative cash inflows equal nominal cumulative cash outflows.) To achieve a positive net present value would require the sale of hundreds more aircraft. Each airplane has a list price of around $216m–$230m, but don't pay too much attention to that, as airlines receive substantial discounts. At full tilt something like 96,000 people will be working on this aircraft.

And yet it could so easily have been abandoned. Boeing decided not to develop a super-jumbo because it estimated the maximum market at 500 as they think that airlines are generally content to continue using the 747. Airbus estimated the market for jumbos and superjumbos at 1,550. It expects to take two-thirds of that business, worth $400bn in today's prices.

It delivered one aircraft in 2007, 12 in 2008 and 14 in 2009.

The managerial art of investment selection

This book places strong emphasis on the formal methods of project appraisal, so a word of warning is necessary at this point. Mathematical technique is merely one element needed for successful project appraisal. The quantitative analysis is only the starting point for decision-making. In most real-world situations there are many qualitative factors that need to be taken into account. The techniques described in Chapter 2 cannot be used in a mechanical fashion. Management is largely an art form with a few useful quantitative techniques to improve the quality of the art. For instance, in generating and evaluating major investments the firm has to take into account the following.

Strategy

The relationship between the proposed project and the strategic direction of the firm is very important. A business unit investment isolated from the main thrust of the firm may be a distraction in terms of managerial attention and financial resources. A project that looks good at divisional level may not be appropriate when examined from the whole-firm perspective. It may even be contradictory to the firm's goals. For example, luxury goods companies are sometimes enticed to produce lower priced items for the mass market or to stretch the brand into unrelated areas. The project, when judged on its own, appears to have a very high NPV. But there is the danger of losing the premium brand strategic position (expensive and exclusive) in the existing product ranges by being associated with something that does not quite fit the image the firm has nurtured.

Social context

The effect on individuals is a crucial consideration. Projects require people to implement them. Their enthusiasm and commitment will be of central importance. Neglecting this factor may lead to resentment and even sabotage. Discussion and consensus on major project proposals may matter more than selecting the mathematically correct option. In many cases, quantitative techniques are avoided because they are precise. It is safer to sponsor a project in a non-quantifiable or judgmental way at an early stage in its development. If, as a result of discussion with colleagues and superiors, the idea becomes more generally accepted and fits into the pervading view on the firm's policy and strategy, the figures are presented in a report. Note here the order of actions. First, general acceptance. Second, quantification. A proposal is usually discussed at progressively higher levels of management before it is 'firmed up' into a project report. One reason for this is that continuing commitment and support from many people will be needed if the project is to succeed. To engender support and to improve the final report it is necessary to start the process in a rather vague way, making room for modifications in the light of suggestions. Some of these suggestions will be motivated by shareholder wealth considerations, others by goals closer to the hearts of key individuals. Allowing adaptability in project development also means that if circumstances change, say, in the competitive environment, the final formal appraisal takes account of this. The sponsor or promoter of a capital investment has to be aware of, and to adjust for, social sub-systems within the organization.

Expense

Sophisticated project evaluation can cost a considerable amount of money. The financial experts' input is costly enough, but the firm also has to consider the time and trouble managers throughout the organization might have to devote to provide good-quality data and make their contribution to the debate. In a firm of limited resources it may be more efficient to search for projects in an informal manner, thus generating a multitude of alternative avenues for growth, rather than analyzing a few in greater quantitative depth.

Stifling the entrepreneurial spirit

Excessive emphasis on formal evaluatory systems may be demotivating to individuals who thrive on free-thinking, fast decision-making and action. The relative weights given to formal approaches and entrepreneurialism will depend on the context, such as the pace of change in the market-place.

A leading businessman describes the problems arising from overemphasis on accounting (that should be finance) numbers – *see* Exhibit 4.1.

Entrepreneur fires broad attack on manufacturers

Peter Marsh

British manufacturers have failed to invest enough in marketing and given too much management control to accountants, according to Edward Atkin, one of the country's most successful engineering entrepreneurs of the past decade ...

Until recently Mr Atkin, was the managing director and majority owner of Avent, one of the world's biggest makers of babies' bottles ...

He sold Avent to a venture capital company for £300m, of which £225m (minus advisers' fees) came to Mr Atkin and his family. The entrepreneur is now weighing up several ideas about ways in which to invest some of the cash in innovative businesses ...

In a speech to the Institution of Electrical Engineers Mr Atkin will say that most successful manufacturers require a stable investment climate and an interest in making world-beating products.

These factors are more likely to be in place if the businesses are owned privately, and also have people with an interest in engineering at the helm, rather than accountants.

'As soon as financial criteria become the main method used for evaluating investment opportunities, the company is almost certainly doomed,' Mr Atkin will say.

He will say that companies subject to the control of investors through a stock market flotation are more likely than private entrepreneurs to be swayed by short-term financial considerations, which are likely to deflect them from decisions linked to building up a global brand on the back of innovative and competitive products.

'It is impossible to forecast variables like volumes, competitive pricing, raw material costs, interest rates or currencies three or five years out,' Mr Atkin will say. 'What is very easy, however, is to appreciate that speeding up a process, reducing waste, eliminating direct labour and improving tolerances and reliability will enhance both the products and their manufacture, as well as the experience of the end-user. These benefits will be long-term and valid, irrespective of the output, exchange rate, raw material costs and all the other variables.' ...

Successful manufacturers such as US semiconductor maker Intel, and BMW and Toyota, two of the world's biggest car producers, have made as a centre of their businesses 'an unbroken trend of consistent [product] development, decade after decade'.

This is a culture, Mr Atkin will say, that makes it relatively easy to build up strong teams of engineering and marketing experts within the company that will stay for long periods. It also makes it easier to establish long-term brand loyalty.

EXHIBIT 4.1

Source: *Financial Times* 17 January 2006, p. 5.

Concentrating on short-term financial goals and presenting these as shareholder wealth maximizing actions can lead to slow pace and market irrelevance. So, being too fastidious in requiring immediately visible and quantifiable returns in an uncertain world can result in the rejection of extremely valuable projects that require a leap into the unknown by a team of enthusiasts. Where would Microsoft be today if in the 1970s it had conducted rigorous NPV analysis on its operating systems when PC sales numbered a few thousand?

Intangible benefits

Frequently, many of the most important benefits that flow from an investment are difficult to measure in money terms. Improving customer satisfaction through better service, quality or image may lead to enhanced revenues, but it is often difficult to state precisely the quantity of the increased revenue flow. For example, new technology often provides a number of intangible benefits, such as reduced time needed to switch machine tools to the production of other products, thereby reducing risk in fluctuating markets, or a quicker response to customer choice. These non-quantifiable benefits can amount to a higher value than the more obvious tangible benefits. An example of how intangible benefits could be allowed for in project appraisal is shown through the worked example of Crowther Precision plc.

> Non-quantifiable benefits can amount to a higher value than the more obvious tangible benefits.

Worked example 4.1
CROWTHER PRECISION PLC

Crowther Precision plc produces metal parts for the car industry, with machinery that is now more than 20 years old. With appropriate maintenance these machines could continue producing indefinitely. However, developments in the machine tool industry have led to the creation of computer-controlled multi-use machines. Crowther is considering the purchase of the Z200 which would provide both quantifiable and non-quantifiable benefits over the old machine. The Z200 costs £1.2m but would be expected to last indefinitely if maintenance expenditure were increased by £20,000 every year for ever.

The quantifiable benefits are:

(a) reduced raw material requirements, due to lower wastage, amounting to £35,000 every year for ever;

(b) labour cost savings of £80,000 every year for ever.

These quantifiable benefits are analyzed using the NPV method.

Incremental net present value analysis of Z200

		Present value, £
Purchase of machine		−1,200,000
Present value of all annual raw material savings	$\dfrac{35,000}{0.1}$	+350,000
Present value of all annual labour savings	$\dfrac{80,000}{0.1}$	+800,000
Less present value of all annual increased maintenance costs	$\dfrac{20,000}{0.1}$	−200,000
Net present value		−250,000

Note: Assume a discount rate of 10%, all cash flows arise at the year ends, zero scrap value of old machine.

Examining the quantifiable elements in isolation will lead to a rejection of the project to buy the Z200. However, the non-quantifiable benefits are:

- reduced time required to switch the machine from producing one version of the car component to one of the other three versions Crowther presently produces;
- the ability to switch the machine over to completely new products in response to changed industry demands, or to take up, as yet unseen, market opportunities in the future;
- improved quality of output leading to greater customer satisfaction.

It is true that the Crowther Precision cash flow analysis has failed to take into account all the relevant factors, but this should not lead to its complete rejection. In cases where non-quantifiable elements are present, the problem needs to be separated into two stages.

1 Analyze those elements that are quantifiable using NPV.
2 If the NPV from Stage 1 is negative, then managerial judgment will be needed to subjectively assess the non-quantifiable benefits. If these are judged to be greater than the 'loss' signaled in Stage 1 then the project is viable. For Crowther, if the management team consider that the intangible benefits are worth more than £250,000 they should proceed with the purchase of the Z200.

This line of thought is continued in Chapter 5, where operational and strategic decisions with options (real options) are considered. As the article in Exhibit 4.2

shows, the decision to commit to an investment means the loss of options. While reading it you might like to relate the ideas presented to Airbus's commitment to the A380 (Case study 4.1). It is committed, while Boeing has greater freedom to act.

Tyranny of time

By their very nature capital investment decisions threaten to place a straight jacket on companies. There is no easy way out.

Peter Martin

When you make a capital investment decision, you freeze time. In fast-moving industries, this may be the most important aspect of the decision – more important than its actual content. But it is rarely assessed in this light.

There is any amount of theory about how to take capital investment decisions ...

All such approaches assume that there are financial and easily quantifiable costs of taking the decision; and less measurable benefits to set against it. The techniques all revolve around ways of making imponderable future benefits more tangible. There is a reason for this: managers usually want to take investment decisions while their superiors usually do not. So the techniques are ever more elaborate ways of capturing the discounted value of blue sky.

But there are also intangible costs of taking the decision, and they are not given the attention they deserve. The cost of freezing time is one of the most important.

Here is how it works. When you make a big capital investment decision, it will usually take between 18 months and five years to bring the plant fully into operation. The cost of tying up capital for that time is reflected in the investment appraisal. But the broader implications of tying up the company are not.

When you have committed yourself to a big new plant, you have not just signed a cheque for the money. You have also sold your soul to this technology, on this scale, in this site. That is what freezing time means. Until the plant is complete, and it is clear whether it works and whether there is a market for its products, time stands still. For you, but not for your rivals.

They are free to react, to adjust technology, to play around with the pricing and volume. You are not. Unless you have built an implausibly flexible new plant, you are on a convergence course with a straitjacket.

Once your new plant is up and running, you can start to adjust the pattern of its output, and strive to reduce its costs. But until then, your options are more limited: press on, or give up.

The semiconductor industry illustrates this dilemma in a big way. In the mid-1990s, the UK looked like a good home for a bunch of new chip plants. Siemens, LG Group and Hyundai all targeted the British regions for big state-of-the-art factories. One of them – Siemens' factory on Tyneside – opened and promptly shut down again. The other two have never made it into production, and look more questionable by the moment: the Asian crisis undermined their parents and their markets simultaneously.

The decisions all three companies had to make were unenviable, because they were all or nothing. Technology had moved on while the plants were being prepared. Once the Siemens plant came into production, it was clear that it was the wrong plant, making the wrong sort of chip, in the wrong place.

So the company shut it down, at vast cost – only to invest another huge sum in a different plant to make different chips in France. For LG and Hyundai the moment of decision comes even before they have had the satisfaction of seeing their plants up and running.

The problem is not so much the risk that a plant's technology may prove inappropriate, or that its markets may not meet expectations: these are the normal risks of doing business in a capital intensive industry. It is more that the process of building the factory shuts out other alternatives, freezing the company's options and its internal clock.

What can companies do to avoid this risk? First, look for investment decisions that can be made piece by piece, and implemented quickly, minimising the freezing effect. Engineers usually hate this approach, because it means they are never designing plants at the cutting edge of the technology, or at maximum efficient scale. That's tough.

Second, once an investment has been approved, managers must resist the temptation to make the decision sacrosanct. It needs revisiting, in the light of changing technology and markets, just as much as plants that are already operating. This is a difficult balance to strike, because every big investment decision usually had to be made in the teeth of the opposition of a faction that wanted something bigger, smaller, older, newer, or somewhere else. This group of dissidents will never be happy with the decision, and they may even be right.

Third, keep a close eye on the relationship between the product cycle time in your industry and the time it takes to get a new plant commissioned.

If the former is shrinking while the latter is lengthening – a common feature of any high-technology industry that has to cater to retail consumers – there will come a point at which the price of freezing time will outstrip the benefits of new plant.

If you cannot keep going by patching the old factory, it is time to think of some revolutionary new process that will replace one big capital investment decision with a lot of small ones. Or give up.

EXHIBIT 4.2

Source: *Financial Times* 1 June 1999, p. 18.

More tricky issues in real-world project appraisal

A fundamental principle in project appraisal is to include only incremental cash flows. These are defined as the cash flows that are dependent on the project's implementation. If a project is accepted only those cash flows which are induced by the investment at time 0 and in subsequent years are regarded at incremental. Some of these cash flows are easy to establish but others are much more difficult to pin down.

INCREMENTAL CASH FLOW	=	CASH FLOW FOR FIRM WITH THE PROJECT	–	CASH FLOW FOR FIRM WITHOUT THE PROJECT

Here are some guide-posts to finding relevant/incremental cash flows:

Include all opportunity costs

The direct inputs into a project are generally easy to understand and measure. However, quite often a project uses resources which already exist within the firm but which are in short supply and which cannot be replaced in the immediate future. That is, the project under consideration may be taking resources

> The project under consideration may be taking resources away from other projects.

away from other projects. The loss of net cash flows from these other projects are termed opportunity costs. For example, a firm may be considering a project that makes use of a factory that at present is empty. Because it is empty we should not automatically assume that the opportunity cost is zero. Perhaps the firm could engage in the alternative project of renting out the factory to another firm. The forgone rental income is a cost of the project under consideration.

Likewise, if a project uses the services of specialist personnel this may be regarded as having an opportunity cost. The loss of these people to other parts of the organization may reduce cash flows on other projects. If they cannot be replaced then the opportunity cost will be the lost net cash flows. If replacements are found then the extra cost imposed, by the additional salaries, etc., on other projects should be regarded as an opportunity cost of the new project under consideration.

For a third example of opportunity cost, imagine your firm bought a stock of platinum to use as a raw material when the price was low. The total cost was £1m. It would be illogical to sell the final manufactured product at a price based on the old platinum value if the same quantity would now cost £3m. An alternative course of action would be to sell the platinum in its existing state, rather than to produce the manufactured product. The current market value of the raw platinum (£3m) would then be the opportunity cost.

Include all incidental effects

It is possible for a new project to either increase or reduce sales of other products or services offered by the company. Take the case of an airline company trying to decide whether to go ahead with a project to fly between the USA and Japan. The direct cash flows, of selling tickets, etc. on these flights, may not give a positive NPV. However, it could be that the new service generates additional net revenue not only for US/Japan flights but also on existing routes as customers switch to this airline because it now offers a more complete world-wide service. If this additional net cash flow is included the project may be viable.

If a clothes retailer opens a second or a third outlet in the same town it is likely to find custom is reduced at the original store. The loss elsewhere in the organization becomes a relevant cash flow in the appraisal of the *new* project, that is, the new shop.

In the soft drinks business, the introduction of a new brand can reduce the sales of the older brands. This is not to say that a company should never risk any cannibalization, only that if a new product is to be launched it should not be viewed in isolation. All incremental effects have to be allowed for including those effects not directly associated with the new product or service.

In the article in Exhibit 4.3, Sir David Rowlands makes a plea for attention to be paid to incidental effects in the evaluation of a new high-speed rail route in the UK.

New lines needed to justify second high-speed rail route

Robert Wright

A new, high-speed rail line in the UK 'may struggle' to justify itself under traditional measures, the man in charge of investigating options for a route admits.

Sir David Rowlands nevertheless looks poised to recommend building a high-speed route from London to Manchester via Birmingham, based on more sophisticated assessment techniques.

Sir David, formerly permanent secretary at the Department for Transport, was put in charge of High Speed 2 – the company set up to investigate options for a new, north–south high-speed line – in January ...

His comments in an interview underline the challenge facing backers of a second dedicated high-speed line in the UK following the completion in 2007 of High Speed 1 from the Channel Tunnel to London St Pancras. As the country's largest population centres are relatively near each other and rapid, frequent trains already have substantial market shares on many routes, traditional economic models produce too few benefits to justify the economic and social costs of construction.

On the prospect of supplementing the southern part of the London-to-Glasgow west coast main line with a dedicated high-speed route, Sir David says: 'Building a business case on a very traditional basis in terms of how transport projects are appraised, it may struggle.'

However, he adds, London Underground's Jubilee Line Extension also failed to justify itself in cost-benefit terms until civil servants started using novel analysis techniques. These measured 'agglomeration benefits' – the improved efficiency and competitiveness gained by connecting people better to each other. That project is now widely recognised as a success.

The case for a high-speed line is likely to be based on factors similar to those for the Jubilee Line, Sir David says, including a new route's ability to free up the existing west coast main line for more freight and commuter traffic.

'For HS2, you need to explore how sensibly you can go beyond existing appraisal techniques,' Sir David says. 'It's something to do with capturing the benefits of reliable train services; it's something to do with the benefits to the existing west coast; and it's something to do with the connectivity benefits that we may generate by drawing Scotland, Yorkshire, the north-west, Midlands and London closer together.' ...

EXHIBIT 4.3

Source: *Financial Times* 15 June 2009, p. 2.

The irrelevance of sunk costs

Do not include sunk costs. For example, the project to build the Concorde involved an enormous expenditure in design and manufacture. At the point where it has to be decided whether or not to put the airplane into service, the costs of development became irrelevant to the decision. Only increment costs and inflows should be considered. The development costs are in the past and are bygones; they should be ignored. The money spent on development is irrecoverable whatever the decision on whether to fly the plane. Similarly with Eurotunnel, the fact that the overspend ran into billions of pounds and the tunnel service is unlikely to make a profit does not mean the incremental cost of using the same electricity to power the trains and the cost of employing train drivers should not be incurred. The £9bn+ already spent is irrelevant to the decision on whether to transport passengers and freight between France and the UK. So long as incremental costs are less than incremental benefits (cash flows when discounted) then the service should operate.

> A common mistake is to regard pre-project survey work as a relevant cost.

A common mistake in this area is to regard pre-project survey work (market demand screening, scientific study, geological survey, etc.) as a relevant cost. After all, the cost would not have been incurred but for the *possibility* of going ahead with the project. However, at the point of decision on whether to proceed, the survey cost is sunk – it will be incurred whether or not implementation takes place, and is therefore not incremental.

Sunk costs can be either costs for intangibles (such as research and development (R&D)), or costs for tangibles that have no other use (such as the costs of the Eurotunnel). When dealing with sunk costs it is sometimes necessary to be resolute in the face of comments such as 'good money is being thrown after bad'. Always remember the 'bad' money outflow happened in the past and is no longer an input factor into a rigorous decision-making process.

Be careful with overhead

Overhead consists of such items as managerial salaries, rent, light, heat, etc. These are costs that are not directly associated with any one part of the firm or one project. An accountant often allocates these overhead costs among the various projects a firm is involved in. When trying to assess the viability of a project we should only include the incremental or extra expenses that would be incurred by going ahead with a project. Many of the general overhead expenses may be incurred regardless of whether or not the project takes place.

There are two types of overhead. The first type is truly incremental costs resulting from a project. For example, extra electricity, rental and administrative staff costs may be incurred by going ahead rather than abstaining. The second type of overhead consists of such items as head office managerial salaries, legal expertise, accounting services, public relations, (R&D) and even the corporate jet. These costs are not directly associated with any one part of the firm or one project and will be incurred whether or not the project under consideration goes ahead. The accountant generally charges a proportion of this overhead to particular divisions and projects. When trying to assess the viability of a project only the incremental costs incurred by going ahead are relevant, those costs which are unaffected are irrelevant.

Dealing with interest

Interest on funds borrowed to invest does represent a cash outflow, but this element should not be included in the cash flow calculations. **To repeat, interest should not be deducted from the net cash flows**. If it were subtracted this would amount to double counting, because the opportunity cost of capital used to discount the cash flows already incorporates a cost of these funds. The net cash flows are reduced to a present value by allowing for the weighted average cost of finance to give a return to shareholders and lenders. If the undiscounted cash flows also had interest deducted there will be a serious understatement of NPV. For more details on the discount rate incorporating the cost of debt finance (interest) see Chapter 10.

Taxation and investment appraisal

Taxation can have an important impact on project viability. If management is implementing decisions that are shareholder-wealth-enhancing, they will focus on the cash flows generated which are available for shareholders. Therefore, they will evaluate the after-tax cash flows of a project. There are two rules to follow in investment appraisal in a world with taxation:

- **Rule 1** If acceptance of a project changes the tax liabilities of the firm, then incremental tax effects need to be accommodated in the analysis.
- **Rule 2** Get the timing right. Incorporate the cash outflow of tax into the analysis at the correct time. For example, it is often the case (for small firms) that tax is paid one year or more after the receipt of the related cash flows.

Tax rates and systems can change rapidly, and any example presented using rates applicable at the time of writing is likely to be soon out of date. We will not get too involved in the details of the UK taxation system but will concentrate on the general principles of how tax is taken into account in project appraisal.

In the UK, HM Revenue and Customs (HMRC) collects corporation tax based on the taxable income of companies. Specific projects are not taxed separately, but if a project produces additional profits in a year, then this will generally increase the tax bill. If losses are made on a project, then the overall tax bill will generally be reduced. Taxable income is rarely the same as the profit reported in the annual reports and accounts because some of the expenses deducted to produce the reported profit are not permitted by HMRC when calculating taxable income. For example, depreciation is not an allowable cost. HMRC permits a 'writing-down' allowance rather than depreciation. So for most plant and machinery in the UK, a writing-down allowance of 25 percent on a declining balance is permitted. In a firm's accounts, such equipment may be depreciated by only, say, 10 percent a year, whereas the tax authorities permit the taxable income to be reduced by 25 percent of the equipment value. Thus, reported profit will often be higher than taxable income. Other types of long-lived assets, such as industrial buildings, have different percentage writing-down allowances – some assets carry a 100 percent writing-down allowance in the year of purchase. *See* Worked example 4.2.

Worked example 4.2
SNAFFLE PLC

Snaffle plc is considering a project which will require the purchase of a machine for £1,000,000 at time zero. This machine will have a scrap value at the end of its four-year life: this will be equal to its written-down value (this simplifying assumption will be dropped later). HMRC permit a 25 percent declining balance writing-down allowance (WDA) on the machine each year. Corporation tax, at a rate of 30 percent of taxable income, is payable. Snaffle's required rate of return is 12 percent.[1] Operating cash flows, excluding depreciation, and before taxation, are forecast to be:

Time (year)	1 £	2 £	3 £	4 £
Cash flows before tax	400,000	400,000	220,000	240,000

Note: All tax flows occur at year ends.

In order to calculate the net present value, first calculate the annual WDA. Note that each year the WDA is equal to 25 percent of the asset value at the start of the year (*see* Table 4.1).

TABLE 4.1
Calculation of writing-down allowances

Point in time (yearly intervals)	Annual writing-down allowance (£)	Written-down value (£)
0	0	1,000,000
1	1,000,000 × 0.25 = 250,000	750,000
2	750,000 × 0.25 = 187,500	562,500
3	562,500 × 0.25 = 140,625	421,875
4	421,875 × 0.25 = 105,469	316,406

[1] If we are dealing with after-tax cash flows, the discount rate will be the after-tax discount rate.

The next step is to derive the project's incremental taxable income and to calculate the tax payments (*see* Table 4.2).

TABLE 4.2
Calculation of corporation tax

Year	1 £	2 £	3 £	4 £
Net income before writing-down allowance and tax	400,000	400,000	220,000	240,000
Less writing-down allowance	250,000	187,500	140,625	105,469
Incremental taxable income	150,000	212,500	79,375	134,531
Tax at 30% of incremental taxable income	45,000	63,750	23,813	40,359

Finally, the total cash flows and NPV are calculated (*see* Table 4.3).

TABLE 4.3
Calculation of cash flows

Year	0 £	1 £	2 £	3 £	4 £
Incremental cash flow before tax	–1,000,000	400,000	400,000	220,000	240,000
Sale of machine					316,406
Tax		0	–45,000	–63,750	–23,813	–40,359
Net cash flow	–1,000,000	355,000	336,250	196,187	516,047

Discounted cash flow

$$-1,000,000 + \frac{355,000}{1.12} + \frac{336,250}{(1.12)^2} + \frac{196,187}{(1.12)^3} + \frac{516,047}{(1.12)^4}$$

$$-1,000,000 \quad +316,964 \quad +268,056 \quad +139,642 \quad +327,957$$

Net present value = +£52,619

Note: tax is payable in the same year that the income was earned in this case; this is generally the position for larger UK firms.

The assumption that the machine can be sold at the end of the fourth year, for an amount equal to the written-down value, may be unrealistic. It may turn out that the machine is sold for the larger sum of £440,000. If this is the case, a *balancing charge* will need to be made, because by the end of the third year HMRC has already permitted write-offs against taxable profit such that the machine is shown as having a written-down value of £421,875. A year later its market value is found to be £440,000. The balancing charge is equal to the sale value at Time 4 minus the written-down book value at Time 3, viz:

£440,000 – £421,875 = £18,125

Taxable profits for Year 4 are now:

	£
Pre-tax cash flows	240,000
Plus balancing charge	18,125
	258,125

This results in a tax payment of £258,125 × 0.30 = £77,438 rather than £40,359.

Of course, the analyst does not have to wait until the actual sale of the asset to make these modifications to a proposed project's projected cash flows. It may be possible to estimate a realistic scrap value at the outset.

An alternative scenario, where the scrap value is less than the Year 4 written-down value, will require a balancing allowance. If the disposal value is £300,000, then the machine cost the firm £700,000 (£1,000,000 – £300,000) but the tax writing-down allowances amount to only £683,594 (£1,000,000 – £316,406). The firm will effectively be overcharged by HMRC. In this case a balancing adjustment, amounting to £16,406 (£700,000 – £683,594), is made to reduce the tax payable (see Table 4.4).

TABLE 4.4
Year 4 taxable profits

	£
Pre-tax cash flows	240,000
Less annual writing-down allowance	105,469
Less balancing allowance	16,406
Taxable profits	118,125
Tax payable @ 30%	35,438

The stages of investment decision-making

There is a great deal more to a successful investment programme than simply project appraisal. As Figure 4.1 demonstrates, project appraisal is one of a number of stages in the investment process. The emphasis in the academic world on ever more sophistication in appraisal could be seriously misplaced. Attention paid to the evolution of investment ideas, their development and sifting may produce more practical returns. Marrying the evaluation of

> The emphasis in the academic world on ever more sophistication in appraisal could be seriously misplaced.

FIGURE 4.1

The investment process

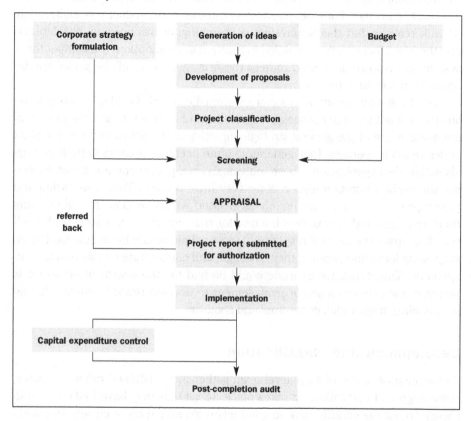

projects once screened with strategic, resource and human considerations may lead to avoidance of erroneous decisions. Following through the implementation with a review of what went right, what went wrong, and why, may enable better decision-making in the future.

Investment by a firm is a process often involving large numbers of individuals up and down an organizational hierarchy. It is a complex and infinitely adaptable process that is likely to differ from one organization to another. However, we can identify some common threads.

Generation of ideas

A firm is more likely to founder because of a shortage of good investment ideas than because of poor methods of appraisal. A good investment planning process requires a continuous flow of ideas to regenerate the organization through the exploitation of new opportunities. Thought needs to be given to the development of a system for the encouragement of idea generation and subsequent communication through the firm. Indeed, one of the central tasks of senior management is to nurture a culture of search for and sponsorship of ideas. In the absence of a well-functioning system, the danger remains that investment proposals only arise in a reactive manner. For example, a firm examines new product possibilities only when it realizes that the old product is becoming, or has become, obsolete. Or else the latest technology is installed in reaction to its adoption by a competitor. A system and culture is needed to help the firm 'get ahead of the game' and be proactive rather than reactive.

One of the main inputs into a more systematic search for ideas is likely to be an environment scanning process. It is also helpful if all potential idea-generators are made aware of the general strategic direction of the firm and the constraints under which it operates. Idea generators often become sponsors of their proposals within the organization. These individuals, in a poorly operating system, can see themselves taking a high risk for very little reward. Their reputation and career prospects can be intimately associated with a project. If it goes badly then they may find themselves blamed for that failure. In a system with such poor incentives the natural response of most people would be to hold back from suggesting ideas and pushing them through, and concentrate on day-to-day management. This defensive attitude could be bad for the organization and it is therefore incumbent on senior management to develop reward systems that do not penalize project idea generators and sponsors.

Development and classification

As the sponsor or the division-level team gather more data and refine estimates, some degree of early filtering takes place. Ideas that may have looked good in theory do not necessarily look so good when examined more closely. In a well-functioning system, idea generation should be propagated in an unstructured, almost random manner, but the development phase starts to impose some degree of order and structure. Many firms like to have a bottom-up approach, with ideas coming from plant level and being reviewed by divisional management before being presented to senior management. At the development stage the sponsor elaborates and hones ideas in consultation with colleagues. The divisional managers may add ideas, ask for information and suggest alternative scenarios.

Ideas that may have looked good in theory do not necessarily look so good when examined more closely.

There may also be division-level projects that need further consideration. As the discussions and data gathering progress, the proposal generally starts to gain commitment from a number of people who become drawn in and involved.

The classification stage involves matching projects to identified needs. Initially, there may be a long list of imaginative project ideas or solutions to a specific problem, but this may be narrowed down in these early stages to two or three. Detailed evaluation of all projects is expensive. Some types of project do not require the extensive search for data and complex evaluation that others do. The following classification may allow more attention to be directed at the type of project where the need is greatest:

- **Equipment replacement** Equipment obsolescence can occur because of technological developments which create more efficient alternatives, because the old equipment becomes expensive to maintain or because of a change in the cost of inputs, making an alternative method cheaper (for example, if the oil price quadruples, taxi firms may shift to smaller cars).

- **Expansion or improvement of existing products** These investments relate to increasing the volume of output and/or improving product quality and market position.

- **Cost reduction** A continuous process of search and analysis may be necessary to ensure that the firm is producing at lowest cost. Small modifications to methods of production or equipment, as well as the introduction of new machines, may bring valuable incremental benefits.

- **New products** Many firms depend on a regular flow of innovatory products to permit continued expansion. Examples are Intel, GlaxoSmithKline and 3M. These firms have to make huge commitments to R&D, market research and promotion. Vast investments are needed in new production facilities around the world.

- **Statutory and welfare** Investments may be required by law for such matters as safety, or pollution control. These do not, generally, give a financial return and so the focus is usually to satisfy the requirement at minimum cost. Welfare investments may lead to some intangible benefits which are difficult to quantify, such as a more contented work-force. The Arnold and Hatzopoulos (2000) survey showed that 78 percent of the firms undertook non-economic projects directed at health and safety issues; 74 percent accepted projects motivated by legislation; and 54 percent had paid for uneconomic projects for social and environmental reasons.

The management team need to weigh up the value of a more comprehensive analysis against the cost of evaluation. Regular equipment replacement, cost reduction and existing product expansion decisions are likely to require less documentation than a major strategic investment in a new product area. Also, the information needs are likely to rise in proportion to the size of the investment. A £100m investment in a new pharmaceutical plant is likely to be treated differently to a £10,000 investment in a new delivery vehicle.

Screening

At this stage, each proposal will be assessed to establish whether it is sufficiently attractive to receive further attention through the application of
sophisticated analysis. Screening decisions should be made with an awareness
of the strategic direction of the firm and the limitations imposed by the financial,
human and other resources available. There should also be a check on the technical feasibility of the proposal and some preliminary assessment of risk.

- **Strategy** Capital allocation is a pivotal part of the overall strategic
  process. A good investment appraisal system must mesh with the firm's
  long-term plan. The managers at plant or division level may not be able to
  see opportunities at a strategic level, such as the benefits of combining two
  divisions, or the necessity for business unit divestment. The bottom-up flow
  of ideas for investment at plant level should complement the top-down
  strategic planning from the centre. Each vantage point has a valuable contribution to make.

- **Budget** Most large firms prepare capital budgets stretching over many
  years. Often a detailed budget for capital expenditure in the forthcoming
  year is set within the framework of an outline plan for the next five years.

TABLE 4.5

Capital expenditure budgets for UK firms

	Small firms	Medium-sized firms	Large firms
	%	%	%
Outline capital expenditure budgets are prepared for:			
1 year ahead	18	8	–
2 years ahead	18	25	13
3 years ahead	35	50	18
4 years ahead	9	–	5
More than 4 years ahead	21	13	61
Blank	–	4	3
Detailed capital expenditure budgets are prepared for:			
1 year ahead	70	79	55
2 years ahead	21	13	21
3 years ahead	9	4	8
4 years ahead	–	–	5
More than 4 years ahead	–	4	11

Note: 96 firms completed the survey questionnaire.

Source: Arnold and Hatzopoulos (2000).

Individual projects are required to conform to the corporate budget. However, the budget itself, at least in the long run, is heavily influenced by the availability of project proposals. The Arnold and Hatzopoulos (2000) survey shows the use of budgets by UK firms (*see* Table 4.5).

Appraisal

It is at the appraisal stage that detailed cash flow forecasts are required as inputs to the more sophisticated evaluation methods, such as net present value. Manuals provide detailed checklists that help the project sponsor to ensure that all relevant costs and other factors have been considered. These manuals may explain how to calculate NPV and IRR and may also supply the firm's opportunity cost of capital. (If risk adjustment is made through the discount rate there may be more than one cost of capital and the sponsor then has to classify the project into, say, high, medium or low risk categories – see Chapter 5.) The project promoter may seek the aid of specialists, such as engineers, accountants and economists, in the preparation of the formal analysis.

Report and authorization

Many firms require that project proposals are presented in a specific manner through the use of capital appropriation request forms. These detail the nature of the project and the amount of finance needed, together with the forecasted cash inflows and the NPV, IRR, ARR or payback. Some analysis of risk and a consideration of alternatives to the proposed course of action may also be required.

Expenditure below a threshold, say £100,000, will gain authorization at division level, while that above the threshold will need approval at corporate level. At head office a committee consisting of the most senior officers (chairman, chief executive, finance director, etc.) will meet on a regular basis to consider major capital projects. Very few investment proposals are turned down by this committee, mainly because these project ideas will have already been through a number of stages of review and informal discussion up and down the organization, and the obviously non-viable will have been eliminated. Also, even marginally profitable projects may get approval to give a vote of confidence to the sponsoring management team. The alternative of refusal may damage motivation and may cause loss of commitment to developing other projects. If the senior management had had doubts about a proposal they would have influenced the sponsoring division(s) long before the proposal reached the final report stage. In most cases there is a long period of consultation between head office and division managers, and informal pressures to modify or drop proposals can be both more efficient and politically astute ways of proceeding than refusal at the last hurdle.

Implementation

Capital expenditure controls

Firms must keep track of investment projects so as to be quickly aware of delays and cost differences compared with the plan. When a project is authorized there is usually a specified schedule of expenditure, and the accountants and senior management will keep a watchful eye on cash out-flows. During the installation, purchasing and construction phases, comparisons with original esti-mates will be made on a periodic basis. Divisions may be permitted to overspend by, say, 10 percent before a formal request for more funds is required. A careful watch is also kept on any changes to the projected start and completion dates. Deviations from projected cash flows can be caused by one of two factors:

> Senior management will keep a watchful eye on cash outflows.

- inaccuracy in the original estimate, that is, the proposal report did not reflect reality perfectly;

- poor control of costs.

It is often difficult to isolate each of these elements. However, deviations need to be identified and explained as the project progresses. This may permit correc-tive action to be taken to avoid further overspending and may, in extreme circumstances, lead to the cancellation of the project.

Post-completion audit

Post-completion auditing is the monitoring and evaluation of the progress of a capital investment project through a comparison of the actual cash flows and other costs and benefits with those forecasted at the time of authorization. Companies need a follow-up procedure which examines the performance of projects over a long time span, stretching over many years. It is necessary to iso-late and explain deviations from estimated values. Table 4.6 shows the extent of the use of post-completion audits by UK companies.

TABLE 4.6

Replies to the question: 'Does your company conduct post-audits of major capital expenditure?'

	Small %	Medium-sized %	Large %	Composite %
Always	41	17	24	28
Sometimes/ on major projects	41	67	71	59
Rarely	12	17	5	10
Never	6	–	–	2

Note: 96 companies responded to the survey.

Source: Arnold and Hatzopoulos (2000).

There are three main reasons for carrying out a post-completion audit:

- **Financial control mechanism** This process helps to identify problems and errors evident in a particular project. A comparison with the original projections establishes whether the benefits claimed prior to approval actually materialize. If a problem is encountered then modifications or abandonment may be possible before it is too late.

- **Insight gained may be useful for future capital investment decisions** One benefit of auditing existing projects is that it might lead to the identification of failings in the capital investment process generally. It may be discovered that data collection systems are inadequate or that appraisal methods are poor. Regular post-completion auditing helps to develop better decision-making. For instance, past appraisals may have paid scant regard to likely competitor reaction; once recognized, this omission will be corrected for in all future evaluations.

- **The psychological effect** If potential project sponsors are aware that implemented proposals are monitored and reviewed they may be encouraged to increase their forecasting accuracy. They may also be dissuaded from playing 'numbers games' with their project submission, designed to draw more resources to their divisions or pet schemes unjustifiably. In addition, they may take a keener interest in the implementation phase.

Senior management must conduct a careful balancing act because the post-completion audit may encourage another sort of non-optimal behaviour. For instance, if managers are judged on the extent to which project outcomes exceed original estimates, there will be a tendency to deliberately understate the forecast. Also, if the audit is too inquisitorial, or if it too forcefully apportions blame for results that are only partially under the control of managers, then they may be inclined to suggest only relatively safe projects with predictable outcomes. This may result in a loss of opportunities. Ideally, regular post-completion reviews are needed, but many firms settle for an audit one year after the asset has been put in place. This may be inadequate for projects producing returns over many years. Some firms do manage an annual review of progress, and some even go as far as monthly monitoring during the first year followed by annual reviews thereafter. Many projects involve only minor commitment of resources and are routine in nature. The need for post-completion auditing is not as pressing for these as it would be for strategic projects requiring major organizational resource commitment. Given the costs involved in the auditing process, many firms feel justified in being highly selective and auditing only a small proportion. Another reason for not carrying out a post-completion audit in all cases is the difficulty of disentangling the costs and benefits of a specific project in a context of widespread interaction and interdependence.

Exhibit 4.4 describes the attitude taken by Severin Schwan, CEO of Roche, to encouraging risk-taking and post-event judgement of the decision-takers.

A healthy attitude to risk-taking

Haig Simonian and Andrew Jack

... Since becoming chief executive of Roche in April, the 40-year-old Austrian [Severin Schwan] has been on a whirlwind tour to gauge for himself what is widely viewed as the world's most successful big pharmaceuticals company ...

His career began in finance and continued through administration, including stints at foreign subsidiaries.

... Mr Schwan stresses his suspicion of metrics and the importance of teamwork – both to define his management style and what Roche requires ...

Collaboration is paramount for Roche. The group has a decentralised structure and ... a hands-off relationship with subsidiaries that analysts say has been a major contribution to its success. The federated structure has fostered focused research, with each company concentrating on specific areas, but has also been supple enough for collaboration on marketing.

Development of Avastin, for example, the breakthrough cancer treatment discovered by Genentech, was accelerated by a division of labour between it and Roche, with each concentrating on different types of the disease. Acterma, a novel rheumatoid arthritis treatment discovered by Chugai and already on sale in Japan, is now being prepared by Roche for Europe and the US.

Mr Schwan says such teamwork is essential in a knowledge-based business such as pharmaceuticals, where scientists need the freedom to think. 'When I toured our labs, I grasped the potential and the enthusiasm of our people. We have to capitalise on that. If you tell your people all the time what to do, don't be surprised if they don't come up with new ideas. Innovative people need air to breathe.'

He accepts there has to be broad guidance too and makes clear that teamwork also requires results. 'Our culture of working together at Roche is based on mutual trust and teamwork. An informal, friendly manner supports this: at the same time, this must not lead to negligence or shoddy compromises – goals must be achieved and, at times, tough decisions have to be implemented.'

His strategic priority now as chief executive is to reinforce the co-operation between Roche's scientists involved in discovering new drugs and their counterparts in diagnostics ...

He tried to encourage teamwork when still rising up the ladder in diagnostics. 'But such efforts were largely on a one-off project basis. After taking over diagnostics in 2006, I tried to do things more systematically. And, as chief executive of the group, I now want to do that more than ever.' ...

'This also has to do with encouraging people to take risks: innovation needs courage. And if something goes wrong, let's put the issue on the table, learn from it and resolve it together. In our sort of business, it's extremely important to be willing to celebrate failure.'

Celebrating failure may sound extraordinary coming from the chief executive of a company with SFr46.1bn (£22bn) in sales and SFR11.4bn in net profits. But Mr Schwan uses a recent example to illustrate his point. For much of last year, Roche was locked in a bitter legal dispute with its US rival Amgen over the intellectual property rights to their two competing drugs for anaemia associated with chronic kidney disease.

Roche's lawyers were convinced of the merits of their case and pushed the legal battle to the limits. In the end, a US court sided with Amgen, barring Roche's Mircera drug from the all-important US market.

Mr Schwan did not admonish the lawyers for poor judgment: just the opposite. He cracked open the champagne, congratulating them for pursuing what they believed was the correct outcome. 'No one in group legal has been punished or censured,' he says.

'Risk adversion is typical of the culture of a big company. People believe they'll never advance by sticking their necks out. We want to develop a culture of encouraging risks to distinguish ourselves. We want quality, not quantity.'

EXHIBIT 4.4

Source: *Financial Times* 4 August 2008, p. 14.

Conclusion

The typical student of finance will spend a great deal of time trying to cope with problems presented in a mathematical form. This is necessary because these are often the most difficult aspects of the subject to absorb. However, readers should not be misled into thinking that complex computations are at the centre of project investment in the practical world of business. Managers are often either ignorant of the principles behind discounted cash flow techniques or

> Managers are often ignorant of the principles behind discounted cash flow techniques.

choose to stress more traditional rule-of-thumb techniques, such as payback and accounting rate of return, because of their communicatory or other perceived advantages. These managers recognize that good investment decision-making and implementation require attention to be paid to the social and psychological factors at work within an organization. They also know that formal technical appraisal takes place only after a long process of idea creation and develop-

> The real art of management is in the process of project creation and selection, not in the technical appraisal stage.

ment in a suitably nurturing environment. There is also a long period of discussion and commitment forming, and continuous re-examination and refinement. The real art of management is in the process of project creation and selection, not in the technical appraisal stage.

5

ALLOWING FOR RISK IN
PROJECT APPRAISAL

Two risky ventures . . .

One that will (probably) not pay off . . .

The £200 billion gamble – Wireless Telecommunications

In 2000 the telecom companies of Europe committed themselves to what may prove to be one of the biggest gambles ever. They agreed to pay £80–£100bn to purchase 3G (third generation) licenses from various European governments, enabling them to offer internet access from mobile phones.

The 'winners' of the auctions for licenses, in addition to handing over thousands of millions to government, had to invest another £100bn building the infrastructure needed to deliver the service to the customer supposedly hungry for internet-enabled phones. By the middle of 2001, so great was the outflow of cash that major telecommunication companies had become burdened with extraordinary amounts of debt. For example, in 1998 BT had debts of roughly £1bn. Over the next three years these rose to over £20bn and serious concern was expressed in the City of London about the excessive debt. Shares tumbled as shareholders worried that too much was being paid for projects based on a high degree of optimism. 3G has been a disappointment. It took until 2005 to roll out 3G services actively, and even with the delay the engineers produced a poor customer experience, with low-quality content and few 3G-tailored websites. Furthermore, the level of competition is so intense that the companies may lose money even with millions of customers.

Perhaps, as the new technology develops, applications will be discovered that induce consumers to rush to pay for and the investment projects turn out to be very rewarding for shareholders. (Perhaps Apple is showing the way here.) Perhaps the 3G projects will be superseded by new technology (WiMAX?) before they are properly up and running. The truth is that we will not know for many years. Such is the fun and excitement of real world business decisions!

And one that did . . .

Camelot

Camelot bid for, and won, the right to create the UK's national lottery. They invested in a vast computer network linking 30,000 retail outlets and paid for 300 man-years to develop specialized software. Camelot also had to train 91,000 staff to operate the system, which can handle over 30,000 transactions a minute, and spend large amounts on marketing. The gamble seems to have paid off. It now regularly reports profits of over £50m a year. The owners of Camelot had a political battle on their hands trying to persuade the public and authorities that they took a risk and things happened to turn out well. It could have been so different; they could have made a multi-million pound investment followed by public indifference and enormous losses.

Introduction

Businesses operate in an environment of uncertainty. The 3G gamble and Camelot examples show that managers can never be sure about what will happen in the future. There is the upside possibility of events turning out to be better than anticipated and the downside possibility of everything going wrong. Implementing an investment project requires acceptance of the distinct possibility that the managers have got it wrong; that the project or enterprise will result in failure. However, to avoid any chance of failure means the adoption of a 'play-safe' or 'do-nothing' strategy. This may itself constitute a worse business sin, that of inertia, and will result in greater failure. There has to be an acceptance of risk and of the potential for getting decisions wrong, but this does not mean that risk cannot be analyzed and action taken to minimize its impact.

What is risk?

A key feature of project appraisal is its orientation to the future. Management rarely has precise forecasts regarding the future return to be earned from an investment. Usually the best that can be done is to make an estimate of the range of the possible future inflows and outflows. There are two types of expectations individuals may have about the future: certainty and uncertainty.

- **Certainty** Under expectations of certainty, future outcomes can be expected to have only one value. That is, there is not a variety of possible future eventualities – only one will occur. Such situations are rare, but there are some investments that are a reasonable approximation to certainty, for instance, lending to a reputable government by purchasing three-month Treasury bills. Unless you are very pessimistic and expect catastrophic change over the next three months, such as revolution, war or a major earthquake, then you can be certain of receiving your original capital plus interest. A firm could undertake a project that had almost complete certainty by investing its funds in Treasury bills, and receiving a return of, say, 2 percent per year. Shareholders may not, however, be very pleased with such a low return.

- **Risk and uncertainty** The terms risk and uncertainty are used interchangeably in the subsequent analysis. They both describe a situation where there is not only one possible outcome, but an array of potential returns. Strictly speaking, risk occurs when specific probabilities can be assigned to the possible outcomes. Uncertainty applies in cases when it is not possible to assign probabilities (or even identify all the possible outcomes). The range and distribution of these possible outcomes may be estimated on the basis of either objective probabilities or subjective probabilities (or a combination of the two).

Objective probabilities

An objective probability can be established mathematically or from historical data. The mathematical probability of a tossed coin showing a head is 0.5. The probability of taking the Ace of Hearts from a pack of 52 cards is 0.0192 (or 1/52). A probability of 0 indicates nil likelihood of outcome. A probability of 1 denotes that there is absolute certainty that this outcome will occur. A probability of 0.3 indicates that there is an expectation that in three times out of ten this will occur. The probabilities for all possible outcomes must sum to 1. We will now examine an example of an objective probability assessment based on historical data for the supermarket retailer Safeburys. If the firm is considering a project that is similar to numerous projects undertaken in the past it may be able to obtain probabilities for future profitability. For instance, Safeburys is examining the proposal to build and operate a new supermarket in Birmingham. Because the firm has opened and operated 100 other supermarkets in the past, and has been able to observe their profitability it is able to assign probabilities to the performance of the supermarket it is proposing to build (*see* Table 5.1 and Figure 5.1).

TABLE 5.1
Safeburys' profitability frequency distribution of existing 100 supermarkets

Profitability range (£m)	Frequency (Number of stores)	Probability
–30 to –20.01	1	0.01
–20 to –10.01	3	0.03
–10 to –0.01	11	0.11
0 to 9.99	19	0.19
10 to 19.99	30	0.30
20 to 29.99	20	0.20
30 to 39.99	10	0.10
40 to 49.99	6	0.06
TOTAL	100	1.00

An examination of this sort of historical record may be a useful first step in the process of making a decision. However, it must be borne in mind that the probabilities may have to be modified to take into account the particular circumstances surrounding the site in Birmingham. For instance, demographic trends, road connections and competitor activity may influence the probabilities for profit or loss. Even with large quantities of historical data there is often still a lot of room for subjective assessment in judging the range of possible outcomes.

> Even with large quantities of historical data there is often still a lot of room for subjective assessment.

FIGURE 5.1

Frequency distribution of supermarket profitability

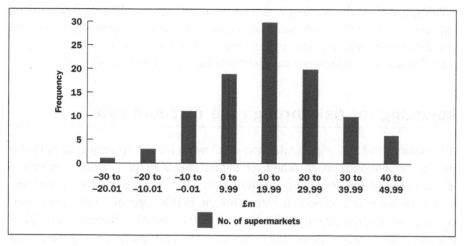

Subjective probabilities

In many project assessments there are no past records to help in the creation of the distribution of probabilities profile. For instance, the product may be completely new, or a foreign market is to be entered. In situations like these, subjective probabilities are likely to dominate, that is, personal judgment of the range of outcomes along with the likelihood of their occurrence. Managers, individually or collectively, must assign probability numbers to a range of outcomes.

It must be acknowledged that the probabilities assigned to particular eventualities are unlikely to be entirely accurate and thus the decision-making that follows may be subject to some margin of error. But consider the alternative of merely stating the most likely outcomes. This can lead to less well-informed decisions and greater errors. For example, a firm might be considering two mutually exclusive projects, A and B. Both projects are expected to be shareholder-wealth-enhancing, based on the estimate of the most likely outcome. The most likely outcome for A is for it to be shareholder-wealth-enhancing, with a 95 percent chance of occurrence. Similarly the most likely outcome for B is a shareholder-wealth-enhancing return, with a 55 percent chance of occurrence (*see* Table 5.2).

TABLE 5.2

Probability outcomes for two projects

Outcome	Project A probability	Project B probability
Shareholder-wealth-enhancing	0.95	0.55
Not shareholder-wealth-enhancing	0.05	0.45

By using probabilities, a more informed decision is made. The project appraiser has been forced to consider the degree of confidence in the estimate of expected viability. It is clear that Project A is unlikely to fail, whereas Project B has a fairly high likelihood of failure. We will examine in detail the use of probability distribution for considering risk later in the chapter, but now turn to more pragmatic, rule-of-thumb and intuitively easier methods for dealing with project risk.

Adjusting for risk through the discount rate

A traditional and still popular method of allowing for risk in project appraisal is the risk premium approach. The logic behind this is simple: investors require a greater reward for accepting a higher risk – the more risky the project the higher the minimum acceptable rate of return. In this approach a number of percentage points (the premium) are added to the risk-free discount rate. (The risk-free rate of return is usually taken from the rate available on government bonds.) The risk-adjusted discount rate is then used to calculate net present value in the normal manner.

An example is provided by Sunflower plc, which adjusts for risk through the discount rate by adding various risk premiums to the risk-free rate depending on whether the proposed project is judged to be low, medium or high risk (*see* Table 5.3). This is an easy approach to understand and adopt, which explains its continued popularity.

Drawbacks of the risk-adjusted discount rate method

The risk-adjusted discount rate method relies on an accurate assessment of the riskiness of a project. Risk perception and judgment are bound to be, to some extent, subjective and susceptible to personal bias. There may also be a high degree of arbitrariness in the selection of risk premiums. In reality it is extremely difficult to allocate projects to risk classes and identify appropriate risk premiums as personal analysis and casual observation can easily dominate.

> Risk perception and judgment are subjective and susceptible to personal bias.

Sensitivity analysis

The net present values calculated in previous chapters gave a static picture of the likely future outcome of an investment project. In many business situations it is desirable to generate a more complete and realistic impression of what may happen to NPV in conditions of uncertainty. Net present value calculations rely on the appraiser making assumptions about some crucial variables: for example

TABLE 5.3

Adjusting for risk – Sunflower plc

Level of risk	Risk-free rate (%)	Risk premium (%)	Risk-adjusted rate (%)
Low	9	+3	12
Medium	9	+6	15
High	9	+10	19

The project currently being considered has the following cash flows:

Point in time (yearly intervals)	0	1	2
Cash flow (£)	−100	55	70

If the project is judged to be low risk:

$$NPV = -100 + \frac{55}{1 + 0.12} + \frac{70}{(1 + 0.12)^2} = +£4.91$$ **Accept**

If the project is judged to be medium risk:

$$NPV = -100 + \frac{55}{1 + 0.15} + \frac{70}{(1 + 0.15)^2} = +£0.76$$ **Accept**

If the project is judged to be high risk:

$$NPV = -100 + \frac{55}{1 + 0.19} + \frac{70}{(1 + 0.19)^2} = -£4.35$$ **Reject**

the sale price of the product, the cost of labour and the amount of initial investment are all set at single values for input into the formula. It might be
enlightening to examine the degree to which the viability of the project changes,
as measured by NPV, as the assumed values of these key variables are altered.
An interesting question to ask might be: If the sale price is raised by 10 percent,
by what percentage would NPV increase? In other words, it would be useful to
know how sensitive NPV is to changes in component values. Sensitivity analysis
is essentially a 'what-if?' analysis – for example, what if labour costs are 5 percent lower? or, what if the raw materials double in price? By carrying out a
series of calculations it is possible to build up a picture of the nature of the risks
facing the project and their impact on project profitability. Sensitivity analysis
can identify the extent to which variables may change (one at a time) before a
negative NPV is produced. A series of 'what-if?' questions are examined in
Worked example 5.1.

Worked example 5.1
ACMART PLC

Acmart plc has developed a new product line called Marts. The marketing department in partnership with senior managers from other disciplines have estimated the likely demand for Marts at 1,000,000 per year, at a price of £1, for the four-year life of the project. (Marts are used in mobile telecommunications relay stations and the market is expected to cease to exist or be technologically superseded after four years.)

If we can assume perfect certainty about the future then the cash flows associated with Marts are as set out in Table 5.4.

TABLE 5.4

Cash flows of Marts

Initial investment	£800,000	
Cash flow per unit		£
Sale price		1.00
Costs		
Labour	0.20	
Materials	0.40	
Relevant overhead	0.10	
		(0.70)
Cash flow per unit		0.30

The finance department have estimated that the appropriate required rate of return on a project of this risk class is 15 percent. They have also calculated the expected net present value.

Annual cash flow = 30p × 1,000,000 = £300,000.

Present value of annual cash flows

= 300,000 × annuity factor for 4 years @ 15%

		£
	= 300,000 × 2.855	= 856,500
Less initial investment		−800,000
Net present value		+56,500

The finance department are aware that when the proposal is placed before the capital investment committee they will want to know how the project NPV changes if certain key assumptions are altered. As part of the report the finance team ask some 'what-if?' questions and draw a sensitivity graph.

■ *What if the price achieved is only 95p (5% below the expected £1) for sales of 1m units (all other factors remaining constant)?*

Annual cash flow = 25p × 1m = £250,000.

	£
250,000 × 2.855	713,750
Less initial investment	800,000
Net present value	−86,250

■ *What if the price rose by 1%?*
Annual cash flow = 31p × 1m = £310,000.

	£
310,000 × 2.855	885,050
Less initial investment	800,000
Net present value	+85,050

■ *What if the quantity demanded is 5% more than anticipated?*
Annual cash flow = 30p × 1.05m = £315,000.

	£
315,000 × 2.855	899,325
Less initial investment	800,000
Net present value	+99,325

■ *What if the quantity demanded is 10% less than expected?*
Annual cash flow = 30p × 900,000 = £270,000.

	£
270,000 × 2.855	770,850
Less initial investment	800,000
Net present value	−29,150

■ *What if the appropriate discount rate is 20% higher than originally assumed (that is, it is 18% rather than 15%)?*
300,000 × annuity factor for 4 years @ 18%.

	£
300,000 × 2.6901	807,030
Less initial investment	800,000
	+7,030

■ *What if the discount rate is 10% lower than assumed (that is, it becomes 13.5%)?*
300,000 × annuity factor for 4 years @ 13.5%.

	£
300,000 × 2.9438	883,140
Less initial investment	800,000
	+83,140

These findings can be summarized more clearly in a sensitivity graph (*see* Figure 5.2).

An examination of the sensitivity graph gives a clear indication of those variables to which NPV is most responsive. This sort of technique can then be extended to consider the key factors that might cause a project to become unviable. This allows the management team to concentrate their analysis, by examining in detail the probability of actual events occurring which would alter the most critical variables. They may also look for ways of controlling the factors to which NPV is most sensitive in any future project implementation. For example, if a small change in material costs has a large impact, the managers may investigate ways of fixing the price of material inputs.

FIGURE 5.2

Sensitivity graph for Marts

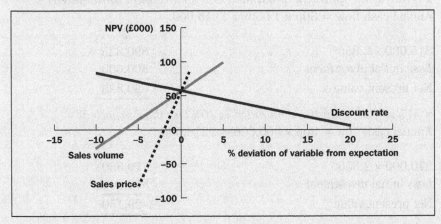

The break-even NPV

The break-even point, where NPV is zero, is a key concern of management. If the NPV is below zero the project is rejected; if it is above zero it is accepted.

The finance team at Acmart now calculate the extent to which some of the variables can change before the decision to accept changes to a decision to reject. (We will not go through all the possible variables.)

■ **Initial investment** If this rises by £56,500 NPV will be at zero (i.e. break-even NPV). A percentage increase of:

$$\frac{£56,500}{£800,000} \times 100 = 7.06\%$$

- **Sales price** The cash flow per unit (after costs), c, can fall to 28p before break-even is reached:

$$800{,}000 = c \times 1{,}000{,}000 \times 2.855$$

$$c = \frac{800{,}000}{2.855 \times 1{,}000{,}000} = 0.2802$$

Thus the price can decline by only 2% from the original price of £1. An alternative approach is to look up the point at which the sales price line crosses the NPV axis in the sensitivity graph.

- **Material cost** If the cash flow per unit can fall to 28p before break-even is reached, 2p can be added to the price of materials before the project produces a negative net present value (assuming all other factors remain constant). In percentage terms the material cost can rise by 5% (($2 \div 40$) × 100) before break-even is reached.

- **Discount rate** One approach is to calculate the annuity factor that will lead to the four annual inflows of £300,000 equaling the initial outflow of £800,000 after discounting.

300,000 × annuity factor   = 800,000
Annuity factor (four-year annuity) = 800,000/300,000 = 2.667

The interest rate corresponding to a four-year annuity factor of 2.667 is approximately 18.5%. This is a percentage rise of 23.33%.

$$\frac{18.5 - 15}{15} \times 100 = 23.33$$

This project is relatively insensitive to a change in the discount rate but highly responsive to a change in the sales price. This observation may lead the managers to request further work to improve the level of confidence in the sales projections.

Advantages of using sensitivity analysis

Sensitivity analysis has the following advantages:

- **Information for decision-making** At the very least it allows the decision-makers to be more informed about project sensitivities, to know the room they have for judgmental error and to decide whether they are prepared to accept the risks.

- **To direct search** It may lead to an indication of where further investigation might be worthwhile. The collection of data can be time consuming and expensive; if sensitivity analysis points to some variables being more crucial than others, then search time and money can be concentrated.

■ **To make contingency plans** During the implementation phase of the investment process the original sensitivity analysis can be used to highlight those factors that have the greatest impact on NPV. Then these parameters can be monitored for deviation from projected values. The management team can draw on contingency plans if the key parameters differ significantly from the estimates. For example, a project may be highly sensitive to the price of a bought-in component. The management team after recognising this from the sensitivity analysis prepare contingency plans to: (a) buy the component from an alternative supplier, should the present one increase prices excessively, (b) produce the component in-house, or (c) modify the product so that a substitute component can be used. Which of the three is implemented, if any, will be decided as events unfold.

Drawbacks of sensitivity analysis

The absence of any formal assignment of probabilities to the variations of the parameters is a potential limitation of sensitivity analysis. For Marts the discount rate can change by 23.33 percent before break-even NPV is reached, whereas the price can only change by 2 percent. At first glance, you would conclude that NPV is more vulnerable to the price changes than to variability in the discount rate. However, if you are now told that the market price for Marts is controlled by government regulations and there is a very low probability of the price changing, whereas the probability of the discount rate rising by more than 23.33 percent is high, you might change your assessment of the nature of the relative risks. This is another example where following the strict mathematical formula is a poor substitute for judgment. At the decision-making stage the formal sensitivity analysis must be read in the light of subjective or objective probabilities of the parameter changing.

> Strict mathematical formula is a poor substitute for judgment.

Another drawback of sensitivity analysis is that each variable is changed in isolation while all other factors remain constant. In the real world it is perfectly possible that a number of factors will change simultaneously. For example, if inflation is higher then both anticipated selling prices and input prices are likely to be raised. The next section presents a partial solution to this problem.

Scenario analysis

With sensitivity analysis we change one variable at a time and look at the result. Managers may be especially concerned about situations where a number of factors change. They are often interested in establishing a worst-case/best-case scenario. That is, what NPV will result if all the assumptions made initially turned out to be too optimistic? And, what would be the result if, in the event, matters went extremely well on all fronts?

Table 5.5 describes a worst-case/best-case scenario for Marts.

TABLE 5.5

Acmart plc: Project proposal for the production of Marts – worst-case and best-case scenarios

Worst-case scenario

Sales	900,000 units
Price	90p
Initial investment	£850,000
Project life	3 years
Discount rate	17%
Labour costs	22p
Material costs	45p
Overhead	11p

		£
Cash flow per unit		
Sale price		0.90
Costs		
Labour	0.22	
Material	0.45	
Overhead	0.11	
		0.78
Cash flow per unit		0.12

	£
Annual cash flow = 0.12 × 900,000 = £108,000	
Present value of cash flows 108,000 × annuity factor (annuity factor 3 years @ 17%) 108,000 × 2.2096	238,637
Less initial investment	–850,000
Net present value	–611,363

Best-case scenario

Sales	1,200,000 units
Price	120p
Initial investment	£770,000
Project life	4 years
Discount rate	14%
Labour costs	19p
Material costs	38p
Overhead	9p

Cash flow per unit		£
Sale price		1.20
Costs		
Labour	0.19	
Material	0.38	
Overhead	0.09	
		0.66
Cash flow per unit		0.54

Annual cash flow = 0.54 × 1,200,000 = £648,000

	£
Present value of cash flows 648,000 × annuity factor	
(4 years @ 14%) 648,000 × 2.9137	1,888,078
Less initial investment	–770,000
Net present value	1,118,078

Having carried out sensitivity, break-even NPV and scenario analysis the management team have a more complete picture of the project. They then need to apply the vital element of judgment to make a sound decision.

Probability analysis

A further technique to assist the evaluation of the risk associated with a project is to use probability analysis. If management have obtained, through a mixture of objective and subjective methods, the probabilities of various outcomes this will help them to decide whether to go ahead with a project or to abandon the idea. We will look at this sort of decision-making for the firm Pentagon plc.

Pentagon plc is trying to decide between five mutually exclusive one-year projects (*see* Table 5.6).

Proposals 1 and 2 represent perfectly certain outcomes. Project 2 has a higher NPV and is the obvious preferred choice.[1] In comparing Project 2 with Projects 3, 4 and 5 we have a problem: which of the possible outcomes should we compare with Project 2's outcome of £20m? Take Project 3 as an example. If the outcome is –£16m then clearly Project 2 is preferred. However, if the outcome is £36m, or even better, £48m, then Project 3 is preferred to Project 2.

TABLE 5.6

Pentagon plc: Use of probability analysis

		Net present value, NPV	Probability of return occurring
Project 1		16	1.0
Project 2		20	1.0
Project 3	Recession	−16	0.25
	Growth	36	0.50
	Boom	48	0.25
Project 4	Recession	−8	0.25
	Growth	16	0.50
	Boom	24	0.25
Project 5	Recession	−40	0.10
	Growth	0	0.60
	Boom	100	0.30

Expected return

A tool that will be useful for helping Pentagon choose between these projects is the expected NPV. This is the mean or average outcome calculated by weighting each of the possible outcomes by the probability of occurrence and then summing the result. That is, multiply the outcome by the probability expressed as a number between 0 and 1; then, add up all the numbers calculated. This is shown in Table 5.7.

The preparation of probability distributions gives the management team some impression of likely outcomes. The additional calculation of expected NPVs adds a further dimension to the informed vision of the decision-maker. Looking at expected NPVs is more enlightening than simply examining the single most likely outcome, which is significantly different from the expected NPV of £26m, for Project 5; the most likely outcome of 0 is not very informative and does not take into account the range of potential outcomes.

It is important to appreciate what these statistics are telling you. The expected NPV represents the outcome expected if the project is undertaken many times. If Project 4 is undertaken 1,000 times, then on average the NPV will be £12m. If the project is undertaken only once, as is the case in most business situations, there would be no guarantee that the actual outcome would equal the expected outcome.

TABLE 5.7
Pentagon plc: Expected NPV

Pentagon plc		Expected NPV, £m
Project 1	16 × 1	16
Project 2	20 × 1	20
Project 3	−16 × 0.25 = −4	
	36 × 0.50 = 18	
	48 × 0.25 = 12	
		26
Project 4	−8 × 0.25 = −2	
	16 × 0.50 = 8	
	24 × 0.25 = 6	
		12
Project 5	−40 × 0.1 = −4	
	0 × 0.6 = 0	
	100 × 0.3 = 30	
		26

The projects with the highest expected NPV turn out to be Projects 3 and 5, each with an expected NPV of 26. However, we cannot get any further in our decision-making by using just the expected NPV formula, because the formula fails to take account of risk. Risk is concerned with the likelihood that the actual performance might diverge from what is expected. Note that risk in this context has both positive and negative possibilities of diverging from the mean, whereas in everyday speech 'risk' usually has only negative connotations. If we plot the possible outcomes for Projects 3 and 5 against their probabilities of occurrence we get an impression that the outcome of Project 5 is more uncertain than the outcome of Project 3 (*see* Figure 5.3).

FIGURE 5.3
Pentagon plc: Probability distribution for Projects 3 and 5

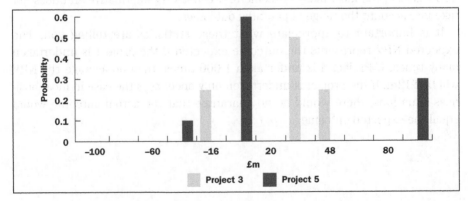

The range of possible outcomes is relatively narrow for Project 3 and presents an impression of lower risk. This is only a general indication. We need a more precise measurement of the dispersion of possible outcomes. This is provided by the standard deviation.

Standard deviation

The standard deviation, σ, is a statistical measure of the dispersion around the expected value. To calculate the standard deviation we first need to calculate the variance σ^2; then take the square root of the variance.

Calculating the variance is straightforward if you take it in stages:

Stage 1 First obtain the deviation of each potential outcome from the expected outcome $(x_i - \bar{x})$. So, in the case of Project 3 the first outcome is –16 (this is our x_i) and the expected outcome $(\bar{x})$ is 26. So, subtracting the second number from the first we have –42.

Stage 2 Square the result from stage 1 for each of the outcomes $(x_i - \bar{x})^2$. So, for the first outcome of Project 3 we take the –42 and multiply by itself: $-42 \times -42 = 1{,}764$.

Stage 3 Multiply the number generated in stage 2 by the probability of that outcome occurring. In the case of the first outcome of Project 3 we multiply 1,764 by 0.25 = 441. That is, $(x_i - \bar{x})^2\, p_i$.

Stage 4 Finally, add together the results of all these calculations for that particular project. So, for Project 3 we add 441 to 50 to 121. Which gives a variance of 612 (*see* Table 5.8).

Note that the variance is a very large number compared with the original potential outcome: for Project 3 these were –16, 36 and 48, whereas the variance is over 600, because the variance measures in pounds squared or NPVs squared, etc. The next stage is to obtain the standard deviation, σ, by taking the square root of the variance. This measures variability around the expected value in straightforward pound or return terms. The standard deviation provides a common yardstick to use when comparing the dispersions of possible outcomes for a number of projects. So, for Project 3 the standard deviation is 24.7.

TABLE 5.8
Pentagon plc: Calculating the standard deviations for the five projects

	Outcome (NPV)	Probability	Expected NPV, £m	Deviation	Deviation squared	Deviation squared times probability
Project	x_i	p_i	$\bar{x}$	$x_i - \bar{x}$	$(x_i - \bar{x})^2$	$(x_i - \bar{x})^2 p_i$
1	16	1.0	16	0	0	0
2	20	1.0	20	0	0	0
3	−16	0.25	26	−42	1,764	441
	36	0.5	26	10	100	50
	48	0.25	26	22	484	121
					Variance	= 612
					Standard deviation	= 24.7
4	−8	0.25	12	−20	400	100
	16	0.5	12	4	16	8
	24	0.25	12	12	144	36
					Variance	= 144
					Standard deviation	= 12
5	−40	0.1	26	−66	4,356	436
	0	0.6	26	−26	676	406
	100	0.3	26	74	5,476	1,643
					Variance	= 2,485
					Standard deviation	= 49.8

If we now put together the two sets of measurements about the five projects we might be able to make a decision on which one should be selected (*see* Table 5.9).

TABLE 5.9
Pentagon plc: Expected NPV and standard deviation

	Expected NPV, $\bar{x}$	Standard deviation, σ
Project 1	16	0
Project 2	20	0
Project 3	26	24.7
Project 4	12	12
Project 5	26	49.8

Project 1 would not, presumably, be chosen by anyone because it is dominated by Project 2. Also, Project 4 is obviously inferior to Project 2 because it has both a lower expected NPV and it is more risky (as defined by its higher standard deviation). That leaves us with Projects 2, 3 and 5. To choose between these we need to think about attitudes to the risk return trade off. Most people and organizations when faced with two projects offering the same NPV (expected NPV) but different levels of risk (variability around the expected NPV) would choose the less risky option. This assumption of *risk aversion* allows us to eliminate Project 5 because it offers the same expected NPV as Project 3, but it has a higher standard deviation. *See* Figure 5.4.

FIGURE 5.4

Pentagon plc: Expected NPVs and standard deviations

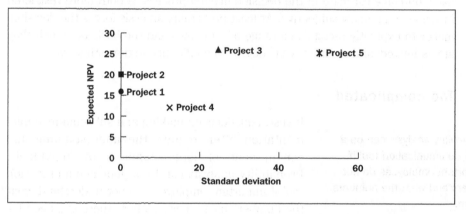

Projects 1, 4 and 5 are recognizably inferior, leaving a choice between Projects 2 and 3. From this point on there is no simple answer. The solution depends on the risk-return preferences of the decision-maker. This is fundamentally a matter for subjective judgment and different management teams will make different choices. When the author has put the choice between Projects 2 and 3 to MBA classes of middle and senior managers, approximately one-half take the safe option of Project 2. However, others in the class say that for the sake of a little more risk, Project 3 gives a significantly higher NPV and so should be accepted. The board of directors of Pentagon need to weigh up the risk preferences of the owners of the company and choose one project or the other. In doing so they may like to consider how this new project fits with the rest of the company's projects. If the firm already has a broad set of projects (operations, strategic business units, product lines, etc.) and many of these projects tend to do well in circumstances when Project 3 does badly, and *vice versa*, they may consider the benefits of diversification make them inclined to accept this investment.

Problems with using probability analysis

Too much faith can be placed in quantified subjective probabilities

When dealing with events occurring in the future, managers can usually only make informed guesses as to likely outcomes and their probabilities of occurrence. A danger lies in placing too much emphasis on analysis of these subjective estimates once they are converted to numerical form. It is all too easy to carry out detailed computations with accuracy to the nth degree, forgetting that the fundamental data usually have a small objective base. Again, mathematical purity is no substitute for thoughtful judgment.

The alternative to the assignment of probabilities, that of using only the most likely outcome estimate in the decision-making process, is both more restricted in vision and equally subjective. At least probability analysis forces the decision-maker to explicitly recognize a range of outcomes and the basis on which they are estimated, and to express the degree of confidence in the estimates.

Too complicated

Probability analysis can be a poor communication tool if important employees do not understand what the numbers mean.

Investment decision-making and subsequent implementation often require the understanding and commitment of large numbers of individuals. Probability analysis can be a poor communication tool if important employees do not understand what the numbers mean. Perhaps here there is a need for education combined with good presentation.

Projects may be viewed in isolation

The context of the firm may be an important variable, determining whether a single project is too risky to accept, so a project should never be viewed in isolation. Take a firm with a large base of stable low-risk activities. It may be willing to accept a high-risk project because the overall profits might be very large and even if the worst happened the firm will survive. On the other hand, a small firm that already has one highly risky activity may only accept further proposals if they are low risk.

Evidence of risk analysis in practice

UK firms have increased the extent of risk analysis in project appraisal over the past 20 years. Table 5.10 summarizes the use of these techniques. This trend has been encouraged by a greater awareness of the techniques and aided by the availability of computing software. Sensitivity and scenario analysis remain the most widely adopted approaches. Probability analysis is now used more widely than in the past but few smaller firms use it on a regular basis. Beta analysis, based on the capital-asset pricing model (discussed in Chapter 10) is rarely used. Simple, rule-of-thumb approaches have not been replaced by the more complex methods. Firms tend to be pragmatic and to use a number of techniques in a complementary fashion.

TABLE 5.10
Risk analysis techniques used in UK firms

	Arnold and Hatzopoulos				Alkaraan and Northcott
	Small %	Medium %	Large %	Total %	%
Sensitivity/scenario analysis	82	83	89	85	89
Shorten the payback period	15	42	11	20	75
Raise the required rate of return	42	71	50	52	82
Probability analysis	27	21	42	31	77
Beta analysis	3	0	5	3	43
Subjective assessment	44	33	55	46	–

Source: Arnold and Hatzopoulos (2000), sample of 96 firms: 34 small, 24 medium, 38 large. Survey date July 1997. Alkaraan and Northcott (2006). A total of 83 large companies returned questionnaires in 2002.

Real options (managerial options)

Traditional project appraisal, based on the calculation of NPV, generally implicitly assumes that the investment being analyzed is a straightforward go-now-or-don't-go-ever decision and that you either accept the project in its entirety at the outset or forget about the whole idea. So, if a company is considering a project with cash flow spread over, say eight years it would estimate the expected cash flows and discount all eight of them (usually following a probability analysis to allow for uncertainty). Under this view of decision-making there is only the initial decision to accept or reject; and if accepted the project is persisted with for the full term analyzed (say, eight years).

Some business decisions are like this. For example, if the project is to build a bridge for a government, then once you have signed the contract, regardless of what happens in the future, you are obligated to deliver a bridge. You cannot delay the start date; nor can you abandon the project halfway through if new information is received indicating that the worst-case scenario is now likely to happen (say, building costs double).

However, with most projects the managers are not making all-or-nothing decisions at the outset. They are able to respond to changing circumstances as they unfold over the life the project. For example, if events turn out badly the managers can react by abandoning the project. So a company that goes ahead with wind-powered electricity machinery production on the basis of a positive NPV given the government's current support for subsidizing renewable energy may abandon the project if government policy changes two years later. The option to abandon rather than be forced to persist has value. This value is usually ignored in traditional NPV analysis.

Sometimes it is the option to expand if events turn out well that is extremely valuable. On other occasions the decision to go ahead or not go ahead is not now-or-never but to consider a range of dates for going ahead; this year, next year or the year after. That is, the company has the option to defer the project, e.g. developing a copper mine only when the world market price of copper rises sufficiently. Going ahead now would destroy value at current low copper prices (a negative NPV) but the *option* to develop has value. The ability to abandon, expand or defer a project can add considerable value compared with a project without one of these flexibilities.

The real options perspective takes into account future managerial flexibility whereas the traditional NPV framework tends to assume away such flexibility.

Real options ('capital investment options') give the right, but not the obligation, to take an action in the future. They give value by presenting managers with the opportunity to exploit an uncertain future in which conditions change unpredictably, making one decision choice better than the other(s). By holding a real option we have the right to select whatever decision suits us best at the time. They differ from financial options traded in the market (*see* Chapter 19) in that their value does not depend on the movement of a financial security or instrument, such as a share or currency rate, but depends on the cash flows of real investment projects within the firm.

Some simple examples of valuable real options

Firms sometimes undertake projects which apparently have negative NPV's. They do so because an option is thereby created to expand, should this be seen to be desirable. The value of the option outweighs the loss of value on the project. For example, many Western firms have set up offices, marketing and production operations in China that run up losses. This has not led to a pull-out because of the long-term attraction to expand within the world's largest market. If they withdrew they would find it very difficult to re-enter and would therefore sacrifice the option to expand. This option is considered to be so valuable that some firms are prepared to pay the price of many years of losses.

Another example would be where a firm has to decide whether to enter a new technological area. If it does it may make losses, but at least it has opened up the choices available to the firm. To have refused to enter at all on the basis of a crude NPV calculation could close off important future avenues for expansion. Microsoft it thought to have lost $4bn on the original X-Box. However, three assets were created (options to expand): a prominent market position,

some strong franchises (e.g. 'Halo' series of games) and the online-gaming service. Subsequent X-Box launches exercise these options to grow. The
pharmaceutical giants run dozens of research programmes showing apparent
negative NPVs: they do so for what is often described as 'strategic reasons'. We
might alternatively call this intuitive option analysis. Perhaps the drugs that a
company is currently developing in a field of medicine, say, for the treatment of
Alzheimer's disease, show negative NPVs when taken in isolation. However, by
undertaking this activity the firm builds capabilities within this specialism,
allowing the firm to stay in the game and participate in future generations of
drugs which may have very high payoffs.

If a property developer purchases a prime site near a town centre there is, in
the time it takes to draw up plans and gain planning permission, the alternative
option of selling the land (abandonment option). Flexibility could also be incorporated in the construction process itself – for example, perhaps alternative
materials can be used if the price of the first choice increases. Also, the buildings could be designed in such a way that they could be quickly and cheaply
switched from one use to another (switching option), for example from offices
to flats, or from hotel to shops. At each stage there is an option to abandon plan
A and switch to plan B. Having plan B available has value. To have only plan A
leaves the firm vulnerable to changing circumstances.

Perhaps in the example of the property developer it may be possible to create
more options by creating conditions that do not compel the firm to undertake
investment at particular points in time. If there was an option to wait a year, or
two years, then the prospects for rapid rental growth for office space *vis-à-vis*
hotels, flats and shops could be more accurately assessed (deferral option or
timing option). Thus a more informed, and in the long run more value-creating,
decision can be made.

True NPV

Thus we need to raise the sophistication of NPV analysis by allowing for the
value of flexibility during the life of the project. A project in which there is the
ability to take further action after uncertainty has been resolved or reduced significantly is more valuable than one that is rigid.

> True NPV = Crude NPV + NPV of expansion option + NPV of the option to
> abandon + NPV of timing option + NPV of other option possibilities

Note: some of these options may be mutually exclusive, e.g. the option to expand and the option to
abandon.

An example of option use – the option to abandon

Imagine you are the chief executive of a company that designs, creates and
sells computer games. A film studio is about to start shooting a major action
thriller film. It will reach the box office in one year from now. The film company

has contacted you offering the right to develop and market a game based on the film (with film clips and voice-overs from the principal actors). You would have to pay £10m now for this. From previous experience you estimate that there is a 50:50 chance of the film being a success or a box-office flop. If it is a success the present value of all the future cash flows for the game will amount to £50m. If, however, it is a flop the high costs of development and promotion will mean a present value of all the future cash flows associated with the game will be negative £50m.

Should you pay £10m now for the game rights?

Conventional NPV analysis is likely to mislead you in this decision. You would set out the cash flows and their probabilities and calculate an expected NPV from them, which will be –£10m (*see* Figure 5.5). Hence you would reject the project.

FIGURE 5.5

Conventional NPV calculation

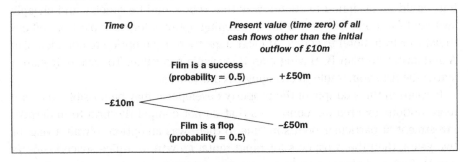

Film is a success   (–£10m + £50m) 0.5 = +£20m
Film is a failure   (–£10m – £50m) 0.5 = –£30m
Expected NPV   = –£10m

The fact that you would be purchasing merely an option to develop the game, without the obligation to do so, is very significant in the valuation of this project. You can abandon the whole plan in one year's time when you have some vital information: how the film performs at the box office after release. If it is success then continue. If it is a failure then do not invest any more than the original £10m and save yourself £50m.

With this flexibility built in, your cash flows in the future are +£50m if the film is well received, and zero if it hammered by the critics and audiences stay away. Each of these has a 50 percent chance of occurring (*see* Figure 5.6).

FIGURE 5.6

Options approach

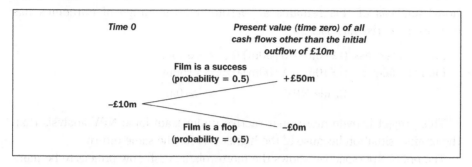

Film is a success $(-£10m + £50m)\ 0.5 = +£20m$
Film is a failure $(-£10m - £0m)\ 0.5\ \ = \ \ -£5m$
Expected NPV $= \underline{+£15m}$

The important point is that we don't view the project as a take-it-now-in-its-entirety-or-forget-it-deal, but rather consider the possibility of future managerial choices. In other words, managers are not passive but are active over the life of the project. There are contingent future decisions which can boost NPV. We need to allow for these possibilities now, when deciding whether to buy the game rights.

The payoff when the real option to abandon is considered is $+£15m$ and it is correct to pay £10m for the game rights now.

The value of the option to abandon is calculated as the difference between the NPV if obligated to go ahead with the entire project and the NPV with the option to abandon.

NPV with option – NPV if there is no option
    $+£15 - (-£10m) = £25m$

Welcoming risk

In traditional NPV analysis the greater the degree of uncertainty about the future cash flows, the lower the value of the project. The higher standard deviation is offputting to a risk-adverse shareholder and their agents, the managers.

Real option analysis takes a different perspective. Uncertainty provides value because the opportunity to exercise the option to take action later becomes all the more precious. To illustrate, let us double the range of the present value of the cash flows after the initial payment. So there is now a 50 percent chance of +£100m and a 50 percent change of –£100m. The expected NPV under traditional analysis of this remains at –£10m but the range of outcomes has increased, i.e. risk has risen.

Film is a success (–£10m + £100m) 0.5 = +£45m
Film is a failure   (–£10m – £100m) 0.5 = –£55m

Crude NPV   = –£10m

This project is even more unattractive under traditional NPV analysis than the original situation because of the higher risk for the same return.

The options perspective shows the more volatile cash flow project to be more valuable than the less volatile one because managers can avoid the downside risk by simply abandoning the project if the news turns out to be bad in one year's time. Risk is no longer symmetrical – that is, with equal probabilities of negative outcomes and positive outcomes around the expected return. It is asymmetrical: you benefit if things go well and do not lose if things go badly (at least you lose no more than you put down as a 'premium' to purchase the option in the first place).

Film is a success (–£10m + £100m) 0.5   = £45m
Film is a failure   (–£10m + 0) 0.5   = –£5m

Option perspective NPV = £40m

Uncertainty can therefore be a good thing, if you hold an option to exploit the change in circumstances as time goes on. If you do not have flexibility to respond then uncertainty is a bad thing and reduces value. Traditional NPV analysis assumes away the possibility of response to contingencies, resulting in a symmetric risk profile. Thus traditional NPV can seriously underestimate the true NPV of many capital investments.

Difficulties with real option analysis

- **Complexity of the valuation process** This book has explained real options using very simple mathematical examples. Analysts in this field actually make use of complex models. This complexity means that most managers are unable to participate in the valuation process in an informed manner without extensive training. The danger is that untrained managers treat the exercise as black-box decision-making: supplying some inputs, e.g. standard deviation of key cost or revenue components, and then handing the numbers over to the financial wizards who put them into the model and out pops the answer. The managers are totally unable critically to assess the machinations within the black box. It may be necessary to question the assumptions behind the calculations but the key managers are not empowered to do so. This could lead to poor decision-making because the quality of inputs is often poor (*see* next point) and to cynicism about the real options approach throughout the organization.

- **Measuring uncertainty** There is a practical constraint of not being able to measure the degree of uncertainty, and therefore the value of an option. Historical data is usually used (where available), e.g. past volatility of oil prices for an oil exploration and development project. A leap of faith is then made in assuming that future standard deviations will be like those in the past. In many cases the option valuer clutches at straws to provide inputs to the calculations – giving the impression of scientific rigour, when the foundations are in fact very weak. Standard deviation numbers are often derived from a source related only tangentially to the project, e.g. average standard deviation of technology company share-price movements may be used as a proxy for the standard deviation of outcomes for a new project initiated by a new company in a new technological field.

- **Overoptimism** In circumstances of very high uncertainty, e.g. when there is brand new technology such as the internet in the 1990s, there is a tendency to be overoptimistic about the value of expanding. In 1999 new 'dotcom' companies joined the stock market proclaiming that once their model was established the potential for scaling up was almost limitless. The market was so huge, they said, that even if the company had an 80 percent chance of complete failure it was still worth backing as it might be the one left standing with options to expand to control the industry standard (the one most visited by travellers, pet owners, book buyers, etc.). These companies presented 'analysis' from 'independent' experts on the growth of internet connections (usually exponential) and the revenues in this field (again exponentially rising). Sadly too many people believed the hype. Similar hype can be exhibited by junior and middle managers about a growth area they are particularly enthusiastic about. Senior managers need to view the high ranges of likely outcomes presented to them with scepticism. In particular they should ask whether the firm's competitors are really going to do nothing while they take all this market for themselves.

- **What is the life of an option?** It may not be clear how long the option value will be available to the firm. For example, a pharmaceutical company may have invested considerably in cardiovascular drug R&D, providing it with potential competitive advantages for many years to come through its options to expand to new generations of drugs. But it is impossible to be precise on how many years the option to develop more drugs in this field will be valuable: is it three years? Five or 20 years? The life of the option depends on so many variables, e.g. developments in surgery or competitors' actions.

Perhaps it is because of these difficulties that only 3.6 percent of large UK firms say that a real options approach to investment analysis is 'important' – none replied that it was 'very important' and 56.6 percent said it was 'not important' (Alkaraan and Northcott, 2006).

Conclusion

This chapter has dealt with some of the more sophisticated aspects of project analysis. It has, hopefully, encouraged the reader to consider a wider range of factors when embarking on investment appraisal. Greater realism and more information clears away some of the fog which envelops many capital investment decision-making processes.

However, this chapter has focused primarily on the technical/mathematical aspects of the appraisal stage of the investment process sequence. While these aspects should not be belittled, as we ought to improve the analysis wherever we can, it should be noted that a successful programme of investment usually rests far more on quality management of other stages in the process. Issues of human communication, enthusiasm and commitment are as vital to investment returns as assessing risk correctly.

Notes

1 These projects, with different returns for zero risk, exist only in an inefficient market environment because in an efficient, well-functioning market you should find increased return is available only by accepting increased risk.

Section II:

SHAREHOLDER VALUE

6

VALUE MANAGED VS EARNINGS MANAGED COMPANIES

Introduction

The first few chapters of this book linked together the objective of shareholder wealth maximization and acceptance or otherwise of proposed projects. This required knowledge of the concepts of the time value of money and the opportunity cost of investors' funds placed into new investments. If managers fail to achieve returns at least as high as those available elsewhere for the same level of risk then, as agents for investors, they are failing in their duty. If a group of investors place £1m in the hands of managers who subsequently generate annual returns of 10 percent those managers would in effect be destroying value for those investors if, for the same level of risk, a 14 percent return is available elsewhere. With a future project the extent of this value destruction is summarized in the projected negative NPV figure.

This technique, and the underlying concepts, are well entrenched throughout modern corporations. However, the full potential of their application is only now dawning on a few particularly progressive organizations. Applying the notion of opportunity cost of capital and focusing on the cash flow of new projects rather than profit figures is merely skimming the surface. Since the mid-1980s a growing band of corporations, ranging from Pepsi in the USA to Lloyds TSB bank in the UK, have examined their businesses in terms of the following questions:

- How much money has been (or will be) placed in this business by investors?
- What rate of return is being (or will be) generated for those investors?
- Is this sufficient given the opportunity cost of capital?

These questions can be asked about past performance or about future plans. They may be asked about the entire organization or about a particular division, strategic business unit or product line. If a line of business does not create value on the capital invested by generating a return greater than the minimum required then managerial attention can be directed to remedying the situation. Ultimately every unit should be contributing to the well-being of shareholders.

The pervasiveness of the value approach

The examination of an organization to identify the sources of value may not seem particularly remarkable to someone who has absorbed the concepts discussed in Chapters 1 to 5, but to many managers steeped in the traditions of accounting-based performance measures such as profits, return on investment and earnings per share, they have revolutionary consequences.

The ideas themselves are not revolutionary or even particularly new. It is the far-reaching application of them to create a true shareholder-value-oriented company that can revolutionize almost everything managers do.

- Instead of working with *plans* drawn up in terms of accounting budgets, with their associated distorted and manipulable view of 'profit' and 'capital investment', managers are encouraged to think through the extent to which their new strategies or operational initiatives will produce what shareholders are interested in: a discounted inflow of cash greater than the cash injected.

- Instead of being *rewarded* in terms of accounting rates of return (and other 'non-value' performance measures, such as earnings per share and turnover) achieved in the short term, they are rewarded by the extent to which they contribute to shareholder value over a long-term horizon. This can radically alter the incentive systems in most firms.

- Instead of directors accepting a low *cash flow on the (market value of) assets tied up* in a poorly performing subsidiary because the accounting profits look satisfactory, they are forced to consider whether greater wealth would be generated by either closure and selling off the subsidiary's assets or selling the operation to another firm which can make a more satisfactory return.

- There then follows a second decision: should the cash released be invested in other activities or be given back to shareholders to invest elsewhere in the stock market? The answers when genuinely sought can sometimes be uncomfortable for executives who prefer to expand rather than contract the organisation.

Dealing with such matters is only the beginning once an organisation becomes value based. Mergers must be motivated and evaluated on the criterion of the extent to which a margin above the cost of capital can be achieved given the purchase price. Strategic analysis does not stop at the point of often vague and woolly qualitative analysis, it goes on to a second phase of valuation of the strategies and quantitative sensitivity analysis. The decisions on the most appropriate debt levels and the dividend payout ratios have as their core consideration the impact on shareholder wealth. In the field of human resources, it is accepted that all organizations need a committed workforce. But committed to what? Shareholder value-based management provides an answer, but also places an onus on managers to communicate, educate and convert everyone else to the process of value creation. This may require a shift in culture, in systems and procedures as well as a major teaching and learning effort.

Value-based management brings together the way in which shares are valued by investors with the strategy of the firm, its organizational capabilities and the finance function (*see* Figure 6.1).

FIGURE 6.1

Components of shareholder value-based management

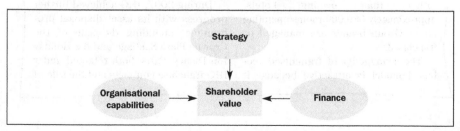

Value-based management is much more than a technique employed by a few individuals who are 'good with numbers'. The principles behind it must pervade the organization – it touches almost all aspects of organisational life.

Value-based management is a managerial approach in which the primary purpose is long-run shareholder wealth maximisation. The objective of the firm, its systems, strategy, processes, analytical techniques, performance measurements and culture have as their guiding objective long-term shareholder wealth maximisation.

> The objective of the firm, its systems, strategy and culture have as their guiding objective shareholder wealth maximization.

Intercontinental Hotels are very aware of the three key questions at the heart of value-based management (How much money? What rate of return? Is this sufficient given the opportunity cost of capital?). The managers are focused on generating high returns from every pound employed in the business. They have gradually withdrawn from the business of owning hotel buildings, which requires large amounts of capital for little reward, and built up a service business of managing hotels, allowing them to release vast amounts of money to give back to shareholders – *see* Exhibit 6.1.

Creating value with every pound at Intercontinental Hotels

Hotels owners are increasingly recognising the benefits of working with a group such as IHG which can offer a portfolio of brands to suit the different real estate opportunities an owner may have, together with effective revenue delivery through global reservation channels. Furthermore, hotel ownership is increasingly being separated from hotel operations, encouraging hotel owners to use third parties such as IHG to manage or franchise their hotels ... IHG seeks to deliver enduring top quartile shareholder returns, when measured against a broad global hotel peer group. IHG's future growth will be achieved predominantly by managing and franchising rather than owning hotels. Approximately 580,000 rooms operating under Group brands are managed or franchised.

The managed and franchised fee-based model is attractive because it enables the Group to achieve its goals with limited capital investment at an accelerated pace. For this reason, the Group has executed a disposal programme for most of its owned hotels, releasing capital and enabling the return of funds to shareholders as well as targeted investment in the business.

A key characteristic of the managed and franchised business is that it generated more cash than is required for investment in the business, with a high return on capital employed. Currently 86% of continuing earnings before regional and central overheads, exceptional items, interest and tax is derived from managed and franchised operations.

During 2007, IHG achieved further progress with its asset disposal programme, including the sale of the Crowne Plaza Santiago and the Holiday Inn Disney, Paris, both retained under IHG franchise contracts and the sale of the InterContinental Montreal retained under an IHG management agreement. In total these transactions generated £49m in proceeds before transaction costs ... In 2007, IHG paid a £709m special dividend, completed a third £250m share buyback and commenced a £150m share buyback. At the year-end, £100m of this buyback was outstanding. Since March 2004, IHG has returned £3.5bn to shareholders.

EXHIBIT 6.1

Source: Intercontinental Hotels Annual Report 2007.

Case study: Compass Group

Perhaps we can gain a glimpse of what shareholder value is by considering the 2006–10 crisis and revival at the worldwide catering company Compass. Sir Roy Gardner was appointed chairman by shareholders to sort out the mess at this 40,000-employee company in 2006. Over the previous four years the share price had halved as the company suffered from one subsidiary after another reporting difficulties; there was even one subsidiary, which feeds UN peace-keepers around the globe, being investigated for corruption at the UN. In the UK catering businesses (e.g. supplying school dinners) there were many loss-making contracts, problems with suppliers and collapsing profit margins.

Sir Roy quickly identified poor decision-making processes; lack of controls (to allow managers to see what was going on in the business and then direct action); poor control of working capital; and a flawed operational structure. He said, 'The previous management concentrated far too much on growing the business, through acquisition. They should have stopped and made sure what they had acquired delivered the expected results'.[1] The acquisition spree resulted in an odd collection of businesses often with little in common. For example, it owned a single hotel, the Strand Palace: 'We don't need one hotel and you have to ask yourself why have we got this'.[2]

A plan was formulated involving organisational restructuring, disposals and cost savings. In the 2007–09 period the company was cut down to focus on its core contract catering business (and to a lesser extent on the support services business). The hotel was quickly sold. Select Service Partner, its travel conces-sions group, was sold for £1.8bn and the proceeds used to reduce its debt and pension deficit. Selecta, the European vending machine business, was sold for £772.5m. Compass withdrew from more than one-third of the countries it oper-ated in, bringing the total down to around 55. The pull-outs were from countries where little or no profit was being made and where operations were small. It also decided to cease the UN business.

'I will not rule out further disposals. At the end of the day it's about share-holder value. If there are businesses that are producing low returns we will consider divesting them,' Sir Roy said.[3] A new management performance pro-gramme has been put in place to change the operational culture. Tighter accounting and audit processes were also introduced to get a grip on where value is being lost. Shareholders received £400m through the company using cash raised from disposals to buy back their shares in the company.

By 2010 it had such strength in its balance sheet and such formidable posi-tive cash flow that it was making a number of major investments in its existing businesses and adding some more by 'in-fill' acquisitions.

> We believe that the key to creating shareholder value is the delivery of strong cash flow. Our aim is to deliver this through revenue growth and operating efficiency, sup-ported by disciplined use of capital expenditure and working capital. The delivery of strong cash flow provides us with the opportunity to reinvest that cash to grow the business and to reward shareholders.
>
> We have a clear and well-focused strategy. Our combined food and support serv-ices offer positions us to take advantage of the continued growth in outsourcing ... Our approach has been to build scale within countries to enable us to drive efficien-cies, combining local market knowledge with the global reach necessary to meet the needs of multinational clients.[4]

The share price has started to rise as investors perceive a greater shareholder value focus throughout the firm – *see* Figure 6.2.

FIGURE 6.2

Compass plc share return performance compared with the FTSE All Share Index

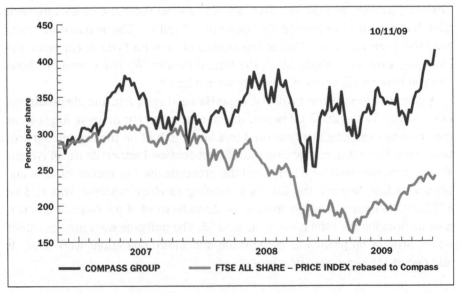

Source: Datastream

Why shareholder value?

It is clear that many commercial companies put shareholder value in second or third place behind other objectives. So why should we feel justified in holding up shareholder wealth maximisation as the banner to follow? Isn't growth in sales or market share more worthy? And what about the return to the labour force and to society generally?

What follows is a brief recap and extension of some of the comments made in Chapter 1 about the objectives of the firm in a competitive market environment that has responsibilities to shareholders.

There are several reasons why shareholder value is gaining momentum. One of these is the increasing threat of takeover by teams of managers searching for poorly managed businesses. Perhaps these individuals are at present running a competitor firm or are wide-ranging 'corporate raiders' ready to swoop on under-managed firms in any industry which, through radical strategic change, divestiture and shifting of executive incentives, can create more value for shareholders.

The owners of businesses have a right to demand that directors act in their best interests, and are increasingly using their powers to remove the stewards of their savings if they fail to do their utmost. To feel truly safe in their jobs managers should aim to create as much wealth as possible.

Arguably society as a whole will benefit if shareholder-owned firms concentrate on value creation. In this way scarce resources can be directed to their most valuable uses. Maximising the productivity of resources enables high economic growth and higher standards of living.

Confusing objectives

Some managers claim that there are measures of performance that are synonymous with, or good proxies for, shareholder wealth – such as customer satisfaction, market leadership or lowest-cost producer. These are then set as 'strategic objectives'. In many cases achieving these goals does go hand in hand with shareholder returns but, as Figure 6.3 shows, the pursuit of these objectives can be taken too far. There is frequently a trade-off between shareholder

FIGURE 6.3

Market share as a strategic objective can be taken too far

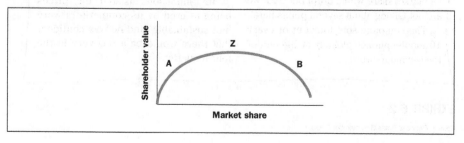

value and these proxy goals. Taking market share as an example: it is apparent that for many firms increasing market share will bring greater economies of scale, create barriers to entry for potential competitors and help establish brand loyalty, among other benefits. This sort of situation is demonstrated by moving from A to Z in Figure 6.3. High market share is clearly an important factor in many industries but some firms seem to become trapped in an obsessive quest for market share.

The car industry is notorious for its very poor returns to shareholders combined with addiction to market share data. For example, the car manufacturers rarely produce double-figure returns on capital. Indeed, a large proportion produce losses. Perhaps some in the industry have taken matters too far and ended up at point B in Figure 6.3. Enormous investment in plant capacity, marketing and price promotions has created a situation where the risk-adjusted returns on the investment are lower than the optimum.

Nokia has indicated that it will not engage in a price war to gain market share – *see* Exhibit 6.2.

Nokia warning surprises investors

David Ibison

Nokia, the world's largest mobile phone maker, yesterday warned that its market share would shrink in the third quarter, bringing to an end a period of almost uninterrupted growth and wiping almost 10 per cent off its share price.

The Finnish company stood by its earlier forecast that industry-wide unit sales for the full year would increase, but admitted for the first time that aggressive moves by its competitors were pricing it out of the market.

The warning surprised investors, who had come to believe the industry juggernaut was immune to the global economic downturn. ...

Rick Simonson, Nokia's chief financial officer, declined to reveal by how much its market share would drop, but said 'we are not talking about several points here'.

The company sold four out of every 10 mobile phones globally at the end of the second quarter. ...

Nokia stressed the decline in its market share was due to a decision not to participate in a price war for low-end phone sales being waged by competitors such as Samsung of South Korea.

'Nokia's strategy is to take market share only when the company believes it to be sustainably profitable in the longer term,' it said. In spite of this commitment to profitability, the announcement has made clear for the first time that Nokia is not impervious to competitive pressures.

It raises doubts about the sustainability of Nokia's business model of building market share, especially in large emerging markets, and increasing its profits while being able to reduce the prices of its handsets.

Mr Simonson insisted the prices being offered by its competitors were 'not sustainable' and he was confident that there would be a recovery in the fourth quarter.

EXHIBIT 6.2

Source: *Financial Times* 6 September 2008, p. 13.

Three steps to value

There are three steps to creating shareholder value (*see* Figure 6.4). First, obtain awareness of, and a genuine commitment to, a shareholder-wealth-enhancing mission throughout the organization. Second, put in place techniques for measuring whether value is being created at various organizational levels. Make sure everyone understands and respects the measures adopted. Third, ensure that every aspect of management is suffused with the shareholder value objective, from human resource management to research and development.

> Ensure that every aspect of management is suffused with the shareholder value objective, from human resource management to research and development.

It is clearly important to have a management team that both understand and are fully committed to shareholder value. To implement true shareholder wealth maximisation, managers need to know how to measure the wealth-creating potential of their actions. Before turning to appropriate methods of evaluating value creation we will examine some of the more popular and increasingly dated measurement techniques used to guide (or misguide) a business.

FIGURE 6.4

The three steps of value-based management

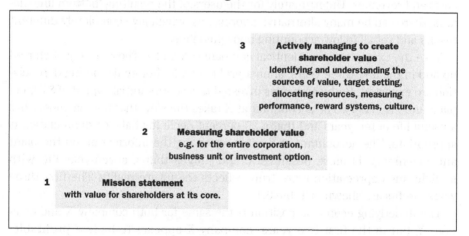

Earnings-based management's failings

The *Financial Times*'s Lex column expressed a view on the traditional accounting-based performance measure of earnings (profits) per share:

> How do you know a company is doing well? When earnings per share (eps) are growing rapidly, would be the standard reply. Eps is the main valuation yardstick used by investors; it has also become something of a fixation within companies. Rentokil, most famously among UK companies, has a target of boosting eps by at least 20 percent

a year. One of the reasons it gobbled up rival services group, BET, was to keep that growth rate going a few more years. But eps is not a holy grail in determining how well a company is performing. This is not merely because management still have latitude in deciding what earnings to report; it is because eps growth says little about whether a company is investing shrewdly and managing its assets effectively. It may, for example, be possible to boost eps by stepping up the rate of investment. But unless the return on investment exceeds the cost of capital, a company will be destroying value.

Financial Times 7 May 1996.

There are many reasons why earnings can mislead in the measurement of value creation, some of which are:

- accounting is subject to distortions and manipulations;
- the investment made is often inadequately represented;
- the time value of money is excluded from the calculation;
- risk is not considered.

The trouble with accounting numbers

When drawing up profit and loss accounts and balance sheets accountants have to make judgments and choose a basis for their calculations. They try to match costs and revenues. Unfortunately for the users of the resulting 'bottom line' figures, there can be many alternative approaches, which give completely different results and yet all follow accounting body guidelines.

Take the example of the identical companies X and Y. These have just started up and in the first three years, annual profits of £3m before deducting depreciation are expected. Both companies invested their entire initial capital of £10m in plant and machinery. The accountant at X takes the view that the machinery has a useful life of ten years and that a 25 percent declining balance depreciation is appropriate. The accountant at Y, after reviewing the information on the plant and machinery, is more pessimistic and judges that a seven-year life with straight-line depreciation more truly reflects the future reality. The first three years' profits are shown in Table 6.1.

The underlying economic position is the same for both company X and company Y, but in the first two years, company X appears to be less profitable. Outside observers and management comparing the two companies may gain a distorted view of quality of stewardship and the potential of the firm. Investment decisions and incentive schemes based on profit figures can lead to sub-optimal decisions and behaviour. They may also lead to deliberate manipulation. There are several arbitrary accounting allocations that make comparisons and decisions difficult. These concern, for example, goodwill and provisions, extraordinary and exceptional items and the treatment of research and development expenditure.

TABLE 6.1

Companies X and Y: Profits for the first three years

	Year (£000s)		
	1	2	3
Company X			
Pre-depreciation profit	3,000	3,000	3,000
Depreciation	2,500	1,875	1,406
Earnings	500	1,125	1,594
Company Y			
Pre-depreciation profit	3,000	3,000	3,000
Depreciation	1,429	1,429	1,429
Earnings	1,571	1,571	1,571

Ignoring the investment money sacrificed

Examining earnings per share growth as an indicator of success fails to take account of the investment needed to generate that growth. Take the case of companies A and B (*see* Table 6.2), both of which have growth in earnings of 10 percent per year and are therefore equally attractive to an earnings-based analyst or manager.

TABLE 6.2

Companies A and B: Earnings

	Year (£000s)		
	1	2	3
Earnings of A	1,000	1,100	1,210
Earnings of B	1,000	1,100	1,210

To a value-oriented analyst A is much more interesting than B if we allow for the possibility that less additional investment is needed for A to create this improving profits pattern. For example, both firms need to offer credit terms to their customers: however B has to offer much more generous terms than A to gain sales; so it has to invest cash in supporting higher debtor balances. B is also less efficient in its production process and has to invest larger amounts in inventory for every unit increase in sales.

When B's accounts are drawn up the additional debtors and inventory are included as an asset in the balance sheet and do not appear as a cost element in the profit and loss account. This results in the costs shown in the profit and loss account understating the cash outflow during a period.

If we examine the cash flow associated with A and B (*see* Table 6.3) we can see immediately that A is generating more shareholder value (assuming the pattern continues and all other factors are the same) because it creates more cash for shareholders.

Table 6.3 illustrates the conversion from earnings to cash flow figures.

TABLE 6.3

Companies A and B: Earnings and cash flow

	Company A £000s			Company B £000s		
Year	1	2	3	1	2	3
Profit (earnings)	1,000	1,100	1,210	1,000	1,100	1,210
Increase in debtors	0	20	42	0	60	126
Increase in inventory	0	30	63	0	50	105
Cash flow before tax	1,000	1,050	1,105	1,000	990	979
Percentage change		+5%	+5.2%		–1%	–1.1%

If B also has to invest larger amounts in vehicles, plant, machinery and property for each unit increase in sales and profit than A the difference in the relative quality of the earnings growth will be even more marked.

Time value

It is possible for growth in earnings to destroy value if the rate of return earned on the additional investment is less than the required rate. Take the case of a team of managers trying to decide whether to make a dividend payment of £10m. If they retained the money within the business both earnings and cash flow would rise by £1,113,288 for each of the next ten years. Managers motivated by earnings growth might be tempted to omit the dividend payment. Future earnings would rise and therefore the share price would also rise on the announcement that the dividend would not be paid. Right? Wrong! Investors in this firm are likely to have a higher annual required rate of return on their £10m than the 2 percent offered by this plan. The share price (in a rational market) will fall and shareholder value will be destroyed. What the managers forgot was that money has a time value and investors value shares on the basis of *discounted* future cash flows.

It seems so obvious that a 2 percent rate of return on invested money is serving shareholders badly. Yet how many companies do you know holding tens or hundreds of millions of cash rather than giving back to shareholders to invest elsewhere? Sure, it gives managers a greater sense of security to have all that cash around – how can the company be liquidated and they lose their jobs? – but shareholders would rather this money was used more effectively. Any money that cannot be used to generate good returns should be handed back to them. If earnings per share are rising what have the shareholders got to complain about? retort the managers. The thundering reply is: it is easy to increase earnings per share just by holding onto ever-larger quantities of money; what shareholders want is a return greater than the opportunity cost of capital (the time value of money) – the return available elsewhere for the same level of risk.

A variation on the theme of growing eps by investing large sums is to acquire other companies. In the case of Vodafone shareholders have been worried that managers were incentivised to increase eps with insufficient attention paid to the amount of investment required by shareholders to boost these accounting numbers. The directors and senior executives were granted large share options if eps growth exceeded 15 percent a year over inflation. Investors thought this could be achieved by acquiring companies on lower price-earnings ratios regardless of the effect of this on shareholder value.

Ignoring risk

Focusing purely on the growth in earnings fails to take account of another aspect of the quality of earnings: risk. Increased profits that are also subject to higher levels of risk require a higher discount rate. Imagine a firm is contemplating two alternative growth options with the same expected earnings, of £100,000 per year to infinity. Each strategy is subject to risk but S has a wider dispersion of possible outcomes than T (*see* Table 6.4).

Investors are likely to value strategy T more highly than strategy S. Examining crude profit figures, either historic or projected, often means a failure to adequately allow for risk. In a value-based approach it is possible to raise the discount rate in circumstances of greater uncertainty – more on this in Chapter 10.

TABLE 6.4

Probabilities of annual returns on strategies S and T

	Strategy S		Strategy T	
	Outcome earnings (profits) £	Probability	Outcome earnings (profits) £	Probability
	–100,000	0.10	80,000	0.10
	0	0.20	90,000	0.15
	100,000	0.40	100,000	0.50
	200,000	0.20	110,000	0.15
	300,000	0.10	120,000	0.10
Expected outcome	**£100,000**		**£100,000**	

Worked example 6.1
EARNINGS GROWTH AND VALUE

Earnings and earnings per share growth can lead to higher shareholder value in some circumstances. In others it can lead to value destruction. Shareholder value will rise if the return obtainable on new investment is at least as great as the required rate of return for the risk class. Consider EPSOS plc, financed entirely with equity capital and with a required rate of return of 15%. To make the example simple we assume that EPSOS does not need to invest in higher levels of working capital if sales expand. EPSOS pays shareholders its entire earnings after tax every year and is expected to continue doing this indefinitely. Earnings and cash flow amount to £100m per year. (The amount charged as depreciation is just sufficient to pay for investment to maintain sales and profits.) The value of the company given the opportunity cost of shareholders' money of 15% is £100m/0.15 = £666.67m.

	£m
Sales	300.00
Operating expenses	157.14
Pre-tax profit	142.86
Taxes @ 30%	42.86
Profits and cash flow after tax	100.00

Now imagine that EPSOS takes the decision to omit this year's dividend. Shareholders are made poorer by £100m now. However, as a result of the additional investment in its operations for the next year and every subsequent year sales, earnings, eps and cash flows after tax will rise by 20%. This is shown below.

	£m
Sales	360.00
Operating expenses	188.57
Pre-tax profit	171.43
Taxes @ 30%	51.43
Profits and cash flow after tax	120.00

Earnings have grown by an impressive 20%. Also value has been created. The extra £20m cash flow per annum stretching into the future is worth £20m/0.15 = £133.33m. This is achieved with a £100m sacrifice now. Here a growth in earnings has coincided with an increase in value. £33.33m of value is created.

Now consider a scenario in which sales growth of 20% is achieved by using the £100m to expand the business, but this time the managers, in going for sales growth, push up operating expenses by 32%. Earnings and cash flow increase by a respectable 6.81%, but, crucially, value falls.

	£m
Sales	360.00
Operating expenses 157.14 × 1.32	207.42
Pre-tax profit	152.58
Taxes @ 30%	45.77
Profits and cash flow after tax	**106.81**

The incremental perpetual cash flow is worth a present value of £6.81m/0.15 = £45.4m. But the 'cost' of achieving this is the sacrifice of £100m of income now. Overall shareholder value has been destroyed despite earnings and eps growth. It is surprising how often senior managers make this basic error.

For an example of a real company growing earnings (profits carefully defined as before the deduction of interest, tax, depreciation and amortization) but producing poor returns on invested capital we turn to Vodafone – *see* Exhibit 6.3. Perhaps we should not focus exclusively on income over a few recent years. Perhaps this near term sacrifice is worth it. Perhaps net cash flows will rocket once the basic infrastructure is in place. Perhaps. (Over the six years following the publication of this article, Vodafone shares fell slightly (much the same as the market), which does not indicate delayed fruit-bearing.)

A wake-up call for bean counters

John Plender

There was something faintly surreal about the accounts of telecom companies in the 1990s bubble, with their multiple definitions of profit and their customary invitation to ignore the bottom line loss. Now that the bubble has burst there is still a hint of surrealism about, as I found when thumbing through Vodafone's figures last week.

Vodafone is now the 13th largest company in the world measured by stock market capitalisation. The obvious pertinent question is whether, when Vodafone's managers talk of 'enlarging our footprint', they are employing a euphemism for size for size's sake or whether they are creating real value.

The preliminary announcement contains a welter of figures, including a loss for the year of £9.8bn. ('Once again we have delivered excellent results,' says Lord MacLaurin, the chairman.) Then you have operating profit before goodwill amortisation and exceptional items; adjusted earnings per share; earnings before interest; tax, depreciation and amortisation (ebitda); and free cash flow.

These numbers are more flattering. Understandably enough, they are also the ones on which Sir Christopher Gent, Vodafone's outgoing chief executive, chooses to dwell.

I emphasise that this is no criticism of Sir Christopher or Vodafone, which observes the normal reporting conventions, but of the conventions themselves. Despite the shareholder value movement, traditional disclosure is hopelessly deficient in explaining the efficiency with which companies deploy capital.

Ebitda, earnings per share, free cash flow and the rest mean nothing without adequate information on the capital used to generate them. Yet nobody has had the wit to ask the quoted companies to report routinely their weighted average cost of capital along with some sensible measure of return on capital.

For that you have to turn to a securities analyst like Mustapha Omar at brokers Collins Stewart. His figures will tell you that Vodafone's cash flow return on investment stopped covering its cost of capital in 2000. Given the wholesale destruction of value since then, he worries that Arun Sarin, the incoming chief executive, is already talking about those damned footprints again ... Forcing companies, analysts and investors to focus on whether a surplus is being earned over the cost of capital could do wonders for value creation.

EXHIBIT 6.3

Source: *Financial Times* 13/14 September 2003.

Return on capital employed (ROCE) has failings

It is becoming clear that simply examining profit figures is not enough for good decision-making and performance evaluation. Obviously the amount of capital invested has to be considered alongside the income earned. This was recognized long before the development of value-based management, as signified by the widespread use of a ratio of profits to assets employed. There are many variations on this theme: return on capital employed (ROCE), return on investment (ROI), return on equity (ROE) and accounting rate of return (ARR), but they all have the same root. They provide a measure of return as a percentage of resources devoted. The major problem with using these metrics of performance is that they are still based on accounting data. The profit figure calculations are difficult enough, but when they are combined with balance sheet asset figures we have a recipe for unacceptable distortion. The *Financial Times* puts it this way:

> Unfortunately, the crude figures for return on capital employed – operating profit/capital employed – that can be derived from a company's accounts are virtually useless. Here the biggest problem is not so much the reported operating profit as the figures for capital employed contained in the balance sheet. Not only are assets typically booked at historic cost, meaning they can be grossly undervalued if inflation has been high since they were acquired; the capital employed is also often deflated by goodwill write-offs. Once balance sheets have been shrunk, pedestrian profits translate into fabulous returns.

Financial Times 7 May 1996.

Added to the list of problems is the issue of capitalisation. That is the extent to which an item of expenditure is written off against profits as an expense or taken onto the balance sheet and capitalised as an asset. For example, firms differ in their treatment of R&D; companies that spend significant sums on R&D and then have a policy of writing it off immediately are likely to have a lower asset value than those which do not always write it off against profits in the year of expenditure. Cross-company comparisons of profits/assets can therefore be very misleading.

Focusing on accounting rates of return can lead to short-termism. Managers who are judged on this basis may be reluctant to invest in new equipment as this will raise the denominator in the ratio, producing a poor ARR in the short term. This can destroy value in the long term. Fast-growing companies needing extensive investment in the short term with the expectation of reaping rich rewards in the long term should not be compared with slow-growth and low-investing firms on the basis of ARR.

Focusing on earnings is not the same as value

One of the most pervasive myths of our time is: '**But our shareholders do focus on eps and ARR, don't they?**' – and it is easy to see why. Senior executives when talking with institutional shareholders and analysts often find the conversation reverting to a discussion of short-term earnings forecasts. If a merger is announced directors feel the need to point out in press releases that the result will not be 'earnings dilutive' in the forthcoming year.

This surface noise is deceiving. Intelligent shareholders and analysts are primarily interested in the long-term cash flow returns on shares. The earnings attributable to the next couple of years are usually an insignificant part of the value of a share. Over two-thirds of the value of a typical share is determined by income to be received five or more years hence (see Chapter 13 for these calculations). Knowledge of this or next year's earnings is not particularly interesting in itself. It is sought because it sheds light on the medium- and long-term cash flows.

There are hundreds of quoted companies that do not expect to produce any positive earnings at all in the next two to five years and yet often these shares are among the most highly valued in the market. There are dozens of biotechnology companies that have tapped shareholders for funds through rights issues and the like for years. Some have become massive concerns and yet have never made a profit or paid a dividend. The same applies to internet companies and, in the past, it was true of satellite television operators (for example BSkyB) which have now reached the phase of high cash generation. Exhibit 6.4 describes what investors are looking for.

Investment community piles on pressure for better returns

Nigel Page

Tapping into the booming liquidity of global capital markets is the corporate ideal – but the gatekeepers of that liquidity, the global investor and analyst communities, are basing their investment strategies on increasingly focused information. In this environment, the historical reporting model is living on borrowed time – investors, who typically base share price valuations on their forecasts of future cash flows, demand forward-looking information to feed into their valuation models.

Management is increasingly sensitive to the stark fact that the use of equity capital is not 'free' – it has been invested in the hope of earning a return. It is this required return . . . that defines the company's cost of equity capital. Management can only create value for shareholders if the company consistently generates a return on capital greater than its cost of capital . . .

For companies, the challenge must be to use this escalating value focus in their strategic planning, and in measuring performance. Once the internal systems are in place, the priority is to establish effective communication into the marketplace. . . .

Historical cost accounting measures are becoming less relevant, with more companies using value-based information and non-financial indicators to judge performance internally. Greater disclosure in these areas will allow investors to make more informed decisions on the potential future of companies.

The international investment community is well aware of the limitations of annual reports, which provide emphasis on accounting profit – itself no real indicator of the creation of economic value . . .

Analysts and institutional investors focus much of their research on company strategy and the 'value platforms' underlying that strategy and recent surveys of investors' demand for, and use of, information confirm their desire for more forward-looking information, as well as the importance of drivers of future performance to their investment decisions.

EXHIBIT 6.4

Source: *Financial Times* 10 December 1999, FT Director (special section), p. VIII.

How a business creates value

Value is created when investment produces a rate of return greater than that required for the risk class of the investment. Shareholder value is driven by the four factors shown in Figure 6.5.

The difference between the second and third elements in Figure 6.5 creates the *performance spread*. The performance spread is measured as a percentage spread above or below the required rate of return, given the finance provider's opportunity cost of capital. Value is destroyed if 3 is greater than 2, and is created when 2 is greater than 3.

FIGURE 6.5

The four key elements of value creation

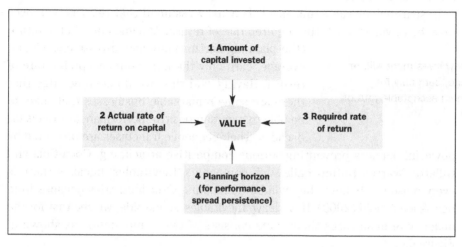

The absolute amount of value generated is determined by the quantity of capital invested multiplied by the performance spread. So, for example, if Black plc has a required rate of return of 14 percent per annum and actually produces 17 percent on an investment base of £1,000,000 it will create £30,000 of value per year:

$$
\begin{aligned}
\text{Annual value creation} \quad &= \quad \text{Investment} \times (\text{actual return} - \text{required return}) \\
&= \quad I\,(r - k) \\
&= \quad £1,000,000 \times (0.17 - 0.14) = £30,000
\end{aligned}
$$

The fourth element in Figure 6.5 needs more explanation. It would be unreasonable to assume that positive or negative return spreads will be maintained forever. If return spreads are negative, presumably managers will (eventually) take the necessary action to prevent continued losses. If they fail to respond then shareholders will take the required steps through, say, sackings or the acceptance of a merger offer. Positive spreads arise as a result of a combination of the attractiveness of the industry and the competitive strength of a firm within that industry (see Chapter 7). High returns can be earned because of market imperfections. For example, a firm may be able to prevent competitors entering its market segment because of economies of scale, brand strength or legal exclusion through patents. However most firms will sooner or later experience increased competition and reduced margins. The higher the initial performance spread the more attractive market entry seems to potential competitors (or substitute product developers). Examples of industries that were at one time extremely profitable and which were penetrated to the point where

> The higher the initial performance spread the more attractive market entry seems to potential competitors.

they have become highly competitive include personal computers and mobile phone manufacture.

In shareholder value analysis it is usually assumed that returns will, over time, be driven towards the required rate of return. At some point in the future (the planning horizon) any new investment will, on average, earn only the minimum acceptable rate of return. Having said this, we do acknowledge that there are some remarkable businesses that seem to be able to maintain positive performance spreads for decades. Their economic franchises are protected by powerful barriers preventing serious competitive attack, e.g. Coca-Cola and Gillette. Warren Buffett calls such companies 'Inevitables' because there is every reason to believe they will be dominating their industries decades from now – see Arnold (2009). If we leave Inevitables to one side, we see that for the majority of businesses their value consists of two components, as shown in Figure 6.6.

Any new investment will, on average, earn only the minimum acceptable rate of return.

FIGURE 6.6
Corporate value

Corporate value = **Present value of cash flows within planning horizon** + **Present value of cash flows after planning horizon**

In the second period (after the planning horizon), even if investment levels are doubled, corporate value will remain constant, as the discounted cash inflows associated with that investment exactly equal the discounted cash outflows.

If it is assumed that Black plc can maintain its 3 percent return spread for ten years and pays out all income as dividends then its future cash flows will look like this:

Years:	1 → 10	11 → infinity
Cash flow:	£170,000	£140,000

The value of the firm is the discounted value of these cash flows.

The discounted cash flow within the planning horizon is:

£170,000 × annuity factor (10 years, 14%) = £170,000 × 5.2161

$$= £886,737$$

plus the discounted cash flow after the planning horizon:

First discount to time 10: £140,000/0.14 = £1,000,000.

This is then discounted back 10 years:

$$\frac{1,000,000}{(1 + 0.14)^{10}} = \underline{£269,744}$$

Value of the firm	£1,156,481
Less initial investment	(£1,000,000)
Value created	**£156,481**

The value of the firm = Capital (£1,000,000) + Value created (£156,481)

$$= £1,156,481$$

An alternative approach: The value of the firm is equal to the initial investment in the firm (£1,000,000) plus the present value of all the values created annually.

Investment	+	Value created within planning horizon	+	Value created after planning horizon
£1,000,000	+	£30,000 × 5.2161	+	£1,000,000 (0.14 – 0.14)
		£30,000 × Annuity factor (10 years, 14%)		
£1,000,000	+	£156,481	+	0 = **£1,156,481**

The five actions for creating value

Good growth occurs when an expanding business unit or an entire corporation obtains a positive spread. Bad growth, the bane of shareholders, occurs when managers invest in strategies that produce negative return spreads. This can so easily happen if the focus of attention is on sales and earnings growth. To managers encouraged to believe that their job is to expand the business and improve the bottom line, acceptance of the notion of bad growth in profits is a problem. But, as we have seen, it is perfectly possible to show growing profits on a larger investment base producing an incremental return less than the incremental cost of capital.

Figure 6.7 shows the options open to managers. This model can be applied at the corporate, business unit or product line level.

It has already been demonstrated that overall Black plc produces a more than satisfactory return on investment. Now assume that the firm consists of two divisions: a clothing factory and a toy import business. Each business is making use

FIGURE 6.7

To expand or not to expand?

	Grow	Shrink
Positive performance spread	Value creation	Value opportunity forgone
Negative performance spread	Value destruction	Value creation

of £500,000 of assets (at market value). The clothing division is expected to produce an 11 percent return per annum over the next ten years whereas the toy
division will produce a 23 percent per annum return over the same period. After
the ten-year planning horizon both divisions will produce returns equal to their
risk-adjusted required return: for the clothing division this is 13 percent and for
the more risky toy division this is 15 percent.

The cash flows are:

Year	$1 \rightarrow 10$	$11 \rightarrow$ infinity
Clothing	£55,000	£65,000
Toys	£115,000	£75,000

The annual value creation within the planning horizon is:

$$I \times (r - k)$$

Clothing	£500,000 × (0.11 − 0.13) = −£10,000
Toys	£500,000 × (0.23 − 0.15) = +£40,000

Despite the higher return required in the toy division, it creates value (calculating required rates of return is covered in Chapter 10). For the next ten years a
15 percent return is achieved plus a shareholder bonus of £40,000. This division
could fit into the top left box of Figure 6.7. The management team may want to
consider further investment in this unit so long as the marginal investment can
generate a return greater than 15 percent. To pass up positive return spread
investments would be to sacrifice valuable opportunities and enter the top right
box of Figure 6.7.

The clothing operation does not produce returns sufficient to justify its present level of investment. Growth in this unit would only be recommended if such
a strategy would enable the division to somehow transform itself so as to
achieve a positive spread. If this seems unlikely then the best option is probably
a scaling down or withdrawal from the market. This will release resources to be
more productively employed elsewhere, either within or outside of the firm.
Such shrinkage would create value by reducing the drag this activity has on the
rest of the firm.

This line of thought can assist managers at all levels to allocate resources. At the corporate level knowledge of potential good growth and bad growth investments will help the selection of a portfolio of businesses. At the business unit level, product and customer groups can be analyzed to assess the potential for value contribution. Lower down, particular products and customers can be ranked in terms of value. A simplified example of corporate level value analysis is shown in Figure 6.8.

In Figure 6.8, strategic business unit A (SBU$_A$) is a value destroyer due to its negative return spread. Perhaps there is over-investment here and shareholders would be better served if resources were transferred to other operations. Many managerial teams pay insufficient attention to the amount of capital devoted to an activity: factory space is retained but rarely or lightly used; inventory levels are double what they need to be; expensive offices in town centres are retained, when an out-of-town block would be adequate; large cash reserves are held. A positive performance spread may be available simply by reducing the capital used by the SBU. Coca-Cola reduced dramatically the required return charge as capital when it separated and sold off capital-intensive bottling and distribution businesses, releasing capital and allowing it to focus on capital-light elements of the business, such as producing syrup concentrate. SBU$_B$ produces a small positive spread and decisions on its future will depend on the expected longevity of its contribution. SBU$_C$ produces a lower return spread than SBU$_E$, but manages to create more value because of its higher future investment levels. Some businesses have greater potential than others for growth while maintaining a positive spread. For example, SBU$_E$ might be a niche market player in fine china where greatly expanded activity would reduce the premium paid by customers for the exclusivity of the product – quickly producing negative spread on the marginal production. Strategic business unit C might be in mid-priced tableware

FIGURE 6.8

Value creation and strategic business unit (SBU) performance spreads

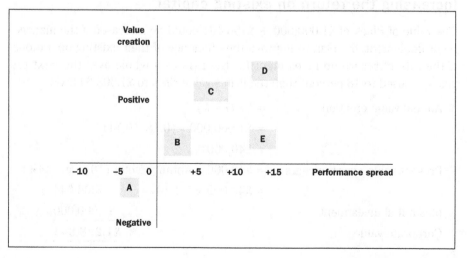

competing on design where investment in the design and marketing teams might produce positive spread growth. Strategic business unit D is capable of high spreads and high investment producing the largest overall gain in value. Drugs with lengthy patent rights often produce high positive spreads for many years, leading to high value creation over their lifetimes.

The five actions available for increasing value are shown in the value action pentagon (Figure 6.9). The five actions in the value action pentagon could be applied to Black plc.

FIGURE 6.9
The value action pentagon

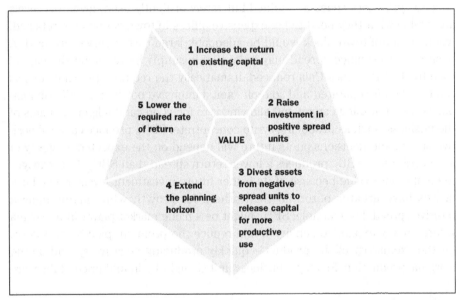

Increasing the return on existing capital

The value of Black of £1,000,000 + £156,481 could be increased if the management implemented a plan to improve the efficiency of their existing operations. If the rate of return on investment for the firm as a whole over the next ten years is raised to 18 percent then the firm's value rises to £1,208,644, viz:

Annual value creation	$= I \times (r - k)$
	$= £1,000,000 \times (0.18 - 0.14)$
	$= £40,000$
Present value over ten years	$= £40,000 \times$ Annuity factor (10 years, 14%)
	$= £40,000 \times 5.2161 \approx$ £208,644
plus initial investment	£1,000,000
Corporate value	**£1,208,644**

An increase of £52,163 (£1,208,644 – £1,156,481) in value is available for every 1 percent improvement in return spread.

Raise investment in positive spread units

If Black could obtain a further £500,000 from investors with a required rate of return of 15 percent to invest in the toy division to produce a 23 percent return the value of the firm would rise to £1,847,242 (£500,000 being the new capital invested).

Annual value creation on clothing	=	–£10,000
Annual value creation on toys = £40,000 × 2	=	£80,000
		£70,000

Over ten years

Clothing:	–£10,000 × Annuity factor (10 years, 13%)		
Toys:	£80,000 × Annuity factor (10 years, 15%)		
Clothing:	–£10,000 × 5.4262	=	–£54,262
Toys:	£80,000 × 5.0188	=	£401,504
			£347,242

plus the initial investment	£1,500,000
Corporate value	**£1,847,242**

Divest assets

If Black could close its clothing division, release £500,000 to expand the toy division and achieve returns of 23 percent on the transferred investment then value increases dramatically:

Annual value creation	$= I \times (r - k)$
	= £1,000,000 × (0.23 – 0.15)
	= £80,000
Present value over ten years	= £80,000 × Annuity factor (10 years, 15%)
	= £80,000 × 5.0188 = £401,504
plus initial investment	£1,000,000
Corporate value	**£1,401,504**

Kingfisher (B&Q etc.) released £440m by selling its Italian operations, which had produced low returns compared with the alternative uses for the money – *see* Exhibit 6.5.

Cheshire's eastern promise

Andrew Hill

The 'Gang of Four' went down in history as the group responsible for the worst excesses of China's Cultural Revolution. They got their comeuppance in the mid 1970s, following the death of Mao. That has not deterred Ian Cheshire of Kingfisher from dubbing his top team 'The Gang of Five' – the chief executive, his finance director, and his three regional heads – as he attempts to salvage his lossmaking operation in the Middle Kingdom.

When he stepped into the top job at Europe's largest home improvement chain slightly more than a year ago, Mr Cheshire looked at his portfolio and decided that, while his profitable Italian business was not worth keeping, his toehold in China was.

In Italy, Kingfisher owned an asset that rivals wanted to buy. The returns on capital were fine at 7 percent, but the business, number two in a mature market, was worth more to others than it was to Kingfisher. It was sold for £440m last August.

China is different. At best, Kingfisher will spend £30m restructuring the business, get it back into the black in 2011, and can then wait for the £29bn home improvement market to pick up before restarting its expansion.

EXHIBIT 6.5

Source: *Financial Times* 27 March 2009, p. 16.

Extend the planning horizon

Sometimes steps can be taken to exploit a competitive advantage over a longer period than originally expected. For example, perhaps the toy division could negotiate a long-term exclusive import license with the supplier of an established premium-priced product, thus closing the door on the entry of competitors. If we suppose that the toy division will now produce a return spread of 23 percent for a 15-year period rather than 10 years the value of the company rises to £1,179,634, viz:

Annual value creation on clothing = –£10,000

Annual value creation on toys   =   £40,000

Present value over 10 years (clothing)

= –£10,000 × Annuity factor (10 years, 13%)

$$= -£10,000 \times 5.4262$$

$$= -£54,262$$

Present value over 15 years (toys) = £40,000 × Annuity factor (15 years, 15%)

$$= £40,000 \times 5.8474 = £233,896$$

Total value creation	= £233,896 – £54,262 =	£179,634
plus initial investment		£1,000,000
Corporate value		**£1,179,634**

Lower the required rate of return

It may be possible to lower the required rate of return by adjusting the proportion of debt to equity in the capital structure or by reducing business risk.[5] (Capital structure is examined in more detail in Chapters 10 and 18.) Suppose that Black can lower its required rate of return by shifting to a higher proportion of debt, so that the overall rate falls to 12 percent. Then the value of the firm rises to £1,282,510.

Annual value creation	$=$	$I \times (r - k)$
	$=$	$1,000,000 \times (0.17 - 0.12)$
	$=$	£50,000
Present value over ten years	$=$	£50,000 × Annuity factor (10 years, 12%)
Total value creation	$=$	£50,000 × 5.6502 = £282,510
plus initial investment		£1,000,000
Corporate value		**£1,282,510**

(Many companies tend to borrow little. They finance their businesses almost entirely through equity (shareholders') money. The motivation is often to reduce the risk of financial distress. This may be due to a desire to serve the interests of shareholders, but more often it is because managers want to avoid financial distress for their own safety. They can become too cautious and forgo the opportunity of reducing the overall cost of capital (discount rate) by not using a higher proportion of cheaper debt finance.)

Conclusion

The switch from management by accounting numbers to management using financial concepts such as value, the time value of money and opportunity cost is only just beginning. Some highly successful firms are leading the way in insisting that each department, business unit and project add value to shareholders' investment. This has required a re-examination of virtually all aspects of management, ranging from performance measurement systems and strategic planning to motivational schemes and training programmes. The rest of this section of the book builds on the basic principles behind value-based management discussed in this chapter.

Notes

1 Quoted in *Financial Times* article, 'Problems kept coming out of the woodwork' by Salamander Davoudi, 19 January 2007, p. 19.
2 *Ibid.*
3 *Ibid.*
4 Richard Cousins, Group Chief Executive, writing in Compass's 2008 Annual Report.
5 Business risk can be reduced by, for example, reducing operating gearing (i.e. reducing the proportion of costs that are fixed, thus lowering the break-even point); or by encouraging customers (e.g. through advertising) to regard your products as essential rather than discretionary; or by matching assets and liabilities better, in terms of maturity and currency.

7

VALUE THROUGH STRATEGY

Introduction

Transforming a corporation from one that is earnings based to one which is focused on value has profound effects on almost all aspects of organisational life. New light is cast on the most appropriate portfolio of businesses making up the firm, and on the strategic thrust of individual business units. Acquisition and divestment strategies may be modified to put shareholder wealth creation centre stage. Capital structure (proportion of debt relative to equity capital) and dividend payout policy are predicated on the optimal approach from the shareholders' point of view, not by 'safety first' or earnings growth considerations. Performance measures, target setting and managerial compensation become linked to the extent that wealth is created rather than the vagaries of accounting numbers.

To unite the organisation in pursuit of wealth creation an enormous educational and motivational challenge has to be met. A change in culture is often required to ensure that at all levels, the goal is to create value. Retraining and new reward systems are needed to help lift eyes from the short-term to long-term achievements.

This chapter gives a taste of the pervading nature of value-based managerial thinking. Later chapters consider some specific aspects of value-based management such as the employment of metrics to gauge the extent of achievement in value terms, the way to calculate the opportunity cost of capital and the value to be destroyed or gained through mergers.

Value principles touch every corner of the business

Figure 7.1 summarizes some of the most important areas where value-based management impacts on the firm. To describe them all fully would require a book as long as this one, so only the most important points are discussed below.

The firm's objective

The firm has first to decide what it is that is to be maximised and what will merely be satisfied. In value management the maximisation of sales, market share, employee satisfaction, customer service excellence, and so on, are rejected as the objective of the firm. All of these are important and there are levels of achievement for each which are desirable in so far as they help to maximising shareholder wealth, but they are not *the* objective. It is important that there is clarity over the purpose of the firm and crystal-clear guiding principles for managers making strategic and operational decisions. Objectives stated in terms of a vague balance of interests are not appropriate for a commercial organisation in a competitive environment. The goal of maximising discounted cash flows to shareholders brings simplicity and direction to decision-making.

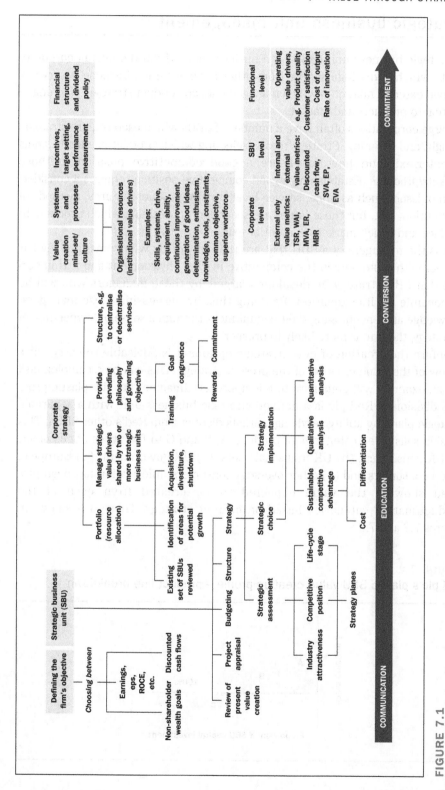

FIGURE 7.1

Value principles influence most aspects of management

Strategic business unit management

A strategic business unit (SBU) is a business unit within the overall corporate entity which is distinguishable from other business units because it serves a defined external market in which management can conduct strategic planning in relation to products and markets.

Large corporations often have a number of SBUs which each require strategic thought and planning. Strategy means selecting which product or market areas to enter/exit and how to ensure a good competitive position in those markets/products. Establishing a good competitive position requires a consideration of issues such as price, service level, quality, product features, methods of distribution, etc., but these issues are secondary to deciding which products to produce and which markets to enter or exit.

It is the managers of a SBU that are the individuals who come into regular contact with customers in the competitive market environment and it is important that SBU strategy be developed largely by those managers who will be responsible for its execution. By doing this, by harnessing these managers' knowledge and encouraging their commitment through a sense of 'ownership' of a strategy, the firm is more likely to prosper.

Before the creation of new strategic options it is advisable to carry out a review of the value creation of the present strategy. This can be a complex task but an example will demonstrate one approach. Imagine that the plastic products division of Red plc is a defined strategic business unit with a separable strategic planning ability servicing markets distinct from Red's other SBUs. This division sells three categories of product, A, B and C to five types of customer: (a) UK consumers, (b) UK industrial users, (c) UK government, (d) European Union consumers and (e) other overseas consumers. Information has been provided showing the value expected to be created from each of the product/market categories based on current strategy. These are shown in Figures 7.2 and 7.3.

FIGURE 7.2

Red plc's plastic SBU value creation profile – product line breakdown

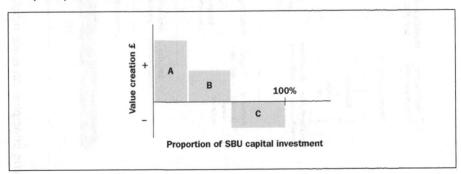

FIGURE 7.3

Red plc's plastic SBU value creation profile – customer breakdown

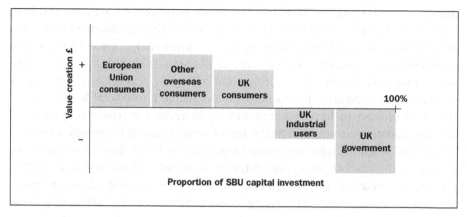

Product line C is expected to destroy shareholder value while absorbing a substantial share of the SBU's resources. Likewise this analysis has identified sales to UK industry and government as detrimental to the firm's wealth. This sort of finding is not unusual: many businesses have acceptable returns at the aggregate level but hidden behind these figures are value-destructive areas of activity. The analysis could be made even more revealing by showing the returns available for each product and market category; for example, product A in the UK consumer market can be compared with product A in the European market.

Warren Buffett, the financier, has made some pithy comments on the tendency for firms to fail to identify and root out value-destructive activities:

> Many corporations that consistently show good returns both on equity and on overall incremental capital have, indeed, employed a large portion of their retained earnings on an economically unattractive, even disastrous, basis. Their marvellous core businesses, however, whose earnings grow year after year, camouflage repeated failures in capital allocation elsewhere (usually involving high-priced acquisitions of businesses that have inherently mediocre economics). The managers at fault periodically report on the lessons they have learned from the latest disappointment. They then usually seek out future lessons. (Failure seems to go to their heads.)

Berkshire Hathaway 1984 Annual Report. © Warren Buffett, reproduced with the permission of the author.

To get a clear line of sight from the customer to the shareholder many businesses need to build an entirely new fact base showing the full economic cost and cash flows associated with customers and product markets. Recognising that some activities are far more valuable than others prepares the ground for a shift of strategic resources. Attention can be directed at restructuring or eliminating value destructive operations, while building up value creative aspects of the business.

Furthermore, project appraisal, budgeting systems and the organizational structure of each SBU must be in harmony with the principle of value-based management. Project appraisal will be carried out using discounted cash flow techniques. Budgeting will not rely solely on accounting considerations, but will have value-based metrics (methods of measurement) – some of these are described in the next chapter. The lines of decision-making authority and communication will be the most appropriate given the market environment to achieve greatest returns. For example in a dynamic unpredictable market setting it is unwise to have a bureaucratic, hierarchical type structure with decision-making concentrated at the top of long chains of command. Devolved power and responsibility are likely to produce a more flexible response to change in the market-place, and initiative with self-reliance are to be highly prized and rewarded. In less dynamic environments low cost, close command and control management with an emphasis on continuous improvement is likely to be most appropriate.

Strategic analysis can be seen as having three parts.[1]

1 **Strategic assessment** In which the external environment and the internal resources and capability are analyzed to form a view on the key influences on the value-creating potential of the organisation.

2 **Strategic choice** In which strategic options are developed and evaluated.

3 **Strategic implementation** Action will be needed in areas such as changes in organizational structure and systems as well as resource planning, motivation and commitment.

Strategic assessment

There are three primary strategic determinants of value creation.

Industry attractiveness

The economics of the market for the product(s) have an enormous influence on the profitability of a firm. In some industries firms have few competitors, and there is low customer buying power, low supplier bargaining power and little threat from new entrants or the introduction of substitute products. Here the industry is likely to be attractive in terms of the returns accruing to the existing players, which will on average exhibit a positive performance spread. Other product markets are plagued with over-capacity, combined with reluctance on the part of the participants to quit and apply resources in another product market. Prices are kept low by the ability of customers and suppliers to 'put the squeeze on' and by the availability of very many close-substitute products. Markets of this kind tend to produce negative performance spreads.[2]

The strength of resources

Identifying a good industry is only the first step. Value-based companies aim to beat the average rates of return on capital employed within their industries. To beat the averages, companies need something special. That something special comes from the bundle of resources that the firm possesses. Most of the resources are ordinary. That is, they give the firm competitive parity. However, the firm may be able to exploit one or two extraordinary resources – those that give a competitive edge. An extraordinary resource is one which, when combined with other (ordinary) resources enables the firm to outperform competitors and create new value-generating opportunities. Critical extraordinary resources determine what a firm can do successfully.

The ability to generate value for customers is crucial for superior returns. High shareholder returns are determined by the firm either being able to offer the same benefits to customers as competitors, but at a lower price; or being able to offer unique benefits that more than outweigh the associated higher price.

Ordinary resources provide a threshold competence. They are vital to ensure a company's survival. In the food retail business, for example, most firms have a threshold competence in basic activities, such as purchasing, human resource management, accounting control and store layout. However, the large chains have resources that set them apart from the small stores: they are able to obtain lower-cost supplies because of their enormous buying power; they can exploit economies of scale in advertising and in the range of produce offered.

Despite the large retailers having these advantages it is clear that small stores have survived, and some produce very high returns on capital invested. These superior firms provide value to the customer significantly above cost. Some corner stores have a different set of extraordinary resources compared with the large groups: personal friendly service could be valued highly; opening at times convenient to customers could lead to acceptance of a premium price; the location may make shopping less hassle than traipsing to an out-of-town hypermarket. The large chains find emulation of these qualities expensive. If they were to try and imitate the small store they could end up losing their main competitive advantages, the most significant of which is low cost.

The extraordinary resources possessed by the supermarket chains as a group when compared with small shops are not necessarily extraordinary resources in the competitive rivalry *between* the chains. If the focus is shifted to the 'industry' of supermarket chains factors like economies of scale may merely give competitive parity – scale is needed for survival. Competitive advantage is achieved through the development of other extraordinary resources, such as the quality of the relationship with suppliers, a very sophisticated system for collecting data on customers combined with target marketing, ownership of the best sites. However, even these extraordinary resources will not give superior competitive position forever. Many of these can be imitated. Long-term competitive advantage may depend on the capabilities of the management team to continually innovate and thereby shift the ground from under the feet of competitors.

The extraordinary resource is then the coherence, attitude, intelligence, knowledge and drive of the managers in the organisational setting.

Many successful companies have stopped seeing themselves as bundles of product lines and businesses. Instead they look at the firm as a collection of resources. This helps to explain the logic behind some companies going into apparently unconnected product areas. The connection is the exploitation of extraordinary resources. So, for example, Honda has many different product areas: motor boat engines, automobiles, motorcycles, lawn mowers and electric generators. These are sold through different distribution channels in completely different ways to different customers. The common root for all these products is Honda's extraordinary resource that led to a superior ability to produce engines. Likewise, photocopiers, cameras and image scanners are completely different product sectors and sold in different ways. Yet, they are all made by Canon – which has extraordinary capabilities and knowledge of optics, imaging and microprocessor controls.

The analyst should not be looking for a long list of extraordinary resources in any one firm. If one can be found, that is good – it only takes one to leap ahead of competitors and produce super-normal returns. If two are found then that is excellent. It is very unusual to come across a company that has three or more extraordinary resources. Coca-Cola is an exception with an extraordinary brand, a distribution system with connected relationships and highly knowledgeable managers.

The TRRACK system

To assist the thorough analysis of a company's extraordinary resource I have developed the TRRACK system. This classifies extraordinary resources into six categories – *see* Figure 7.4.

FIGURE 7.4
The TRRACK system

T	Tangible
R	Relationships
R	Reputation
A	Attitude
C	Capabilities
K	Knowledge

Notice that the vast majority of extraordinary resources are intangible. They are qualities that are carried within the individuals that make up organizations, or are connected with the interaction between individuals. They are usually developed over a long time rather than bought. These qualities cannot be scientifically evaluated to provide objective quantification. Despite our inability to be precise it is usually the case that these people-embodied factors are the most important drivers of value creation and we must pay most attention to them.

Tangible

Occasionally physical resources provide a sustainable competitive advantage. These are assets that can be physically observed and are often valued (or misvalued) in a balance sheet. They include real estate, materials, production facilities and patents. They can be purchased, but if they were easily purchased they would cease to be extraordinary because all competitors would go out and buy. There must be some barrier preventing other firms from acquiring the same or similar assets for them to be truly valuable in the long run. Microsoft's ownership of its operating system and other standards within the software industry gives it a competitive edge. McDonald's makes sure that it takes the best locations on the busiest highways, rather than settle for obscure secondary roads. Many smaller businesses have found themselves, or have made smart moves to ensure they are, the owners of valuable real estate adjacent to popular tourist sites. Pharmaceutical companies, such as Merck, own valuable patents giving some protection against rivalry – at least temporarily.

Relationships

Over time companies can form valuable relationships with individuals and organizations that are difficult or impossible for a potential competitor to emulate. Relationships in business can be of many kinds. The least important are the contractual ones. The most important are informal or implicit. These relationships are usually based on a trust that has grown over many years. The terms of the implicit contract are enforced by the parties themselves rather than through the court – a loss of trust can be immensely damaging. It is in all the parties' interests to cooperate with integrity because there is the expectation of reiteration leading to the sharing of collective value created over a long period. South African Breweries (SAB) has 98 percent of the beer market in South Africa. It has kept out foreign and domestic competitors because of its special relationships with suppliers and customers. It is highly profitable. Most of South Africa's roads are poor and electricity supplies are intermittent. To distribute its beer it has formed some strong relationships. The truck drivers, many of whom are former employees, are helped by SAB to set up their small trucking businesses. *Shebeens* sell most of the beer. These are unlicensed pubs. Often, they are tiny – no more than a few benches. SAB cannot sell directly to the illegal *shebeens*. Instead it maintains an informal relationship via a system of wholesalers. SAB makes sure that distributors have refrigerators and, if necessary, generators. A new entrant to the market would have to develop its own special relationship with truck drivers, wholesalers and retailers. In all likelihood it would have to establish a completely separate and parallel system of distribution. Even then it would lack the legitimacy that comes with a long-standing relationship. Relationships between employees, and between employees and the firm, can give a competitive edge. Some firms seem to possess a culture that creates wealth through the cooperation and dynamism of the employees. Information is shared, knowledge is developed, innovative activity flows, rapid response to market change is natural and respect for all pervades. The quality of the relationships with government can be astonishingly important to a company. Defence contractors cultivate a special relationship with various organs of government. The biggest firms often attract the best ex-government people to take up directorships or to head liaison with government. Their contacts and knowledge of the inside workings of purchasing decisions, with the political complications, can be very valuable. A similar logic often applies to pharmaceutical companies, airlines and regulated companies.

Reputation

Reputations are normally made over a long period. Once a good reputation is established it can be a source of very high returns (assuming that all the necessary ordinary resources are in place to support it). With car hire in a foreign country the consumer is unable to assess quality in advance. Hertz provide certification for local traders under a franchise arrangement. These local car hirers would see no benefit to providing an above-average service without the certification of Hertz because they would not be able to charge a premium price.[3] It is surprising how much more consumers are willing to pay for the assurance of reliable and efficient car hire when they travel abroad compared with the hiring of a car from an unfranchised local. Companies pay a large premium to hire Goldman Sachs when contemplating an issue of securities or a merger. They are willing to pay for 'emotional reassurance'.[4] The CEO cannot be sure of the outcome of the transaction. If it were to fail the penalty would be high – executives may lose bonuses and, perhaps, their jobs, shareholders lose money. The CEO therefore hires the best that is available for such once-in-a-lifetime moves. The cost of this hand-holding is secondary. Once an adviser has a history of flawless handling of large and complex transactions it can offer a much more effective 'emotional comfort-blanket'[5] to CEOs than smaller rivals. This principle may apply to pension fund advisers, management consultants and advertising agencies as well as top investment bankers. Perhaps the most important manifestation of the importance of reputation is branding. Branded products live or die by reputation. A strong brand can be incredibly valuable.

Attitude

Attitude refers to the mentality of the organisation. It is the prevalent outlook. It is the way in which the organisation views and relates to the world. Terms such as disposition, will and culture are closely connected with attitude. Every sports coach is aware of the importance of attitude. The team may consist of players with the best technique in the business or with a superb knowledge of the game, they may be the fastest and the most skilful, but without a winning attitude they will not succeed. There must be a will to win. Attitude can become entrenched within an organisation. It is difficult to shake off a negative attitude. A positive attitude can provide a significant competitive edge. Some firms develop a winning mentality based on a culture of innovation, others are determinedly oriented towards customer satisfaction while some companies are quality driven. 3M has a pervasive attitude of having-a-go. Testing out wild ideas is encouraged. Employees are given time to follow up a dreamed-up innovation, and they are not criticized for failing. Innovations such as 'Post-it' notes have flowed from this attitude. Canon has the attitude of *Tsushin* – 'heart-to-heart and mind-to-mind communication' between the firm and its customers. In this way trust is developed.

Capabilities

Capabilities are derived from the company's ability to undertake a set of tasks. The term skill can be used to refer to a narrow activity or a single task. Capability is used for the combination of a number of skills.[6] For example, a company's capability base could include abilities in narrow areas such as market research, innovative design and efficient manufacturing that, when combined, result in a superior capability in new product development. A capability is more than the sum of the individual processes – the combination and coordination of individual processes may provide an extraordinary resource. Sony developed a capability in miniaturization. This enabled it to produce a string of products from the Walkman to the Playstation.

Knowledge

Knowledge is the awareness of information, and its interpretation, organisation, synthesis and prioritisation, to provide insights and understanding. The retention, exploitation and sharing of knowledge can be extremely important in achieving and maintaining competitive advantage. All firms in an industry share basic knowledge. For example, all publishers have some knowledge of market trends, distribution techniques and printing technology. It is not this common knowledge that I am referring to in the context of extraordinary resources. If a publisher builds up data and skills in understanding a particular segment of the market, say investment books, then its superior awareness, interpretation, organisation, synthesis, and prioritisation of information can create competitive advantage through extraordinary knowledge. The company will have greater insight than rivals into this segment of the market. There are two types of organisational knowledge. The first, *explicit* knowledge, can be formalized and passed on in codified form. This is objective knowledge that can be defined and documented. The second, *tacit* knowledge, is ill- or undefined. It is subjective, personal and context specific. It is fuzzy and complex. It is hard to formalise and communicate. Examples of explicit knowledge include costing procedures written in company accounting manuals, formal assessment of market demand, customer complaint data and classification. Explicit knowledge is unlikely to provide competitive advantage: if it is easily defined and codified it is likely to be available to rivals. Tacit knowledge, on the other hand, is very difficult for rivals to obtain. Consider the analogy of baseball: explicit knowledge of tactics is generally available; what separates the excellent from the ordinary player is the application of tacit knowledge, e.g. what becomes an instinctive ability to recognize types of pitches and the appropriate response to them. Tacit knowledge is transmitted by doing, the main means of transferring knowledge from one individual to another is through close interaction to build understanding, as in the master-apprentice relationship.

If you would like to delve more deeply into competitive resource analysis there are fuller discussions in Chapter 10 of *The Financial Times Guide to Value Investing*, Arnold (2009) and Chapter 15 of *The Financial Times Guide to Investing*, Arnold (2010).

Life-cycle stage of value potential

A competitive advantage in an attractive industry will not lead to superior long-term performance unless it provides a *sustainable* competitive advantage and the economics of the industry *remain* favourable. Rival firms will be attracted to an industry in which the participants enjoy high returns and sooner or later competitive advantage is usually whittled away. The longevity of the competitive advantage can be represented in terms of a life cycle with four stages: development, growth, maturity and decline (*see* Figure 7.5). In the development phase during which competitive advantage (and often the industry) is established, perhaps through technological or service innovation, the sales base will be small. As demand increases a growth phase is entered in which competitive strength is enhanced by factors such as industry leadership, brand strength and patent rights. A lengthy period of competitive advantage and high return can be expected. Eventually the sources of advantage are removed, perhaps by competitor imitation, or by customers and suppliers gaining in bargaining power. Other possibilities pushing towards the maturity stage are technological breakthroughs by competitors able to offer a superior product, or poor management leading to a loss of grip on cost control. Whatever the reason for the reduction in the performance spread, the firm now faces a choice of three routes, two of which can lead to a repositioning on the life cycle; the third is to enter a period of negative performance spreads. The two positive actions are (a) to erect barriers and deterrents to the entry of firms to the industry. Barriers put in the path of the outsiders make it difficult for those insects to advance on your honey pot. Also, a clear message could go out to the aspiring entrant that if they did dare to cross the threshold then they will be subject to a massive retaliatory attack until they are driven out again, and (b) to continually innovate and improve the SBU's product offering to stay one step ahead of the competitors. An example of the simultaneous use of those two actions is provided by Microsoft. It is able to dominate the operating software market and the application market because of the high costs for users switching to a competitor's software, the network effect of Office being a standard system used throughout the world, and its close working relationships with hardware producers; this makes life very difficult for any potential new entrant. It is also pumping billions into new products – it has thousands of software engineers. But even Microsoft will find its business units eventually fall into a terminal decline phase of value creation because of a loss of competitive advantage. When it does, even though it will be extremely difficult for it to do so, the company must withdraw from value-destructive activities and plow the capital retrieved into positive performance-spread SBUs.

FIGURE 7.5

The life-cycle stages of value creation

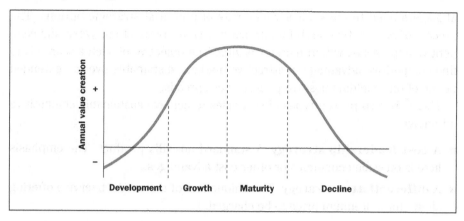

Strategy planes

The three elements of strategic assessment can be summarised on a strategy planes chart like the one shown in Figure 7.6 for Red plc which, besides the plastics SBU, also has a young internet games division, a coal-mining subsidiary, a publishing group with valuable long-term copyrights on dozens of best sellers, a supermarket chain subject to increasingly intense competition in an over-supplied market and a small airline company with an insignificant market share.

The strategy planes framework can be used at the SBU level or can be redrawn for product/customer segments within SBUs.

FIGURE 7.6

Strategy planes

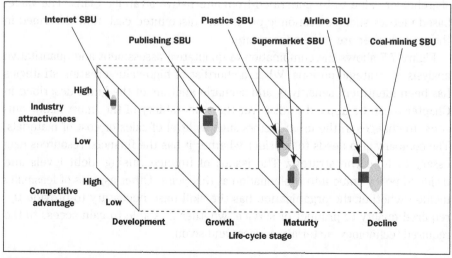

Note: The size of the circle represents the proportion of the firm's assets devoted to this SBU. The size of the rectangle represents the current performance spread. If the spread is negative it is shown outside the circle.

Strategic choice

Managers need to consider a wide array of potential strategic options. The process of systematic search for alternative market product entry/exit and competitive approaches within markets is vital. The objective of such a search is to find competitive advantage in attractive markets sustainable over an extended period of time yielding positive performance spreads.

There are two proven types of strategies to achieve sustainable competitive advantage:

- **A cost leadership strategy** A standard no-frills product. The emphasis here is on scale economies or other cost advantages.

- **A differentiation strategy** The uniqueness of the product/service offering allows for a premium price to be charged.

To fall between these two stools can be disastrous.

Once a sufficiently wide-ranging search for possible strategic directions has been conducted the results that come to the fore need to be evaluated. They are usually considered in broad descriptive terms using qualitative analysis with written reports and reflective thought. This qualitative thinking has valuable attributes such as creativity, intuition and judgment in the original formulation of strategic options, the assessment of their merits and in the subsequent reiterations of the process. The qualitative strategy evaluation is complemented by a quantitative examination for which accounting terms such as profit, earnings per share (eps), return on capital employed (ROCE) and balance sheet impact are traditionally used. This has the advantage of presenting the strategic plans in the same format that the directors use to present annual results to shareholders. However these metrics do not accurately reflect the shareholder value to be generated from alternative strategic plans. The value-based metrics such as economic profits and discounted cash flow described in the next chapter are more appropriate.

Figure 7.7 shows the combination of qualitative assessment and quantitative analysis of strategic options. When a shortlist of high-value-creating strategies has been identified, sensitivity and scenario analysis of the kinds described in Chapter 5 can be applied to discover the vulnerability of the 'most likely' outcome to changes in the input factors such as level of sales or cost of materials. The company also needs to consider whether it has the financial resources necessary to fund the strategy. The issues of finance raising, debt levels and dividend policy come into the equation at this point. Other aspects of feasibility include whether the organization has the skill base necessary to provide the required quality of product or service, whether it is able to gain access to the required technology, materials, services and so on.

FIGURE 7.7
Strategy formulation and evaluation

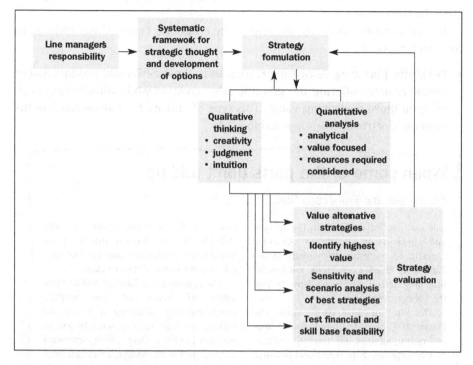

Strategy implementation

Making the chosen strategy work requires the planned allocation of resources and the reorganisation and motivation of people. The firm's switch to value-based principles has an impact on these implementation issues. Resources are to be allocated to units or functions if it can be shown that they will contribute to value creation after taking into account the quantity of resources used. Managers are given responsibilities and targets set in accordance with value creation.

What use is the head office?

So far the firm has been described as consisting of a group of strategic business units. So where does the head office fit into this picture if each of these units has a separately identifiable market and is capable of independent strategic action?

We know that companies need to apply value-based principles to all its activities and so this must include the centre. Everything the head office does must create value for shareholders. This means awareness of the quantity of assets used in each task and the return generated by those assets in that task. Many companies fail to think this through; head office costs spiral as new activities are taken to the centre to add to those traditionally carried out, without thought as to whether these tasks are (a) necessary, or (b) if necessary, most efficiently executed by the centre.

In a value-based company the role of the corporate centre (head office) has four main aspects:

■ **Portfolio planning** Allocating resources to those SBUs and product and/or customer areas offering the greatest value creation while withdrawing capital from those destroying value. This type of activity is demonstrated in the General Electric article – *see* Exhibit 7.1.

When some of the parts don't add up

Justin Baer and Francesco Guerrera

It is rare for Jeffrey Immelt, the urbane and personable head of General Electric, to voice his displeasure at the back-seat chief executives who offer him unsolicited advice on how to run the US conglomerate.

But in an interview with the Financial Times, Mr Immelt found himself railing against the 'trading culture' that has spread from Wall Street to corporate America.

'People think that running GE is like driving a stagecoach: if horse number three breaks down, take it out and shoot it,' he said during a November 2006 interview. 'It is a lousy way to run a company like GE.'

Sometimes, though, even chief executives like Mr Immelt have to pull the trigger in shedding a beloved workhorse.

GE said last month it would be likely to spin off its consumer and industrial division. A proud part of the company's heritage – the electric toaster, washing machine and the incandescent light bulb were all invented there – the division's focus on low-margin businesses turned it into a laggard within the portfolio. And its drag on the company's overall growth rates had worsened amid the US economy's slowdown.

While GE could have made the investments necessary to revive the division's prospects, such as expanding a distribution network for selling appliances outside the US, Mr Immelt and his team found more productive uses for that capital in other parts of the company.

The dilemma is a familiar one to managers of many of the world's conglomerates. Showing a knack for making the right calls on what to add or subtract is what defines a conglomerate's success and is its leaders' principal duty. Indeed, conglomerates have traditionally been built on the premise that their diverse set of businesses will enable them to outperform less diverse companies.

As Chris Zook, head of the global strategy practice at Bain, the management consultancy, says: 'Conglomerates tend to have around a third of their divisions in businesses they have no long-term logical reason to be in.'

For executives, it is also knowing when to let go that counts. Supplanted long ago by energy, aviation and financial services as the drivers of GE's profits, the C&I division nonetheless held more than just sentimental value to Mr Immelt and his predecessor, Jack Welch. The businesses made money, reliably churning out cash GE could plough into faster-growing operations or use to fund long-term research projects or finance acquisitions.

'The more you want to focus on those businesses and invest in those businesses, the more you look around at the others and say, 'Hey, does this really fit the profile?' says Pam Daley, GE's senior vice-president of corporate business development. 'Then you have to make some tough decisions.'

In his seven years at the helm, Mr Immelt has jettisoned more than $50bn in businesses. Gone are insurance, plastics and industrial supply, among others. 'This is a 130-year-old company, and it does evolve,' Ms Daley says.

Other conglomerates have, too. ... At Textron, whose interests range from golf carts to Cessna corporate jets, each business is measured by its ability to increase its value by 15 per cent annually.

'When you have a portfolio as diverse as ours, there is really no other way to compare businesses on an equal footing,' says Stuart Grief, vice-president of strategy and business development. 'We use the exact same lens to look at acquisition targets.' ...

Collective input plays a part in adding to portfolio of businesses

Every month, the slide presentations arrive in Pam Daley's e-mail inbox.

They come from each of General Electric's business leaders, offering updated lists of their leading candidates for acquisitions and partnerships.

Initiated in 2001 by Jeffrey Immelt, chief executive, the process requires division heads to submit five of each, says Ms Daley ...

'None of these guys can count to five,' Ms Daley says. 'You get lists of 20 from some, which is exactly what you want if the opportunities are there.'

At GE, the process of adding to its portfolio of businesses is as stringent as the one that determines what is subtracted. The similarities reflect the fact that any company, even one with pockets as deep as GE, has only so much capital to invest.

The business heads then travel to GE's Fairfield, Connecticut, headquarters for a meeting with the company's senior executives to discuss changes to their so-called pipeline list and, when necessary, seek Mr Immelt's blessing to enter negotiations or make a bid.

Very few items escape Mr Immelt's radar, Ms Daley notes; managers need their boss's approval to pursue any deal worth more than $3m (£1.5m).

Then after the business heads have made their pitches and left the room, Mr Immelt, Ms Daley and other corporate officers stay behind to discuss the other pipeline – those businesses GE thinks might be better off owned by another company.

EXHIBIT 7.1

Source: *Financial Times* 7 August 2008, p. 10.

- **Managing strategic value drivers shared by two or more SBUs** These crucial extraordinary resources, giving the firm competitive advantage, may need to be centrally managed or at least coordinated by the centre to achieve the maximum benefit. An example here could be strong brand management or technological knowledge. The head office needs to ensure adequate funding of these and to achieve full, but not over-exploitation.

- **Provide the pervading philosophy and governing objective** Training, goal setting, employee rewards and the engendering of commitment are all focused on shareholder value. A strong lead from the centre is needed to avoid conflict, drift and vagueness.

- **The overall structure of the organization** This needs to be appropriate for the market environment and designed to build value. Roles and responsibilities are clearly defined with clear accountability for value creation.

We can apply the principles of portfolio planning to Red plc. The corporate centre could encourage and work with the plastics division in developing ideas for reducing or eliminating the value losses being made on some of its products and markets – recall that it is destroying value in product line C and in sales to UK industrial customers and the UK government. Once these have been fully evaluated head office could ensure that resources and other services are provided to effectively implement the chosen strategy. For example, if the highest value-creating option is to gradually withdraw capital from product line C and to apply the funds saved to product line A, the management team at C are likely to become demotivated as they reduce the resources under their command and experience lower sales (and profit) rather than, the more natural predisposition of managers, a rising trend. The centre can help this process by changing the targets and incentives of these managers away from growth and empire building towards shareholder value.

On the level of corporate-wide resource allocation, the directors of Red plc have a great deal of work to do. The publishing division is already creating high value from its existing activities, yet it is still in the early growth phase. The subsidiary management team believe that significant benefits would flow from buying rights to other novels and children's stories. By combining these with its present 'stable' it could enter more forcefully into negotiations with book retailers, television production companies wishing to make screen versions of its stories and merchandising companies intending to put the image of some of the famous characters on articles ranging from T-shirts to drink cans. This strategy will involve the purchase of rights from individual authors as well as the acquisition of firms quoted on the stock exchange. It will be costly and require a substantial shift of resources within the firm. But, as can be seen from Figure 7.8, the value created makes the change attractive.

The internet division has been put on a tight rein in terms of financial resources for its first three years because of the high risk attached to businesses involved in speculative innovation in this market. However, the energetic and able managers have created a proven line of services that have a technological lead over competitors, a high market share and substantial barriers to entry in the form of copyrights and patents. The directors decide to expand this area.

The plastics division as a whole is in a mature market with positive but gradually declining performance spreads. Here the strategic approach is to reduce the number of product lines competing on cost and transfer resources to those niche markets where product differentiation allows a premium price to be charged. The intention is to move gradually to a higher competitive advantage overall but accept that industry attractiveness will decline. Overall resources dedicated to this division will remain approximately constant, but the directors will be watching for deterioration greater than that anticipated in the current plan.

FIGURE 7.8

Using strategy plane analysis: Red plc's shifting strategy planes

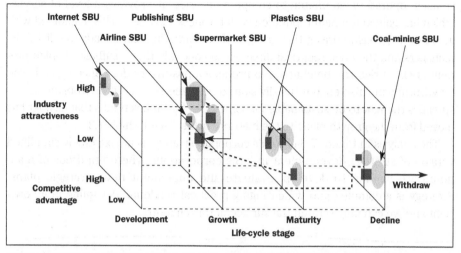

Note: The size of the circle represents the proportion of the firm's assets devoted to this SBU. The size of the rectangle represents the current performance spread. If the spread is negative it is shown outside the circle.

The supermarket division is currently producing a positive performance spread but a prolonged price war is forecast for the industry, to be followed by a shake-out, leading to a withdrawal of many of the current firms. Some directors are in favour of supporting this division vigorously through the troublesome times ahead in the expectation that when many of the weaker players have left the field, margins will rise to abnormally high levels – producing large perform-ance spreads and high value in the long run. In terms of the value-creating life cycle this SBU would be shifted from the maturity strategy plane to the growth plane (shown in Figure 7.8). Other directors are not willing to take the risk that their firm will not be one of the survivors from the battle for market share. Furthermore, they argue that even if they do win, the enormous resources required, over the next five years, will produce a value return less than that on the publishing or internet SBUs. Therefore, if financial resources are to be con-strained, they should put money into these 'star' divisions.

The coal-mining division is haemorrhaging money. The industry is in terminal decline because of the high cost of coal extraction and the increasing tendency for the electricity-generating companies to source their coal needs from abroad. Moreover Red is a relatively small player in this market and lacks the economies of scale to compete effectively. To add insult to injury a large proportion of the corporation's capital is tied up in the coal stockpiles required by the electricity firms. The decision is taken to withdraw from this industry and the best approach to achieve this is investigated – sale to a competitor or liquidation.

The airline operation has never made a satisfactory return and is resented by the managers in other divisions as a drain on the value they create. However, the recent deregulation of air travel and especially the opening up of landing slots at major European airports has presented a major new opportunity. Despite being one of the smallest operators, so unable to compete on price, it provides a level of service which has gained it a high reputation with business travellers. This, combined with its other major value driver, the strength of its marketing team, leads the divisional managers and the once sceptical directors to conclude that a sufficiently high premium ticket price can be charged to produce a positive performance spread. The new European rules enable the division to be placed on the growth plane as the spread is thought to be sustainable for some time. Sir Stelios thinks that easyJet has moved from the growth plane to the maturity plane – *see* Exhibit 7.2.

The analysis in Figure 7.8 of Red's corporate strategy is an extremely simplified version of strategy development in large corporations where hundreds of man-hours are needed to develop, evaluate and implement new strategic plans. Strategy is a complex and wide-ranging practical academic discipline in its own right and we can only scratch the surface in this chapter.

Sir Stelios spells out fears for EasyJet

Kevin Done

Sir Stelios Haji-Ioannou, the founder and largest shareholder in EasyJet, yesterday dug in his heels in his public disagreement with the rest of the airline's board over its future growth strategy in the midst of the deepening recession.

In an interview with the Financial Times, he said he was engaging with other shareholders and with financial analysts to explain his concern that the group was not sufficiently focused on conserving cash and on limiting its big capital expenditure commitments. ...

'The real issue is the Airbus contract,' he said, under which EasyJet is committed to taking delivery of 109 new A320 family short-haul jets during the next four years with a total value of $5.1bn (£3.4bn) at list prices before heavy discounts.

'I am keen to focus the debate on how much they cost, and how they are to be paid for, rather than on passenger numbers,' he said.

Sir Stelios, who founded EasyJet in 1995, has been a pioneer, alongside Ireland's Ryanair, of the low-cost business model in Europe. It has been built on capturing large chunks of market share from the legacy carriers as well as on stimulating market growth by offering much lower fares and by having a lower cost base than the traditional airlines.

The rapidly expanding low-cost carriers have traditionally been given a valuation premium as growth stocks, but Sir Stelios said he believed this era was over. 'At the heart the question is are we a growth company or a mature company. I think it [EasyJet] is a mature company.'

EasyJet management, backed by the rest of the board, said last week it was already taking a cautious approach, but Sir Stelios, a non-executive director, told investors he believed that the group's approach was 'based on optimistic assumptions about future revenues'. ...

EXHIBIT 7.2

Source: *Financial Times* 24 November 2008, p. 21.

Targets and motivation

The remaining aspects of management affected by a switch from an earnings-based approach to a value-based approach shown in Figure 7.1 have already been touched on and, given the scope of this book, will not be explained any further here. The interested reader can consult some of the leading writers in this area (*see* McTaggart *et al.* (1994), McKinsey (2005), Rappaport (1998), Stewart (1991) and Reimann (1989)). The financial structure debate concerning the proportion of debt in the overall capital mix of the firm is discussed in Chapters 10 and 18 and the dividend payout ratio debate is described in Chapter 14.

One final point to note with regard to Figure 7.1 is the importance of having different types of value-creating targets at different levels within the organization. At board room and senior executive level it seems reasonable that there should be a concern with overall performance of the firm as seen from the shareholders' perspective and so total shareholder return, Wealth Added Index, Market Value Added, Excess Return and market to book ratio (metrics described in Chapter 9) would be important guides to performance, and incentive schemes

Case study 7.1

Strategy, planning and budgeting at Lloyds bank

Although business units are responsible for their own strategy development, the Lloyds banking group provides guidelines on how strategy should be developed. ... These unit plans are then consolidated into an aggregate plan for the value centre. The process undertaken is then subjected to scrutiny by the centre. The strategic planning process consists of five stages:

1. **Position assessment** Business units are required to perform a value-based assessment of the economics of the market in which the business operates and of the relative competitive position of the business within that market. Market attractiveness and competitive position must include a numerical rather than a purely qualitative assessment.
2. **Generate alternative strategies** Business units are required to develop a number of realistic and viable alternatives.
3. **Evaluate alternative strategies** Business units are required to perform shareholder value calculations in order to prioritise alternatives. Even if a potential strategy has a high positive net present value, this does not necessarily mean that it will be accepted. An assessment of project risk or do-ability is overlaid across the net present value calculations.
4. **Agree chosen strategy with the centre** Whilst it is perceived to be vital that the managers who best understand their business are given sufficient authority to develop strategies which they consider to be most appropriate, it is nevertheless considered equally important that there is a challenge mechanism at the centre to ensure that appropriate analyses have been performed and assumptions made are credible.
5. **The chosen strategy becomes a contract** Once the preferred strategy has been agreed with the centre, resource allocation and milestones are agreed. Budgetary performance targets are derived from the projections included within the strategic plan. Beyond this, however, business unit managers are free to choose whatever structures and performance indicators are considered to be relevant and appropriate.

Source: 'Lessons from practice: VBM at Lloyds TSB', by M. Davies in G. Arnold and M. Davies (eds), *Value-Based Management*. 2000 © John Wiley & Sons Limited. Reproduced with permission.

would be (at least partially) based upon them. Economic profit, Economic Value Added and discounted cash flow are also useful guides for senior managers. These metrics are described and critically assessed in the next chapter.

Moving down the organisation, target setting and rewards need to be linked to the level of control and responsibility over outcomes. Strategic business unit performance needs to be expressed in terms of value metrics such as discounted cash flow, economic profit, and Economic Value Added. Outcomes are usually under the control of divisional and other middle-ranking managers and so the reward system might be expressed in terms of achieving targets expressed in these metrics. At the operating level where a particular function contributes to value creation but the managers in that function have no control over the larger value centre itself, perhaps the emphasis should shift to rewarding high performance in particular operational value drivers such as throughput of customers, reduced staff turnover, cost of production, faster debtor turnover, etc.

Key rule: All managers should agree to both short- and long-term targets. This counters the natural tendency in all of us to focus on short-term goals that might not be optimal in the long run.

Conclusion

A commercial organization that adopts value principles is one that has an important additional source of strength. The rigorous thought process involved in the robust application of these principles will force managers to review existing systems and product and market strategies and to bring an insistence on a contribution to shareholder value from all parts of the company. A firm that has failed to ask the right questions of its operating units or use the correct metrics in measuring performance will find its position deteriorating *vis-à-vis* its competitors.

Notes

1 See Johnson and Scholes (2007) for more detail.
2 For more detail on market attractiveness analysis consult Arnold, G. (2009) *The Financial Times Guide to Value Investing*. London: Financial Times Prentice Hall (Chapter 9), Arnold, G. (2010) *The Financial Times Guide to Investing*, 2nd edn. London: Financial Times Prentice Hall (Chapter 14) or any major textbook on strategy. Michael Porter is a leading writer in the field of strategy.
3 Kay, J. (1993) *Foundations of Corporate Success*. New York: Oxford University Press. A study of corporate strategy.
4 Martin, P. (1998) 'Goldman's goose', *Financial Times*, 11 August, p. 14. Why Goldman Sachs can charge a large amount for advice.
5 *Ibid.*
6 De Wit, B. and Meyer, R. (2004) *Strategy: Process, Content, Context*. 3rd edn. Cincinnati, OH: South Western College Publishers.

8

MEASURES OF VALUE CREATION

Introduction

Managers at all levels need to establish plans for future actions. In drawing up these plans they need reliable measures of value to choose between alternative paths. The metrics discussed in this chapter are useful for this purpose.

Then, as strategic moves at both the corporate level and the business unit level unfold, managers need to monitor progress to see if they are still on-track to create value. Again, these metrics can be useful. Targets can be set, and, as milestones are passed, incentive schemes can bestow a share of the value created on those responsible. The aim is to make sure every member of staff understands what value is, and each person becomes fully committed to creating it.

At each level of responsibility there should be knowledge of how much of the finance provider's cash has been used in an SBU, product line or project and the required rate of return on that capital. Everyone should know that extra rewards flow to those that help achieve returns above the required rate of return.

The metrics discussed in this chapter quantify the plan, targets and incentives to encourage high performance from the boardroom to the shop floor. They can be used to judge the entire firm or just a small part of it.

Using cash flow to measure value

We discuss a number of measures of value in this and the next chapter. There is a hot debate between rival consultants as to which is the best for guiding managers seeking to create value. However, they all agree that the measure that lies at the theoretical heart of all the others is discounted cash flow.

In Chapter 2 the value of an investment is described as the sum of the discounted cash flows (NPV). This principle was applied to the assessment of a new project: if the investment produced a rate of return greater than the finance provider's opportunity cost of capital it is wealth enhancing. The same logic can be applied to a range of different categories of business decisions, including:

- resource allocation
- business unit strategies
- corporate level strategy
- motivation, rewards and incentives.

Consider the figures for Gold plc in Table 8.1. These could refer to the entire company. Alternatively the figures could be for business unit returns predicated on the assumption of a particular strategy being pursued, or they could be for a product line. (Note: to understand this chapter the reader needs the concepts and tools developed in Chapter 2 and its appendix. You may want to refresh your knowledge of basic discounted cash flow analysis before proceeding.)

TABLE 8.1

Gold plc forecast cash flows

Required rate of return = 12% per annum

Year	1	2	3	4	5	6	7	8 and subsequent years
	£	£	£	£	£	£	£	£
Forecast profits	1,000	1,100	1,100	1,200	1,300	1,450	1,600	1,600
Add book depreciation and other non-cash items (e.g. amortization of goodwill)	500	600	800	800	800	800	800	800
Less fixed capital investment	–500	–3,000	–600	–600	–300	–600	–800	–800
Less additional investment in working capital*								
Inventory	50	–100	–70	–80	–50	–50	–50	0
Debtors	–20	–20	–20	–20	–20	–20	–20	0
Creditors	10	20	10	10	20	20	30	0
Cash	–10	–10	–10	–10	–10	–10	–10	0
Add interest previously charged to profit and loss account	100	150	200	200	200	200	200	200
Taxes	–300	–310	–310	–420	–450	–470	–550	–550
Cash flow	830	–1,570	1,100	1,080	1,490	1,320	1,200	1,250

Discounted cash flow

$$\frac{830}{1.12} \quad - \frac{1,570}{(1.12)^2} + \frac{1,100}{(1.12)^3} + \frac{1,080}{(1.12)^4} + \frac{1,490}{(1.12)^5} + \frac{1,320}{(1.12)^6} + \frac{1,200}{(1.12)^7} + \frac{1,250}{0.12} \times \frac{1}{(1.12)^7}$$

741	–1,252	783	686	845	669	543	4,712

*A positive figure for inventory, debtors and cash floats indicates cash released from these forms of investment. A negative figure indicates additional cash devoted to these areas. For creditors a positive figure indicates higher credit granted by suppliers and therefore a boost to cash flows.

Table 8.1 starts with forecasted profit figures and then makes a number of adjustments to arrive at cash flow figures. This method is valuable because it reflects the corporate reality that forward estimates for business units are usually in the form of accounting budgets rather than cash flows, and managers need to know how to work from these numbers toward cash flow rather than starting from scratch to obtain reliable cash flow projections.

Profit figures are created after a number of deductions, such as depreciation, that do not affect the company's cash flow for the year. When an item is depreciated in the accounts profits are reduced but no cash is lost. It is only when capital items are paid for that cash actually flows out, so depreciation is added to the profit figures. Instead of depreciation we take away the amount that actually flows out each year for investment in fixed capital equipment such as factories, machinery and vehicles (fixed capital investment).

In drawing up the profit figures the accountant does not recognize the using-up of shareholder's cash when inventory (e.g. raw materials stock) or debtors (granting credit to customers) are increased. The accountant observes one asset (cash in hand) being replaced by another (inventory, money owed by customers) and so there is no expense to deduct. However, the cash flow analyst sees cash being used for these items as the business grows and so makes an adjustment to the profit figures when deriving the cash flow numbers.

Similarly, if cash is tied up in cash floats to run the business (e.g. cash in the tills of a betting shop or food retailer) the fact that this cash is no longer available to shareholders needs to be recognized. So, if shareholders had to supply extra cash floats in a period this is deducted from the profit numbers when trying to get at cash flow.

Whether suppliers send input goods and services to this firm for payment on 'cash on delivery terms' or 'credit terms' the accountant, rightly, records the value of these as an expense, and deducts this from the profit and loss account, in the year of delivery and use. The cash flow analyst needs to make an adjustment here because the full amount of the expense may not yet have flowed out in cash. So, if creditor balances increase we need to recognize that the profit and loss account has overstated the outflow of cash. We need then to add back the extent to which the creditor amount outstanding has increased from the beginning of the year to the end to arrive at the cash flow figure.

We also add back the interest charged to the profit because the 12 percent discount rate already includes an allowance for the required return to lenders (see Chapter 10). To include a deduction for interest in calculating cash flow would be to double count this element.

The cash flow figures at the bottom of the columns are sometimes referred to as 'free cash flow'. That is they represent the amount that is free to be paid out to the firm's investors (shareholders and debt holders). These amounts could be paid out without affecting future cash flows because the necessary investment for future growth in the form of fixed capital items and working capital (inventory, debtor, cash floats less trade credit) is already allowed for.

The total of the discounted cash flows provides us with a value of the SBU (or firm, etc.) after taking into account all the cash inflows/outflows and reducing those distant cash flows by the required rate of return (the opportunity cost of capital). This discount rate is based on a blend of the required return to shareholders capital and the required return to debt holders capital. Chapter 10 describes the logic behind the derivation of the discount rate, which is a weighted average of the required returns to equity and debt – the Weighted Average Cost of Capital, or WACC.

By examining the discounted cash flow the SBU management and the firm's managing director can assess the value contribution of the SBU. The management team putting forward these projected cash flows could then be judged and rewarded on the basis of performance targets expressed in cash flow terms. On the other hand, the cash flows may refer to a particular product line or specific customer(s). At each of these levels of management a contribution to overall corporate value is expected.

The planning horizon[1] is seven years and so the present value of the future cash flows is:

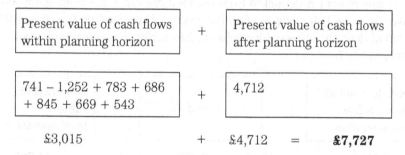

In analysis of this kind it is not unusual to find that most of the value arises after the planning horizon. However, bear in mind that it is the actions (strategic positioning etc.) and the investments made within the planning horizon that create the platform for these high post-planning horizon free cash flows.

Note that in the case of Gold we have not shown a large initial cash outflow, in contrast to the NPV calculations described in the first part of the book. This is to illustrate how you can use discounted cash flow analysis to analyze the present value of the future cash flows (not *net* present value) of an SBU etc. that was established years before, and you do not have the start-up costs to consider – this type of analysis only considers the future cash inflows and outflows, not the bygone (sunk) costs.

The value shown in the calculation based on one particular strategic direction (say the result from Table 8.1) can be compared with alternatives to see which is likely to provide the highest value. You could also conduct sensitivity and scenario analysis (see Chapter 5) to highlight areas of concern and in order that managerial attention may be directed to reduce the probability of a poor outcome.

Corporate value

If the SBU that we are valuing has other assets that are not used in the creation of free cash flow and those assets have a market value then we add this to the total of the discounted operational cash flow to arrive at the total firm value. For example, many firms hold portfolios of shares or bonds as investments with no connection to the firm's operations. The market value of these adds to the value of the firm derived from the operational free cash flow. Likewise, if a company owns an empty and unused factory which could be sold its value can be added to the total.

Corporate value (enterprise value)	=	Present value of free cash flow from operations	+	Value of non-operating assets

Shareholder value from operations

If the value of debt is deducted from the total present value from operations we derive the value belonging to shareholders. So, if we assume that this SBU has £3,000 of debt the shareholder value before taking account of non-operational assets is £4,727.

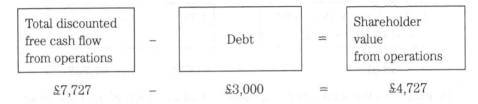

Total discounted free cash flow from operations	–	Debt	=	Shareholder value from operations
£7,727	–	£3,000	=	£4,727

The term 'debt' here extends beyond interest bearing debt to include finance lease obligations, underfunded pension plans and contingent liabilities.

If we now assume that this SBU has £800 of government bonds held as investments, separate from its operations, and £600 of equity investments, then total shareholder value amounts to £6,127:

Total shareholder value	=	Shareholder value from operations	+	Value of non-operating assets
£6,127	=	£4,727	+	£1,400

Comparing the discounted free cash flows with alternatives

The figure of £7,727 is the present value of all the future operating cash flows. An alternative course of action is to sell off the SBU's assets, either piecemeal or as a whole. We should compare these alternatives with the present value of continuing to own and run the business. The opportunity cost of following the strategy is the value of the best forgone alternative.

Real management is not about precise numbers – it's about what lies behind the numbers

By embarking on cash flow based analysis (or shareholder value analysis or economic profit analysis or economic value added analysis), the decision-maker is forced to investigate and understand the underlying business. Only by thorough examination is he/she going to put realistic numbers into the future projection table. This means a knowledge of the competitive environment and the extraordinary resources that the firm possesses to produce high returns in its chosen industry(ies) – see Chapter 7. In other words, the decision-maker needs to investigate the key 'value drivers' in the company and the industry.

However there is a trap here for the unwary and ill-informed. A manager lacking the intellectual tools, theoretical frameworks and facts to carry out high quality strategic analysis will produce simplistic and misleading input numbers to the cash flow forecasts: GIGO – garbage in/garbage out.

Value-based management is not a mechanical discipline. It is not about inputting a few numbers to a computer program and then waiting until *the* answer pops out. It is a process requiring judgment every step of the way; it requires careful reflection on the results and their sensitivity to the input numbers. Deep thought is required to appreciate the impact of making slightly (or greatly) different judgments on the input variables; and in assessing the probabilities of variations occurring. Value-based management is a decision-making-in-a-haze-of-

---

Investment after the planning horizon

After the planning horizon annual cash flows may well differ from the figure of £1,250 due to additional investment in fixed and working capital items but this will make no difference to present *value* as any new investment made (when discounted) will be the same as the discounted value of the future cash inflows from that investment. In other words, the company is able to earn merely the required rate of return from Year 8 onwards so no new investment can create value. For example, suppose that Gold raised additional funds of £1,000 and at the end of Year 9 invested this in a project generating a perpetual annual net cash inflow of £120 starting at time 10. When these figures are discounted to time 0 the NPV is zero:

Present value of cash outflow $\qquad \dfrac{-£1,000}{(1.12)^9} = -360.61$

Present value of cash inflows $\qquad \dfrac{£120/0.12}{(1.12)^9} = +360.61$

Thus incremental investment beyond the planning horizon generates no incremental value and so can be ignored for value calculations.

uncertainty discipline. How can it be otherwise if it is to be useful in the real world of unpredictability and vagueness. But it gives us a framework and the tools for navigating the best judged route given these circumstances.

A premium is put on people who can make good judgment calls despite the imprecision. These people search for more data to try to see through the haze of the future. More data also leads to thought and action designed to reduce the range of probable outcomes.

The connection with stock market valuation

The kind of discounted cash flow analysis illustrated in Table 8.1 is used by financial institutions to value shares. (In these cases interest paid to lenders is subtracted to determine the cash flow attributable to shareholders which is then discounted at the required return for shares of that risk class – not a weighted average cost of capital including the return to debt holders – see Chapter 13.) Given the emphasis by the owners of the firm on cash flow generation it would make sense for managers when evaluating strategies, projects, product lines and customers to use a similar method.

Shareholder value analysis

Alfred Rappaport (1998) has taken the basic concept of cash flow discounting and developed a simplified method of analysis. In the example of Gold plc (see Table 8.1) the component elements of the cash flow did not change in a regular pattern. For example, fixed capital investment was ten times as great in Year 2 as in Year 5. Rappaport's shareholder value analysis assumes relatively smooth change in the various cash flow elements from one year to the next as they are all taken to be related to the sales level. Rappaport's seven key factors which determine value are as set out in Figure 8.1.

FIGURE 8.1
Rappaport's value drivers

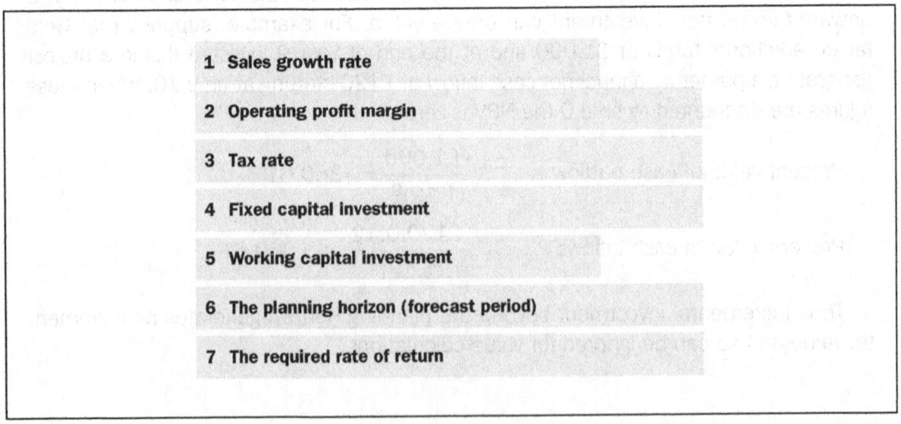

1 Sales growth rate
2 Operating profit margin
3 Tax rate
4 Fixed capital investment
5 Working capital investment
6 The planning horizon (forecast period)
7 The required rate of return

Rappaport calls the seven key factors value drivers, and this can be confusing given that other writers describe a value driver as a factor that enables some degree of competitive advantage. To distinguish the two types of value driver the quantitative seven listed in Figure 8.1 will be referred to as Rappaport's value drivers. To estimate future cash flows Rappaport assumes a constant percentage rate of growth in sales. The operating profit margin is a constant percentage of sales. Profit here is defined as profit before deduction of interest and tax, PBIT. The tax rate is a constant percentage of the operating profit. Fixed capital and working capital investment are related to the *increase* in sales.

So, if sales for the most recent year amount to £1m and are expected to continue to rise by 12 percent per year, the operating profit margin on sales[2] is 9 percent, taxes are 31 percent of operating profit, the incremental investment in fixed capital items is 14 percent of the *change* in sales, and the incremental working capital investment is 10 percent of the *change* in sales, the cash flow for the next year will be as set out in Table 8.2.

TABLE 8.2
Silver plc: sales, operating profit and cash outflows for next year

Sales in year 1

= Sales in prior year × (1 + Sales growth rate)

= 1,000,000 × 1.12

1,120,000

Operating profit

= Sales × Operating profit margin

= 1,120,000 × 0.09

100,800

Taxes

= Operating profit × 31%

= 100,800 × 0.31

−31,248

Incremental investment in fixed capital

= Increase in sales × Incremental fixed capital investment rate

= 120,000 × 0.14

−16,800

Incremental investment in working capital

= Increase in sales × Working capital investment rate

= 120,000 × 0.10

−12,000

Operating free cash flow   £40,752

Using shareholder value analysis to value an entire company

Corporate value is the combined value of the debt portion and equity portion of the overall capital structure:

$$\text{Corporate value} = \text{Debt} + \text{Shareholder value}$$

The debt element is the market value of debt, such as long-term loans and overdrafts, plus the market value of quasi-debt liabilities, such as preference shares. In practical shareholder value analysis the balance sheet book value of debt is often used as a reasonable approximation to the market value. The above equation can be rearranged to derive shareholder value:

$$\text{Shareholder value} = \text{Corporate value} - \text{Debt}$$

Rappaport's corporate value has three elements, due to his separation of the discounted cash flow value of marketable securities – these are assets not needed in operations to generate the business's cash flows – from the cash flows from operations (*see* Figure 8.2). The value of the marketable securities is expressed as their current market price.

FIGURE 8.2
Rappaport's corporate value

| Corporate value | = | Present value of operating cash flows within the planning horizon ('forecast period') | + | Present value of operating cash flows after the planning horizon | + | The current value of marketable securities and other non-operating investments, e.g. government bonds |

Free cash flow is the operating cash flow after fixed and working capital investment; that which comes from the *operations* of the business. It excludes cash flows arising from, say, the sale of shares by the company or bond issue. It also excludes payments of interest or dividends (*see* Figure 8.3).

A closer look at depreciation and investment in fixed capital

Investment in plant, machinery, vehicles, buildings, etc. consists of two parts.

■ **Type 1** Annual investment to replace worn-out equipment and so on, leaving the overall level of assets constant.

■ **Type 2** Investment that adds to the stock of assets, presumably with the intention of permitting growth in productive capacity. This is called incremental fixed-capital investment.

A simplifying assumption often employed in shareholder value analysis is that the 'depreciation' figure in the profit and loss account is equal to the Type 1 investment. This avoids the necessity of first adding back depreciation to operating profit figures and then deducting Type 1 capital investment. It is only necessary to account for that extra cash outflow associated with incremental fixed capital investment. Free cash flow therefore is as defined in Figure 8.3.

FIGURE 8.3
Rappaport's free cash flow

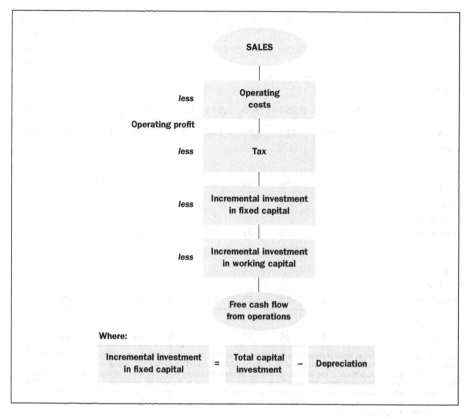

Illustration

We can calculate the shareholder value of Silver plc by using Rappaport's seven value drivers if we assume a planning horizon of eight years and a required rate of return of 15 percent (*see* Tables 8.3 and 8.4).

The company also has £60,000 of investments in foreign and domestic shares and £50,000 in long-term fixed interest rate securities. These are assets not required to produce operating profit and can be sold off with the proceeds given to their owners, i.e. the shareholders. Corporate value is as set out in Figure 8.4.

TABLE 8.3
Rappaport's value drivers applied to Silver plc

1	Sales growth	12% per year
2	Operating profit margin	9% of sales
3	Taxes	31% of operating profit
4	Incremental fixed capital investment	14% of the change in sales
5	Incremental working capital investment	10% of the change in sales
6	The planning horizon (forecast period)	8 years
7	The required rate of return	15% per year

TABLE 8.4

An example of shareholder value analysis – cash flow calculation

Year	0	1	2	3	4	5	6	7	8	9 and sub-sequent years
£000s										
Sales	1,000	1,120	1,254	1,405	1,574	1,762	1,974	2,211	2,476	2,476
Operating profits		101	113	126	142	159	178	199	223	223
Less taxes		−31	−35	−39	−44	−49	−55	−62	−69	−69
Less incremental investment in fixed capital		−17	−19	−21	−24	−26	−30	−33	−37	0
Less incremental working capital investment		−12	−13	−15	−17	−19	−21	−24	−27	0
Operating free cash flow		41	46	51	57	65	72	80	90	154

Note: All figures are rounded to whole numbers. There is no additional investment in fixed assets and working capital after year 8 shown. This indicates that the perpetual cash flow of 154 can be produced without expanding the physical capacity of the firm (no new factories, etc.). However, investment in the form of replacement of existing facilities subject to wear and tear is taking place, equal to the depreciation amount deducted before the figure for operating profits is input to the analysis. Investment above and beyond this replacement investment may take place, but it has no impact on the value calculation because investment after the planning horizon generates a return equal to the required rate of return, i.e. there is no performance spread for these assets, and so such investment is ignored for the calculation of firm value.

The required rate of return in shareholder value analysis is the weighted average required return on debt and equity capital (the WACC) which allows for a return demanded by the debt holders and shareholders in proportion to their provision of capital (see Chapter 10). This explains why cash flows before deduction of interest are discounted rather than just those attributable to shareholders: some of those cash flows will go to debt holders. The discounted cash flows derived in this way are then summed to give the corporate value (sometimes called enterprise value). When debt, in this case, £200,000, is deducted, shareholder value is obtained.

Shareholder value = Corporate value – Debt
Shareholder value = £705,000 – £200,000 = £505,000

Again, this kind of analysis can be used at a number of different levels:

- whole business
- division/SBU

FIGURE 8.4

Corporate value

Present value of operating cash flows within the planning horizon (forecast period)	$\dfrac{41}{1.15} + \dfrac{46}{(1.15)^2} + \dfrac{51}{(1.15)^3} + \dfrac{57}{(1.15)^4}$ $+ \dfrac{65}{(1.15)^5} + \dfrac{72}{(1.15)^6} + \dfrac{80}{(1.15)^7} + \dfrac{90}{(1.15)^8}$	= 259
+		
Present value of operating cash flows after the planning horizon	$\dfrac{154}{0.15} = 1{,}027$ then discount result by eight years $\dfrac{1{,}027}{(1.15)^8} =$	336
+		
The current value of marketable securities and other non-operating investments	60+50	= 110
CORPORATE VALUE		705 or £705,000

- operating unit
- project
- product line or customer.

Strategy valuation using shareholder value analysis

The quantitative evaluation of alternative strategies in terms of value creation can assist strategic choice. It is advisable when applying shareholder value analysis to a business unit or corporate level strategy formulation and evaluation to consider at least four alternative strategic moves:

- a continuation of current strategy – 'base-case' strategy;
- liquidation;
- trade sale (selling the entire business to another firm) or spin-off (selling a business unit, while perhaps retaining a stake);
- new operating strategy.

Imagine that the company we have been using to explain shareholder value analysis is involved in the production of plastic guttering for houses and the shareholder value figure of £505,000 represents the base-case strategy, consisting of relatively low levels of incremental investment and sales growing at a slow rate.

Alternatives

■ The company has recently been approached by a property developer interested in purchasing the company's depot and offices for the sum of £400,000. Other assets (vehicles, inventory, machinery) could be sold to raise a further £220,000 and the marketable securities could be sold for £110,000. This liquidation would result in shareholders receiving £530,000 (£400,000 + £220,000 + £110,000 − £200,000). This liquidation option produces slightly more than the base-case strategy.

■ The third possibility is a trade sale or spin-off. Companies can sell separable businesses to other firms or float off strategic business units or groups of SBUs on the stock market. Cadbury Schweppes split itself in 2008 into a confectionery business and a soft drinks business. In the case of the fictional guttering firm, it is too small to obtain a separate quotation for component parts, and its operations are too well integrated to allow a trade sale of particular sections. However, in the past shareholders have been approached by larger competitors to discuss the possibility of a takeover. The three or four major industry players are trying to build up market share with the stated aim of achieving 'economies of scale and critical mass' and there is the distinct impression that they are being over-generous to selling shareholders in smaller firms – they are paying 'silly prices'. The management judge that if they could get a bidding war going between these domineering larger firms they could achieve a price of about £650,000 for shareholders.

■ The fourth possibility involves an expansion into a new product area of multi-coloured guttering. This will require large-scale investment but should result in rapidly rising sales and higher operating margins. The expected Rappaport value drivers are as set out in Table 8.5. Note the increased investment in capital items. Also note the higher risk of this strategy compared with the base-case is reflected in the increased discount rate from 15 to 16 percent.

The guttering firm's shareholder value under the new strategy is as set out in Table 8.6. This shows that there are lower cash flows in the first three years with this strategy compared with the base-case strategy because of the increased investment, yet the overall expected shareholder value rises from £505,000 to £1,069,000.

TABLE 8.5

Rappaport's value drivers applied to an expansion of Silver plc

1	Sales growth	25% per year
2	Operating profit margin	11% of sales
3	Taxes	31% of operating profit
4	Incremental fixed capital investment	15% of the change in sales
5	Incremental working capital investment	10% of the change in sales
6	The planning horizon (forecast period)	8 years
7	The required rate of return	16% per year

TABLE 8.6

The guttering firm's shareholder value under the new strategy

Year	0	1	2	3	4	5	6	7	8	9 and subsequent years
£000s										
Sales	1,000	1,250	1,563	1,953	2,441	3,052	3,815	4,768	5,960	5,960
Operating profits		138	172	215	269	336	420	524	656	656
Less taxes		−43	−53	−67	−84	−104	−130	−162	−203	−203
Less incremental investment in fixed capital		−38	−47	−59	−73	−92	−114	−143	−179	0
Less incremental working capital investment		−25	−31	−39	−49	−61	−76	−95	−119	0
Operating free cash flow		32	41	50	63	79	100	124	155	453

$$\text{Discounted cash flows within planning horizon} \quad \frac{32}{1.16} + \frac{41}{(1.16)^2} + \frac{50}{(1.16)^3} + \frac{63}{(1.16)^4} + \frac{79}{(1.16)^5} + \frac{100}{(1.16)^6} + \frac{124}{(1.16)^7} + \frac{155}{(1.16)^8} = 295$$

Discounted cash flow beyond planning horizon 453/0.16 = 2,831, then 2,831/(1.16)^8	= 864
Marketable securities	= 110
Corporate value	1,269

Shareholder value   = Corporate value − Debt

= £1,269,000 − £200,000

= £1,069,000

Sensitivity and scenario analysis

(These comments apply to cash flow analysis as well.)

To make a more informed choice the directors may wish to carry out a sensitivity and scenario analysis (see Chapter 5 for an introduction to this technique).

A worst-case and a best-case scenario could be constructed and the sensitivity to changes in certain variables could be scrutinized. For example, alternative discount rates and incremental investment in fixed capital rates could be examined for the multi-coloured product strategy as shown in Table 8.7.

One observation that may be made from Table 8.7 is that even if the amount of incremental capital investment required rises to 20 percent of the increase in sales and the discount rate moves to 17 percent this strategy produces the highest value of all the four options considered. The management team may wish to consider the consequences and the likelihood of other variables changing from the original expected levels.

TABLE 8.7
Shareholder value for the guttering firm under different discount and capital investment rates

£000s		Discount rate		
		15%	16%	17%
Incremental fixed capital investment rates	15%	1,205	1,069	951
	20%	1,086	955	843

Targets, rewards and alignment of managerial effort

Following an initial shareholder value analysis it can be useful to breakdown each of the seven Rappaport value drivers into more detail. So, for example, if the operating profit margin is 20 percent you could investigate what proportion of the 80 percent of income from sales flows out in the form of wages, or material costs, or overheads, etc. This will permit focus of managerial attention. It also allows performance measures and targets to be more detailed. The production manager can be set targets in terms of raw material wastage and shop floor employee efficiency. These operating targets can then be fed into the goal to improve the operating margin and the ultimate goal of shareholder wealth maximization. Similarly, managers with responsibility for fixed and working capital investment can agree targets that are aligned with all the other managers in terms of being focused on value.

Another use of this analytical method: the value drivers (and their component parts) can be used to benchmark the company against competitors. So, if you find that your firm has the highest level of work-in-progress inventory per unit of sales you may want to see if there are efficiency gains to be made.

Problems with shareholder value analysis

There are some disadvantages to the use of shareholder value analysis.

- Constant percentage increases in value drivers lack realism in some circumstances; in others it is a reasonable simplification.

- It can be misused in target setting, for example if managers are given a specific cash flow objective for a 12-month period they may be dissuaded from necessary value-enhancing investment (i.e. using cash) to achieve the short-term cash flow target. Alleviate this problem by setting both short- and long-term targets. The short-term ones may show negative cash flows.

- Data availability – many firms' accounting systems are not equipped to provide the necessary input data. The installation of a new cash flow orientated system may be costly.

Economic profit

Economic profit, EP (also called residual income) has an advantage over shareholder value analysis because it uses the existing accounting and reporting systems of firms by focusing on profit rather than cash flow information. This not only reduces the need to implement an overhaul of the data collecting and reporting procedures but also provides evaluatory and performance measurement tools which use the familiar concept of profit. Managers used to 'bottom line' figures are more likely to understand and accept this metric than one based on cash flow information.

> Economic profit for a period is the amount earned by a business after deducting all operating expenses and a charge for the opportunity cost of the capital[3] employed.

A business only produces an economic profit if it generates a return greater than that demanded by the finance providers given the risk class of investment. There are two versions of economic profit.

The entity approach to EP

One version of EP is based on profit after tax is deducted but before interest is deducted.[4] There are two ways to calculate this EP.

The profit less capital charge method

Here a charge for the use of capital equal to the invested capital multiplied by the return required by the share and debt holders (which is a weighted average cost of the debt and the equity, WACC) is deducted from the operating profits after tax:

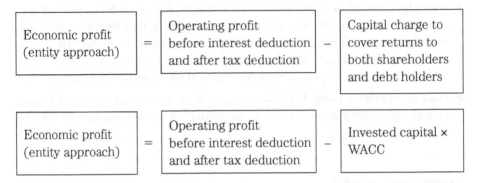

The 'performance spread' method

The difference between the return achieved on invested capital and the weighted average cost of capital (WACC), i.e. the required rate of return, is the performance spread. This percentage figure is then multiplied by the quantity of invested capital to obtain EP:

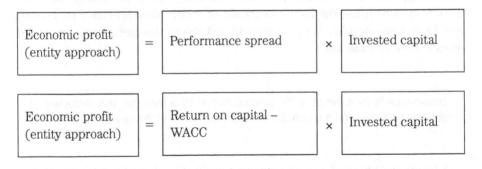

The WACC allows for an appropriate risk-adjusted return to each type of finance provider (debt and equity) – see Chapter 10 for a calculation of this. As can be seen from the following Illustration either method leads to the same EP.

Illustration

EoPs plc has a weighted average cost of capital (required rate of return) of 12% and has used £1m of invested capital (share and debt) to produce an operating profit before interest and after tax of £180,000 during the past year.

Profit less capital charge:

EP = Operating profits before interest and after tax – (Invested capital × WACC)

  = £180,000 – (£1,000,000 × 0.12)

  = £60,000

Performance spread approach:

EP = (Return on capital – WACC) × Invested capital

  = (18% – 12%) × £1,000,000

  = £60,000

The equity approach to EP

This entity EP approach, based on operating profit before the deduction of interest, calculates the surplus above the return to all the finance providers to the business entity including the debt holders. The alternative is the 'equity approach'. With this, interest is deducted from the profit figure so we obtain the profit that belongs to the shareholders. Also the required return is the return demanded on the equity capital only. So, EP is the profit attributable to shareholders after a deduction for the implicit cost of employing shareholders' capital.

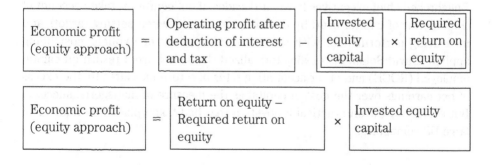

Illustration

In the case of EoPs let us assume that one-half the £1m of capital is equity and the other half debt. The equity required rate of return is 15% and the debt required rate of return is 9% (i.e. £45,000 per year), therefore the weighted average cost of capital is 12%.

Profit less capital charge:
Deducting £45,000 of interest from the operating profit figure we have £135,000.

$$\text{EP (equity)} = \text{Operating profits after interest and tax} - (\text{Invested equity capital} \times \text{Required return on equity})$$
$$= £135,000 - (£500,000 \times 0.15)$$
$$= £60,000$$

Performance spread approach:
The return on equity[5] is 27% (£135,000/£500,000).

$$\text{EP (equity)} = (\text{Return on equity} - \text{Required return on equity}) \times \text{Invested equity capital}$$
$$= (27\% - 15\%) \times £500,000$$
$$= £60,000$$

A short history of economic profit

The principles behind economic profit have a long antecedence. For at least a century economists have been aware of the need to recognize the minimum return to be provided to the finance provider as a 'cost' of operating a business. Enlightened chief executives have for decades, if not centuries, taken account of the amount of capital used by divisional managers when setting targets and measuring performance, with some sort of implicit, or explicit, cost being applied. David Solomons (1965) formalized the switch from return on capital employed (ROCE) and other accounting rates of return measures to 'the excess of net earnings over the cost of capital as the measure of managerial success'. But even he drew on practical innovation that had taken place in a number of large US companies.

The use of economic profit is becoming more widespread

For over two decades major US firms, including Walt Disney, Quaker Oats and AT&T, have been switching to using economic profit as a guiding concept. The focus of economic profit on the productive use of capital can have profound consequences. Roberto Goizueta, CEO of Coca-Cola, put the basic philosophy this way: 'We raise capital to make concentrate, and sell it at an operating profit. Then we pay the cost of that capital. Shareholders pocket the difference'.[1]

Barclays Bank adopted the technique in 2000 declaring their aim to double economic profit every four years. 'Economic Profit (EP) ... is profit after tax and minority interests less a capital charge (average shareholders' equity and goodwill excluding minority interests multiplied by the Group cost of capital). Barclays believes that economic profit encourages both profitable growth and the efficient use of capital. Barclays has a set of four year performance goals for the period 2008 to 2011 inclusive. The primary goal is to achieve compound annual growth in economic profit in the range of 5% to 10% (£9.3bn to £10.6bn of cumulative economic profit) over the 2008 to 2011 goal period. Given the increase in the cost of capital and regulatory capital requirements in 2008 we intend to publish new goals in 2009.' (Barclays Annual report, 2008.) In 2008 Barclays reported that it produced economic profit of £1.7bn (it used the equity method with 'average shareholder's equity for economic profit purposes' of £27,400m and cost of equity of 10.5 percent. The capital charge was £2,876m).

When Xerox adopted Six Sigma, an approach to problem solving developed by General Electric that emphasizes small teams, measurement and economic return, it found significant improvement. 'Six Sigma is very rigid and disciplined ... Every project is managed with economic profit metrics. There is none of the squishy stuff ... The learning process begins with taking out waste, working out where value gets added and where it does not', says Xerox manager Anne Mulcahy.[2]

[1] Quoted in Tully (1993), p. 93.
[2] *Financial Times* 23 September 2005, p. 13.

Usefulness of economic profit

A focus on EP rather than the traditional accounting profit has the advantage that every manager down the line is encouraged (rewarded) for paying close attention to the cost associated with using capital in a business unit, project, product line or the entire corporation. The introduction of EP targets has resulted in some dramatic reductions in money tied-up wastefully in assets such as raw material stocks, and in significant reductions in requests for major fixed capital expenditure. Managers who are judged on profits may not be as keen to reduce capital employed as those judged on EP.

Economic profit can be used to evaluate strategic options which produce returns over a number of years. For example, Spoe plc is considering the investment of £2m in a new division that is expected to produce a constant operating profit after tax of £300,000 per year to infinity without the need for any further investment in fixed capital or working capital in subsequent years. The company has a required rate of return on capital of 13 percent. The extra 'value' created on top of the initial investment of £2m is:

$$\text{Economic profit (entity) per year} = (\text{Return on capital} - \text{WACC}) \times \text{Invested capital}$$

$$= (15\% - 13\%) \times £2,000,000$$

$$= £40,000$$

The present value of this perpetuity is:

£40,000/0.13 = £307,692

This £307,692 is the additional value, in present terms, of economic profit. [Of course, we can only call this value if we make the bold assumption that profit numbers bear a close resemblance to cash flow numbers (an assumption too frequently and too glibly made by consultants and writers in this area). See below for challenges to this assumption]. To obtain the total value of this division we add to this the initial investment:

$$\text{Value of new division} = \text{Present value of economic profit} + \text{Initial investment}$$

$$= £307,692 + £2,000,000 = £2,307,692$$

Having expressed the new strategy in terms of EP, in implementing it EP targets can be set annually and rewards granted for achieving (exceeding) those targets.

Economic profit has an advantage over shareholder value analysis in that it can be used to look back at how the firm (unit) has performed relative to the amount of capital used each year as well as creating future targets in terms of EP. (Shareholder value analysis is generally used only in forward-looking mode. Having said that however, once the shareholder value analysis estimates have been made for a strategy it is possible to set interim targets, which, as time passes, are examined for deviation. So, in this sense it can be used in backward looking mode, i.e. within a plan.) With EP it is possible to go to a firm and examine past performance from scratch, without the need for established EP targets within a plan.

Economic profit per unit can be calculated. For example, economic profit per square foot or economic profit per unit of output. Economic profit sends a more powerful signal because it is expressed in absolute amounts of money generated for shareholders above the minimum required, e.g. £1.20 EP per unit sold, rather than a percentage, e.g. profit margin of 14 percent. Profit margins fail to allow for the size of the capital commitment.

Difficulties with economic profit

There are, however, some disadvantages to the use of economic profit.

The balance sheet does not reflect invested capital

Balance sheets are not designed to provide information on the present economic value of assets being used in a business. Assets are generally recorded at original cost less depreciation, amortization (reduction in intangibles) and depletion (e.g reduction in oil reserves). With or without inflation it does not take many years for these balance sheet values to deviate dramatically from the theoretically correct capital employed figures for most firms. Generally balance sheets significantly understate the amount of capital employed, and this understatement causes EP to appear high. Moreover, many businesses invest in assets that never find their way to a balance sheet. For example, some firms pour vast sums into building up brand images and do so with the, often correct, belief that shareholders' money is being well invested, with the pay-off arising years later. Nevertheless, accounting convention insists on such expenditures being written off against profits rather than being taken into the balance sheet. The same problem applies to other 'investments' such as business reputation and management training. The early theorists in value measurement suggested using current values of assets. Following them I would be tempted in certain circumstances to use the either (a) the sum of the resale value of individual assets, or (b) replacement cost. Much depends on the objective of the analysis:

- If the objective is to monitor past performance in terms of examining the efficiency with which money was invested the historical amount invested seems somewhat relevant as the 'capital' figure. However, there will be many circumstances where a distinctly unsatisfactory capital figure is derived from a balance sheet, e.g. when assets were acquired decades before the current period.

- If you are monitoring current (this year) performance perhaps the current replacement value or the sum of the resale value of individual assets may be most useful. Sometimes the resale value is very low when the assets are highly specific with little secondary market, so relying on the resale value alone would give an artificially low asset value. In other circumstances the replacement value is clearly way above the level that any manager would actually replace at and so a more informed decision can be made by using resale value as it represents the opportunity cost of using the assets this year.

- If the asset value is needed to make future oriented decisions about where to invest assets presently owned by the firm then the sum of the resale value of the individual assets would be most useful because this would capture the opportunity cost – the firm could sell off these assets as an alternative. The sunk costs associated with past investment are not relevant in such a decision and so balance sheet values are not very useful.

- If the decision concerns the obtaining of new assets to implement a project/strategy then the cost of obtaining them is relevant.

Note that we use the 'sum of the resale value of individual assets' rather than the current market value of all-the-assets-when-welded-together-as-a-coherent-whole for the corporation/SBU because to use the latter would eliminate any value by definition. For example, if a firm starts up with £1m of capital and a brilliant idea, as soon as the strategy is put in place to exploit the idea the resale value of the firm as an operating entity rises to, say, £10m. That is, the resale value of the firm is equal to the initial capital plus the present value of the future cash flows or EP. The £10m current market value of all-the-assets-when-welded-together-as-a-coherent-whole includes £9m of value, but the value of the sum of the individual assets is in the region of £1m.

Manipulation and arbitrariness

The difficulties caused by relying on accounting data are exacerbated by the freedom available to manipulate such figures as well as the degree of subjectivity involved in arriving at some of the figures in the first place. For example, if a business has sold goods on credit some customers are likely to fail to pay on the due date. The problem for the accountant (and managers) is to decide when to accept that particular debts will never be paid; is it after three months, six months or a year? Until they are declared 'bad debts' they are recorded as an asset – perhaps they will turn out to be worth something, perhaps they won't. At each balance sheet date judgment is required to establish an estimate of the value of the debtor balance to the firm. Similar problems of 'flexibility' and potential for manipulation are possible with the estimate of the length of life of an asset (which has an effect on annual depreciation), and with R&D expenditure or inventory valuation.

Having a wide range of choice of treatment of key inputs to the profit and loss account and balance sheets makes comparability over time, and between companies, very difficult.

High economic profit and negative NPV can go together

There is a danger of over-reliance on EP. For example, imagine a firm has become a convert to economic profit and divisional managers are judged on annual economic profit. Their bonuses and promotion prospects rest on good performance spreads over the next 12 months. This may prompt a manager to accept a project with an impressive EP over the short term whether or not it has a positive NPV over its entire life. Projects that produce poor or negative EPs in the first few years, for example biotechnology investments, will be rejected even if they will enhance shareholder wealth in the long term.

Also, during the life of a project, managers may be given specific EP targets for a particular year. They may be tempted to ensure the profit target is met by cutting down on certain expenditures such as training, marketing and maintenance. The target will be achieved but long-term damage may be inflicted.

The CEO of Siemens, Klaus Kleinfield, was quoted in the *Financial Times* (6 November 2006, p. 24) saying that 'management pay is based on the "economic value added" each division provides against each year's budget.' But a former senior director says this has led to a lack of investment in some parts of the business as managers look to earn as much as possible.

A third value-destroying use of EP occurs when managers are demotivated by being set EP targets. For example, if managers have no control over the capital employed in their part of the business, they may become resentful of and cynical about value-based management if they are told nevertheless to achieve certain EP targets.

Care must be taken by external observers when examining the EP (or EVA) to judge performance, particularly in annual league tables. Misleading impressions are frequent over periods as short as one year because some firms that are on a high value creating path often have years where EP is low (or nil). Then there are firms on a value destructive path which report high current year EP. You can only judge performance over a number of years. When EP is used internally, however, it frequently does make sense to produce annual (or even six-monthly) EP figures to compare with a plan to see if the value creation strategy is on target. Within the plan there will probably be periods of negative EP (e.g. in the start-up phase), as well as periods of high surpluses over the cost of capital.

Difficult to allocate revenues, costs and capital to business units, products, etc.

To carry out EP analysis at the sub-firm level it is necessary to measure profit and capital invested separately for each area of the business. Many costs and capital assets are shared between business units, product lines and customers. It is very difficult in some situations to identify the proportion of the cost, debt or asset that is attributable to each activity. It can also be expensive. Consultants tend to be overoptimistic about the ability of accountants and managers to do this in a theory-compliant and precise manner.

Economic value added (EVA®)

EVA, developed and trademarked by the US consultants Stern Stewart and Co., is a variant of EP that attempts to overcome some of the problems outlined above. Great energy has been put into its marketing and it is probably the most widely talked about value metric.

EVA = Adjusted invested capital × (Adjusted return on capital – WACC)

or

EVA = Adjusted operating profits after tax – (Adjusted invested capital × WACC)

The adjustments to profit and capital figures are meant to refine the basic EP.[6] Stern Stewart suggest that up to 164 adjustments to the accounting data may be needed. For example, spending on marketing and R&D helps build value and so these are added back to the balance sheet as assets (and amortized over the period expected to benefit from these expenditures). Goodwill on acquisitions previously written off is also returned and is expressed as an asset, thus boosting both profits and the balance sheet.

There are a number of difficulties with these adjustments – for example, over what period should these reconstituted 'assets' be amortized? Should you make adjustments for events up to five years ago, ten years ago, or the whole life of the firm?

EVA, like the generic EP, has the virtue of being based on familiar accounting concepts and it is arguably more accurate than taking ordinary accounting figures. However, critics have pointed out that the adjustments can be time-consuming and costly, and many are based on decisions that are as subjective as the original accountant's numbers. There also remains the problem of poorly, if enthusiastically, implemented EVA reward systems producing results that satisfy targets for EVA but which produce poor decisions with regard to NPV. Furthermore, the problem of allocating revenue, costs and capital to particular business units and products is not solved through the use of EVA.

Also the Stern Stewart definition of capital is 'the sum of all the cash that has been invested in a company's net assets over its life' (Stewart (1991), p. 86). Imagine the difficulties in establishing this given that most invested 'cash' put in will be in the form of many years of retained earnings which leads us back to the difficulties of accounting numbers and the dubiousness of making 'adjustments' to the raw numbers. Added to this problem is the issue of accepting this capital figure as relevant for many decisions. For example, in judging future strategic plans, perhaps the opportunity cost of those assets (the sum of the individual resale values) would be more relevant than what was paid for them, much of which may have become a sunk cost years ago (see Chapter 3). So, if Eurotunnel is contemplating a new strategy in 2011, should its 'capital invested' figure be £9bn (its cost of building, etc.) when calculating projected annual EVAs? Of course not. What is relevant is the opportunity cost of capital – the value of those assets in their best alternative use today (2011), not the money invested in the 1980s. Likewise if you are monitoring managers' performance this year the historic cost of assets they are using may be totally irrelevant to the analysis of their efficiency, whereas the money that they could have raised through the alternative of selling off the assets rather than operating them might be of enormous interest, as this may be the best alternative use.

Despite the outstanding problems companies are seeing benefits from introducing EVA.

> It's not rocket science, but it is good lingua franca that does indeed get everyone back to basics, makes them understand better the cash consequences of their own actions and, further, makes them address other departments' problems, not just their

own. Within each of our businesses we don't incentivise, for example, the sales director on sales and we don't incentivise the finance director on cash generation. The whole management team is incentivised on EVA and that means they are all pulling in the same direction and have to liaise better.

Mike Ashton, Finance Director of BWI.[7]

The CEO of Brambles, the world's biggest supplier of pallets, said that a big factor in the company's recovery has been the introduction of 'Brambles Value Added'. This concept – derived from economic value added – measures performance as profit minus the cost of capital and is used to evaluate investment, to report on performance and reward managers. 'The objective was to ensure that management had an absolute incentive to count capital employed as a cost of doing business.'[8]

The use of EVA is spreading around the world. Sony, in Japan, has invited Stern Stewart to work with the company. In Germany Volkswagen has attempted to align managerial interests with those of shareholders by making up to 40 percent of their annual bonuses dependent on achieving EVA targets.

Conclusion

This chapter has described a number of value-based metrics used to guide organizations. This is a field dominated by consultancy organizations each with a particular approach to sell. The foundation for all of them is discounted cash flow allowing for a suitable return on the money shareholders contribute to the business. I suggest that, rather than selecting one internal value metric, a better approach, for both strategic investment discussion and performance targeting and measurement, is to set both cash flow and economic profit targets. This would counter a number of problems of using each separately and would help to alleviate the tendency of managers to take action to achieve particular short-term targets at the expense of long-term wealth.

Notes

1 Discussed in Chapter 6.
2 Operating profit margin on sales is sales revenue *less* cost of sales and all selling and administrative expenses before deduction of tax and interest.
3 The meaning of the word 'capital' used here is different from its meaning in accounting. 'Capital' in accounting is a part of the shareholders' equity of the company ('capital issued', 'paid-in capital', etc.). 'Capital' in the present context means the sum of shareholders' equity (and of the borrowings of the company in the first version of EP) – *see* note 5 for a fuller discussion.
4 There are a few technical complications ignored here, but this is the essence of EP. For more detail consult McTaggart *et al.* (1994) or Stewart (1991).

5 The entity EP and the equity EP give the same annual EP figures but can give different equity values if calculated with a WACC determined by the initial proportions of debt and equity (i.e. those amounts put into the business by shareholders and debt holders). This is apparent in the following illustration (to be read after absorbing the fundamentals of WACC in Chapter 10). Valucrazee plc is set up with £50m from shareholders and £50m of debt capital. Equity at this risk level requires a rate of return of 20 percent, while debt requires 10 percent, therefore the WACC (based on initial proportions of debt and equity) = 15 percent. The company is expected to produce cash flow available for all the finance providers (i.e. before deduction of interest but after tax) of £25m per year to infinity.

Value under the entity approach:

Annual EP	=	Profit after tax before interest	−	Capital × Required rate of return	
Annual EP	=	£25m	−	(£100m × 15%)	= £10m

Corporate value	=	Initial total capital	+	Present value of annual economic profit	
Corporate value	=	£100m	+	£10m/0.15	= £166.67m

Equity value = Corporate value − debt value = £166.67m − £50m = £116.67m

Value under the equity approach:

Annual EP	=	Profit after tax and interest − Equity capital × Required rate of return
Annual EP	=	(£25m − £5m) − (£50m × 20%) = £10m

Equity value	=	Initial equity + Present value of annual equity economic profit	
Equity value	=	£50m + £10m/0.20	= £100m

The reason for the £16.67m difference is that the surplus cash flow above the minimum required is discounted at different rates. In the first case the £10m surplus cash flow (which must all be attributable to shareholders as the debt holders are satisfied with the 'required rate of return' deduction) is discounted at 15 percent, whereas in the second case it is discounted at 20 percent.

To make the two equity values equal we need to follow the rule when calculating WACC of using market value weights for debt and equity (i.e. what the total value of the shares in the company are after going ahead) rather than original book (balance sheet) values. The market value of debt remains the same if a value-enhancing project is accepted – that is, £50m. However, the market value of the equity is significantly higher than the amount first put in by the shareholders.

The annual cash flow to equity of £20m when discounted at 20 percent is £100m. Therefore, the weights used to calculate the WACC are:

Debt	£50m	Weight: £50m/£150m = 0.333
Equity	£100m	Weight: £100m/£150m = 0.667
Total capital	£150m	

$$\text{WACC} = K_e W_E + K_D W_D = 0.2 \times 0.667 + 0.1 \times 0.333 = 16.67\%$$

This changes the valuation under the entity approach:

Annual EP	=	Profit after tax before interest –	Capital × Required rate of return	
Annual EP	=	£25m	– (£100m × 16.67%)	= £8.33m

Corporate value = Initial total capital + Present value of annual economic profit
Corporate value = £100m + £8.33m/0.1667 = £150m

Equity value = Corporate value – debt value = £150m – £50m = £100m (the same as under the equity approach)

Under the WACC-adjusted-for-market-value-of-equity approach we observe a fall in the annual EP when using the entity approach from £10m to £8.33m because we, correctly, require 20 percent return on two-thirds (£100m) of capital employed out of a total of £150m (at market values).

What is the practical manager to do? In theory you should be using the market value proportions of debt and equity that are optimal for your firm for all projects, SBUs and for valuing the entire firm. That is, the firm should have target levels of debt relative to the equity base that produces the lowest WACC (see Chapter 10).

The reality in most firms is that the optimum mix of debt and equity is unlikely to be known with any precision as the factors determining the optimum, at base, can only be quantified through subjective probability estimates, e.g. the chance of financial distress (see Chapter 18). So, it is reasonable to think of the optimum proportions of debt and equity as a range rather than a pin-point percentage. For most firms the reasonable range is quite large. It could easily run from 50:50 gearing to 33:66 gearing. The advice to think in terms of a range for the WACC is reinforced by the many difficulties in other inputs to the WACC calculation, from the cost of equity (what is the risk premium? Is beta the appropriate adjustment for risk?) to the risk free rate of return – *see* Chapter 10.

Given the complications with the WACC under the entity approach many analysts would simply plump for the equity approach in the first place.

6 Notice that EVA is derived from the entity EP rather the equity EP because the WACC contains an allowance for a return to all finance providers, including debt holders. Therefore the 'adjusted invested capital' is equity plus debt.

7 Quoted in *Management Today*, January 1997, p. 45.

8 David Turner, CEO of Brambles, quoted in the *Financial Times* 27 December 2005, p. 13.

9

ENTIRE FIRM VALUE MEASUREMENT

Introduction

This chapter describes five 'market-based' measures of value performance. The feature common to all these measures is the focus on the stock market's valuation of the company. Total shareholder return (TSR) measures the rise or fall in the capital value of a company's shares combined with any cash payment, e.g. dividends, received by shareholders over particular periods of time, be it one year, three years or ten years. This gets to the heart of the issue for owners of companies – what return do I get on my shares from the activities of the managers hired to steward the resources entrusted to them?

The Wealth Added Index (WAI[1]) examines the change in share values after allowance for the required rate of return over the period of time examined. Two other metrics, Market Value Added (MVA[2]) and Market to book ratio (MBR), also examine the current share price in the market (together with the value of debt). However, rather than track share return performance through time these metrics relate the current market values to the amount of capital put into the business by the share owners (and lenders) since its foundation. If the company's strategic and operational actions have been robust in the pursuit of shareholder value then the current market value of the equity and debt should be significantly greater than the amount placed in the directors' hands by the purchasers of shares, through the retention of profits and the lending of debt capital. If, however, the market currently values the shares and the debt at less than the amount put in we know for sure that value has been destroyed.

The observation of a positive difference between current valuation and amount injected may or may not mean value has been generated. This depends on whether the investment made by shareholders and debt holders produced a sufficient *rate* of return given the time period over which the money was held in the stewardship of the directors. So, for example, if a firm founded 15 years ago with £1m of shareholder capital and £1m of debt paid out no dividends and received no more funds from finance providers is now valued at £3.56m for its shares and £1m for its debt, we need to know the required rate of return on equity for this risk class given the shareholders' opportunity cost to judge whether the annual rate of return of around 8.8 percent is sufficient. (Chapter 10 discusses how to calculate required rates of return.) Excess return, ER, is a modified MVA, allowing for this opportunity cost of capital over the period.

These five metrics can only be used for 'entire firm' assessments for a select group of companies – those with a stock market price quote (around 3,000 UK companies). Also note that these metrics cannot be used for analysis of parts of the business, such as a strategic business unit, due to the absence of a share price for a section of a company.

The metrics discussed in the previous chapter, on the other hand, can be used both for disaggregated analysis and for the entire firm. So it makes sense to think in terms of there being at least nine whole-firm value metrics available. These should not be thought of as mutually exclusive but complementary if calculated and viewed with sufficient informed thought.

Total shareholder return (TSR)

Shareholders are interested in the total return earned on their investment relative to general inflation, a peer group of firms, and the market as a whole. Total returns includes dividend returns and share price changes over a specified period. For one-period TSR:

$$TSR = \frac{\text{Dividend per share} + (\text{Share price at end of period} - \text{Initial share price})}{\text{Initial share price}} \times 100$$

Consider a share that rises in price over a period of a year from £1 to £1.10 with a 5p dividend paid at the end of the year. The TSR is 15 percent.

$$TSR = \frac{d_1 + (P_1 - P_0)}{P_0} \times 100$$

$$TSR = \frac{0.05 + (1.10 - 1.00)}{1.00} \times 100 = 15\%$$

When dealing with multi-period TSRs we need to account for the dividends received in the interim years as well as the final dividend. The TSR can be expressed either as a total return over the period or as an annualized rate.

So, for example if a share had a beginning price of £1, paid annual dividends at the end of each of the next three years of 9p, 10p and 11p respectively and had a closing price of £1.30, the total average annual return (assuming dividends are reinvested in the company's shares immediately on receipt) is calculated via internal rate of return (see Chapter 2 for an introduction to IRR):

Time	0	1	2	3
Price/cash flow (p)	−100	9	10	11+130

$$-100 + \frac{9}{1 + r} + \frac{10}{(1 + r)^2} + \frac{141}{(1 + r)^3} = 0$$

At:

$r = 19\%: -1.7037$

$r = 18\%: 0.6259$

$$\text{The internal rate of return} = 18 + \frac{0.6259}{0.6259 + 1.7037} = 18.27\%$$

The annualised TSR is 18.27%.

The total shareholder return over the three years $= (1 + 0.1827)^3 - 1 = 65.4\%$.

TSRs for a number of periods are available from financial data organizations such as Datastream and on most financial websites (e.g. www.advfn.com).

TSR (often referred to simply as 'total return') has become an important indicator of managerial success:

Performance against this type of measure is now used as the basis for calculating the major component of directors' bonuses in over half of FTSE 100 companies . . . TSR reflects the measure of success closest to the hearts of a company's investors: what they have actually gained or lost from investing in one set of executives rather than in another.

(*Management Today*, March 1997, p. 48.)

Exhibit 9.1 shows the one-year TSR for a number of US and European companies.

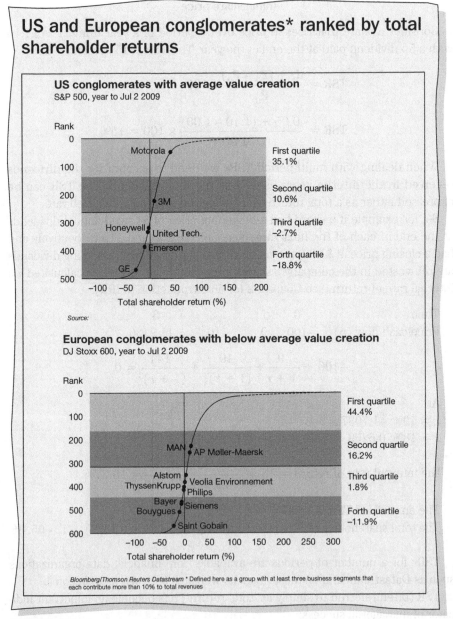

US and European conglomerates* ranked by total shareholder returns

US conglomerates with average value creation
S&P 500, year to Jul 2 2009

| | Rank | Total shareholder return (%) |
| First quartile 35.1% |
| Second quartile 10.6% |
| Third quartile −2.7% |
| Forth quartile −18.8% |

Motorola
3M
Honeywell   United Tech.
Emerson
GE

Source:

European conglomerates with below average value creation
DJ Stoxx 600, year to Jul 2 2009

First quartile 44.4%
Second quartile 16.2%
Third quartile 1.8%
Forth quartile −11.9%

MAN   AP Møller-Maersk
Alstom   Veolia Environnement
ThyssenKrupp   Philips
Bayer   Siemens
Bouygues
Saint Gobain

Bloomberg/Thomson Reuters Datastream * Defined here as a group with at least three business segments that each contribute more than 10% to total revenues

EXHIBIT 9.1

Source: *Financial Times* 13 July 2009, p. 21.

In Table 9.1 the TSRs of the ten largest UK companies are shown for one year and for five years. Some perform better over one year relative to the others in the group, others perform better over five. The 'dividend yield plus capital gain' metric needs to be used in conjunction with a benchmark to filter out economy-wide or industry-wide factors. So, it would make sense to compare the TSR for HSBC with the TSR for the Banking sector to be able to judge whether a particular performance is due to factors lifting the entire sector or is attributable to good management in the firm.

TSR has taken off as a key performance measure. In 2008 BP announced that its top executives are to be rewarded based on total shareholder return relative to the other four 'supermajor' international oil companies (the executives thus shared in the pain of the decline in the shares after the Gulf oil spill). In the same year Smiths Group announced an incentive plan in which basic salaries are frozen, but, if total shareholder return is over and above the median return of the FTSE 100 the executives will receive shares in the company. Ford has said it was 'setting a new objective of providing a total shareholder return – dividend plus share price appreciation – in the top quartile of the S&P500 group of companies over time'.[3]

Thoughtful use of TSR

There are five issues to be borne in mind when making use of TSR:

- **Relate return to risk class** Two firms may have identical TSRs and yet one may be subject to more risk due to the greater volatility of earnings as a result, say, of the economic cycle. The risk differential must be allowed for in any comparison. This may be particularly relevant in the setting of incentive schemes for executives. Managers may be tempted to try to achieve higher TSRs by taking greater risk.

TABLE 9.1

TSRs for the ten largest UK quoted companies over one year and five years to November 2009

	TSR 1 year %	TSR 5 years %
HSBC	28	19
BP	24	39
Vodafone	14	19
Royal Dutch Shell	9	24
GlaxoSmithKline	6	28
Rio Tinto	66	193
BHP Billiton	122	260
British American Tobacco	21	172
Astra Zeneca	2	37
B.G. Group	37	228

Source: Datastream.

■ **Reliance on TSR assumes efficient share pricing** It is difficult to assess the extent to which share return outperformance is due to management quality and how much is due to exaggerated (or pessimistic) expectations of investors at the start and end of the period being measured. If the market is not efficient in pricing shares and is capable of being swayed by irrational optimism and pessimism then TSRs can be an unreliable guide to managerial performance.

■ **TSR is dependent on the time period chosen** A TSR over a three-year period can look very different from a TSR measured over a one-year or ten-year period. Consider the annual TSRs for Company W in Table 9.2. Measured over the last two years the TSR of company W is very good. However over five years a £1m investment grows to only £1,029,600, an annual rate of return of 0.6 percent.

TABLE 9.2
Annual TSRs for company W

	Annual TSR	Value of £1m investment made at the end of 2005
2006	+10%	£1,100,000
2007	−20%	£880,000
2008	−40%	£528,000
2009	+30%	£686,400
2010	+50%	£1,029,600

■ **If managerial pay/bonus is linked to company TSR** over, say, a one-year period, executives can become resentful if the stock market is going through a downturn. This happened in 2008, when shares fell across the board and managers missed out on bonuses through no fault of their own. They might have performed very well, as individuals and as a company, and yet their take-home renumeration was lower than in a year when the stock market rose. This problem can be alleviated by relating bonuses to TSR relative to peer group.

■ **TSR is useless in the case of companies not quoted on a stock market** (over 99 per cent of firms).

TSRs must be used carefully. Fund managers are increasingly wary of using them in managerial incentive schemes because performance bonuses dependent on one-year TSRs may result in managers being rewarded for general stock market movements beyond their control. Even worse would be the encouragement of the selective release of information to boost short-term TSR so that managers can trigger higher bonuses.

Wealth Added Index (WAI)

The Wealth Added Index, developed by consultant firm Stern Stewart, measures the increase in shareholders' wealth through dividends received and share capital gains (or losses) over a period of time, say five years, after deducting the 'cost of equity', defined as the return required for shares of that risk class. It thus addresses one of the key criticisms of TSR by checking whether an impressive looking TSR has actually produced a return greater than the investor's opportunity cost given the length of time over which the TSR is measured.

To calculate the WAI first observe the rise in market capitalization (value of all the shares) over say five years. Deduct the rise that is due to the firm obtaining more money from shareholders in this period, for example from a rights issue. Then add back cash returned to shareholders in the form of dividends and share buy-backs. Then deduct the required return on the money shareholders committed to the company for the relevant period – this is the equity opportunity cost. (See Chapter 10 for a discussion on how this might be calculated.)

Under WAI analysis those companies whose share values grow more than the return required by investors create value. Those that return less than the required return destroy value. Take the case of Vodafone over the five years to September 2007 (case study 9.1) for an example of a positive WAI.

Points to consider when using WAI

- Stern Stewart rely on the capital asset pricing model to calculate the required return on share capital. There are serious problems with this – *see* Chapter 10 for a discussion of the subject.

- There is an assumption that stock markets price shares correctly given company prospects at both the start and end dates. The experience of the tech bubble around the turn of the millennium and the crash of 2008 should have raised doubts here, let alone the evidence of share mispricing in the academic literature. So, one has to be sceptical as to whether outperformance is due to managerial skill or market movements. Volatile markets can turn an apparent 'wealth creator' company into an apparent 'wealth destroyer company, which may have little to do with managerial performance.

- Critics say that the WAI, in most circumstances, is no better than the use of an appropriately benchmarked TSR (i.e. benchmarked against a group of peers). Certainly, in a period of declining share prices (e.g. 2000–03, or 2008) you will find that the vast majority of companies show depressingly negative WAI because the deduction of required returns remains so high (usually between 8 percent and 11 percent per year). Comparing total return performance against peers (e.g. industry group) may be quicker, more informative and more just to the managers. At the heart of the problem is the artificiality of requiring companies to achieve increases in market capitalization above a theoretical minimum rate in all market conditions and regardless of whether all similar companies are experiencing an industry or market-wide shock.

- Because the WAI measures in cash terms rather than percentages, the biggest companies appear at the top (and bottom) of the league tables pushing out smaller companies with higher percentage rates of return on shareholders' capital.

Vodafone's Wealth Added Index

Vodafone had a market capitalization of £61,685m on 18 September 2002. By 18 September 2007 this had grown to £88,291m. This seems an impressive rise, but we do not know yet whether shareholders put more money into the company in the intervening five years, nor whether the company had paid out vast sums to shareholders in the form of dividends and share buy-backs. Also, we do not know whether the gain is more than or less than the required rate of return given that these shares are risky. The WAI takes into account these factors.

To calculate the WAI we could consult the annual reports to establish the amount paid to the company by shareholders buying more shares. This is £802m over the five years. We could also examine the accounts to find the amounts paid to shareholders in dividends and share buy-backs. This is a very large sum because of the policy in 2004–06 of large buy-backs (£20,628m). Together with dividends shareholders received £31,278m.

If we use the CAPM to calculate the required rate of return (see chapter 10) we need to do some investigation. The 10-year UK government bond yield in September 2002 was 4.41 per-cent (from Datastream) – we'll take this as our risk-free rate of return (see Chapter 10 for a discussion on this). Beta is more tricky because ideally we need to know the beta in 2002. We could search for a database which had historic betas, but given our scepticism about the valid-ity of CAPM beta for risk adjustment we'll simply take 1.0 as the value (Datastream showed a beta of 1.12 in 2007). The equity risk premium can be taken as 3.5 percent – see Chapter 10 for a discussion on this). Thus the rate of return over one year is:

$$r_i = r_f + \beta(RP) = 4.41 + 1(3.5) = 7.91\%$$

Over five years:

$$(1 + 0.0791)^5 - 1 = 0.46 \text{ or } 46\%$$

	£m
Change in market capitalization over five years	26,606
Less the rise due to additional money injected by shareholders[1]	–802
Plus dividends, share buy-backs, etc.	31,278
Less required rate of return over five years £61,685 × 0.46	–28,375
Wealth Added Index	28,707

Thus Vodafone added wealth to shareholders above their required rates during this five-year period. However, to put this into perspective the total return (dividends + capital gains) on the UK stock market as a whole in the five years was over 100 percent. Also, Vodafone's market capitalization stood at over £90,000m in 2001.

[1] To follow Stern Stewart's recommendations strictly we should recognize that any new funds raised from shareholders over the period require a rate of return. Thus the CAPM cost of equity capital should be applied to the new funds from share-holders, from the date that the money was raised to the end date – thus there should be a further deduction which is not shown to keep the example reasonably simple.

Market Value Added (MVA)

Stern Stewart & Co. has also developed the concept of Market Value Added (MVA). This looks at the difference between the total amount of capital put into the business by finance providers (debt and equity) and the current market value of the company's shares and debt. It provides a measure of how executives have performed with the capital entrusted to them. A positive MVA indicates value has been created. A negative MVA indicates value has been destroyed.

$$MVA = \text{Market value} - \text{Invested capital}$$

where:

Market value = Current value of debt, preference shares and ordinary shares.

Invested capital = All the cash raised from finance providers or retained from earnings to finance new investment in the business, since the company was founded. In practice, balance sheet asset values (with a few adjustments) are used.

Managers are able to push up the conventional yardstick, total market value of the business, simply by investing more capital. MVA, by subtracting capital injected or retained from the calculation, measures net value generated for shareholders.

Illustration

MerVA plc was founded 20 years ago with £15m of equity finance. It has no debt or preference shares. All earnings have been paid out as dividends. The shares in the company are now valued at £40m. The MVA of MerVA is therefore £25m:

$$MVA = \text{Market value} - \text{Capital}$$

$$MVA = £40m - £15m = £25m$$

If the company now has a rights issue raising £5m from shareholders the market value of the firm must rise to at least £45m for shareholder wealth to be maintained. If the market value of the shares rose to only £44m because shareholders are doubtful about the returns to be earned when the rights issue money is applied within the business (that is, a negative NPV project) shareholders will lose £1m of value. This is summarized below:

	Before rights issue	After rights issue
Market value	£40m	£44m
Capital	£15m	£20m
MVA	£25m	£24m

According to Stern Stewart if a company pays a dividend both the 'market value' and the 'capital' parts of the equation are reduced by the same amount and MVA is unaffected. Imagine an all-equity financed company with an equity market value of £50m at the start of the year, which increased to £55m by the end of the year after generating £10m of post-tax profit in the year and the payment of a £6m dividend. The capital put into the firm by shareholders over the company's life by purchasing shares and retained earnings amounted to £20m at the start of the year.

	Start of year		End of year
Market value	£50m		£55m
Capital	£20m	£20m	
	plus earnings	£10m	
	less dividend	−£6m	
			£24m
MVA	£30m		£31m

If the company had not paid the dividend then, according to Stern Stewart both the market value and the capital rise by £6m and MVA would remain at £31m. Thus:

	Start of year	End of year
Market value	£50m	£61m
Capital	£20m	£30m
MVA	£30m	£31m

This dividend policy irrelevance argument is challenged in Chapter 14, where it is shown that increasing or decreasing the dividend may add value. The point to take from this section is that profits produced by the business are just as much part of the ownership capital as money raised through the sale of shares to owners at the foundation of the business or in later years. If £1 is to be retained rather than paid out to shareholders then market capitalisation should rise by £1 to avoid loss of shareholder value. If it does not, then that £1 can be put to a better use outside of the firm.

A short cut

In the practical application of MVA analysis it is often assumed that the market value of debt and preference shares equals the book value of debt and preference shares. This permits the following version of MVA, cutting out the necessity to obtain data for the debt levels (market value or balance sheet value) or the preference share values:

$$\text{MVA} = \text{Ordinary shares market value} - \text{Capital supplied by}$$
$$\text{ordinary shareholders}$$

Judging managerial performance by MVA

The absolute level of MVA is perhaps less useful for judging performance than the change in MVA over a period. Alistair Blair, writing in *Management Today*,[4] is quite scathing about crude MVA numbers:

> An MVA includes years old and now irrelevant gains and losses aggregated on a pound-for-pound basis with last year's results and today's hope or despair, as expressed in the share price. Surely, what we are interested in is current performance, or if we're going to be determinedly historic, performance since the current top management team got its hands on the controls.

What Alistair Blair seems to be proposing is that we convert MVA into a period (say five years) measure of performance so we can isolate the value-creating contribution of a particular span of years under the leadership of a team of managers.

Points to consider when using MVA

There are a number of issues to be borne in mind when using MVA:

Estimating the amount of cash invested

Measuring the amount of capital put into and retained within a business after it has been trading for a few years is fraught with problems. For example, does R&D expenditure produce an asset (i.e. become part of shareholders' funds) or is it an expense to be written off the profit and loss account? How do you treat goodwill on acquisitions? The accountants' balance sheet is not designed for measuring capital supplied by finance providers, but at least it is a starting point. Stern Stewart make use of a proxy measure called 'economic book value'. This is based on the balance sheet capital employed figure, subject to a number of adjustments. It has been pointed out by critics that these adjustments are rather arbitrary and complex, making it difficult to claim that economic book value equals the theoretically correct 'capital' in most cases.

When was the value created?

The fact that a positive MVA is produced is often of limited use when it comes to evaluating the quality of the current managers. For a company that is a few decades old the value drivers may have been put in place by a previous generation of directors and senior managers. The MVA measure can be considered crude in that it measures value created over the entire life of the firm but fails to pinpoint when it was created. Nor does it indicate whether value creation has stopped and the firm is living off accumulated fat in terms of strong market positions, patents, etc. Ideally we need to know whether new value creating positions are being constructed rather than old ones being eroded.

Is the rate of return high enough?

It is difficult to know whether the amount of MVA generated is sufficiently in excess of capital used to provide a satisfactory return relative to the risk-adjusted time value of money. Positive MVA companies can produce poor rates of return. Take company B in the following example. It has a much lower rate of return on capital than A and yet it has the same MVA.

	A	B
MVA	£50m	£50m
Market value	£100m	£100m
Capital	£50m	£50m
Age of firm	3 years	30 years

(Both firms have paid out profits each year as dividends, therefore the capital figure is the starting equity capital.)

Inflation distorts MVA

If the capital element in the equation is based on a balance sheet figure then during times of inflation the value of capital employed may be understated. If capital is artificially lowered by inflation *vis-à-vis* current market value for companies where investment took place a long time ago then MVA will appear to be superior to that for a similar firm with recently purchased assets.

Trusting that the stock market prices shares correctly at all times

This is a very dubious assumption. It is not even required for pricing efficiency, which is based on the notion of there being no bias in the errors of pricing, not on the perfect pricing of all shares at all times.

The MVA is an absolute measure

Judging companies on the basis of absolute amounts of pounds means that companies with larger capital bases will tend to be at the top (and bottom) of the league tables of MVA performance. Size can have a more significant impact on the MVA than efficiency. This makes conparison between firms of different sizes difficult. The market to book ratio, MBR, described below, is designed to alleviate this problem.

Two companies showing the same MVA can produce different levels of real wealth for shareholders

See the example of AVerseM in the next section.

Excess return (ER)

Two of the major drawbacks of the MVA are illustrated in the case of AVerseM. This company was established five years ago with £10m of equity capital (assume no debt throughout the example). At that time equity put at this level of risk was required to produce a return of 10 percent per year. The company made after-tax profits of £1m in its second year and £1m in its third year (zero in the other years). These profits were paid out as dividends in the year of occurrence. AVerseM now has a market capitalization of £11m and is therefore showing a respectable MVA of £1m.

$$\text{MVA} = \text{Market value} - \text{Invested capital}$$

$$\text{Invested capital} = \text{Original capital} + \text{Retained earnings} = £10m + £0m$$

$$\text{MVA} = £11 - £10m = £1m$$

[Stern Stewart and Co. actually define capital as 'essentially a company's net assets (total assets less non-interest-bearing current liabilities)' (Stewart (1991), p. 744) rather than strictly the amount of money put into the business by investors. They make three major groups of adjustments to the raw balance sheet numbers, such as adding the capital value of leases and adding back R&D expenses previously written off, to try to get closer to the amount put into the business by investors, but using balance sheet numbers for a firm that has operated for a number of year must be considered crude.]

If the original £10m put into AVerseM had been invested elsewhere to yield its required rate of return for the same risk, 10 percent, today shareholders would hold an investment worth £16.1m:

$$10 (1 + 0.1)^5 = £16.1m$$

Determining whether AVerseM has achieved shareholder wealth creation is far from clear with the MVA, even if we had a precise 'invested capital' figure. Notice how the MVA has ignored the value of dividends. If there was another company that also started with £10m of capital and has a current market capitalization of £11m, but has made no profits and paid no dividends over the five years, it would also show an identical MVA of £1m, despite the fact that it has not generated as much wealth for shareholders as AVerseM.

Also notice that the time value of money is not allowed for (the third problem listed for the MVA). To cope with these two problems we could use Excess return, ER.[5] This metric examines the amount of capital invested in previous years and then charges the company for its use over the years. It also credits companies for the returns shareholders can make from the money paid to them (e.g. as dividends) when re-invested in the market:

Excess return expressed in present value terms = Actual wealth expressed in present value terms – Expected wealth expressed in present value terms

Expected wealth is calculated as the value of the initial investment in present value terms if it had achieved the required rate of return over the time it has been invested in the business. So, for AVerseM this is £16.1m. (Of course, if AVerseM had raised more money from shareholders, in, say, the fourth year, through a rights issue, we would include that here too.)

Actual wealth is the present values of cash flows received by shareholders, plus the current market value of the shares. Each cash flow received in past years needs to be compounded up to the present:

Present value of dividends if the money received was invested at the required rate of return between receipt and present time

Received 3 years ago	£1m $(1 + 0.1)^3 = $ £1.331m
Received 2 years ago	£1m $(1 + 0.1)^2 = $ £1.210m
Current market value of shares (market capitalization)	£11.000m
Actual wealth	£13.541m

Excess return = Actual wealth – Expected wealth
Excess return = £13.541 – £16.1m = –£2.559m

Value has been destroyed as the return achieved is less than 10 percent per year.

Expected return suffers from many of the other drawbacks associated with the MVA, such as finding the figure for the capital injected by shareholders for a company that has traded for many years, faith that the market will price the shares correctly and the fact that because it is an absolute measure rather than a percentage it favours larger firms. There is also the difficulty of selecting the required rate of return (*see* Chapter 10).

Also if inflation turned out to be much higher than anticipated when the bulk of the capital was invested, ER will be distorted as nominal returns on the stock market rise, lifting current market value of shares.

Market to book ratio (MBR)

Rather than using the arithmetical difference between the capital raised and the current value, as in MVA, the MBR is the market value divided by the capital invested. If the market value of debt can be taken to be the same as the book value of debt then a version of the MBR is the ratio of the market value of the company's ordinary shares to the amount of capital provided by ordinary share-holders (if preference share capital can be regarded as debt for the purpose of value-based management).

There is, of course, the problem of estimating the amount of capital supplied, as this usually depends on adjusted balance sheet net asset figures. For example, goodwill write-offs and other negative reserves are reinstated, as in MVA. It is also suggested that asset values be expressed at replacement cost so that the MBR is not too heavily distorted by the effects of inflation on historic asset figures.

Illustration

MaBaR plc has an equity market value of £50m, its book debt is equal to the market value of debt, and the adjusted replacement cost of assets attributable to ordinary shareholders amounts to £16m.

Market value	£50m
Capital	£16m
MVA	£34m
MBR £50m/£16m	= 3.125

MaBaR has turned every pound put into the firm into £3.125.

The rankings provided by MBR and MVA differ sharply. The largest companies dominating the MVA ranks generally have lower positions when ordered in terms of MBR.

Care must be taken when using MBR for performance measurement and target setting because if it is wrongly applied it is possible for positive NPV projects to be rejected in order for MBR to be at a higher level. Take the case of a company with an MBR of 1.75 considering fundraising to make an investment of £10m in a project estimated to produce a positive NPV of £4m. Its market to book ratio will fall despite the project being shareholder wealth enhancing.

		Before project		After project acceptance
Value of firm		£70m	(70 + 10 + 4)	£84m
Capital		£40m		£50m
MVA		£30m		£34m
MBR	70/40 =	1.75	84/50 =	1.68

The new project has an incremental MBR of 1.4 (14/10 = 1.4). This is less than the firm's original overall MBR of 1.75, which is dragged down by accepting the project. This effect should be ignored by managers motivated by shareholder wealth enhancement. They will focus on NPV.

Conclusion

TSR, WAI, MVA, ER and MBR should be seen not as competitors, but as complementary, especially as each has serious drawbacks. Relying on one indicator is unnecessarily restrictive. It is perfectly possible to use all these measures simultaneously, thereby overcoming many of the weaknesses of each individually. And don't forget that the measures described in the previous chapter may be used alongside these in the assessment of value creation by the entire firm.

Notes

1 Wealth Added Index and WAI are both registered trademarks of the consulting firm Stern Stewart.
2 Market Value Added and MVA are both registered trademarks of the consulting firm Stern Stewart.
3 Nikki Tait, 'Ford aims to slash $1bn from cash base this year', *Financial Times*, 8 January 1999, p. 17.
4 Alistair Blair, *Management Today*, January 1997, p. 44.
5 This method is promoted by Young and O'Byrne (2001) in their book.

10

WHAT IS THE COMPANY'S COST OF CAPITAL?

Introduction

Until this point a cost of capital (required rate of return) has been assumed for, say, a project or a business unit strategy, but we have not gone into much detail about how an appropriate cost of capital is calculated. This vital issue is now addressed.

The objective set for management in a value-based organization is the maximization of long-term shareholder wealth. This means achieving a return on invested money that is greater than shareholders could obtain elsewhere for the same level of risk. Shareholders, and other finance providers, have an opportunity cost associated with putting money into your firm. They could withdraw the money placed with you and invest it in a comparable company's securities. If, for the same risk, the alternative investment offers a higher return than your firm's shares, then as a management team you are destroying shareholder wealth.

> **The cost of capital is the rate of return that a company has to offer finance providers to induce them to buy and hold a financial security.**

The cost of capital is the rate of return that a company has to offer finance providers to induce them to buy and hold a financial security. This rate is determined by the returns offered on alternative securities with the same risk.

Using the correct cost of capital as a discount rate is important. If it is too high investment will be constrained, firms will not grow as they should and shareholders will miss out on value-enhancing opportunities. There can be a knock-on effect to the macroeconomy and this worries politicians. For example, the one-time President of the Board of Trade, Michael Heseltine, complained:

> Businesses are not investing enough because of their excessive expectations of investment returns ... The CBI tells me that the majority of firms continue to require rates of return above 20 percent. A senior banker last week told me his bank habitually asked for 30 percent returns on capital.[1]

This chapter focuses on the question of how to measure the returns available on a variety of financial securities at different risk levels. This will be developed into an overall cost of capital for the firm and provide a method for calculating the benchmark rate for the firm, SBUs and projects.

A word of warning

Too often, the academics and consultants give the impression of scientific preciseness when calculating a firm's cost of capital. The reality is that behind any final number generated lies an enormous amount of subjective assessment or, worse, opinion. Choices have to be made between competing judgments on a range of issues, including the appropriate risk premium, financial gearing level and risk measure. Good decision-making comes from knowing the limitations of the input variables to the decision. Knowing where informed judgment has been employed in the cost of capital calculation is required to make value-enhancing decisions and thus assist the art of management. In short, the final number for the required rate of return is less important than knowledge of the factors behind the calculation and the likely size of the margin of error. Precision is less important than knowledge of what is a reasonable range.

The required rate of return

The capital provided to large firms comes in many forms. The main forms are equity and debt capital, but there are a number of hybrids, such as convertible bonds. When a finance provider chooses to supply funds in the form of debt finance, there is a deliberate attempt to reduce risk. This can be achieved in a number of ways: by imposing covenants on management which, for example, restrict the gearing (proportion of debt to share capital) level or maintain an interest cover ratio (e.g. annual profit must remain four times greater than annual interest); accept assets as security; by ensuring that the lenders are ahead of other finance providers (particularly ordinary and preference holders) in terms of annual pay-outs and in the event of liquidation.

A lender to a corporation cannot expect to eliminate all risk and so the required rate of return is going to be above that of lending to a reputable State such as the USA or the UK. Placing your savings with the UK government by buying its bonds in return for the promise of regular interest and the payment of a capital sum in a future year is the closest you are going to get to risk-free lending. The rate of return offered on government bonds and Treasury bills (lending that is repaid in a few months) is the bedrock rate that is used to benchmark other interest rates. It is called the risk-free rate of return, or given the symbol r_f.

A stable well-established company with a relatively low level of borrowing and low risk operations might have to pay a slightly higher rate of return on debt capital than the UK government. Such a company, if it issued a corporate bond with a high credit rating (low risk of default), would pay, say, an extra 100 basis points (i.e.1%) per year. This is described as the risk premium (RP) on top of the risk-free rate. Then, the cost of debt capital, k_D, is:

$$k_D = r_f + RP$$

If the current risk free rate is 6 percent, then k_D = 7 percent.

If the firm already has a high level of debt and wishes to borrow more it may need to offer as much as 800 basis points above the risk-free rate. The credit rating is likely to be below investment grade (below BBB- by Standard and Poor's and Baa3 by Moody's – see Chapter 16 for more details) and therefore will be classified as a high-yield (or junk) bond. So the required return might be 14 percent.

$$k_D = r_f + RP = 6 + 8 = 14\%$$

If the form of finance provided is equity capital then the investor is accepting a fairly high probability of receiving no return at all on the investment. The firm has no obligation to pay annual dividends, and other forms of capital have prior claims on annual cash flows. If the firm does less well than expected then it is, generally, ordinary shareholders who suffer the most. If the firm performs well very high returns can be expected. It is the expectation of high returns that causes ordinary shareholders to accept high risk – a large dispersion of returns.

Different equities have different levels of risk, and therefore returns. A shareholder in Tesco is likely to be content with a lower return than a shareholder in, say, an internet start-up, or a company quoted on the Russian Stock Exchange. Thus we have a range of financial securities with a variety of risk and associated return – *see* Figure 10.1.

Two sides of the same coin

The issues of the cost of capital for managerial use within the business and the value placed on a share (or other financial security) are two sides of the same coin. They both depend on the level of return. The holders of shares make a valuation on the basis of the returns they estimate they will receive. Likewise, from the firm's perspective, it estimates the cost of raising money through selling shares (or retaining earnings) as the return that the firm will have to pay to shareholders to induce them to buy and hold the shares. The same considerations apply to bondholders, preference shareholders and so on. If the future cash flowing from the form of finance is anticipated to fall from a previously assumed level then the selling price of the share, bond, etc. goes down until the return is at the level dictated by the returns on financial securities of a similar type and risk. If a company fails to achieve returns that at least compensate finance providers for their opportunity cost it is unlikely to survive for long. Figure 10.2, taking shares as an example, illustrates that valuing a share and the cost of equity capital are two sides of the same coin.

FIGURE 10.1
Risk-return – hypothetical examples

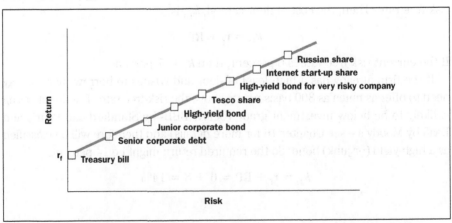

FIGURE 10.2
Two sides of the same coin

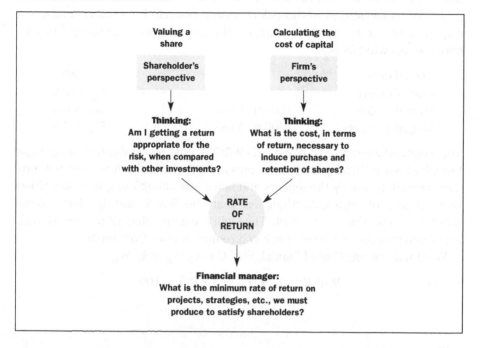

The weighted average cost of capital (WACC)

We have established that firms need to offer returns to finance providers commensurate with the risk they are undertaking. The amount of return is determined by what those investors could get elsewhere at that risk level (e.g. by investing in other companies). If we take a firm that is financed entirely by share capital (and this is the optimal capital structure) then the required rate of return to be used in value analysis, e.g. a project or SBU appraisal, is the required return demanded by investors on the company's shares. However, this is only true if the new project (or division) has the same level of risk as the existing set of projects.

The stock market prices shares on the basis of the current riskiness of the firm. This is determined by the activities it undertakes. A company can be seen as merely a bundle of projects from the perspective of ordinary shareholders. If these projects are, on average, of high risk then the required return will be high. If the proposed project (or division) under examination has the same risk as the weighted average of the current set then the required return on the company's equity capital is the rate appropriate for this project (if the company received all its capital from shareholders and none from lenders). If the new project has a lower risk, the company-wide cost of capital needs to be adjusted down for application to this project.

If, however, we are dealing with a company that has some finance in the form of debt and some in the form of equity the situation becomes a little more complicated. Imagine that a corporation is to be established by obtaining one-half of its £1,000m of capital from lenders, who require an 8 percent rate of return for an investment of this risk class, and one-half from shareholders, who require a 12 percent rate of return for the risk they are accepting. Thus we have the following facts:

Cost of debt		$k_D = 8\%$
Cost of equity		$k_E = 12\%$
Weight of debt	£500m / £1bn	$W_D = 0.5$
Weight of equity	£500m / £1bn	$W_E = 0.5$

The weighted average cost of capital (WACC) must be established to calculate the minimum return needed on an investment within the firm, that will produce enough to satisfy the lenders and leave just enough to give shareholders their 12 percent return. Anything less than this WACC and the shareholders will receive less than 12 percent. They will recognize that 12 percent is available elsewhere for that level of risk and remove money from the firm.

Weighted Average Cost of Capital, WACC $= k_E W_E + k_D W_D$

$$WACC = 12 \times 0.5 + 8 \times 0.5 = 10\%$$

Illustration

Imagine the firm invested £100,000 in a project that produced a net cash flow per year of £10,000 to infinity (assuming a perpetuity makes the example simple). The first call on that cash flow is from the debt holders, who effectively supplied £50,000 of the funds. They require £4,000 per annum. That leaves £6,000 for equity holders – an annual return of 12 percent on the £50,000 they provided. Thus an overall return of 10 percent (the WACC) provides an 8 percent return on the capital supplied by lenders and 12 percent on the capital supplied by shareholders.

If things go well and a return of £11,000 (i.e. 11 percent) is generated, then debt holders still receive the contracted amount of £4,000, but the equity holders get a return significantly above the minimum they require, at 14 percent return: £7,000 is left to pay out to shareholders on their £50,000 capital input to this project.

Of course, this example assumes that all new projects use the same proportions of debt and equity finance as the firm as a whole; that is, 50 percent of its capital comes from debt. The issue of whether you should use different types (or weights) of finance for different projects (say, borrow all the £100,000 for this particular project at 8 percent) rather than use the 50:50 mixture is discussed later.

Lowering the WACC and increasing shareholder returns

Examining the WACC formula we see an apparently simple way of reducing the required rate of return, and thus raise the value of a project, division or the entire firm: change the weights in the formula in favour of debt. In other words, alter the capital structure of the firm by having a higher proportion of its capital in the form of cheaper debt. The jargon referring to levels of debt relative to equity capital is 'financial gearing' or 'leverage' (used in the USA) – there is more on gearing in Chapter 18.

For example, if the company is expected to produce £100m cash flow per year (to infinity) and its WACC is 10 percent its total corporate value ('enterprise' value that is, the value of the debt and equity) is:

$$£100m / 0.10 = £1,000m$$

Let us try to lower the WACC.

Imagine that instead of the firm being established with 50 percent debt in its overall capital, it is set up with 70 percent debt. The proportion of total capital in the form of equity is therefore 30 percent. *If* (a big if) the equity holders remain content with a 12 percent return while the debt holders accept an 8 percent annual return the WACC will fall, and the value of the firm will rise.

$$WACC = k_E W_E + k_D W_D$$

$$WACC = 12 \times 0.3 + 8 \times 0.7 = 9.2\%$$

$$\text{Firm value} = £100m / 0.092 = £1,086.96m$$

Why don't all management teams increase the proportion of debt in the capital structure and magic-up some shareholder value? The fly in the ointment for many firms is that equity investors are unlikely to be content with 12 percent returns when their shares have become more risky due to the additional financial leverage. The key question is: how much extra return do they demand? The financial economists and Nobel laureates Franco Modigliani and Merton Miller (MM) presented the case that in a perfect capital market (all participants such as shareholders and managers have all relevant information, all can borrow at same interest, etc.) the increase in k_E would exactly offset the benefit from increasing the debt proportion, to leave the WACC constant so increasing the debt proportion does not add to shareholder value – the only factor that can add value is the improvement in the underlying performance of the business, i.e. its cash flows. According to this view (that there is no single optimal capital structure that will maximize shareholder wealth) there is no point in adjusting the debt or equity proportions.

In this stylized world k_D remains at 8 percent, but k_E moves to 14.67 percent, leaving WACC, firm value, and shareholder value constant.

$$WACC = k_E W_E + k_D W_D$$

$$WACC = 14.67 \times 0.3 + 8 \times 0.7 = 10\%$$

However, there is hope for managers trying to improve shareholder wealth by adjusting the capital structure because in constructing a perfect world Modigliani and Miller left out at least two important factors: tax and financial distress.[2]

The benefit of tax

First tax. A benefit of financing through debt is that the annual interest can be used to reduce taxable profit thus lowering the cash that flows out to the tax authorities. In contrast, the annual payout on equity (dividends) cannot be used to reduce the amount of profit that is taxed. The benefits gained from being able to lower the tax burden through financing through debt reduces the effective cost of this form of finance. (Note that this reduction is valid only if the company is profitable and paying corporation tax.)

To illustrate: Firm A is a company in a country that does not permit interest to be deducted from taxable profit. Firm B is in a country that does permit interest to be deducted. For both companies the interest is 8 percent on £500m. Observe the effect on the amount of profit left for distribution to shareholders:

	Firm A £m	Firm B £m
Profits before interest and tax	100	100
Interest		−40
Taxable profit	100	60
Amount taxed @ 30%	−30	−18
Interest	−40	
Amount available for distribution shareholders	30	42

The extra £12m for Firm B reduces the effective cost of debt from 8 percent to only $8(1 - T)$, where T = the corporation tax rate, 30 percent. The cost of debt capital falls to $8(1 - 0.3) = 5.6$, or £28m on £500m of debt. The taxman, by taking £12m less from the company purely because the tax rules allow the deductibility of interest from taxable profit, lowers the effective cost of the debt.

So including the 'tax shield' effect we find a reduction in the WACC that leads to an increase in the amount available for shareholders. In our example, if we assume tax on corporate profits at 30 percent then the effective cost of debt falls to 5.6 percent. Resulting in the WACC becoming 8.8 percent.

So, if:

$$k_{DBT} = \text{cost of debt before tax benefit} = 8\%$$

$$k_{DAT} = \text{cost of debt after tax benefit} = 8(1 - T) = 8(1 - 0.30) = 5.6\%$$

If we assume a 50:50 capital structure the WACC is:

$$\text{WACC} = k_E W_E + k_{DAT} W_D$$

$$WACC = 12 \times 0.5 + 5.6 \times 0.5 = 8.8\%$$

Investment project cash flows discounted at this lower rate will have a higher present value than if discounted at 10 percent. Given that the debt holders receive only their contractual interest and no more this extra value flows to shareholders.

But, financial distress constrains gearing

The introduction of the tax benefit strongly pushes the bias towards very high gearing levels to obtain a lower WACC and higher value. However, such extreme gearing is not observed very often in real world companies. There are a number of reasons for this, the most important of which is the increasing risk to the finance providers (particularly equity capital holders) of financial distress and, ultimately, liquidation. (See Chapter 18 for more reasons.)

As gearing rises so does the probability of equity investors receiving a poor (no) return. So they demand higher expected returns to compensate. At first, the risk premium rises slowly, but at high gearing levels it rises so fast that it more than offsets the benefit of increasing debt in the capital structure. This is demonstrated in Figure 10.3, in which the WACC at lower levels of debt is primarily influenced by the increasing debt proportion in the capital structure, and at higher levels by the rising cost of equity (and eventually debt).

The conclusion drawn from the capital structure literature is that there is an optimal gearing level that achieves the lowest WACC and highest firm value – discussed in more detail in Chapter 18. When companies are calculating their WACC they should use this target gearing ratio and not a gearing ratio they happen to have at the time of calculation.

So, if in our example case the required return on equity rises from 12 percent to 13 percent when the proportion of the debt in the capital structure rises to 65 percent from 50 percent and the effective rate of return payable on debt is 5.6 percent after the tax shield benefit (i.e. remaining at 8 percent before the tax benefit) then the WACC falls and the value available for shareholders rises.

FIGURE 10.3

Cost of capital with different capital structures (including consideration of the tax shield and financial distress)

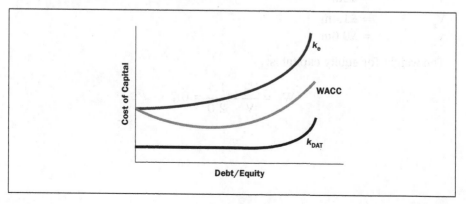

$$\text{WACC} = k_E W_E + k_{DAT} W_D$$

$$\text{WACC} = 13 \times 0.35 + 5.6 \times 0.65 = 8.19\%$$

Taking financial gearing too far

For this particular company we will assume that 65 percent gearing is the optimum debt/equity ratio. If we go to 80 percent debt we find this reduces shareholder wealth because the firm's projects (in aggregate) are now discounted at a higher rate of return reducing their present value. The main reason the discount rate rises significantly is that the required return on shares rises to, say, 30 percent as investors fear massive potential loss due to the large commitment of the firm to pay out interest whether or not the firm is doing well. The debt holders also worry about increased financial distress risk – i.e. they might not receive their capital or interest – and so they increase their required rate of return to 10 percent before the tax shield benefit, which is an effective cost to the firm of 7 percent after allowing for the tax shield benefit.

$$\text{WACC} = k_E W_E + k_{DAT} W_D$$

$$\text{WACC} = 30 \times 0.2 + 7 \times 0.8 = 11.6\%$$

Worked example 10.1
Poise plc

The rate of return offered to debt holders of Poise plc before considering the benefit to shareholders of the tax shield, k_{DBT}, is 10%, whereas the required return on equity is 20%. The total amount of capital in use (equity + debt), V, is £2m. Of that, £1.4m represents the market value of its equity, V_E, and £600,000 equals the market value of its debt, V_D. These are the optimum proportions of debt and equity.

Thus:

k_{DBT}	= 10%
k_E	= 20%
V	= £2m
V_E	= £1.4m
V_D	= £0.6m

The weight for equity capital is:

$$W_E = \frac{V_E}{V} = \frac{1.4}{2.0} = 0.7$$

The weight for debt is:

$$W_D = \frac{V_D}{V} = \frac{0.6}{2.0} = 0.3$$

The corporate tax rate is 30% and therefore the after-tax cost of debt is:

$$k_{DAT} = k_{DBT} (1 - T)$$
$$k_{DAT} = 10 (1 - 0.30) = 7\%$$

The weighted average cost of capital for Poise is:

$$\begin{aligned} \text{WACC} \quad &= k_E W_E + k_{DAT} W_D \\ &= 20\% \times 0.7 + 7\% \times 0.3 \\ &= \mathbf{16.1\%} \end{aligned}$$

This is the rate of return Poise needs to achieve on new business projects if they are of the same risk as the average risk of the current set of projects. If the new projects are of higher or lower risk an adjustment needs to be made to the discount rate used – this is discussed later in the chapter.

If Poise is considering a project that requires an investment of £1m at time 0 and then produces after tax annual cash flows before interest payments of £161,000 as a perpetuity (i.e. it achieves a 16.1% rate of return) then the net cost of satisfying the debt holders after the tax shield benefit is £21,000. (The debt holders supplied 30% of the £1m invested, i.e. £300,000; and the cost to the firm of satisfying them is £300,000 × 7% = £21,000.) The remainder of the annual cash flows go to the shareholders; so they receive £140,000 per year which is a 20% return on the £700,000 they supplied.

If the project produces a much lower annual cash flow of £100,000 (a rate of return of 10%) then the debt holders still receive £21,000, leaving only £79,000 for the shareholders. These investors could have achieved a return of 20% by investing in other companies at this level of risk. An annual return of £79,000 represents a mere 11.3% return (£79,000/£700,000). Thus shareholders suffer a loss of wealth relative to the forgone opportunity.

The cost of equity capital

A shareholder has in mind a minimum rate of return determined by the returns available on other shares of the same risk class. Managers, in order to maximize shareholder wealth, must obtain this level of return for shareholders from the firm's activities. If a company does not achieve the rate of return to match the investor's opportunity cost it will find it difficult to attract new funds and will become vulnerable to take-over or liquidation.

With debt finance there is generally a specific rate payable for the use of capital. In contrast, ordinary shareholders are not explicitly offered specific payments. However, an implicit rate of return must be offered to attract investors – it is the expectation of high returns that causes ordinary shareholders to accept high risk.

Investors in shares require a return that provides for two elements. First, they need a return equal to the risk-free rate (usually taken to be that on government securities). Second, there is the risk premium, which rises with the degree of systematic risk (systematic risk is explained below).

Rate of return on shares = Risk-free rate + Risk premium

$$k_E = r_f + RP$$

The risk-free rate gives a return sufficient to compensate for both impatience to consume and inflation (see Chapter 2).[3] To estimate the relevant risk premium on a company's equity there are two steps.

- Step one estimates the average extra return demanded by investors above the risk-free return to induce them to buy a portfolio of average-risk level shares. We look back at the returns shareholders have actually received on average-risk shares above the risk-free return in the past and make the assumption that this is what they also demanded before the event – *ex ante* in the jargon.[4] The average annual risk premium actually obtained by shareholders can only be calculated over an extended period of time (many decades) as short-term returns on shares can be distorted (they are often negative for a year, for example). The risk premium is expressed as the difference between the market return, r_m, and the risk-free return, r_f, that is $(r_m - r_f)$.

- Step two adjusts the risk premium for a typical (average-risk level) share to suit the risk level for the particular company's shares under consideration. If the share is more risky than the average then $(r_m - r_f)$ is multiplied by a systematic risk factor greater than 1. If it is less risky it may be multiplied by a systematic risk factor of, say, 0.8 to reduce the risk premium.

To understand the origin of the most popular method of calculating the cost of equity capital, the capital asset pricing model, it is necessary to first of all deal with the issues of shareholder diversification, the elimination of unsystematic risk and the focus on the variable called beta.

Diversification

If an investor only has one company's shares in their 'portfolio' then risk is very high. Adding a second reduces risk. The addition of a third and fourth continues to reduce risk but by smaller amounts. This sort of effect is demonstrated in Figure 10.4. The reason for the risk reduction is that security returns generally do not vary with perfect positive correlation. That is, returns do not go up together and down together by the same percentages at the same time. At any one time the good news about one share is offset to some extent by bad news about another.

Generally within a portfolio of shares if one is shooting up, others are stable, going down or rising. Each share movement depends mostly on the particular news emanating from the company. News is generally particular to companies and we should not expect them each to report good (or bad) news on the same day. So, if on a day one share in the portfolio reports the resignation of brilliant chief executive we might expect that share to fall. But, because the portfolio owner is diversified the return on the portfolio will not move dramatically downward. Other companies are reporting marketing coups, big new contracts, or whatever, pushing up their share prices. Others (the majority?) are not reporting any news and their share prices do not move much at all. The point is that by not having all your eggs in one basket you reduce the chance of the collective value of your investments falling off a cliff. The risk, or volatility, of the value of the portfolio, as measured by standard deviation, is reduced. The greater the extent of diversification, the lower the standard deviation (see Chapter 5 for a discussion of standard deviation).

So, despite the fact that returns on individual shares can vary dramatically a portfolio will be relatively stable. The type of risk being reduced through diversification is referred to as unsystematic risk (unique, or idiosyncratic, or specific risk – you wouldn't expect financial economists to make things easy by having one word for it, would you?). This element of variability in a share's return is due to the specific circumstances of the individual firms. In a portfolio these individual ups and downs tend to cancel out. Another piece of jargon applied to this type of risk is that it is 'diversifiable'. That is, it can be eliminated simply by holding a sufficiently large portfolio.

Systematic risk

However, no matter how many shares are held there will always be an element of risk that cannot be cancelled out by broadening the portfolio. This is called systematic (or market) risk. There are some risk factors common to all firms to a greater or lesser extent. These include macroeconomic movements such as economic growth, inflation and exchange rate changes. No firm is entirely immune from these factors. For example, a deceleration in GDP growth or a rise in tax rates is likely to impact on the returns of all firms within an economy.

Note, however, that while all shares respond to these system-wide risk factors they do not all respond equally. Some shares will exhibit a greater sensitivity to these systematic risk elements than others. The revenues of the luxury goods sectors, for example, are particularly sensitive to the vicissitudes of the economy. Spending on electrical goods and sports cars rises when the economy is in

FIGURE 10.4

Systematic and unsystematic risk

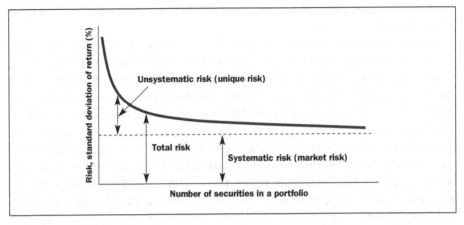

a strong growth phase but falls off significantly in recession. On the other hand, some sectors experience limited variations in demand as the economy booms and shrinks; the food producing and food retailing sectors are prime examples here. People do not cut down significantly on food bought for home consumption despite falling incomes.

It is assumed, quite reasonably, that investors do not like risk. If this is the case then the logical course of action is going to be to eliminate as much unsystematic risk as possible by diversifying. Most of the shares in UK companies are held by highly diversified institutional investors such as pension funds, insurance funds, unit trusts and investment trusts. While it is true that many small investors are not fully diversified it is equally true that the market, and more importantly, market returns are dominated by the actions of fully diversified investors. These investors ensure that the market does not reward investors for bearing some unsystematic risk.

To understand this imagine that by some freak accident a share offered a return of say 50 percent per annum which includes compensation for both unsystematic and systematic risk. There would be a mad scramble to buy these shares, especially by the major diversified funds which don't care about the unsystematic risk on this share – they have other share returns to offset the oscillations of this new one. The buying pressure would result in a rise in the share price. This process would continue until the share offered the same return as other shares with that level of systematic risk (the cash flows, e.g. dividends, expected from the company remain constant but the share price rises therefore returns on the purchase price of the share fall).

Let us assume that the price doubles and therefore the return offered falls to 25 percent. The undiversified investor will be dismayed that they can no longer find any share that will compensate for what they perceive as the relevant risk for them, consisting of both unsystematic and systematic elements.

In the financial markets the risk that matters is the degree to which a particular share tends to move when the market as a whole moves. This is the only issue of concern to the investors that are fully diversified because ups and downs due to specific company events do not affect the return on the portfolio – only market-wide events affect the portfolio's return.

This is leading to a new way of measuring risk. For the diversified investor the relevant measure of risk is no longer standard deviation of returns, it is its systematic risk.

Beta

The capital asset pricing model (CAPM) defined this systematic risk as beta.[5] Beta, β, measures the covariance between the returns on a particular share with the returns on the market as a whole (usually measured by a market index, FTSE All Share index). That is, the beta value for a share indicates the sensitivity of that share to general market movements. A share with a beta of 1.0 tends to have returns that move broadly in line with the market index. A share with a beta greater than 1.0 tends to exhibit amplified return movements compared to the index. For example, Barclays has a beta of 1.83 and, according to the CAPM, when the market index return rises by say 10 percent the returns on Barclays' shares will tend to rise by 18.3 percent. Conversely if the market falls by 10 percent then Barclays' shares' returns will tend to fall by 18.3 percent.

Shares with a beta of less than 1.0, such as M&S with a beta of 0.72, will vary less than the market as a whole. So, if the market is rising shares in M&S will not enjoy the same level of upswing. However should the market ever suffer a downward movement for every 10 percent decline in shares generally M&S will give a return decline of only 7.2 percent, it is therefore less risky than a share in Barclays according to CAPM. (*Note*: These co-movements are to be taken as statistical expectations rather than precise predictions – thus over a large sample of return movements M&S's returns will move by 7.2 percent for a 10 percent market movement, if beta is a correct measure of company to market returns. On any single occasion the co-movements may not have this relationship.) Table 10.1 displays the betas for some large UK companies.

TABLE 10.1
Betas as measured in 2009

Share	Beta	Share	Beta
BT	0.99	Barclays Bank	1.83
Sainsburys (J)	0.70	Marks and Spencer	0.72

Source: Datastream

The basic features of beta are:

When

$\beta = 1$ A 1% change in the market index return generally leads to a 1% change in the return on a specific share

$0 < \beta < 1$ A 1% change in the market index return generally leads to a less than 1% change in the returns on a specific share

$\beta > 1$ A 1% change in market index return generally leads to a greater change than 1% on a specific company's share.

The security market line (SML)

Risk has been redefined for a fully diversified investor in an efficient market as systematic risk because this is the risk that cannot be diversified away and so a higher return is required if an investor is to bear it. In the CAPM the relationship between risk as measured by beta and expected return is shown by the *security market line* as in Figure 10.5. Shares perfectly correlated with the market return (r_m) will have a beta of 1.0 and are expected to produce an annual return of 9.5 percent in the circumstances of a risk-free rate of return at 6 percent and the risk-premium on the market portfolio of shares over safe securities at 3.5 percent (we will examine the origin of this number later). Shares that are twice as risky, with a beta of 2, will have an expected return of 13 percent (that is the risk-free return of 6 percent plus two times the risk premium on averagely risky shares of 3.5 percent). Shares that vary half as much as the market index are expected to produce a return of 7.75 percent (which is 6 percent plus one-half of 3.5 percent) *in this particular* hypothetical risk-return line.

To find the level of return expected for a given level of beta risk the following equation can be used:

$$\boxed{\text{Expected return}} \;=\; \boxed{\text{risk-free rate}} \;+\; \text{beta} \times \; \boxed{\begin{array}{l}\text{The average risk} \\ \text{premium for shares} \\ \text{(expected return on} \\ \text{the market minus the} \\ \text{risk-free rate)}\end{array}}$$

or

$$k_E = r_f + \beta (r_m - r_f)$$

For a share with a beta of 1.55 when the risk-free return is 6 percent the expected return will be:

$$k_E = 6 + 1.55\,(9.5 - 6) = 11.4\%$$

The better way of presenting this is to place the risk premium (RP) in the brackets rather than r_m and r_f separately because this reminds us that what is important in the risk premium is the required extra return over the risk-free rate as revealed by investors over many years – not the current market returns and risk-free rate. It is amazing how often financial journalists get this wrong and

FIGURE 10.5

A hypothetical security market line (SML)

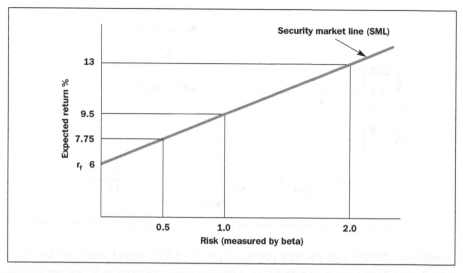

fixate on recent and current r_m and r_f rather than the long-term historical difference between the two. The market risk premium $(r_m - r_f)$ is fairly stable over
time as it is taken from a long-term historical relationship. Indeed, taking a short
period to estimate this would result in wild fluctuations from year to year, none of
which would reflect the premiums investors demand for holding a risky portfolio
of shares compared with a risk-free security. It is only over long periods that we
get a clearer view of returns required by shareholders as an acceptable premium.

Thus the better presentation is:

$$k_E = r_f + \beta(RP)$$

$$k_E = 6 + 1.55(3.5) = 11.4\%$$

Shifting risk-return relationships

At any one time the position of the SML depends primarily on the risk-free rate
of return. If the interest rate on government securities rises by say two percentage points the SML lifts upwards by 2 percent (*see* Figure 10.6).

Risk premiums across the world

Table 10.2 shows estimates of the extra annual return received by investors for holding a portfolio of shares compared with government bonds over various time periods.
It is clear that the extra return over periods as short as one year can give a distorted
picture – we cannot possibly assume that the negative return on shares in 2008 represents the normal 'additional' return demand by investors above a risk-free

FIGURE 10.6

Shifts in the SML – a 2 percent point rise in the risk-free rate

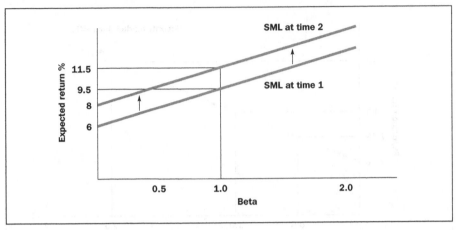

investment. Notice that the risk premium received for holding shares rather than government bonds has generally been in the range of 2 percent to 5 percent for the 17 countries listed. This gives us a strong indication of the likely future risk premium demanded by investors today. Therefore using a risk premium in this range for cost of equity capital calculation could be defended on these grounds. But note the assumption you would be making: that the returns investors actually received after the event (e.g. over the twentieth century) reflect the return they would have been demanding before the event (e.g. start of the twentieth century) for investing in shares rather than bonds.

To state definitively the return premium share investors generally receive over government bond and Treasury bill investors is obviously impossible as it depends on the period of time studied. What we can do is apply a principle when trying to establish a usable figure for the 'equity risk premium'. We would look at data for a long time period because the relationship between the returns on shares and bonds (or bills) is subject to a great deal of fluctuation in the short term (witness 2008 when shares fell). If we used the two longest periods in Table 10.2 we would say the extra return on shares is around 3.5 percent (for the UK and a number of other countries). For the remainder of this book we will, for practical purposes, assume an historic premium for shares over reputable government bond securities of 3.5 percent.[6]

However, this is a contentious area. Many informed thinkers (e.g. Dimson et al., 2009) believe that an equity risk premium for US, UK and world equities today lies in the region of 3 percent to 3.5 percent. Fama and French (2002) suggest an equity premium of 2.5 percent to 4.3 percent for US shares, while many old textbooks (e.g. Brealey, Myers and Allen, 2006) stick to higher numbers (5 percent to 8 percent). Considering how crucial this number is to many areas of finance theory, it may surprise you to find that there is so much room for choosing the equity risk premium.

TABLE 10.2
Equity risk premiums

	% per annum
UK	
109 years 1900–2008	3.6
50 years 1959–2008	3.4
10 years 1999–2008	–3.9
Other countries	
Australia 109 years 1900–2008	5.7
Belgium 109 years 1900–2008	2.0
Canada 109 years 1900–2008	3.7
Denmark 109 years 1900–2008	1.5
France 109 years 1900–2008	3.4
Germany 109 years 1900–2008[1]	4.7
Ireland 109 years 1900–2008	2.4
Italy 109 years 1900–2008	3.7
Japan 109 years 1900–2008	5.0
Netherlands 109 years 1900–2008	3.2
Norway 109 years 1900–2008	2.0
South Africa 109 years 1900–2008	5.2
Spain 109 years 1900–2008	2.1
Sweden 109 years 1900–2008	4.6
Switzerland 109 years 1900–2008	1.5
USA 109 years 1900–2008	3.8
World 109 years 1900–2008	3.4

[1] For Germany the years 1922–23 are excluded.

Sources: Elroy Dimson, Paul Marsh, Mike Staunton and Jonathan Wilmot (2009) *Credit Suisse Global Investment Returns Yearbook*, Credit Suisse Research Institute, Zurich (available online free of charge). The risk premiums presented are relative to government bonds rather than government bills.

Estimating some expected returns

To calculate the returns investors require from particular shares you need to obtain three numbers using the CAPM: (i) the risk-free rate of return, r_f, (ii) the risk premium for the market portfolio, $(r_m - r_f)$, and (iii) the beta of the share. Betas are available from free financial websites. In 2010 the returns on long-term UK government securities are about 4 percent. For the purpose of illustration we will take a risk premium of 3.5 percent. We have to acknowledge our imprecision at this point (even though some consultants will give a cost of equity capital to a tenth of a percentage point). Table 10.3 calculates the returns required on shares of some leading UK firms using beta as the only risk variable influencing returns.

TABLE 10.3

Returns expected by investors based on CAPM

Share	Beta (β)	Expected returns
		$r_f + \beta(r_m - r_f)$
BT	0.99	4 + 0.99 (3.5) = 7.47%
Sainsburys (J)	0.70	4 + 0.7 (3.5) = 6.45%
Barclays Bank	1.83	4 + 1.83 (3.5) = 10.4%
Marks and Spencer	0.72	4 + 0.72 (3.5) = 6.52%

Calculating beta

To make CAPM work for making decisions concerning the future it is necessary to calculate the *future* beta. That is, how more or less volatile a particular share is going to be relative to the market. Investors want extra compensation for relative volatility over the period when they hold the share – i.e. time still to come. Obviously, the future cannot be foreseen, and so it is difficult to obtain an estimate of the likely co-movements of the returns on a share and the market portfolio. One approach is to substitute subjective probability beliefs, but this has obvious drawbacks. The most popular method is to observe the historic relationship between returns and to assume that this co-variance will persist into the future.

Figure 10.7 shows a simplified and idealized version of this sort of analysis. Twelve monthly observations for, say, 2009 are shown (commercially supplied beta calculations are often based on at least 60 monthly observations stretching back over five years). Each plot point in Figure 10.7 expresses the return on the market index portfolio r_m for a particular month and the return on the specific shares r_j being examined in that same month.

In such an analysis the market portfolio will be represented by some broad index containing many hundreds of shares. In this highly idealized example the relative returns plot along a straight line referred to as the *characteristic line*. The example shown here is a perfect statistical relationship, there is no statistical 'noise' causing the plot points to be placed off the line. The characteristic line has a form described by the following formula

$$r_j = a + \beta_j r_m$$

where:

r_j = rate of return on the jth share

r_m = rate of return on the market index portfolio

FIGURE 10.7
The characteristic line – no unsystematic risk

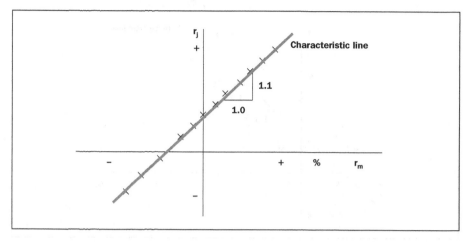

a = alpha. The regression line intercept

β_j = the beta of security j.

The slope of the characteristic line is the beta for share j. That is:

$$\frac{\text{Change in r}_j}{\text{Change in r}_m} = \beta$$

In this case the slope is 1.1 and therefore $\beta = 1.1$.

A more realistic representation of the relationship between the monthly returns on the market and the returns on a specific share are shown in Figure 10.8. Here very few of the plot points fall on the fitted regression line (the line of best fit). The reason for this scatter of points is because unsystematic risk effects in any one month may cause the returns on a specific share to rise or fall by a larger or smaller amount than it would if the returns on the market were the only influence. The slope of the best fit line is 1.2, therefore beta is 1.2.

Gordon growth model method for estimating the cost of equity capital

The most influential model for calculating the cost of equity in the early 1960s (and one which is still used today) was created by Gordon and Shapiro (1956), and further developed by Gordon (1962). Suppose a company's shares priced at P produce earnings of E per share and pay a dividend of d per share. The company has a policy of retaining a fraction, b, of its earnings each year to use for internal investments. If the rate of return (discount or capitalization rate) required on shares of this risk class k_E then, under certain restrictive conditions, it can be shown that earnings, dividends and reinvestment will all grow continuously, at a rate of $g = br$, where r is the rate of return on the reinvestment of earnings, and we have:

FIGURE 10.8

The characteristic line – with unsystematic risk

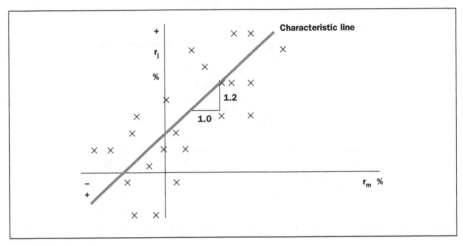

$$P = \frac{d_1}{k_E - g}$$

Solving for k_E we have:

$$k_E = \frac{d_1}{P} + g$$

where d_1 is the dividend to be received next year.

That is, the rate of return investors require on a share is equal to the prospective dividend yield (d_1/P) *plus* the rate at which the dividend stream is expected to grow (g).

Gordon and Shapiro said that there are other approaches to the estimation of future dividends than the extrapolation of the current dividend on the basis of the growth rate explicit in b and r, so we can derive g in other ways and still the k_E formula remains valid.

A major problem in the practical employment of this model is obtaining a trustworthy estimate of the future growth rate of dividends to an infinite horizon. Gordon and Shapiro (1956) told us to derive this figure from known data in an objective manner, using common sense and with reference to the past rate of growth in a corporation's dividend. In other words, a large dose of judgment is required. The cost of equity capital under this model is very sensitive to the figure put in for g, and yet there is no reliable method of estimating it for the *future*, all we can do is make reasoned estimates and so the resulting k_E is based merely on an informed guess. Using past growth rates is one approach, but it means that it is assumed that the future growth of the company's earnings and dividends will be exactly the same as in the past – often an erroneous supposition. Professional analysts' forecasts could be examined, but their record of predicting the future is generally a poor one – especially for more than two years ahead. (Remember this model requires us to estimate g for all future years, to an infinite horizon.) The rate of growth, g, is discussed further in Chapter 13, in the context of share valuation.

The cost of retained earnings

The most important source of long-term finance for most corporations is retained earnings (profits that the company has made and has not paid out as dividends). There are many large companies that rarely, if ever, go to their share-holders to raise new money, but rely on previous years' profits. There is a temptation to regard retained earnings as 'costless' because it was not neces-sary for the management to go out and persuade investors to invest by offering a rate of return.

However, retained earnings should be seen as belonging to the shareholders. They are part of the equity of the firm. Shareholders could make good use of these funds by investing in other firms and obtaining a return. These funds have an opportunity cost. We should regard the cost of retained earnings as equal to the expected returns required by shareholders buying new shares in a firm. There is a slight modification to this principle in practice because new share issues involve costs of issuance and therefore are required to give a marginally higher return to cover the costs of selling the shares.

The cost of debt capital

The cost of debt is generally determined by the following factors:

- the prevailing interest rates
- the risk of default (and expected rate of recovery of lenders' funds in the event of default)
- the benefit derived from interest being tax deductible.

There are two types of debt capital. The first is debt that is traded, that is, bought and sold in a security market. The second is debt that is not traded.

Traded debt

In the UK, bonds are normally issued by companies to lenders with a nominal value of £100. Vanilla bonds carry an annual coupon rate until the bonds reach maturity when the nominal or par value of £100 is paid to the lender (*see* Chapter 16 for more details). The rate of return required by the firm's creditors, k_D, is represented by the interest rate in the following equation which causes the future discounted cash flows payable to the lenders to equal the current market price of the bond P_D. We know the current price P_D of the bond in the market and the annual cash flow that will go to the lenders in the form of interest, i, and we know the cash to be received, R_n, when the bond is redeemed at the end of its life. The only number we don't yet have is the rate of return, k_D. This is found in the same way as the internal rate of return is found. (If IRR is alien to you, re-reading Chapter 2 may be beneficial.)

$$P_D = \sum_{t=1}^{n} \frac{i}{(1+k_D)^t} + \frac{R_n}{(1+k_D)^n}$$

where:

i = annual nominal interest (coupon payment) receivable from year 1 to year n;

R_n = amount payable upon redemption;

k_D = cost of debt capital (before the tax shield benefit);

$\sum_{t=1}^{n}$ means add up the results of all the $\dfrac{i}{(1 + k_D)^t}$ from next year (year 1) to the n number of years of the bond's life.

For example, Elm plc issued £100m of bonds six years ago carrying an annual coupon rate of 8 percent. They are due to be redeemed in four years for the nominal value of £100 each. The next coupon is payable in one year and the current market price of a bond is £93. The cost of this redeemable debt can be calculated by obtaining the internal rate of return, imagining that a new identical set of cash flows is being offered to the lenders from a new (four-year) bond being issued today. The lenders would pay £93 for such a bond (in the same risk class) and receive £8 per year for four years plus £100 at the end of the bond's life. Thus the cash flows from the firm's perspective are:

Year	0	1	2	3	4
	+£93	–£8	–£8	–£8	–£108

Thus the rate of return being offered is calculated from:

$$+93 - \frac{8}{1 + k_D} - \frac{8}{(1 + k_D)^2} - \frac{8}{(1 + k_D)^3} - \frac{108}{(1 + k_D)^4} = 0$$

With k_D at 11 percent the discounted cash flow = + £2.307.

With k_D at 10 percent the discounted cash flow = – £0.66.

Using linear interpretation the IRR can be found:

$$k_D = 10\% + \frac{0.66}{2.307 + 0.66}(11-10) = 10.22\%$$

Even though the bonds were once worth a total of £100m in the market (if they were sold at par value), this is no longer their value because they are now selling at £93 each. The total market value of the bonds, V_D, is calculated as follows:

$$V_D = \pounds 100m \times \frac{\pounds 93}{\pounds 100} = \pounds 93m$$

We are concerned with finding the cost to a company of the various types of capital it might use to finance its investment projects, strategic plans, etc. It would be wrong to use the coupon rate of 8 percent on the bond. This was the required rate of return six years ago (assuming the bond was sold for £100). A rate of 10.22 percent is appropriate because this is the rate of return bond investors are demanding in the market today. The cost of capital is the best available return elsewhere for the bondholders for the same level of risk. Managers are charged with using the money under their command to produce a return at least equal to the opportunity cost. If the cash flows attributable to these lenders for a project or SBU are discounted at 8 percent then a comparison of the resulting net present value of the investment with the return available by taking the alternative of investing the cash in the capital markets at the same risk is not being made. However, by using 10.22 percent for the bond cost of capital we can compare the alternatives available to the lenders in the financial markets.

Irredeemable bonds

The rate of return on irredeemable bonds (those that pay interest every year to an indefinite horizon) is easy. They have interest payments which form a perpetuity, therefore:

$$k_D = \frac{i}{P_D}$$

For example, a bond currently trading at £110 offering a £7 annual coupon is giving a rate of return of £7/£110 = 6.36 percent.

Tax effects

As explained earlier in the chapter, a firm is able to offset debt interest against a corporation tax liability. It is the cost of debt after the benefit of the tax shield that is of interest to firms as this is the effective cost of this form of finance – assuming they have taxable profits which can be reduced by the interest charge.

In the calculation for Elm plc taxation has been ignored and so the above calculation of 10.22 percent should be properly defined as the cost of debt before tax, k_{DBT}. An adjustment is necessary to establish the true cost of the bond capital to the firm.

If T is the rate of corporate tax, 30 percent, then the cost of debt after tax, k_{DAT} is:

$$k_{DAT} = k_{DBT}(1 - T)$$

$$k_{DAT} = 10.22(1 - 0.30) = 7.15\%$$

A short cut

We have calculated the yield to redemption on a very simple bond from first principles, to illustrate the key elements. In reality, most bonds offer coupon payments
every six months – this complicates the type of analysis shown above. However,
yields to redemption on bonds of different risk classes are available commercially,
which avoids effort. The *Financial Times* displays the yields ('bid yield') offered
on a range of frequently traded bonds of various risk classes (*see* the tables 'Global
Investment Grade' and 'High Yield and Emerging Market Bonds'). Two useful
websites for bond yields are *Investors Chronicle* (www.investorschronicle.
co.uk/bonds) (produced with FixedIncomeInvestor) and the *Financial Times*
(www.ft.com/bonds&rates). These sources may not be able to provide the yield to
redemption for the particular bond that interests you, but you can discover the
rates payable for bonds of different credit ratings. So if you know or can estimate
the credit rating of the company under examination, you can obtain an approximate rate of return (before the tax shield benefit K_{DBT}).

Untraded debt

Most debt capital, such as bank loans, is not traded and repriced regularly on a
financial market. We need to find the rate of interest that is the opportunity cost
of lenders' funds – the current 'going rate' of interest for the risk class. The easi-
est way to achieve this is to look at the rate being offered on similar tradeable
debt securities.

Floating-rate debt

Most companies have variable-rate debt in the form of either bonds or bank
loans. Usually the interest payable is set at a margin over a benchmark rate
such as bank base rate or LIBOR (see Chapter 15). For practical purposes the
current interest payable can be taken as the before-tax rate of return (k_{DBT})
because these rates are the market rates. There is a theoretical argument
against this simple approach based on the difference between short- and long-
term interest rates. For example, it may be that a firm rolls over a series of
short-term loans and so in effect will be using this as long-term finance. In this
case the theoretically correct approach is to use the long-term interest rate and
not the current short-term rate because the former more accurately reflects
what is likely to be required to be paid over the life of the loan.

The cost of preference share capital

Preference shares have some characteristics in common with debt capital (e.g. a
specified annual payout of higher ranking than ordinary share dividends) and

some characteristics in common with equity (dividends may be missed in some circumstances, and the dividend is not tax deductible) – *see* Chapter 17 for more details. If the holders of preference shares receive a fixed annual dividend and the shares are irredeemable the perpetuity formula may be used to value the security:

$$P_P = \frac{d_1}{k_p}$$

where P_P is the price of preference shares, d_1 is the annual preference dividend, k_p, is the investors' required rate of return. Therefore, the cost of this type of preference share is given by:

$$k_p = \frac{d_1}{P_P}$$

Hybrid securities

Hybrid securities can have a wide variety of features – e.g. a convertible bond is a combination of a straight bond offering regular coupons and an option to convert the bond to shares in the company. It is usually necessary to calculate the cost of capital for each of the component elements separately. This can be complex and is beyond the scope of this chapter.

Calculating the weights

Book (balance sheet) values for debt, equity and hybrid securities should not be used in calculating the weighted average cost of capital. Market values should be used. For example if £100m was raised by selling perpetual bonds (coupons promised without a definite cease date) when interest rates were 5 percent, but these bonds now offer a 10 percent return and, therefore, are selling at half the original value, £50m, then this figure should be used in the weightings. The rationale for using market values is that we need to generate a return for the finance providers on the basis of their current contribution to the capital of the firm and in relation to the current opportunity cost – accounting values have little relevance to this. Investors in bonds right now are facing an opportunity cost of £50m (i.e. they could sell the bonds and release £50m of cash) so this is the figure that managers should see as the amount sacrificed by these finance providers, not the £100m that the bonds once traded at.

With equity capital it is correct to use the market capitalization figure (current share price multiplied by number of shares issued to investors). This is the amount that current investors are sacrificing to invest in this company today – the shares could be sold in the market-place at that value. The balance sheet value for equity shareholders funds is not relevant. It is likely to be very different to the market capitalization. Balance sheets consist of a series of historical accounting entries that bear little relation to the value placed on the shares by investors. Market capitalization figures are available in Monday editions of the *Financial Times* for quoted companies. Most financial websites provide market capitalization, e.g. www.londonstockexchange.com.

The WACC with three or more types of finance

The formula becomes longer, but not fundamentally more difficult when there are three (or more) types of finance. For example, if a firm has preference share capital as well as debt and equity the formula becomes:

$$\text{WACC} = k_E W_E + k_{DAT} W_D + k_p W_p$$

where W_p is the weight for preference shares,

$$W_E = \frac{V_E}{V_E + V_D + V_P}, \ W_D = \frac{V_D}{V_E + V_D + V_P} \text{ and } W_P = \frac{V_P}{V_E + V_D + V_P}.$$

The weight for each type of capital is proportional to market values – and, of course, $W_E + W_D + W_p$ totals to 1.0.

Classic error

Managers are sometimes tempted to use the cost of the latest capital raised to discount projects, SBUs etc. This is wrong. Also do not use the cost of the capital you might be about to raise to finance the project.

The latest capital raised by a company might have been equity at, say, 12 percent, or debt at a cost of, say, 8 percent. If the firm is trying to decide whether to go ahead with a project that will produce an IRR of, say, 10.5 percent the project will be rejected if the latest capital-raising exercise was for equity and the discount rate used was 12 percent. On the other hand the project will be accepted if, by chance, the latest funds raised happen to be debt with a cost of 8 percent. The WACC should be used for all projects – at least, for all those of the same risk class as the existing set of projects. The reason is that a firm cannot move too far away from its optimum debt to equity ratio level. If it does its WACC will rise. So, although it may seem attractive for a subsidiary manager to promote a favoured project by saying that it can be financed with borrowed funds and therefore it needs only to achieve a rate of return above the interest rate it must be borne in mind that the next capital-raising exercise after that will have to be for equity to maintain an appropriate financial gearing level.

What about short-term debt?

Short-term debt should be included as part of the overall debt of the firm when calculating WACC. The lenders of this money will require a return. However, to the extent that this debt is temporary or is offset by cash and marketable securities held by the firm it may be excluded.

Applying the WACC to projects and SBUs

The overall return on the finance provided to a firm is determined by the portfolio of current projects. Likewise the risk (systematic) of the firm is determined by the collection of projects it is currently committed to. If a firm made an additional capital investment that has a much higher degree of risk than the average in the existing set then it is intuitively obvious that a higher return than the normal rate for this company will be required. On the other hand if an extraordinarily low risk activity is contemplated this should require a lower rate of return than usual.

Some multi-divisional firms make the mistake of demanding that all divisions achieve the same rate of return or better. This results in low risk projects being rejected when they should be accepted and high risk projects being accepted when they should be rejected.

Figure 10.9 is drawn up for an all-equity financed firm, but the principle demonstrated applies to firms financed by a mixture of types of capital. Given the firm's normal risk level the market demands a return of 11 percent. If another project is started with a similar level of risk then it would be reasonable to calculate NPV on the basis of a discount rate of 11 percent. This is the opportunity cost of capital for the shareholders – they could obtain 11 percent by investing their money in shares of other firms in a similar risk class. If however the firm invested in project A with a risk twice the normal level management would be doing their shareholders a disservice if they sought a mere 11 percent rate of return. At this risk level shareholders can get 16 percent on their money elsewhere. This sort of economic decision-making will result in projects being accepted when they should have been rejected. Conversely project B if discounted at the standard rate of 11 percent will be rejected when it should have been accepted. It produces a return of 8.5 percent when all that is required is a return of 7.5 percent for this risk class. It is clear that this firm should accept any project lying on or above the sloping line and reject any project lying below this line.

The rule discussed earlier (that a firm should accept any project that gives a return greater than the opportunity cost of capital) now has to be refined. This rule can only be applied if the marginal project has the same risk level as the existing set of projects. Projects with different risk levels require different levels of return.

Just how high the discount rate has to be is as much a matter for managerial judgment as it is based on the measures of risk and return developed by theorists.

FIGURE 10.9

Rates of return for projects of different systematic risk levels

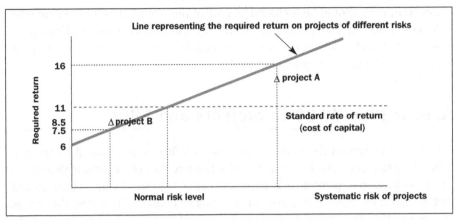

The CAPM provides a starting point, a framework for thinking about risk premiums, but judging the viability of a project or division is still largely an art which requires experience and perceptive thought, not least because it is very difficult to quantify the likely risk of, say, a SBU developing an internet business. It may be possible to classify projects into broad categories say, high, medium and low, but precise estimation is difficult. What is clear is that the firm should not use a single discount rate for all its activities. UBS was ridiculed in the *Financial Times* for making this mistake: 'UBS ... allocated capital to divisions using the group cost of capital, rather than adjusting for that division's risk. It is hard to imagine a serious industrial company being this primitive' (*Financial Times* 22 April 2008, p. 20).

What do managers actually do?

Academic literature promotes forcefully the use of the WACC. But to what extent have UK firms adopted the recommended methods? In 1983 Richard Pike expressed a poor opinion of the techniques used by business people to select the cost of capital: 'the methods commonly applied in setting hurdle rates are a strange mixture of folk-lore, experience, theory and intuition'. In 1976 Westwick and Shohet reported that less than 10 percent of the firms they studied used a WACC. The position has changed significantly. Arnold and Hatzopoulos (2000), in a study of 96 UK firms, found that the majority now calculate a WACC – *see* Table 10.4.

Despite years of academic expounding on the virtues of WACC and extensive managerial education, a significant minority of firms do not calculate a WACC for use in capital investment appraisal. Furthermore, as Tables 10.5 and 10.6 show, many firms that calculate a WACC do not follow the prescribed methods. Further evidence of a light grasp of textbook procedure was demonstrated in some of the statements made by respondents: 'Above is a minimum [WACC]. A hurdle rate is also used which is the mid-point of the above [WACC] and the lowest rate of return required by venture capitalists.' 'WACC + safety margin', 'Weighted average cost of capital plus inflation'.

TABLE 10.4

Replies to the question: How does your company derive the discount rate used in the appraisal of major capital investments? (percentage of respondents)

Method used	Category of company			
	Small (%)	Medium (%)	Large (%)	Composite (%)
WACC	41	63	61	54
The cost of equity derived from the capital asset pricing model is used	0	8	16	8
Interest payable on debt capital is used	23	8	1	11
An arbitrarily chosen figure	12	4	3	6
Dividend yield on shares plus estimated growth in capital value of share	0	0	3	1
Earnings yield on shares	3	0	0	1
Other	12	8	11	10
Blank	9	8	5	7

Source: Arnold and Hatzopoulos (2000). The 'large' category represents the largest 100 companies in the UK as measured by capital employed. The 'medium-sized' companies are ranked between 250 and 400, and the 'small' firms are ranked 820 and 1000. The capital employed ranged between £1.3bn and £24bn for the large firms, £207m and £400m for the medium-sized firms and £40m and £60m for the small companies.

TABLE 10.5

Method of calculating the weighted average cost of capital (percentage of respondents that use WACC)

Method	Category of company			
	Small (%)	Medium (%)	Large (%)	Composite (%)
Using the CAPM for equity and the market rate of return on debt capital	50	68	79	70
Cost of the equity calculated other than through the CAPM with the cost of debt derived from current market interest rates	50	32	18	29
Other	0	0	3	1

Source: Arnold and Hatzopoulos (2000).

TABLE 10.6

If the weighted average cost of capital is used, then how are the weights defined? (percentage of respondents)

	Category of company			
Method of defining weights	Small (%)	Medium (%)	Large (%)	Composite (%)
A long-term target debt and equity ratio	19	26	39	30
The present market values of debt and equity	44	47	42	44
Balance sheet ratios of debt and equity	37	26	19	26

Source: Arnold and Hatzopoulos (2000).

Gregory and Rutterford (1999) and Rutterford (2000) carried out a series of in-depth interviews with 18 FTSE-100 company finance directors or heads of corporate finance. They found that 14 of the companies made use of the capital asset pricing model to estimate the equity cost of capital, five used the dividend yield plus growth method (Gordon's growth model), four used the historic real rate of return on equity and five used more than one method.

Risk-free rate and betas used

In terms of the risk-free rate most firms (12 out of 14 using the CAPM) used the yield on UK government bonds – they generally chose a bond with a maturity of between seven and 20 years. The remainder used a real (excluding inflation) rate of interest. None used the Treasury bill rate.

Betas were sourced from financial databases, such as that of the London Business School, or from financial advisers – most firms used more than one source. Many interviewees felt that any fine-tuning of the beta estimate would have less impact on the k_E estimate than would the choice of the equity risk premium.

Risk premiums used

Two out of the 13 firms which estimated an equity risk premium chose a figure from a mid-1990s Barclays Capital Equity Gilt Study. This was based on a different time period to the study of Dimson, Marsh and Staunton. The Barclays studies published in the mid-1990s tracked returns from 1918 only rather than from January 1900 (the more recent Equity Gilt studies go back to 1900). The figures picked up by companies from these reports, at around 7.5 percent, are much higher than those used earlier in this chapter. The other 11 firms chose a number in a narrow range of 4.5 percent to 6 percent. The firms concerned admitted that their estimates were a 'gut feel' choice 'that came from our planning manager. He's an MBA and a lot of his MBA work was on the cost of capital. Five percent is a figure he's plucked out of the air based on his experience and knowledge' (Company O: Gregory and Rutterford, 1999, p. 43). Alternatively, managers tended to rely on advice from their bankers that the current equity risk premium was lower than at any time in the past – this had the effect of reducing the WACC estimate by almost two percentage points (compared with using a risk premium of 7.5 percent) in most cases. This intuitive approach has subsequently been borne out by the downward revision of historical risk premiums in empirical studies, as we saw in Credit Suisse data (Table 10.2).

Cost of debt

All 11 firms that explicitly consider the cost of debt allowed for the corporate tax rate to reduce the effective cost. All the companies used the cost of long-term debt rather than the Treasury (three-month lending) rate advocated in some textbooks. The majority chose to base the cost of debt on the cost of government debt and either take this as the cost of debt or add a credit risk premium. Three companies took the yield on their own outstanding bonds and the remainder chose a long-term bond yield 'based on experience'. 'We do not put in our real cost of debt. There are certain, for example tax driven, vehicles which give us actually quite a low cost of debt . . . So we tend to ignore those. That does build up a nice margin of safety within the target (cost of capital) of course' (Company C: Gregory and Rutterford, 1999, p. 46).

Debt/equity ratios

Ten out of 15 firms that calculated the WACC used a long-run target debt/equity ratio, five used the actual debt/equity ratio and one used both. For firms using a target ratio, this was taken as 20 percent, 25 percent or 30 percent, and was at least as high as the current actual debt/equity ratio, in some cases substantially higher – one firm with a cash surplus nevertheless chose a ratio of 20 percent.

Ten companies chose to estimate a nominal (including inflation) WACC (average value of 11.67 percent). Five used a real (excluding inflation) WACC (average value of 8.79 percent) and three used both a nominal and a real WACC. Rutterford (2000) comments: 'differences in data inputs for the equity risk premium (from 4 percent to 7.5 percent) and the choice of debt/equity ratio (from 0 percent to 50 percent) meant that the final WACC estimate was a fairly subjective estimate for each firm'.

Hurdle rates

Corporations seem to make a distinction between WACC and the hurdle rate. Gregory and Rutterford found that the average *base* hurdle rate was

0.93 percent higher than the average WACC. The base hurdle rate is defined as the rate for standard projects, before any adjustments for divisional differences in operating risk, financial risk or currency risk. Most of the firms had a range of hurdle rates, depending on project or the risk factors.

However, there was no consensus among the firms on how to adjust the differential project risk. Fourteen out of 18 made some adjustment for different levels of risk, with nine of those 14 making some adjustment for country risk or foreign exchange risk as well as for systematic risk. Note however that in 17 out of 18 cases the adjustment was made to the base hurdle rate and not to the more theoretically appropriate WACC. There was a general impression of sophistication in attaining the WACC in the first place, followed by a rule-of-thumb-type approach when making risk adjustments: 'The comment I make in terms of the hurdle rates for investment purposes is that we do it relatively simplistically in terms of low risk, high risk, country-specific risk' (Company P: Gregory and Rutterford, 1999, p. 53).

Methods range from adding two percentage point increments, to having two possible hurdle rates, say, 15 percent and 20 percent. Fifteen firms had premiums of 0 percent to 8 percent over the base hurdle rate, while three firms added more than ten percentage points for the highest-risk projects.

Some way to go yet

Even when the textbook model is accepted a range of WACCs can be estimated for the same firm: 'for example, altering the choice of target debt/equity ratio or equity risk premium can have an impact of 2 percent or more on the resulting WACC figure. Furthermore, little work has yet been done to extend the complex analysis for the firm's WACC to the divisional level' (Rutterford, 2000, p. 149). This lack of sophistication was confirmed in another study, carried out by Francis and Minchington (2000) that discovered 24 percent of firms (of varied sizes) used a divisional cost of capital that reflects the cost of debt capital only significantly underestimating the cost of capital. Furthermore, 69 percent did not use a different rate for different divisions to reflect levels of risk.

Pre-tax and post-tax WACC

The method we use throughout the book is the 'post-tax approach' in which the cost of equity is calculated as a return required after tax deductions on returns and the cost of debt after the tax shield effect. This is to be used when the cash flows of the project or company to be discounted are calculated after tax has been deducted.

Alternatively the 'pre-tax approach' could be used in which the cost of equity is 'grossed up' by 1–T (T = corporation tax rate):

$$k_{E \text{ pre-tax}} = \frac{k_{E \text{ post-tax}}}{1-T}$$

Then post-tax WACC = pre-tax WACC $(1 - T)$.

This pre-tax WACC can be used for cash flows before a deduction for tax is made. Case study 10.1 shows Henkel's use of a pre-tax WACC applied to earnings before deduction of interest and tax, EBIT.

Regulators such as those for energy supply (OFGEM) often use a third WACC. This is called 'vanilla WACC'. The required return is set equal to a weighted average of post-tax cost of equity (e.g. normal CAPM calculation shown in this chapter) and pre-tax cost of debt. Tax is estimated and allowed for separately in a similar way as other elements of operating expenditure.

Case study 10.1

Henkel's calculation of WACC and its use for performance measurement

The German home care, personal care and adhesives company Henkel set out on their website how they calculate WACC – reproduced below. (See Chapter 8 for a description of EVA.)

Note that, as for the calculation of the cost of equity capital in this chapter, Henkel first calculate and use an after-tax return to the equity holders. They later state what the WACC would have been if the required return on equity is calculated at the rate that shareholders expect *before* the tax authorities deduct their amounts (thus dividends, for example, are taxed and this reduces the return to shareholders).

The 'WACC before tax' includes the 'cost of debt before tax', and not the cost of debt after allowing for the tax shield effect. In using WACC for EVA calculations Henkel focuses on earnings before deduction of interest and tax (EBIT), which makes sense when they are using the 'before tax deducted' version of WACC.

Performance measurement

To make achievement of our growth targets measurable, we have adopted a modern system of metrics with which we calculate value-increase and return ratios in line with capital market practice.

We use economic value added (EVA®)[1] as a central performance management parameter to assess growth to date and to appraise future plans. EVA® is a measure of the additional financial value created by a company in a given reporting period. A company creates economic value added if its operating profit exceeds its cost of capital, the latter being defined as the return on capital employed expected by the capital market.

Operational business performance is measured on the basis of operating profit (EBIT). The capital employed figure is calculated from the assets side of the balance sheet.

The cost of capital employed is calculated as a weighted average of the cost of capital (WACC) comprising both equity and debt. In fiscal 2008, we applied a WACC after tax of 7.5 percent. Before tax, the figure was 11 percent. We regularly review our cost of capital in order to reflect changing market conditions. Starting in fiscal 2009, therefore, we have adopted a WACC of 11.5 percent before tax and 8.0 percent after tax.

We further apply different WACC rates depending on the business sector involved, based on sector-specific beta factors. In the year under review, this resulted in a WACC before tax of 10.5 percent (7.5 percent after tax) for both Laundry & Home Care and Cosmetics/Toiletries, and of 12.0 percent before tax (8.5 percent after tax) for Adhesive Technologies. Since the start of 2009, we have been applying a WACC for Adhesive Technologies of 12.5 percent (8.5 percent after tax), while the values for the other two business sectors have remained unchanged.

At Henkel, EVA® is calculated as follows:

EVA® = EBIT – (Capital Employed × WACC)

EVA® serves to promote value-added decisions and profitable growth in all our business sectors. Operations exhibiting consistently negative value contributions with no prospect of positive EVA® values in the future are divested or otherwise discontinued.

[1] EVA® is a registered trademark of Stern Stewart & Co.

Weighted average cost of capital (WACC)

	2008	since 2009
Risk-free interest rate	4.8%	4.8%
Market risk premium	4.5%	4.5%
Beta factor	0.90	1.00
Cost of equity after tax	**8.9%**	**9.4%**
Cost of debt capital before tax	5.6%	5.3%
Tax shield (30%)	–1.7%	–1.6%
Cost of debt capital after tax	**3.9%**	**3.7%**
Share of equity[1]	75%	75%
Share of debt capital[1]	25%	25%
WACC after tax[2]	**7.5%**	**8.0%**
Tax rate	30%	30%
WACC before tax[2]	**10.0%**	**11.5%**

[1] A market values.
[2] Rounded.

WACC before tax by business sector

	2008	since 2009
Laundry & Home Care	10.5%	10.5%
Cosmetics/Toiletries	10.5%	10.5%
Adhesive Technologies	12.0%	12.5%

EVA® and ROCE by business sector

In million euros	Laundry & Home care	Cosmetics/ Toiletries	Adhesive Technologies	Corporate	Group
EBIT	439	376	658	–694	779
Capital employed	2,604	2,151	6,590	–24	11,321
WACC[2]	**273**	**226**	**791**	**–3**	**1,245[3]**
EVA® 2008	**166**	**150**	**–132**	**–692**	**–466[3]**
EVA® 2007	183	149	253	–116	469
ROCE® 2008	**16.9**	**17.5**	**10.0**	–	**6.9**
ROCE® 2007	16.7	16.7	16.9	–	15.4

[1] Calculated on the basis of units of 1,000 euros.
[2] Calculated on the basis of the different sector-specific WACC rates applied.
[3] Calculated on the basis of the WACC rate of 11.0 percent for the Henkel Group.

Source: http://www.henkel.com/SID-0AC8330A-30F020C3/about-henkel/performance-measurement-11917.htm.

Implementation issues

How large is the equity risk premium?

To understand the controversy over the equity risk premium we need to appreciate that it can only ever be a subjective estimate. The reason for this is that we are trying to figure out how much additional annual return investors in an averagely risky share require above the risk-free rate today. Investors when deciding this are looking at the future, not the past. Each investor is likely to have a different assessment of the appropriate extra return compared with the risk-free investment. We need to assess the weighted average of investors' attitudes.

Using historical returns to see the size of the premium actually received may be a good starting point, but we must be aware that we are making a leap of faith to then assume that the past equity risk premium is relevant for today's analysis with its future focus. In using historic data we are making at least two implicit assumptions:

■ there has been no systematic change in the risk aversion of investors over time

■ the index being used as a benchmark has had an average riskiness that has not altered in a systematic way over time.

Differing views

Some City analysts believe that things have changed so radically in terms of the riskiness of ordinary shares for a fully diversified investor that the risk premium is now very small – some plump for 2 percent while extremists say that over the long run shares are no more risky than gilts, so say that the premium is zero. To justify their beliefs they point to the conquest of inflation, the lengthening of economic cycles, the long bull market (an argument weakened recently) and the increasing supply of risk capital as ageing industrial societies start to save more for retirement.

Even Barclays Capital dramatically revised the equity risk premium from over seven percentage points greater than gilts to around 4 percent in their Equity Gilt studies (an annual publication). The Competition Commission tends to take a range of between 2.5 and 4.5 percent. Ofcom uses 4.5 percent as an input to the cost of capital calculations for regulated telecom and media companies. OFWAT uses a range of between 3 percent and 4 percent. OFGEM (the UK gas and electricity regulator) uses a range of between 2.5 percent to 4.5 percent. The regulators calculate the amount of capital these firms are using and then allow prices charged to the consumer to be at a level which targets an appropriate rate of return (WACC) on the money invested in the business. Note that in their negotiating stance the regulators are likely to take a range that is as low as possible. (*See* Exhibit 10.1)

Water bill cuts put customers first

David Fickling

Water bills in the UK will drop by an average of £14, or 4 per cent, by 2014, under a five-year pricing plan by Ofwat, the regulator, that will heavily curtail water companies' investment programmes.

The regulator bowed to political pressure to put consumers first. The last price review, in 2004, was widely seen as having been too generous to the water companies. ...

At the end of five years, average water bills will be 12 per cent lower than requested by Severn Trent, 11 per cent lower for South West Water, 10 per cent lower for Northumbrian Water and 11 per cent lower for United Utilities. But the result comes at the expense of spending on the water network, with the companies' £24.2bn spending plans, equivalent to £1,024 per property, cut to £20.8bn, or £881 per property. ...

The regulator also gave an unexpectedly low estimate of companies' financing costs, raising the question of how they will cope if energy costs, inflation or credit markets deviate from Ofwat's expectations.

Ofwat calculated that companies would have a cost of capital of 4.5 per cent over the period, compared with a range of 4.7 per cent to 5.25 per cent estimated by the utilities.

Some companies, including Thames, have previously warned that if their cost of capital were underestimated it could threaten their ability to finance their activities, leading to a credit downgrade or possibly an appeal to the Competition Commission.

Investors in the UK's 24 water businesses, which had almost universally been seeking permission to increase bills above the rate of inflation, reacted with disappointment. The proportion of net profits paid as dividends by water companies is almost double that of the broader market.

Shares in United Utilities fell as much as 5.5 per cent to 475p in morning trading ...

EXHIBIT 10.1

Source: *Financial Times* 24 July 2009, p. 3.

An opinion

In my view, equities have not become as safe as gilts. For equities the last two decades of the twentieth century were a charmed period. Shareholders have now learnt the hard way that one can lose a great deal of money in stock markets. It is possible for returns to be negative for an entire decade or more. I believe the prudent investor needs to examine a long period of time, in which rare, but extreme, events have disrupted the financial system (wars, depressions, manias and panics) to gain an impression of the riskiness of shares.

What is clear is that obtaining the risk premium is not as scientific as some would pretend. The range of plausible estimates is wide and the effect of choosing 2 percent rather than 3.5 percent, or even 7.5 percent can have a significant effect on the acceptance or rejection of capital investment projects within the firm, or the calculation of value performance metrics. One of the respondents to the Arnold and Hatzopoulos survey expressed the frustration of practitioners by pointing out that precision in the WACC method is less important than to have reliable basic data: 'The real issue is one of risk premium on equity. Is it 2% or 8%?!'

Which risk-free rate?

The risk-free rate is a completely certain return. For complete certainty two conditions are needed:

- the risk of default is zero
- when intermediate cash flows are earned on a multi-year investment there is no uncertainty about reinvestment rates.

The return available on a zero coupon government bond[8] which has a time horizon equal to the cash flow (of a project, an SBU, etc.) being analyzed is the closest we are going to get to the theoretically correct risk-free rate of return.

Business projects usually involve cash flows arising at intervals, rather than all at the end of an investment. Theoretically, each of these separate cash flows should be discounted using different risk-free rates. So, for the cash flows arising after one year on a multi-year project, the rate on a one-year zero-coupon government bond should be used as part of the calculation of the cost of capital. The cash flows arising in year five should be discounted on the basis of a cost of capital calculated using the five-year zero-coupon rate and so on. However, this approach is cumbersome, and there is a practical alternative that gives a reasonable approximation to the theoretical optimum. It is considered acceptable to use a long-term government rate on all the cash flows of a project that has a long-term horizon. Furthermore, the return on a government bond with coupons, rather than a zero coupon bond, is generally taken to be acceptable. The rule of thumb seems to be to use the return available on a reputable government security having the same time horizon as the project under consideration – so for a short-term project one should use the discount rate which incorporates the short-term government security rate, for a 20-year project use the 20-year government bond yield-to-maturity.[9]

How reliable is CAPM's beta?

There are many problems with the use of the CAPM's beta in the cost of equity capital calculation. We will consider two of them here:

The use of historic betas for future analysis

The mathematics involved in obtaining an historical beta is straightforward enough; however it is not clear whether using weekly data is more appropriate than monthly, or whether the historical data on the returns on the market and the return on a particular share should be recorded over a one-, three-, five- or ten-year period. Each is likely to provide a different estimate of beta. Even if this is resolved the difficulty of using an historical measure for estimating a future relationship is very doubtful. Betas tend to be unstable over time. This was discovered as long ago as the early 1970s. If the requirement is to compensate investors for the risk class of the share they hold surely we need a measure of risk that is not volatile, otherwise managers will be rejecting projects in one year that they accept in another purely because of the different time period over which beta was measured (and whether weekly or monthly data are used). Table 10.7 gives an impression of the variability of the betas for some UK firms – some have been stable, while others have changed significantly.

TABLE 10.7
Betas as measured for the five years to 1997, 2000, 2004 and 2009

	1997	2000	2004	2009
Barclays Bank	1.22	1.55	1.11	1.83
BT	0.91	0.94	1.62	0.99
Marks and Spencer	0.95	0.44	0.50	0.72
J. Sainsbury	0.60	0.19	0.80	0.70

Source: Datastream.

One potential explanation for the shifting betas is that the risk of the security changes – firms change the way they operate and the markets they serve. A company that was relatively insensitive to general market change two years ago may now be highly responsive – but have the companies in Table 10.7 really changed the nature (riskiness) of their businesses that much over these periods? I doubt it. Alternatively, the explanation may lie in measurement error – large random errors cause problems in producing comparable betas from one period to another. To add to this problem we have a wide variety of market indices (such as FTSE-100, FTSE All Share) to choose from when calculating the historical co-variability of a share with the market (its beta).

The breakdown in the relationship between beta and return

The fundamental point about the CAPM is that investors demand higher returns on shares that are more volatile relative to the market index. Investors require that a share with a beta of 1.5 should provide a higher return than a share with a beta of 1. When the model was first developed in the 1960s this was nothing more than an assertion based on theorizing. In the 1970s and 1980s tests were performed to see if, in practice, portfolios of shares having shown a high beta produce higher returns in future than portfolios of shares with a low beta. In theory, the returns on share portfolios with different betas would lie along the security market line (SML). So, if you purchased a portfolio made up of shares with a beta of 2.0 (historically these shares have been twice as volatile as the market) you would expect it to produce much higher returns over the next five years than a portfolio made up of shares that have shown a low beta in their historic relationship with market returns, say, a beta of 0.5. If beta is the only risk that investors care about (the nub of the CAPM) then this is the only factor for raising the equity cost of capital. If the historical evidence shows that investors have not received this extra return then one has to doubt whether beta risk is a (or the only) form of risk that investors require compensation for. And, if they don't require compensation for taking on this extra risk why should managers try to achieve higher returns for higher beta activities? So, are investors really bothered about beta risk?

The results of early studies generally showed a positive relationship between beta and subsequent returns. Investors got a higher return for bearing beta risk – it seems reasonable to presume that this is because they *demanded* this premium. This demand was transmitted via the buying and selling of shares on the stock market. By influencing share prices investors influence returns – for shares with the same level of projected cash flows the high beta ones are bid down because investors are more reluctant to hold them.

However, the evidence of the early studies was not perfectly in support of the CAPM. The extent to which returns rose with beta was significantly less than the theoreticians expected. Low-risk shares tended to show rates of return higher than the theory would suggest, and high beta shares show lower returns than the CAPM predicts.

The debate moved in the late 1980s and 1990s to whether the CAPM and beta were any use at all. The question 'Is beta dead?' has caused heated debate in the academic world just at the time, ironically, of its greatest adoption by practitioners. Fischer Black (1993) discovered that while returns on US shares did vary in relation to beta in the period 1931–91, there appeared to be no relationship at all in the period 1966–91. His Portfolio 1 (consisting of those shares with the top 10 percent of betas, average beta of 1.50) showed the same return as portfolio 10 (average beta of 0.51).

The publication of Eugene Fama and Kenneth French's (1992) empirical study of US share returns over the period 1963–90 was a further blow to the CAPM. They found 'no reliable relation between β and average return'.[10] They continue: 'The Sharpe-Lintner-Black model [CAPM] has long shaped the way academics and practitioners think about average return and risk ... In short, our tests do not support the most basic prediction of the SLB model, that average stock returns are positively related to market βs ... Our bottom-line results are: (a) β does not seem to help explain the cross-section of average stock returns, and (b) the combination of size and book-to-market equity [do].' (Fama and French's later paper (2006) reports that higher beta did not lead to higher returns over the 77 years to 2004.) In other words, beta has not been able to explain returns whereas two other factors have. A firm's total market value has had some effect on returns – the larger the firm (market capitalization), the lower the return. Also the ratio of the firm's book (balance sheet) value to its market value (total value of all shares issued) has had some explanatory power – if book value is high *vis-à-vis* market value then returns tend to be higher. This particular onslaught on CAPM has caused great consternation and reaction in the academic world.

Louis Chan and Josef Lakonishok (1993) breathed a little life into the now dying beta. They looked at share returns over the period 1926–91 and found a faint pulse of a relationship between beta and returns but were unable to show statistical significance because of the 'noisy' data. More vibrant life can be witnessed if the share return data after 1982 is excluded – but, then, shouldn't it work in all periods? They also argued that beta may be a more valid determinant of return in extreme market circumstances, such as a stock market crash and therefore should not be written off as being totally 'dead'.

Beta has been brought to its knees by the punches delivered by American researchers, it was kicked again while it was down by the damaging evidence drawn from the European share markets. For example Albert Corhay and co-researchers Gabriel Hawawini and Pierre Michel (1987) found that investors in stocks (shares) trading in the USA, the UK and Belgium were not compensated with higher average returns for bearing higher levels of risk (as measured by beta) over the 13-year sample period. Investors in stocks trading on the Paris Stock Exchange were actually penalized rather than rewarded – they received below average rates of return for holding stocks with above-average levels of risk. Strong and Xu (1997) show that UK shares during the period 1973–92 displayed a *negative* relationship between average returns and beta!

It is plain that even if the CAPM is not dead, it has been severely wounded. Beta may or may not have some explanatory power for returns. That debate will rage for many years yet. What we can conclude from the evidence presented is that there appears to be more to risk than beta.

Fundamental beta

Instead of using historical betas calculated through a regression of the firm's returns against a proxy for the market portfolio (eg. FTSE 100) some analysts calculate a 'fundamental beta'. This is based on the intuitive underpinning of the risk-return relationship: if the firm (or project) cash flows are subject to more (systematic) variability then the required return should be higher. What causes greater systematic variability? Three factors have been advanced:

- **The type of business in which the company (SBU or project) is engaged** Some businesses are more sensitive to market conditions than others. The turnover and profits of cyclical industries change a great deal with macroeconomic fluctuations. So, for example, the sale of yachts, cars or designer clothes rises in a boom and crashes in decline. On the other hand, non-cyclical industries, such as food retailing or tobacco, experience less variability with the economic cycle. Thus, in a fundamental beta framework cyclical businesses would be allocated a higher beta than non-cyclical businesses. If the purchase of the product can be delayed for months, years or even indefinitely (i.e. it is discretionary) then it is more likely to be vulnerable to an economic downturn.

- **Degree of operating gearing** If the firm has high fixed costs compared with variable costs of production its profits are highly sensitive to output (turnover) levels. A small percentage fall in output and revenue can result in a large percentage change in profits. The higher variability in profit means that a higher beta should be allocated.

- **Degree of financial gearing** If the company has high borrowings, with a concomitant requirement to pay interest regularly, then profits attributable to shareholders are likely to be more vulnerable to shocks. So the beta will rise if the company has higher financial gearing (or leverage). The obligation to meet interest payments increases the variability of after-interest profits. In a recession profits can more easily turn into losses. Financial gearing exacerbates the underlying business risk.

The obvious problem with using the fundamental beta approach is the difficulty of deriving the exact extent to which beta should be adjusted up or down depending on the strength of the three factors.

Some thoughts on the cost of capital

Progress

There have been a number of significant advances in theory and in practice over the last 40 years. No longer do most firms simply use the current interest rate, or adjust for risk in an entirely arbitrary manner. There is now a theoretical base to build on, both to determine a cost of capital for a firm, and to understand the limitations (or qualities) of the input data and modelling.

It is generally accepted that a weighted average of the costs of all the sources of finance is to be used. It is also accepted that the weights are to be based on market values (rather than book values), as market values relate more closely to the opportunity cost of the finance providers. Furthermore, it is possible that the WACC may be lowered and shareholder value raised by shifting the debt/equity ratio.

Even before the development of modern finance it was obvious that projects (or collections of projects, as firms are) that had a risk higher than that of investing in government securities require a higher rate of return. A risk premium must be added to the risk-free rate to determine the required return. However, modern portfolio theory (MPT) has refined the definition of risk, so the analyst need only consider compensation (additional return) for systematic risk.

Outstanding issues

Despite the progress, considerable difficulties remain. Practitioners need to be aware of both the triumphs of modern financial theory as well as its gaps. The area of greatest controversy is the calculation of the cost of equity capital. In determining the cost of equity capital we start with the following facts.

■ The current risk-free rate is the bedrock. It is acceptable to use the rate on a government bond with the same maturity as the project, SBU, etc.

■ The return should be increased to allow for the risk of a share with average systematic risk. (Add a risk premium to the risk-free rate return.) As a guide, investors have received a risk premium of around 2 to 5 percent for accepting the risk level equivalent to that on the average ordinary share over the past century or so, depending on the country.

■ A particular company's shares do not carry average equity risk, therefore the risk premium should be increased or decreased depending on the company's systematic risk level.

So, if the project or SBU under examination has a systematic risk which is lower than that on the average share it would seem sensible that the returns attributable to shareholders on this project should be somewhere between the risk-free rate and the risk-free rate plus, say, 3.5 percent. If the project has a systematic risk greater than that exhibited by shares generally then the returns required for shareholders will be more than the risk-free rate plus, say, 3.5 percent.

The main difficulty is in calculating the systematic risk level. In the heyday of the CAPM this was simple: beta was all you needed. Today we have to allow for the possibility that investors want compensation for a multiplicity of systematic risk factors. Not unnaturally many business people are unwilling to adopt such a burdensome approach and fall back on their 'judgment' to adjust for the risk of a project. In practice it is extremely difficult to state precisely the risk of a project – we are dealing with future uncertainties about cash flows from day-to-day business operations subject to sudden and unforeseen shocks. The pragmatic approach is to avoid precision and simply place each proposed project into one of three risk categories: low, medium or high. This neatly bypasses the complexities laid out by the theorists and also accurately reflects the fact that decisions made in the real world are made with less than complete knowledge. Mechanical decision-making within the firm based on over-simplistic academic models is often a poor substitute for judgment that recognizes the imperfections of reality.

One thing is certain: if anyone ever tells you that they can unequivocally state a firm's cost of capital to within a tenth of a percentage point, you know you are talking to someone who has not quite grasped the complexity of the issue.

Conclusion

A firm that asks an unreasonably high rate of return will be denying its shareholders wealth-enhancing opportunities and ceding valuable markets to competitors. One that employs an irrationally low cost of capital will be wasting resources, setting managers targets that are unduly easy to reach and destroying wealth.

This chapter has described the academic foundations for calculating a company's cost of capital. It has also pointed out the practical difficulties of calculating real world discount rates. The difficulties are severe, but please don't throw your hands up and conclude that the economists and finance theorists have taken us on a long, arduous road back to where we started. We are not at square one. We have a set of rules to provide a key management number. We now know that judgment is required at many stages in the process and where those particular points are. This allows us to view any number produced by our own calculations or those of the finance team, with the required amount of reasoned scepticism. And, when making decisions on whether to invest in that new factory or close down a division we have some grasp of the degree to which there is room for error in the value calculation. This part of the book reinforces that in this uncertain world we should think in terms of a range of possible outcomes, with all too imprecise subjective probabilities, not in terms of cut-and-dried pin-point precision. The arguments in this chapter should, I hope, allow you to estimate the boundaries for the range of values you feel comfortable with. Returns falling below the acceptable range can be easily rejected, those with a good margin above are simple decisions. Management at these extremes is survivable even for the humdrum executive. Those projects that give returns lying in the middle require insightful judgment: that is the art of management and call for leaders.

Notes

1 Quoted in Philip Coggan and Paul Cheeseright, *Financial Times*, 8 November 1994.
2 Modigliani and Miller did not ignore tax and financial distress in their work, but did downplay them in the formulation of their early model.
3 This is assuming that future inflation is included in the projected cash flows. That is, we are using nominal cash flows and a nominal interest rate. An alternative method is to use real cash flows and a real discount rate (i.e. with inflation removed).
4 An alternative is the 'Forward looking approach' in which the analyst tries to obtain estimates of what extra future annual return investors require at this time for investing in an averagely risky share. There are some serious doubts about the subjective nature of the inputs to these calculations.
5 Other models of risk and return define systematic risk in other ways.
6 3.5 percent would be well within the confidence interval for the equity risk premium range shown in the most recent serious studies.

7   An excellent discussion of the calculation of the cost of capital by regulators is to be found in Lockett, M. (2001) Calculating the cost of capital for the regulated electricity distribution companies, Aston University MBA Project Dissertation and in a later paper: Lockett, M. (2002), Calculating the cost of capital for the regulated electricity distribution companies. *Power Engineering Journal*, October, pp. 251–63.

8   A zero-coupon bond is one that promises the owner a capital sum at the end of its life, say ten years down the line, but does not offer any income between now and then. These sell for much less than the amount promised at the end. So a 'zero' with ten years to run offering £100 on redemption might currently be selling for £40. As a holder you have no income, but you do receive a large capital gain.

9   Lockett (2002) describes the increasing popular approach of using the rate of return offered on a UK government index-linked gilt in a WACC calculation that is based on real rates of return and real cash flows. That is, with inflation removed from both. This would appear to be a method used by regulators such as OFGEM, OFWAT and the Competition Commission. This generally provides a figure of around 1 percent as the required return in the absence of inflation or risk. However, this has fluctuated so widely over the past 15 years (from 5 percent to under 1 percent) that a number of the regulators refuse to use the prevailing index-linked gilt yield if it is unusually low and substitute their judgment as to what a 'normal' rate is (so much for mathematical precision!). If you are conducting an analysis with actual projected cash flows (i.e. with inflation built into the assumptions) then you need to add an estimated inflation rate, which will take you back (approximately) to the rate on the conventional government bond of the same time to maturity.

10 There is some controversy over their interpretation of the data, but nevertheless this is a very serious challenge to the CAPM.

11

MERGERS: IMPULSE, REGRET AND SUCCESS

Introduction

The topic of mergers is one of those areas of finance that attracts interest from the general public as well as finance specialists and managers. There is nothing like an acrimonious bid battle to excite the press, where one side is portrayed as 'David' fighting the bullying 'Goliath', or where one national champion threatens the pride of another country by taking over a key industry. Each twist and turn of the campaign is reported on radio and television news broadcasts, and, finally, there is a victor and a victim. So many people have so much hanging on the outcome of the conflict that it is not surprising that a great deal of attention is given by local communities, national government, employees and trade unionists. The whole process can become emotional and over-hyped to the point where rational analysis is sometimes pushed to the side.

This chapter examines the reasons for mergers ranging from the gaining of economies of scale to managerial empire building. Then a major question is addressed: do shareholders of acquiring firms gain from mergers? Evidence is presented which suggests that in less than one-half of corporate mergers do the shareholders of the acquiring firm benefit. To help the reader understand the causes of this level of failure the various managerial tasks involved in achieving a successful (that is, a shareholder wealth-enhancing) merger, including the 'soft' science issues, such as attending to the need to enlist the commitment of the newly acquired workforce, are discussed.

In the next chapter the merger process itself is described, along with the rules and regulations designed to prevent unfairness. Also discussed is the way in which mergers are financed.

The merger decision

Expanding the activities of the firm through acquisition involves significant uncertainties. Very often the acquiring management seriously underestimate the complexities involved in merger and post-merger integration.

Theoretically the acquisition of other companies should be evaluated on essentially the same criteria as any other investment decision, that is, using NPV. As Rappaport states: 'The basic objective of making acquisitions is identical to any other investment associated with a company's overall strategy, namely, to add value'.[1]

In practice, the myriad collection of motivations for expansion through merger, and the diverse range of issues such an action raises, means that mergers are usually extremely difficult to evaluate using discounted cash flow techniques. Consider these two complicating factors.

- The benefits from mergers are often difficult to quantify. The motivation may be to 'apply superior managerial skills' or to 'obtain unique technical capabilities' or to 'enter a new market'. The fruits of these labours may be real, and directors may judge that the strategic benefits far outweigh the cost, and yet these are difficult to express in numerical form.

- Acquiring companies often do not know what they are buying. If a firm expands by building a factory here, or buying in machinery there, it knows what it is getting for its money. With a merger, information is often sparse – especially if it is a hostile bid in which the target company's managers are opposed to the merger. Most of the value of a typical firm is in the form of assets which cannot be expressed on a balance sheet, for example the reservoir of experience within the management team, the reputation with suppliers and customers, competitive position and so on. These attributes are extremely difficult to value, especially from a distance, and when there is a reluctance to release information. Even the quantifiable elements of value, such as stock, buildings and free cash flow, can be miscalculated by an 'outsider'.

You say acquisition, I say merger

Throughout this book the word merger will be used to mean the *combining of two business entities under common ownership*.

Many people, for various reasons, differentiate between the terms merger, acquisition and takeover – for example, for accounting and legal purposes. However, most commentators use the three terms interchangeably, and with good reason. It is sometimes very difficult to decide if a particular unification of two companies is more like a merger, in the sense of being the coming together of roughly equal-sized firms on roughly equal terms, in which the shareholders remain as joint owners and both teams of executives share the managerial duties, or whether the act of union is closer to what some people would say is an acquisition or takeover – a purchase of one firm by another with the associated implication of financial and managerial domination. In reality it is often impossible to classify the relationships within the combined entity as a merger or a takeover. The literature is full of cases of so-called mergers of equals that turn out to be a takeover of managerial control by one set of managers at the expense of the other.[2] Jürgen Schrempp, the chairman of DaimlerChrysler, shocked the financial world with his honesty on this point. At the time of the union of Chrysler with Daimler Benz in 1998 it was described as a merger of equals. However, in 2000 Schrempp said, 'The structure we have now with Chrysler [as a standalone division] was always the structure I wanted. We had to go a roundabout way but it had to be done for psychological reasons. If I had gone and said Chrysler would be a division, everybody on their side would have said: "There is no way we'll do a deal."'[3] Jack Welch, the well-respected industrialist, supports Schrempp: 'This was a buy-out of Chrysler by Daimler. Trying to run it as a merger of equals creates all kinds of problems ... There is no such thing as a merger of equals ... There has to be one way forward and clear rules.'[4] Lord Browne, chief executive of BP, at the time of the mergers with Amoco and Arco, also has strong views on this subject: 'There is a big cultural problem with mergers of equals ... in the end there has to be a controlling strain from the two companies.'[5] This book will use the terms merger, acquisition and takeover interchangeably.

Types of merger

Mergers have been classified into three categories: horizontal, vertical and conglomerate.

Horizontal

In a horizontal merger two companies engaged in similar lines of activity are combined. Recent examples include the merger of Lloyds TSB and HBOS and Wm Morrison and Safeway. One of the motives advanced for horizontal mergers is that economies of scale can be achieved. But not all horizontal mergers demonstrate such gains. Another major motive is the enhancement of market power resulting from the reduction in competition. Horizontal mergers often attract the attention of government competition (anti-trust) agencies such as the Office of Fair Trading and the Competition Commission in the UK.

Vertical

Vertical mergers occur when firms from different stages of the production chain amalgamate. So, for instance, if a manufacturer of footwear merges with a retailer of shoes this would be a (downstream) vertical merger. If the manufacturer then bought a leather producer (an upstream vertical merger) there would be an even greater degree of vertical integration. The major players in the oil industry tend to be highly vertically integrated. They have exploration subsidiaries, drilling and production companies, refineries, distribution companies and petrol stations. Vertical integration often has the attraction of increased certainty of supply or market outlet. It also reduces costs of search, contracting, payment collection, advertising, communication and co-ordination of production. An increase in market power may also be a motivation: this is discussed later.

Conglomerate

A conglomerate merger is the combining of two firms which operate in unrelated business areas. For example, General Electric is a conglomerate buying companies from a wide range of industries, e.g. financial services, avionics and medical imaging. Some conglomerate mergers are motivated by risk reduction through diversification; some by the opportunity for cost reduction and improved efficiency. Others have more complex driving motivations – many of which will be discussed later.

Merger statistics

Figure 11.1 shows that merger activity has occurred in waves, with peaks in the early 1970s, late 1980s, late 1990s and 2007. The vast majority (over 95 percent) of these mergers were agreed ('friendly'), rather than opposed by the target (acquired) firm's management ('hostile'). Only a small, but often noisy, fraction enter into a bid battle stage.

The phenomenon of merger activity rising to very high levels for a few years and then subsiding to more pedestrian levels for a long time has been observed in many countries. Peaks in merger activity tend to occur at peaks in economic activity following a sustained period of growth, which is usually accompanied by stock market exuberance, e.g. 1929, 1971–72, 1988–89 and 2000. In the USA, for example, there were bursts of activity in the following periods: 1890–1905 (creating monopoly power from oligopolistic and near-competitive industries); 1920–1929 (oligopoly power sought); 1965–1971 (rapid growth, many conglomerates, shift towards greater diversification); 1986–1990 (restructuring to core businesses – 'focus strategy' – away from conglomerate structures; assistance from leveraged finance); and 1997–2000 (focus strategy on core extraordinary resources, dotcom, telecoms and media mania, globalisation, deregulation of some industries, consolidation of fragmented industries).

Europe also experienced high merger activity in the early 1970s, late 1980s and late 1990s, as globalisation assisted the synchronisation of booms and busts. Globalisation is also demonstrated by the increasing proportion of mergers that are cross-border combinations. The UK has a particularly high level of merger activity compared with the rest of Europe. This is assisted by the UK governments' more *laissez-faire* attitude towards mergers and the greater influence of the stock market in society – similar to many other 'Anglo Saxon' economies.

Merger waves may occur because a merger mania strikes a particular industry (e.g. new technology changes the most efficient scale). This merger mania may be a managerial behavioural phenomenon (e.g. managers see a number of mergers in their industry and so rush to merge before they are acquired). Alternatively, managers and investors become very optimistic about the value-generating potential of mergers during periods of economic and stock market growth. Those that have experienced success in the recent past continue to expand via acquisition, believing the power of their talent to improve target companies – much of this is hubris, as revealed in the economic downturn that follows boom. Another reason for merger waves is that suppliers of finance suffer bouts of irrational exuberance in economic and market booms too, supplying plentiful cheap finance and going easy on things like debt covenants, financial gearing and interest cover ratios.

Figure 11.1(b) shows that in the late 1990s shares became a more important means of payment as the stock market boomed. In the first part of the 1980s merger boom (1985–89) ordinary shares tended to be the preferred method of payment. However, for most years cash is the dominant form of consideration.

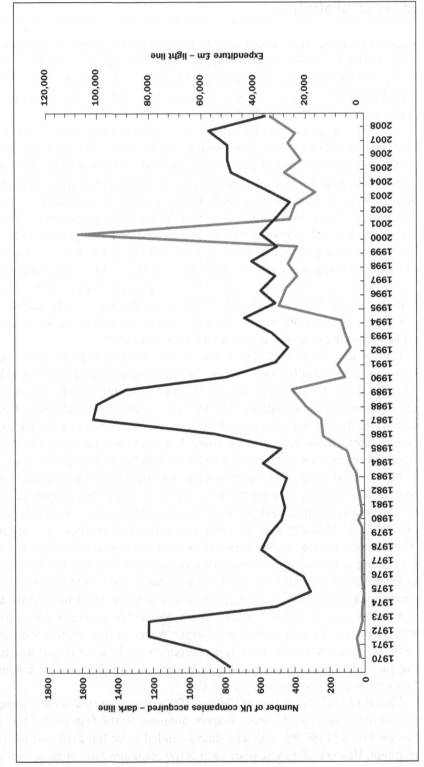

FIGURE 11.1 (continued)

(b) UK mergers – method of payment, 1970–2008

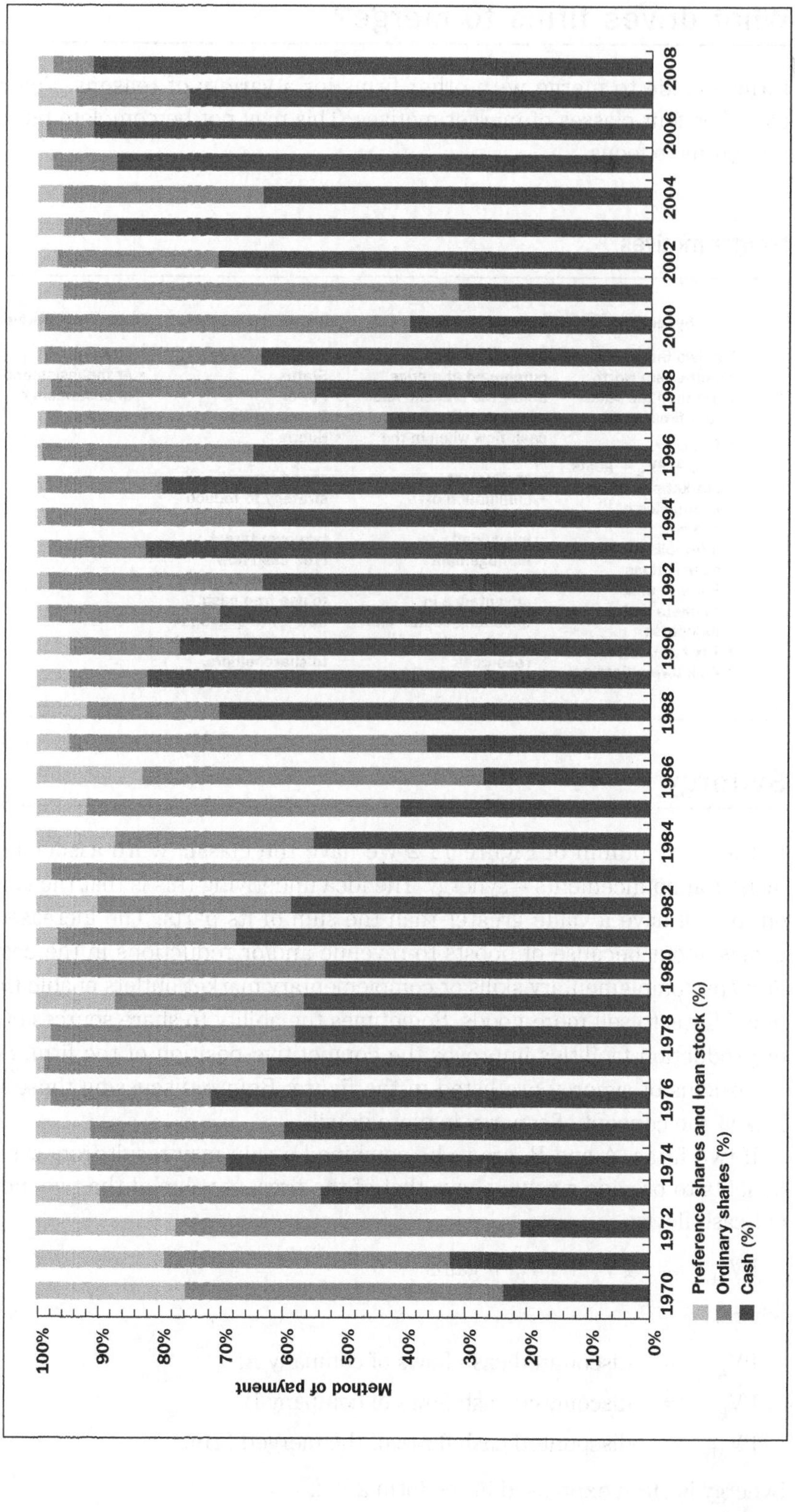

What drives firms to merge?

Firms decide to merge with other firms for a variety of reasons. Figure 11.2 identifies four classes of merger motives. This may not be complete but at least it helps us to focus.

FIGURE 11.2
Merger motives

Synergy	Superior management	Managerial motives	Third party motives
The two firms together are worth more than the value of the firms apart	Target can be purchased at a price below the present value of the target's future cash flow when in the hands of new management.	• Empire building • Status • Power • Remuneration • Hubris • Survival: speedy growth strategy to reduce probability of being takeover target • Free cash flow: management prefer to use free cash flow for acquisitions rather than return it to shareholders.	• Advisers. • At the insistence of customers or suppliers.
• $PV_{AB} =$ $PV_A + PV_B +$ gains • Market power • Economies of scale • Internalisation of transactions • Entry to new markets and industries • Tax advantages • Risk diversification.	• Elimination of inefficient and misguided management • Conglomerate's advantages in allocating capital and in using extraordinary resources. • Under-valued shares.		

Synergy

In the first column of Figure 11.2 we have the classic word associated with merger announcements – synergy. The idea underlying this is that the combined entity will have a value greater than the sum of its parts. The increased value comes about because of boosts to revenue and/or reductions in the cost base. Perhaps complementary skills or complementary market outlets enable the combined firms to sell more goods. Sometimes the ability to share sources of supply or production facilities improves the competitive position of the firm. Some of the origins of synergy are listed in the figure. Before discussing these we will look at the concept of synergy in more detail.

If two firms, A and B, are to be combined a gain may result from synergistic benefits to provide a value above that of the present value of the two independent cash flows:

$$PV_{AB} = PV_A + PV_B + \text{gains}$$

where:

PV_A = discounted cash flows of company A;

PV_B = discounted cash flows of company B;

PV_{AB} = discounted cash flows of the merged firm.

Synergy is often expressed in the form $2 + 2 = 5$.

Value is created from a merger when the gain is greater than the transaction costs. These usually comprise advisers' fees, underwriters' fees, legal and accounting costs, stock exchange fees, public relations bills and so on. So if we assume that A and B as separate entities have present values of £20m and £10m respectively, the transaction costs total £2m and the value of the merged firms is £40m (£42m before paying transaction costs), then the net (after costs) gain from merger is £10m:

$$£40m = £20m + £10m + \text{gain}$$

But who is going to receive this extra value? The incremental value may be available for the acquirer or the target, or be split between the two. If company A is the acquirer, it might pay a price for B which is equal to the PV of B's cash flows (£10m), in which case all of the gain from the merger will accrue to A. However, this is highly unlikely. Usually an acquiring firm has to pay a price significantly above the pre-bid value of the target company to gain control – this is called the acquisition premium, bid premium or control premium.

If it is assumed that before the bid B was valued correctly on the basis of its expected future cash flows to shareholders then the bid premium represents the transferring of some of the gains to be derived from the created synergy. For example, if A paid £15m for B (and absorbed the £2m of costs) then B's shareholders receive £5m of the gain. If A has to pay £20m to acquire B then A receives no gain.

Kraft expected to make large synergistic savings and revenue gains by its merger with Cadbury (*see* Exhibit 11.1).

Also, note another possibility known as the 'winner's curse' – the acquirer pays a price higher than the combined present value of the target and the potential gain. The winner's curse is illustrated by a number of examples mentioned in the article by John Plender (*see* Exhibit 11.2).

Market power

One of the most important forces driving mergers is the attempt to increase market power. This is the ability to exercise some control over the price of the product. It can be achieved through either (a) monopoly, oligopoly or dominant producer positions, etc., or (b) collusion or de facto cooperation (no formal agreement but signals are sent to competitors to avoid price competition).

If a firm has a large share of a market it often has some degree of control over price. It may be able to push up the price of goods sold because customers have few alternative sources of supply. Even if the firm does not control the entire market, a reduction in the number of participating firms to a handful makes collusion easier. Whether openly or not, the firms in a concentrated market may agree among themselves to charge customers higher prices and not to undercut each other. The regulatory authorities are watching out for such socially damaging activities and have fined a number of firms for such practices, for example in the cement, vitamins and chemicals industries.

Kraft/Cadbury

The LEX column of the *Financial Times*

Putting Kraft Foods and Cadbury together makes a mouth-watering confection. But Kraft will have to make its proposal sweeter still to take the candy; its 745p-a-share approach, rejected by Cadbury and already overtaken by the market, is a mere starting point. Rivals could also launch a grab.

A tie-up would tick several strategic boxes. Cadbury brings emerging-market strength that Kraft has long lacked, thanks to its British Commonwealth heritage and 2003 acquisition of Adams, a gum business big in Latin America. The combined group would be a significant force in Brazil, Russia and India. Elsewhere, joining Kraft's clout with grocers, such as Wal-Mart, to Cadbury's mastery of 'instant consumption' outlets

– convenience stores and newsagents – should pump up the top line. Estimated cost synergies of $625m look achievable; taxed and capitalised, they are worth some $4.4bn. That alone covers Kraft's 31 per cent premium.

Yet Kraft, a food conglomerate struggling to grow, needs the deal more than Cadbury. Kraft says absorbing Cadbury would increase its revenue growth target by a percentage point to 5 per cent, and earnings per share by two percentage points – though Cadbury is only a quarter its size. But Kraft is offering an enterprise value of only 13 times 2009 earnings before interest, tax, depreciation and amortisation, below recent big food industry deals. ...

EXHIBIT 11.1

Source: *Financial Times* 8 September 2009, p. 16.

Market power is a motivator in vertical as well as horizontal mergers. Downstream mergers are often formed in order to ensure a market for the acquirer's product and to shut out competing firms. Upstream mergers often lead to the raising or creating of barriers to entry or are designed to place competitors at a cost disadvantage.

Even conglomerate mergers can enhance market power. For example, a conglomerate may force suppliers to buy products from its different divisions under the threat that it will stop buying from them if they do not comply. It can also support each division in turn as it engages in predatory pricing designed to eliminate competitors. Or it may insist that customers buy products from one division if they want products from another.

According to the European Commission, General Electric, in trying to merge with Honeywell, was attempting to put competitors at a disadvantage. In the end the Competition Commissioner blocked the bid, much to the annoyance of GE and US politicians, including George W. Bush – *see* Exhibit 11.3.

A winner's curse that haunts the banking behemoths

John Plender

As governments across the world roll out their plans to re-regulate the financial system, one aspect of the financial debacle receives far too little attention. This is the speed with which great institutions of national importance can be destroyed by ill-judged takovers.

The phrase 'winner's curse' barely does justice to the plight of Bank of America after its takeover of Merrill Lynch. So, too, with Royal Bank of Scotland's acquisition of ABN Amro; and even more so with Lloyds TSB, where the disastrous purchase of HBOS came after years of prudent behaviour and pedestrian performance.

This is not, of course, a phenomenon that occurs exclusively in the financial world, although the systemic consequences there are often worse because banks are highly leveraged. In the previous cycle, two great pillars of the British industrial establishment, Marconi and Imperial Chemical Industries, reduced themselves to shadows of their former selves with injudicious, badly financed takeovers. At much the same time in the dotcom bubble, Time Warner saw multibillion value destruction as a consequence of the merger with AOL.

A recurring feature of such disasters is that they are often associated with an overly dominant chief executive. Because of the age-old problem of information asymmetry, it is always difficult for non-executive directors to check and balance a determined chief executive. When the chief executive is in charge of a complex international financial institution, it is even harder, especially where he has stocked the board with people who lack experience in high finance and cannot understand the financial plumbing.

If it is difficult for non-executives, it is even more so for shareholders who are at one remove from the board. Keith Skeoch of Standard Life, who chairs the UK's Institutional Shareholders Committee, says the shareholder agenda needs to be robust on these issues. Yet it is a measure of how difficult it is for shareholders to restrain a dominant chief executive that at RBS most institutions voted in favour of the ABN Amro deal in spite of the fact that the banking crisis provided an excuse to retreat or renegotiate. In the case of Marconi, the institutions notoriously egged on the management in carrying out the risky North American cash acquisitions that wrecked the company.

Did banks' risk committees highlight the dangers of rushed acquisitions and inadequate due diligence? Maybe Sir David Walker's review of the corporate governance of financial institutions, which will make its first pronouncements this week, will cast light on this. But not all banks had risk committees. And one of the problems of these bodies is that they tend to be dominated by accountants who produce splendid matrices of all manner of risks, neatly categorised into hierarchies and pigeonholes.

The danger here is that common sense discussion of the obvious can give way to detailed technical discussion that is remote from the real threats. How many bank risk or audit committees asked simple questions on what had happened to leverage and whether the marked increase in leverage over the past decade posed a serious threat? Another simple, obvious question relates to banks' capacity for collective memory loss. In cycle after cycle, real estate has provided an easy but lethal opportunity for banks to expand loan books. For all the complexity of the current crisis, it remains substantially rooted in real estate. And while the issues to do with toxic paper continue to fester, we are now reaching the point where bad debts in conventional residential and commercial property are exacerbating an already dangerous situation.

What needs to be done to prevent mergers and acquisitions wreaking further damage? First, we need to recognise that it is a very peculiar feature of the so-called Anglo-American model of capitalism that it puts so much resource into an activity that countless academic studies have shown to be generally value destroying for the acquiring shareholders. The evidence seems to suggest that the net effect of M&A is wealth distribution from buyer to seller rather than the efficient capital allocation that its proponents claim. Yet as Lord Myners, City minister, points out, the thrust of the UK Takeover Code is overwhelmingly directed at protecting shareholders in the target company, not those in the acquirer.

In banking, the economic costs of M&A can be even greater because, as currently, it can increase concentration and produce banks that are too big to fail or, as in the combined Travelers-Citicorp, too big to be managed effectively.

Part of the solution lies in robust competition policy. Yet non-executive directors and institutional shareholders also need to raise their game. A key to doing that is to recognise M&A for what it is: a very high risk business activity. That is not to say that good takeovers are a chimera. Sir Fred Goodwin did, after all, do a fine job with the acquisition of NatWest. But that led to hubris, which takes us back to where we started.

EXHIBIT 11.2

Source: *Financial Times* 13 July 2009, p. 16.

GE to face call for Gecas separation

Deborah Hargreaves

The European Commission is expected to press General Electric to separate the accounts and management of Gecas, its aircraft leasing arm, as a condition of giving the go-head to its $41bn (£29bn) deal to buy Honeywell.

The Commission is also believed to be looking for some divestment of part of Honeywell's avionics business and its regional jet engines business . . .

Gecas offers aircraft financing, leasing and fleet management. Brussels has been concerned about GE's ability to bundle products when offering equipment to airlines – for example, by offering a cheaper engine if an airline agrees to take Honeywell avionics – and its use of Gecas' market power to kit out airlines with GE products.

The Commission's statement of objections to the deal says: 'Gecas is therefore used by GE to influence the outcome of airlines' airframe purchasing decisions and act as a promoter of GE-powered airframes to the detriment of GE's engine manufacturer competitors and eventually results, through the use of its disproportionate power, in excluding competing engine sales.'

Gecas will specify the use of a GE engine in aircraft it wants to buy. Brussels is worried that the leasing arm will do the same for Honeywell's avionics and other aircraft equipment.

EXHIBIT 11.3

Source: *Financial Times* 6 June 2001

Economies of scale

An important contributor to synergy is the ability to exploit economies of scale. Larger size often leads to lower cost per unit of output (or may lead to increased sales efficiency). Rationalising and consolidating manufacturing capacity at fewer, larger sites can lead to economies of production utilising larger machines. Economies in marketing can arise through the use of common distribution channels or joint advertising. There are also economies in administration, research and development and purchasing.

Even with mergers of the conglomerate type managers claim achievable economies of scale. They identify savings from the sharing of central services such as administrative activities, advertising and accounting. Also the development of executives might be better at a large firm with a structured programme of training and access to a wider range of knowledgeable and experienced colleagues. Financial economies, such as being able to raise funds more cheaply in bulk, are also alluded to.

Many businesses possess assets such as buildings, machinery or people's skills that are not used to their full limits. For example, banks and building societies own high street sites. In most cases neither the buildings nor the employees are being used as intensively as they could be. Hence we have one of the motivating forces behind bank and building society mergers. Once a merger is completed, a number of branches can be closed, to leave one rather than two in a particular location. Thus the customer flow to the remaining branch will be, say, doubled, with the consequent saving on property and labour costs.

Another synergistic reason for financial service industry mergers is the ability to market successful products developed by one firm to the customers of the other. Economies of scope arise when costs are spread over an inceased range of products or services (or sales benefit from offering an increased range of products). For example, the unit delivery costs (trucks, etc.) of tinned soup can be reduced if the truck also carries baked beans. On the sales side, Kraft wanted to take over Cadbury partly in order to gain access to its valuable distribution channels in many countries.Other brands can be pushed through the sales, marketing and distribution networks.

Case study 11.1 on the oil industry demonstrates the importance of even greater size in an industry that already had giants.

Internalisation of transactions

By bringing together two firms at different stages of the production chain an acquirer may achieve more efficient co-ordination of the different levels. The focus here is on the costs of communication, the costs of bargaining, the costs of monitoring contract compliance and the costs of contract enforcement. Vertical integration reduces the uncertainty of supply or the prospect of finding an outlet. It also avoids the problems of having to deal with a supplier or customer in a strong bargaining position. Naturally, the savings have to be compared with the extra costs that may be generated because of the loss of competition

Economies of scale in oil

Around the turn of the millennium there was a great deal of merger activity in the oil industry. Exxon and Mobil merged; as did Chevron and Texaco; Total, Fina and Elf; and B.P., Amoco and Arco, to name a few. The financial markets encouraged the trend, seeing the benefits from economies of scale. Greater size allows the possibility of cutting recurring costs, particularly in overlapping infrastructure. It also means access to cheaper capital. However, the most important advantage it gives is the ability to participate in the difficult game of twenty-first-century exploration and production. The easily accessible oil of the world has long been tapped. Today's oil companies have to search in awkward places like the waters off West Africa and China. The capital costs are enormous and risks are high. Only large companies can put up the required money and absorb the risk of a series of failed explorations. In addition, bigger oil companies have more political clout, which was particularly the case in George W. Bush's Washington, but also in developing country capitals around the world.

between suppliers – managers of units may become complacent and inefficient because they are assured of a buyer for their output.

Across Europe the heavy building materials industry is vertically integrated. The manufacturers of cement also own ready-mix concrete divisions and/or aggregates businesses. 'Cement represents the main cost item in the production of ready mix concrete, so there are powerful incentives for ready mix suppliers to secure access to supplies of cement to add to their existing supplies of aggregates.'[6]

Entry to new markets and industries

If a firm has chosen to enter a particular market but lacks the right know-how, the quickest way of establishing itself may be through the purchase of an existing player in that product or geographical market. To grow into the market organically, that is, by developing the required skills and market strength through internal efforts alone, may mean that the firm, for many years, will not have the necessary critical size to become an effective competitor. During the growth period losses may well be incurred. Furthermore, creating a new participant in a market may generate over-supply and excessive competition, producing the danger of a price war and thus eliminating profits. An example of a market-entry type of merger is Cadbury Schweppes' takeover of Adams in the USA. As a result Cadbury quickly established a position in the gum (Stimorol/Trident/Dentyne chewing gum) and cough sweet (Hall's) markets and captured an effective distribution operation without creating additional capacity.

Many small firms are acquired by large ones because they possess particular technical skills. The small firm may have a unique product developed through the genius of a small team of enthusiasts, but the team may lack the interest and the skills to produce the product on a large scale, or to market it effectively. The purchaser might be aware that its present range of products are facing a declining market or are rapidly becoming obsolescent. It sees the chance of applying its general managerial skills and experience to a cutting-edge technology through a deal with the technologically literate enthusiasts. Thus the two firms are worth more together than apart because each gains something it does not already have. Many biotechnology companies have been bought by pharmaceutical giants for this reason – *see* Exhibit 11.4.

Another reason for acquiring a company at the forefront of technology might

Pharma spending spree could swallow biotech

Lina Saigol and Andrew Jack

Some of the world's biggest pharmaceuticals companies are likely to embark on a buying spree as imminent patent expiries combine with a greater willingness from biotechs to sell out.

The leading pharma companies are seeking to compensate for an estimated drop of more than $100bn in sales over the next five years on blockbusters such as Pfizer's Lipitor, Wyeth's Effexor, Merck's Singulair and Eli Lilly's Zyprexa.

'There are multi-layers of M&A going on at the moment as the big pharma companies look for ways in which to get their share prices up – and these companies are deploying a wider range of strategies to do so than ever before,' said Richard Girling, global co-head of healthcare at Merrill Lynch.

Several chief executives, including Andrew Witty at GlaxoSmithKline and Bernard Poussot at Wyeth, have already said they are suspending share buybacks

to take advantage of the dislocation in the markets to acquire assets.

They have been helped in the short term by the relative outperformance of pharma stocks, easing pressure from investors to return cash. More importantly, with valuations down more than 30 per cent, it looks more attractive to acquire biotechs rather than negotiate complex licensing deals.

About half of European biotech companies could face severe financial distress during the next two years, forcing many into takeovers to survive. Those that could be open to deals include Zeltia, Allergy Therapeutics, Vernalis and GPC Biotech.

A second important category of acquisitions will be in niches. GlaxoSmithKline and Sanofi-Aventis are among those compaies that look set to expand their interest in the purchase of generic drug companies ...

EXHIBIT 11.4

Source: *Financial Times* 6 January 2009, p. 22.

be to apply the talent, knowledge and techniques to the parent company's existing and future product lines to give them a competitive edge. Many Asian companies have acquired companies in the west for this reason.

Tax advantages

In some countries, if a firm makes a loss in a particular year, this can be used to reduce taxable profit in a future year. More significantly, for this discussion about mergers, not only can past losses be offset against current profits within one firm in one line of business, past losses of an acquired subsidiary can be used to reduce present profits of the parent company and thus lower tax bills. There is an incentive to buy firms which have accumulated tax losses.

In the UK the rules are more strict. The losses incurred by the acquired firm before it becomes part of the group cannot be offset against the profits of another member of the group. The losses can only be set against the future profits of the acquired company. Also that company has to continue operating in the same line of business.

Risk diversification

One of the primary reasons advanced for conglomerate mergers is that the overall income stream of the holding company will be less volatile if the cash flows come from a wide variety of products and markets. At first glance the pooling of unrelated income streams would seem to improve the position of shareholders. They obtain a reduction in risk without a decrease in return.

The problem with this argument is that investors can obtain the same risk reduction in an easier and cheaper way. They could simply buy a range of shares in the independent separately quoted firms. In addition, it is said that conglomerates lack focus – with managerial attention and resources being dissipated.

A justification on more solid theoretical grounds runs as follows. A greater stability of earnings will appeal to lenders, thus encouraging lower interest rates (and higher levels of debt). Because of the reduced earnings volatility there is less likelihood of the firm producing negative returns and so it should avoid defaulting on interest or principal payments. The other group that may benefit from diversification is individuals who have most of their income eggs in one basket – that is, the directors and other employees.

Superior management

The first column of Figure 11.2 (see p. 288) deals with the potential gains available through the combining of two firms' trading operations. The second column shows benefits which might be available to an acquiring company which has a management team with superior ability, either at running a target's operations, or at identifying undervalued firms which can be bought at bargain prices.

Inefficient management

If the management of Firm X is more efficient than the management of Firm Y then a gain could be produced by a merger if X's management is dominant after the unification. Inefficient management may be able to survive in the short run but eventually the owners will attempt to remove it by, say, dismissing the senior directors and management team through a boardroom coup. Alternatively the shareholders might invite other management teams to make a bid for the firm, or simply accept an offer from another firm that is looking for an outlet for its perceived surplus managerial talent.

A variation on the above theme is where the target firm does have talented management but they are directing their efforts in their own interests and not in the interests of shareholders. In this case the takeover threat can serve as a control mechanism limiting the degree of divergence from shareholder wealth maximisation.

A conglomerate's superior efficiency in allocating capital and in using an extraordinary resource

In less well developed markets, where banking, stock markets, accounting and legal infrastructures are weak, investors are wary of providing capital to young companies for growth. Conglomerates can often step in here as they are able to allocate capital to businesses better than if they were individual businesses seeking capital in the external markets (banks, bonds and equity). Internal assessment and monitoring will suffer from fewer information asymmetry problems, leading to a lower cost of capital than if external finance is used. Also internal finance might be able to take a longer term perspective.

Some companies possess an extraordinary resource that allows them to outperform competitors. Often, this resource is under-utilised. By merging with another company the resource can be shared with little additional cost to the parent. For example, film studios buy theme parks and allow the parks to make use of their film characters to develop rides and in marketing. Or a brand is extended into another product line through merger, e.g. Virgin moves into TV.

Undervalued shares

Many people believe that stock markets occasionally underestimate the true value of a share. It may well be that the potential target firm is being operated in the most efficient manner possible and productivity could not be raised even if the most able managerial team in the world took over. Such a firm might be valued low by the stock market because the management are not very aware of the importance of a good stock market image. Perhaps they provide little information beyond the statutory minimum and in this way engender suspicion and uncertainty. Investors hate uncertainty and will tend to avoid such a firm. On the other hand, the acquiring firm might be very conscious of its stock market image and put considerable effort into cultivating good relationships with the investment community.

In many of these situations the acquiring firm has knowledge which goes beyond that which is available to the general public. It may be intimately acquainted with the product markets, or the technology, of the target firm and so can value the target more accurately than most investors. Or it may simply be that the acquirer puts more resources into information searching than anyone else. Alternatively they may be insiders, using private information, and may buy shares illegally.

Managerial motives

The reasons for merger described in this section are often just as rational as the ones which have gone before, except, this time, the rational objective may not be shareholder wealth maximization.

One group which seems to do well out of merger activity is the management team of the acquiring firm. When all the dust has settled after a merger they end up controlling a larger enterprise. And, of course, having responsibility for a larger business means that the managers *have* to be paid a lot more money. Not only must they have higher monthly pay to induce them to give of their best, they must also have enhanced pension contributions and myriad perks. Being in charge of a larger business and receiving a higher salary also brings increased status. Some feel more successful and important, and the people they rub shoulders with tend to be in a more influential class.

As if these incentives to grow rapidly through mergers were not enough, some people simply enjoy putting together an empire – creating something grand and imposing gives a sense of achievement and satisfaction. To have control over ever-larger numbers of individuals appeals to basic instincts: some measure their social position and their stature by counting the number of employees under them. Warren Buffett comments, 'The acquisition problem is often compounded by a biological bias: many CEO's attain their positions in part because they possess an abundance of animal spirits and ego. If an executive is heavily endowed with these qualities – which, it should be acknowledged, sometimes have their advantages – they won't disappear when he reaches the top. When such a CEO is encouraged by his advisors to make deals, he responds much as would a teenage boy who is encouraged by his father to have a normal sex life. It's not a push he needs.'[7]

John Kay points out that many managers enjoy the excitement of the merger process itself:

> For the modern manager, only acquisition reproduces the thrill of the chase, the adventures of military strategy. There is the buzz that comes from the late-night meetings in merchant banks, the morning conference calls with advisers to plan your strategy. Nothing else puts your picture and your pronouncements on the front page, nothing else offers so easy a way to expand your empire and emphasise your role.[8]

These first four managerial motives for merger – empire building, status, power and remuneration – can be powerful forces impelling takeover activity. But, of course, they are rarely expressed openly, and certainly not shouted about during a takeover battle.

Hubris

The fifth reason, hubris, is also very important in explaining merger activity. It may help particularly to explain why mergers tend to occur in greatest numbers when the economy and companies generally have had a few good years of growth, and management are feeling rather pleased with themselves.

Richard Roll in 1986 spelt out his hubris hypothesis for merger activity. Hubris means over-weaning self-confidence, or less kindly, arrogance. Managers commit errors of over-optimism in evaluating merger opportunities due to excessive pride or faith in their own abilities. The suggestion is that some acquirers do not learn from their mistakes and may be convinced that they can see an undervalued firm when others cannot. They may also think that they have the talent, experience and entrepreneurial flair to shake up a business and generate improved profit performance (*see* Exhibit 11.5).

On toads and princesses

Warren Buffett

Many managements apparently were overexposed in impressionable childhood years to the story in which the imprisoned handsome prince is released from the toad's body by a kiss from the beautiful princess. Consequently, they are certain that the managerial kiss will do wonders for the profitability of Company T(arget). Such optimism is essential. Absent that rosy view, why else should the shareholders of Company A(cquisitor) want to own an interest in T at the 2X takeover cost rather than at the X market price they would pay if they made direct purchases on their own? In other words, investors can always buy toads at the going price for toads. If investors instead bankroll princesses who wish to pay double for the right to kiss a toad, those kisses had better pack some real dynamite. We've observed many kisses, but very few miracles. Nevertheless, many managerial princesses remain serenely confident about the future potency of their kisses – even after their corporate backyards are knee-deep in unresponsive toads.

EXHIBIT 11.5

Source: Berkshire Hathaway, Annual Report, 1981. Reprinted by kind permission of Warren Buffett. © Warren Buffett.

Note that the hubris hypothesis does not require the conscious pursuit of self-interest by managers. They may have worthy intentions but can make mistakes in judgement.

Survival

It has been noticed by both casual observers and empiricists that mergers tend to take place with a large acquirer and a smaller target. Potential target managements may come to believe that the best way to avoid being taken over, and then sacked or dominated, is to grow large themselves, and to do so quickly. Mergers can have a self-reinforcing mechanism or positive feedback loop – the more mergers there are, the more vulnerable management feel and the more they are inclined to carry out mergers. Firms may merge for the survival of the management team and not primarily for the benefit of shareholders.

Free cash flow

Free cash flow is defined as cash flow in excess of the amount needed to fund all projects that have positive NPVs. In theory, firms should retain money within the firm to invest in any project which will produce a return greater than the investors' opportunity cost of capital. Any cash flow surplus to this should be returned to shareholders (*see* Chapter 14).

However Jensen (1986) suggests that managers are not always keen on simply handing back the cash which is under their control. This would reduce their power. Also, if they needed to raise more funds the capital markets will require justification concerning the use of such money. So instead of giving shareholders free cash flow the managers use it to buy other firms. Peter Lynch is more blunt: '[I] believe in the bladder theory of corporate finance, as propounded by Hugh Liedtke of Pennzoil: The more cash that builds up in the treasury, the greater the pressure to piss it away.'[9]

Third-party motives

Advisers

There are many highly paid individuals who benefit greatly from merger activity. Advisers charge fees to the bidding company to advise on such matters as identifying targets, the rules of the takeover game, regulations, monopoly references, finance, bidding tactics, stock market announcements, and so on. Typical fees are between 0.125 percent and 0.5 percent of the value of the target company for advisory work. Fees for helping to raise finance e.g. underwriting a rights issue, could be 4 percent of the amount raised. Advisers are also appointed to the target firms.

Other groups with a keen eye on the merger market include accountants and lawyers. In the Mittal and Arcelor merger, the investment bankers took away around $100m in fees, much of it for raising €10.8bn of new loans. Exhibit 11.6 gives some impression of the level of fees paid.

There is also the press, ranging from tabloids to specialist publications. Even a cursory examination of them gives the distinct impression that they tend to have a statistical bias of articles which emphasise the positive aspects of mergers. It is difficult to find negative articles, especially at the time of a takeover. They like the excitement of the merger event and rarely follow up with a consid-

Banking fees are facing a backlash

Lina Saigol

Rio Tinto says it ditched the Chinalco deal because everything in the market has changed since February.

One thing that hasn't changed, however, are the M&A and capital markets fees the Anglo-Australian miner is paying its advisers and bookrunners.

Insiders estimate that, including the fees it spent acquiring and financing Alcan, the Canadian aluminium producer in 2007, Rio has clocked up an investment banking bill of close to $1bn.

That's serious money, but do shareholders care? They haven't until now.

When markets are booming, banks can charge what they want for their services and companies are so terrified of not getting the best corporate finance available that they pay up without question.

But at a time when investors are being deprived of dividends as they instruct their boards to watch how they spend every penny, investment banking fees are starting to come under scrutiny.

This year, investors in BHP Billiton grumbled at the $280m costs the miner rang up relating to its failed hostile takeover of Rio Tinto – the bulk of which was tied to an expensive $55bn debt facility never used.

Others have complained about the increase in underwriting fees – with as much as 3 per cent of proceeds from capital raisings going to the banks, compared with 2 per cent during a typical bull market. ...

EXHIBIT 11.6

Source: *Financial Times* 8 June 2009, p. 20.

ered assessment of the outcome. Also the press reports generally portray acquirers as dynamic, forward-looking and entrepreneurial.

It seems reasonable to suppose that professionals engaged in the merger market might try to encourage or cajole firms to contemplate a merger and thus generate turnover in the market. Some provide reports on potential targets to try and tempt prospective clients into becoming acquirers.

Of course, the author would never suggest that such esteemed and dignified organisations would ever stoop to promote mergers for the sake of increasing fee levels alone. You may think that, but I could not possibly comment.

Suppliers and customers

In 2005 Rolls Royce, the aircraft engine maker, called for consolidation of the aerospace parts sector. The company announced it would like to reduce the number of suppliers to as few as 40 companies, including 25 'first tier' suppliers (compared with 70 previously). This led to mergers amongst its suppliers. When Bosch merged with American Allied Signal and Lucas with Varity in the late 1990s there was pressure from the customers – the car producers. They were intent on reducing the number of car-parts suppliers and put increased responsibility on the few remaining suppliers. Instead of buying in small mechanical parts from dozens of suppliers and assembling them themselves into, say, a braking system, the assemblers wanted to buy the complete unit. To provide a high level of service Bosch, which is skilled in electronics, needed to team up with Allied Signal for its hydraulics expertise. Similarly Lucas, which specializes in mechanical aspects of braking, needed Varity's electronic know-how. Ford announced that it was intent on reducing its 1,600 suppliers to about 200 and is 'even acting as marriage broker to encourage smaller suppliers to hitch-up with bigger, first-tier suppliers'.[10] These suppliers would then be world players with the requisite financial, technical and managerial muscle.

An example of suppliers promoting mergers is at the other end of the car production chain. Motor dealers in the UK in the late 1990s were sent a clear message from the manufacturers that a higher degree of professionalism and service back-up is required. This prompted a flurry of merger activity as the franchisees sought to meet the new standards.

Figure 11.2 provided a long list of potential merger motives (*see* p. 288). This list is by no means complete. Examining the reasons for merger is far from straightforward. There is a great deal of complexity, and in any one takeover, perhaps half a dozen or more of the motives discussed are at play.

Do the shareholders of acquiring firms gain from mergers?

Some of the evidence on the effects of acquisitions on the shareholders of the bidding firm is that in slightly over half of the cases shareholders benefit. However, most studies show that acquiring firms give their shareholders poorer returns on average than firms that are not acquirers. Even studies which show a gain to acquiring shareholders tend to produce very small average gains – *see* Table 11.1.

KPMG sent a report to the Press in November 1999 showing the poor performance of cross-border mergers in terms of shareholder value. They then, embarrassed, tried to retrieve the report before it received publicity. Many commentators said that the evidence, that only 17 percent of cross-border mergers increased shareholder value, would not help KPMG win business assisting firms conducting such mergers.

Much of the recent research has drawn attention to differences in post-acquisition performance of acquirers that are highly rated by investors at the time of the bid ('glamour shares') and the post-acquisition performance of low rated acquirer ('value shares'), e.g. low price earnings ratios or low share price relative to balance sheet net asset value. This over-valuation of glamorous shares seems to be at least a partial explanation for subsequent under-performance. Over time investors reassess the price premium placed on the glamour shares bringing their prices down – whether they are acquirers or not.

TABLE 11.1

Summary of some of the evidence on merger performance from the acquiring shareholders' perspective

Study	Country of evidence	Comment
Meeks (1977)	UK	At least half of the mergers studied showed a considerable decline in profitability compared with industry averages.
Firth (1980)	UK	Relative share price losses are maintained for three years post-merger.
Government Green Paper (1978) (A review of monopolies and mergers policy) (1978)	UK	At least half or more of the mergers studied have proved to be unprofitable.
Ravenscraft and Scherer (1987)	USA	Small but significant decline in profitability on average.
Limmack (1991)	UK	Long-run under-performance by acquirers.
Franks and Harris (1989)	UK and USA	Share returns are poor for acquirers on average for the two years under one measurement technique, but better than the market as a whole when the CAPM is used as a benchmark.
Sudarsanam, Holl and Salami (1996)	UK	Poor return performance relative to the market for high-rated (judged by price to earnings ratio) acquirers taking over low-rated targets. However some firms do well when there is a complementary fit in terms of liquidity, slack and investment opportunities.
Manson, Stark and Thomas (1994)	UK	Cash flow improves after merger, suggesting operating performance is given a boost.
Gregory (1997)	UK	Share return performance is poor relative to the market for up to two years post-merger, particularly for equity-financed bids and single (as opposed to regular) bidders.
Loughran and Vijh (1997)	USA	In the five post-merger years firms that offer shares as payment show negative returns relative to the market. Those that offer cash show positive market-adjusted returns.
Rau and Vermaelen (1998)	USA	Acquirers under-perform post-merger. This is due to over-optimism by investors leading to over-pricing of some acquirers regarded as glamour stocks at the time of the merger.

TABLE 11.1 (continued)

Study	Country of evidence	Comment
Sudarsanam and Mahate (2003)	UK	Generally acquirers under-perform. Cash acquirers generate higher returns than equity payment acquirers. High price to earnings ratio (and low book to market ratio) acquirers do not perform as well as low PER acquirers and low book to market ratio acquirers.
Powell and Stark (2005)	UK	Takeovers result in modest improvements in operating performance of acquirers.
Goergen and Renneboog (2004)	Europe-wide study	On average bidder performance is roughly the same as the market during the four months around the merger announcement date. Bids financed by equity produce better announcement period returns than those financed by cash.
Conn, Cosh, Guest and Hughes (2005)	UK	Quoted companies acquiring UK companies results in poor returns around the announcement date and over the subsequent three years an average (–22 percent). UK acquirers in cross-border mergers of quoted companies are also poor performers. However, private UK (not on stock market) acquirers tend to produce zero post-acquisition returns on average.
Gregory (2005)	UK	Acquirers under-perform the market by 19.9 percent over 60 months. Acquirers with a high level of free cash flow perform better than acquirers with low free cash flow in the five years following merger as measured by total return.
Moeller, Schingemann and Stulz (2005)	USA	On average acquirer shareholders experience a poor return in the few days around acquisition announcement – particularly in 1998–2001 (hi-tech boom period).
Cosh, Guest and Hughes (2006)	UK	The larger the holding of shares in the company by the chief executive, the better the post-merger long-term share returns.

Managing mergers

Many mergers fail to produce shareholder wealth and yet there are companies that pursue a highly successful strategy of expansion through mergers. This section highlights some of the reasons for failure and some of the requirements for success.

The three stages

There are three phases in merger management. It is surprising how often the first and third are neglected while the second is given great amounts of managerial attention. The three stages are:

- preparation
- negotiation and transaction
- integration.

In the preparation stage strategic planning predominates. A sub-set of the strategic thrust of the business might be mergers. Targets need to be searched for and selected with a clear purpose – shareholder wealth maximisation in the long term. There must be a thorough analysis of the potential value to flow from the combination and tremendous effort devoted to the plan of action which will lead to the successful integration of the target. The negotiation and transaction stage has two crucial aspects to it.

- Financial analysis and target evaluation; this evaluation needs to go beyond mere quantitative analysis into fields such as human resources and competitive positioning.
- Negotiating strategy and tactics; it is in the area of negotiating strategy and tactics that the specialist advisers are particularly useful. However the acquiring firm's management must keep a tight rein and remain in charge.

The integration stage is where so many mergers come apart. It is in this stage that the management need to consider the organisational and cultural similarities and differences between the firms. They also need to create a plan of action to obtain the best post-merger integration. The key elements of these stages are shown in Figure 11.3.

Too often the emphasis in managing mergers is firmly on the 'hard' world of identifiable and quantifiable data. Here economics, finance and accounting come to the fore. There is a worrying tendency to see the merger process as a series of logical and mechanical steps, each with an obvious rationale and a clear and describable set of costs and benefits. This approach all but ignores the potential

FIGURE 11.3

The progression of a merger

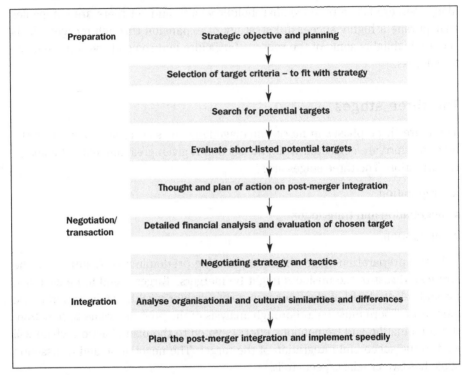

Preparation	Strategic objective and planning
	↓
	Selection of target criteria – to fit with strategy
	↓
	Search for potential targets
	↓
	Evaluate short-listed potential targets
	↓
	Thought and plan of action on post-merger integration
	↓
Negotiation/transaction	Detailed financial analysis and evaluation of chosen target
	↓
	Negotiating strategy and tactics
	↓
Integration	Analyse organisational and cultural similarities and differences
	↓
	Plan the post-merger integration and implement speedily

for problems caused by non-quantifiable elements, for instance, human reactions and interrelationships. Matters such as potential conflict, discord, alienation and disloyalty are given little attention.[11] There is also a failure to make clear that the nature of decision-making in this area relies as much on informed guesses, best estimates and hunches as on cold facts and figures.

The organizational process approach

The organisational process approach takes into account the 'soft' aspects of merger implementation and integration. Here the acquisition process, from initial strategic formulations to final complete integration, is perceived as a complex, multi-faceted programme with the potential for a range of problems arising from the interplay of many different hard and soft factors. Each merger stage requires imaginative and skilled management for the corporate objective to be maximised (Sudarsanam (2003) is an excellent guide).

Problem areas in merger management

We now examine some of the areas where complications may arise.

The strategy, search and screening stage

The main complicating element at the stage of strategy, search and screening is generated by the multitude of perspectives regarding a particular target candidate. Each discipline within a management team may have a narrow competence and focus, so there is potential for a fragmented approach to the evaluation of targets. For example, the marketing team may focus exclusively on the potential for marketing economies and other benefits, the research and development team on the technological aspects and so on. Communication between disparate teams of managers can become complicated and the tendency will be to concentrate the communication effort on those elements which can be translated into the main communicating channel of business: quantifiable features with 'bottom lines' attached. This kind of one-dimensional communication can, however, all too easily fail to convey the full nature of both the opportunities and the problems. The more subtle aspects of the merger are likely to be given inadequate attention.

Another problem arises when senior managers conduct merger analysis in isolation from managers at the operating level. Not only may these 'coal-face' managers be the best informed about the target, its industry and the potential for post-merger integration problems; their commitment is often vital to the integration programme.

There is an obvious need to maximise the information flow effort, both to obtain a balanced, more complete view of the target, and to inform, involve and empower key players in the successful implementation of a merger strategy.

The bidding stage

Once a merger bid is under way a strange psychology often takes over. Managers seem compelled to complete a deal. To walk away would seem like an anticlimax, with vast amounts of money spent on advisers and nothing to show for it. Also they may feel that the investment community will perceive this management as being one unable to implement its avowed strategic plans. It may be seen as 'unexciting' and 'going nowhere' if it has to retreat to concentrate on its original business after all the excitement and promises surrounding a takeover bid.

Managers also often enjoy the thrill of the chase and develop a determination to 'win'. Pay, status and career prospects may hinge on rapid growth. Additionally, acquirers may be impelled to close the deal quickly by the fear of a counter-bid by a competitor, which, if successful, would have an adverse impact on the competitive position of the firm.

Thus mergers can take on a momentum that is difficult to stop. This is often nurtured by financial advisers keen on completing a transaction.

These phenomena may help to explain the heavy emphasis given to the merger transaction to the detriment of the preparation and integration stages. They may also go some way to explaining merger failure – in particular, failure to enhance shareholder value as a result of the winner's curse.

Exhibit 11.7 describes the problems presented to would-be acquiring managers when a merger attempt fails. Knowing the cost of failure may push some managers to over-pay.

A match made in recession

Julie MacIntosh

When Peter Huntsman and his family accepted a $6.5bn takeover offer last summer for the chemicals company they founded, they assumed the deal would have closed by now.

Instead, Huntsman Corporation has spent months soothing investors and employees and convincing customers to stick around while battling buy-out firm Apollo in court over the deal, which finally collapsed late on Sunday.

'Selling a business is not easy, and in today's market it's darn near impossible,' Mr Huntsman, chief executive of the company, says.

As the year's tally of broken mergers and dropped takeover bids grows, dozens of executives who spent months preaching the merits of a proposed deal are now scrambling to re-draft their strategies and explain why their companies will be just fine on their own.

It is an uphill battle both for proposed acquirers and their jilted targets. One chief executive – Jeffrey Rein of the pharmacy chain Walgreens – recently stepped down after an attempted takeover of a rival fell through.

The credit crunch, however, is giving most corporate leaders who might otherwise have lost credibility a chance to lay blame elsewhere. That may soften the blow to their reputations and egos. But it hardly lets them off the hook with shareholders, employees and customers.

Executives at companies ranging from failed acquirers Microsoft, Electronic Arts and BHP Billiton, to abandoned targets Corn Products and Alpha Natural now face the challenge of having to rally their constituencies around a new plan of action.

The difficulty of each company's about-face depends on how important the deal was to their strategy, why it broke apart, and the strength of both companies' next-best options.

For an acquirer, the biggest peril of a broken deal may be having to argue – or pretend – that in spite of publicly lusting after a certain assets for months and claiming it is critical to your success, you do not actually need it. The plight of an abandoned target can be even tougher, however – particularly if customers have started switching away their business, or employees have headed for the exit.

'When the deal falls apart, it's usually the company that was going to be acquired that is hurt more,' says Robert Joffe, a partner at law firm Cravath, Swaine & Moore. 'Usually, they end up looking around frantically for another deal.'

Finding another suitor at an acceptable price is tougher in this market, however, and a drawn-out search for an alternate acquirer could do more damage than good.

'I don't think you can be in a perpetual "for sale" mode,' said Mr Huntsman. 'Who wants to work for a company or buy a company that doesn't have a sure future?'

Many former targets are instead hunkering down to shore up their businesses while, in some cases, trying to dodge low-ball bids from opportunitistic rivals.

After Microsoft dropped its unsolicited bid for Yahoo, for example, Yahoo tried to appease growth-minded investors by forming a partnership with Google before former chief Jerry Yang ultimately resigned.

In some cases, even acquirers feel the need to review their defences. Cleveland-Cliffs, which some shareholders felt should have sold itself rather than trying unsuccessfully to buy coal miner Alpha Natural adopted a 'poison pill' anti-takeover device before the deal was cancelled.

'Any time you get involved in a deal, you basically put yourself in play,' said Michael Quillen, chief executive of Alpha Natural. 'You've told the world what you're thinking about doing, and it is the acquired and acquirer that fall into that category.'

A company's vulnerability ultimately depends on its back-up options. Weak target companies that had been counting on a particular deal for salvation tend to be worst off, executives and their advisers say.

Rescue deals to sell Merrill Lynch, Wachovia, Washington Mutual, and parts of Lehman have grabbed headlines recently. But such situations would also include the broken acquisition of LandAmerica Financial by Fidelity National, which now-bankrupt LandAmerica had hoped would keep it from having to file for Chapter 11 protection.

'If you're selling a company out of weakness and something falls apart, and people knew you had to sell it, that's a totally different scenario than it you're selling it out of strength,' said Mr Huntsman.

Huntsman's biggest challenge, perhaps, was fighting claims by Apollo that Huntsman could become insolvent if its proposed merger was consummated. Solvency concerns also prompted the record-breaking takeover of Canadian telecommunications giant BCE to collapse.

'We're obviously in a very grey area here,' Mr Huntsman said. 'How do you stop a rumour from speading once that rumour is out?'

'We've got some bridges to mend,' he said. 'We've built this business from essentially nothing, and we're fighters and are going to keep building the business.'

Alpha Natural's Mr Quillen said many of his shareholders had believed his company's takeover was not likely to close in the first place, thanks to opposition by a key Cleveland-Cliffs investor, and have already 'moved on'.

He said: 'Hoepfully, we didn't lose a lot of credibility as a management team. In our mind, we've never felt like we had a "for sale" sign out on the front lawn.'

Alpha, like other companies with a cushion of cash, is considering share buybacks, a dividend, or even an acquisition of its own as it retools its strategy. 'But until this thing settles down, it's really a difficult time to make the right decision,' Mr Quillen said. 'It's best being cautious for right now.'

If anything, the past few months may have taught executives that caution is warranted not just after a deal falls apart but far earlier – when the transaction is announced.

Microsoft, for example, highlighted its weaknesses when it professed that it needed Yahoo to compete on the web. Other companies that similarly evangelise about a certain asset, claiming that it will fill a gaping hole in their product or service portfolio, are often left with a heap of questions to answer if the deal disintegrates.

United Technologies, on the other hand, began to stress with increased frequency as its unsuccessful courtship of Diebold dragged on that the deal was not a 'must-have'.

Such restrained messages are not likely to inspire acquisition fervour from shareholders, but they may prevent shareholder uprisings if a deal is scrapped.

'It's very important in designing your message to think about what you're saying about your portfolio, in case the deal were to fall apart,' Cravath's Mr Joffe says. 'It's hard to bridle the enthusiasm of businesspeople. They always want to paint things in the brightest of colours, but sometimes that's self-defeating.'

EXHIBIT 11.7

Source: *Financial Times* 16 December 2008, p. 14.

Expectations of the acquiring firm's operational managers regarding the post-merger integration stage

Clarity and planning are needed to avoid conflict and disappointment among managers. For example, the integration strategy may outline a number of different tasks to be undertaken in the 12–24 months following an acquisition. These may range from disposal of assets and combining operating facilities to new product development and financial reconstruction. Each of these actions may be led by a different manager. Their expectations regarding the speed of implementation and the order in which each of these actions will be taken may be different. A clear and rational resource-planning and allocation mechanism will reduce ambiguity and improve the co-ordination of decision-making.

Aiming for the wrong type of integration

There are different degrees of integration when two firms come together under one leadership. At one extreme is the complete *absorption* (or *integration*) of the target firm and the concomitant fusing of two cultures, two operational procedures and two corporate organizations. At the other, is the *holding company, preservation* or *portfolio approach* where the degree of change of the acquired subsidiary may amount merely to a change in some financial control procedures, but otherwise the target firm's management may continue with their own systems, unintegrated operations and culture.

The complete absorption approach is usually appropriate in situations where production and other operational costs can be reduced through economies of scale and other synergies, or revenues can be enhanced through, say, combined marketing and distribution. The preservation approach is most suitable when it is recognized that the disbenefits of forcing organizations together outweigh the advantages, for example when the products and markets are completely different and the cultures are such that a fusion would cause an explosive clash. These arm's-length mergers are typical of the acquisitive conglomerates. In such mergers general management skills are transferred along with strict financial performance yardsticks and demanding incentive schemes, but little else has changed.

With *symbiosis-based* mergers there is a need to keep a large degree of difference, at least initially, in culture, organization and operating style, but at the same time to permit communication and cross-fertilization of ideas. There may also be a need to transfer skills from one part of the combined organization to another, whether through training and teaching or by personnel reassignment. An example might be where a book publisher acquires an internet service provider; each is engaged in a separate market but there is potential for profitable co-operation in some areas. As well as being aware of the need for mutual assistance, each organisation may be jealous of its own way of doing things and does not want its *esprit de corps* disrupted by excessive integration.

Why do mergers fail to generate value for acquiring shareholders?

A definitive answer as to why mergers fail to generate value for acquiring shareholders cannot be provided, because mergers fail for a host of reasons. However there do appear to be some recurring themes.

The strategy is misguided

History is littered with strategic plans that turned out to be value destroying rather than value creating. Daimler-Benz in combining Mercedes with Fokker and Dasa tried to gain synergies from an integrated transport company, then it tried to become a global car producer by merging with Chrysler. Marconi sold off its defence businesses to concentrate on telecommunication equipment. It spent a fortune buying companies at the forefront of technology only to slam into the hi-tech recession in 2001 – its shares lost 98 percent of their value. At the turn of the millennium, Time Warner thought it needed to pay a very high price to merge with AOL so that it could take a leading part in the convergence of media and information/communication technology. Major British banks went on a shopping spree in 2006–07 only to find that the competition regulators insisted they break themselves up in 2009–10 because they had market shares that were dominating and they endangered the financial system because the were 'too big to fail'.

Over-optimism

Acquiring managers have to cope with uncertainty about the future potential of their acquisition. It is possible for them to be over-optimistic about the market economics, the competitive position and the operating synergies available. They may underestimate the costs associated with the resistance to change they may encounter, or the reaction of competitors. Merger fever, the excitement of the battle, may lead to openness to persuasion that the target is worth more than it really is (*see* Exhibit 11.8). A common mistake is to underestimate the investment required to make a merger work, particularly in terms of managerial time.

Failure of integration management

One problem is the over-rigid adherence to prepared integration plans. Usually plans require dynamic modification in the light of experience and altered circumstances. The integration programme may have been based on incomplete information and may need post-merger adaptation to the new perception of reality.

Common management goals and the engendering of commitment to those goals is essential. The morale of the workforce can be badly damaged at the time of a merger. The natural uncertainty and anxiety has to be handled with understanding, tact, integrity and sympathy. Communication and clarity of purpose are essential as well as rapid implementation of change. Cultural differences need to be tackled with sensitivity and trust established. Lord Browne, of BP, advises quick integration: 'It's very important to mix the cultures early on. If the

On masquerading skimmed milk, lame horses and sexy deals

We believe most deals do damage to the shareholders of the acquiring company. Too often, the words from *HMS Pinafore* apply: 'Things are seldom what they seem, skim milk masquerades as cream.' Specifically, sellers and their representatives invariably present financial projections having more entertainment value than educational value. In the production of rosy scenarios, Wall Street can hold its own against Washington.

In any case, why potential buyers even look at projections prepared by sellers baffles me. Charlie and I never give them a glance, but instead keep in mind the story of the man with an ailing horse. Visiting the vet, he said: 'Can you help me? Sometimes my horse walks just fine and sometimes he limps.' The Vet's reply was pointed: 'No problem – when he's walking fine, sell him.' ...

Talking to *Time Magazine* a few years back, Peter Drucker got to the heart of things: 'I will tell you a secret: Dealmaking beats working. Dealmaking

is exciting and fun, and working is grubby. Running anything is primarily an enormous amount of grubby detail work ... dealmaking is romantic, sexy. That's why you have deals that make no sense.'

... I can't resist repeating a tale told me last year by a corporate executive. The business he grew up in was a fine one, with a long-time record of leadership in its industry. Its main product, however, was distressingly glamorless. So several decades ago, the company hired a management consultant who – naturally – advised diversification, the then-current fad. ('Focus' was not yet in style.) Before long, the company acquired a number of businesses, each after the consulting firm had gone through a long – and expensive – acquisition study. And the outcome? Said the executive sadly, 'When we started we were getting 100% of our earnings from the original business. After ten years, we were getting 150%.'

EXHIBIT 11.8

Source: Letter to shareholders, *Berkshire Hathaway Annual Report 1995*. © Warren Buffett.

entities that existed previously still exist, then there is great reluctance to change anything.' He also suggests using a third party to help select the best managers. Following the merger with Amoco, BP sent 400 top executives to an independent recruitment agency for assessment. 'When you merge with a company, you basically play with half a deck [of cards] because you know all your people, and they know all theirs. So how do you find a way of actually knowing everything about everyone – the answer is get a third party in.'[12]

The absence of senior management commitment to the task of successful integration severely dents the confidence of target and acquired managers.

Coopers & Lybrand, the international business advisers, conducted 'in-depth interviews with senior executives of the UK's top 100 companies covering 50 deals'. Some factors emerged which seem to contribute to failure, and others which are critical for raising the chances of success. These are shown in Figure 11.4.

FIGURE 11.4

Survey on the reasons for merger failure and success – Coopers & Lybrand

The most commonly cited causes of failure include:		The most commonly cited reasons for success include:	
Target management attitudes and cultural differences	85%	Detailed post-acquisition plans and speed of implementation	76%
Little or no post-acquisition planning	80%	A clear purpose for making acquisitions	76%
Lack of knowledge of industry or target	45%	Good cultural fit	59%
Poor management and poor management practices in the acquired company	45%	High degree of management co-operation	47%
Little or no experience of acquisitions	30%	In-depth knowledge of the acquiree and his/her industry	41%

The ten rules listed in Figure 11.5 are NOT recommended for shareholder wealth-oriented managers.

FIGURE 11.5

Arnold's ten golden rules for alienating 'acquired' employees

1. Sack people in an apparently arbitrary fashion.
2. Insist (as crudely as possible) that your culture is superior. Attack long-held beliefs, attitudes, systems, norms, etc.
3. Don't bother to find out the strengths and weaknesses of the new employees.
4. Lie to people – some old favourites are:
   - 'there will not be any redundancies';
   - 'this is a true merger of equals'.
5. Fail to communicate your integration strategy:
   - don't say why the pain and sacrifice is necessary, just impose it;
   - don't provide a sense of purpose.
6. Encourage the best employees to leave by generating as much uncertainty as possible.
7. Create stress, loss of morale and commitment, and a general sense of hopelessness by being indifferent and insensitive to employees' need for information.
8. Make sure you let everyone know that you are superior – after all, you won the merger battle.
9. Sack all the senior executives immediately – their knowledge and experience and the loyalty of their subordinates are cheap.
10. Insist that your senior management appear uninterested in the boring job of nuts-and-bolts integration management. After all, knighthoods and peerages depend upon the next high-public-profile acquisition.

Conclusion

At a minimum this chapter should have made it clear that following a successful merger strategy is much more than simply 'doing the deal'. Preparation and integration are usually of greater significance to the creation of value than the negotiation and transaction stage. And yet, too often, it is towards this middle stage that most attention is directed.

Doubts have been raised about the purity of the motives for mergers but we should restrain ourselves from being too cynical as many mergers do create wealth for shareholders and society. Industries with a shifting technological or market base may need fewer larger firms to supply goods at a lower cost. The savings from superior managerial talent are genuine and to be praised in many cases. Restructuring, the sharing of facilities, talent and ideas, and the savings from the internalization of transactions are all positive outcomes and often outweigh the negative effects.

Like many tools in the armory of management, growth through mergers can be used to create or destroy.

Websites

www.berkshirehathaway.com   Berkshire Hathaway
www.ft.com   Financial Times
www.londonstockexchange.com   London Stock Exchange
www.thetakeoverpanel.org.uk   The Takeover Panel

Notes

1 Rappaport, A. (1998) *Creating Shareholder Value*, p. 138. New York: Free Press.
2 For example, *see* Cartwright, S. and Cooper, C. (1992) *Mergers and Acquisitions: The Human Factor*. Oxford: Butterworth Heinemann; Buono, A. and Bowditch, J. (1989) *The Human Side of Mergers and Acquisitions*. San Francisco: Jossey-Bass.
3 Burt, T. and Lambert, R. 'The Schrempp Gambit …', *Financial Times*, 30 October 2000, p. 26.
4 Burt, T. 'Steering with his foot to the floor', *Financial Times*, 26 February 2001, p. 12.
5 Buchan, D. and Buck, T. 'Refining BP's management', *Financial Times*, 1 August 2002, p. 21.
6 Batchelor, C. 'Vertical integration sets building materials debate', *Financial Times*, 17 December 1999, p. 26.
7 Buffett, W. *Berkshire Hathaway Annual Report*, 1994.
8 Kay, J. 'Poor odds on the takeover lottery', *Financial Times*, 26 January 1996.
9 Lynch (1990), p. 204.
10 *The Economist*, 8 June 1996, pp. 92–3.

11 For a more thorough consideration of the human side of mergers consult Haspeslagh, P. and Jemison, D. (1991) *Managing Acquisitions*. New York: Free Press; Cartwright, S. and Cooper, C. (1992) *Mergers and Acquisitions The Human Factor*. Oxford: Butterworth Heinemann; Buono, A. and Bowditch, J. (1989) *The Human Side of Mergers and Acquisitions*. San Francisco: Jossey-Bass.

12 Lord Browne quoted in Buchan, D. and Buck, T. 'Refining BP's management', *Financial Times*, 1 August 2002, p. 21.

12

THE MERGER PROCESS

Introduction

This chapter focuses on two aspects of mergers. It first covers the middle stage of the merger process: that is, the deal-making stage, particularly in the circumstances of a hostile takeover. We look at the restraining rules and regulatory bodies that attempt to prevent unfairness.

Second, the chapter examines the question of what type of payment to make for the shares of the target firm. Should the acquirer offer cash, shares in itself or some other form of payment?

The City Code on Takeovers and Mergers

The City Panel on Takeovers and Mergers provides the main governing rules for companies engaged in merger activity. It is often referred to as the 'Takeover Panel' or simply the 'Panel'. Its rules are expressed in the City Code on Takeovers and Mergers (the 'Takeover Code' or 'Code'),

The Takeover Panel was set up by City institutions, bankers, accountants, the London Stock Exchange (LSE) and the Bank of England as a self-regulatory non-statutory organization in 1968. It was viewed as a model of self-regulation around the world because it could be very quick in making and enforcing decisions. Also, because it was run by very knowledgeable practitioners from the City, it could maintain a high degree of flexibility, e.g. it could quickly change the rules to meet new challenges – especially when clever financiers thought they had found a way around the current restrictions. It could also maintain a degree of informality in providing companies with guidance on what is acceptable and what is not – a 'word in the ear' or a 'raised eyebrow' could prevent many actions that would have been against the spirit of the Panel's rules. The alternative approach (adopted in many countries), one based on statute and lawyers, was seen as bureaucratic, expensive and slow.

Somehow the Panel has managed to hold on to its old speed, flexibility and informality despite it now having statutory backing (under the Companies Act 2006 and the EU's Directive on Takeover Bids). It has some strong legal powers, such as the right to insist on receiving information from anyone involved in a bid. Panel decisions are legally enforceable. However, it still operates with a high degree of self-regulation and independence from the state; for example, it can amend its own rules.

It also still relies on an informal relationship with the regulated community, and uses subtle power and influence, rather than a rigid set of statutory rules subject to constant challenge in the courts. Even now it very rarely goes to court to enforce or defend a decision – the courtroom is seen very much as a last resort. The litigation culture that bedevils a lot of other countries is something the City and the government have tried to avoid.

Thus, we still have a 'light-touch' regulatory system, with the Panel seen as approachable for consultation, guidance and negotiation, rather than a heavy-handed rule-enforcer.

The sanctions the Panel employs are largely the same as those used before it received statutory backing. These range from private or public reprimands (embarrassing and potentially commercially damaging to bidder, target or adviser) to the shunning of those who defy the Code by regulated City institutions – the Financial Services Authority (FSA) demands that no regulated firm (such as a bank, broker or adviser) should act for a client firm that seriously breaks the Panel's rules ('cold-shouldering'). Practitioners in breach of the Code may be judged not fit and proper persons to carry on investment business by the FSA, so there is considerable leverage over City institutions that might otherwise be tempted to assist a rule-breaker. The Panel may give a ruling restraining a person from acting in breach of its rules. It may also insist on compensation being paid. The FSA can also take legal action under market abuse legislation, e.g. when there is share-price manipulation. In rare cases the Panel may temporarily remove voting rights from particular shareholders.

Note, however, that the Panel does not offer a view on either the commercial merit of the bid or on competition or other public policy issues that might arise.

As well as having regulatory power over companies quoted on public markets, the Panel can regulate the behaviour of all other public limited companies.

The fundamental objective of the Takeover Panel regulation is to ensure fair and equal treatment for all shareholders. The main areas of concern are:

- shareholders being treated differently, for example large shareholders getting a special deal;
- insider dealing (control over this is assisted by statutory rules);
- management action that is contrary to its shareholders' best interests; for example, the advice to accept or reject a bid must be in the shareholders' best interest, not that of the management;
- lack of adequate and timely information released to shareholders;
- artificial manipulation of share prices; for example an acquirer offering shares cannot make the offer more attractive by getting friends to push up its share price;
- the bid process dragging on and thus distracting management from their proper tasks.

The Office of Fair Trading (OFT) also takes a keen interest in mergers to ensure that they do not produce 'a substantial lessening of competition'. The OFT has the power to clear a merger. A small minority of proposed mergers may, after an OFT initial screening, be followed by a Competition Commission (CC) investigation. The CC is the ultimate arbiter in deciding if a substantial lessening of competition is likely. It conducts full detailed investigations and can insist on major changes to the merged entity. For example William Morrison was required to sell a number of

Safeway supermarkets following their merger in 2004.[1] A CC inquiry may take several months to complete, during which time the merger bid is put on hold. There is some confusion as to where the jurisdiction boundaries of the OFT and the CC lie because competitors of the merging firms can ask a tribunal (Competition Appeal Tribunal) to overturn a clearance by the OFT and insist on a CC referral, casting doubt on the power of the OFT. Another hurdle in the path of large intra-European Union mergers is their scrutiny by the European Commission in Brussels. This is becoming increasingly influential.

The combination of Friends Reunited and Genes Reunited was thought by the OFT to endanger competition and so it referred the bid to the Competition Commission – *see* Exhibit 12.1.

Friends site sale hits obstacle

Tim Bradshaw and Ben Fenton

The sale of Friends Reunited hit a stumbling block yesterday when it was referred to the Competition Commission over concerns it could damage the online genealogy market.

ITV had agreed to sell the networking site for £25m to Brightsolid, a division of DC Thomson & Co, the newspaper and magazine publisher, in August.

Brightsold is particularly interested in combining the family history arm of Friends, Genes Reunited, with its own genealogy properties, 1911census.co.uk and FindMyPast.com.

However, the Office of Fair Trading said the deal would lead to reduced competition in a fast-growing market.

Amelia Fletcher, the OFT's senior director of mergers, said: 'The proposed acquisition would see the three main providers of online genealogy services reduced to two, and we are concerned this could lead to a reduction in choice or service for consumers.'

The OFT ruling is likely to provoke further criticism among businessmen and politicians frustrated at what they see as damaging regulatory intervention in developing new media markets, say people involved in a series if emergent campaigns.

EXHIBIT 12.1

Source: *Financial Times* 3 November 2009, p. 17.

Action before the bid

Figure 12.1 shows the main stages of a merger. The acquiring firm usually employs advisers to help make a takeover bid. Most firms carry out mergers infrequently and so have little expertise in-house. The identification of suitable targets may be one of the first tasks of the advisers. Once these are identified there would be a period of appraising the target. The strategic fit would be considered and there would be a detailed analysis of what would be purchased. The product markets and types of customers could be investigated and there would be a financial analysis showing sales, profit and rates of return history. The assets and liabilities would be assessed and non-balance sheet assets such as employees' abilities would be considered.

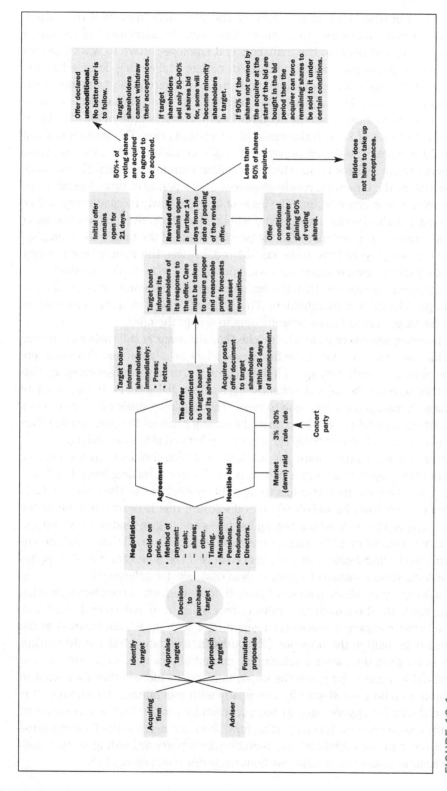

FIGURE 12.1
The merger process

If the appraisal stage is satisfactory the firm may approach the target. Because it is often cheaper to acquire a firm with the agreement of the target management, and because the managers and employees have to work together after the merger, in the majority of cases discussions take place designed to produce a set of proposals acceptable to both groups of shareholders and managers.

During the negotiation phase the price and form of payment need to be decided upon. In most cases the acquirer has to offer a bid premium. This tends to be in the range of 20 to 100 percent of the pre-bid price. The average is about 30 to 50 percent. The timing of payment is also considered. For example, some mergers involve 'earn-outs' in which the selling shareholders (usually the same individuals as the directors) receive payment over a period of time dependent on the level of post-merger profits. The issue of how the newly merged entity will be managed will also be discussed – who will be chief executive? Which managers will take particular positions? Also the pension rights of the target firm's employees and ex-employees have to be considered, as does the issue of redundancy, especially the removal of directors – what pay-offs are to be made available?

If agreement is reached then the acquirer formally communicates the offer to the target's board and shareholders. This will be followed by a recommendation from the target's board to its shareholders to accept the offer.

If, however, agreement cannot be reached and the acquirer still wishes to proceed a hostile bid is created. One of the first stages might be a 'dawn raid'. This is where the acquirer acts with such speed in buying the shares of the target company that the raider achieves the objective of obtaining a substantial stake in the target before the target's management has time to react. The acquirer usually offers investors a price which is significantly higher than the closing price on the previous day. This high price is only offered to those close to the market and able to act quickly.

An important trigger point for disclosure of shareholdings in a company, whether the subject of a merger or not, is the 3 percent holding level. If a 3 percent stake is owned then this has to be publicly declared to the company (it is posted on free financial websites). This disclosure rule is designed to allow the target company to know who is buying its shares and to give it advance warning of a possible takeover raid. The management can then prepare a defence and present information to shareholders should the need arise. (The 3 percent rule also applies to a holding via derivatives of shares such as contracts for difference).

If a company builds up a stake of more than 30 percent of the shares carrying voting rights the Takeover Panel rules usually oblige it to make a cash bid for all of the target company's shares (or a share offer with a cash alternative) at the highest price paid in the previous 12 months (a 'mandatory bid'). A 30 percent stake often gives the owner a substantial amount of power. It is thought that the shareholders need to be given the opportunity to decide whether they want to continue to hold their shares in a company with a dominant shareholder. It is very difficult for anyone else to bid successfully for the firm when someone already has 30 percent. It is surprising how often one reads in the financial press that a company or individual has bought a 29.9 percent holding so that they have as large a stake as possible without triggering a mandatory bid.

Sometimes, in the past, if a company wanted to take over another it would, to avoid declaring at the 3 percent level (or 5 percent as it was then), or to avoid bidding at the 30 percent level, sneak up on the target firm's management and shareholders. It would form a 'concert party' by persuading its friends, other firms and individuals to buy stakes in the target. Each of these holdings would be below the threshold levels. When the acquirer was ready to pounce it would already have under its control a significant, if not a majority, controlling interest. Today all concert party holdings are lumped together for the purposes of disclosure and trigger points. The concert party rules were perceived as reducing the potential for shareholders to work together to correct a bad management or bad strategy. These rules have now been relaxed for non-bid situations – see Exhibit 12.2.

FSA clarifies position on activist investors

Brooke Masters and Kate Burgess

Investors can work actively together to oust a chief executive or change corporate strategy without falling foul of European Union and UK rules against market abuse and acting in concert, the Financial Services Authority said.

But such alliances must be based on specific corporate issues rather than a long-term agreement to vote together, and the investors cannot trade on information they may glean while working together, the City watchdog added.

The FSA said it was clarifying what hedge funds and other activist investors can do because it supported recent proposals from Sir David Walker to increase shareholder engagement. Lord Myners, the City minister, has also criticised institutions for failing to engage with bank leaders.

Some investors have said they were reluctant to work together for fear of falling foul of 2007 guidance from the FSA that warned activist investors not to collude. Knight Vinke, the activist group, said it began its 2007 public campaign against HSBC by outlining its views in a newspaper advertisement because of concerns about that guidance.

The Institutional Shareholders Committee sought clarification, which the FSA provided yesterday.

Sally Dewar, FSA managing director for wholesale markets, wrote: 'We do not believe that our regulatory requirements prevent collective engagement by institutional shareholders designed to raise legitimate concerns on particular corporate issues, events or matters of governance with the management of investee companies.'

The clarification comes as EU rules make it easier for dissident shareholders to challenge management. Under UK law changes passed in July, investors need to amass control of 5 per cent of voting shares to call a general meeting, down from 10 per cent.

The 2007 guidance is still in effect, including a warning to investors not to avoid disclosure requirements by purchasing smaller stakes and working together. Trading on non-public information about another investor's undeclared activist strategy could still be considered market abuse. ...

EXHIBIT 12.2

Source: *Financial Times* 20 August 2009, p. 17.

Once a company becomes a bid target, any dealings in the target's shares by the bidder (or an associate) must be publicly disclosed no later than midday on the business day following the transaction. Furthermore, once an offer is under way, any holder of 1 percent or more of either the bidder or the target must publicly disclose dealings by midday of the next business day. An investor holding 1 percent must disclose any dealings in the bidder's or target's shares, warrants, convertibles, contracts for difference, options, other derivatives and all other securities in the company. As Exhibit 12.3 shows, this disclosure at the 1 percent level has been extended to shares in any 'other company involved in the bid', including the bidder.

Takeover Panel to force more disclosure over shareholdings

Adrian Cox and Lina Saigol

The Takeover Panel is proposing to force investors to reveal more about their shareholdings during takeover battles.

At the moment investors only have to disclose their holdings if they trade shares and own more than 1 per cent.

However, the UK mergers and acquisitions watchdog is concerned that the current disclosure rules of not cover shareholdings accumulated before a bid begins and do not apply to other investments and types of securities that may affect the outcome.

'To understand who controls the votes in a company is to have a better angle on what's going on and how the transaction is going to turn out,' Tony Pullinger, deputy director general of the Takeover Panel, said.

The proposals would mean that investors holding more than 1 per cent of target company's shares during a paper bid would have to reveal their position.

That would extend not only to shares in the company being bid for but also in any other company involved in the bid.

If adopted, the regime would help investors find out which shareholders

were building a stake in a target company and which were merely taking a financial gamble on the success or failure of the bidding.

Typically, merger arbitrageurs simultaneously purchase stock in a target company and sell stock in its potential acquirer, hoping to make a profit from the spread, or difference, between a target company's share price after a takeover announcement and the closing price at completion of the deal.

This is because during a takeover, the stock of the acquiring company usually falls while the stock of the target company rises.

The Panel said for the time being it would not extend the disclosure rules to short selling in a takeover, when investors sell borrowed stock in a bet that the price will fall.

However, it will monitor whether companies that borrow or lend securities should disclose the details, in part to eliminate potential double-counting of holdings. Even so, it said, the cost of new rules would currently outweigh the benefits.

EXHIBIT 12.3

Source: *Financial Times* 9 May 2009, p. 14.

A tactic that has become common recently is for a potential bidder to announce that they are thinking of making a bid rather than actually doing it –

they make an '*indicative offer*' (dubbed a virtual bid) saying they might bid but not committing themselves to the expense and strict timetable of a formal offer. Shareholders in targets may gain from having potential bidders announce an interest in buying their shares and are in favour of allowing time for the bid to be put together. On the other hand, it is not in the shareholders' interest for the management to continually feel under siege. The Takeover Panel permits indicative offers, but after a few weeks (generally six to eight) without a genuine offer emerging it declares that the potential bidder has to 'put up or shut up' before a deadline date. Once that period has expired the virtual bidder must walk away for at least six months.

Kraft made an informal bid for Cadbury on 7 September 2009. It was not until 30 September that the Takeover Panel set a deadline for a formal offer – *see* Exhibit 12.4.

Kraft given deadline for Cadbury bid

Jenny Wiggins and Jonathan Birchall

Kraft is under pressure to make a former takeover bid for Cadbury after the UK's Takeover Panel gave the US food group less than six weeks to put an offer on the table or walk away.

The Panel yesterday set a deadline of November 9 for Kraft to come forward with a formal offer after the UK confectionery group approached it with a 'put up or shut up' request last week.

If Kraft does not make a formal offer by November 9 it will not be allowed to bid for Cadbury for six months unless another bidder enters the fray. Kraft yesterday said it had 'noted' the decision and understood the implications.

Roger Carr, Cadbury's chairman, said the company had not changed its view on Kraft, and stood by its rejection of the £10.2bn approach. ...

Kraft's options include formalising its current offer, which values Cadbury at 719p a share, returning with a higher one or walking away.

Cadbury investors have supported the board's decision to reject Kraft's indicative offer and want the US group to return with one that values Cadbury at about 850p a share.

The shareholders also want Kraft to increase the cash portion of its offer from 40 per cent to about 50 per cent. ...

EXHIBIT 12.4

Source: *Financial Times* 1 October 2009, p. 19.

Traps for bidders to avoid

If the bidder purchases shares carrying 10 percent or more of the voting rights in the offer period or in the previous 12 months of a bid, the offer must include a cash alternative at the highest price paid by the bidder. A potential bidder should be careful not to buy any shares at a price higher than a fair value.

If the bidder buys shares in the target at a price above the offer price during a bid the offer must be increased to that level. So, be careful of topping up acceptances by offering a high price to a few shareholders.

The bid

In both a friendly and a hostile bid the acquirer is required to give notice to the target's board and its advisers that a bid is to be made. The press and the Stock Exchange are usually also informed. The target management must immediately inform their shareholders (and the Takeover Panel). This is done through an announcement to the Stock Exchange and a press notice (disseminated on numerous free financial websites), which must be quickly followed by a letter explaining the situation. In a hostile bid the target management tend to use phrases like 'derisory offer' or 'wholly unacceptable'.

Within 28 days of the initial notice of an intention to make an offer the offer document has to be posted to each of the target's shareholders. Details of the offer, the acquirer and its plans will be explained. If the acquisition would increase the total value of the acquirer's assets by more than 15 percent the acquirer's shareholders need to be informed about the bid. If the asset increase is more than 25 percent then shareholders must vote in favor of the bid proceeding. They are also entitled to vote on any increase in authorized share capital.

The target management have 14 days in which to respond to the offer document. Assuming that they recommend rejection, they will attack the rationale of the merger and the price being offered. They may also highlight the virtues of the present management and reinforce this with revised profit forecasts and asset revaluations. There follows a period of attack and counter-attack through press releases and other means of communication. Public relations consultants may be brought in to provide advice and to plan tactics.

The offer remains open for target shareholders to accept for 21 days from the date of posting the offer document. If the offer is revised it must be kept open for a further 14 days from the posting date of the revision.[2] However, to prevent bids from dragging on endlessly the Panel insists that the maximum period for a bid is 60 days from the offer document date (posting day). The final offer date is day 46, which allows 14 days for acceptances. There are exceptions: if another bidder emerges, then it has 60 days, and its 60th day becomes the final date for both bidders; or if the Board of the target agrees to an extension; if the bid is referred to the CC the Panel can 'stop the clock'. If the acquirer fails to gain control within 60 days then it is forbidden to make another offer for a year to prevent continual harassment.

After the bid

Usually an offer becomes unconditional when the acquirer has bought, or has agreed to buy, between 50 and 90 percent of the target's shares. Prior to the declaration of the offer as unconditional the bidding firm would have said in the offer documents that the offer is conditional on the acquirer gaining (usually) 90 percent (or whatever figure they select) of the voting shares. This allows the bidding firm to receive acceptances from the target shareholders without the obligation to buy.[3] Once the bid is declared unconditional the acquirer is making a firm offer for the shares that it does not already have, and indicating that no better offer is to follow. Before the announcement of unconditionality those target shareholders who accepted the offer are entitled to withdraw their acceptance – after it, they are forbidden to do so.

Usually in the days following unconditionality the target shareholders who have not already accepted quickly do so. The alternative is to remain a minority shareholder – still receiving dividends (if management and the majority share-holders choose to pay dividends) but with power concentrated in the hands of a majority shareholder. There is a rule to avoid the frustration of having a small group of shareholders stubbornly refusing to sell. If the acquirer has bought nine-tenths of the shares it bid for, it can, within three to six months of the original offer, insist that the remaining shareholders sell at the final offer price.

If the bid has lapsed or not been declared unconditional the bidder cannot bid again for a 12-month period. However, the bidder is allowed to bid again if a bid is made by another company or the bidder's renewed offer is recommended by the target management.

Scheme of arrangement

There is a quick and cheap way of combining two companies called a scheme of arrangement, whereby the target managers and the acquiring managers agree to allow the target shareholders to vote on a merger. If three-quarters of them vote in favour, and the arrangement is sanctioned by a court, then the scheme is binding on all shareholders. All the target shareholders are then required to sell to the acquirer. Thus the acquirer can avoid have a rump minority hanging on to their shares.

Defence tactics

Roughly one-half of UK hostile bids are unsuccessful. Here are a few of the tactics employed by target managers to prevent a successful bid or to reduce the chances of a bid occurring.

Before bidding starts

- **Eternal vigilance** Be the most effective management team and educate share-holders about your abilities and the firm's potential. Cultivate good relationships with unions, work force and politicians. Polish social image.
- **Defensive investments** Your firm buys a substantial proportion of the shares in a friendly firm, and it has a substantial holding of your shares.
- **Forewarned is forearmed** Keep a watch on the share register for the accumulation of shares by a potential bidder.

After bidding has started

- **Attack the logic of the bid** Also attack the quality of the bidder's management.
- **Improve the image of the firm** Use revaluation, profit projections, dividend promises, public relations consultants.
- **Attack the value creating (destroying) record of the bidder.**
- **Try to get an OFT block or Competition Commission inquiry.**
- **Encourage unions, the local community, politicians, customers and suppliers to lobby on your behalf.**
- **White knight** Invite a second bid from a friendly company.
- **Lobby your major shareholders.**
- **Buy another business to make the firm too big or incompatible with the bidder.**
- **Arrange a management buyout of your company.**
- **Begin litigation against the bidder** Bidders sometimes step over the legal boundary in their enthusiasm – e.g. false statements, gaining private information – a court case could be embarrassing.
- **Employee share ownership plans (ESOPs)** These can be used to buy a substantial stake in the firm and may make it more difficult for a bidder to take it over.
- **Share repurchase** Reduces the number of shares available in the market for bidders.
- **Grey knight** A new bidder who is a rival to the hostile bidder launches a bid. The rivalry may produce a higher takeover price.

The following tactics are likely to be frowned upon or banned by the Takeover Panel in the UK, but are used in the USA and in a number of continental European countries.

- **Poison pills** Make yourself unpalatable to the bidder by ensuring additional costs should it win – for example, target shareholders are allowed to buy shares in target or acquirer at a large discount should a bid be successful. 'Shareholder rights plans' trigger the issuance of new shares or allow investors to sell at a premium.
- **Crown jewels defence** Sell off the most attractive parts of the business.
- **Pac-Man defence** Make a counter-bid for the bidder.
- **Asset lock-up** A friendly buyer purchases those parts of the business most attractive to the bidder.
- **Stock lock-up (white squire)** Target shares are issued to a friendly company or individual(s).
- **Golden parachutes** Managers get massive pay-offs if the firm is taken over.
- **Give in to greenmail** Key shareholders try to obtain a reward (for example, the repurchase of their shares at premium) from the company for not selling to a hostile bidder or for not becoming a bidder themselves. (Green refers to the colour of a US dollar.)
- **Limit voting rights** In some European states the management has the ability to limit voting rights to say a maximum of 15 percent regardless of the actual share holding.
- **Sell shares that carry multiple voting rights to friendly parties, e.g. employees.**
- **Change of control covenant** This, in effect, forces a company to default on its debt due to a takeover that management disapprove of.

Paying for the target's shares

Figure 11.1(b) in Chapter 11 showed the relative importance of alternative methods of paying for the purchase of shares in another company over three decades. The relative popularity of each method has varied considerably over the years but in most years cash is the most attractive option, followed by shares, and finally the third category, comprising mostly debentures, loan stocks, convertibles and preference shares.

The figures given in Figure 11.1(b) tend to give a slightly distorted view of the financial behaviour of acquiring firms. In many cases where cash is offered to the target shareholders the acquirer does not borrow that cash or use cash reserves. Rather, it raises fresh funds through a rights issue of shares before the takeover bid.

The table may also be misleading in the sense that a substantial proportion of mergers do not fall neatly into the payment categories. Many are mixed bids, providing shareholders of the target firms with a variety of financial securities or offering them a choice in the consideration they wish to receive, for example cash or shares, shares or loan stock. This is designed to appeal to the widest range of potential sellers.

Cash

One of the advantages of using cash for payment is that the acquirer's shareholders retain the same level of control over their own company. That is, new shareholders from the target have not suddenly taken possession of a proportion of the acquiring firm's voting rights, as they would if the target shareholders were offered shares in the acquirer. Sometimes it is very important to shareholders that they maintain control over a company by owning a certain proportion of the firm's shares. Someone who has a 50.1 percent stake may resist attempts to dilute that holding to 25 percent even though the company may more than double in size.

The second major advantage of using cash is that its simplicity and preciseness give a greater chance of success. The alternative methods carry with them some uncertainty about their true worth. Cash has an obvious value and is therefore preferred by vendors, especially when markets are volatile.

From the point of view of the target's shareholders, cash has the advantage – in addition to being more certain in its value – that it also allows the recipients to spread their investments through the purchase of a wide-ranging portfolio. The receipt of shares or other securities means that the target shareholder either keeps the investment or, if diversification is required, has to incur transaction costs associated with selling the shares.

A disadvantage of cash to the target shareholders is that they may be liable for capital gains tax (CGT). This is payable when a gain is 'realised'. If the target shareholders receive cash on shares which have risen in value they may pay tax. If, on the other hand, the target shareholders receive shares in the acquiring firm then their investment gain is not regarded as being realised, so no capital gains tax is payable at that time. The tax payment will be deferred until the time of the sale of the new shares – assuming an overall capital gain is made. (Note that some investment funds, e.g. pension funds do not pay CGT and so this problem does not arise. Also, CGT can be reduced by tax free allowances and capital losses on other investments and so many shareholders will not consider CGT a burden.)

Offering cash may put a strain on the acquiring company's cash flow.

In certain circumstances the Takeover Panel insists on a cash offer or a cash alternative to an all-share offer.

Another consideration: with cash, any risk of misvaluing the target rests wholly with the acquirer – if shares in the acquirer are accepted by the target shareholders, then they take some of the misvaluation risks. Also borrowing cash that is then paid out for the target's shares may be a way of adjusting the financial gearing (debt to equity ratio) of the firm. On the other hand, the firm may already have high borrowings and be close to breaching loan covenants and so is reluctant to borrow more.

Shares

There are two main advantages to target shareholders of receiving shares in the acquirer rather than cash. First, capital gains tax can be postponed because the investment gain is not realised. Second, they maintain an interest in the combined entity. If the merger offers genuine benefits the target shareholders may wish to own part of the combined entity.

To the acquirer, an advantage of offering shares is that there is no immediate outflow of cash. In the short term, this form of payment puts less pressure on cash flow. However the firm may consider the effect on the capital structure of the firm and the dilution of existing shareholders' positions.

Another reason for using shares as the consideration is that the price–earnings ratio (PER) game can be played. Through this companies can increase their earnings per share (EPS) by acquiring firms with lower PERs than their own. The share price can rise (under certain conditions) despite there being no economic value created from the merger.

Imagine two firms, Crafty plc and Sloth plc. Both earned £1m last year and had the same number of shares. Earnings per share on an historic basis are identical. The difference between the two companies is the stock market's perception of earnings growth. Because Crafty is judged to be a dynamic go-ahead sort of firm with management determined to improve earnings per share by large percentages in future years it is valued at a high PER of 20.

Sloth, on the other hand, is not seen by investors as a fast-moving firm. It is considered to be rather sleepy. The market multiplies last year's earnings per share by only a factor of 10 to determine the share price – see Table 12.1.

TABLE 12.1

Illustration of the price to earnings ratio game – Crafty and Sloth

	Crafty	Sloth
Current earnings	£1m	£1m
Number of shares	10m	10m
Earnings per share	10p	10p
Price to earnings ratio	20	10
Share price	£2	£1

Because Crafty's shares sell at a price exactly double that of Sloth it would be possible for Crafty to exchange one of its shares for two of Sloth's. (This is based on the assumption that there is no bid premium, but the argument that follows works just as well even if a reasonable bid premium is paid.)

If Crafty buys all the shares in Sloth its share capital rises by 50 percent, from ten million shares to 15 million shares. However EPS are one-third higher. If the stock market still puts a high PER on Crafty's earnings, perhaps because investors believe that Crafty will liven up Sloth and produce high EPS growth because of their more dynamic management, then the value of Crafty increases and Crafty's shareholders are satisfied.

Each old shareholder in Crafty has experienced an increase in earnings per share and a share price rise of 33 percent. Also, previously Sloth's shareholders owned £10m of shares in Sloth; now they own £13.33m of shares (*see* Table 12.2).

TABLE 12.2

Crafty after an all-share merger with Sloth

	Crafty
Earnings	£2m
Number of shares	15m
Earnings per share	13.33p
Price to earnings ratio	20
Share price	267p

This all seems rational and good, but shareholders are basing their valuations on the assumption that managers will deliver on their promise of higher earnings growth through operational efficiencies, etc. Managers of companies with a high PER may see an easier way of increasing EPS and boosting share price. Imagine you are managing a company which enjoys a high PER. Investors in your firm are expecting you to produce high earnings growth. You could try to achieve this through real entrepreneurial and/or managerial excellence, for example by product improvement, achieving economies of scale, increased operating efficiency, etc. Alternatively you could buy firms with low PERs and not bother to change operations. In the long run you know that your company will produce lower earnings because you are not adding any value to the firms that you acquire, you are probably paying an excessive bid premium to buy the present earnings and you probably have little expertise in the new areas of activity.

However, in the short run, EPS can increase dramatically. The problem with this strategy is that to keep the earnings on a rising trend you must continue to keep fooling investors. You have to keep expanding at the same rate to receive regular boosts. One day expansion will stop; it will be revealed that the underlying economics of the firms bought have not improved (they may even have worsened as a result of neglect), and the share price will fall rapidly. This is another reason to avoid placing too much emphasis on short-term EPS figures. The Americans call this the boot strap game. It can be very lucrative for some managers who play it skilfully. However there can be many losers – society, shareholders, employees.

Three other considerations when using shares as payment: it may pull the company away from the optimum financial gearing ratio; it may reduce near-term earnings per share (which may worry managers targeting these), even though the deal will increase shareholder value; and managers (or dominant shareholders) who own a high proportion of the acquirer may be reluctant to allow an issue of shares that will dilute their control.

There are some significant dangers in paying shares for an aquisition, as Buffett makes clear in Exhibit 12.5.

Wealth for shareholders from mergers: the view of Warren Buffett

Our share issuances follow a simple basic rule: we will not issue shares unless we receive as much intrinsic business value as we give. Such a policy might seem axiomatic. Why, you might ask, would anyone issue dollar bills in exchange for fifty-cent pieces? Unfortunately, many corporate managers have been willing to do just that.

The first choice of these managers in making acquisitions may be to use cash or debt. But frequently the CEO's cravings outpace cash and credit resources (certainly mine always have). Frequently, also, these cravings occur when his own stock [shares] is selling far below intrinsic business value. This state of affairs produces a moment of truth. At that

point, as Yogi Berra has said, 'You can observe a lot just by watching.' For shareholders then will find which objective the management truly prefers – expansion of domain or maintenance of owners' wealth.

The need to choose between these objectives occurs for some simple reasons. Companies often sell in the stock market below their intrinsic business value. But when a company wishes to sell out completely, in a negotiated transaction, it inevitably wants to – and usually can – receive full business value in whatever kind of currency the value is to be delivered. If cash is to be used in payment, the seller's calculation of value received couldn't be easier. If stock [shares] of the buyer is to be currency, the seller's calculation is still relatively easy: just figure the market value in cash of what is to be received in stock.

Meanwhile, the buyer wishing to use his own stock as currency for the purchase has no problems if the stock is selling in the market at full intrinsic value.

But suppose it is selling at only half intrinsic value. In that case, the buyer is faced with the unhappy prospect of using a substantially undervalued currency to make its purchase.

Ironically, were the buyer to instead be a seller of its entire business, it too could negotiate for, and probably get, full intrinsic business value. But when the buyer makes a partial sale of itself – *and that is what the issuance of shares to make an acquisition amounts to* – it can customarily get no higher value set on its shares than the market chooses to grant it.

The acquirer who nevertheless barges ahead ends up using an undervalued (market value) currency to pay for a fully valued (negotiated value) property. In effect, the acquirer must give up $2 of value to receive $1 of value. Under such circumstances, a marvelous business purchased at a fair sales price becomes a terrible buy. For gold valued as gold cannot be purchased intelligently through the utilization of gold – or even silver – valued as lead.

If, however, the thirst for size and action is strong enough, the acquirer's manager will find ample rationalizations for such a value-destroying issuance of stock. Friendly investment bankers will reassure him as to the soundness of his actions. (Don't ask the barber whether you need a haircut.)

A few favorite rationalizations employed by stock-issuing managements follow:

(a) 'The company we're buying is going to be worth a lot more in the future.' (Presumably so is the interest in the old business that is being traded away; future prospects are implicit in the business valuation process. If 2X is issued for X, the imbalance still exists when both parts double in business value.)

(b) 'We have to grow.' (Who, it might be asked, is the 'We'? For present share-holders, the reality is that all existing businesses shrink when shares are issued. Were Berkshire to issue shares tomorrow for an acquisition, Berkshire would own everything that it now owns plus the new business, but *your* interest in such hard-to-match businesses as See's Candy Shops, National Indemnity, etc. would automatically be reduced. If (1) your family owns a 120-acre farm and (2) you invite a neighbor with 60 acres of comparable land to merge his farm into an equal partnership – with you to be managing partner, then (3) your managerial domain will have grown to 180 acres but you will have permanently shrunk by 25% your family's ownership interest in both acreage and crops. Managers who want to expand their domain at the expense of owners might better consider a career in government.) ...

... There are three ways to avoid destruction of value for old owners when shares are issued for acquisitions. One is to have a true business-value-for-business-value merger, ... Such a merger attempts to be fair to shareholders of *both* parties, with each receiving just as much as it gives in terms of intrinsic business value ... It's not that acquirers wish to avoid such deals, it's just that they are very hard to do.

The second route presents itself when the acquirer's stock sells at or above its intrinsic business value. In that situation, the use of stock as currency actually may enhance the wealth of the acquiring company's owners ...

... The third solution is for the acquirer to go ahead with the acquisition, but then subsequently repurchase a quantity of shares equal to the number issued in the merger. In this manner, what originally was a stock-for-stock merger can be converted, effectively, into a cash-for-stock acquisition. Repurchases of this kind are damage-repair moves. Regular readers will correctly guess that we much prefer repurchases that directly enhance the wealth of owners instead of repurchases that merely repair previous damage. Scoring touchdowns is more exhilarating than recovering one's fumbles.

The language utilized in mergers tends to confuse the issues and encourage irrational actions by managers. For example, 'dilution' is usually carefully calculated on a pro forma basis for both book value and current earnings per share. Particular emphasis is given to the latter item. When that calculation is negative (dilutive) from the acquiring company's standpoint, a justifying explanation will be made (internally, if not elsewhere) that the lines will cross favorably at some point in the future. (While deals often fail in practice, they never fail in projections – if the CEO is visibly panting over a prospective acquisition, subordinates and consultants will supply the requisite projections to rationalize any price.) Should the calculation produce numbers that are immediately positive – that is, anti-dilutive – for the acquirer, no comment is thought to be necessary.

The attention given this form of dilution is overdone: current earnings per share (or even earnings per share of the next few years) are an important variable in most business valuations, but far from all-powerful.

There have been plenty of mergers, non-dilutive in this limited sense, that were instantly value-destroying for the acquirer. And some mergers that have diluted current and near-term earnings per share have in fact been value-enhancing. What really counts is whether a merger is dilutive or anti-dilutive in terms of intrinsic business value (a judgment involving consideration of many variables). We believe calculation of dilution from this viewpoint to be all-important (and too seldom made).

A second language problem relates to the equation of exchange. If Company A announces that it will issue shares to merge with Company B, the process is customarily described as 'Company A to Acquire Company B', or 'B Sells to A'. Clearer thinking about the

matter would result if a more awkward but more accurate description were used: 'Part of A sold to acquire B' or 'Owners of B to receive part of A in exchange for their properties'. In a trade, what you are giving is just as important as what you are getting …

… Managers and directors might sharpen their thinking by asking themselves if they would sell 100% of their business on the same basis they are being asked to sell part of it. And if it isn't smart to sell all on such a basis, they should ask themselves why it is smart to sell a portion. A cumulation of small managerial stupidities will produce a major stupidity – not a major triumph. (Las Vegas has been built upon the wealth transfers that occur when people engage in seemingly-small disadvantageous capital transactions.) …

… Finally, a word should be said about the 'double whammy' effect upon owners of the acquiring company when value-diluting stock issuances occur. Under such circumstances, the first blow is the loss of intrinsic business value that occurs through the merger itself. The second is the downward revision in market valuation that, quite rationally, is given to that now-diluted business value. For current and prospective owners understandably will not pay as much for assets lodged in the hands of a management that has a record of wealth-destruction through unintelligent share issuances as they will pay for assets entrusted to a management with precisely equal operating talents, but a known distaste for anti-owner actions. Once management shows itself insensitive to the interests of owners, shareholders will suffer a long time from the price/value ratio afforded their stock (relative to other stocks), no matter what assurances management gives that the value-diluting action taken was a one-of-a-kind event.

EXHIBIT 12.5

Source: Warren Buffett's letter to shareholders in the *Berkshire Hathaway Annual Report* 1982.

Other types of finance

Alternative forms of consideration including debentures, loan stock, convertibles and preference shares (described in Chapters 16 and 17) are unpopular, largely because of the difficulty of establishing a rate of return on these securities that will be attractive to target shareholders. Also, these securities often lack marketability and voting rights over the newly merged company.

Deferred payment

Deferred payment, in which the total to be paid over the next few years depends on performance targets being achieved, is a useful way of tying in key personnel to the combined company (they might be offered an 'earn-out' deal). Another advantage of deferring payment is the reduced cash flow strain.

Conclusion

The bid process is fairly complex with rules to be obeyed by both the bidder and the target. It is understandable that many company managements feel the necessity of holding hands with the experts in the investment banks. Be careful though; the cost of this advice can be exorbitant. It is interesting that Philip Green, the billionaire owner of BHS and Arcadia, generally prefers to talk directly with the management and shareholders of potential targets rather than pay M&A specialists to suggest strategic moves, analyse and negotiate for him, speeding up the process and saving money – when you are using your own money the pain of the £1m cheque is more acutely felt – although he brings the bankers in for specific tasks later.

> The bid process is fairly complex with rules to be obeyed by both the bidder and the target.

Investment banks can be useful for key activities, including certain stages in the negotiations. They can advise on the type of finance to be used to purchase the target's shares. More significantly, they can assist with the raising of fresh funds, e.g. a bond or share issue – the underwriting fees on these can be high, so be wary of signing blank cheques. They can guide you through the Takeover Panel rules. Finally, the City experts may be able to help with the valuation of the target. The next chapter will allow you to understand the rationale and drawbacks of the techniques they are likely to use.

Websites

www.berkshirehathaway.com   Berkshire Hathaway
www.ft.com   Financial Times
www.kpmg.co.uk   KPMG

www.londonstockexchange.com　　London Stock Exchange
www.thetakeoverpanel.org.uk　　The Takeover Panel
www.competition-commission.org.uk　Competition Commission
www.oft.gov.uk　　Office of Fair Trading

Notes

1　This was actually negotiated between the OFT and Morrisons following the Competition Commission's ruling.

2　If an offer is revised all shareholders who accepted an earlier offer are entitled to the increased payment.

3　If 90 percent of the target shares are offered, the bidder must proceed (unless there has been a material adverse change of circumstances). At lower levels of acceptance, it has a choice of whether to declare unconditionality.

13

VALUING COMPANIES

Introduction

Managers must become acquainted with the main influences on the valuation of entire companies and how to value individual shares in companies. If they are to be given the responsibility of maximizing the wealth of shareholders managers need knowledge of the factors influencing that wealth, as reflected in the share price of their own company. Without this understanding they will be unable to determine the most important consequence of their actions – the impact on share value. Managers need to appreciate share price derivation because the

> Managers need to appreciate share price derivation because the change in their company's share value is one of the key factors by which they are judged.

change in their company's share value is one of the key factors by which they are judged. It is also useful for them to know how share prices are set if the firm plans to gain a flotation on a stock exchange, or when it is selling a division to another firm. In mergers an acquirer needs good valuation skills so as not to pay more than necessary, and a seller needs to ensure that the price is fair.

This chapter describes the main methods of valuing shares: net asset value, dividend valuation models, price earnings ratio models and cash flow models. There is an important subsection in the chapter that shows how the valuation of shares differs if the purchase would give managerial control from the valuation of shares which provide only a small minority stake.

The two skills

Two skills are needed to be able to value shares. The first is analytical ability, to be able to understand and use mathematical valuation models. Second, and most importantly, good judgment is needed, because the majority of the inputs to the mathematical calculations are factors, the precise nature of which cannot be defined with absolute certainty, so great skill is required to produce reasonably accurate results. The main problem is that the determinants of value occur in the future, for example future cash flows, dividends or earnings.

The monetary value of an asset is what someone is prepared to pay for it. Assets such as cars and houses are difficult enough to value with any degree of accuracy. At least corporate bonds generally have a regular cash flow (coupon)

> The monetary value of an asset is what someone is prepared to pay for it.

and an anticipated capital repayment. This contrasts with the uncertainties associated with shares, for which there is no guaranteed annual payment and no promise of capital repayment. The difficulties of share valuation are amply represented by the case of Amazon.com in Case study 13.1.

Case study 13.1

Amazon.com

Amazon, the internet retailer, has never made a profit. In fact it lost over $700m in 1999 and offered little prospect of profits in the near term. So, if you were an investor in early 2000 what value would you give to a company of this calibre? Anything at all? Amazingly, investors valued Amazon at over $30bn in early 2000 (more than all the traditional book retailers put together). The share price had gained 6,000 percent in 30 months since its stock market flotation in 1997. The brand was well established and the numbers joining the online community rose by thousands every day. Investors were confident that Amazon would continue to attract customers and produce a rapid rate of growth in revenue. Eventually, it was thought, this revenue growth would translate into profits and high dividends. When investors had calmed down after taking account of the potential for competition and the fact that by 2001 Amazon was still not producing profits, they reassessed the value of Amazon's likely future dividends. In mid-2001, they judged the company to be worth only $4bn – it had run up losses of $1.4bn in 2000, indicating that profits and dividends were still a long way off. However, by 2010 the company was generating free cash flow and positive operating profit. It had broadened its offering beyond books. It had even developed its own hardware – the Kindle electronic book reader. The market now valued its shares at $32bn, which was 36 times estimates for 2009 profits after tax. This was taking a lot of future growth on trust.

Valuation using net asset value (NAV)

The balance sheet seems an obvious place to start when faced with the task of valuation. In this method the company is viewed as being worth the sum of the value of its net assets. The balance sheet is regarded as providing objective facts concerning the company's ownership of assets and obligations to creditors. Here fixed assets are recorded along with stocks, debtors, cash and other liquid assets. With the deduction of long-term and short-term creditors from the total asset figure we arrive at the net asset value (NAV).

An example of this type of calculation is shown in Table 13.1 for Cadbury.

The NAV of over £3bn of Cadbury compares with a market value placed on all the shares when totalled of £10bn (market capitalization figures are available in Monday editions of the *Financial Times*). This great difference makes it clear that the shareholders of Cadbury are not rating the firm on the basis of balance sheet net asset figures. This point is emphasized by an examination of Table 13.2.

Three of the four firms listed in Table 13.2 have very small balance sheet values in comparison with their total market capitalization. The exception is Vodafone, which boosted its balance sheet by buying many other companies producing over £74bn intangible assets in the form of goodwill (amount paid for target above the fair value of the assets acquired) and other intangible assets.

Analysts may adjust values shown on balance sheets to replacement cost or realizable values, e.g. a property asset bought 5 years go and valued on the balance sheet at cost may be adjusted to its current market value. However, even with many alterations of this kind for most companies market value will remain a long way from NAV.

For most companies, investors look to the income flow to be derived from a holding. This flow is generated when the balance sheet assets are combined with assets impossible to quantify: these include the unique skills of the workforce, the relationships with customers and suppliers, the value of brands, the reservoir of experience within the management team, and the competitive positioning of the firms' products. Assets, in the crude sense of balance sheet values, are only one dimension of overall value. Investors in the market generally value intangible, unmeasurable assets more highly than those that can be identified and recorded by accountants (see Figure 13.1).

> Investors in the market generally value intangible, unmeasurable assets more highly than those that can be identified and recorded by accountants.

Criticizing accountants for not producing balance sheets which reflect the true value of a business is unfair. Accounts are not usually designed to record up-to-date market values. Land and buildings are frequently shown at cost rather than market value; thus the balance sheet can provide a significant over- or under-valuation of these assets' current value. Plant and machinery is shown at the purchase price less

TABLE 13.1

Cadbury Abridged Balance Sheet 31 December 2008

		£m
Fixed assets		5,990
Current assets		
	Inventories (stocks)	767
	Tax recoverable	35
	Trade and other receivables	1,067
	Investments (short-term)	247
	Cash and cash equivalents	251
	Derivative financial instruments	268
		2,635
Assets held for sale		270
Current liabilities		(3,388)
Non-current liabilities		(1,973)
Net assets		3,534
Shareholders' funds		3,522

Source: Cadbury Report & Accounts 2008.

TABLE 13.2

Net asset values and total capitalization of some firms

Company (Accounts year)	NAV £m	Total capitalization (market value of company's shares) £m
GlaxoSmithKline (2008)	8,318	66,045
Unilever (2008)	9,948	22,935
BSkyB (2009)	Negative 64	9,536
Vodafone (2009)	84,777	70,800

Source: Annual reports and accounts; *Financial Times*, 23 November 2009; www.advfn.com.

FIGURE 13.1

What creates value for shareholders?

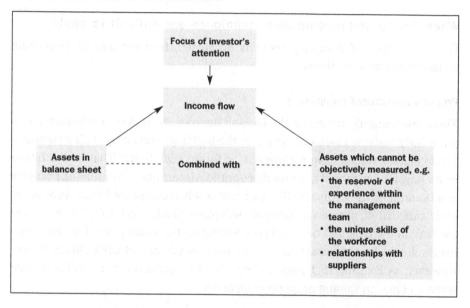

a depreciation amount. Inventory (stock) is valued at the lower of cost or net realizable value – this can lead to a significant under-estimate, as the market value can appreciate to a figure far higher than either of these. The list of balance sheet entries vulnerable to subjective estimation, arbitrary method and even cynical manipulation is a long one: goodwill, provisions, merger accounting, debtors, intangible brand values and so on.

When asset values are particularly useful

The accounts-based approach to share value is fraught with problems but there are circumstances in which asset backing is correctly given more attention.

Firms in financial difficulty

The shareholders of a firm in financial difficulty may pay a great deal of attention to the asset backing of the firm. They may weigh up the potential for asset sales or asset-backed borrowing. In extreme circumstances they may try to assess the break-up value. Here the liquidation value is key: what could be realized by selling the assets and paying off all the liabilities, after allowing for liquidation expenses such as redundancy payments, tax and legal costs. Liquidation value may be far below NAV.

Takeover bids

In a takeover bid shareholders will be reluctant to sell at less than NAV even if the prospect for income growth is poor. A standard defensive tactic in a takeover battle is to revalue balance sheet assets to encourage a higher price.

When discounted income flow techniques are difficult to apply

For some types of company there is no straightforward way of employing income-flow-based methods:

Property investment companies

These are primarily valued on the basis of their assets. It is generally possible to put a fairly realistic up-to-date price on the buildings owned by such a company. These market values have a close link to future cash flows. That is, the future rents payable by tenants, when discounted, determine the value of property assets and thus the company. If higher rent levels are expected than were previously anticipated, chartered surveyors will place a higher value on the asset, and the NAV in the balance sheet will rise, forcing up the share price. For such companies, future income, asset values and share values are all fairly closely linked. However, as Exhibit 13.1 makes clear, there remains much room for debate when it comes to valuing property companies.

Valuations complicated by lack of functioning market

Daniel Thomas

The recent spate of fundraising in the property sector has again raised the thorny problem about the accuracy of valuations in a rapidly changing market.

Most companies have so far managed to fit rights issues around interim results and at least a December year-end valuation. However, any forth-coming issues may have a problem basing equity raisings on numbers more than six weeks old.

Land Securities was given the impression that the listings authorities may not have been happy even with a December year-end valuation when it launched its issue last week, which was why it had been conducting frequent valuation updates that eventually saw the use of end-January numbers.

Indeed, financial authorities have taken a keen interest in the valuations debate. The Bank of England has recently called certain property professionals to talk about the problems that valuers are having ascribing accurate prices to property assets.

As can be seen from the recent rights issues, these concerns are warranted as valuations lie at the heart of property as an asset class. A collapse of confidence in the value of property undermines the position of countless property companies, investment funds and private holdings, not to mention the banks that own the loans that support these property portfolios.

To take the most public consequence so far, the use of caveats by valuers over the accuracy of their statements has led to concerns by auditors about signing off the full-year accounts of property companies.

According to IPD, four-fifths of commercial property valuations had risk statements attached at the end of last year, and the Royal Institution of Chartered Surveyors has had to make it clear that these cannot be considered warnings needing any qualification of accounts.

At the heart of the problem is a lack of a functioning market – with few willing buyers or sellers, judging the market value of a property becomes difficult. Circumstances of distress clearly skew the final sale price. For some companies, selling at far below the nominal book value is acceptable in order to generate cash.

Would another seller get that same price if they were not in such distress? Probably not. So does that make it the market value? There lies the problem.

Some think yes, that property should be marked to market. But others think there should be a mark to some more theoretical model of longer-term fair value. And between these lies a grey area, such as whether market sentiment and future forecasts should be taken into account.

The strength of a tenant in a building, which has a market effect on its value given the reliability of income, has also thrown up issues. The valuers for the Lehman brothers' buildings would never have anticipated a tenant default, in one of the most extreme examples to date.

But even with difficulties in a highly volatile market, valuers should not feel pressurised to use guidance notes – there needs to be confidence in their market expertise.

DTZ's Robert Peto, a former chairman of the RICS valuation faculty, said that complaining that evidence is skewed because of a lack of a 'willing buyer' is a misconception of how valuations work. 'Values have to be through the eyes of the buyers, not the vendors. There is nothing wrong with marking to a stressed market,' he says.

In reality, there is little alternative to the mark-to-market approach as long as the property industry wants to remain a respected asset class. Investors need the ability to compare accurate and as current as possible pricing with other asset classes, which will invariably be valued at their own market levels.

Banks need to know whether loans are in breach – and, if so, how much – before they can take action.

Once you get over the fact that investment levels are down substantially from previous years, there are plenty of transactional data that can be used – about £4.3bn in the final quarter of 2008 according to Atisreal. Values are not theoretical – they are what one would be able to buy a building for today.

Tape measures and books of rules should never have allowed the situation to become controversial and the speed of the correction so far shows that valuers have, in fact, been doing a fairly good job in keeping up with changes, even with a noticeable lag.

Compare the UK with certain other markets in Europe, where investors complain that a lack of transparency has kept them from committing to any meaningful activity.

Valuers should be applauded for keeping as abreast as possible in most cases in the UK – and having marked down property preparing themselves for the bounce back. The first to spot the floor will be a popular person.

EXHIBIT 13.1

Source: *Financial Times* 24 February 2009, p. 20.

Investment trusts

The future income of investment trusts comes from the individual shareholdings. The shareholder in a trust would find it extremely difficult to calculate the future income to be received from each of the dozens or hundreds of shares held. An easier approach is simply to take the current share price of each holding as representing the future discounted income. The share values are aggregated to derive the trust's NAV and this has a strong bearing on the price at which the trust shares are traded.

Resource-based companies

For oil companies, mineral extractors, mining houses and so on, the proven or probable reserves have a significant influence on the share price (*see* Exhibit 13.2).

Income flow is the key

The value of a share is usually determined by the income flows that investors expect to receive in the future from its ownership. Information about the past is only of relevance to the extent that it contributes to an understanding of expected future performance. Income flows will occur at different points in the future and so they have to be discounted. There are three classes of income valuation models:

- dividend-based models
- earnings-based models
- cash flow-based models.

NAV valuation sparks dispute

Timon Day

A row had broken out between oil company LASMO and HSBC Securities over the broker's sharp cut in its estimation of LASMO's net asset value from 132p to 98p a share. It knocked £48m off LASMOs stock market value driving its shares down 5p to 123p. This is a particularly sensitive time because LASMO is in the middle of an all-share offer for Monument Oil & Gas – whose former broker is HSBC ...

Most of the dispute over the valuation centres on Algeria where LASMO has a 12 percent stake in 14 oil fields operated by US group Anadarko. Mr Perry does not accept LASMO's valuation of between £300m and £500m for its Algerian interests, putting a price of just £210m on them.

EXHIBIT 13.2

Source: *Investors Chronicle* 11 June 1999.

Dividend valuation methods

The dividend valuation models (DVMs) are based on the premise that *the market value of ordinary shares represents the sum of the expected future dividend flows, to infinity, discounted to present value.*

The only cash flows that investors ever receive from a company are dividends. This holds true if we include a 'liquidation dividend' upon the sale of the firm or on formal liquidation, and any share repurchases can be treated as dividends. Of course, an individual shareholder is not planning to hold a share forever to gain the dividend returns to an infinite horizon. An individual holder of shares will expect two types of return:

- income from dividends and
- a capital gain resulting from the appreciation of the share and its sale to another investor.

The fact that the individual investor is looking for capital gains as well as dividends to give a return does not invalidate the models' focus on all dividends to an infinite horizon. The reason for this is that when a share is sold by that investor, the purchaser is buying a future stream of dividends, so the price paid is determined by future dividend expectations.

To illustrate this, consider the following: A shareholder intends to hold a share for one year. A single dividend will be paid at the end of the holding period, d_1 and the share will be sold at a price P_1 in one year.

To derive the value of a share at time 0 to this investor (P_0), the future cash flows, d_1 and P_1, have to be discounted at a rate which includes an allowance for the risk class of the share, k_E.

$$P_0 = \frac{d_1}{1 + k_E} + \frac{P_1}{1 + k_E}$$

Example

An investor is considering the purchase of some shares in Willow plc. At the end of one year a dividend of 22p will be paid and the shares are expected to be sold for £2.43. How much should be paid if the investor judges that the rate of return required on a financial security of this risk class is 20 percent?

Answer

$$P_0 = \frac{d_1}{1 + k_E} + \frac{P_1}{1 + k_E}$$

$$P_0 = \frac{22}{1 + 0.2} + \frac{243}{1 + 0.2} = 221p$$

The dividend valuation model to infinity

The relevant question to ask to understand DVMs is: Where does P_1 come from? The buyer at time 1 estimates the value of the share based on the present value of future income given the required rate of return for the risk class. So if the second investor expects to hold the share for a further year and sell at time 2 for P_2, the price P_1 will be:

$$P_1 = \frac{d_2}{1 + k_E} + \frac{P_2}{1 + k_E}$$

Returning to the P_0 equation we are able to substitute discounted d_2 and P_2 for P_1. Thus:

$$P_0 = \frac{d_1}{1 + k_E} + \frac{P_1}{1 + k_E}$$

$$P_0 = \frac{d_1}{1 + k_E} + \frac{d_2}{(1 + k_E)^2} + \frac{P_2}{(1 + k_E)^2}$$

If a series of one-year investors bought this share, and we in turn solved for P_2, P_3, P_4, etc., we would find:

$$P_0 = \frac{d_1}{1 + k_E} + \frac{d_2}{(1 + k_E)^2} + \frac{d_3}{(1 + k_E)^3} + \ldots + \frac{d_n}{(1 + k_E)^n}$$

Even a short-term investor has to consider events beyond his or her time horizon because the selling price is determined by the willingness of a buyer to purchase a future dividend stream. If this year's dividends are boosted by short-termist policies such as cutting out R&D and brand-support marketing the investor may well lose significantly because other investors push down the share price as their forecasts for future dividends are lowered.

Example

If a firm is expected to pay dividends of 20p per year to infinity and the rate of return required on a share of this risk class is 12% then:

$$P_0 = \frac{20}{1 + 0.12} + \frac{20}{(1 + 0.12)^2} + \frac{20}{(1 + 0.12)^3} + \ldots + \frac{20}{(1 + 0.12)^n}$$

$$P_0 = 17.86 + 15.94 + 14.24 + \ldots + \ldots +$$

Given this is a perpetuity there is a simpler approach:

$$P_0 = \frac{d_1}{k_E} = \frac{20}{0.12} = 166.67p$$

The dividend growth model

In contrast to the situation in the above example, for most companies dividends are expected to grow from one year to the next. To make DVM analysis manageable simplifying assumptions are usually made about the patterns of growth in dividends. Most managers attempt to make dividends grow more or less in line with the firm's long-term earnings growth rate. They often bend over backwards to smooth out fluctuations, maintaining a high dividend even in years of poor profits or losses. In years of very high profits they are often reluctant to increase the dividend by a large percentage for fear that it might have to be cut back in a downturn.[1] So, given management propensity to make dividend payments grow in an incremental or stepped fashion it seems that a reasonable model could be based on the assumption of a constant growth rate. (Year to year deviations around this expected growth path will not materially alter the analysis.) See Worked examples 13.1 and 13.2 for use of the constant dividend growth model.

> Given management propensity to make dividend payments grow in an incremental or stepped fashion it seems that a reasonable model could be based on the assumption of a constant growth rate.

Worked example 13.1
A CONSTANT DIVIDEND GROWTH VALUATION: SHHH PLC

If the last dividend paid was d_0 and the next is due in one year, d_1, then this will amount to $d_0(1 + g)$ where g is the growth rate of dividends.

For example, if Shhh plc has just paid a dividend of 10p and the growth rate is 7% then:

d_1 will equal $d_0(1 + g) = 10(1 + 0.07) = 10.7$p

and

d_2 will be $d_0(1 + g)^2 = 10(1 + 0.07)^2 = 11.45$p

The value of a share in Shhh will be all the future dividends discounted at the risk-adjusted discount rate of 11%:

$$P_0 = \frac{d_0(1 + g)}{1 + k_E} + \frac{d_0(1 + g)^2}{(1 + k_E)^2} + \frac{d_0(1 + g)^3}{(1 + k_E)^3} + \ldots + \frac{d_0(1 + g)^n}{(1 + k_E)^n}$$

$$P_0 = \frac{10(1 + 0.07)}{1 + 0.11} + \frac{10(1 + 0.07)^2}{(1 + 0.11)^2} + \frac{10(1 + 0.07)^3}{(1 + 0.11)^3} + \ldots + \frac{d_0(1 + g)^n}{(1 + k_E)^n}$$

Using the above formula could require a lot of time. Fortunately it is mathematically equivalent to the following formula,[2] which is much easier to employ.

$$P_0 = \frac{d_1}{k_E - g} = \frac{d_0(1 + g)}{k_E - g} = \frac{10.7}{0.11 - 0.07} = 267.50\text{p}$$

Note that, even though the shortened formula only includes next year's dividend all the future dividends are represented.

A further illustration is provided by the example of Pearson plc.

Worked example 13.2
PEARSON PLC

Pearson plc, the publishing, media and education group, has the following dividend history:

Year	Net dividend per share (p)
1996	16.1
1997	17.4
1998	18.8
1999	20.1
2000	21.4
2001	22.3
2002	23.4
2003	24.2
2004	25.4
2005	27.0
2006	29.3
2007	31.6
2008	33.8

The average annual growth rate, g, over this period has been:

$$g = \sqrt[12]{\frac{33.8}{16.1}} - 1 = 0.064 \; or \; 6.4\%$$

If (a big if) it is assumed that this historical growth rate will continue into the future and 10% is taken as the required rate of return, the value of a share can be calculated.

$$P_0 = \frac{d_1}{k_E - g} = \frac{33.8(1 + 0.064)}{0.10 - 0.064} = 999p$$

In fact, in late 2009 Pearson's shares stood at 850p. Perhaps analysts were anticipating a slower rate of growth in future than in the past. Perhaps we employed an unreasonably low discount rate given the risks facing the company. Or perhaps the market consensus view of Pearson's growth prospects was over-pessimistic.

Non-constant growth

Firms tend to go through different phases of growth. If they have a strong competitive advantage in an attractive market they might enjoy super-normal growth. Eventually, however, most firms come under competitive pressure and growth becomes normal. Ultimately, many firms fail to keep pace with the market environmental change in which they operate and growth falls to below that for the average company.

To analyze companies that go through different phases of growth a two-, three- or four-stage model may be used. In the simplest case of two-stage growth the share price calculation requires the following:

1 Calculate each of the annual dividends in the first period.

2 Estimate the share price at the point at which the dividend growth shifts to the new permanent rate.

3 Discount each of the dividends in the first period and the share price given in 2. Add all the discounted numbers to obtain the current value.

Worked example 13.3
NORUCE PLC

You are given the following information about Noruce plc.

The company has just paid an annual dividend of 15p per share and the next is due in one year. For the next three years dividends are expected to grow at 12% per year. This rapid rate is caused by a number of favourable factors: an economic upturn, the fast acceleration stage of newly developed products and a large contract with a government department.

After the third year the dividends will grow at only 7% per annum, because the main boosts to growth will, by then, be absent.

Shares in other companies with a similar level of systematic risk to Noruce produce an expected return of 16% per annum.

What is the value of one share in Noruce plc?

Answer

Stage 1 Calculate dividends for the super-normal growth phase.

$$d_1 = \quad 15(1 + 0.12) \quad = \quad 16.8$$
$$d_2 = \quad 15(1 + 0.12)^2 \quad = \quad 18.8$$
$$d_3 = \quad 15(1 + 0.12)^3 \quad = \quad 21.1$$

Stage 2 Calculate share price at time 3 when the dividend growth rate shifts to the new permanent rate.

$$P_3 = \frac{d_4}{k_E - g} = \frac{d_3(1 + g)}{k_E - g} = \frac{21.1(1 + 0.07)}{0.16 - 0.07} = 250.9$$

Stage 3 Discount and sum the amounts calculated in Stages 1 and 2.

$$\frac{d_1}{1 + k_E} = \frac{16.8}{1 + 0.16} = 14.5$$

$$+ \quad \frac{d_2}{(1 + k_E)^2} = \frac{18.8}{(1 + 0.16)^2} = 14.0$$

$$+ \quad \frac{d_3}{(1 + k_E)^3} = \frac{21.1}{(1 + 0.16)^3} = 13.5$$

$$+ \quad \frac{P_3}{(1 + k_E)^3} = \frac{250.9}{(1 + 0.16)^3} = \underline{160.7}$$

$$202.7\text{p}$$

What is a normal growth rate?

Growth rates will be different for each company but for corporations taken as a whole dividend growth will not be significantly different from the growth in nominal gross national product (real GNP plus inflation) over the long term. If dividends did grow in a long-term trend above this rate then they would take an increasing proportion of national income – ultimately squeezing out the consumption and government sectors. This is, of course, ridiculous. Thus, in an economy with expected long-term inflation of 2 percent per annum and growth of 2.5 percent, we might expect the long-term growth in dividends to be about 4.5 percent. Also, it is unreasonable to suppose that a firm can grow its earnings and dividends forever at a rate significantly greater than that for the economy as a whole. To do so is to assume that the firm eventually becomes larger than the economy. There will be years, even decades, when average corporate dividends do grow faster than the economy as a whole and there will always be companies with much higher projected growth rates than the average for periods of time. Nevertheless the real GNP + inflation growth relationship provides a useful benchmark.

> There will be years, even decades, when average corporate dividends do grow faster than the economy as a whole.

Companies that do not pay dividends

Some companies, for example Dell, Apple and Warren Buffett's Berkshire Hathaway, do not pay dividends. This is a deliberate policy as there is often a well-founded belief that the funds are better used within the firms than they would be if the money is given to shareholders. This presents an apparent problem for the DVM but the measure can still be applied because it is reasonable to suppose that one day these companies will start to pay dividends. Perhaps this will take the form of a final break-up payment, or perhaps when the founder is approaching retirement he/she will start to distribute the accumulated resources. At some point dividends must be paid, otherwise there would be no attraction in holding the shares. Microsoft is an example of a company that did not pay a dividend for 28 years. However, in 2003 it decided that it would start a process of payout of some of its enormous pile of cash and now pays an annual dividend.

Some companies do not pay dividends for many years due to regular losses. Often what gives value to this type of share is the optimism that the company will recover and that dividends will be paid in the distant future.

Problems with the dividend growth valuation model

Dividend valuation models present the following problems.

1 They are highly sensitive to assumptions. Take the case of Pearson above. If we change the growth assumption to 7 percent and reduce the required rate of return to 9.5 percent, the value of the share leaps to over £14.

$$P_0 = \frac{d_1}{k_E - g} = \frac{33.8(1 + 0.07)}{0.095 - 0.07} = 1{,}447\text{p}$$

2 The quality of input data is often poor. The problems of calculating an appropriate required rate of return on equity are discussed in Chapter 10. Added to this is great uncertainty about the future growth rate.

3 If g exceeds k_E a nonsensical result occurs. This is a problem for those who would use the model in a mechanical way by simply using the historical growth rate for g. However, in intelligent use of the model we replace the short-term super-normal growth rate followed by a lower rate after the super-normal period with a g which is some weighted average growth rate reflecting the return expected over the long run. This is unlikely to result in a g more than one or two percentage points greater than the growth rate for the economy as a whole (because the greatest weight will be given to the near term super-normal growth period, we may allow a growth rate slightly higher than the economy). Alternatively, for those periods when g is greater than k, one may calculate the specific dividend amounts and discount them as in the non-constant growth model (e.g. the two-stage model). For the years after the super-normal growth occurs, the usual growth formula may be used, as we did for Noruce plc in Worked example 13.3.

The difficulties of using the DVMs are real and yet the methods are to be favoured, less for the derivation of a single number than for the understanding of the principles behind the value of financial assets that the exercise provides. They demand a disciplined thought process that makes the analyst's assumptions about key variables explicit (about earnings and dividend growth, about reasonable required rates of

> DVMs demand a disciplined thought process that makes the analyst's assumptions about key variables explicit.

return, etc.) This allows the analyst to question the validity and robustness of any final number produced. The analyst is also made aware of the possibility of a range of values depending on the assumptions made.

How do you estimate future growth?

The most influential variable, and the one subject to most uncertainty, on the value of shares is the growth rate expected in dividends. Accuracy here is a much sought-after virtue. While this book cannot provide readers with a perfect crystal ball for seeing future dividend growth rates, it can provide a few pointers.

Determinants of growth

Three factors influence the rate of dividend growth.

- **The quantity of resources retained and reinvested within the business** This relates to the percentage of earnings not paid out as dividends. The more a firm invests the greater its potential for growth.
- **The rate of return earned on those retained resources** The efficiency with which retained earnings are used will influence value.
- **Rate of return earned on existing assets** This concerns the amount earned on the existing baseline set of assets, that is, those assets available before reinvestment of profits. This category may be affected by a sudden increase or decrease in profitability. If the firm, for example, is engaged in oil exploration and production, and there is a worldwide increase in the price of oil, profitability will rise on existing assets. Another example would be if a major competitor is liquidated, enabling increased returns on the same asset base due to higher margins because of an improved market position.

In addition to using retained earnings, investment funds can be raised and future value can be boosted just so long as the firm has positive net present value projects.

There is a vast range of influences on the future return from shares. One way of dealing with the myriad variables is to group them into two categories: at firm and economy level.

Focus on the firm

A dedicated analyst would want to examine numerous aspects of the firm, and its management, to help develop an informed estimate of its growth potential. These will include the following.

■ **Strategic analysis** The most important factor in assessing the value of a firm is its strategic position. We need to consider the attractiveness of the industry, the competitive position of the firm within the industry and the firm's position on the life cycle of value creation to appreciate the potential for increased dividends. (This topic is covered very briefly in Chapter 7. For a fuller discussion consult Arnold (2009) *The Financial Times Guide to Value Investing* or Arnold (2010) *The Financial Times Guide to Investing*.)

■ **Evaluation of management** Running a close second in importance for the determination of a firm's value is the quality of its management. A starting point for analysis might be to collect factual information such as their level of experience and education. But this has to be combined with far more important evaluatory variables which are unquantifiable, such as judgment, and even gut-feeling about issues such as competence, integrity, intelligence and so on. Having honest managers with a focus on increasing the wealth of shareholders is at least as important for valuing shares as the factor of managerial competence. Investors downgrade the shares of companies run by the most brilliant managers if there is any doubt about their integrity – highly competent crooks can destroy shareholder wealth far quicker than any competitive action, just ask the shareholders in Enron or Bernard Madoff's investors. (For a fuller discussion of the impact of managerial competence and integrity on share values, see Arnold (2009).)

■ **Using the historical growth rate of dividends** For some firms the past growth may be extrapolated to estimate future dividends. If a company demonstrated a growth rate of 6 percent over the past ten years it might be reasonable to use this as a starting point for evaluating its future potential. This figure may have to be adjusted for new information such as new strategies, management or products – that is the tricky part.

■ **Financial statement evaluation and ratio analysis** An assessment of the firm's profitability, efficiency and risk through an analysis of accounting data can be enlightening. However, adjustments to the published figures are likely to be necessary to view the past clearly, let alone provide a guide to the future. Warren Buffett comments:

> When managers want to get across the facts of the business to you, it can be done within the rules of accounting. Unfortunately when they want to play games, at least in some industries, it can also be done within the rules of accounting. If you can't recognise the differences, you shouldn't be in the equity-picking business.[3]

Accounts are valuable sources of information, but they have three drawbacks:

– they are based in the past when it is the future which is of interest,

– the fundamental value-creating processes within the firm are not identified and measured in conventional accounts, and

– they are frequently based on guesses, estimates and judgments, and are open to arbitrary method and manipulation.

Armed with a questioning frame of mind the analyst can adjust accounts to provide a truer and fairer view of a company. The analyst may wish to calculate three groups of ratios to enable comparisons:

■ Internal liquidity ratios permit some judgment about the ability of the firm to cope with short-term financial obligations – quick ratios, current ratios, etc.

■ Operating performance ratios may indicate the efficiency of the management in the operations of the business – asset turnover ratio, profit margins, debtor turnover, etc.

■ Risk analysis concerns the uncertainty of income flows – sales variability over the economic cycle, operational gearing (fixed costs as a proportion of total), financial gearing (ratio of debt to equity), cash flow ratios, etc.

Ratios examined in isolation are meaningless. It is usually necessary to compare with the industry, or the industry sub-group comprising the firm's competitors. Knowledge of changes in ratios over time can also be useful.

Focus on the economy

All firms, to a greater or lesser extent, are influenced by macroeconomic changes. The prospects for a particular firm can be greatly affected by sudden changes in government fiscal policy, the central bank's monetary policy, changes in exchange rates, etc. Forecasts of macroeconomic variables such as GNP are easy to find, for example *The Economist* publishes a table of forecasts every week. Finding a forecaster who is reliable over the long term is much more difficult. Perhaps the best approach is to obtain a number of projections and through informed judgment develop a view about the medium-term future. Alternatively, the analyst could recognize that there are many different potential futures and then develop analyses based on a range of possible scenarios – probabilities could be assigned and sensitivity analysis used to provide a broader picture.

It is notable that the great investors (e.g. Benjamin Graham, Philip Fisher, Warren Buffett, Charles Munger, Peter Lynch) pay little attention to macroeconomic forecasts when valuing companies. The reason for this is that value is determined by income flows to the shareholder over many economic cycles stretching over decades, so the economists' projection (even if accurate) for this or that economic number for the next year is of little significance.

Price–earnings ratio (PER) model

The most popular approach to valuing a share is to use the price-to-earnings (PER) ratio. The historical PER compares a firm's share price with its latest earnings (profits) per share. Investors estimate a share's value as the amount they are willing to pay for each unit of earnings. If a company produced earnings per share of

10p in its latest accounts and investors are prepared to pay 20 times historical earnings for this type of share it will be valued at £2.00. The historical PER is calculated as follows:

$$\text{Historical PER} = \frac{\text{Current market share of price}}{\text{Last year's earnings per share}} = \frac{200\text{p}}{10\text{p}} = 20$$

So, the retailer Marks and Spencer which reported earnings per share of 32.3p with a share price of 394p in November 2009 had a PER of 12.2 (394p/32.3p). PERs of other retailers are shown in Table 13.3.

Investors are willing to buy Dunelm's shares at 21.7 times last year's earnings compared with only 14.7 times last year's earnings for Greggs. One explanation for the difference in PERs is that companies with higher PERs are expected to show faster growth in earnings in the future. Dunelm may appear expensive relative to Greggs based on historical profit figures but the differential may be justified when forecasts of earnings are made. If a PER is high investors expect profits to rise. This does not necessarily mean that all companies with high PERs are expected to perform to a high standard, merely that they are expected to do significantly better than in the past. Few people would argue that Laura Ashley has performed well in comparison with Dunelm, and yet it stands at a higher historical PER, reflecting the market's belief that Laura Ashley has more growth potential from its low base than Dunelm.

> If a PER is high investors expect profits to rise.

So using the historical PER can be confusing because a company can have a high PER because it is usually a high-growth company or because it has recently had a reduction of profits from which it is expected to recover soon.

TABLE 13.3
PERs for retailers

Retailer	PER
Laura Ashley	27.2
Clinton Cards	6.8
Debenhams	8.7
Dunelm	21.7
Greggs	14.7
JJB Sport	10.4
Marks and Spencer	12.2
Next	12.3

Source: *Financial Times* 19 November 2009.

PERs are also influenced by the uncertainty of the future earnings growth. So, perhaps, Next and JJB Sport have the same expected growth rate but the growth at JJB is subject to more risk and therefore the market assigns a lower earnings multiple.

FIGURE 13.2

PERs for the UK and USA (S&P 500) stock markets 1970–2009

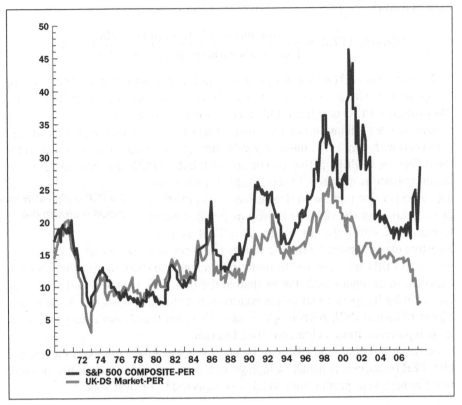

Source: DATASTREAM.

PERs over time

There have been great changes over the years in the market's view of what is a reasonable multiple of earnings to place on share prices. What is excessive in one year is acceptable in another. This is illustrated in Figure 13.2.

The crude and the sophisticated use of the PER model

Some analysts use the historical PER (P_0/E_0), to make comparisons between firms without making explicit the considerations hidden in the analysis. They have a view of an appropriate PER based on current prevailing PER for other firms in the

> Analyzing through comparisons lacks intellectual rigor.

same industry. So, for example, in 2010 Tesco with a PER of 15.5 may be judged to be priced correctly relative to similar firms – Sainsbury had a PER of 10.8 and Morrisons 11.7. Analyzing through comparisons lacks intellectual rigor. First, the assumption that the 'comparable' companies are correctly priced is a bold one. It is easy to see how the market could be pulled up (or down) by its own bootstraps and lose touch with fundamental considerations by this kind of thinking (say, telecommunication shares in the 1998–2000 bubble). Second, it fails to provide a framework for the analyst to test the important implicit input assumptions – for example, the growth rate expected in earnings in each of the companies, or the difference in required rate of return given the different risk level of each. These elements are probably in the mind of the analyst, but there may be benefits in making these more explicit. This can be done with the more complete PER model, which is forward-looking and recognizes both risk levels and growth projections.

The infinite dividend growth model can be used to develop the more complete PER model because they are both dependent on the key variables of growth, g (in dividends or earnings), and the required rate of return, k_E. The dividend growth model is:

$$P_0 = \frac{d_1}{k_E - g}$$

If both sides of the dividend growth model are divided by the expected earnings for the next year, E_1, then:

$$\frac{P_0}{E_1} = \frac{d_1/E_1}{k_E - g}$$

Note this is a *prospective* PER because it uses next year's earnings E_1, rather than an historic PER, which uses E_0.

In this more complete model the appropriate multiple of earnings for a share rises as the growth rate, g, goes up; and falls as the required rate of return, k_E, increases. The relationship with the ratio d_1/E_1 is more complicated. If this payout ratio is raised it will not necessarily increase the PER because of the impact on g – if more of the earnings are paid out less financial resource is being invested in projects within the business, and therefore future growth may decline.

Worked example 13.4
RIDGE PLC

Ridge plc is anticipated to maintain a payout ratio of 48% of earnings. The appropriate discount rate for a share for this risk class is 14% and the expected growth rate in earnings and dividends is 6%.

$$\frac{P_0}{E_1} = \frac{d_1/E_1}{k_E - g}$$

$$\frac{P_0}{E_1} = \frac{0.48}{0.14 - 0.06} = 6$$

The spread between k_E and g is the main influence on an acceptable PER. A small change can have a large impact. Taking the case of Ridge, if we now assume a k_E of 12% and g of 8% the PER doubles.

$$\frac{P_0}{E_1} = \frac{0.48}{0.12 - 0.08} = 12$$

If k_E becomes 16% and g 4% then the PER reduces to two-thirds its former value:

$$\frac{P_0}{E_1} = \frac{0.48}{0.16 - 0.04} = 4$$

Worked example 13.5
WHIZZ PLC

You are interested in purchasing shares in Whizz plc. This company produces high-technology products and has shown strong earnings growth for a number of years. For the past five years earnings per share have grown, on average, by 10% per annum.

Despite this performance and analysts' assurances that this growth rate will continue for the foreseeable future you are put off by the exceptionally high prospective price earnings ratio (PER) of 25.

In the light of the more complete forward-looking PER method, should you buy the shares or place your money elsewhere?

Whizz has a beta of 1.8 which may be taken as the most appropriate systematic risk adjustment to the risk premium for the average share (*see* Chapter 10).

The risk premium for equities over government bonds has been 5% over the past few decades, and the current risk-free rate of return is 7%.

Whizz pays out 50% of its earnings as dividends.

Answer

Stage 1 Calculate the appropriate cost of equity

$$k_E = r_f + \beta(r_m - r_f)$$

$$k_E = 7 + 1.8 \, (5) = 16\%$$

Stage 2 Use the more complete PER model

$$\frac{P_0}{E_1} = \frac{d_1/E_1}{k_E - g} = \frac{0.5}{0.16 - 0.10} = 8.33$$

The maximum multiple of next year's earnings you would be willing to pay given the growth rate of dividends hereafter of 10% is 8.33. This is a third of the amount you are being asked to pay, therefore you will refuse to buy the share.

FIGURE 13.3

Prospective PERs for various risk classes and dividend growth rates

$$\text{Assumed payout ratio} = \frac{d_1}{E_1} = 0.5$$

Discount rate, k_E

		8	9	10	12
Growth	0	6.3	5.6	5.0	4.2
rate, g	4	12.5	10.0	8.3	6.3
	5	16.7	12.5	10.0	7.1
	6	25.0	16.7	12.5	8.3
	8	–	50.0	25.0	12.5

Prospective PER varies with *g* and *k*~E~

If an assumption is made concerning the payout ratio, then a table can be drawn up to show how PERs vary with k_E and g – see Figure 13.3.

A payout ratio of 40–50 percent of after tax earnings is normal for UK shares, although in periods of profit declines companies tended to maintain dividends thus pushing up the proportion of earnings paid out.

We can draw out the implicit key elements hidden in the crude PER model by using the more complete model – see Figure 13.4.

The more complete model can help explain the apparently perverse behaviour of stock markets. If there is 'good' economic news such as a rise in industrial output or a fall in unemployment the stock market often falls. The market likes the increase in earnings that such news implies, but this effect is often outweighed by the effects of the next stage. An economy growing at a fast pace is vulnerable to rises in inflation and the market will anticipate rises in interest rates to reflect this. Thus the r_f and the rest of the SML are pushed upward. The return required on shares, k_E, will rise, and this will have a depressing effect on share prices.

Exhibit 13.3 shows that the use of discounted earnings to value a key asset (and therefore the company) is far from uncontroversial: which earnings are to be discounted – those estimated by the current owners as those estimated by potential buyers?

FIGURE 13.4

The more complete PER model makes explicit key elements hidden in the crude PER model

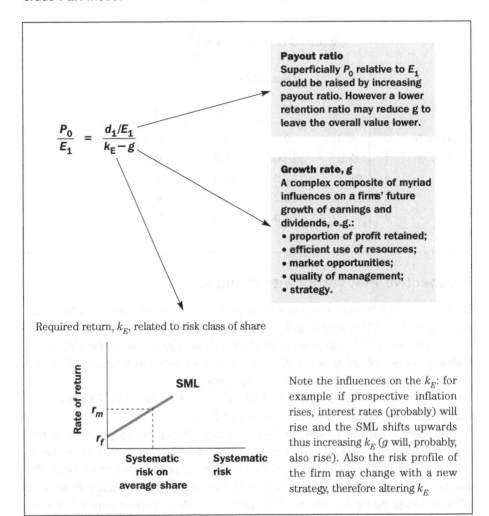

$$\frac{P_0}{E_1} = \frac{d_1/E_1}{k_E - g}$$

Payout ratio
Superficially P_0 relative to E_1 could be raised by increasing payout ratio. However a lower retention ratio may reduce g to leave the overall value lower.

Growth rate, g
A complex composite of myriad influences on a firms' future growth of earnings and dividends, e.g.:
• proportion of profit retained;
• efficient use of resources;
• market opportunities;
• quality of management;
• strategy.

Required return, k_E, related to risk class of share

Rate of return

SML

r_m

r_f

Systematic risk on average share

Systematic risk

Note the influences on the k_E: for example if prospective inflation rises, interest rates (probably) will rise and the SML shifts upwards thus increasing k_E (g will, probably, also rise). Also the risk profile of the firm may change with a new strategy, therefore altering k_E.

New valuation method for ships triggers inflation fears

Robert Wright in London

Concerns have been raised about whether big shipping banks will start inflating the value of billions of euros of their assets after two endorsed a new valuation method producing ship values well above market rates. ...

The Hamburg Shipbrokers' Association, which devised the method, believes several other banks are preparing to start using the method, which values ships according to their likely future earnings, rather than their market value.

The Hamburg standard's proponents argue it gives a fairer picture than traditional assessments based on the prices fetched by similar ships. Such sales give a false idea of ships' value during the current shipping downturn, the new standard's proponents argue, because the few sales going through are forced sales by financially distressed owners.

The initiative has nevertheless attracted fierce criticism from bankers and brokers who believe it is delaying banks' inevitable recognition of falls in most ships' market value, some of more than 50 percent.

'Assets have a value,' one London-based shipbroker said. 'The value is what people will pay for them.'

It remains unclear whether banks backing the new standard will use it for all accounting, including financial reporting. Some may use it only to decide whether shipowners are complying with clauses in their loan agreements that demand the ships involved remain above a set, minimum value. ...

Dagfinn Lunde, head of shipping at Rotterdam-based DVB Bank, another significant shipping lender, criticised the thinking behind the method. Current market prices, he said, accurately reflected current shipping markets, where many ships are laid up out of use.

'Would you buy a ship today if you could not have the price so low that you could afford to lay it up for at least two years before you earn any money?' he said.

Standard change risks rocking the boat

Robert Wright

Earlier this year the Delmas Abuja, a small container ship owned by Hamburg-based Claus-Peter Offen, was leased to France's CMA CGM and worked services between the Mediterranean and the west coast of Africa.

Now the ship, renamed the Santa Giulietta, is unemployed and moored on the River Fal in the west of England waiting for better times.

The dispute about efforts by some German shipbrokers and banks to introduce a new method of ship valuation revolves around how to value a vessel such as the Santa Giulietta.

Advocates of the Hamburg model – such as Thomas Rehder, chairman of the Hamburg Shipbrokers' Association – point out that it remains self-evidently the same ship, with similar long-term prospects, as before.

It would be misleading to write the ship's value down to a market price depressed by short-term factors.

The Hamburg system's critics worry what will happen if owners of ships in the Santa Giulietta's position find themselves forced by financial pressure to sell them. Worse still, what will happen if the owner's lenders end up seizing the ship as collateral for outsanding debts? If the ship has been valued under the new system, they argue, either the ship owner or bank could face the prospect of having suddenly to recognise millions of dollars of unrecognised losses. ...

At least some of the ships in those portfolios could be worth twice as much under the Hamburg method as a market-based method. There are already reports of a ship valued at $28m under the Hamburg system selling for $14m.

A change to the new method would matter, one London shipbroker argues, even if the system is being used only for banks' internal accounting, rather than published accounts. Banks risk not recognising when ships' values have fallen so far they are worth less than has been secured against them, he argues.

However, Thomas Rehder ... the main force behind the new standard, insists market-based valuations are appropriate only where an owner is answering the question of what he would obtain in an immediate sale.

'You can ask a different question,' he says. 'What is the investment amount that I can justify in my balance sheet if I don't want to sell but want to be sure I make money over the remaining life of the investment?' Then I have to look at the expected cash flow.'

The Hamburg standard involves complex calculations including the ship's age, likely future operating costs, scrap value and its past earning record.

Mr Rehder also points out the negative consequences of a market-based method. Banks can demand payments from borrowers – which can sometimes push the borrowers into insolvency – if assets' market values fall below set levels against the loan amount. Banks also have to set aside extra equity for loans against vessels that have fallen in value.

Yet many ships currently fetching low prices are all but certain to have years of profitable life ahead.

'We know we're in a cyclical market in this business,' Mr Rehder says. 'It's completely unrealistic to expect that over the next 20 years ships will only earn operating expenses or ships idle.'

The Hamburg method's opponents, however, believe it could slow down the sector's recognition of the depth of the current crisis and risks inflating balance sheets and propping up market participants for whom there is little hope of rescue.

It will be up to banks and their regulators to balance that risk against the risk that the current method exacerbates the crisis.

EXHIBIT 13.3

Source: *Financial Times* 26 October 2009, p. 25.

Valuation using cash flow

The third and the most important valuation method is cash flow. In business it is often said that 'cash is king'. From the shareholders' perspective the cash flow relating to a share is crucial – they hand over cash and are interested in the ability of the business to return cash to them. John Allday, head of valuation at Ernst and Young, says that discounted cash flow 'is the purest way. I would prefer to adopt it if the information is there'.[4]

The interest in cash flow is promoted by the limited usefulness of published accounts. Scepticism about the accuracy of earnings figures, given the flexibility available in their construction, prompts a switch of attention to a purer valuation method than PER.

The cash flow approach involves the discounting of future cash flows. These cash flows are defined as the cash generated by the business after deduction of investment in fixed assets and working capital to fully maintain its long-term competitive position and its unit volume and to make investment in all new value-creating projects. To derive the cash flow attributable to shareholders, any interest paid in a particular period is deducted as well as taxation. The process of the derivation of cash flow from profit figures is shown in Figure 13.5.

An example of a cash flow calculation is shown in Table 13.4. The difference between profit and cash flows is particularly stark in the case of 2011 – the earnings number is much larger than the cash flow because of the large capital investment in fixed assets. Earnings are positive because only a small proportion of the cost of the new fixed assets is depreciated in that year.

FIGURE 13.5

Cash flow calculation from projected profit figures

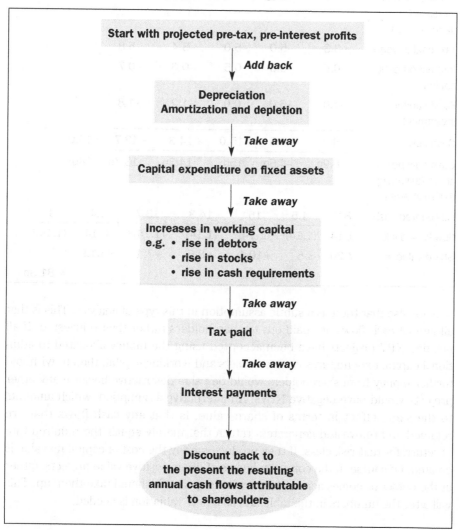

TABLE 13.4

Cash flow-based share valuation

£m age	2010	2011	2012	2013	2014	Estimated aver-annual cash flow for period beyond planning horizon 2015–infinity
Forecast pre-tax, pre-interest profits	+11.0	+15.0	+15.0	+16.0	+17.0	
Add depreciation, amortization and depletion	+1.0	+2.5	+5.5	+4.5	+4.0	
Working capital increase (–) decrease (+)	+1.0	–0.5	0.0	+1.0	+1.0	
Tax (paid in year)	–3.3	–5.0	–5.0	–5.4	–5.8	
Interest on debt capital	–0.5	–0.5	–0.5	–0.6	–0.7	
Fixed capital investment	–1.0	–16.0	0.0	–1.2	–1.8	
Cash flow	+8.2	–4.5	+15.0	+14.3	+13.7	+14.0
Cash flow per share (assuming 100m shares)	8.2p	–4.5p	15p	14.3p	13.7p	14p

Discounted cash flow $k_E = 14\%$

$$\frac{8.2}{1.14} - \frac{4.5}{(1.14)^2} + \frac{15}{(1.14)^3} + \frac{14.3}{(1.14)^4} + \frac{13.7}{(1.14)^5} + \frac{14}{0.14} \times \frac{1}{(1.14)^5}$$

Share value = 7.20 –3.5 +10.1 +8.5 +7.1 +51.9

= 81.3p

Note also that there is a subtle assumption in this type of analysis. This is that all annual cash flows are paid out to shareholders rather than reinvested. If all positive NPV projects have been accepted using the money allocated to additional capital expenditures on fixed assets and working capital, then to withhold further money from shareholders would be value destructive because any other projects would have negative NPVs. An alternative assumption, which amounts to the same effect in terms of share value, is that any cash flows that are retained and reinvested generate a return that merely equals the required rate of return for that risk class. If they produce merely the cost of capital no value is created. Of course, if the company knows of other positive value projects, either at the outset or comes across them in future years, it should take them up. This will alter the numbers in the table and so a new valuation is needed.

The definition of cash flow used here (which includes a deduction of expenditure on investment in fixed and working capital to maintain long-term competitive position, unit volume and make all new value creating projects) is significantly different to many accountant's and analyst's definitions of cash flow. They often neglect to allow for one or more of these factors. Be careful if you are presented with alternative cash flow numbers based on a different definition of cash flow.

Valuation using owner-earnings

A simplified version of cash flow analysis is owner earnings.[5] For shares, intrinsic value is the discounted value of the owner earnings that can be taken out of a business during its remaining life. These correspond with standard cash flow analysis except that we calculate a sustainable level of owner earnings for a typical year (subject to a steady growth) rather than a unique cash flows for each of the future years.

Future owner earnings are determined by the strength and durability of the economic franchise (attractiveness of the industry plus competitive position of the firm in the industry), the quality of management and the financial strength of the business. In the following analysis we make use of Warren Buffett's definition of owner earnings, but with the additional factor in (c) and (d) of 'investment in all new value-creating projects'.

Owner earnings are defined as:

- earnings after tax and interest; *plus*

- depreciation, depletion (e.g. of oil reserves), amortization (of intangible assets, such as brand value) and certain other non-cash charges; *less*

- the amount of expenditures for plant and machinery, etc. that a business requires to fully maintain its long-term competitive position and its unit volume and to make investment in all new value-creating projects; *less*

- any extra amount for working capital that is needed to maintain the firm's long-term competitive position and unit volume and to make investment in all new value-creating projects.

Note that there are two types of investment. First, that which is needed to permit the firm to continue to maintain its existing competitive position at the current level of output. Second, investment in value-creating growth opportunities beyond the current position.

So, for example, Cotillo plc has reported earnings after tax for the most recent year of £16.3m. In drawing up the income (profit and loss) account deductions of £7.4m were made for depreciation, £152,000 for the amortization of intangible assets and £713,000 of goodwill was written off. It is estimated that an annual expenditure of £8.6m on plant, machinery, etc. will be required for the company to maintain its long-term competitive position and unit volume. For the sake of simplicity we will assume that no further monies will be needed for extra working capital to maintain long-term competitive position and unit volume. Also, Cotillo has no new value-creating projects.

The trading record of Cotillo plc has been remarkably stable in the past and is unlikely to alter in the future. It is reasonable to use the above figures for all future years. This would result in an estimated annual owner earnings of £15.965m (*see* Table 13.5).

TABLE 13.5

Cotillo plc, owner earnings

		£000s
(a)	Reported earnings after tax and interest	16,300
	Plus	
(b)	Depreciation, depletion, amortization and other non-cash charges (7,400 + 152 + 713)	8,265
		24,565
	Less	
(c) and (d)	Expenditure on plant, equipment, working capital, etc. required to maintain long-term competitive position, unit volume and investment in new projects	
		8,600
		15,965

If we regard last year's owner earnings as the sustainable level for all future years then the discounted value of a perpetuity of £15.965m is £159.65m, if we take the discount rate to be 10 percent:

$$\text{Intrinsic value} = \frac{£15.965m}{0.10} = £159.65m$$

Intrinsic value is determined by the owner earnings that can be *taken out* of the business during its remaining life. Logically the management of Cotillo should pay out the full £15.956m each year to shareholders if the managers do not have investment projects within the firm that will generate returns of 10 percent or more because shareholders can get 10 percent return elsewhere for the same level of risk as holding a share in Cotillo. If the managers come across another project that promises a return of exactly 10 percent shareholder wealth will be unchanged whether the company invests in this or chooses to ignore the project and continues with the payment of all owner earnings each year. If the management discover, in a future year, a value-creating project that will produce, say, a 15 percent rate of return (for the same level of risk as the existing projects) then shareholders will welcome a reduction in dividends during the years of additional investment. The total value of discounted future owner earnings will rise and intrinsic value will be greater than £159.65m if such a project is undertaken.

Now let us assume that Cotillo has a series of new value-creating (i.e. generating returns greater than 10 percent for the same risk) projects it can invest in. By investing in these projects owner earnings will rise by 5 percent year on year (on the one hand owner earnings are decreased by the need for additional investment under (c) and (d), but, on the other hand reported earnings are boosted under (a), to produce a net 5 percent growth). The intrinsic value becomes £335.26m viz:

Next year's owner earnings = £15.965m(1+g) = £15.965m(1+0.05) = £16.763m

$$\text{Intrinsic value} = \text{next year's owner earnings}/(k_E - g) = \frac{16.763}{0.10 - 0.05} = £335.26m$$

It is legitimate to discount owner earnings because they amount to that which can be paid out to shareholders after all value-creating projects are financed and payments have been made for the investment to maintain the firm's competitive position and unit volume. It would not be legitimate to discount conventional accounting earnings. These are much larger than dividends because part of these earnings is ploughed back into the business for capital items and working capital. Owner earnings are much smaller than conventional earnings and are, in general, closer to the dividend level than to the conventional earnings figure, much of which could not be paid out to shareholders without jeopardizing the future income flows of the business.

EBITDA

EBITDA is classified by some commentators as a cash flow measure of value. EBITDA means earnings before (deduction of) interest, taxation, depreciation and amortization. Many financiers and press reporters use EBITDA in a ratio with enterprise value, EV (market value of equity + market value of debt – cash in the business). It is compared to EV, rather than equity value, because it includes the interest element.

$$\frac{EV}{EBITDA} = \frac{\text{Market value of equity + market value of debt – cash}}{EBITDA}$$

The common use is to compare the EV/EBITDA multiple of the company that the commentator is examining with the multiples currently shown for comparable companies. For instance, when Kraft tried to take over Cadbury in 2009 the press looked at the EV/EBITDA multiple Kraft was offering in the light of the multiples paid for other recently acquired food companies and in the light of the current multiples for stock market quoted comparable firms.

There are a number of benefits claimed for the use of EBITDA in valuation:

- EBITDA is close to cash flow. We cannot say this. It does not take account of tax payments or the need to invest in working capital, for example. It is still vulnerable to a wide range of accrual accounting adjustments, e.g. the valuation of debtors.

- Because the estimation of depreciation, amortization and other non-cash items is vulnerable to judgment error, we can be presented with a distorted profit number; by focusing on profit before these elements are deducted, we can get at a truer estimation of cash flow claim EBITDA's advocates. When making comparisons between firms and discovering a wide variety of depreciation methods being employed (leading to poor comparability), this argument does have some validity: to remove all depreciation, amortization etc. may allow us to compare the relative performances more clearly. However, this line of reasoning can take us too far away from accural accounting. If we accept the need for accrual accounting to provide us with more useful earnings numbers, then we simply cannot dispose of major accrual items when it suits us. By using EBITDA we distort the comparison anyway, because high capital expenditure firms are favoured by the removal of their non-cash item deductions.

- Another argument: If we are focused on future income from the firm's operations we need not allow for the depreciation and amortization because this is based on historical investment in fixed assets that has little relationship with the expected future capital expenditure. While alighting on a truth, the substitution of EBITDA for conventional profit (or for proper cash flow numbers) is wrong because it fails to take into account the need for investment in fixed capital items (and working capital). In the real world, directors (and valuers) cannot ignore (however much they would want to) the cost of using up and wearing out equipment and other assets or the fact that interest and tax need to be paid. Warren Buffett made the comment: 'References to EBITDA make us shudder – does management think the tooth fairy pays for capital expenditures?[6]

- EBITDA is more useful for valuing companies that do not currently make profits, thus enlarging the number of companies that can be analyzed. But note, that all the methods described in this chapter can be used for companies that are currently loss-making – we simply forecast future cash flows, dividends or earnings. EBITDA does not really have an edge over the others in this regard.

- A final argument: When comparing firms with different levels of borrowing, EBITDA is best because it does not deduct interest. It is true EBITDA increases comparability of companies with markedly different financial gearing, but it is also true that the less distortionary EBIT (earnings before interest and tax deduction) can do the same without the exclusion of depreciation or amortisation.

There will be no promoting of EBITDA as a useful measure of valuation in this book, because it can lead to some very distorted thinking. EBITDA (pronounced e-bit-dah) became a very popular measure of a company's performance in the late 1990s. It was especially popular with managers of firms that failed to make a profit. Managers liked to emphasize this measure in their communications to shareholders because large positive numbers could be shown. Some cynics have renamed it 'earnings before I tricked the dumb auditor'.

If you run an internet company that makes a £100m loss and the future looks pretty dim unless you can persuade investors and bankers to continue their support, perhaps you would want to add back all the interest (say £50m), depreciation on assets that are wearing out or becoming obsolete (say £40m), and the declining value of intangible assets, such as software licences and goodwill amortization of, say, £65m, so that you could show a healthy positive number on EBITDA of £55m. And if your loss seems to get worse from one year to the next as your acquisition strategy fails to pay off, it is wonderfully convenient to report and emphasize a stable or rising EBITDA.

The use of EBITDA by company directors can make political spin doctors look like amateurs by comparison. EBITDA is not covered by any accounting standards so companies are entitled to use a variety of methods – whatever shows the company in the best light, I guess.

Another ratio that is calculated is market capitalization (market value of all the ordinary shares) divided by EBITDA. The problem here is that the numerator is an equity measure whereas the denominator relates to income flowing to both debt and equity holders. Those companies with very high debt burdens will look reasonably priced on this measure, when in fact they might be overpriced.

Having listed the drawbacks of the use of EBITDA in valuation, it is important to point out its role in another area; that is, in judging the financial stability and liquidity of the firm. A key measure is the EBITDA to interest ratio. That is how many times greater are the earnings of the company than the gross annual interest bill:

$$\text{EBITDA interest coverage} = \frac{\text{EBITDA}}{\text{Gross interest}}$$

This is used to judge short-term ability to pay interest if the firm could stop paying out for fixed capital items. But, there might still be taxes to pay above and beyond this. Also note that while capital item expenditure may be stopped in the short run, if the company wants to maintain competitive position it will need to keep up with rivals.

Regular users of EBITDA are the private equity firms, particularly when trying to sell a company that they have been running for a while. Long-term capital expenditure to maintain the firm's competitive position, unit volume and invest in positive NPV projects may not be their highest priority when preparing a company for sale – so remember, *caveat emptor*.

Bright House is a company that rents TVs and sofas to poor people. It directed journalists to its EBITDA figures (suitably positive). If any company is going to have a large depreciation item in its accounts as sofas and so on deteriorate, it is BrightHouse. Net profit is not prominent in press releases. Guess what? It is owned by a private equity fund. Do you think they might want to sell it on to a stock exchange soon? *See* Exhibit 13.4.

Double-digit growth for BrightHouse

Esther Bintliff

BrightHouse, which rents high-end consumer durables to people who cannot get credit, enjoyed double-digit revenue and profit growth in the six months to September. The lift came as rising unemployment and economic uncertainty helped widen the company's customer base.

The privately owned retail chain, which rents out top-of-the-range televisions sets, washing machines and sofas without requiring large deposits or credit ratings, is due to report today that revenues surged 15.6 per cent to £94.6m in the six months to September 30.

Sales were helped by the opening of 11 new stores in the period, bringing the nationwide total to 188, although like-for-like revenue also rose 9.9 per cent.

Profits advanced even faster than sales, with earnings before interest, tax, depreciation and amortisation of £14.6m, up 23.7 per cent from the same six-month period in 2008.

Leo McKee, BrightHouse chief executive, said that the flexibility of the rent-to-own model had proved attractive to consumers facing uncertain financial conditions. About half of BrightHouse's customers are wholly or partially reliant on benefits, and the average customer pays £23 a week for three or four products.

Mr McKee said: 'Where the rent-to-own proposition works really well is that if you come in and you decide to rent a telly or a sofa, if in six months you want to return it, you can and there's no charge. If you're a poorer person, you avoid the debt trap.'

BrightHouse, which saw its customer base expand by 14.7 per cent to 156,000 in the first half, also takes a pragmatic approach to consumers who find it difficult to keep up with their weekly payments.

'We have a flexible range of options,' said Mr McKee. 'We might say, don't pay us anything for six weeks and we'll put it all in the end of the period payment.'

'Or we can say, give us that product back and we'll hold it for you for up to a year.'

Mr McKee insisted that in spite of witnessing strong growth during the downturn, the company, which is owned by Vision Capital, the private equity fund, was 'not just for recessionary times', and would target further expansion in spite of indications that the downturn is easing. ...

EXHIBIT 13.4

Source: *Financial Times* 9 November 2009, p. 23.

Valuing unquoted shares

The principles of valuation are the same for companies with a quoted share price on an exchange and for unquoted firms. The methods of valuation discussed above in relation to shares quoted on an exchange may be employed, but there may be some additional factors to consider in relation to unquoted firms' shares.

■ **There may be a lower quality and quantity of information** The reporting statements tend to be less revealing for unquoted firms. There may also be a managerial reluctance to release information – or managers may release information selectively so as to influence value, for example, in merger discussions.

- **These shares may be subject to more risk** Firms at an early stage in their life cycle are often more susceptible to failure than are established firms.

- **The absence of a quotation usually means the shares are less liquid** That is, there is a reduced ability to sell quickly without moving the price. This lack of marketability can be a severe drawback and often investors in unquoted firms, such as venture capitalists, insist on there being a plan to provide an exit route within say five years, perhaps, through a stock market float. But that still leaves a problem for the investor within the five years should a sale be required.

- **Cost of tying-in management** When a substantial stake is purchased in an unquoted firm, for the existing key managers to be encouraged to stay they may be offered financial incentives such as 'golden hand-cuffs' which may influence value. Or the previous owner-managers may agree an 'earn-out' clause in which they receive a return over the years following a sale of their shares (the returns paid to these individuals will be dependent on performance over a specified future period).

- **Owner/director compensation** When considering a takeover price for an unquoted company, the reported figures need to be examined carefully because it is often the case that the owner-directors have been over-paying themselves from company coffers. Therefore an upward adjustment is needed to the profit/cash flow numbers. On the other hand, owner-directors may have under-paid themselves and a takeover would mean their replacements would need to be paid considerably more.

Unquoted firms' shares tend to sell at significantly lower prices than those of quoted firms. The BDO Stoy Hayward/Acquisitions Monthly Private Company Price Index (www.bdo.co.uk) shows unquoted firms being sold at an average PER of under two-thirds that for quoted shares.

Unusual companies

Obtaining information to achieve accuracy with discounted income flow methods is problematic for most shares. But in industries subject to rapid technological innovation it is extraordinarily difficult. While discounted income flow remains the ultimate method of valuation some analysts use more immediate proxies to estimate value. (A less scientific-sounding description is 'rules of thumb'.) For example, Gerry Stephens and Justin Funnell, media and telecoms analysts at NatWest Markets, describe the approach often adopted in their sector:[7]

> Rather than DCF (discounted cash flow), people are often more comfortable valuing telemedia project companies using benchmarks that have evolved from actual market prices paid for similar assets, being based on a comparative measure or scale such as per line, per subscriber, per home or per pop (member of population). For example, an analyst might draw conclusions from the per-pop price that Vodaphone trades at

to put a price on the float of Telecom Italia Mobile. The benchmark prices will actually have originated from DCF analysis and the price paid can give an element of objective validation to the implied subjective DCF.

Other sectors difficult to value directly on the basis of income flow include: advertising agencies, where a percentage of annual billings is often used as a proxy; mobile phone operators, where ARPU (average revenue per user) is used; fund managers, where value of funds under management is used; hotels, where star ratings may be combined with number of rooms and other factors such as revenue per available room; cement companies, where their annual production capacity (or sales) in metric tons is multiplied by a number thought to have validity to the analyst; car parking companies, where the number of car parking spaces is multiplied; and insurance companies, where the annual premiums payable is multiplied.

Managerial control changes the valuation

The value of a share can change depending on whether the purchaser gains a controlling interest in the firm. The purchase of a single share brings a stream of future dividends without any real influence over the level of those dividends. However, control of a firm by, say, purchasing 50 percent or more of the shares, permits the possibility of changing the future operations of the firm, thus enhancing returns. A merger may allow economies of scale and other synergies, or future earnings may be boosted by the application of superior management skills.

The difference in value between a share without management control and one with it helps to explain why we often witness a share price rise of 30–50 percent in a takeover bid battle. There are two appraisals of the value of the firm, both of which may be valid depending on the assumption concerning managerial control. Figure 13.6 shows that extra value can be created by merging the operations of two firms.

Figure 13.6 is not meant to imply that the acquiring firm will pay a bid premium equal to the estimated merger benefits. The price paid is subject to negotiation and bargaining. The acquirer is likely to try to offer significantly less than the combined amount of the target firm's value 'as is' and the merger benefits. This will enable it to retain as much as possible of the increased value for itself rather than pass value on to the target shareholders. (*See* Chapter 12 for more detail.)

The merger of British Airways and Iberia will provide a framework for illustrating possible use of the income flow model when managerial control is obtained. In 2009 the two companies claimed that by merging they could save €400m annually by cutting staff, ending overlapping routes and pushing up yields or average fares.

In the absence of a takeover the value of a share in either company is:

$$P_0 = \frac{d_1}{k_E - g}$$

FIGURE 13.6

Value creation through merger

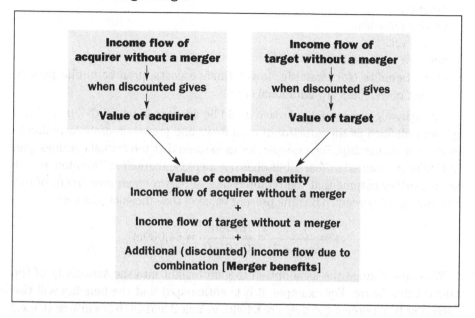

This is where d_1 and g are generated by the existing structure and strategy.

Alternatively, we could examine the entire cash flow of the company (available to be paid out to shareholders after maintaining the firm's competitive position, unit volume and investing in all value generating projects) rather than that relating to a single share.

$$V = \frac{C_1}{k_E - g_c}$$

where:

V   = value of the entire firm;
C_1 = total cash flows at time 1 expected to continue growing at a constant rate of g_c in future years.

If there is a new strategy the values in the equations change:

$$P_0 = \frac{d_1^*}{k_E - g^*}$$

or, for the entire cash flow:

$$V = \frac{C_1^*}{k_E - g_c^*}$$

$d_1{}^*, C_1{}^*, g^*, g_c{}^*$ allow for the following:

> synergy;
> cutting out costs;
> tax benefits;
> superior management;
> other benefits (for example, lower finance costs, greater public profile, market power) less any additional costs.

Alternatively, a marginal approach could be adopted in which $C_1{}^*, d_1{}^*, g^*$ and $g_c{}^*$ are redefined as the *additional* cash flows and growth in cash flows due to changes in ownership. For example, let us assume that the annual earnings gain of €400m is obtained in Year 1 but does not increase thereafter. Therefore $g = 0$. Let us further assume that the required rate of return on an investment of this risk class is 10 percent. Thus the present value of the efficiency gains is:

$$V = \frac{C_1{}^*}{k_E - g_c{}^*} = \frac{€400m}{0.10 - 0} = €4,000m$$

We could change the assumption to gain insight into the sensitivity of the added value figure. For example, if it is anticipated that the benefits will rise each year by 2 percent (so they are €408m in Year 2 and €416.2m in Year 3, etc.) then the maximum bid premium will rise:

$$V = \frac{C_1{}^*}{k_E - g_c{}^*} = \frac{€400m}{0.10 - 0.02} = €5,000m$$

On the other hand, the management of the two companies might have been carried away with the excitement of the bid battle and the €400m quoted might have come from hype or hubris, and, in fact, the difficulties of integration produce negative incremental cash flows.

Allowing for real option values

The expected income flows to be received by shareholders are the foundation for share valuation. But what about companies that have no projected income flows? Take an oil company that has fallen on hard times. It has shut down all of its oil wells because the cost of extraction is greater than current market price of oil. In fact, the oil price would have to double to make it worthwhile reopening the wells. So there is little that the analyst can put into, say, a discounted cash flow calculation because the chances are that the company will never produce income again. However, this is not to say that there is no value. The company has the right but not the obligation to start taking oil from its wells when it wants to. This can be worth a lot of money if an event happens, e.g. the price of oil triples.

The same logic applies to parts of a firm. There may be little prospect of the asset producing an income flow for the shareholders and yet there is value because of the existence of an option someday to implement the project should circumstances change. Thus to the value of identifiable income flows we should add the value of the collection of options that the firm may be holding, ranging from expansion options, delaying options to the option to quit. This area of finance is known a *contingent claim valuation*: cash flows are to some extent contingent on the occurrence or non-occurrence of some event and therefore the asset being valued is greater than the present value of the expected cash flows. BT owns thousands of patents, some of which may be worth millions, if not billions, when the time is ripe. Indeed, we may discover at some point in the future that one or two of the inventions and innovations produced in the labs and currently hidden away in the vaults are worth more than all the currently projected cash flows on its existing business. We will not know until the contingent event happens (e.g. a complementary technological breakthrough) and the new business is created. Another example: if you were a song writer in the 1970s and you were smart you would have held on to the rights to use your music in any form. Even though you could not at that time value those rights for use in devices you could not even imagine (mobile phone ringtones, MP3 players, etc.), you did figure out that circumstances change and options to do something can suddenly become amazingly valuable.

Knowing that real options are important is one thing, but valuing them is quite another. Most are very difficult to value. Be cautious: people can come up with very suspect numbers vulnerable to bias. Chapter 5 discusses real options.

Worked example 13.6
THINGAMEES

Big plc has made it clear to the widget industry that it is willing to sell its subsidiary, Little plc, a manufacturer of thingamees. You are a member of the strategy management team at Thingamees International plc, the largest producers of thingamees in the UK. Your firm is interested in acquiring Little and as a first step has obtained some information from Big plc.

Little plc balance sheet

	£m
Fixed assets	10
Current assets	
Cash	0.5
Stock	1.5
Debtors	3.0
	5
Current liabilities	(6)
Bank loan	(4)
Net assets	5

Trading record

Year	Earnings, £m (Owner earnings)
2009	1.86
2008	1.70
2007	1.65
2006	1.59
2005	1.20
2004	1.14
2003	1.01

Additional information

By combining the logistical departments you estimate that transport costs could be lowered by £100,000 per annum, and two secretarial posts eliminated, saving £28,000 p.a.

The closure of Little's head office would save £400,000 p.a. in staffing and running costs, but would also mean an additional £250,000 p.a. of administration costs at Thingamees plc to undertake some crucial tasks. The office building is situated in a good location and would raise a net £5m if sold immediately. A potential liability not displayed in Little's balance sheet is a possible legal claim of £3m relating to an earlier disposal of an asset. The plaintiff and Little's board have not yet reached agreement (Little's board is adamant that there is no liability).

Your appraisal of Little's management team is that it is a mixed bunch – some good, some very bad. Profits could be raised by £500,000 per year if you could impose your will quickly and remove poor managers. However, if you have to take a more gradual 'easing out' approach, operating profits will rise by only £300,000 per year.

The problems connected with a quick transition are: a sacking left, right and centre may cause disaffection among the good managers, encouraging hostility, departures and (a) profits collapse, and (b) Big plc is keen that you provide a commitment to avoid large-scale redundancies.

Big, Little and Thingamees International all have a beta of 1.9, which is representative of the appropriate adjustment to the risk premium on the average share given the systematic risk. The risk-free rate of return is 8% and the historical risk premium of share portfolios over safe securities has been 3.5%.

The increased market power available to Thingamees International after purchasing Little would improve margins in Thingamees International's existing business to provide an additional £100,000 per annum. Assume that tax is irrelevant.

Required

(a) Calculate the value of Little plc in its present form, assuming a continuation of its historical growth rate.
(b) Calculate the value of Little plc if you were unable to push for maximum management redundancies and Little continued with its historical growth rate for its owner earnings (that is, the earnings before merger benefits). Include the annual merger benefits assuming that they are constant for all future years to an infinite horizon, that is, there is no growth in these.
(c) Calculate the value of Little plc on the assumption that you are able to push through the rapid management changes and the pre-acquisition earnings continue on their historical growth path. (Add on the annual merger savings assuming these are the same for every future year.)
(d) Discuss the steps you would take to get around the obstacles to shareholder wealth maximization.

Answers

(a) First calculate the required rate of return:

$$k_E = r_f + \beta \, (r_m - r_f)$$

$$= 8 + 1.9 \, (3.5) = 14.65\%$$

(The required rate of return is discussed in Chapter 10.)

■ Then calculate growth rate of cash flows:

$$g = \sqrt[6]{\frac{1.86}{1.01}} - 1 = 10.71\%$$

■ Then calculate the value of Little plc:

$$V = \frac{C_1}{k_E - g} = \frac{1.86(1 + 0.1071)}{0.1465 - 0.1071} = \pounds52.264m$$

The value of Little to its shareholders under its present strategy and managers is £52,264m.

(b) Calculate the present value of the future cash flows. These come in three forms:

(i) Those cash flows available immediately from selling assets, etc., less the amount due on a legal claim (taking the most conservative view):

Time 0 cash flows

Sale of head office	£5m
Less legal claim	£3m
	£2m

(ii) Merger benefit cash flow – constant for all future years:

	£m
Transport	0.100
Secretaries	0.028
Head office	0.150
Managerial efficiency	0.300
Market power	0.100
Boost to cash flow	0.678

This is a perpetuity which has a present value of:

$$\frac{0.678}{0.1465} = \pounds4.628m$$

(iii) The present value of Little under its existing strategy, £52.264m. Add these values together:

	£2.000m
	£4.628m
	£52.264m
Total value if unable to sack poor managers	**£58.892m**

(c) Value of business in existing form   £52.264m
plus value of annual savings and benefits

$$\frac{678{,}000 + 200{,}000}{0.1465}$$ £5.993m

plus Time 0 cash flows   £2.000m

Total value if able to sack poor managers   £60.257m

Thingamees International now has a bargaining range for the purchase of Little. Below £52.264m the existing shareholders will be reluctant to sell. Above £60.257m, Thingamees may destroy value for its own shareholders even if all poor managers can be removed.

(d) Some ideas: One possible step to reduce risk is to insist that Big plc accepts all liability relating to the legal claim. Another issue to be addressed in the negotiation phase is to avoid being hamstrung by redundancy commitments. Also plan the process of merger integration. In the period before the merger explain your intentions to Little's employees. After the transfer do not alienate the managers and other employees by being capricious and secretive – be straight and honest. If pain is to be inflicted for the good of the firm, be quick, rational and fair, communicate and explain (*see* Chapter 11 for more detail).

Exhibit 13.5 discusses some of the practical difficulties in valuation.

The black art of valuation is fraught with dangers

Tony Jackson

In fraught times like these, it is natural for investors to reach for the basic tools of valuation by way of reassurance. Sadly, such times also remind us how brittle those tools really are. ...

In formal terms, at least, DCF lies at the root of all investment decisions – whether to buy a share, acquire a company or build a factory. It is a simple three-step process; determine the sum of future cash flows, reduce them to present value through a discount rate, and compare the result with today's price.

Warren Buffett, the world's most successful portfolio investor – and a noted acquirer of companies – has argued repeatedly that DCF is not just the main, but the only valuation tool. Price/earnings ratios, dividend yields and even growth rates are irrelevant, except insofar as they help clarify the scale and timing of future cash flows.

But Mr Buffett is a special case. What if, for the rest of us, DCF is a fantasy?

One thoughtful if jaundiced observer of the science, James Montier of Société Générale, effectively argues just that.

First, he says, analysts are hopeless at forecasting. And the further out they go, the more hopeless they get.

I have some sympathy with that.

As a novice analyst some three dea-cades ago, I was aghast at the notion of five or 10-year forecasts. Mere 12-month projections of earnings, balance sheets and cash flows seemed daunting enough.

Second, the discount rate used by analysts – though not, one imagines, by Mr Buffett – is essentially subjective.

Spurred on by financial theory, they use at least three components: the risk-free rate (usually the Treasury bond yield), the equity risk premium and the stock's beta.

The first seems fair enough. The second is a notional figure which can be calculated all sorts of ways – by sector, by market, ex post or ex ante and so on.

More to the point, the figure arrived at is typically 3 to 4 per cent – which, given the huge risks and uncertainties in the forecast itself, is bogus precision.

The stock's beta, meanwhile, is arguably a red herring, as we shall see in a moment. But first, what would Mr Buffett say to all that?

'Even an experienced and intelligent analyst,' he wrote some years ago, 'can go wrong in estimating future cash flow.

'The answer is to stick to businesses which are relatively simple and stable in character.'

Mr Buffett explicitly rules out busi-nesses or industries that are new, unstable or subject to rapid change, such as investment banking or technology.

Without wishing to put words into the great man's mouth, this seems to include most of the market.

Taken as a simple syllogism, this is rather daunting. It says that 1) the only rational valuation method is DCF; 2) DCF is not applicable to most busi-nesses, and therefore 3) most businesses cannot be rationally valued.

And yet business people go on making valuation decisions every day. How come?

Part of the answer, I suspect, is that executives proceed much more cau-tiously than analysts. Their cash-flow projections are lower, their discount rates higher. This makes sense.

If a fund manager buys a stock on false assumptions, he can dump it. If an executive builds a plant on the same basis, he is stuck.

The other part of the answer is that the market works as a kind of blunder-ing average. The point is not that it is setting the right price, but that it is set-ting a price at all.

This is what Mr Buffett means when he says 'Mr Market' is there to serve you, not to guide you. It is also why he rejects the use of beta. Suppose a stock that normally tracks the market sud-denly collapses for no good reason. Should you not buy it, just because its beta has gone up?

Alas, for the average fund manager the answer is normally yes. If the market says a stock is risky, so it is. And if DCF says a stock is cheap but its market price is falling, end of story.

The head of research at a London stockbroking firm tells me his first lesson to young analysts is that their job is to forecast not a company's earnings, but its share price.

If this sounds cynical, it is also sober realism. If analysts think a stock is cheap but DCF says different, they will in practice fiddle the forecast and/or dis-count rate until it gives the right answer.

In other words, build DCF models to your heart's content, but do not expect the market to agree with you.

Or not within the time available, at any rate.

EXHIBIT 13.5

Source: *Financial Times* 15 September 2008, p. 24.

Conclusion

There are two points about valuation worth noting. First going through a rigorous process of valuation is more important than arriving at *an* answer. It is the understanding of the assumptions and an appreciation of the nature of the inputs to the process that give insight, not a single number at the end. It is the recognition of the qualitative, and even subjective, nature of key variables in an apparently quantitative analysis that leads to knowledge about values. We cannot escape the uncertainty inherent in the valuation of a share – what someone is

> Going through a rigorous process of valuation is more important than arriving at *an* answer.

willing to pay depends on what will happen in the future – and yet this is no excuse for rejecting the models as unrealistic and impractical. They are better than the alternatives: guessing, or merely comparing one share with another with no theoretical base to anchor either valuation. At least the models presented in this chapter have the virtue of forcing the analyst to make explicit the fundamental considerations concerning the value of a share.

The second point leads on from the first. It makes sense to treat the various valuation methods as complementary rather than as rivals. Obtain a range of values in full knowledge of the weaknesses of each approach and apply informed judgment to provide an idea of the value region.

Notes

1 *See* discussion in Chapter 14 based on evidence from Lintner (1956) and 3i (1993) – details of these sources are in Chapter 14 References and Further Reading.

2 If the dividends continue to grow at the rate g in perpetuity.

3 Warren Buffett seminar held at Columbia University Business School. 'Investing in equity markets', 13 March 1985, Transcript, p. 23. Reproduced in Janet Lowe (1997).

4 Quoted by Robert Outram (1997), p. 70.

5 Warren Buffett developed this method. A modified version is shown here which incorporates the investment in value generating projects rather than steady state owner earnings (see Arnold (2009) *The Financial Times Guide to Value Investing* for more details).

6 Warren Buffett, in a letter to shareholders attached to the *Annual Report of Berkshire Hathaway Inc* (2000). Reprinted with kind permission of Warren Buffett. © Warren Buffett.

7 Stephens and Funnell (1995), p. 20.

14

WHAT PAY-OUTS SHOULD WE MAKE TO SHAREHOLDERS?

Dividend policy is often reported to shareholders, but seldom explained. A company will say something like, 'Our goal is to pay out 40% to 50% of earnings and to increase dividends at a rate at least equal to the rise in the CPI.'[1] And that's it – no analysis will be supplied as to why that particular policy is best for the owners of the business. Yet, allocation of capital is crucial to businesses and investment management. Because it is, we believe managers and owners should think hard about the circumstances under which earnings should be retained and under which they should be distributed.

> Managers and owners should think hard about the circumstances under which earnings should be retained and under which they should be distributed.

Source: Warren Buffett, a letter to shareholders attached to the *Annual Report of Berkshire Hathaway Inc* (1984). © Warren Buffett.

Introduction

After 60 years of observing managers Warren Buffett's comments may be viewed as a sad indictment of the quality of managerial thought on the issue of dividend policy. On the central issue of whether to retain profits, or distribute them to shareholders to use elsewhere, there appears to be vagueness and confusion. He has suggested that the issue is addressed at a superficial level with the employment of simple rules of thumb and no analysis. This conclusion may or may not be unfair – this chapter is not designed to highlight managerial failings in the depth of thought department. What it can do, however, is point out the major influences on the level of the dividend decision in any one year. Some of these are fully 'rational' in the sense of the economist's model, others are less quantifiable, and stem more from the field of psychology.

The conclusion reached is that managers have to weigh up a range of forces – some pulling them in the direction of paying out either a high proportion of earnings or a low one; other forces pulling them to provide a stable and consistent dividend, and yet others pulling them to vary the dividend from year to year.

These are, of course, merely the range of forces influencing managers who are fully committed to shareholder wealth maximisation and thinking 'hard about the circumstances under which earnings should be retained'. If we admit the possibility that managers have other goals, or that they make little intellectual effort, the possible outcomes of the annual or semi-annual boardroom discussion on the dividend level can range widely.

Defining the problem

Dividend policy is the determination of the proportion of profits paid out to shareholders – usually periodically. The issue to be addressed is whether shareholder wealth can be enhanced by altering the *pattern* of dividends not the size of dividends overall. Naturally, if dividends over the lifetime of a firm are larger, value will be greater. So in the forthcoming analysis we will assume that:

- the underlying investment opportunities and returns on business investment are constant; and

- the extra value that may be created by changing the capital structure (debt–equity ratio) is constant.

Therefore only the pattern of dividend payments may add or subtract value. For example, perhaps a pattern of high pay-outs in the immediate future, with a consequential reduction in dividend growth thereafter, may be superior to a policy of zero or small dividends now followed by more rapid growth over time.

Another aspect of the pattern question is whether a steady, stable dividend growth rate is better than a volatile one which varies from year to year depending on the firm's internal need for funds.

Some background

UK-quoted companies usually pay dividends every six months. In each financial year there is an *interim* dividend related to the first half year's trading, followed by the final dividend after the financial year-end. The board of directors are empowered to recommend the *final* dividend level but it is a right of shareholders as a body to vote at the annual general meeting whether or not it should be paid. Not all companies follow the typical cycle of two dividends per year: a few pay dividends quarterly and others choose not to pay a dividend at all.

Dividends may only be paid out of accumulated distributable profits and not out of capital. This means that companies which have loss-making years may still pay dividends, but only up to the point that they have retained profits from previous years.[2] This rule is designed to provide some protection to creditors by putting a barrier in the way of shareholders looking to remove funds from the firm, and thereby withdrawing the cushion of capital originally provided by shareholders. Further restrictions may be placed on the firm's freedom of action with regard to dividend levels by constraints contained in bond, preference share and bank-loan agreements.

The proportion of after-tax earnings paid as dividends varies greatly between firms, from zero percent to more than 100 percent. The average for companies quoted on the London Stock Exchange is usually around 40–50 percent, but it has risen to 70 percent or more.

Theorists in their hypothetical world

According to an important 1961 paper by Miller and Modigliani (MM), if a few assumptions can be made, dividend policy is irrelevant to share value. The determinant of value is the availability of projects with positive NPVs and the pattern of dividends makes no difference to the acceptance of these. The share price would not move if the firm declared either a zero dividend policy or a policy of high near-term dividends. The conditions under which this was held to be true included:

- There are no taxes.
- There are no transaction costs, for example:
  - investors face no brokerage costs when buying or selling shares,
  - companies can issue shares with no transaction costs.
- All investors can borrow and lend at the same interest rate.
- All investors have free access to all relevant information.
- Investors are indifferent between dividends and capital gains on shares.

Given these assumptions, dividend policy can become irrelevant. For example, a firm which had plentiful positive NPV projects but nevertheless paid all profits each year as dividends would not necessarily be destroying shareholder wealth because in this ideal world any money paid out could quickly be replaced by having a new issue of shares, e.g. through a rights issues.[3] The investors in these shares would willingly pay a fair price because of their access to all relevant information. The shares can be issued by the firm without costs of underwriting or merchant banks' fees, etc., and bought by the shareholders without brokers' fees or costs associated with the time spent filling in forms, etc. That is, there are no transaction costs.

If a company chose not to pay any dividends at all and shareholders required a regular income then this could be achieved while leaving the firm's value intact. 'Homemade dividends' can be created by shareholders selling a portion of their shares to other investors – again, as there are no costs of transactions and no taxation the effect is identical to the receipt of cash in the form of an ordinary dividend from the firm.

Take the example of Belvoir plc, an all-equity company which has a policy of paying out all annual net cash flow as dividend. The company is expected to generate a profit of £1m to an infinite horizon. Given the cost of equity capital is 12 percent we can calculate the value of this firm using the dividend valuation model (with zero growth – *see* Chapter 13 for details).

$$P_0 = d_0 + \frac{d_1}{k_E} = £1m + \frac{£1m}{0.12} = £9.333m$$

This includes £1m of dividend due to be paid immediately, plus the £1m perpetuity.

Now suppose that the management have identified a new investment opportunity. This will produce additional cash flows of £180,000 per year starting in one year. However the company will be required to invest £1m now. There are two ways in which this money for investment could be found. First, the managers could skip the present dividend and retain £1m. Second, the company could maintain its dividend policy for this year and pay out £1m, but simultaneously launch a new issue of shares, say a rights issue, to gain the necessary £1m.

It will now be demonstrated that in this perfect world, with no transaction costs, shareholder value will be the same whichever dividend policy is adopted. What *will* increase shareholder value is the NPV of the project.

$$\text{NPV} = -\pounds 1\text{m} + \frac{\pounds 180,000}{0.12} = \pounds 500,000$$

The value of the firm is raised by £500,000, by the acceptance of the project and not because of the dividend policy. If the project is financed through the sacrifice of the present dividend the effect on shareholder wealth is:

Year	0	1	2	3 etc.
Cash flow to				
shareholders	0	1,180,000	1,180,000	1,180,000

$$\text{Shareholders' wealth} = \frac{1,180,000}{0.12} = \pounds 9.833\text{m}$$

Shareholders' wealth is increased by £500,000.

If the project is financed through a rights issue (selling more shares to existing shareholders – *see* Chapter 17) while leaving the dividend pattern intact the effect on shareholder wealth is the same – an increase of £500,000.

Year	0	1	2	3
Cash flow to				
shareholders:				
Receipt of dividend	+£1,000,000			
Rights issue	–£1,000,000			
	0	1,180,000	1,180,000	1,180,000

$$\text{Shareholders' wealth} = \frac{1,180,000}{0.12} = \pounds 9.833\text{m}$$

Shareholders' wealth is enhanced because £1m of shareholders' money is invested in a project which yields more than 12 percent. If the incremental cash inflows amounted to only £100,000 then the wealth of shareholders would fall, because a 10 percent return is insufficient given the opportunity cost of shareholders' money:

$$\frac{\pounds 1,100,000}{0.12} = \pounds 9.167\text{m}$$

If the new investment produces a 12 percent return shareholders will experience no loss or gain in wealth. The critical point is that in this hypothetical, perfect world the pattern of dividend makes no difference to shareholders' wealth. This is determined purely by the investment returns. If a firm chose to miss a dividend for a year, because it had numerous high-yielding projects to invest in, this would not decrease share values, because the perfectly well-informed investors are aware that any cash retained will be going into positive NPV projects which will generate future dividend increases for shareholders. If a shareholder needs income this year, they can sell a portion of shares held to create a 'homemade dividend' confident in the knowledge that a fair price would be obtained in this perfect world, which takes into account the additional value from the project.

The other extreme – dividends as a residual

Now we take another extreme position. Imagine that the raising of external finance (for example rights issues) is so expensive that to all intents and purposes it is impossible. The only source of finance for additional investment is earnings. Returning to the example of Belvoir, it is obvious that under these circumstances, to pay this year's dividend will reduce potential shareholder value by £500,000 because the new project will have to be abandoned.

In this world dividends should only be paid when the firm has financed all its positive NPV projects. Once the firm has provided funds for all the projects which more than cover the minimum required return, investors should be given the residual. They should receive this cash because they can use it to invest in other firms of the same risk class, which provide an expected return at least as great as the required return on equity capital, k_E. If the firm kept all the cash flows and continued adding to its range of projects the marginal returns would be likely to decrease, because the project with the highest return would be undertaken first, followed by the one with the next highest return, and so on, until returns became very low.

In these circumstances dividend policy becomes an important determinant of shareholder wealth:

■ If cash flow is retained and invested within the firm at less than k_E, shareholder wealth is destroyed; therefore it is better to raise the dividend payout rate.

■ If retained earnings are insufficient to fund all positive NPV projects shareholder value is lost, and it would be beneficial to lower the dividend.

What about the world in which we live?

We have discussed two extreme positions so far and have reached opposing conclusions. In a perfect world the dividend pattern is irrelevant because the firm can always fund itself costlessly if it has positive NPV projects, and shareholders can costlessly generate 'homemade dividends' by selling some of their shares. In a world with no external finance the pattern of dividends becomes crucial to shareholder wealth, as an excessive pay-out reduces the take-up of positive NPV projects; and an unduly low pay-out means value destruction because investors miss out on investment opportunities elsewhere in the financial securities market.

In our world there are transaction costs to contend with. If a firm pays a dividend to keep to its avowed dividend pattern and then, in order to fund projects, takes money from shareholders through a rights issue, this is not frictionless: there are costs. The expense for the firm includes the legal and administrative cost of organising a rights issue or some other issue of shares; it may be necessary to prepare a prospectus and to incur advertising costs; underwriting fees alone can be as much as 4 percent of the amount raised. The expense for the shareholder of receiving money with one hand only to give it back with the other might include brokerage costs and the time and hassle involved. Taxes further complicate the issue by imposing additional costs.

It is plain that there is a powerful reason why dividend policy might make some difference to shareholder wealth: the investment opportunities within the firm obviously have some effect. This may help to explain why we witness many young rapidly growing firms with a need for investment finance having a very low dividend (or zero) pay-outs, whereas mature 'cash cow' type firms choose a high payout rate.

The relationship between investment opportunity and dividend policy is a far from perfect one and there are a number of other forces pulling on management to select a particular policy. These will be considered after some more down-to-earth arguments from Warren Buffett (*see* Exhibit 14.1).

Berkshire Hathaway Inc

'Earnings should be retained only when there is a reasonable prospect – backed preferably by historical evidence or, when appropriate by a thoughtful analysis of the future – *that for every dollar retained by the corporation, at least one dollar of market value will be created for owners* [italics in original]. This will happen only if the capital retained produces incremental earnings equal to, or above, those generally available to investors.'

Warren Buffett says that many managers think like owners when it comes to demanding high returns from subordinates but fail to apply the same principles to the dividend payout decision:

'The CEO of multi-divisional company will instruct Subsidiary A, whose earnings on incremental capital may be expected to average 5%, to distribute all available earnings in order that they may be invested in Subsidiary B, whose earnings on incremental capital are expected to be 15%. The CEO's business school oath will allow no lesser behavior. But if his own long-term record with incremental capital is 5% – and market rates are 10% – he is likely to impose a dividend policy on shareholders of the parent company that merely follows some historic or industry-wide payout pattern. Furthermore, he will expect managers of subsidiaries to give him a full account as to why it makes sense for earnings to be retained in their operations rather than distributed to the parent-owner. But seldom will he supply his owners with a similar analysis pertaining to the whole company ... shareholders would be far better off if earnings were retained only to expand the high-return business, with the balance paid in dividends or used to repurchase stock [shares].'

EXHIBIT 14.1

Source: Letter to shareholders, *Annual Report of Berkshire Hathaway Inc* (1984). Reproduced by kind permission of Warren Buffett. ©
Warren Buffett.

Shareholders are willing to accept that dividends should be lowered if companies are going through hard times when the survival of the firm or the acceptance of positive NPV project is at risk – *see* Exhibit 14.2.

New fears emerge on dividend pay-outs

Kate Burgess

Fresh worries that the downturn in the global economy will force more dividend cuts were raised yesterday after two further companies reduced pay-outs.

Enterprise Inns and Stobart became the latest in a line of UK companies to cut pay-outs to preserve cash.

Imperial Tobacco, a company traditionally known for the consistency of its pay-outs, also suggested it could reduce future dividend growth to take into account the restructuring costs of its acquisition of Altadis.

BT is widely expected to cut its dividend tomorrow and doubts hang over Marks and Spencer's pay-out when the retailer announces its results next week. BP signalled in March that it was freezing its pay-out this year for the first time in a decade.

The scale of the dividend cuts is hitting investors, for whom dividends are an important component of returns.

Richard Batty, global investment strategist at Standard Life Investments, said: 'In this downturn investors have been willing to forgo dividends for the sake of the longer-term survival of a company. Investor attitudes may be changing.'

He added that current dividend forecasts were pricing in too pessimistic an outlook for equity markets. Derivative markets had priced in 'savage cuts' of a 50 per cent fall in FTSE 100 dividends between 2009 and 2010.

Standard Life said UK dividends cuts, in the worst case, could be 35 per cent in 2009–11. Mr Batty added that 'these would still be the severest cuts in dividends on record, bar 1918–19 at the end of the first world war when the UK economy was effectively bankrupt'.

Other analysts expect further cuts of 10–20 per cent in UK dividends in the next two years.

The bulk of dividend cuts has come from banks. Now cuts from non-financial companies are expected to follow suit as earnings come under pressure.

EXHIBIT 14.2

Source: *Financial Times* 13 May 2009, p. 1.

HMV handed cash back to its shareholders when it had cash surplus to its investment requirements because that is 'the responsible thing to do' – *see* Exhibit 14.3.

Double boost for HMV shareholders

Sophy Buckley

HMV, the music, book and film retailer, is increasing the return to its shareholders with a 31 per cent jump in its interim dividend and a 12-month share buy-back programme that could be worth about £50m.

The group, which includes the Waterstone's book chain, said the moves reflected its confidence despite showing a degree of caution about slowing sales growth.

The shares dipped $3\frac{1}{2}$p to 251p as analysts shaved their profits forecasts.

Alan Giles, chief executive, said: 'We are very comfortable with the level of gearing in the business – if you talk to analysts most think we will be debt free by the end of this financial year.'

'We can very comfortably fund £60m–65m on our ongoing organic expansion and still have £50m plus left over. Obviously the responsible thing to do with that is to return it to shareholders.' ...

EXHIBIT 14.3

Source: *Financial Times* 19 January 2005, p. 24.

Some muddying factors

Clientele effects

Some shareholders prefer a dividend pattern that matches their desired consumption pattern. There may be natural clienteles for shares which pay out a high proportion of earnings, and another clientele for shares which have a low payout rate. For example, retired people, living off their private investments, may prefer a high and steady income, so they would tend to be attracted to firms with a high and stable dividend yield. Likewise, some pension funds need regular cash receipts to meet payments to pensioners.

Shareholders who need a steady flow of income, could, of course, generate a cash flow stream by selling off a proportion of their shares on a regular basis as an alternative to investing in firms with a high payout ratio. But this approach will result in transaction costs (brokerage, marketmakers' spread and loss of interest while waiting for cash after sale). Also it is time-consuming and inconvenient to regularly sell off blocks of shares; it is much easier to receive a series of dividend cheques through the post.

> It is time-consuming and inconvenient to regularly sell off blocks of shares; it is much easier to receive a series of dividend cheques through the post.

Furthermore, people often acknowledge self-control problems and so make rules for themselves, such as 'we will live off the income but never touch the capital.' They are afraid of starting down a slippery slope of selling off a proportion of shares each year in case they are tempted to over-indulge. Thus, shares with high dividends are attractive because they give income without the need to dig into capital.

Another type of clientele are people who are not interested in receiving high dividends in the near term. These people prefer to invest in companies with good growth potential – companies which pay low dividends and use the retained money to invest in projects with positive NPVs within the firm. The idea behind such practices is that capital gains (a rising share price) will be the main way in which the shareholder receives a return. An example of such a clientele group might be wealthy middle-aged people who have more than enough income from their paid employment for their consumption needs. If these people did receive large amounts of cash in dividends now they would probably only reinvest it in the stock market. A cycle of receiving dividends followed by reinvestment is inefficient.

It seems reasonable to argue that a proportion of shareholders choose to purchase particular shares at least partially because the dividend policy suits them. This may place pressure on the management to produce a stable and consistent dividend policy because investors need to know that a particular investment is going to continue to suit their preferences. Inconsistency would result in a lack of popularity with any client group and would depress the share price. Management therefore, to some extent, target particular clienteles.[4]

The clientele force acting on dividend policy at first glance seems to be the opposite of the residual approach. With the clientele argument, stability and consistency are required to attract a particular type of clientele, whereas with the residual argument, dividends depend on the opportunities for reinvestment – the volume of which may vary in a random fashion from year to year, resulting in fluctuating retentions and dividends. Most firms seem to square this circle by having a consistent dividend policy based on a medium- or long-term view of earnings and investment capital needs. The shortfalls and surpluses in particular years are adjusted through other sources of finance: for example, borrowing or raising equity through a rights issue in years when retained earnings are insufficient; paying off debt or storing up cash when retentions are greater than investment needs. There are costs associated with such a policy, for example the costs of rights issues, and these have to be weighed against the benefit of stability.

Exhibit 14.4 hints at strong clientele effects – unfortunately BP was forced by US politicians to cut its dividends in 2010 following the oil spill.

The clientele effect is often reinforced by the next factor we will examine, taxation. The consistent dividend pattern policy is encouraged by the information aspect of dividends – discussed after that.

Taxation

The taxation of dividends and capital gains on shares is likely to influence the preference of shareholders for receiving cash either in the form of a regular payment from the company (a dividend) or by selling shares (in the market to create home-made dividends or in a share buy-back – *see* later in the chapter). If shareholders are taxed more heavily on dividends than on capital gains they are more likely to

Companies strive to keep investors sweet

Tom Burgis

The ghost of traumatic AGMs past hovered over Peter Sutherland last week as he recalled 'several years of buffeting' at the hands of BP's shareholders over the size of their dividends.

BP raised its quarterly dividend by 31 per cent, after five years of annual rises of only 10 per cent or so. The veteran chairman knows only too well the attachment of British investors to their regular pay-outs.

'It's almost sacrosanct in the UK: you do not cut the dividend,' says Graham Secker, equity strategist at Morgan Stanley. 'But in times of strife cutting the dividend is not such a bad idea.'

Another analyst complains that dividend increases are too often based on 'CEOs' egos'; rather than business fundamentals. ...

... the bulls' devotion to dividends may be about to cool. ... The rise of hedge funds, private equity and other new types of investor has diluted the sway of pension funds, traditionally dividends' biggest fans. Changes to capital gains tax mean that it is becoming more profitable for many investors to make returns through the appreciation of the share price than through dividends.

That may anger the breed of shareholder that harangues Mr Sutherland at BP meetings. But according to research by Morgan Stanley's Mr Secker, an end to the dividend-cutting taboo might, on balance, be no bad thing for investors. ...

EXHIBIT 14.4

Source: *Financial Times* 22 April 2008, p. 23.

favour shares which pay lower dividends. In the past, UK and US dividends were taxed at a higher rate than that which applied to the capital gains made on the sale of shares for those shareholders subject to these taxes. However, in recent years, the difference has been narrowed significantly.

Elton and Gruber (1970) found evidence that there was a statistical relationship between the dividend policy of firms and the tax bracket of their shareholders – shareholders with higher income tax rates were associated with low-dividend shares and those with lower income tax rates with high-dividend shares.

Gordon Brown, when chancellor, changed the tax system explicitly to encourage lower dividends and greater investment within firms. He said:

> The present system of tax credits encourages companies to pay out dividends rather than reinvest their profits. This cannot be the best way of encouraging investment for the long term as was acknowledged by the last government. Many pension funds are in substantial surplus and at present many companies are enjoying pension holidays, so this is the right time to undertake long-needed reform. So, with immediate effect, I propose to abolish tax credits paid to pension funds and companies.[5]

Information conveyance

Dividends appear to act as important conveyors of information about companies. An unexpected change in the dividend is regarded as a sign of how the directors view the future prospects of the firm. An unusually large increase in the dividend is often taken to indicate an optimistic view about future profitability. A declining dividend often signals that the directors view the future with some pessimism.

> Dividends appear to act as important conveyors of information about companies.

The importance of the dividend as an information-transferring device occurs because of a significant market imperfection – information asymmetry. That is, managers know far more about the firm's prospects than do the finance providers. Investors are continually trying to piece together scraps of information about a firm. Dividends are one source that the investor can draw upon. They are used as an indicator of a firm's sustainable level of income. It would seem that managers choose a target dividend payout ratio based on a long-term earnings trend.[6] It is risky for managers' career prospects for them to increase the dividend above the regular growth pattern if they are not expecting improved business prospects. This sends a false signal and eventually they will be found out when the income growth does not take place.

It is the increase or decrease over the *expected* level of dividends that leads shareholders to revise expectations. Character Group raised its dividends to send a signal – *see* Exhibit 14.5.

Confidence call by Character

Tom Burgis

Character Group raised its dividend yesterday in spite of a fall in profits, in a move designed to signal confidence that the toymaker was on the road to recovery following a product recall and a bleak Christmas.

Pre-tax profit tumbled to £3.25m for the six months to the end of February, against £7m last time, on revenue of £48.6m (£56.2m).

The shares fell 7p to 110p. A slump to a low of 68½p last year knocked about £170m off its market capitalisation and followed a recall of the Bindeez beads range after they were found to contain a chemical that acted similarly to a dangerous date-rape drug when ingested, and a pre-Christmas warning that festive sales would be disappointing.

Richard King, executive chairman, said cash of £10m and no debt justified the pay-out increase of 10 per cent to 2.2p.

EXHIBIT 14.5

Source: *Financial Times* 30 April 2008, p. 22.

Exhibit 14.6 contains the comments of a respected investor. He certainly looks to dividends for signals.

Dividends can be the best reward

John Lee

... I have been a consistent fan of dividends for all my investing life and never deserted them as others did during the absurd years of internet madness.

When I hear of a company's results in my 8.15am daily broker's call, the first question I ask is about the dividend; for me the dividend decision usually says it all – it is a reflection of the results for the past year, the directors' view of the coming year and, very importantly, the financial strength/liquidity of the business.

Most boards recognise the importance of endeavouring to maintain if not increase dividends annually – providing more certainty for investors. Only the short-sighted cut their dividend unless they really have to ...

A dividend yield also provides a prop to a share price and gives an annual return to investors when perhaps capital growth is hard to come by. Sometimes when talking to a chairman or chief executive after a poor trading statement, I encourage them to maintain their dividend – often they express surprise that I need to question this as they have every intention of doing so ...

EXHIBIT 14.6

Source: *Financial Times* 2/3 December 2006, p. 10.

Generally company earnings fluctuate to a far greater extent than dividends. This smoothing of the dividend flow is illustrated in Table 14.1 where Cadbury has shown a rise and a fall in earnings per share but has a steadily rising dividend.

A reduction in earnings is usually not followed by a reduction in dividends, unless the earnings fall is perceived as likely to persist for a long time. Ever since Lintner's (1956) survey on managers' attitudes to dividend policy in the 1950s, researchers have shown that directors are aware that the market reacts badly to dividend downturns and they make strenuous efforts to avoid a decline. Almost every day the financial press reports firms making losses and yet still paying a dividend. By continuing the income stream to shareholders the management signal that the decline in earnings is temporary and that positive earnings are expected in the future.

When times are good and profits are bounding ahead directors tend to be cautious about large dividend rises. To double or treble dividends in good years increases the risk of having to reduce dividends should the profit growth tail off and losing the virtue of predictability and stability cherished by shareholders.

Signals are funny things. A number of the large US technology companies started paying dividends for the first time in 2000–2004. In many cases the share price fell. The reason: investors took the dividends as a signal that the companies have run out of growth opportunities.

Signals are funny things.

TABLE 14.1

Cadbury earnings and dividend, 16-year record (pence per share)

Year	Earnings	Dividends
1993	14.7	6.9
1994	16.1	7.5
1995	16.2	8.0
1996	16.9	8.5
1997	34.0	9.0
1998	17.1	9.5
1999	32.0	10.0
2000	24.8	10.5
2001	27.0	11.0
2002	27.4	11.5
2003	18.2	12.0
2004	23.3	12.5
2005	33.9	13.0
2006	31.6	14.0
2007	19.4	15.5
2008	22.8	16.4

Source: Cadbury report and accounts.

Resolution of uncertainty

Myron Gordon (1963) has argued that investors perceive that a company, by retaining and reinvesting a part of its current cash flow, is replacing a certain dividend flow to shareholders now with an uncertain more distant flow in the future. Because the returns from any reinvested funds will occur in the far future they are subject to more risk and investors apply a higher discount rate than they would to near-term dividends. The market places a greater value on shares offering higher near-term dividends. Investors are showing a preference for the early resolution of uncertainty. Under this model investors use a set of discount rates which rise through time to calculate share values; therefore the dividend valuation model becomes:

$$P_0 = \frac{d_1}{1 + k_{E1}} + \frac{d_2}{(1 + k_{E2})^2} + \ldots \frac{d_n}{(1 + k_{En})^n}$$

where:

d = dividend

k_{E1} = required return on equity capital by shareholder

significantly $k_{E1} < k_{E2} < k_{E3} \ldots$

The dividends received in Years 2, 3 or 4 are of lower risk than those received seven, eight or nine years hence.

The crucial factor here may not be actual differences in risk between the near and far future, but *perceived risk*. It may be that immediate dividends are valued more highly because the investors' perception of risk is not perfect. They overestimate the riskiness of distant dividends and thus undervalue them. However, whether the extra risk attached to more distant dividends is real or not, the effect is the same – investors prefer a higher dividend in the near term than they otherwise would and shareholder value can be raised by altering the dividend policy to suit this preference – or so the argument goes.

There have been some impressive counter-attacks on what is described as the 'bird-in-the-hand fallacy'. The riskiness of a firm's dividend derives from the risk associated with the underlying business and this risk is already allowed for through the risk-adjusted discount rate, k_E. To discount future income even further would be excessive. Take a company expected to produce a dividend per share of £1 in two years and £2 in ten years. The discount rate of, say, 15 percent ensures that the £2 dividend is worth, in present value terms, less than the dividend received in two years, and much of this discount rate is a compensation for risk.

$$\text{Present value of £1 dividend} = \frac{£1}{(1.15)^2} = 75.6\text{p}$$

$$\text{Present value of £2 dividend} = \frac{£2}{(1.15)^{10}} = 49.4\text{p}$$

Alternatively, take a company that pays out all its earnings in the hope of raising its share price because shareholders have supposedly had resolution of uncertainty. Now, what is the next move? We have a company in need of investment finance and shareholders wishing to invest in company shares – as most do with dividend income. The firm has a rights issue. In the prospectus the firm explains what will happen to the funds raised: they will be used to generate dividends in the future. Thus shareholders buy shares on the promise of future dividends; they discount these dividends at a risk-adjusted discount rate determined by the rate of return available on alternative, equally risky investments, say, 15 percent (applicable to *all* the future years). To discount at a higher rate would be to undervalue the shares and pass up an opportunity of a good investment.

Agency effects

Many people take the view that UK firms pay out an excessive proportion of their earnings as dividends. The argument then runs that this stifles investment because of the lower retention rate. However, set alongside this concern should go the observation that many firms seem to have a policy of paying high dividends, and then, shortly afterwards, issuing new shares to raise cash for investment. This is a perplexing phenomenon. The cost of issuing shares can be burdensome and shareholders generally pay tax on the receipt of dividends. One possible answer is that it is the signaling (information) value of dividends that drives this policy. However, the costs are so high that it cannot always be explained by this. A second potential explanation lies with agency cost.

Managers (the agents) may not always act in the best interests of the owners (the principals). One way for the owners to regain some control over the use of their money is to insist on relatively high payout ratios. Then, if managers need funds for investment they have to ask. A firm that wishes to raise external capital will have its plans for investment scrutinised by a number of experts, including:

■ investment bankers who advise on the issue;

■ underwriters who, like investment bankers, will wish to examine the firm and its plans as they are attaching their good name to the issue;

■ analysts at credit-rating agencies;

■ analysts at stockbroking houses who advise shareholders and potential shareholders;

■ shareholders.

In ordinary circumstances the firm's investors can only influence managerial action by voting at a general meeting (which is usually ineffective due to apathy and the use of proxy votes by the board), or by selling their shares. When a company has to ask for fresh capital investors can tease out more information and can examine managerial action and proposed actions. They can exercise some control over their savings by refusing to buy the firm's securities if they are at all suspicious of managerial behaviour. Of particular concern is the problem of investment in projects with negative NPV for the sake of building a larger managerial empire.

A more generous view, from the field of behavioural finance, is that managers are merely over-optimistic and over-confident about their ability to invest money wisely and so it is best to limit the amount left in the business for them to invest.

Scrip dividends

A scrip dividend gives shareholders an opportunity to receive additional shares in proportion to their existing holding instead of the normal cash dividend. The shareholders can then either keep the shares or sell them for cash. From the company's point of view scrip dividends have the advantage that *cash does not leave the company*. This may be important for companies going through difficult trading periods or as a way of adjusting the gearing (debt to equity) ratio. Shareholders may welcome a scrip dividend because they can increase their holdings without brokerage costs and other dealing costs.

> From the company's point of view scrip dividends have the advantage that *cash does not leave the company.*

An enhanced scrip dividend is one where the shares offered are worth substantially more than the alternative cash payout. Such an offer is designed to encourage the take-up of shares and is like a mini-rights issue.

Share buy-backs and special dividends

An alternative way to return money, held within the company, to the owners is to repurchase issued shares. Microsoft bought back $12bn of its shares in 2007 and started a further $40bn buy-back in 2008. Buying its own shares was seen as a better way of returning money to shareholders than raising the dividend to an extraordinary high level.

Buy-backs are a useful alternative when the company is unsure about the sustainability of a possible increase in the normal cash dividend. A stable policy may be pursued on dividends, then, as and when surplus cash arises, shares are repurchased. This two-track approach avoids sending an over-optimistic signal about future growth through underlying dividend levels.

> This two-track approach avoids sending an over-optimistic signal.

A second possible approach to returning funds without signalling that all future dividends will be raised abnormally is to pay a special dividend. This is the same as a normal dividend but usually bigger and paid on a one-off basis – *see* Exhibit 14.7 for an example.

Share repurchases have been permitted in the UK since the Companies Act 1981 came into force, subject to the requirement that the firm gain the permission of shareholders as well as warrant holders, option holders or convertible holders. The rules of the London Stock Exchange (and especially the Takeover Panel) must also be obeyed. These are generally aimed at avoiding the creation of an artificial market in the company's shares.

Special dividend at Hargreaves

Philip Stafford

Hargreaves Lansdown is to pay shareholders a special dividend for a second consecutive year as the UK's largest independent financial adviser reported a 20 per cent rise in profit for the year to June 30.

But the group warned investors not to count on the continuation of special pay-outs, as it expected income from interest to be 'materially reduced'.

'It's not guaranteed,' said Stephen Lansdown, executive chairman and co-founder of the group which floated in 2007. 'It's important that people don't take is as read, as we may need the cash to support the business in other ways in the future.' ...

The special dividend of 2.807p a share comes on top of an increase in the final dividend from 2.42p to 4.229p, giving an overall pay-out of 10.101p a share. This represents a rise of almost 30 per cent over the previous year. ...

EXHIBIT 14.7

Source: *Financial Times* 3 September 2009, p. 18.

A special dividend has to be offered to all shareholders. However a share repurchase may not always be open to all shareholders as it can be accomplished in one of three ways:

- purchasing shares in the stock market;
- all shareholders are invited to tender some or all of their shares;
- an arrangement with particular shareholders.

Share buy-backs have the advantage over special dividends in giving shareholders a choice in whether they wish to sell their shares and receive cash. Perhaps tax considerations mean that they prefer to hold on to the shares anticipating a rising earnings per share and share price as other investors sell to the company.

Buy-backs are often a good way for directors to distribute money that the firm cannot use as effectively as the shareholders. A buy-back is often seen as a signal that the managerial team is not holding on to cash to empire-build for their own glory and income. However, in the 1990s–2000s, share buy-backs became a management fad with the aim of providing short-term boosts to the share price and earnings per share rather than for rational long-term shareholder wealth enhancement reasons. This was overlaid with another fad – that for high borrowings relative to the equity capital of the business. This can enhance returns to shareholders in stable circumstances but can be very risky if the underlying cash flows of the business decline – as they did for many in 2009. Thus we had the spectacle of 2007 (boom time) buy-backs at, say, £5 per share, followed by a desperate attempt to reinforce the business through selling shares at, say, £1 per share in 2009 (the crash). Existing shareholders were not pleased when a portion of the company was handed over to outsiders for such a small amount.

Exhibit 14.8 discusses research that says that price at which the shares are bought is crucially important to whether a buy-back is shareholder wealth-enhancing.

Ill-judged buy-backs are 'collectively destroying billions in shareholder value'

Chris Hughes

The extra investment performance created by share buy-backs has dwindled to 'negligible' levels, with many companies destroying shareholder value by ill-judged share purchases, according to new research.

Share buy-backs have become increasingly popular in recent years as the expanding economy has strengthened corporate cash-flow and boards have bowed to perceived investor pressure to hand cash back. The relatively low level of debt carried by listed companies has also provided scope to take on more leverage and return cash through share buy-backs.

When a company pursues a share buy-back, it nominates a broker to buy its shares in the stock market. Normally these shares are then cancelled, so the company's earning are then distributed less widely, and this boosts earnings per share (EPS).

It is estimated that in 2007 almost 15 per cent of Europe's large and mid-cap companies have undertaken buy-backs exceeding 2 per cent of their market capitalisation.

However, Collins Stewart, the broker, says many companies are ignoring the 'essential valuation criteria' that determine whether or not a buy-back creates value for a company's investors.

It says companies focus too much on boosting EPS, when the fundamental question should be the price at which shares are repurchased. It also blames investment banks for advising companies to do ill-judged buy-backs just for the fees.

'We find numerous examples where the rationale for a buy-back – usually involving EPS enhancement – ignores the basic principles that will best ensure positive returns to shareholders,' says Collins Stewart. 'A substantial number of buy-backs are, collectively, destroying billions in shareholder value through ill-judged decisions.'

The research found that in aggregate, there was less than a 50 per cent chance that a share buy-back would now lead to a company's share price outperforming.

The general problem, Collins Stewart argues, is that shares are less cheap than they used to be. ...

Next, the retailer dubbed by Collins Stewart as the 'buy-back junkies par excellence', destroyed a notional £70m of value on its buy-back this year – in spite of a good record in previous years.

Tate & Lyle says its buy-back was launched with the support of its shareholders.

'They welcomed it because it made efficient use of our balance sheet after our sale of European starch assets. Less than 20 per cent of the buy-back had been completed when the share price fell in the autumn. Since our results announcement in October, we have resumed the buy-back with the full support of our shareholders,' he says.

Next is also unapologetic. The retailer says: 'Next has a stated policy, the board firmly believes that it is by improving EPS over a period of time that drives the share price and shareholder value. Next does have quite a lot of rules about the circumstances for buying back shares.' ...

Collins Stewart says an emphasis on EPS-based performance hurdles in executive bonuses could create an incentive for boards to sanction share buy-backs even when their share price is too high.

It blames guidance from the Association of British Insurers, dating back to 1990, that share buy-backs are

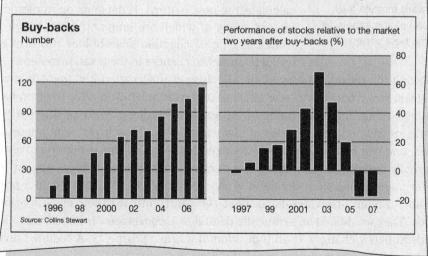

Buy-backs
Number

Performance of stocks relative to the market two years after buy-backs (%)

Source: Collins Stewart

to be exercised only 'if to do so would result in an increase in earnings per share and is in the best interests of shareholders generally'.

The study says the ABI's guidance is 'like a red rag to a bull for managements who may find it, perhaps coincidentally, to be closely aligned with their own interests.'

However, Peter Montagnon, head of investment affairs at the ABI, rejects the accusation and says Collins Stewart is jumping to conclusions that are not justified, especially given that the ABI guidance stresses that buy-backs should always be in shareholders' interest.

'It is simply wrong to say we are encouraging buy-backs and falling into the trap of encouraging executives to use them to meet their performance hurdles,' he says.

EXHIBIT 14.8

Source: *Financial Times* 15 December 2007, p. 16.

A round-up of the arguments

There are two questions at the core of the dividend policy debate.

Question 1 Can shareholder wealth be increased by changing the pattern of dividends over a period of years?

Question 2 Is a steady, stable dividend growth rate better than one which varies from year to year depending on the firm's internal need for funds?

The answer to the first question is 'yes'. The accumulated evidence suggests that shareholders for one reason or another value particular patterns of dividends across time. But there is no neat, simple, straightforward formula into which we can plug numbers to calculate the best pattern. It depends on numerous factors, many of which are unquantifiable, ranging from the type of clientele shareholder the firm is trying to attract to changes in the taxation system.

> There is no neat, simple, straightforward formula into which we can plug numbers to calculate the best pattern.

Taking the residual theory alone, the answer to Question 2 is that the dividend will vary from year to year because it is what is left over after the firm has retained funds for investment in all available projects with positive NPV. Dividends will be larger in years of high cash flow and few investment opportunities, and will be reduced when the need for reinvestment is high relative to internally generated cash flow. However, in practice, shareholders appear to prefer stable, consistent dividend growth rates. Many of them rely on a predictable stream of dividends to meet (or contribute to) their consumption needs. They would find an erratic dividend flow inconvenient. Investors also use dividend policy changes as an indication of a firm's prospects. A reduced dividend could send an incorrect signal and depress share prices.

FIGURE 14.1

The forces pulling management in the dividend decision

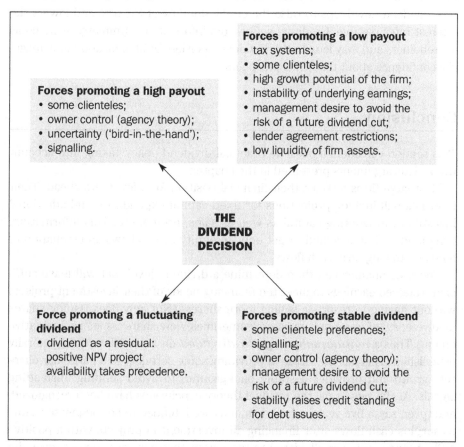

So many factors influence dividend policy that it is very difficult to imagine that someone could develop a universally applicable model which would allow firms to identify an optimal payout ratio. Figure 14.1 shows the range of forces pulling managers towards a high payout rate, and other forces pulling towards a low payout rate. Simultaneously, their own forces encourage a fluctuating dividend and other factors promote a stable dividend.

Most of the factors in Figure 14.1 have already been explained, but there are two which need a comment here: liquidity and credit standing. Dividends require an outflow of cash from firms; therefore companies with plentiful liquid assets, such as cash and marketable securities, are more able to pay a dividend. Other firms, despite being highly profitable, may have very few liquid assets. For example, a rapidly growing firm may have a large proportion of its funds absorbed by fixed assets, inventory and debtors. Thus some firms may have greater difficulty paying cash dividends than others.

Lenders generally prefer to entrust their money to stable firms rather than ones that are erratic, as this reduces risk. It could be speculated that a consistent dividend flow helps to raise the credit standing of the firm and lowers the interest rates payable. Creditors suffer from information asymmetry as much as shareholders and may look to this dividend decision for an indication of managerial confidence about the firm's prospects.

Conclusion

This section considers a possible practical dividend policy, taking into account the various arguments presented in the chapter.

Most large firms forecast their financial position for a few years ahead. Their forecasts will include projections for fixed capital expenditure and additional investment in working capital as well as sales, profits, etc. This information, combined with a specified target debt to equity ratio, allows an estimation of medium- to long-term cash flows.

These companies can then determine a dividend level that will leave sufficient retained earnings to meet the financing needs of their investment projects without having to resort to selling more shares. (Not only does issuing shares involve costs of issue but investors sometimes view share issues as a negative omen.) Thus a *maintainable regular dividend* on a growth path is generally established. This has the virtue of providing some certainty to a particular clientele group and provides a stable background, to avoid sending misleading signals. At the same time the residual theory conclusions have been recognized, and (over, say, a five-year period) dividends are intended to be roughly the same as surplus cash flows after financing all investment in projects with a positive NPV. Agency costs are alleviated to the extent that managers do not, over the long run, store up (and misapply) cash flows greater than those necessary to finance high-return projects.

The future is uncertain and so companies may consider their financial projections under various scenarios. They may focus particularly on the negative possibilities. Dividends may be set at a level low enough that, if poorer trading conditions do occur, the firm is not forced to cut the dividend. Thus a margin for error is introduced by lowering the payout rate.

Companies that are especially vulnerable to macroeconomic vicissitudes, such as those in cyclical industries, are likely to be tempted to set a relatively low maintainable regular dividend so as to avoid the dreaded consequences of a reduced dividend in a particularly bad year. In years of plenty directors can pay out surplus cash in the form of special dividends or share repurchases. This policy of low regular payouts supplemented with irregular bonuses allows shareholders to recognise that the payouts in good years might not be maintained at the extraordinary level. Therefore they do not interpret them as a signal that profits growth will persist at this high level.

If a change in dividend policy becomes necessary then firms are advised to make a gradual adjustment, as a sudden break with a trend can send an erroneous signal about the firms' prospects. And, of course, the more information shareholders are given concerning the reasons behind a change in policy, the less likelihood there is of a serious misinterpretation.

Firms in different circumstances are likely to exhibit different payout ratios. Those with plentiful investment opportunities will, in general, opt for a relatively low dividend rate compared with that exhibited by companies with few such opportunities. Each type of firm is likely to attract a clientele favouring its dividend policy. For example investors in fast-growth, high-investment firms are prepared to accept low (no) dividends in return for the prospect of higher capital gains.

A suggested action plan

A suggested action plan for a dividend policy is as follows.

1 Forecast the 'surplus' cash flow resulting from the subtraction of the cash needed for investment projects from that generated by the firm's operations over the medium to long term.

2 Pay a maintainable regular dividend based on this forecast. This may be biased on the conservative side to allow for uncertainty about future cash flows.

3 If cash flows are greater than projected for a particular year, keep the maintainable regular dividend fairly constant (ideally with stable growth), but pay a special dividend or initiate a share repurchase programme. If the change in cash flows is permanent, gradually shift the maintainable regular dividend while providing as much information to investors as possible about the reasons for the change in policy.

Notes

1 The CPI, consumer price index, is the main US measure of inflation.

2 A company cannot pay a dividend, even in a profitable year, if there are accumulated losses brought forward from earlier years that remain uncovered by previous years' profits in the balance sheet.

3 The complicating effect of capital structure on firms' value is usually eliminated by concentrating on all-equity firms.

4 The following researchers present evidence on the clientele effect: Elton and Gruber (1970), Pettit (1977), Lewellen, Stanley, Lease and Schlarbaum (1978), Litzenberger and Ramaswamy (1982), Crossland, Dempsey and Moizer (1991).

5 Gordon Brown, Chancellor of the Exchequer, Budget Speech, 2 July 1997.

6 Lintner (1956) and 3i (1993) survey, in which 93 percent of finance directors agreed with the statement that 'dividend policy should follow a long-term trend in earnings'.

Section III:

FINANCE RAISING

15

DEBT FINANCE AVAILABLE TO FIRMS OF ALL SIZES

Introduction

For many firms, especially smaller ones, a combination of overdrafts and loans, trade credit, leasing and hire purchase make up the greater part of the funding needs. Large companies have access to stock markets, bond markets and syndicated loan facilities. These are often closed to the smaller firm, so, to pursue their expansion programmes, they turn to the local banks and the finance houses as well as their suppliers for the wherewithal to grow. The giants of the corporate world have access to dozens of different types of finance, but they too value the characteristics, cheapness and flexibility of the forms discussed in this chapter.

All the forms of finance discussed in this chapter are described as either short- or medium-term finance (with the exception of some bank loans). The definitions of short-term and medium-term finance are not clear-cut. Usually finance repayable within a year is regarded as short, whereas that due for repayment between one and seven years is taken to be medium. But these cut-offs are not to be taken too seriously. Quite often an overdraft facility, which is due for repayment in, say, six months or one year, is regularly 'rolled over' and so may become relied upon as a medium-term, or even long-term, source of funds. Leasing, which is usually classified as a medium-term source, can be used for periods of up to 15 years in some circumstances; in others it is possible to lease assets for a period of only a few weeks, for example, a computer or photocopier. The forms of finance we will examine in this chapter are listed in Figure 15.1.

FIGURE 15.1

The main forms of short-term and medium-term finance

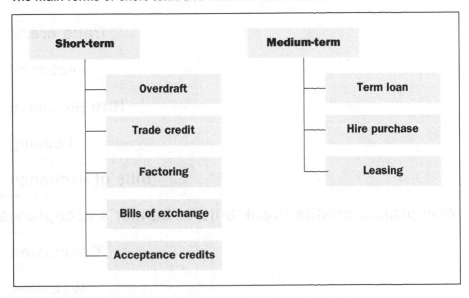

Contrasting debt finance with equity

What is debt?

Put at its simplest, debt is something that has to be repaid. Corporate debt repayments generally take the form of interest and capital payments, but they can be more exotic compensations such as commodities and shares. The usual method is a combination of a regular interest, with capital (principal) repayments either spread over a period or given as a lump sum at the end of the borrowing.

> **Debt is something that has to be repaid.**

Cost of debt

Debt finance is less expensive to the firm than equity (ordinary shares) finance, not only because the costs of raising the funds (for example, arrangement fees with a bank or the issue costs of a bond) are lower, but because the rate of return required to attract investors is less than for equity. This is because investors recognize that investing in a firm via debt finance is less risky than investing via shares. It is less risky because interest has a higher claim than equity holders on income generated by the company – interest has to be paid even if that means there is nothing left to pay the shareholders a dividend. There is thus a greater certainty of receiving a return than there is for equity holders. Also, if the firm goes into liquidation, the holders of a debt type of financial security are paid back from the sale of the assets before shareholders receive anything. Thus we say that debt holders 'rank' higher than equity holders for annual payouts and liquidation proceeds.

Extraordinary profits go to shareholders

Offsetting these plus-points for debt (from the debt holders point of view) is the fact that lenders do not, generally, share in the value created by an extraordinarily successful business. They usually receive the contractual minimum and no more, whereas shareholders can gain much more than the minimum required because they are the recipients of any surplus the firm generates. In the case of high performing businesses this can result in an initial share investment of a few thousand pounds being turned into many millions. For example, a garage owner, Iain McGlinn, put £4,000 into a small retail venture by purchasing some shares. When the Body Shop was eventually sold to L'Oréal in 2006 he received nearly £150m for his 23 percent stake.

Voting rights

Another disadvantage with debt is that the lenders do not, in normal circumstances, have any voting power over the company's direction, for example, choosing the directors, agreeing to a merger or voting for a dividend payment. Having said this, debt holders are able to protect their position to some extent through rigorous lending agreements and if these are breached they may be able to take control of a company. These lending agreements may, for instance, insist that the company does not exceed certain debt level relative to the amount shareholders hold in the company, or that annual interest does not exceed a stated multiple of annual profits. Debt covenants are discussed in Exhibit 15.1.

Covenants in spotlight as banks reduce 'headroom' on company debt

Anousha Sakoui

Mark Pain describes it as one of the most difficult periods of his 25-year career – involving round-the-clock work at an incredible intensity.

The finance director of Barratt Developments is referring to four months spent renegotiating the housebuilder's finances, at a time when the UK property market has nosedived.

It is an experience being lived by a growing number of companies having to face the fact that they can no longer refinance themselves out of trouble, unlike previous years, when debt financing was abundant and on easy terms. ...

Many companies are already in talks with lenders to ease debt terms, in particular waiving or resetting so-called covenants as earnings deteriorate. ...

Covenants are financial ratios or limits that provide lenders with red flags warning of any sign that a company may start to struggle to meet debt repayments. ...

Barratt agreed with lenders to reset covenants, including swapping its interest cover-based covenant with a cash-flow covenant, highlighting banks' growing focus on the ability of companies to generate cash as they try to ride through the next few years, rather than profitability.

Barratt also had its leverage covenant and minimum tangible net worth covenants relaxed, which would allow it to make writedowns on its land bank.

Other covenants in the spotlight are based on the size of the loan relative to the value of the assets. Property companies are at risk of breaching these triggers as real estate prices plunge. ...

Banks balance the need to set those covenants tight enough to keep a grip on performance but loose enough to avoid breaches. Mr Duncan says initial breaches are more likely to be waived and covenants reset for a fee. A second breach is more of an issue. ...

Once a company realises it is close to breaching, or has breached, tests it is thrown into talks with banks in an attempt to get waivers.

In the Barratt example, the board was taken aback by a big drop in orders in the first week of April. Concerned about a £400m debt refinancing due in 12 months, Mr Pain started talking to banks ...

For banks, though, the growing concern is that many existing financings carry so few, or such loose, covenants that by the time a company is forced into talks it will be too late.

Because covenants and the negotiations around them are carried out behind closed doors, the scale of the problem is hidden. Some believe the number of companies struggling with covenants could be double what has been reported in the press.

Covenant measures

- **Leverage** – a measure of borrowings relative to earnings. For an investment grade company, debt divided by earnings before interest, tax, depreciation and amortisation (Ebitda) typically has to be kept below 3.5–3.75. For a leveraged buy-out for example, with more speculative grade debt, it can be much higher

- **Interest cover** – the ratio of interest cost to earnings before interest and tax. ... Ensures that profitability is enough to ensure a company can meet interest payments.

- **Capex** – places a restriction on the amount a company can spend on capital expenditure over a period of time. More common in buy-out financing

- **Debt service or cash flow** – monitors that a company has enough cash to cover both principal and interest repayments on debt. More common in buy-out financing

- **Tangible net worth** – measures the value of a company's tangible assets

EXHIBIT 15.1

Source: *Financial Times* 21 August 2008, p. 18.

Shock absorption

The fact that debt finance usually requires regular cash outlays in the form of interest and the repayment of a capital sum means that the firm is obliged to maintain payments through bad times as well as good, or face the possibility of the lenders taking action to recover their dues by forcing the sale of assets or liquidation. High debt levels therefore pose a risk to the existence of the company – a poor performance over a few years can wipe out shareholders' wealth as the firm digs into the equity base to pay the debt obligations (for a consideration of when debt levels become too great *see* Chapters 10 and 18). The fact that shares carry no right to pay a dividend or to ever repay the capital allows them to act as shock absorbers for the company. When losses are made the company does not have the problem of finding money for a dividend.

> High debt levels therefore pose a risk to the existence of the company.

Tax deductibility

When a company pays interest the tax authorities regard this as a cost of doing business and it can be used to reduce the taxable profit. This lowers the effective cost to the firm of servicing the debt compared with servicing equity capital through dividends, which are not tax deductible (*see* Chapter 10). To the attractions of the low required return on debt we must add the benefit of tax deductibility.

Collateral and restrictions

Institutions providing debt finance often try to minimise the risk of not receiving interest and their original capital. They do this by first of all looking to the earning ability of the firm, that is, the pre-interest profits in the years over the period of the loan. As a back-up they often require that the loan be secured against assets owned by the business, so that if the firm is unable to pay interest and capital from profits the lender can force the sale of the assets to receive their legal entitlement. The matter of security has to be thought about carefully before a firm borrows capital. It could be very inconvenient for the firm to grant a bank a fixed charge on a specific asset – say a particular building – because the firm is then limiting its future flexibility to use its assets as it wishes. For instance, it will not be able to sell that building, or even rent it without the consent of the bank or the bondholders.

Bank borrowing

For most companies and individuals banks remain the main source of externally (i.e. not retained profits) raised finance.

Borrowing from banks is attractive for companies for the following reasons:

- **It is quick** The key provisions of a bank loan can be worked out speedily and the funding facility can be in place within a matter of hours. Contrast this with a bond issue or arranging factoring (see below) which both require a lot of preparation.

- **It is flexible** If the economic circumstances facing the firm should change during the life of the loan banks are generally better equipped – and are more willing – to alter the terms of the lending agreement than bondholders. If the firm does better than originally expected a bank overdraft (and some loans) can be repaid without penalty. Contrast this with many bonds with fixed redemption dates, or hire purchase/leasing agreements with fixed terms. Negotiating with a single lender in a crisis has distinct advantages (with bond finance there might be thousands of lenders – *see* next chapter).

- **It is available to small firms** Bank loans are available to firms of almost any size whereas the bond or money markets are for the big players only.

- **Administrative and legal costs are low** Because the loan arises from direct negotiation between borrower and lender there is an avoidance of the marketing, arrangement, regulatory and underwriting expenses involved in a bond issue (*see* Chapter 16).

Factors for a firm to consider

There are a number of issues a firm needs to address when considering bank borrowing.

Costs

The borrower may be required to pay an arrangement fee, say 1 percent of the loan, at the time of the initial lending, but this is subject to negotiation and may be bargained down.[1] The interest rate can be either fixed for the entire term of the loan (or part of it) or floating. If it is floating then the rate will generally be a certain percentage above the bank's base rate or the London Inter-Bank Offered Rate (LIBOR). LIBOR is the rate at which very safe banks lend to each other in the financial markets. This can be lending for as short as a few hours (overnight LIBOR) or for much longer periods, say three or six months.

Customers in a good bargaining position may be able to haggle so that they pay only 1 or 2 percent 'over base', or over say, 'three-month LIBOR'. In the case of the three-month LIBOR benchmark rate the interest payable changes every three months depending on the rates in the market for three-month lending between high quality banks. Because the borrowing corporation is not as safe as a high quality bank borrowing in the interbank market it will pay 1 percent (or 100 basis points), 2 percent (200 basis points) or some other number of basis points per year more than the high quality bank would. In the case of base-rate related lending the interest payable changes immediately the bank announces a change in its base rate. This moves at irregular intervals in response to financial market conditions, which are heavily influenced by the Bank of England in its attempts to control the economy.

For customers in a poorer bargaining position, offering a higher risk proposal, the rate could be 5 percent or more over the base rate or LIBOR. The interest rate will be determined not only by the riskiness of the undertaking and the bargaining strength of the customer but also by the degree of security for the loan and the size of loan. Furthermore, economies of scale in lending mean that large borrowers pay a lower interest rate.

A generation ago it would have been more normal to negotiate fixed-rate loans but sharp movements of interest rates in the 1970s and 1980s meant that banks and borrowers were less willing to make this type of long-term commitment. Most loans today are 'variable rate'. Floating-rate borrowings have advantages for the firm over fixed-rate borrowings:

- if interest rates fall the cost of the loan falls;
- at the time of arrangement fixed rates are usually above floating rates (to allow for lenders' risk of misforecasting future interest rates);
- returns on the firm's assets may go up at times of higher interest rates and fall at times of low interest rates, therefore the risk of higher rates is offset. For example, a bailiff firm may prosper in a high interest rate environment and can cope with higher interest charged to its business borrowing.

However floating rates have some disadvantages:

- the firm may be caught out by a rise in interest rates if, as with most businesses, its profits do not rise when interest rates rise. Many have failed because of a rise in interest rates at an inopportune time;

■ there will be uncertainty about the precise cash outflow impact of the interest payable. Firms need to plan ahead; in particular, they need to estimate amounts of cash coming in and flowing out, not least so that they can pay bills on time. If the firm has large amounts of floating rate debt it has an extra element of uncertainty in estimating cash flows and thus greater difficulty in managing the business efficiently.

Security

When banks are considering the provision of debt finance for a firm they will be concerned about the borrower's competence and honesty. They need to evaluate the proposed project and assess the degree of managerial commitment to its success. The firm will have to explain why the funds are needed and provide detailed cash forecasts covering the period of the loan. Between the bank and the firm stands the classic gulf called 'asymmetric information' in which one party in the negotiation is ignorant of, or cannot observe, some of the information that is essential to the contracting and decision-making process. The bank is unable to accurately assess the ability and determination of the managerial team and will not have a complete understanding of the market environment in which they propose to operate.

> Between the bank and the firm stands the classic gulf called 'asymmetric information'.

Companies may overcome bank uncertainty to some degree by providing as much information as possible at the outset and keeping the bank informed of the firm's position as the project progresses.

The finance director and managing director need to consider both the quantity and quality of information flows to the bank. An improved flow of information can lead to a better and more supportive relationship. Firms with significant bank financing requirements to fund growth will be well advised to cultivate and strengthen understanding and rapport with its bank(s). The time to lay the foundations for subsequent borrowing is when the business does not need the money so that when loans are required there is a reasonable chance of being able to borrow the amount needed on acceptable terms.

Another way for a bank to reduce its risk is to ensure that the firm offers sufficient collateral for the loan. Collateral provides a means of recovering all or the majority of the bank's investment should the firm fail. The bank's loan can be secured by either a fixed or a floating charge against the firm's assets. A fixed charge means that specific assets are used as security which, in the event of default, can be sold at the insistence of the lender(s) and the proceeds used to repay them. A floating charge means that the loan is secured by a general charge on all the assets of the corporation. In this case the company has a large degree of freedom to use its assets as it wishes, such as sell them or rent them out, until it commits a default which 'crystallizes' the floating charge. If this happens a receiver will be appointed with powers to dispose of assets and to distribute the proceeds to the creditors. Even though floating-charge lenders can force liquidation, fixed-charge lenders rank above floating-charge debt holders in the payout after insolvency –

they get paid first, if there is anything left then the floating charge lenders receive something.

Collateral can include stocks, debtors and equipment as well as land, buildings and marketable investments such as shares in other companies. In theory banks often have this strong right to seize assets or begin proceedings to liquidate. In practice they are reluctant to use these powers because the realisation of full value from an asset used as security is sometimes difficult and such Draconian action can bring adverse publicity.

Banks are careful to create a margin for error in the assignment of sufficient collateral to cover the loan because, in the event of default, assigned assets usually command a much lower price than their value to the company as a going concern. A quick sale at auction produces bargains for the buyers of liquidated assets and, usually, little for the creditors.

Another safety feature applied by banks is the requirement that the firm abide by a number of loan covenants which place restrictions on managerial action, for example insisting that annual profits be at least four times annual interest in every year while the loan is outstanding. (*See* debt covenants discussion in Exhibit 15.1).

Finally, lenders can turn to the directors of the firm to provide additional security. They might be asked to sign personal guarantees that the firm will not default. Personal assets (such as homes) may be used as collateral. This erodes the principle of limited liability status and is likely to inhibit risk-taking productive activity. However for many smaller firms it is the only way of securing a loan and at least it demonstrates the commitment of the director to the success of the enterprise.[2]

Repayment

A firm must carefully consider the period of the loan and the repayment schedules in the light of its future cash flows. It could be disastrous, for instance, for a firm engaging in a capital project which involved large outlays for the next five years followed by cash inflows thereafter to have a bank loan which required significant interest and principal payments in the near term. For situations like these, repayment holidays or grace periods may be granted, with the majority of the repayment being made once cash flows are sufficiently positive.

It may be possible for a company to arrange a mortgage-style repayment schedule in which monthly payments from the borrower to the lender are constant throughout the term.

The terms of a loan are usually tailored to the specific needs of the individual borrower and these are capable of wide variation. A proportion of the interest and the principal can be repaid monthly or annually and can be varied to correspond with the borrower's cash flows. It is rare for there to be no repayment of the principal during the life of the loan but it is possible to request that the bulk of the principal is paid in the later years. Banks generally prefer self-amortizing term loans with a high proportion of the principal paid off each year. This has the advantage of reducing risk by imposing a programme of debt reduction on the borrowing firm and allows the lender to check on the company's continued financial soundness by observing whether there is difficulty in obtaining any of the scheduled payments from the company.

The repayment schedule agreed between bank and borrower is capable of infinite variety – four possibilities are shown in Table 15.1.

The retail banks are not the only sources of long-term loans. Insurance companies and other specialist institutions will also provide long-term debt finance.

TABLE 15.1

Example of loan repayment arrangements

£10,000 borrowed, repayable over four years with interest at 10% pa (assuming annual payments, not monthly)

(a)	Time period (years)	1	2	3	4
	Payment (£)	3,155	3,155	3,155	3,155
(b)	Time period (years)	1	2	3	4
	Payment (£)	1,000	1,000	1,000	11,000
(c)	Time period (years)	1	2	3	4
	Payment (£)	0	0	0	14,641
(d)	Time period (years)	1	2	3	4
	Payment (£)	0	1,000	6,000	6,831

Overdraft

Usually the amount that can be withdrawn from a bank account is limited to the amount put in. However business and other financial activity often requires some flexibility in this principle, and it is often useful to make an arrangement to take more money out of a bank account than it contains – this is an overdraft.

An overdraft is a permit to overdraw on an account up to a stated limit.

Overdraft facilities are usually arranged for a period of a few months or a year and interest is charged on the excess drawings.

Advantages

Overdrafts have the following advantages.

■ **Flexibility** The borrowing firm is not asked to forecast the precise amount and duration of its borrowing at the outset but has the flexibility to borrow up to a stated limit. Also the borrower is assured that the moment the funds are no longer required they can be quickly and easily repaid without suffering a penalty.

- **Cheapness** Banks usually charge two to five percentage points over base rate (or LIBOR) depending on the creditworthiness, security offered and bargaining position of the borrower. There may also be an arrangement fee of, say, 1 percent of the facility. These charges may seem high but it must be borne in mind that overdrafts are often loans to smaller and riskier firms that would otherwise have to pay much more for their funds. Large and well-established borrowers with low gearing and plenty of collateral can borrow on overdraft at much more advantageous rates. A major saving comes from the fact that the banks charge interest on only the daily outstanding balance. So, if a firm has a large cash inflow one week it can use this to reduce its overdraft, temporarily lowering the interest payable, while retaining the ability to borrow more another week.

Drawbacks

A major drawback to an overdraft is that the bank retains the right to withdraw the facility at short notice. Thus, a heavily indebted firm may receive a letter from the bank insisting that its account be brought to balance within a matter of days. This right lowers the risk to the lender because it can quickly get its money out of a troubled company (if the firm has the money), which allows it to lower the cost of lending. However, it can be devastating for the borrower and so firms are well advised to think through the use to which finance provided by way of an overdraft is put. It is not usually wise to use the money for an asset that cannot be easily liquidated; for example, it could be problematic if an overdraft is used for a bridge-building project which will take three years to come to fruition.

> It is not usually wise to use the money for an asset that cannot be easily liquidated.

With overdrafts the bank may take either a fixed or a floating charge over the firm's assets. It will also be on the look out for other forms of security, e.g. a personal guarantee from the directors or owners of the business (if the company defaults the bank can force the directors to pay off the loan from their own resources). When Sir Richard Branson borrowed from Lloyds TSB the bank took shares owned by Sir Richard in Virgin Atlantic as security. Also, unusually, the overdraft facility extended to three years.

Conditions of lending

A bank will generally examine the following factors before lending to a firm:

- **Cash flow projections** A healthy set of projected cash flows will usually be required showing sufficient profitability and liquidity to pay off the overdraft at the end of the agreed period.

- **Creditworthiness** This goes beyond examining projected future cash flows and asset backing and considers important factors such as the character and talents of the individuals leading the organisation.

- **The amount that the borrower is prepared to put into the project or activity, relative to that asked from the bank** If the borrower does not show commitment by putting their money into a scheme, banks can get nervous and stand-offish.

- **Security** The back-up of specific assets or a charge over a large body of general assets will help to reassure a lender that it will be repaid one way or another. Bankers may look at a firm or a project on two levels. First, they might consider a 'liquidation analysis' in which they think about their position in a scenario of business failure. Second, they will look at a firm or project on the assumption that it is a going concern, where cash flows rather than assets become more important.

Seasonal businesses

Overdrafts are particularly useful for seasonal businesses because the daily debit-balance interest charge and the absence of a penalty for early repayment mean that this form of finance can be cheaper than a loan. Take the case of Fruit Growers plc (Worked example 15.1).

Worked example 15.1
FRUIT GROWERS PLC

The management of Fruit Growers plc are trying to decide whether to obtain financing from an overdraft or a loan. The interest on both would be 10% per year or 2.5% per quarter. The cash position for the forthcoming year is represented in Figure 15.2.

Option 1. A loan for the whole year

A loan for the whole year has the advantage of greater certainty that the lending facility will be in place throughout the year. A total loan of £0.5m will be needed, and this will be repaid at the end of the year with interest. At the beginning of the year Fruit Growers' account is credited with the full £500,000. For the months when the business does not need the £500,000 the surplus can be invested to receive a return of 2% per quarter.

FIGURE 15.2

Monthly cash flow balance for Fruit Growers plc

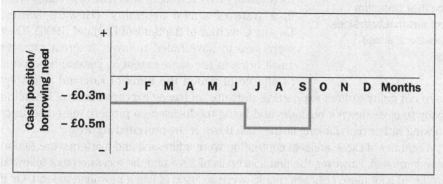

Cost of a loan for the whole year

Interest charged 500,000 × 10%	=	£50,000
Less interest receivable when surplus funds earn 2% per quarter		
January–June 200,000 × 4%	=	£8,000
October–December 500,000 × 2%	=	£10,000
Total cost of borrowing	=	£32,000

Option 2. An overdraft facility for £500,000

An overdraft facility for £500,000 has the drawback that the facility might be withdrawn at any time during the year – however, it is cheaper.

Costs of an overdraft facility for £500,000

1st quarter (J, F & M) 300,000 × 2.5%	=	£7,500
2nd quarter (A, M & J) 300,000 × 2.5%	=	£7,500
3rd quarter (J, A & S) 500,000 × 2.5%	=	£12,500
4th quarter (O, N & D)	=	£0
Total cost of borrowing	=	£27,500

Note: We will ignore the complications of compounding intra-year interest.

Criticism of banks

The risk of a sudden withdrawal of an overdraft facility for most firms is very slight: banks do not generate goodwill and good publicity by capriciously and lightly cancelling agreed overdrafts. The high street banks came in for strong criti-

> 'The best that could be said about the relationship between banks and their small firm customers was that both sides were in a state of armed neutrality.'

cism in the early 1990s: 'In 1993 the best that could be said about the relationship between banks and their small firm customers was that both sides were in a state of armed neutrality' (Howard Davies, Deputy Governor of the Bank of England, 1996). They were said to have failed to lower interest rates to small firms to the same extent as general base rates (a charge of which the Bank of England said they were not guilty), of not supporting start-ups, of having excessive fees, of being too ready to close down a business and being too focused on property-based security backing rather than looking at the cash flows of the proposed activity.

A number of these areas of contention were addressed and matters were said to have improved. However, the financial crisis of 2008 and the recession that followed produced a lot more criticism. Banks were accused of being unwilling to lend. Or, if they did lend, the charges and interest rates were so high that it was uneconomic for companies to borrow. (They also demanded much more collateral).

The government has stepped in to help. It encourages banks to lend to small and medium-sized enterprises by guaranteeing that it will recompense the lender up to 75 percent of the loan if the borrower fails to repay. The scheme is called Enterprise Finance Guarantee (EFG). It is used when there is a sound business proposition, but the loan may otherwise be declined due to a lack of security for the lender. However, this deal does not come for free – the UK government charges a 2 percent annual fee on the outstanding balance of the loan. Up to £1m is available to businesses with a turnover under £25m (for more details, see www.businesslink.gov.uk).

Term loans

A term loan is a loan of a fixed amount for an agreed time and on specified terms. These loans are normally for a period of between three and seven years, but they can range from one to 20 years. The specified terms will include provisions regarding the repayment schedule. If the borrower is to apply the funds to a project which will not generate income for perhaps the first three years it may be possible to arrange a grace period during which only the interest is paid, with the capital being paid off once the project has a sufficiently positive cash flow. Other arrangements can be made to reflect the pattern of cash flow of the firm or project: for example a 'balloon' payment structure is one when only a small part of the capital is repaid during the main part of the loan period, with the majority repayable as the maturity date approaches. A 'bullet' repayment arrangement takes this one stage further and provides for all the capital to be repaid at the end of the loan term.

Not all term loans are drawn down in a single lump sum at the time of the agreement. In the case of a construction project which needs to keep adding to its borrowing to pay for the different stages of development, an instalment arrangement might be required with, say, 25 percent of the money being made available immediately, 25 percent at foundation stage and so on. This has the added attraction to the lender of not committing large sums secured against an

asset not yet created. From the borrower's point of view a drawdown arrangement has an advantage over an overdraft in that the lender is committed to
providing the finance if the borrower meets prearranged conditions, whereas
with an overdraft the lender can withdraw the arrangement at short notice.

The interest charged on term loans can be either at fixed or floating rates. In
addition to the interest rate, the borrower will pay an arrangement fee which
will largely depend on the relative bargaining strength of the two parties.

A term loan often has much more accompanying documentation than an overdraft because of the lengthy bank commitment. This will include a set of
obligations imposed on the borrowing firm such as information flows to the bank as
well as financial gearing (debt to equity capital ratio) and liquidity (availability of
funds to meet claims) constraints. If these financial ratio limits are breached or
interest and capital is not paid on the due date the bank has a right of termination,
in which case it could decide not to make any more funds available, or, in extreme
cases, insist on the repayment of funds already lent. Even if a firm defaults the
bank will usually try to reschedule or restructure the finance of the business (e.g.
grant a longer period to pay) rather than take tough enforcement action.

With term loans there is often a restriction reducing the borrower's ability to repay
prior to the scheduled maturity without paying an expensive 'break-fee'. But even
without a break-fee clause in the agreement, term loans suffer from the disadvantage
that any monies repaid will not be available to be utilised again. As Exhibit 15.2
describes, there are many ways of raising debt finance other than going to a bank.

SMEs tap alternative lenders

Hugo Greenhalgh

The continuing reluctance of high street banks to increase business lending has forced many entrepreneurs to become far more innovative in their approach to financing.

Charles Armstong, chief executive of Trampoline Systems, a social analytics company, said the collapse in conventional finance models had served as a catalyst for people to try alternative strategies. 'Not just informal friends and family routes, but new formal approaches too,' he said. Crowdfunding – raising small stakes from a large number of investors – was becoming more mainstream, he noted.

Knomo, a London-based bag design and manufacturing company, raised £500,000 in October from friends, family and a regional growth fund. 'The declining economy and retail market made this incredibly challenging,' co-founder Howard Harrison said.

According to a survey by Opinium Research conducted for the Financial Times, 63 per cent of the 217 small and medium-sized enterprise (SME) respondents with fewer than 249 employees said they were simply not borrowing. Of those that were or actively considering borrowing, 24 per cent had secured a loan against personal or company assets, 16 per cent had taken out a personal loan or used their credit cards, and 13 per cent had accepted loans from friends and family. Ten per cent had remortgaged their homes.

Clive Lewis, head of enterprise at the Institute of Chartered Accountants in England and Wales, said a large number of SMEs were managing with their existing bank lending 'for fear of having facilities reduced or withdrawn', and were resorting to personal credit cards to fund business costs.

The high street banks' continuing refusal to increase lending to SMEs has exacerbated the situation. Bank of England figures revealed lending to non-financial companies fell £14.7bn between April and June compared with the previous three months.

'The banks' behaviour gets people out looking for alternatives like peer-to-peer and micro-credit,' said Rafael Gomes, director of strategic services at Exclusive Analysis, a risk forecasting company.

For Emmett Kilduff, founder of cmypitch, an online business network, the fact that more enterpreneurs were 'bootstrapping' and looking for sums from contacts and family proved their resourcefulness.

'Entreprenuers have always sought creative means of funding their dreams,' said William Flatau, founder of First Funding, a brokerage for private debt deals. 'Friends and families have always been a first stop for start-ups. Business angel networks, however, are seeing vastly increased levels of inquiries as other forms of finance have dried up – but many angels are not in a position to invest.' He stressed the importance of linking private lenders with business borrowers. 'The message is clear: businesses can borrow from people, not banks.'

EXHIBIT 15.2

Source: *Financial Times* 8 August 2009, p. 30.

Revolving credit facility

A revolving credit facility (RCF) provides the borrower with some of the benefits of an overdraft and some of the benefits of a term loan. The RCF is set up by a bank for a fixed period, say five years, during which time the borrower may borrow up to a fixed amount. So, say the borrower draws the maximum permitted under the agreement for, say, a one-year period and then repays a large part of it, it then has the ability to borrow again up to the maximum at any point within the five years without the need to renegotiate with the bank, so it is a useful back-up facility. The advantages it has over the term loan are that any repayments before the five years are up do not incur a 'break-fee' for repaying early, and any monies repaid will be available to be utilised again (within the period of the facility). Thus, the borrower has a flexible loan, with the lender committed to satisfying the short-term funding needs of the firm. This flexibility does not come for free – the borrower will pay a 'commitment fee' to the bank for allowing access to the funds, even if no funds are actually drawn.

Trade credit

The simplest and most important source of short-term finance for many firms is trade credit. This means that when goods or services are delivered to a firm for use in its production they are not paid for immediately. These goods and services can then be used to produce income before the invoice has to be paid.

The writer has been involved with a number of small business enterprises, one of which was a small retail business engaged in the selling of crockery and glassware – Crocks. Reproduced, as Figure 15.3, is an example of a real invoice (with a few modifications to hide the identity of the supplier). When we first started buying from this supplier we, as a matter of course, applied for trade credit. We received the

FIGURE 15.3

A typical invoice

Supplier XYZ plc	Invoice number 501360
54 West Street, Sussex	Date 29/02/98
Invoice address	Branch address
Crocks	Crocks
Melton Mowbray	Grantham
Leics	Lincolnshire
LE13 1XH	

INVOICE

Account	Customer order No.	Sales order	Carrier	AEP	Despatch No.	Due date	Page
TO2251	81535	TO1537		090	000067981	28/03/98	1

Item	Part code	Description	Unit of sale	Quantity despatched	Unit price	%	Amount	VAT code
1	1398973	Long glass	Each	12	0.84	0.00	10.08	0
2	12810357	Tumbler	Each	12	0.84	0.00	10.08	0
3	1395731	Plate	Each	60	1.10	0.00	66.00	0
4	1258732	Bowls	Each	30	4.23	0.00	126.90	0
5	1310102	Cup	Each	1	4.24	0.00	4.24	0
		VAT 0: 217.30 @ 17.5%						

	Nett goods	217.30
	Charges	0.00
	VAT	38.03
		255.33

Note our settlement terms: $2\frac{1}{2}$% discount may be deducted for payment within 14 days of invoice date; otherwise due 30 days strictly nett.

usual response, that the supplier requires two references vouching for our trust-worthiness from other suppliers that have granted us trade credit in the past, plus a reference from our bankers. Once these confidential references were accepted by the supplier we were granted normal credit terms for retailers of our type of product, that is, 30 days to pay from the date of delivery. One of the things you learn in business is that agreements of this kind are subject to some flexibility. We found that this supplier does not get too upset if you go over the 30 days and pay around day 60: the supplier will still supply to the business on normal credit terms even if you do this on a regular basis.

Each time supplies were delivered by this firm we had to make a decision about when to pay. Option 1 is to pay on the 14th day to receive $2\frac{1}{2}$ percent discount – see note at the bottom of the invoice. Option 2 is to take 60 days to pay. (Note: with Option 1 the $2\frac{1}{2}$ percent deduction is on the 'nett goods' amount which is the value of the invoice before value added tax (VAT) is added, that is £217.30.)

Option 1

$$£217.30 \times 0.025 = £5.43$$

So, we could knock £5.43 off the bill if we paid it 14 days after delivery. This looks good but we do not yet know whether it is better than the second option.

Option 2

This business had an overdraft, so if we could avoid taking money from the bank account the interest charge would be less. How much interest could be saved by taking an additional 46 days (60 days – 14 days) to pay this invoice? Assuming the annual percentage rate (APR) charged on the overdraft is 10 percent the daily interest charge is:

$$(1 + d)^{365} = 1 + i$$

where:

d = daily interest, and i = annual interest

$$d = \sqrt[365]{(1 + i)} - 1$$

$$\sqrt[365]{(1 + 0.1)} - 1 = 0.00026116$$

Interest charge for 46 days:

$$(1 + 0.00026116)^{46} - 1 = 0.01208 \text{ or } 1.208\%$$

If we go for the early settlement discount and pay on day 14, we would have to borrow £255.33 minus the discount of £5.43 over a 46-day period at 10 percent per annum interest.

$$(255.33 - 5.43) \times 0.01208 = £3.02$$

Thus £3.02 interest is saved by delaying payment to the 60th day, compared with a saving of over £5 on the option of paying early.[3] In this particular case taking extended trade credit is not the cheapest source of finance; it is cheaper to use the overdraft facility.

Many suppliers to our business did not offer a discount for early settlement. This gives the impression that trade credit finance is a free source of funds, so the logical course of action is to get as much trade credit as possible. The system is therefore open to abuse. However, a supplier will become tired of dealing with a persistent late payer and will refuse to supply, or will only supply on a basis of payment in advance. Another point to be borne in mind is that gaining a bad reputation in the business community may affect relationships with other suppliers.

Advantages

Trade credit has the following advantages.

- **Convenient/informal/cheap** Trade credit has become a normal part of business in most product markets.

- **Available to companies of any size** Small companies, especially fast-growing ones, often have a very limited range of sources of finance to turn to and banks frequently restrict overdrafts and loans to the asset backing available. It is important to note that trade credit is a vital source of finance for the largest companies in the world as well as the smallest. For example, Tesco and Asda typically have over twice as much owing to suppliers at any one time as the value of all the goods on their shelves. The suppliers don't just provide food, etc.; they supply much of the money needed for the rest of Tesco's and Asda's operations. Some suppliers are getting fed up with it – *see* Exhibit 15.3.

Factors determining the terms of trade credit

Tradition within the industry

Customs have been established in many industries concerning the granting of trade credit. Individual suppliers are often unwise to step outside these traditions because they may lose sales.

Bargaining strength of the two parties

If the supplier has numerous customers, each wanting to purchase the product in a particular region, and the supplier wishes to have only one outlet then it may decide not to supply to those firms which demand extended trade credit. On the other hand, if the supplier is selling into a highly competitive market where the buyer has many alternative sources of supply, credit might be used to give a competitive edge.

Product type

Products with a high level of turnover relative to stock levels carried by firms are generally sold on short credit terms, for example food. The main reason is that these products usually sell on a low profit margin and the delay in payment can cause the money tied up in trade credit to grow to a very large sum very quickly. This can have a large impact on the cash resources and profit margin of the supplier. (*See* the Tesco example in Exhibit 15.3.)

Tesco accused of putting small suppliers at risk

Elizabeth Rigby

A leading consumer-goods maker has accused Tesco of forcing suppliers to wait almost two months to be paid, warning that some smaller operators could be forced out of business.

Bart Becht, chief executive of Reckitt Benckiser, told the Financial Times this week that the move by the biggest retailer this month to extend the time it would take to pay for goods from 30 to 60 days could be damaging.

'The question is [if] in the long term they drive the smaller suppliers out of business, that is the key question and it might happen,' he said in an unusual public comment on one of his biggest customers.

The only reason Mr Becht could see that Tesco might ask Reckitt and others for more favourable payment terms was to 'squeeze more out of the suppliers'.

Mr Becht, who supplies companies such as Tesco with products ranging from Airwick air freshners to Nurofen headache pills, said it would be unreasonable for the retailer to ask suppliers in high turnover categories such as household cleaning products, toiletries and personal care goods, to wait longer.

'I don't think it is reasonable – no, it is not,' said Mr Becht. 'There is absolutely no logic to that. They turn over the inventory [in] much less [time]

than 60 days, so why should they have 60 day payment terms?'

Tesco said last night that it had only asked 300 of its suppliers to accept the new terms for goods such as television sets, books, kettles and clothing.

Reckitt made clear that it had not been approached by Tesco to make any changes to its payment terms. Mr Becht said he could not comment on whether it would make sense for Tesco to change its terms for goods that had a lower turnover.

Asked about its decision to make some suppliers wait up to 60 days to be paid, Tesco said: 'This is a measured move affecting only a small proportion of our suppliers. We compare well with our competitors and are keen to deliver the best possible value to our customers in today's challenging climate. We are especially mindful of the impact on our small suppliers and stand ready to discuss any problems with them.'

Tesco's relations with suppliers have become increasingly fraught since the retailer decided to demand more favourable payment terms in its fight to see off rivals such as Aldi and Lidl.

Many suppliers have been quietly complaining about changes to terms but have shied away from airing grievances publicly for fear of retribution. ...

EXHIBIT 15.3

Source: *Financial Times* 31 October 2008, p. 1.

Credit standing of individual customers

A less risky customer may be granted longer periods to pay.

Factoring

To receive trade credit is a bonus for customer firms. However, this common practice also brings a burden to the firms supplying this form of finance. For many companies the amount owed by customers at any one time (debtor balances) is a multiple of their monthly turnover. For a medium-sized firm this can amount to millions of pounds. Costs, e.g. wages, have flowed out but customers are yet to pay – which can impose a severe strain on the ability of the firm to meet its obligations as they fall due.

Factoring (or 'invoice finance') companies provide three services to firms with outstanding debtors, the most important of which, in the context of this chapter, is the immediate transfer of cash. This is provided by the factor on the understanding that when invoices are paid by customers the proceeds will go to them. Factoring is increasingly used by companies of all sizes as a way of meeting cash flow needs induced by rising sales and debtor balances. About 80 percent of factoring turnover is handled by the clearing bank subsidiaries, e.g. HSBC Invoice Finance, Lloyds TSB and Royal Bank of Scotland Corporate Banking. However there are dozens of smaller factoring companies. Three closely related services are offered by factors. These are: the provision of finance, sales ledger administration and credit insurance.

The provision of finance

At any one time a typical business can have one-fifth or more of its annual turnover outstanding in trade debts: a firm with an annual turnover of £5m may have a debtor (trade receivables) balance of £1m. These large sums create cash difficulties that can pressurise an otherwise healthy business. Factors step in to provide the cash needed to support stock levels, to pay suppliers and generally aid more profitable trading and growth. The factor will give an advanced payment on the security of outstanding invoices. Normally about 80 percent of the invoice value can be made available to a firm immediately (with some factors this can be as much as 90 percent). The remaining 20 percent is transferred from the factor when the customer finally pays up. Naturally the factor will charge a fee and interest on the money advanced. The cost will vary between clients depending on sales volume, the type of industry and the average value of the invoices. The charge for finance is comparable with overdraft rates (1.5–3 percent over base rate). As on an overdraft the interest is calculated on the daily outstanding balance of the funds that the borrowing firm has transferred to their business account. Added to this is a service charge that varies between 0.2 and

3 percent of invoiced sales. This is set at the higher end if there are many small invoices or a lot of customer accounts or the risk is high. Figure 15.4 shows the stages in a typical factoring transaction. First, goods are delivered to the customer and an invoice is sent. Second, the supplier sells the right to receive the invoice amount to a factor in return for, say, 80 percent of the face value now. Third, some weeks later the customer pays the sum owing, which goes to the factor and finally, the factor releases the remaining 20 percent to the supplier less interest and fees.

Factors frequently reject clients as unsuitable for their services. The factor looks for 'clean and unencumbered debts' so that it can be reasonably certain of receiving invoice payments. It will also want to understand the company's business and to be satisfied with the competence of its management. Figure 15.5 shows how a factor might calculate the amount to be advanced.

This form of finance has some advantages over bank borrowing. The factor does not impose financial ratio covenants (e.g. profits as a multiple of interest) or require fixed asset backing. Also the fear of instant withdrawal of a facility (as with an overdraft) is absent as there is usually a notice period. The disadvantages are the raised cost and the unavailability of factoring to companies with many small-value transactions. Also, some managers say it removes a safety margin: instead of spending frugally while waiting for customers to pay, they may be tempted to splurge the advance.

FIGURE 15.4
Stages in a factoring deal

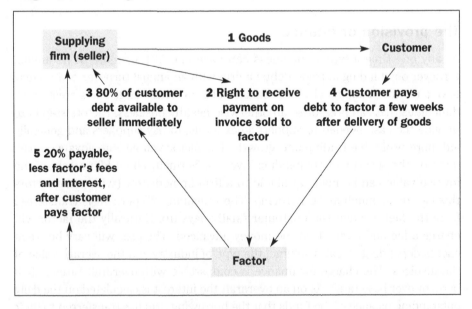

FIGURE 15.5

Amount available from a factor

A supplying firm has £1m of outstanding invoices, £40,000 are so old that the factor will not consider them, £60,000 are rejected as poor quality or are export sales and £30,000 are subject to a dispute between the supplier and the customer. The factor is prepared to advance 80% of suitable invoices:

Total invoices		£1,000,000
Less:		
Debts excessively old	£40,000	
Non-approved	£60,000	
In dispute	£30,000	
		(130,000)
		£870,000

The amount the factor is willing to provide to the supplier immediately is 80% of £870,000, or £696,000 (69.6% of total invoices).

Sales ledger administration

Companies, particularly young and fast-growing ones, often do not want the trouble and expense of setting up a sophisticated system for dealing with the collection of outstanding debts. For a fee (0.75–2.5 percent of turnover) factors will take over the functions of recording credit sales, checking customers' creditworthiness, sending invoices, chasing late payers and ensuring that debts are paid. The fees might seem high, say £100,000 for a firm with a turnover of £5m, but the company avoids the in-house costs of an administrative team and can concentrate attention on the core business. Moreover, factors are experienced professional payment chasers who know all the tricks of the trade (such as 'the cheque is in the post' excuse) and so can obtain payment earlier. With factoring sales ledger administration and debt collection generally come as part of the package offered by the finance house, unlike with invoice discounting (see overleaf).

Credit insurance

The third service available from a factor is the provision of insurance against the possibility that a customer does not pay the amount owed. The charge for this service is generally between 0.3 and 0.5 percent of the value of the invoices.

Trade credit insurance hit the headlines in 2008 and 2009 when it was claimed that the withdrawal of insurance cover for invoices sent to certain customers (e.g. Woolworths) led to their demise – see Exhibit 15.4.

Atradius to widen trade credit cover

Paul J Davies

Atradius, one of the world's biggest insurers of trade credit, offered a drop of oil to the wheels of the UK economy after it said it would extend more cover to 13,000 businesses following an underwriting review. ...

Trade credit insurers were thrown into the spotlight when the economy ground to a halt in the final quarter of 2008 after companies blamed a widespread reduction in insurance cover for the seizing up of their supply chains.

Trade credit insurance pays out if a company goes bust before it pays for goods or services. Retailers were especially hard hit, and Woolworths said the removal of credit insurance and the resulting problems with its supply chain helped push it into administration.

Shaun Purrington, Atradius's UK and Ireland director, said retail was one of the few sectors that would not benefit from his company's increased risk appetite. 'We see a difficult outlook for retail in the fourth quarter and the first quarter of next year,' he said. ...

Mr Purrington said the increase in capacity had been driven by more transparency on the part of companies wanting insurance rather than a big improvement in the economic outlook. 'This is not about the economy improving,' he said. 'It's about better information sharing between insurers and companies, which has helped us to better identify the risks we feel comfortable with.' ...

'We are now prepared to consider risks that we would have avoided in the nine previous months, but we will still be cautious because we think another wave of insolvencies could materialise,' he said. ...

EXHIBIT 15.4

Source: *Financial Times* 5 November 2009, p. 21.

Recourse and non-recourse

Most factoring arrangements are made on a non-recourse basis, which means that the factor accepts the risk of non-payment by the customer firm. For accepting this risk the factor will not only require a higher return but also want control over credit assessment, credit approval and other aspects of managing the sales ledger to ensure payment. Some firms prefer recourse factoring in which they retain the risk of customer default but also continue to maintain the relationship with their customers through the debt collection function without the sometimes overbearing (and more costly) intervention of the factor. With confidential invoice factoring the customer is usually unaware that a factor is the ultimate recipient of the money paid over, as the supplier continues to collect debts, acting as an agent for the factor.

Invoice discounting

Firms with an annual turnover under £10m typically use factoring (with sales ledger administration) whereas larger firms tend to use invoice discounting. Here, invoices are pledged to the finance house in return for an immediate payment of up to 90 percent of the face value. The supplying company guarantees to pay the amount represented on the invoices and is responsible for collecting the debt. The customers are generally totally unaware that the invoices have been discounted. When the due date is reached it is to be hoped that the customer has paid in full. Regardless of whether the customer has paid, the supplying firm is committed to handing over the total invoice amount to the finance house and in return receives the remaining 10 percent less service fees and interest. Note that even invoice discounting is subject to the specific circumstances of the client agreement and is sometimes made on a non-recourse basis.

The finance provider usually only advances money under invoice discounting if the supplier's business is well established and profitable. There must be an effective and professional credit control and sales ledger administration system. Charges are usually lower than for factoring because the sales ledger administration is the responsibility of the supplying company. Fees are 0.2 to 0.8 percent of company sales plus interest comparable with business overdraft rates. Invoice discounting has the advantage over factoring of maintaining the relationship between customer and supplier without the intervention of a finance house. Thus customer records are kept confidential, the customer does not get nervous about its supplier using a factor – often seen (usually wrongly) as a desperate act, indicating financial troubles – and the customer is not excessively pressurised by a forceful debt collector.

The idea of raising funds using unpaid invoices has been taken a step further with supply chain financing (SCF), which increases funds to both the customer and supplier – *see* Exhibit 15.5.

New lease of life for supply chain financing

Jennifer Hughes

Companies are increasingly using their own unpaid invoices – known as receivables – to secure financing and achieve lower funding costs as their usual lenders have become more reluctant to provide conventional lending facilities in the wake of the credit crunch.

So-called supply chain financing (SCF) was already a growing business before the credit crisis stuck, but its use has spread rapidly as financial conditions have worsened. SCF is designed to raise cash against company assets known as receivables, which mainly consist of unpaid invoices.

Banks have reported a 65 per cent increase in the volumes being funded through SCF over the last year, according to a survey from Demica, a consultancy. More than 90 per cent of top banks offer SCF to their corporate clients, up from just a half a year ago, Demica said.

SCF involves companies and their suppliers agreeing to extend the payment period to the supplier, who still obtains early payment from the buyer's bank. The buyer gets the benefit of longer payment times, the supplier lowers it working capital costs, which it can then pass back to the buyer in lower prices. The bank in the middle has the invoices to secure its lending and earns a margin on the loan. ...

EXHIBIT 15.5

Source: *Financial Times* 27 May 2008, p. 16.

Hire purchase

With hire purchase the finance company buys the equipment that the borrowing firm needs. The equipment (plant, machinery, vehicles, etc.) belongs to the hire purchase (HP) company. However the finance house allows the 'hirer' firm to use the equipment in return for a series of regular payments. These payments are sufficient to cover interest and contribute to paying off the principal. While the monthly instalments are still being made the HP company has the satisfaction and security of being the legal owner and so can take repossession if the hirer defaults on the payments. After all payments have been made the hirer becomes the owner, either automatically or on payment of a modest option-to-purchase fee. Nowadays, consumers buying electrical goods or vehicles have become familiar with the attempts of sales assistants to also sell an HP agreement so that the customer pays over an extended period. Sometimes the finance is provided by the same organization, but more often by a separate finance house. The stages in an HP agreement are as in Figure 15.6, where the HP company buys the durable good which is made available to the hirer firm for immediate use. A series of regular payments follows until the hirer owns the goods.

Some examples of assets that may be acquired on HP are as follows:

- Plant and machinery
- Business cars
- Commercial vehicles
- Agricultural equipment

- Hotel equipment
- Medical and dental equipment
- Computers, including software
- Office equipment

FIGURE 15.6
The hire purchase sequence

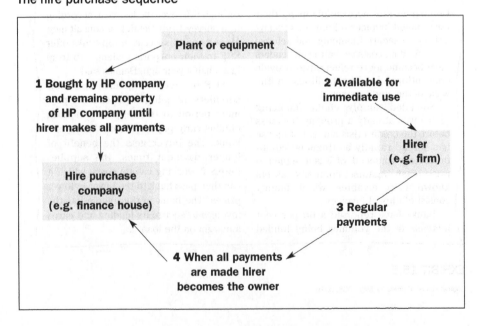

The main advantages of this form of finance are as follows:

- **Small initial outlay** The firm does not have to find the full purchase price at the outset. A deposit followed by a series of instalments can be less of a cash flow strain. The funds that the company retains by handing over merely a small deposit can be used elsewhere in the business for productive investment. Set against this is the relatively high interest charge and the additional costs of maintenance and insurance.

- **Easy to arrange** Usually at point of sale, allowing immediate use of the asset.

- **Certainty** This is a medium-term source of finance that cannot be withdrawn provided contractual payments are made, unlike an overdraft. On the other hand the commitment is made for a number of years and it could be costly to terminate the agreement. There are also budgeting advantages to the certainty of a regular cash outflow.

- **HP is often available when other sources of finance are not** For some firms the equity markets are unavailable and banks will no longer lend to them, but HP companies will still provide funds as they have the security of the asset to reassure them.

- **Fixed-rate finance** In most cases the payments are fixed throughout the HP period. While the interest charged will not vary with the general interest rate throughout the life of the agreement the hirer has to be aware that the HP company will quote an interest rate which is significantly different from the true annual percentage rate. The HP company tends to quote the flat rate. So, for example, on a £9,000 loan repayable in equal instalments over 30 months the flat rate might be 12.4 percent. This is calculated by taking the total interest charged over the two and a half years and dividing by the original £9,000. The monthly payments are £401.85 and therefore the total paid over the period is £401.85 × 30 = £12,055.50. The flat interest is:

$$^{2.5}\sqrt{(12{,}055.50/9{,}000)} - 1 = 0.1240 \text{ or } 12.4\%$$

This would be the true annual rate if the entire interest and capital were repaid at the end of the 30th month. However, a portion of the capital and interest is repaid each month and therefore the annual percentage rate (APR) is much higher than the flat rate. As a rough rule of thumb the APR is about double the flat rate. Ask what the APR is.

- There are fewer and more flexible covenants than with bank loans.

- **Tax relief** The hirer qualifies for tax relief in two ways:
  - The asset can be subject to a writing-down allowance (WDA) on the capital expenditure. For example, if the type of asset is eligible for a 25 percent WDA and originally cost £10,000 the using firm can reduce its taxable profits by £2,500 in the year of purchase; in the second year tax-

able profits will be lowered by £7,500 × 0.25 = £1,875. If tax is levied at 30 percent on taxable profit the tax bill is reduced by £2,500 × 0.30 = £750 in the first year, and £1,875 × 0.3 = £562.50 in the second year. Note that this relief is available despite the hirer company not being the legal owner of the asset.

■ Interest payments (an element of the monthly instalment) are deductible when calculating taxable profits.

The tax reliefs are valuable only to profitable companies. Many companies do not make sufficient profit for the WDA to be worth having. This can make HP an expensive form of finance. An alternative form of finance, which circumvents this problem (as well as having other advantages) is leasing.

Leasing

Leasing is similar to HP in that an equipment owner (the lessor) conveys the right to use the equipment in return for regular rental payments by the equipment user (the lessee) over an agreed period of time. The essential difference is that the lessee never becomes the owner – the leasing company retains legal title.[4] Subsidiaries of clearing banks dominate the UK leasing market, but the world's biggest leasing companies are owned by vehicle manufacturers.

Figure 15.7 shows that a typical lease transaction involves a firm wanting to make use of an asset approaching a finance house which purchases the asset and rents it to the lessee.

It is important to distinguish between operating leases and finance leases.

FIGURE 15.7
A leasing transaction

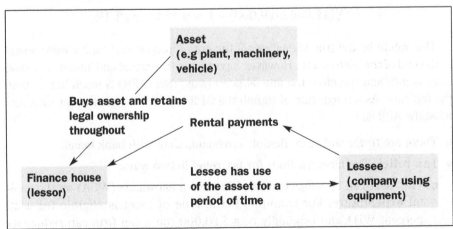

Operating lease

Operating leases commit the lessee to only a short-term contract or one that can be terminated at short notice. These are certainly not expected to last for the entire useful life of the asset and so the finance house has the responsibility of finding an alternative use for the asset when the lessee no longer requires it. Perhaps the asset will be sold in the secondhand market, or it might be leased to another client. Either way the finance house bears the risk of ownership. If the equipment turns out to have become obsolete more quickly than was originally anticipated it is the lessor that loses out. If the equipment is less reliable than expected the owner (the finance house) will have to pay for repairs. Usually, with an operating lease, the lessor retains the obligation for repairs, maintenance and insurance. It is clear why equipment which is subject to rapid obsolescence and frequent breakdown is often leased out on an operating lease. Photocopiers, for example, used by a university department are far better leased; so, if they break down the university staff do not have to deal with the problem. In addition the latest model can be quickly installed in the place of an outdated one. The same logic applies to computers, facsimile machines and so on. The most common form of operating lease is contract hire. These leases are often used for a fleet of vehicles. The leasing company takes some responsibility for the management and maintenance of the vehicles. A residual price for the item is agreed at the start of the contract and is paid by the lessor, say 36 months after the lease payment starts.

Operating leases are also useful if the business involves a short-term project requiring the use of an asset for a limited period. For example construction companies often use equipment supplied under an operating lease (sometimes called plant hire). Operating leases are not confined to small items of equipment. There is a growing market in leasing aircraft and ships for periods less than the economic life of the asset, thus making these deals operating leases. Many of Boeing's and Airbus's aircraft go to leasing firms – *see* Exhibit 15.6.

Lessors take evasive action in difficult market

Tracy Alloway

The global aircraft-leasing business is facing upheaval as the industry struggles to cope with a lack of funding and an airline customer base which itself is grappling with the most severe recession to hit the aviation sector.

The extent of the damage inflicted on the aircraft leasing sector, which has grown rapidly over the past two decades, could lead to a dramatic reshaping of the industry as big questions hang over the future of its traditional funding model. ...

The number of lessors up for sale means that a total portfolio of about 1,800 aircraft is coming on to the market at a time when the sector's traditional business model is threatened by the lack of financing and aircraft values are extremely depressed.

	Year of manufacture	Purchase value Sep 09 ($m)	Change since Jan	Monthly lease rate, Sep 09 ($'000)*	Change since Jan
New aircraft					
Boeing 737–800 (narrow-body)	2009	39.5	▼–7%	340	▼–6%
Airbus A330–200 (wide-body)		82.0	▼–7%	700	▼–16%
Used aircraft					
Boeing 737–300 (narrow-body)	1999	9.6	▼–9%	115	▼–26%
Boeing 747–400 (wide-body)		43.3	▼–16%	590	▼–11%

Source: Ascend   * Based on five-year lease

Top ten leasing companies

By fleet value	Value ($bn)	Fleet
GE Capital Aviation Services	36.36	1,834
International Lease Finance	34.69	1,075
RBS Aviation Capital	6.81	228
CIT Aerospace	6.49	238
Babcock & Brown Aircraft Management	6.10	283
AerCap**	5.65	358
AWAS	4.41	210
Aviation Capital Group	4.27	234
Aircastle Advisor	3.12	130
Macquarie AirFinance	2.60	125

** After proposed Genesis acquisition

The global aircraft leasing industry is crucial to airlines and airlines manufacturers alike. It controls a fleet of almost 6,900 aircraft – about a third of the world's commercial aircraft in service – and accounts for about two-thirds of new orders won by aircraft manufacturers last year. Airlines rely extensively on leasing to offset the high cost of aircraft ownership.

Like so many other sectors crippled by the financial crisis the aircraft leasing industry is facing the sternest test since its inception in the mid-1960s. Lessors have historically aimed to use economies of scale – pitting aircraft manufacturers against each other for big orders – and access to inexpensive debt, often acquired by piggybacking on their parent companies' credit ratings, to build their portfolios. In return it often allowed airlines to access cheaper financing for aircraft than buying direct as well as greater flexibility in expanding and managing their fleets. ...

The uncertainty and poor state of the global airline industry has also hit resale values of aircraft. 'We've got passenger traffic, cargo traffic and capacity down, a record number of parked aircraft, and Boeing and Airbus are still producing at record rates,' said Richard Aboulafia, vice-president of analysis at Teal Group, a

Virginia-based aerospace consultant. 'That means asset prices are getting clobbered.'

Market values for a new Boeing 737 or Airbus A320 have fallen almost 10 per cent in the last nine months. Values of older, longer-range models have dropped even further.

If all those factors are not enough to put off potential buyers of an aircraft lessor, sellers face the additional problem of trying to find someone with pockets deep enough to fund a leasing business, which relies on rolling over debt to fund aircraft purchases. ...

EXHIBIT 15.6

Source: *Financial Times* 24 September 2009, p. 25.

Finance lease

Under a finance lease (also called a capital lease or a full payout lease) the finance provider expects to recover the full cost (or almost the full cost) of the equipment, plus interest, over the period of the lease. With this type of lease the lessee usually has no right of cancellation or termination. Despite the absence of legal ownership the lessee will have to bear the risks and rewards that normally go with ownership: the lessee will usually be responsible for maintenance, insurance and repairs and suffer the frustrations of demand being below expectations or the equipment becoming obsolete more rapidly than anticipated. Most finance leases contain a primary and a secondary period. It is during the primary period that the lessor receives the capital sum plus interest. In the secondary period the lessee pays a very small 'nominal', rental payment.

Advantages

The advantages listed for hire purchase also apply to leasing: small initial outlay, certainty, available when other finance sources are not, fixed-rate finance, tax relief, and fewer, more flexible covenants than on term loans. There is an additional advantage of operating leases and that is the transfer of obsolescence risk to the finance provider.

The tax advantages for leasing are slightly different from those for HP. The rentals paid on an operating lease are regarded as tax deductible and so this is relatively straightforward. For financial leases, however, the tax treatment is linked to the modern accounting treatment. This is designed to prevent some creative accounting which under the old system allowed a company to appear to be in a better gearing (debt/equity ratio) position if it leased rather than purchased its equipment. In the old days a company could lower its apparent gearing ratio and therefore improve its chances of obtaining more borrowed funds by leasing. Take the two companies X and Y, which have identical balance sheets initially, as shown in Figure 15.8.

FIGURE 15.8
Balance sheets of companies X and Y

Initial balance sheet for both X and Y	
Shareholders' funds (net assets)	£1,000,000
Debt capital	£1,000,000
Total assets	£2,000,000

Now, if X borrows a further £1m to buy equipment, while Y leases £1m of equipment the balance sheets appear strikingly different under the old accounting rules.

	Company X	Company Y
Shareholders' funds (net assets)	1,000,000	1,000,000
Debt capital	2,000,000	1,000,000
Total assets	3,000,000	2,000,000

Company X has a debt/equity ratio of 200 percent whereas Y has obtained the use of the asset 'off-balance sheet' and so has an apparent gearing ratio of only 100 percent. A superficial analysis of these two firms by, say, a bank lender, may lead to the conclusion that Y is more capable of taking on more debt. In reality Y has a high level of fixed cash outflow commitments stretching over a number of years under the lease and is in effect highly geared. Under these rules Y could also show a higher profit to asset ratio.

Today finance leases have to be 'capitalised' to bring them on to the balance sheet. The asset is stated in the balance sheet and the obligations under the lease agreement are stated as a liability. Over subsequent years the asset is depreciated and, as the capital repayments are made to the lessor the liability is reduced. The profit and loss account is also affected: the depreciation and interest are both deducted as expenses.

The tax authorities apply similar rules and separate the cost of interest on the asset from the capital cost. The interest rate implicit in the lease contract is tax deductible in the relevant year. The capital cost for each year is calculated by allocating rates of depreciation (capital allowances) to each year of useful life.

These new rules apply only to finance leases and not to operating leases. A finance lease is defined (usually) as one in which the present value of the lease payments is at least 90 percent of the asset's fair value (usually its cash price). This has led to some bright sparks engineering leasing deals which could be categorised as operating leases and therefore kept off balance sheets – some are designed so that 89 percent of the value is paid by the lessee. However the authorities are fighting back as Exhibit 15.7 shows.

A very important tax advantage can accrue to some companies through leasing because of the legal position of the asset not belonging to the lessee. Companies that happen to have sufficient profits can buy assets and then reduce

Companies' balance sheets set to get a new lease of life

Jeremy Grant

At a congressional hearing in Washington last year, Sir David Tweedie, chairman of the International Accounting Standards Board, drew laughter when he said one of his ambitions was 'actually flying in an aircraft that's on an airline's balance sheet before I die'.

He has long been frustrated by the ability of airlines to run their fleets using certain types of leases whose costs do not have to be fully reflected in their financial statements – preventing investors from seeing the full extent of an airline's debt profile.

But last week, the world's accounting standard-setters signalled an end to this smoke-and-mirrors approach to lease accounting, heralding the first overhaul of the accounting treatment in the multibillion-dollar leasing business since the 1970s.

The IASB, which sets global accounting rules, and its US counterpart, the Financial Accounting Standards Board, met to work out new rules that would force not only airlines, but also retailers, restaurant chains and other users of commercial leases to bring lease assets on to their balance sheets for the first time. ...

Take Continental Airlines. At the end of 2005, the aircraft operated 622 aircraft, of which 477 were leased. Long-term debt recorded on Continental's balance sheet was $5bn.

But it also disclosed $11bn in future payments under operating leases for the lifetime of those leases. If this were brought on-balance sheet, Continental's debt could more than double.

With debt off-balance sheet, investors cannot easily see how much capital an airline or retailer is employing, nor the sources of financing for that capital.

Change is coming after a Securities and Exchange Commission report into off-balance sheet financing that discouraged structures 'motivated primarily and largely by accounting and reporting considerations, rather than economics'.

Tom Jones, vice-chairman of the IASB, says: 'There is generally a feeling that lease accounting is very old and not very effective. There's a suspicion that leasing standards have been so carved-up that it's relatively easy to keep stuff off-balance sheet. It's high time standard-setters looked to see if they're appropriate'.

Leasing is an important source of finance, allowing airlines to operate aircraft without owning them, and retailers similarly to operate stores. Under a capital, or finance lease, a company records a liability for rental payments but also records an asset for the property or equipment it is leasing.

But current so-called FAS 13 rules include four criteria that leases can be structured to avoid. This turns the lease into an operating lease – and thus is placed off-balance sheet. Critics say this does not reflect the full extent of the liability that the lessee has taken on. They say operating leases are really a type of long-term debt and this obligation should be reflected on the balance sheet. Companies with a large volume of leases are likely to resist change because bringing leases on to the balance sheet could skew the leverage and financial return ratios that affect market valuations and their ability to borrow. Bank loan covenants may also have to be changed.

The Equipment Leasing and Finance Association challenges the idea that the right to use equipment under a lease should be represented in financial statements as an asset, because the lessee has no control over the asset – to sell it, for example.

Kenneth Bentsen, ELFA president, says a 'true lease' is one where a party agrees to provide an asset for use by another party in return for some consideration. However, that consideration does not amortise the cost of the asset the same way as if that asset had been purchased through a loan.

'We think there are some basic tenets that need to be adhered to. There is a clear difference in many cases between a pure operating lease and a true debt instrument where there is a transfer of ownership. That's a significant economic difference,' he says.

As for the airlines, banks that lend to them and Wall Street credit analysts have been aware of the on-balance sheet implications of their operating lease liabilities for years, according to Phil Baggaley, airline analyst at Standard & Poor's.

'Credit analysts are already capitalising off-balance sheet leases and, to a large extent, the equity analysts are – and certainly the banks that lend to them are,' he says. Such analysts typically estimate an airline's operating lease liabilities by plugging the future off-balance sheet lease payments that are listed in the notes to financial statements into financial models.

But accountants say that these future payment figures do not represent the current value of leases, and until such information is brought on to the balance sheet such modelling is too vague to be of real use to investors.

FASB and IASB are expected next year to produce a draft proposal for public comment. A final document would emerge in 2009. ...

Additional reporting by Barney Jopson in London

EXHIBIT 15.7

Source: *Financial Times* 21 February 2007, p. 28.

their taxable profits by writing off a proportion of the assets' value (say 25 percent on a reducing balance) against income each year. However companies with low profits or those which make a loss are unable to fully exploit these investment allowances and the tax benefit can be wasted. But if the equipment is bought by a finance company with plenty of profits, the asset cost can be used to save on the lessor's tax. This benefit can then be passed on to the customer (the lessee) in the form of lower rental charges. This may be particularly useful to start-up companies and it has also proved of great value to low- or no-profit privatized companies. For example, the railway operating companies often make losses and have to be subsidised by the government. They can obtain the services of rolling stock (trains, etc.) more cheaply by leasing from a profit-generating train-leasing company than by buying. Another advantage is that the leasing agreement can be designed to allow for the handing back of the vehicles should the operating licence expire or be withdrawn (as the train-operating licences are – after seven years or so).

Bills of exchange

A bill is a document that sets out a commitment to pay a sum of money at a specified point in time. The simplest example is an ordinary bank cheque that has been dated two weeks hence. The government borrows by selling Treasury bills which commit it to paying a fixed sum in, say, three months. Local authorities issue similar debt instruments, as do commercial organizations in the form of commercial bills (*see* Chapter 16).

Bills of exchange are mainly used to oil the wheels of overseas trade. They have a long history helping to promote international trade, particularly in the nineteenth and twentieth centuries. The seller of goods to be transported to a buyer in another country frequently grants the customer a number of months in which to pay. The seller will draw up a bill of exchange (called a trade acceptance in international trade) – that is, a legal document is produced showing the indebtedness of the buyer. The bill of exchange is then forwarded to, and accepted by the customer, which means that the customer signs a promise to pay the stated amount and currency on the due date. The due date is usually 90 days later but 30, 60 or 180 days bills of exchange are not uncommon. The bill is returned to the seller who then has two choices, either to hold it until maturity and receive payment under it then, or to sell it to a bank or discount house (the bill is discounted). Under the second option the bank will pay a lower amount than the sum to be received in, say, 90 days from the customer. The difference represents the bank's interest.

For example, if a customer has accepted a bill of exchange that commits it to pay £200,000 in 90 days the bill might be sold by the supplier immediately to a discount house or bank for £194,000. After 90 days the bank will realise a profit of £6,000 on a £194,000 asset, an interest rate of 3.09 percent ((6,000/194,000) × 100) over 90 days. This gives an approximate annual rate of:

$$(1.0309)^4 - 1 = 0.1294 = 12.94\%$$

Through this arrangement the customer has the benefit of the goods on 90 days credit, the supplier has made a sale and immediately receives cash from the discount house amounting to 97 percent of the total due. The discounter, if it borrows its funds at less than 12.9 percent, turns in a healthy profit. The sequence of events is shown in Figure 15.9.

Bills of exchange are normally only used for transactions greater than £75,000. The effective interest rate charged by the discounter is a competitive 1.5 to 4 percent over interbank lending rates (for example, LIBOR) depending on the creditworthiness of the seller and the customer. The bank has recourse to both of the commercial companies: if the customer does not pay then the seller will be called upon to make good the debt. This overhanging credit risk can sometimes be dealt with by the selling company obtaining credit insurance. Despite the simplification of Figure 15.9, many bills of exchange do not remain in the hands of the discounter until maturity but are traded in an active second-

FIGURE 15.9

The bill of exchange sequence

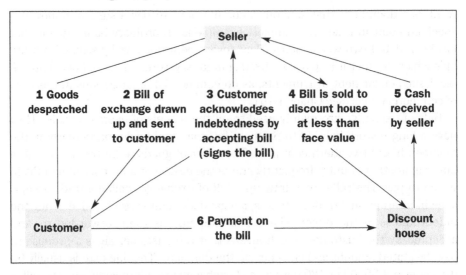

ary market (the money market). Note also that not all bills of exchange are a form of temporary finance. Some are 'sight drafts'; that is, payable on demand without a delay of a few days (as with 'time drafts' as 'term drafts').

Acceptance credits (bank bills or banker's acceptance)

In the case of acceptance credits (bank bills) the company which is in need of finance requests the drawing up of a document which states that the signatory will pay a sum of money at a set date in the future. This is 'accepted' (signed) by a bank rather than by a customer. Simultaneously the company makes a commitment to pay the accepting bank the relevant sum at the maturity date of the bill.

This bank commitment to pay the holder of the acceptance credit can then be sold in the money markets to, say, another bank (a discounter) by the firm to provide for its cash needs. (Alternatively an importing company could give the acceptance credit to its overseas supplier in return for goods – and the supplier can then sell it at a discount if required.)

The acceptance credit is similar to a bill of exchange between a seller and a buyer, but now the organisation promising to pay is a reputable bank representing a lower credit risk to any subsequent discounter. These instruments therefore normally attract finer discount rates than a trade bill. When the maturity date is reached the company pays the issuing bank the value of the bill, and the bank pays the ultimate holder of the bill its face value.

The company does not have to sell the acceptance credit immediately and so can use this instrument to plug finance gaps at opportune times. There are two costs of bank bill finance:

- The bank charges acceptance commission for adding its name to the bill.
- The difference between the discount price and the acceptance credit's due sum.

These costs are relatively low compared with those on overdrafts and there is an ability to plan ahead because of the longer-term commitment of the bank. Unfortunately this facility is only available in hundreds of thousands of pounds and then only to the most credit-worthy of companies.

Figure 15.10 shows the actions taken in an acceptance credit transaction.

FIGURE 15.10
An acceptance credit sequence

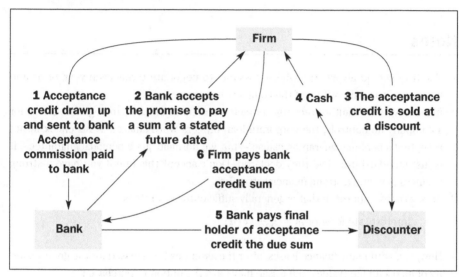

Conclusion

The modern corporation has a rich array of alternative sources of funds available to it. We have considered only short- and medium-term finance in this chapter. The next chapter looks at debt finance available for the long term, mostly finance available to the largest firms with the ability to draw on the financial markets. Chapter 17 describes the various ways of raising share finance for the growing firm.

It is the responsibility of the senior management team to select the most appropriate combination of forms of finance and the proportions of each. Each organisation faces different circumstances and so the most appropriate mixture will change from one entity to another. To help make this judgment we have already considered the advantages and disadvantages of bank overdrafts and loans; trade credit; factoring; hire purchase and leasing, and; trade and bank bills. We now go on to broaden the range of possible types to bonds, convertibles, mezzanine finance, Eurobonds, medium-term notes, commercial paper, project finance, sale and leaseback, preference shares and ordinary shares.

Websites

www.bankofengland.co.uk	Bank of England
www.bba.org.uk	British Bankers Association
www.berr.gov.uk	Department for Business, Enterprise and Regulatory Reform
www.fsb.org.uk	Federation of Small Businesses
www.payontime.co.uk	Better Payments Practice Group
www.fla.org.uk	Finance and Leasing Association
www.factors.org.uk	Factors and Discounters Association

Notes

1 The firm should always try, where possible, to negotiate terms each year, or as and when the financial position of the company improves.

2 Indeed, when the author recently contacted a number of banks to negotiate a loan for a company he controls, the corporate loan officers were amazed at his cheek in not accepting a personal guarantee clause – 'but we normally get a personal guarantee – it is just standard practice' they declared. Don't accept this line if you have a strong business plan and a strong financial structure.

3 An alternative approach that is generally sufficiently accurate is:

$$\text{Interest rate for } n \text{ days} = \frac{i}{365} \times (n)$$

4 However, with many finance leases, after the asset has been leased for the great majority of its useful life (value), the lessee may have the option to purchase it.

16

DEBT FINANCE FROM THE FINANCIAL MARKETS

Introduction

The concept of borrowing money to invest in real assets within a business is a straightforward one, yet in the sophisticated capital markets of today with their wide variety of financial instruments and forms of debt, the borrowing decision can be bewildering. Should the firm tap the domestic bond market or the Eurobond market? And what about syndicated lending, mezzanine finance and high-yield bonds? The variety of methods of borrowing finance is infinite. This chapter outlines the major categories of debt finance from the financial markets and illustrates some of the fundamental issues a firm may consider when selecting its finance mix. As you can see from the detail taken from the annual accounts of GlaxoSmithKline plc (Figure 16.1) a firm may need knowledge and understanding of a great many different debt instruments. The terms bonds, commercial paper, Eurobond, medium-term notes and loan stock mentioned in the extract are explained in this chapter. In addition we cover convertible bonds, foreign bonds, project finance, securitization and sale and leaseback.

> In the sophisticated capital markets of today with their wide variety of financial instruments and forms of debt, the borrowing decision can be bewildering.

FIGURE 16.1

Loans and other borrowings for GlaxoSmithKline plc

	2008 £m	2007 £m
Short-term borrowings:		
3.25% € European Medium Term Note 2009 London Stock Exchange	(481)	–
3.375% € European Medium Term Note 2008 London Stock Exchange	–	(736)
4.875% £ European Medium Term Note 2008 London Stock Exchange	–	(497)
Commercial paper	–	(2,064)
Bank loans and overdrafts	(426)	(161)
Other loans	(1)	(6)
Obligations under finance leases	(48)	(40)
Long-term borrowings:		
3.25% € European Medium Term Note 2009 London Stock Exchange	–	(368)
US$ Floating rate Note 2010 New York Stock Exchange	(694)	–
3.00% € European Medium Term Note 2012 London Stock Exchange	(718)	(548)
5.125% € European Medium Term Note 2012 London Stock Exchange	(2,154)	(1,645)

4.85% US$ US Medium Term Note 2013 New York Stock Exchange	**(1,728)**	–
4.375% US$ US Medium Term Note 2014 London Stock Exchange	**(1,146)**	(746)
5.625% € European Medium Term Note 2017 London Stock Exchange	**(1,193)**	(912)
5.65% US$ US Medium Term Note 2018 New York Stock Exchange	**(1,901)**	–
4.00% € European Medium Term Note 2025 London Stock Exchange	**(709)**	(542)
5.25% £ European Medium Term Note 2033 London Stock Exchange	**(979)**	(978)
5.375% US$ US Medium Term Note 2034 London Stock Exchange	**(344)**	(249)
6.375% US$ US Medium Term Note 2038 New York Stock Exchange	**(1,888)**	–
6.375% £ European Medium Term Note 2039 London Stock Exchange	**(693)**	–
5.25% £ European Medium Term Note 2042 London Stock Exchange	**(984)**	(984)
Loan stock	**(8)**	(9)
Bank loans	**(1)**	(1)
Other loans and private financing	**(3)**	(2)
Obligations under finance leases	**(88)**	(83)

Source: GlaxoSmithKline plc Annual Report 2008.

Bonds

A bond is a long-term contract in which the bondholders lend money to a company. In return the company (usually) promises to pay the bond owners a series of interest payments, known as coupons, until the bond matures. At maturity the bondholder receives a specified principal sum called the par, face or nominal value of the bond. This can be £100, £1,000, £50,000 or any other sum chosen by the issuer. In the USA and Europe the most popular par values ('lot sizes') are $1,000, €5,000 and €50,000. The time to maturity is generally between seven and 30 years although a number of firms, for example Disney, IBM and Reliance of India, have issued 100-year bonds.

Bonds may be regarded as merely IOUs (I owe you) with pages of legal clauses expressing the promises made. Some corporate bonds are sufficiently liquid (many transactions, so traders/owners are able to buy/sell at low cost without moving the price) to trade on the London Stock Exchange, but the vast majority of trading occurs in the over-the-counter (OTC) market directly

> Bonds may be regarded as merely IOUs.

between an investor and a bond dealer. Access to a secondary trading market means that the investor who originally provided the firm with money does not have to hold on to the bond until the maturity date (the redemption date). However, because so many investors buy and then hold to maturity rather than trade in and out bonds generally have thin secondary markets compared with shares. The amount the investor receives in the secondary market might be more or less than what he/she paid. For instance, imagine an investor paid £99.80 for a bond that promised to pay a coupon of 9 percent per year on a par value of £100 and to pay the par value in seven years. If one year after issue interest rates on similar bonds are 20 percent per annum no one will pay £99.80 for a bond agreement offering £9 per year for a further six years plus £100 on the redemption date. We will look at a method for calculating exactly how much they might be willing to pay later in the chapter.

These negotiable (that is tradeable in a secondary market) instruments come in a variety of forms. The most common is the type described above with regular (usually semi-annual) fixed coupons and a specified redemption date. These are known as straight, plain vanilla or bullet bonds. Other bonds are a variation on this. Some pay coupons every three months, some pay no coupons at all (called zero coupon bonds – these are sold at a large discount to the par value and the investor makes a capital gain by holding the bond), some bonds do not pay a fixed coupon but one which varies depending on the level of short-term interest rates (floating-rate or variable-rate bonds), some have interest rates linked to the rate of inflation. In fact, the potential for variety and innovation is almost infinite. Bonds issued in the last few years have linked the interest rates paid or the principal payments to a wide variety of economic events, such as the price of silver, exchange-rate movements, stock market indices, the price of oil, gold, copper – even to the occurrence of an earthquake. These bonds were generally designed to let companies adjust their interest payments to manageable levels in the event of the firm being adversely affected by some economic variable changing. For example, a copper miner pays lower interest on its finance if the copper price falls. In 1999 Sampdoria, the Italian football club, issued a €3.5m bond that paid a higher rate of return if the club won promotion to the 'Serie A' division (2.5 percent if it stayed in Serie B, 7 percent if it moved to Series A). If the club rose to the top four in Serie A the coupon would rise to 14 percent.

Debentures and loan stocks

The most secured type of bond is called a debenture. They are usually secured by either a fixed or a floating charge against the firm's assets. A fixed charge means that specific assets are used as security that, in the event of default, can be sold at the insistence of the debenture bondholder and the proceeds used to repay them. Debentures secured on property may be referred to as mortgage debentures. A floating charge means that the loan is secured by a general charge on all the assets of the corporation (or a class of the firm's assets such as inventory or debtors). In this case the company has a high degree of freedom to use its assets as it wishes, such as sell them (so long as there is enough security left) or rent them out, until it commits a default which 'crystallizes' the floating charge. If this happens a receiver will be appointed with powers to dispose of assets and to distribute the proceeds to the creditors. Even though floating-charge debenture holders can force liquidation, fixed-charge debenture holders rank above floating-charge debenture holders in the payout after insolvency.

The terms bond, debenture and loan stock are often used interchangeably and the dividing line between debentures and loan stock is a fuzzy one. As a general rule debentures are secured and loan stock is unsecured but there are examples which do not fit this classification. If liquidation occurs the unsecured loan stock-holders rank beneath the debenture holders and some other categories of creditors, such as the tax authorities. In the USA and other markets, the definitions are somewhat different and this can be confusing. There a debenture is an unsecured bond and so the holders become general creditors who can only claim assets not otherwise pledged. The secured form of bond is referred to as the mortgage bond and unsecured shorter-dated issues (less than 15 years) are called notes.

Bonds are often referred to collectively as fixed-interest securities. While this is an accurate description for many bonds, others do not offer regular interest payments that are fixed amounts. Nevertheless they are all lumped together as fixed interest to contrast these types of loan instrument with equities that do not carry a promise of a return (Warren Buffett uses the term fixed maturity securities).

Trust deeds and covenants

Bond investors are willing to lower the interest they demand if they can be reassured that their money will not be exposed to a high risk. This reassurance is conveyed by placing risk-reducing restrictions on the firm. A trust deed sets out the terms of the contract between bondholders and the company. A trustee (if one is appointed) ensures compliance with the contract throughout the life of the bond and has the power to appoint a receiver.[1] The loan agreement will contain a number of affirmative covenants. These usually include the requirements to supply regular financial statements, interest and principal payments. The deed may also state the fees due to the lenders and details of what procedures are to be followed in the event of a technical default, for example non-payment of interest.

In addition to these basic covenants are the negative (restrictive) covenants. These restrict the actions and the rights of the borrower until the debt has been repaid in full. Some examples are as follows.

- **Limits on further debt issuance** If lenders provide finance to a firm they do so on certain assumptions concerning the riskiness of the capital structure. They will want to ensure that the loan does not become more risky due to the firm taking on a much greater debt burden relative to its equity base, so they limit the amount and type of further debt issues – particularly debt which is higher ('senior debt') ranking for interest payments and for a liquidation payment. Subordinated debt – with low ranking on liquidation – is more likely to be acceptable.

- **Dividend level** Lenders are opposed to money being taken into the firm by borrowing at one end, while being taken away by shareholders at the other. An excessive withdrawal of shareholder funds may unbalance the financial structure and weaken future cash flows.

- **Limits on the disposal of assets** The retention of certain assets, for example property and land, may be essential to reduce the lenders' risk.

- **Financial ratios** A typical covenant here concerns the interest cover, for example: 'The annual pre-interest pre-tax profit will remain four times as great as the overall annual interest charge'. Other restrictions might be placed on working capital ratio levels, and the debt to net assets ratio. In the case of Wolseley, the threshold is 3.5 for the net debt to earnings (before deduction of interest, tax depreciation and amortization) ratio – *see* Exhibit 16.1.

Wolseley shares plunge as net debt increases

Robert Cookson and David Fickling

Shares in Wolseley lost almost a third of their value yesterday after the building materials group warned that its debt pile, denominated mostly in euros, had swollen by a fifth to £3bn as sterling crumbled.

The rising debt, together with falling profits, stoked fears that Wolseley will breach its ... covenants this year, forcing the company into costly debt renegotiations or a dilutive rights issues.

UBS, its broker, said Wolseley was 'highly likely' to break its covenants when they are tested in July. ...

... Wolseley's covenants require its net debt to be no higher than 3.5 times earnings before interest, tax, depreciation and amortisation. The figure for the full year to July 2008 was 2.7 times. UBS estimates Wolseley's ebitda in July 2009 will be £608m against net debt of £2.56bn.

In an attempt to keep within the 3.5 figure, Wolseley has over the past five months reduced working capital, cut jobs and set up a receivables funding arrangement to raise cash from its pending invoices. The company cut 7,500 jobs over the period, bringing the total to 66,000, and said the receivables arrangement had reduced net debt by £72m.

However, it has become more difficult to meet the net debt covenant as the slide in the pound has caused Wolseley's foreign currency debt to rise in sterling terms. The effect of currency movements has increased net debt over the period by £557m, a 22 per cent jump. ...

... In an attempt to mitigate this, Wolseley moved a total of £1bn of euro and dollar-denominated debt into sterling and set up a currency hedge against further falls in the pound against the euro. ...

The shares fell 85p to 201p.

EXHIBIT 16.1

Source: *Financial Times* 27 January 2009, p. 20.

While negative covenants cannot provide completely risk-free lending they can influence the behaviour of the management team so as to reduce the risk of default. The lenders' risk can be further reduced by obtaining guarantees from third parties (for example, guaranteed loan stock). The guarantor is typically the parent company of the issuer.

Repayments

The principal on many bonds is paid entirely at maturity. However, there are bonds which can be repaid before the final redemption date. One way of paying for redemption is to set up a sinking fund that receives regular sums from the firm that will be sufficient, with added interest, to redeem the bonds. A common approach is for the company to issue bonds where it has a range of dates for redemption; so a bond dated 2018–2022 would allow a company the flexibility to repay a part of the principal in cash over four years. Another way of redeeming bonds is for the issuing firm to buy the outstanding bonds by offering the holder a sum higher than or equal to the amount originally paid. A firm is also able to purchase bonds on the open market.

Some bonds are described as 'irredeemable' as they have no fixed redemption date. From the investor's viewpoint they may be irredeemable but the firm has the option of repurchase and can effectively redeem the bonds.

Bond variations

Bonds which are sold at well below the par value are called deep discounted bonds, the most extreme form of which is the zero coupon bond. It is easy to calculate the rate of return offered to an investor on this type of bond. For example, if a company issues a bond at a price of £60 which is redeemable at £100 in eight years the annualized rate of return (r) is:

$$60(1 + r)^8 = 100$$

$$r = \sqrt[8]{\frac{100}{60}} - 1 = 0.066 \text{ or } 6.6\%$$

(Mathematical tools of this kind are explained in the appendix to Chapter 2.)

These bonds are particularly useful for firms with low cash flows in the near term, for example firms engaged in a major property development that will not mature for many years.

A major market has developed recently called the floating rate note (FRN) market (also called the variable-rate note market). Two factors have led to the rapid growth in FRN usage. First, the oscillating and unpredictable inflation of the 1970s and early 1980s caused many investors to make large real-term losses on fixed-rate bonds as the interest rate fell below the inflation rate. As a result many lenders became reluctant to lend at fixed rates on a long-term basis. This reluctance led to floaters being cheaper for the issuer because it does not need to offer an interest premium to compensate the investor being locked into a fixed rate. Second, a number of corporations, especially financial institutions, hold assets which give a return that varies with the short-term interest rate level and so prefer to hold a similar floating-rate liability. These instruments pay an interest that is linked to a benchmark rate – such as the LIBOR (London Inter-Bank Offered Rate – the rate that safest banks charge each other for borrowed funds). The issuer will pay, say, 70 basis points (0.7 of a percentage point) over LIBOR. The coupon is set for (say) the first six months at the time of issue, after which it is adjusted every six months; so if six-month LIBOR is 5 percent, the FRN would pay 5.7 percent for that particular six months. (There are LIBOR rates for various lengths of time, for example, lending/borrowing between high reputation banks for a few hours (overnight LIBOR) or for three months).

There are many other variations on the basic vanilla bond, two of which will be examined later – high-yield bonds and convertible bonds. We now turn to another major source of long-term debt capital – syndicated bank borrowing.

Syndicated loans

For large loans a single bank may not be able or willing to lend the whole amount. To do so would be to expose the bank to an unacceptable risk of failure on the part of one of its borrowers. Bankers like to spread their lending to gain the risk-reducing benefits of diversification. They prefer to participate in a number of syndicated loans in which a few banks each contribute a portion of the overall loan. So, for a large multinational company loan of, say, £500m, a single bank may provide £30m, with perhaps 100 other banks contributing the remainder. The bank originating the loan will usually manage the syndicate and is called the lead manager (there might be one or more lead banks). This bank (or these banks) may invite a handful of other banks to co-manage the loan who then persuade other banks to supply much of the funding. That is, they help the process of forming the syndicate group of banks in the general syndication – the process of getting other banks to agree to lend – these other banks are called participating banks. The managing banks also underwrite much of the loan – guaranteeing to provide the funds if other banks do not step forward.[2]

Syndicated loans are available at short notice and can be provided discreetly (helpful if the money is to finance a merger bid, for example). They generally offer lenders lower returns than bonds, but as they rank above most bonds on liquidation payouts there is less risk. The loans carry covenants similar to those on bond agreements. The volume of new international syndicated loans now runs into hundreds of billions of pounds per year.

A disadvantage of a syndicated loan is that the borrower may not form a relationship with single bank (a bilateral loan). A single lender with whom it conducts a variety of banking business is more likely to sit down and negotiate with a borrower should it run into difficulties and seek waivers on loan covenant breaches – it may also be more willing to supply additional funds.

Credit rating

Firms often pay to have their bonds rated by specialist credit-rating organisations. The debt rating depends on the likelihood of payments of interest and/or capital not being paid (that is, default) and, in some cases, on the extent to which the lender is protected in the event of a default by the loan contract (the recoverability of the debt). UK government gilts have an insignificant risk of default whereas unsecured subordinated corporate loan stock has a much higher risk. We would expect that firms in stable industries and with conservative accounting and financing policies and a risk-averse business strategy would have a low risk of default and therefore a high credit rating. Companies with a high total debt burden, a poor cash flow position, in a worsening market environment causing lower and more volatile earnings, will have a high default risk and a low credit rating. The dominant credit rating agencies are Moody's, Standard & Poor's (S&P), and Fitch.

The highest rating is AAA or Aaa (triple-A rated). Such a rating indicates very high quality. The capacity to repay interest and principal is extremely strong. Single A indicates a strong capacity to pay interest and capital but there is some degree of susceptibility to impairment as economic events unfold. BBB or Baa indicates adequate debt service capacity but vulnerability to adverse economic conditions or changing circumstances. B and C rated debt has predominantly speculative characteristics. The lowest is D, which indicates the firm is in default or is very likely to default.

Ratings of BBB– (or Baa3 for Moody's) or above are regarded as 'investment grade' – this is important because many institutional investors are permitted to invest in investment grade bonds only (*see* Figure 16.2). Bonds rated below this are called high-yield (or junk) bonds. Generally, the specific loan is rated rather than the borrower. If the loan does not have a rating it could be that the borrower has not paid for one, rather than implying anything sinister.

The rating and re-rating of bonds is followed with great interest by borrowers and lenders and can give rise to some heated argument. Frequently borrowers complain that their ratings are not judged to be as high as they think they should be, resulting in higher interest rates payable on the bonds.

Table 16.1 shows the proportion of corporate bonds that have defaulted 1, 2, 3, 4 and 5 years after issue over the period.

When examining data on default rates it is important to appreciate that default is a wide-ranging term, and could refer to any number of events from a missed payment to bankruptcy. For some of these events all is lost from the investor's perspective. For other events a very high percentage, if not all, of the interest and principal is recovered. Hickman (1958) observed that defaulted publicly held and

FIGURE 16.2

A comparison of Standard & Poor's, Moody's and Fitch's rating scales

Standard & Poor's	Fitch	Moody's	
AAA	AAA	Aaa	
AA+	AA+	Aa1	
AA	AA	Aa2	
AA–	AA–	Aa3	
A+	A+	A1	Investment grade bonds
A	A	A2	
A–	A–	A3	
BBB+	BBB+	Baa1	
BBB	BBB	Baa2	
BBB–	BBB–	Baa3	
BB+	BB+	Ba1	
BB	BB	Ba2	
BB–	BB–	Ba3	
B+	B+	B1	
B	B	B2	Non-investment grade.
B–	B–	B3	High-yield 'junk' bonds
CCC	CCC	Caa	
CC		Ca	
C		C	

traded bonds tended to sell for 40 cents on the dollar. This average recovery rate rule-of-thumb seems to have held over time – in approximate terms – with senior bank loans returning over 60 percent and subordinated bonds under 30 percent.

Examples of ratings on long-term instruments are given in Table 16.2. The ratings here are for December 2009 and will not necessarily be applicable in future years because the creditworthiness and the specific debt issue can change significantly in a short period.

A lot of weight is placed on bond ratings by investors and regulators. Sometimes they feel aggrieved when the analyst's powers of observation and judgment on default likelihood turn out to be limited. The rating agencies were severely criticised in 2009 for not spotting the dangers in a number of bonds which gained their income from thousands of US mortgages – see Exhibit 16.2.

TABLE 16.1

Fitch global corporate finance average cumulative default rates 1990–2008

Percentage	1 year	2 years	3 years	4 years	5 years
'AAA'	0.00	0.00	0.00	0.00	0.00
'AA'	0.04	0.00	0.00	0.02	0.05
'A'	0.09	0.22	0.34	0.44	0.62
'BBB'	0.26	0.77	1.42	2.16	2.86
'BB'	1.42	3.32	4.94	6.43	8.22
'B'	1.83	3.76	5.68	7.54	9.20
'CCC to 'C'	22.30	27.59	30.64	33.33	36.92
Investment grade	0.14	0.35	0.61	0.89	1.16
High yield	2.99	5.22	7.16	8.92	10.81
All Corporates	0.68	1.25	1.77	2.24	2.73

Source: http://www.fitchratings.com/creditdesk/reports/report_frame.cfm?rpt_id=428182

TABLE 16.2

Examples of ratings on long-term instruments in December 2009

	Currency of borrowing	S&P	Moody's	Fitch	Interest (bid yield)
GE Capital	US$	AA+	Aa2	–	4.21
BNP Paribas	US$	AA–	Aa2	AA–	4.10
Citigroup	US$	A	A3	A+	3.16
HSBC	€	A	A3	AA–	2.72
Citigroup	Yen	A	A3	A+	3.70
HSBC	£	A	A2	A	3.29
Xstrata	€	BBB	Baa2	–	3.26
Royal Caribbean Cruises	€	BB–	Ba3	–	10.06
Philippines	US$	BB–	Ba3	BB	5.75
Kazkommerts	US$	B	Ba3	B–	13.83
Argentina	US$	DEF	Ca	D	34.41

Source: Shown in the *Financial Times* daily – see tables headed 'Global Investment Grade' and 'High Yield & Emerging Market Bonds'; particular issue used is 1 December 2009.

Ratings agency model left largely intact

Aline van Duyn and Joanna Chung

Big banks are not the only ones whose income is soaring on the back of commissions and fees from selling and trading the huge amounts of debt being sold by governments, banks and companies.

Credit rating agencies ... have also seen a surge in revenue, as most debt that is issued – government-backed or not – comes with a credit rating for which the borrowers pays a fee.

Indeed, the ratings business is doing so well that some analysts have raised revenues forecasts. ...

The ratings agencies remain central to the debt markets and their business models today remain largely intact, in spite of widespread claims that they exacerbated the credit crisis. The criticism centres on the fact that Moody's, S&P and Fitch gave triple A ratings to hundreds of billions of dollars of bonds backed by risky mortgages – but these securities have since been downgraded and are now in many cases worthless. Ratings continue to be written into the official criteria used by many investors to define what debt they can and cannot buy. They are also still central to risk assessments by regulators and other official agencies.

Ironically, some of the biggest investors and borrowers are suing the rating agencies.

The largest pension fund in the US, the California Public Employees' Retirement System (Calpers), has filed a suit against the three leading rating agencies over potential losses of more than $1bn over what it says are 'wildly inaccurate' triple A ratings. That is just one of many. S&P currently faces around four dozen separate law suits from investors and institutions.

In the past, most lawsuits have failed because rating agencies are protected by the first amendment right to free speech. Their ratings are an 'opinion' and there-fore subject to free speech protections. Whether this will continue to be the case is a key factor in the debate about the future of the industry. ...

Already, rating agencies have themselves undertaken reviews aimed at restoring confidence in their ratings, particularly on the structured finance part of the business which includes bonds backed by loans like mortgages and where most of the controversies have been. ...

... Michael Barr, Treasury's assistant secretary for financial institutitons, portrayed the proposed legislation as an attempt to ensure that better information is put into the market and to encourage the right incentives for the issuance of ratings. Other models, including the investor-paid model also have inherent conflicts of interest that would pose problems, he said.

No matter what the reforms, 'we are not going to be able to eliminate the need for investors to use their own judgment ... The one thing we want to make clear ... no investor should take as a matter of blind faith what the ratings [agency's] judgement is,' Mr Barr said this week.

The SEC, which has created a new group of examiners to oversee the sector, is looking for ways to reduce reliance on credit ratings.

Mary Shapiro, chairman of the SEC, said at a Congressional hearing that new rules would be put forward later this summer. She said one rule would require issuers to disclose preliminary ratings to get rid of 'pernicious' ratings shopping (when a company solicits a preliminary rating from an agency but only pays for and discloses the highest rating it receives); disclose information underlying the ratings; look at sources of revenue disclosure and performance history of ratings over one-, five- and 10-year periods; and see how the SEC could get investors to do additional due diligence of their own.

'While the Administration's proposals are well-intentioned, they are easily criticised as merely cosmetic,' says Joseph Grundfest, a law professor at Stanford University. 'If you really want change you have to recognise that the industry is dominated by two agencies and the SEC should create a new category of agencies owned by investors.'

The status of rating agencies means that they have access to information that is not made public, information they do not need to disclose, and this is one reason they are supposed to have better insights into companies and deals than ordinary investors might. It is this special status that some believe should be targeted.

'When an opinion has regulatory power, which is what ratings have, it has to come with some accountability,' says Arturo Cifuentes, principal with Atacama Partners, a financial advisory firm. 'It is not enough to say it is just an opinion, because it carries more weight than that in the financial system.'

EXHIBIT 16.2

Source: *Financial Times* 23 July 2009, p. 31.

Mezzanine debt and high-yield (junk) bonds

Mezzanine debt is a loan offering a high return with a high risk. It may be either unsecured or secured but ranking behind senior loans for payment of interest and capital. This type of debt generally offers interest rates two to nine percentage points more than that on senior debt and frequently gives the lenders some right to a share in equity values should the firm perform well. It is a kind of hybrid finance ranking for payment below straight debt but above equity – it is thus described alternatively as *subordinated, intermediate*, or *low grade*. One of the major attractions of this form of finance for the investor is that it often comes with equity warrants or share options (*see* Chapter 19) attached which can be used to obtain shares in the firm – this is known as an 'equity kicker'. These may be triggered by an event such as the firm joining the stock market.

> It is a kind of hybrid finance ranking for payment below straight debt but above equity.

Mezzanine finance tends to be used when bank borrowing limits are reached and the firm cannot or will not issue more equity. The finance it provides is cheaper (in terms of required return) than would be available on the equity market and it allows the owners of a business to raise large sums of money without sacrificing control. It is a form of finance which permits the firm to move beyond what is normally considered acceptable debt:equity ratios (gearing or leverage levels).

Crucially, unlike most bank loans, which usually involve annual repayments, mezzanine is often like an interest-only mortgage with no capital repayments until the end of the loan. Also, mezzanine lenders, which are often specialist funds rather than banks, are usually prepared to lend against the company's prospects in terms of expected cash flows, rather than insisting on security (collateral), as banks tend toward.

Bonds with high-risk and high-return characteristics are called high-yield (junk) bonds (they are rated below investment grade by rating agencies with ratings of BBs, Bas, Bs and Cs). These may be bonds that started as apparently safe investments but have now become more risky ('fallen angels') or they may be bonds issued specifically to provide higher-risk finance instruments for investors. This latter type began its rise to prominence in the USA in the 1980s.

> The US junk bond market has grown from almost nothing in the early 1980s to over $100bn of new issues each year.

The US junk bond market has grown from almost nothing in the early 1980s to over $100bn of new issues each year. This money has been used to spectacular effect in corporate America – the most outstanding event was the $25bn takeover of RJR Nabisco using primarily junk bonds. The rise of the US junk bond market meant that no business was safe from the threat of takeover, however large – *see* Case study 16.1.

The high-yield bond is much more popular in the USA than in Europe because of the aversion (constrained by legislation) to such instruments in the major financial institutions. The European high-yield bond market is in its infancy. The first high-yield bonds denominated in European currencies were issued as recently as 1997 when Geberit, a Swiss/UK manufacturer, raised DM 157.5m by selling ten-year bonds offering an interest rate which was 423 basis points (4.23 percent) higher than the interest rate on a ten-year German government bond (bund). Since then there have been over 100 issues. Nevertheless the European high-yield market remains about one-tenth the size of the US one. Exhibit 16.3 shows the size of the European high-yield bond market.

Case study 16.1

The junk bond wizard: Michael Milken

While studying at Wharton Business School in the 1970s Michael Milken came to the belief that the gap in interest rates between safe bonds and high-yield bonds was excessive, given the relative risks. This created an opportunity for financial institutions to make an acceptable return from junk bonds, given their risk level. At the investment banking firm Drexel Burnham Lambert, Milken was able to persuade a large body of institutional investors to supply finance to the junk bond market as well as provide a service to corporations wishing to grow through the use of junk bonds. Small firms were able to raise billions of dollars to take over large US corporations. Many of these issuers of junk bonds had debt ratios of 90% and above – for every $1 of share capital $9 was borrowed. These gearing levels concerned many in the financial markets. It was thought that companies were pushing their luck too far and indeed many did collapse under the weight of their debt. The market was dealt a particularly severe blow when Michael Milken was sentenced for infringing various laws, sent to jail and ordered to pay $600m in fines. Drexel was also convicted, paid $650m in fines and filed for bankruptcy in 1990. The junk bond market was in a sorry state in the early 1990s, with high levels of default and few new issues. However it did not take long for the market to recover.

European high-yield bonds are in demand

Anousha Sakoui

As €10bn ($14.28bn) in orders flooded in from investors for Italian car maker Fiat's junk bond last month, even the company's bankers were surprised by the torrent of demand for a €1.25bn offering of risky debt. Just a few weeks earlier, such a deal might not have been possible.

Indeed, risk aversion levels were so high during the first 18 months of the financial crisis that the European high-yield market was completely closed to new issues.

Yet such has been the change of sentiment in recent weeks that European high-yield bonds have become the best performing fixed income asset class globally – returning almost 50 per cent in 2009, according to Credit Suisse.

So far this year the market has swallowed €6.1bn of euro-denominated junk bonds, according to Société Générale. The total includes a €2.7bn bond from Italian telecom company Wind – the biggest ever unsecured European junk bond – and the Fiat issue. Overall issuance is bigger because it includes other currencies.

Digging down into banks' order books highlights a radical change in the sources of demand for high-yield paper.

With both Wind and Irish bottling company Ardagh Glass, over 70 per cent of orders were from longer term or so-called 'real money' investors, according to analysis by debt information provider CapitalStructure. Before the credit crunch, it was typically hedge funds and structured credit investors which accounted for the bulk of demand in Europe.

Demand now is driven by pension and insurance funds, suggesting a new pool of long-term liquidity is evolving for riskier European borrowers and one which could be more permanent. The buyers include fund management groups such as Threadneedle – as well as investors that have dedicated high-yield funds such as Bluebay Asset Management. Aviva Investors, the asset management arm of the insurance company, is another such investor, having launched a Global High Yield Bond Fund last year.

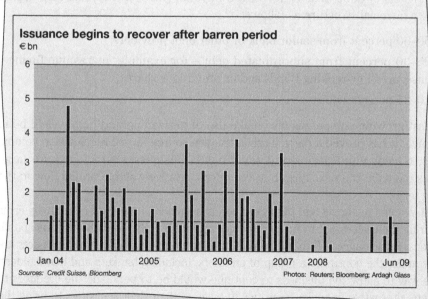

Issuance begins to recover after barren period

€ bn

Sources: Credit Suisse, Bloomberg

Photos: Reuters; Bloomberg; Ardagh Glass

'European high yield has had a number of false dawns but the expectation is that this time it will be more sustainable,' says Dagmar Kent Kershaw, Head of Credit Fund Management at Intermediate Capital Group. 'It is fantastic news for a high-yield market which has been starved of product.'...

The revival in the high-yield market reflects the strong increase in global risk appetite in recent months as well as a view that default levels may fall short of earlier estimates. Partly because of the improvement in the market, Moody's says it now expects the default rate for European speculative grade companies to peak at 12 per cent in the first quarter of 2010, down from an earlier forecast of a peak of 15 per cent by the end of 2009.

While the US junk bond market has been long established, the European high-yield market has only developed over the past decade. Unlike the US, where borrowers have a long tradition of using bond markets to fund themselves, European companies relied heavily on bank debt in the past. ...

According to Barclays Capital, the European junk bond market is set to grow from €100bn currently to €150bn by the end of 2012. The revival in high yield has also sparked interest in the leveraged loan market, which has rallied 25 per cent this year.

EXHIBIT 16.3

Source: *Financial Times* 14 August 2009, p. 29.

> **Mezzanine finance is usually a private rather than publicly traded form of debt.**

Mezzanine finance is usually a private form of debt (e.g. loan) rather than a publicly traded form of debt. However, mezzanine notes are sometimes issued which are tradeable in a secondary market. Mezzanine finance has proved to be particularly useful to managers involved in those management buyouts (MBO) that require high levels of debt, that is, leveraged buyouts (LBOs). A typical LBO would have a financial structure as follows:

- 50–60 percent from senior bank or other debt providers;
- 25–30 percent from subordinated debt – for example, mezzanine finance, unsecured low-ranking bonds and/or preference shares;
- 10–25 percent equity.

Fast-growing companies also make use of mezzanine and highly-yield bond finance. It has proved a particularly attractive source for cable television companies, telecommunications and some media businesses which require large investments in the near term but also offer a relatively stable profits flow in the long term.

Mezzanine financing and high-yield bonds have been employed not only by firms 'gearing themselves up' to finance merger activity but also for leveraged recapitalisations. For instance, a firm might have run into trouble, defaulted and its assets are now under the control of a group of creditors, including bankers and bondholders. One way to allow the business to continue would be to persuade the creditors to accept alternative financial securities in place of their debt securities to bring the leverage to a reasonable level. They might be prepared to accept a mixture of shares and mezzanine finance. The mezzanine instruments permit the holders to receive high interest rates in recognition of the riskiness of the firm, and they open up the possibility of an exceptionally high return from warrants or share options should the firm get back to a growth path. The alternative for the lenders may be a return of only a few pence in the pound from the immediate liquidation of the firm's assets.

Mezzanine finance/junk bond borrowing usually leads to high debt levels, resulting in a high fixed cost on the firm and can be a dangerous way of financing expansion and therefore the use of these types of finance has been criticised. On the other hand, some commentators have praised the way in which high gearing and large annual interest payments have focused the minds of managers and engendered extraordinary performance. Also, without this finance, many takeovers, buyouts and financial restructurings would not take place.

Financing a leveraged buyout

If the anticipated cash flows are reasonably stable then a highly leveraged buyout may give an exceptional return to the shareholders. Take the case of Sparrow, a subsidiary of Hawk plc. The managers have agreed a buyout price of £10m, equal to Sparrow's assets. They are able to raise £1m from their own resources to put into equity capital and have borrowed £9m. The debt pays an interest rate of 14 percent and the corporate tax rate is 25 percent (payable one year after year end). Profits before interest and tax in the first year after the buyout are expected to be £1.5m and will grow at 25 percent per annum thereafter. All earnings will be retained within the business to pay off debt.

> Highly leveraged buyout may give an exceptional return to the shareholders.

Table 16.3 shows the projected cash flows and debt position.

In the first few years the debt burden absorbs a large proportion of the rapidly increasing profits. However it only takes six years for the entire debt to be retired. The shareholders then own a business with assets of over £10m, an increase of over tenfold on their original investment. The business is also producing a large annual profit, which could make a stock market flotation attractive, in which case the value of the shares held by the management will probably be worth much more than £10m.[3]

Convertible bonds

Convertible bonds (or convertible loan stocks) carry a rate of interest in the same way as vanilla bonds, but they also give the holder the right to exchange the bonds at some stage in the future into ordinary shares according to some prearranged formula.[4] The owner of these bonds is not obliged to exercise this right of conversion and so the bond may continue until redemption as an interest-bearing instrument. Usually the *conversion price* is 10–30 percent greater than the share price at the date of the bond issuance. So if a £100 bond offered the right to convert to 40 ordinary shares the conversion price would be £2.50 (that is, £100/40) which, given the current market price of the shares of, say, £2.20, would be a *conversion premium* of:

TABLE 16.3

Sparrow – Profit and Loss Account and Balance Sheet (£000s)

	Years					
	1	2	3	4	5	6
Profit before interest and taxes (after depreciation)	1,500	1,875	2,344	2,930	3,662	4,578
Less interest	1,260	1,226	1,144	999	770	433
	240	649	1,200	1,931	2,892	4,145
Tax	0	60	162	300	483	723
Profits available to pay off debt	240	589	1,038	1,631	2,409	3,422

Balance Sheet

		Year					
	Opening	1	2	3	4	5	6
Equity	1,000	1,240	1,829	2,867	4,498	6,907	10,329
Debt	9,000	8,760	8,171	7,133	5,502	3,093	0
Assets	10,000	10,000	10,000	10,000	10,000	10,000	10,329

Notes: Past tax liabilities have been accepted by Hawk. Money set aside for depreciation is used to replace assets to maintain £10m of assets throughout. Also depreciation equals capital allowances used for tax purposes.

$$\frac{2.50 - 2.20}{2.20} = 0.136 \text{ or } 13.6$$

Venture Production, a North Sea oil explorer, issued convertible bonds in July 2005. The issue raised £29m. The bonds were to be redeemed in 2010 if they had not been converted before then and were issued at a par value of £100. The coupon was set at 4.25 percent and the conversion price was at 474p per share. From this information we can calculate the conversion ratio:

$$\text{Conversion ratio} = \frac{\text{Nominal (par) value of bond}}{\text{conversion price}} = \frac{£100}{£4.74} = 21.1 \text{ shares}$$

Each bond carries the right to convert to 21.1 shares, which is equivalent to paying 474p for each share at the £100 par value of the bond.

Unusually, in this particular case, if the bonds were not converted or redeemed then the holder will receive 110 percent of par value rather than simply the par value in October 2010, to give a total yield to maturity (the properly calculated rate of return – see next section) of 5.904 percent.

The conversion price was set at a premium of 16 percent over the ordinary share price at the time of pricing, which was 408p ((474–408)/408 = 16%). At the time of the issue many investors may have looked at the low interest rate on the convertible and said to themselves that although this was greater than the dividend yield on an average share (3 percent), it was less than that on conventional bonds, but offsetting this was the prospect of capital gains made by converting the bonds into shares. If the shares rose to, say, £6, then each £100 bond could be converted to 21.1 shares worth 21.1 × £6 = £126.6.

The value of a convertible bond (a type of 'equity-linked bond') rises as the value of ordinary shares increases, but at a lower percentage rate. The value could be analysed as a 'debt portion' (which depends on the discounted value of the coupons) and an 'equity portion' (the right to convert is an equity option). If the share price rises above the conversion price the investor may exercise the option to convert if he/she anticipates that the share price will at least be maintained and the dividend yield is higher than the convertible bond yield. If the share price rise is seen to be temporary the investor may wish to hold on to the bond. If the share price falls or rises by only a small amount the value of the convertible will be the same as a straight bond at maturity.

Figure 16.3 provides some of the key technical terms used for convertibles.

FIGURE 16.3
Summary of convertible bond technical jargon

- **Conversion ratio** This gives the number of ordinary shares into which a convertible bond may be converted:

$$\text{Conversion ratio} = \frac{\text{Nominal (par) value of bond}}{\text{Conversion price}}$$

- **Conversion price** This gives the price of each ordinary share obtainable by exchanging a convertible bond:

$$\text{Conversion price} = \frac{\text{Nominal (par) value of bond}}{\text{Number of shares into which bond may be converted}}$$

- **Conversion premium** This gives the difference between the conversion price and the market share price, expressed as a percentage:

$$\text{Conversion premium} = \frac{\text{Conversion price} - \text{Market share price}}{\text{Market share price}} \times 100$$

- **Conversion value** This is the value of a convertible bond if it were converted into ordinary shares at the current share price:

$$\text{Conversion value} = \text{Current share price} \times \text{Conversion ratio}$$

The right to convert may specify a particular date or dates over, say, a four-year period, or any time between two dates.

Most convertible bonds are unsecured but as the Case study on Greenhills shows, this is not always the case – a good thing for Hunter Ground!

SECURED CONVERTIBLE DEBENTURES

Greenhills

The first AIM-traded company to go into receivership was Greenhills, the restaurant operator. A major investor, Hunter Ground, appointed administrative receivers on 4 December 1996. Hunter Ground held secured convertible debentures from Greenhills worth £506,000.

Source: *Investors Chronicle*, 20 December 1996, p. 11. Reprinted with kind permission of the *Investors Chronicle*.

Advantages to the company of convertible bonds

Convertible bonds have the following advantages to the company.

- **Lower interest than on a similar debenture** The firm can ask investors to accept a lower interest on these debt instruments because the investor values the conversion right. This was a valuable feature for many dot.com companies in the late 1990s. Companies such as Amazon and AOL could pay 5–6 percent on convertibles – less than half what they would have paid on straight bonds.

- **The interest is tax deductible** Because convertible bonds are a form of debt the coupon payment can be regarded as a cost of the business and can therefore be used to reduce taxable profit.

- **Self-liquidating** When the share price reaches a level at which conversion is worthwhile the bonds will (normally) be exchanged for shares so the company does not have to find cash to pay off the loan principal – it simply issues more shares. This has obvious cash flow benefits. However the disadvantage is that the other equity holders may experience a reduction in earnings per share and dilution of voting rights.

- **Fewer restrictive covenants** The directors have greater operating and financial flexibility than they would with a secured debenture. Investors accept that a convertible is a hybrid between debt and equity finance and do not tend to ask for high-level security, impose strong operating restrictions on managerial action or insist on strict financial ratio boundaries – notwithstanding the case of Greenhills (*see* Case study 16.2). Many Silicon Valley companies with little more than a web portal and a brand have used convertibles because of the absence of a need to provide collateral or stick to asset: borrowing ratios.

- **Underpriced shares** A company which wishes to raise equity finance over the medium term, but judges that the stock market is temporarily underpricing its shares, may turn to convertible bonds. If the firm does perform as the managers expect and the share price rises, the convertible will be exchanged for equity.

- **Cheap way to issue shares** Graham and Harvey (2001) found that managers favoured convertibles as an inexpensive way to issue 'delayed' equity. Equity is raised at a later date without the high costs of rights issues, etc.

- **Available finance when straight debt and equity are not available** Some firms locked out of the equity markets (e.g. because of poor recent performance) and the straight debt markets because of high levels of indebtedness may still be able to raise money in the convertible market. Firms use convertible debt 'to attract investors unsure about the riskiness of the company' (Graham and Harvey (2001)).

Advantages to the investor

The advantages of convertible bonds to the investor are as follows.

- They are able to wait and see how the share price moves before investing in equity.

- In the near term there is greater security for their principal compared with equity investment, and the annual coupon is usually higher than the dividend yield (annual dividend on shares divided by share price).

Exchangeable bonds

The bonds sold may not give the right to conversion into shares of the issuers, but shares of another company held by the issuer. Note that the term exchangeable bond is probably more appropriate in these cases.

Valuing bonds

Bonds, particularly those traded in secondary markets such as the London Stock Exchange, are priced according to supply and demand. The main influences on the price of a bond will be the general level of interest rates for securities of that risk level and maturity. If the coupon is less than the current interest rate the bond will trade at less than the par value of £100. Take the case of an irredeemable bond (where coupons are paid every year forever) with an annual coupon of 8 percent of the par value, i.e. £8 per year. When the bond was first issued general interest rates for this risk class may well have been 8 percent and so the bond may have been sold at £100. However interest rates change over time. Suppose that the rate demanded by investors is now 10 percent. Investors will no longer be willing to pay £100 for an instrument that yields £8 per year. The current market value of the bond will fall to

£80 (£8/0.10) because this is the maximum amount needed to pay for similar bonds given the current interest rate of 10 percent. If the coupon is more than the current market interest rate the market price of the bond will be greater than the nominal (par) value. Thus if markets rates are 6 percent the irredeemable bond will be priced at £133.33 (£8/0.06).

Notice the inverse relationship between the price of a bond and the rate of return offered on it.

The formula relating the price of an irredeemable bond, the coupon and the market rate of interest is:

$$P_D = \frac{i}{k_D}$$

where

P_D = price of bond

i = nominal annual interest (the coupon rate × nominal (par) value of the bond)

k_D = market discount rate, annual return required on similar bonds

Also:

$$V_D = \frac{I}{k_D}$$

where

V_D = total market value of all the bonds

I = total annual nominal interest payable on all the bonds

We may wish to establish the market rate of interest represented by the market price of the bond. For example, if an irredeemable bond offers an annual coupon of 9.5 percent and is currently trading at £87.50, with the next coupon due in one year, the rate of return is:

$$k_D = \frac{i}{P_D} = \frac{9.5}{87.5} = 0.1086 \text{ or } 10.86\%$$

Redeemable bonds

A purchaser of a redeemable bond buys two types of income promise; first the coupon, second the redemption payment. The amount that an investor will pay depends on the amount these income flows are worth when discounted at the rate of return required on that risk class of debt. The relationships are expressed in the following formulae:

$$P_D = \frac{i_1}{1 + k_D} + \frac{i_2}{(1 + k_D)^2} + \frac{i_3}{(1 + k_D)^3} + \dots \frac{R_n}{(1 + k_D)^n}$$

and:

$$V_D = \frac{I_1}{1 + k_D} + \frac{I_2}{(1 + k_D)^2} + \frac{I_3}{(1 + k_D)^3} + \dots + \frac{R^*_n}{(1 + k_D)^n}$$

where

i_1, i_2 and i_3 = nominal interest per bond in years 1, 2 and 3...up to n years

I_1, I_2 and I_3 = total nominal interest in years 1, 2 and 3...up to n years

R_n and R^*_n = redemption value of a bond, and total redemption of all bonds in year n, at the redemption date, year n.

The Worked example of Blackaby illustrates the valuation of a bond when the market interest rate is given.

Worked example 16.1
BLACKABY PLC

Blackaby plc issued a bond with a par value of £100 in September 2009, redeemable in September 2015 at par. The coupon is 8% payable annually in September. The facts available from this are:

- the bond might have a par value of £100 but this may not be what investors will pay for it;
- the annual cash payment will be £8 (8% of par);
- in September 2015, £100 will be handed over to the bondholder.

Question 1

What is the price investors will pay for this bond at the time of issue if the market rate of interest for a security in this risk class is 7%?

Answer

$$P_D = \frac{8}{1 + 0.07} + \frac{8}{(1 + 0.07)^2} + \frac{8}{(1 + 0.07)^3} + \dots \frac{8}{(1 + 0.07)^6} + \frac{100}{(1 + 0.07)^6}$$

£8 annuity for 6 years @ 7% = 4.7665 × £8   =   38.132

plus $\dfrac{100}{(1 + 0.07)^6}$ =   66.634

$$P_D =$$ £104.766

Question 2

What is the bond's value in the secondary market in September 2012 if interest rates rise by 200 basis points between 2009 and 2012? (Assume the next coupon payment is in one year.)

Answer

P_D = £8 annuity for 3 years @ 9% = 2.5313 × 8		=	20.25
plus $\dfrac{100}{(1 + 0.09)^3}$		=	77.22
			£97.47

Again, note that as interest rates rise the price of bonds falls.

If we need to calculate the rate of return demanded by investors from a particular bond when we know the market price and the coupon amounts we compute the internal rate of return. For example Bluebird plc issued a bond many years ago which is due for redemption at par of £100 in three years. The coupon is 6 percent and the market price is £91. The rate of return now offered in the market by this bond is found by solving for k_D:

$$P_D = \frac{i_1}{1 + k_D} + \frac{i_2}{(1 + k_D)^2} + \frac{R_n + i_3}{(1 + k_D)^3}$$

$$91 = \frac{6}{1 + k_D} + \frac{6}{(1 + k_D)^2} + \frac{106}{(1 + k_D)^3}$$

The skills learned in calculating internal rates of return in Chapter 2 are needed to solve this. At an interest rate (k_D) of 9 percent, the right side of the equation amounts to £92.41. At an interest rate of 10 percent the right-hand side of the equation amounts to £90.05. Using linear interpolation:

Interest rate	9%	?	10%
Value of discounted cash flows	£92.41	£91	£90.05

$$k_D = 9\% + \frac{92.41 - 91}{92.41 - 90.05} \times (10 - 9) = 9.6\%$$

This is the yield-to-maturity (YTM) discussed in the next section.

The two types of interest yield

There are two types of yields used for fixed-interest securities. The *income yield* (also known as the flat yield, interest yield and running yield) is the gross (before tax) interest amount divided by the current market price of the bond expressed as a percentage:

$$\frac{\text{Gross interest (coupon)}}{\text{Market price}} \times 100$$

Thus for a holder of Bluebird's bonds the income yield is:

$$\frac{£6}{£91} \times 100 = 6.59\%$$

This is a gross yield. The after-tax yield will be influenced by the investor's tax position.

$$\text{Net interest yield} = \text{Gross yield } (1 - T),$$

where T = the tax rate applicable to the bondholder.

The income yield is not the true rate of return available to the investor should he/she purchase the bond because it fails to take into account the capital gain (or loss) from holding the bond. At a time when bonds in the same risk class are offering rates of return greater than 6.59 percent it is obvious that any potential purchaser of Bluebird bonds in the market will be looking for a return other than from the coupon. That additional return comes in the form of a capital gain over three years of £9. The investor purchases at £91 and will receive the £100 par value when the bond is redeemed in three years. A rough estimate of this annual gain is $(9/91) \div 3 = 3.3$ percent per year.

When this is added to the income yield we have an approximation to the second type of yield, the yield to maturity (also called the redemption yield). The yield to maturity of a bond is the discount rate such that the present value of all the cash inflows from the bond (interest plus principal) is equal to the bond's current market price. The rough estimate of 9.89 percent (6.59% + 3.3%) has not taken into account the precise timing of the investor's income flows. When this is adjusted for, the yield to maturity is 9.6 percent – the internal rate of return calculated above. Thus the yield to maturity includes both coupon payments and the capital gain or loss on maturity. The *Financial Times* quotes 'bid yields' for the bonds it displays – *see* Table 16.2 on page 457 and Exhibit 16.5 on page 479 and Exhibit 16.4 on page 478. These can be read as the yields to maturity.

The *Investors Chronicle*, in collaboration with Fixed Income Investor, publishes a corporate bond index and shows bond yields (www.investorschronicle.co.uk/bonds). See also www.ft.com/bonds&rates and www.BondMarketPrices.com.

International sources of debt finance

Larger and more creditworthy companies have access to a wider array of finance than small firms. These companies can tap the *Euro-securities markets*, which are informal (unregulated) markets in money held outside its country of origin. For example there is a large market in *Eurodollars*. These are dollar credits (loans) and deposits managed by a bank not

> Euro-securities markets are informal (unregulated) markets in money held outside its country of origin.

resident in the USA. This has the distinct advantage of transactions not being subject to supervision and regulation by the authorities in the USA. So, for example, an Italian firm can borrow dollars from a Spanish bank in the UK and the US regulatory authorities have no control over the transaction.

There is a vast quantity of dollars held outside the USA and this money is put to use by borrowers. The same applies to all the major currencies – the money is lent and borrowed outside its home base, so is beyond the reach of the domestic regulators. Today it is not unusual to find an individual holding a dollar account at a UK bank – a *Eurodeposit* account – which pays interest in dollars linked to general dollar rates. This money can be lent to firms wishing to borrow in Eurodollars prepared to pay interest and capital repayments in dollars. There are large markets in Euro Swiss Francs, Eurosterling and Euroyen.[6] The title 'Euro' is misleading as this market is not limited to the European currencies or European banks and is unconnected with the European single currency, the euro. The title came about because the modern market was established when the Soviet Union transferred dollars from New York to a French bank at the height of the cold war in 1957. The cable address happened to be EUROBANK. The euro currency was not even a gleam in the eye of a euro-enthusiast at the time. Nowadays, Eurosecurities business is transacted daily in all of the major financial centres.

To add a little precision: 'Eurocurrency' is short-term (less than one year) deposits and loans outside the jurisdiction of the country in whose currency the deposit/loan is denominated; 'Eurocredit' is used for the market in medium- and long-term loans in the Euromarkets.

The companies large enough to use the Eurosecurities markets are able to put themselves at a competitive advantage *vis-à-vis* smaller firms. There are at least four advantages:

■ The finance available in these markets can be at a lower cost in both transaction costs and rates of return.

■ There are fewer rules and regulations, such as needing to obtain official authorisation to issue or needing to queue to issue, leading to speed, innovation and lower costs.

■ There may be an ability to hedge foreign currency movements. For example, if a firm has assets denominated in a foreign currency it can be advantageous to also have liabilities in that same currency to reduce the adverse impact of exchange-rate movements (*see* Chapter 21).

■ National markets are often not able to provide the same volume of finance. The borrowing needs of some firms are simply too large for their domestic markets to supply. To avoid being hampered in expansion plans large firms can turn to the international market in finance.

For these internationally recognised firms there are three sources of debt finance:

- the domestic or national market;

- the financial markets of other countries which make themselves open to foreign firms – *the foreign debt market*;

- the Eurosecurities market which is not based in any one country, so is not regulated by any country.

For example, there are three bond markets available to some firms – as shown in Figure 16.4.

FIGURE 16.4
Bond markets

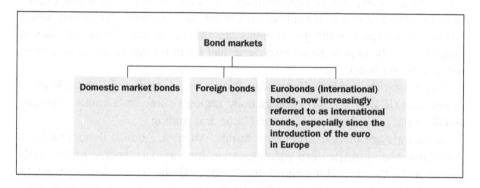

Foreign bonds

A foreign bond is a bond denominated in the currency of the country where it is issued when the issuer is a non-resident. For example, in Japan bonds issued by non-Japanese companies denominated in yen are foreign bonds. (The interest and capital payments will be in yen.) Foreign bonds have been given some interesting names: foreign bonds in Tokyo are known as Samurai bonds, foreign bonds issued in New York and London are called Yankees and Bulldogs respectively. The Netherlands allows foreigners to issue Rembrandt bonds and in Spain Matador bonds are traded. Foreign bonds are regulated by the authorities where the bond is issued. These rules can be demanding and an encumbrance to companies needing to act quickly and at low cost. The regulatory authorities have also been criticised for stifling innovation in the financial markets. The growth of the less restricted Eurobond market has put the once dominant foreign bond market in the shade.

Eurobonds (International bonds)

Eurobonds are bonds sold outside the jurisdiction of the country of the currency in which the bond is denominated. So, for example, the UK financial regulators have little influence over the Eurobonds denominated in sterling, even though the trans-

> Eurobonds are not subject to the rules and regulations which are imposed on foreign bonds.

actions (for example interest and capital payments) are in pounds. They are medium- to long-term instruments with standard maturities of three, five, seven and ten years but there are longer maturities of 15 to 30 years driven by pension fund and insurance company demand for long dated assets. Eurobonds are not subject to the rules and regulations which are imposed on foreign bonds, such as the requirement to issue a detailed prospectus.[7] More importantly they are not subject to an interest-withholding tax. In the UK most domestic bonds are subject to a withholding tax by which basic rate income tax is deducted before the investor receives interest. Interest on Eurobonds is paid gross without any tax deducted – which has attractions to investors keen on delaying, avoiding or evading tax. Moreover, Eurobonds are bearer bonds which means that the holders do not have to disclose their identity – all that is required to receive interest and capital is for the holder to have possession of the bond. In contrast, UK domestic bonds are registered, which means that companies and governments are able to identify the owners. Bearer bonds have to be kept in a safe place as a thief could benefit greatly from possession of a bearer bond.

Despite the absence of official regulation, the International Capital Markets Association (ICMA), a self-regulatory body, imposes some restrictions, rules and standardized procedures on Eurobond issue and trading.

Eurobonds are distinct from euro bonds, which are bonds denominated in euros and issued in the euro currency area. Increasingly, people differentiate between the two by calling Eurobonds 'international bonds' leaving the title euro for the currency introduced in 1999. Of course, there have been euro-denominated bonds issued outside the jurisdiction of the authorities in the euro area. These are euro Eurobonds.

The development of the Eurobond market

In the 1960s many countries, companies and individuals held surplus dollars outside of the USA. They were reluctant to hold these funds in American banks under US jurisdiction. There were various reasons for this. For example, some countries, particularly the former Soviet Union and other communist bloc countries of the cold war era, thought their interests were best served by using the dollars they had on the international markets, away from the powers of the US authorities to freeze or sequestrate (seize) assets. More recently this sort of logic has applied to countries such as Iran. Also in the 1960s the American authorities had some very off-putting tax laws and created a tough regulatory environment in their domestic financial markets. These encouraged investors and borrowers alike to undertake transactions in dollars outside the USA. London's strength as a financial centre, the UK authorities' more relaxed attitude to business, and its position in the global time zones, made it a natural leader in the Euro markets. The first Eurobond was issued in the early 1960s and the market grew modestly through the 1970s and then at a rapid rate in the 1980s. By then the Eurodollar bonds had been joined by bonds denominated in a wide variety of Eurocurrencies. The market was stimulated not only by the tax and anonymity benefits, which brought a lower cost of finance than for the domestic bonds, but also by the increasing demand from transnational companies and governments needing large sums in alternative currencies and with the potential for innovatory characteristics. It was further boosted by the recycling of dollars from the oil-exporting countries.

In 1979 less than $20bn worth of bonds were issued in a variety of currencies. Nowadays the rate of new issuance is over $2,000bn a year, with a total amount outstanding of over $26,000bn. In any one year approximately 40–50 percent of new bonds are denominated in dollars. Euro-denominated issues account for 40–50 percent of issues. The yen is the currency of issue for 5–10 percent of international bonds, with all the other currencies put together making up 10–15 percent. Even though the majority of Eurobond trading takes place through London, sterling is not one of the main currencies, and what is more, it tends to be large US and other foreign banks located in London which dominate the market.

> **Sterling is not one of the main currencies.**

Types of Eurobond

The Eurobond market has been extraordinarily innovative in producing bonds with all sorts of coupon payment and capital repayment arrangements (for example, the currency of the coupon changes half-way through the life of the bond, or the interest rate switches from fixed to floating rate at some point). We cannot go into detail here on the rich variety but merely categorise the bonds into broad types.

- **Straight fixed-rate bond** The coupon remains the same over the life of the bond. These are usually made annually, in contrast to domestic bond semi-annual coupons. The redemption of these bonds is usually made with a 'bullet' repayment at the end of the bond's life.

- **Equity related** These take two forms:
  - **Bonds with warrants attached** Warrants are options which give the holder the right to buy some other asset at a given price in the future. An equity warrant, for example, would give the right, but not the obligation, to purchase shares. There are also warrants for commodities such as gold or oil, and for the right to buy additional bonds from the same issuer at the same price and yield as the host bond. Warrants are detachable from the host bond and are securities in their own right, unlike convertibles.
  - **Convertibles** The bondholder has the right (but not the obligation) to convert the bond into ordinary shares at a preset price.

■ **Floating-rate notes (FRNs)** These have a variable coupon reset on a regular basis, usually every three or six months, in relation to a reference rate, such as LIBOR. The size of the spread over LIBOR reflects the perceived risk of the issuer. The typical term for an FRN is about five to 12 years.

Within these broad categories all kinds of 'bells and whistles' (features) can be attached to the bonds, for example *reverse floaters* – the coupon declines as LIBOR rises; *capped bonds* – the interest rate cannot rise above a certain level; *zero coupon* – a capital gain only is offered to the lender. Many bonds have 'callback features' under which the issuer may buy the bond back after a period of time has elapsed, say five years, at a price specified when the bond was issued. A 'put' feature gives the bondholder the right, but not the obligation, to sell the bond back to the issuer (usually at par value) on designated dates.

The majority of Eurobonds (more than 80 percent) are rated AAA or AA and denominations are usually $1,000, $5,000 or $50,000 (or similar large sums in the currency of issue).

Corporations account for a relatively small proportion of the international bond market. The biggest issuers are the banks. Issues by governments ('sovereign issues') and state agencies in the public sector account for about one-tenth of issues. Also represented are governments and international agencies such as the World Bank, the International Bank for Reconstruction and Development and the European Investment Bank.

> Corporations account for a relatively small proportion of the international bond market. The biggest issuers are the banks.

Issuing Eurobonds

With Eurobonds a bank (lead manager or book runner) or group of banks acting for the issuer invite a large number of other banks or other investors to buy some of the bonds. (Alternatively, in a 'bought deal' the lead manager agrees to buy the entire issue at a specific price and yield. He or she then tries to sell it on in the market.) The managing group of banks is usually responsible for underwriting the issue (guaranteeing to buy if no one else does) and it may enlist a number of smaller institutions to use their extensive contacts to sell the bonds – 'the selling group'.

Eurobonds are traded on the secondary market through intermediaries acting as market makers who quote prices at which they are ready to buy or sell. Most Eurobonds are listed on the London, Dublin or Luxembourg stock exchanges, but the market is primarily an over-the-counter one, that is, most transactions take place outside a recognised exchange. Deals are usually conducted using the telephone, computers, telex and fax, but there are a number of electronic platforms for trading Eurobonds. It is not possible to go to a central source for price information. Most issues hardly ever trade, and those that do take place in private between the customer and the bond dealer – there is no obligation to inform the public about the deal. Figure 16.5 presents the advantages and disadvantages of Eurobonds.

The Saturday edition of the *Financial Times* shows a selection of the most liquid sterling denominated bonds – *see* Exhibit 16.4. About one-half are from governments or quasi-governments, the rest from UK corporations.

The *Financial Times* also publishes a table (Monday–Friday) showing a selection of secondary-market bid prices of actively traded international bonds. This gives the reader some idea of current market conditions and rates of return demanded for bonds of different maturities, currencies and riskiness – *see* Exhibit 16.5.

Each weekday the *Financial Times* also shows a selection of bonds in the high-yield and emerging markets categories – *see* Exhibit 16.6.

FIGURE 16.5

Advantages and drawbacks of Eurobonds as a source of finance for corporations

Advantage	Drawback
1 Large loans for long periods are available.	1 Only for the largest companies – minimum realistic issue size is about £50m.
2 Often cheaper than domestic bonds. The finance provider receives the interest without tax deduction and retains anonymity and therefore supplies cheaper finance.	2 Bearer securities are attractive to thieves and therefore safe storage is needed.
3 Ability to hedge interest rate and exchange-rate risk.	3 Because interest and capital are paid in a foreign currency there is a risk that exchange-rate movements mean more of the home currency is required to buy the foreign currency than was anticipated.
4 The bonds are usually unsecured. The limitations placed on management are less than those for a secure bond.	4 The secondary market can be illiquid.
5 The lower level of regulation allows greater innovation and tailor-made financial instruments.	

STERLING BOND PRICES

Bond price with par value set at 100

Issue	Thur price	Week chge	GRY	Inc yld	Moody rtg	S&P rtg	Issue size	Sprd to gilts
Barclays 6.875 Perpetual	102.2	0.45	6.32	6.73			650	–
EIB 5 1/2 7/12/09	99.7	–0.1	13.26	5.52			3900	–
WORLD BANK 5 3/4 7/12/09	100.2	–0.1	0.2	5.74			400	–
SCOT PWR 6 5/8 10	102.15	–0.08	–8.21	6.49			200	–
TESCO 6 5/8 10	104.4	1.05	1.56	6.35			150	–
Next 5.25 30 Sep 2013	101.3	0.23	4.81	5.18			300	–
Ibrd 5.375 15 Jan 2014	109.85	0.4	2.8	4.89			250	–
M & S 5.625 24 Mar 2014 MTN	102.93	0.92	4.79	5.47			400	–
EIB 6 1/4 15/4/14	113.43	0.5	2.92	5.51			2550	–
SAFEWAY 6 1/2 14	110.48	0.43	3.96	5.88			150	–
Kfw EXCH 5.5 07 Dec 2015 MTN	111.45	0.52	3.34	4.93			2050	–
BgTransco 6.0 07 Jun 2017	109.7	0.73	4.4	5.47			300	–
EIB 8 3/4 25/8/17	132.48	0.67	3.79	6.61			1000	–
HALIFAX 9 3/8 15/5/21	101.4	–3.4	8.96	9.25			500	–
EIB 5 3/8 7/6/21	110.53	1.05	4.16	4.86			1875	–
Ge 5.5 07 Jun 2021 MTN	98.25	1.8	5.63	5.6			360	–
Sevtre 6.125 26 Feb 2024	106.48	1.35	5.38	5.75			300	–
ITALY 6 4/8/28	111.83	1.33	4.95	5.37			1500	–
EIB 6 7/12/28	120.03	0.93	4.37	5			3700	–
Edf 5.875 18 Jul 2031	108.85	0.85	5.12	5.4			650	–

Gross (before deduction of tax) redemption yield, 'yield to maturity'

Income yield

Par value in millions

Change in price over the past week

Bonds shown are selection of those available on the Bondscape service. GRY = Gross Redemption Yield.
Source: Bondscape. Data compiled on: **November 19th 2009**

EXHIBIT 16.4

Source: *Financial Times* 21/22 November 2009.

Issuer: Next, coupon: 5.25 percent, redemption date: 30 September 2013

Medium-term notes (MTNs)

By issuing a note a company promises to pay the holders a certain sum on the maturity date, and in many cases a coupon interest in the meantime. The name 'note' is misleading because they are usually bonds like the others we have discussed in this chapter (domestic bonds or Eurobonds) rather than short-term notes of under one year maturity. These instruments are typically unsecured and may carry floating or fixed interest rates. Medium-term notes (MTN) have been sold with a maturity of as little as nine months and as great as 30 years, so the word 'medium' is a little deceiving. They can be denominated in the domestic currency of the borrower (MTN) or in a foreign currency (Euro MTN). MTNs normally pay an interest rate above LIBOR, usually varying between 0.2 and 3 percent over LIBOR.

BONDS – GLOBAL INVESTMENT GRADE

Standard and Poor's
Moody's
Fitch

Dec 1	Red date	Coupon	Ratings S*	M*	F*	Bid price	Bid yield	Day's chge yield	Mth's chge yield	Spread vs Govts
US$										
Citigroup	01/11	6.50	A	A3	A+	103.73	3.09	−0.08	0.23	2.87
Morgan Stanley	04/12	6.60	A	A2	A	109.08	2.56	−0.05	−1.17	1.89
Household Fin	05/12	7.00	A	A3	AA−	109.23	3.06	0.17	−0.32	2.39
HBOS Treas UK	06/12	5.50	A+	Aa3	AA−	104.45	3.62	0.14	−0.47	2.48
Verizon Global	09/12	7.38	A	A3	A	114.18	2.04	−0.08	−0.36	0.93
Abu Dhabi Nt En	10/12	5.62	NR	Aa2	−	102.50	4.68	−1.12	0.63	3.65
Bank of America	01/13	4.88	A	A2	A+	103.95	3.52	−0.04	−0.34	2.42
Goldman Sachs	07/13	4.75	A	A1	A+	105.27	3.19	−0.19	−0.57	2.09
Hutchison 03/33	01/14	6.25	A−	A3	A−	110.70	3.45	−0.02	−0.63	1.45
Misc Capital	07/14	6.13	A−	A3	−	107.72	4.25	0.02	−0.41	2.24
BNP Paribas	06/15	4.80	AA−	A2	AA−	103.57	4.08	−0.03	−0.29	2.07
GE Capital	01/16	5.00	AA+	Aa2	−	103.95	4.26	0.04	−0.53	1.55
Erste Euro Lux	02/16	5.00	AAA	−	−	60.82	14.47	−	−	11.33
Credit Suisse USA	03/16	5.38	A+	Aa1	AA−	106.67	4.15	0.03	−0.25	1.51
SPI E&G Aust	09/16	5.75	A−	A1	A−	104.99	4.88	−0.05	−0.21	2.19
Abu Dhabi Nt En	10/17	6.17	NR	Aa2	−	100.00	6.16	−0.49	0.16	3.24
Swire Pacific	04/18	6.25	A−	A3	A	106.68	5.25	−	0.15	2.45
ASNA	11/18	6.95	A	A3	A+	101.00	6.80	−	−	3.42
Codelco	01/19	7.50	A	A1	A	119.63	4.82	−	−0.06	1.46
AT & T Wireless	03/31	8.75	A	A2	A	131.67	6.08	−0.02	−0.04	1.88
GE Capital	03/32	6.75	AA+	Aa2	−	89.71	7.72	−	−	3.21
Goldman Sachs	02/33	6.13	A	A1	A+	102.00	5.96	0.01	−0.59	1.76
Euro										
GR Cap Euro Fdg	05/11	4.00	AA+	Aa2	−	102.56	2.16	0.06	0.05	1.19
HSBC Fin	06/12	3.38	A	A3	AA−	101.60	2.70	0.00	0.09	1.39
Xstrata Fin CA	06/12	4.88	BBB	Baa2	−	103.87	3.25	0.04	−0.56	1.65
CCCI	10/12	6.13	A	A1	A+	105.90	3.90	−0.03	−0.16	2.58
Amer Honda Fin	07/13	6.25	A+	A1	−	110.82	3.04	0.08	−0.29	1.06
SNS Bank	02/14	4.63	A	A2	A	102.12	4.06	−0.02	−1.57	2.10
JP Morgan Chase	01/15	5.25	A+	Aa3	AA−	108.35	3.44	−0.07	−0.19	1.12
Hutchison Fin 06	09/16	4.63	A−	A3	A−	100.22	4.58	−0.11	−0.17	1.86
Hypo Alpe Bk	10/16	4.25	−	Aa2	−	82.32	7.64	−0.02	−0.17	4.98
GE Cap Euro Fdg	01/18	5.38	AA+	Aa2	−	104.69	4.67	0.11	−0.08	1.75
Unicredit	01/20	4.38	A	Aa3	A	101.96	4.13	0.00	−0.20	1.94
ENEL	05/24	5.25	A−	A2	A	107.07	4.57	−0.17	−0.29	2.51
Yen										
ORIX 106	03/11	1.46	A−	−	−	97.96	3.11	−0.05	−0.34	2.96
Amer Int	04/12	1.40	A−	A3	BBB	81.88	10.34	0.01	−1.08	10.97
Citi Group 15	09/12	1.11	A	A3	A+	93.50	3.69	−0.01	−0.28	3.44
ACOM 51	06/13	2.07	BBB	A3	A−	88.48	6.06	−0.03	−2.08	5.81
Deutche Bahn Fin	12/14	1.65	AA	Aa1	AA	100.06	1.64	−	−0.09	1.04
Nomura Sec S 3	03/18	2.28	−	−	−	92.52	3.44	−0.06	−0.26	2.49
£ Sterling										
Morgan stanley	04/11	7.50	A	A2	A	105.42	3.29	0.00	−0.26	2.64
HSBC Fin	03/12	7.00	A	A3	AA−	107.09	3.69	−0.11	−0.33	2.35
Slough Estates	09/15	6.25	−	−	A−	101.26	5.90	−0.05	−0.45	3.08
ASIF III	12/18	5.00	A+	A1	A−	75.00	8.99	0.00	0.15	5.44

US $ denominated bonds NY close; all other London close. S* – Standard & Poor's, M* – Moody's.
F* – Fitch
Source: ThomsonReuters

Redemption date: date when the bond will be redeemed (par value paid to lenders)

Price that a bond dealer has/will pay to buy bond

Gross yield to maturity

The spread between the gross yield to maturity paid on this bond (given its current price) and the yield on a government bond with the same length of time to maturity and in the same currency. In this case on additional 2.51% per year.

EXHIBIT 16.5

Source: *Financial Times* 2 December 2009.

BONDS – HIGH YIELD & EMERGING MARKET

Dec 1	Red date	Coupon	S*	Ratings M*	F*	Bid price	Bid yield	Day's chge yield	Mth's chge yield	Spread vs US
High Yield US$										
HSBK Europe	05/13	7.75	B+	Ba2	B+	95.50	9.31	–0.36	–0.68	6.74
Kazkommerts Int	04/14	7.88	B	Ba3	B–	82.75	13.21	–1.71	0.25	11.15
Bertin	10/16	10.25	B–	B1	–	102.00	9.84	–	–0.72	7.16
High Yield Euro										
Royal Carib Crs	01/14	5.63	BB–	Ba3	–	85.50	10.06	0.01	–0.25	8.00
Kazkommerts Int	02/17	6.88	B	Ba3	B–	74.75	12.36	–0.20	–0.15	9.60
Emerging US$										
Bulgaria	01/15	8.25	BBB	Baa3	BBB–	115.25	4.85	0.05	–0.02	2.82
Peru	02/15	9.88	BBB–	Ba1	BBB–	128.25	3.80	–0.33	–0.68	1.77
Brazil	03/15	7.88	BBB–	Baa3	BBB–	118.94	3.86	–0.09	–0.50	1.83
Mexico	09/16	11.38	BBB+	Baa1	BBB	140.00	4.47	–0.29	–0.62	1.73
Argentina	01/17	11.38	DEF	Ca	D	39.85	34.42	0.01	–37.81	31.74
Philippines	01/19	9.88	BB–	Ba3	BB	128.50	5.80	0.05	0.11	2.53
Brazil	01/20	12.75	BBB–	Baa3	BBB–	160.75	5.02	–0.07	–0.39	1.74
Colombia	02/20	11.75	BBB–	Ba1	BB+	145.31	5.81	0.14	–0.40	2.54
Russia	03/20	7.50	BBB	Baa1	BBB	113.19	5.35	–0.09	–0.38	2.62
Mexico	08/31	8.30	BBB+	Baa1	BBB	130.44	5.81	–0.06	–0.21	1.54
Indonesia	02/37	6.63	BB–	Ba2	BB	96.75	6.89	–0.15	–0.06	2.62
Emerging Euro										
Brazil	02/15	7.38	BBB–	Baa3	BBB–	116.00	3.89	–0.05	–0.24	1.66
Poland	02/16	3.63	A–	A2	A–	97.94	4.01	–0.01	–0.04	1.46
Turkey	03/16	5.00	BB–	Ba3	BB–	102.65	4.50	–0.12	–0.08	1.96
Mexico	02/20	5.50	BBB+	Baa1	BBB	103.25	5.08	–	–0.23	1.93

US $ denominated bonds NY close; all other London close. S* – Standard & Poor's, M* – Moody's.
F* – Fitch

Source: ThomsonReuters

EXHIBIT 16.6

Source: *Financial Times* 2 December 2009.

An MTN programme stretching over many years can be set up with one set of legal documents. Then, numerous notes can be issued under the programme in future years. A programme allows greater certainty that the firm will be able to issue an MTN when it needs the finance and allows issuers to by-pass the costly and time-consuming documentation associated with each stand-alone note (bond). The programme can allow for bonds of various qualities, maturities, currencies or type of interest (fixed or floating). Over the years the market can be tapped at short notice in the most suitable form at that time, e.g. US$ rather than £, or redemption in three years rather than two. It is possible to sell in small denominations, e.g. $5m, and on a continuous basis, regularly dripping bonds into the market. The bankers organizing the MTN programme charge a 'commitment fee' (around 10 to 15 basis points) for keeping open the option to borrow under an MTN programme, even if the company chooses not to do so in the end. Management fees will also be payable to the syndication of banks organizing the MTN facility. The costs of setting up an MTN programme are high compared with the costs of a single bond issue (and more expensive than bank debt except for the very best AAA, AA, and some A-rated companies). Many companies set one up because they believe that the initial expense is outweighed by the flexibility and cost savings that a programme provides over time.

The success of an MTN programme depends on the efficiency of the lead manager and the flexibility of the issuer to match market appetite for lending in particular currencies or maturities with the issuer's demands for funds at each point over, say, the five-year life of the MTN programme. The annual cost of running an MTN programme, excluding credit rating agency fees, can be around £100,000. GlaxoSmithKline's current outstanding MTNs are shown at the start of the chapter.

Commercial paper

The issue and purchase of commercial paper is one means by which the largest commercial organisations can avoid paying the bank intermediary a middleman fee for linking borrower and lender. Commercial paper promises to the holder a sum of money to be paid in a few days. The lender buys these short-term IOUs, with an average life of about 40 days (normal range 30–90 days, but can be up to 270 days), and effectively lends money to the issuer. Normally these instruments are issued at a discount rather than the borrower being required to pay interest – thus the face value (amount paid on redemption) will be higher than the amount paid for the paper at issuance. Large corporations with temporary surpluses of cash are able to put that money to use by lending it directly to other commercial firms at a higher rate of effective interest than they might have received by depositing the funds in a bank.

This source of finance is usually only available to the most respected corporations with the highest credit ratings, as it is usually unsecured lending (no collateral), but there are occasional issues that offer security of a specific asset or a guarantee from a bank. Standard & Poor's and Moody's use a different grading system for short-term instruments (e.g. 'A–1' or 'Prime-1' are the highest ratings). The main buyers, such as money market mutual funds, are often restricted to having the bulk of their portfolios in the form of 'top' rated issues. Lower-rated issues do exist, but the demand is very limited.

While any one issue of commercial paper is short term it is possible to use this market as a medium-term source of finance by 'rolling over' issues. That is, as one issue matures another one is launched. A commercial paper programme (a revolving underwriting facility) can be set up by a bank whereby the bank (or a syndicate of banks) underwrites a specified sum for a period of five to seven years. The borrower then draws on this every few weeks or months by the issue of commercial paper to other lenders. If there are no bids for the paper the underwriting bank(s) buys the paper at a specified price. Eurocommercial paper is issued and placed outside the jurisdiction of the country in whose currency it is denominated.

Companies need to be wary of being too reliant on commercial paper. A number have found their credit ratings lowered unexpectedly, making it impossible to obtain roll-over finance from the CP market, resulting in severe disruption to plans, and even to liquidation.

Project finance

A typical project finance deal is created by an industrial corporation providing some equity capital for a separate legal entity to be formed to build and operate a project, for example an oil pipeline, or an electricity power plant. The project finance loan is then provided as bank loans or through bond issues direct to the separate entity. The significant feature is that the loan returns are tied to the cash flows and fortunes of a particular project rather than being secured against the parent firm's assets. For most ordinary loans the bank looks at the credit standing of the borrower when deciding terms and conditions. For project finance, while the parent company's (or companies') credit standing is a factor, the main focus is on the financial prospects of the project itself.

> For project finance the main focus is on the financial prospects of the project itself.

To make use of project finance the project needs to be easily identifiable and separable from the rest of the company's activities so that its cash flows and assets can offer the lenders some separate security. Project finance has been used across the globe to finance power plants, roads, ports, sewage facilities and telecommunications networks. A few recent examples are given in Exhibit 16.7.

Project finance has grown rapidly over the last 25 years. Globally, about £50bn is lent in this form per year. A major stimulus has been the development of oil prospects. For the UK, the North Sea provided a number of project finance opportunities. Many of the small companies which developed fields and pipelines would not have been able to participate on the strength of their existing cash flow and balance sheet, but they were able to obtain project finance secured on the oil or fees they would later generate.

There is a spectrum of risk sharing in project finance deals. At one extreme there are projects where the parent firm (or firms) accept the responsibility of guaranteeing that the lenders will be paid in the event of the project producing insufficient cash flows. This is referred to as *recourse finance* because the lenders are able to seek the 'help' of the parent. At the other extreme, the lenders accept an agreement whereby, if the project is a failure, they will lose money and have no right of recourse to the parent company. If the project's cash flows are insufficient the lenders only have a claim on the assets of the project itself rather than on the sponsors or developers.

Between these two extremes there might be deals whereby the borrower takes the risk until the completion of the construction phase (for example, provides a completion guarantee) and the lender takes on the risk once the project

Project finance has funded ...

A liquefied natural gas project in Qatar

The biggest project-financed facility ever begun is being built in Qatar. Qatargas, the state-controlled energy firm, joined with Exxon and raised $7.6bn from 57 investors in 2005 to build a gas freezing and storage plant. The gas will then be shipped to the UK in tankers. Not only does forming a separate project with a state-controlled company reduce political risk (*see* below) but also it can open doors to lenders in the country.

Developing an oil field

In 2006 Northern Petroleum agreed a €40m project financing facility with Standard Bank to develop a number of onshore oilfields in the Netherlands. Normally a project lender would insist on the sponsoring company or its contractors providing a guarantee that it will be paid back in the event of failure to complete the project construction. However, Standard Bank agreed that Northern Petroleum has the skills to project manage and to forgo the guarantee. In return the bank received options to buy 3 million shares in Northern Petroleum, thus taking some extra reward if the company (project) performs well. (An option gives the right to buy shares at a price already agreed – say, £3 when the current share price is £2. If the company does well the share might move to, say, £4, in which case the options become worth at least £1 each – Chapter 19 has more on options.)

A telephone infrastructure

In 2000 Hutchinson UK 3G raised £3bn by way of project finance to part-fund the building of the UK's fifth mobile network. This was three-year debt without recourse to shareholders.

EXHIBIT 16.7

is in the operational phase. Alternatively, the commercial firm may take some risks such as the risk of cost overruns and the lender takes others such as the risk of a government expropriating the project's assets.

The sums and size of projects are usually large and involve a high degree of complexity and this means high transaction and legal costs. Because of the additional risk to the lenders the interest rates charged tend to be higher than for conventional loans. Whereas a well-known highly creditworthy firm might pay 20 basis points (0.20 percent) over LIBOR for a 'normal' parent company loan, the project company might have to pay 100 basis points (1 percent) above LIBOR.

Advantages of project finance

Project finance has a number of advantages.

- **Transfer of risk** By making the project a stand-alone investment with its own financing, the parent(s) can gain if it is successful and is somewhat insulated if it is a failure, in that other assets and cash flows may be protected from the effects of project losses. This may lead to a greater willingness to engage in more risky activities which may benefit both the firm and society. If there are a number of sponsoring parent companies (because of the sheer size of the project or the need to tap into the resources of more than one firm), then there is the additional risk of incomplete management control for each parent if it is a joint venture. Due to this risk a project finance structure is preferred with a separate legal entity so that the borrowing risk is not borne directly by the parent. Of course, this benefit is of limited value if there are strong rights of recourse.

- **Off-balance-sheet financing** The finance is raised on the project's assets and cash flows and therefore is not always recorded as debt in the parent company's balance sheet. This sort of off-balance-sheet financing is seen as a useful 'wheeze' or ploy by some managers – for example, gearing limits can be bypassed. However, experienced lenders and shareholders are not so easily fooled by accounting tricks. This said, many lenders are willing to allow the project entity to be funded 60–90 percent by debt if the contractual and risk structure of the project company are favourable, e.g. sound government guarantee of annual income for 20 years from a bridge or electricity plant.

- **Political risk** If the project is in a country prone to political instability, with a tendency towards an anti-transnational business attitude and acts of appropriation, a more cautious way of proceeding may be to set up an arm's length (separate company) relationship with some risk being borne by the banking community, particularly banks in the host country. An example of this sort of risk is given in Exhibit 16.8.

- **Simplifies the banking relationship** In cases where there are a number of parent companies, it can be easier to arrange finance for a separate project entity than to have to deal with each of the parent companies separately.

- **Managerial incentives** Managers of projects may be given an equity stake in the project if it is set up as a separate enterprise. This can lead to high rewards for exceptional performance.

- **Avoiding borrowing restrictions** The parent firm's funding lines might be constrained or fully utilised for its general business activities.

Enron

In 1995 the state of Maharashtra in India suddenly revoked the contract it had with Enron for the construction of a power project, creating major problems for Enron and its bankers.

EXHIBIT 16.8 'Regulatory risk' exists in many parts of the world ...

Sale and leaseback

If a firm owns buildings, land or equipment it may be possible to sell these to another firm (for example a bank, insurance company or specialised leasing firm) and simultaneously agree to lease the property back for a stated period under specific terms. The seller receives cash immediately but is still able to use the asset. However the seller has created a regular cash flow liability for itself. For example in 2000 Abbey National, the mortgage bank, sold its branch network and its Baker Street head office (221b Baker Street – the home of Sherlock Holmes) totalling 6.5m sq.ft. The 722 branches and head office will be occupied by Abbey National under leases as short as one year, and as long as 20. The objective was to obtain flexibility in accommodation so that the bank can change with its customers and with the industry. It allowed the firm to 'concentrate on banking rather than being property developers, which is not our job'.[8]

> The seller receives cash immediately but is still able to use the asset.

In 2007 Tesco completed a sale and leaseback for £650m with British Land. The initial rent was £29m per year (a yield of 4.5 percent). The rents will rise by a rate linked to inflation, with a maximum of 3.5 percent per year. Most of the proceeds are to be used to pay for the opening of more Tesco stores. A number of other retailers have used their extensive property assets for sale and lease-back transactions so that they could plough the proceeds into further expansion.

In many countries the tax regime encourages sale and leaseback transactions. For example, some property owners are unable to use depreciation and other tax allowances (usually because they do not have sufficient taxable profits). The sale of the asset to an organization looking to reduce taxable profits through the holding of depreciable assets enables both firms to benefit. Furthermore, the original owner's subsequent lease payments are tax deductible.

A sale and leaseback has the drawback that the asset is no longer owned by the firm, so any capital appreciation has to be forgone. (However, clawback arrangements are possible, which allow the seller to receive a share of any increase in the value of the property, e.g. if say a factory site was granted planning permission for houses.) Also long lease arrangements of this kind usually provide for the rental payments to increase at regular intervals, such as every three or five years. There are other factors limiting the use of sale and leaseback as a financial tool. Leasing can involve complex documentation and large legal fees, which often make it uneconomic to arrange leases for less than £20m. There is also a degree of inflexibility: for example, unwinding the transaction if, say, the borrower wanted to move out of the property, can be expensive. Another disadvantage is that the property is no longer available to be offered as security for loans.

The case of Woolworths (Exhibit 16.9) highlights one of the perils of sale and leaseback.

Seeds of Woolworths' demise sown long ago

Elizabeth Rigby

At Woolworths' annual meeting this summer a perennially cheerful Trevor Bish-Jones cut a rather forlorn figure as he told his audience that making '£3bn of [group] sales for £30m of net profit is hard work this side of the fence'.

The imperturbable chief executive could be forgiven for feeling a little sorry for himself. Mr Bish-Jones had just been ousted from the variety retailer having laboured for six-and-a-half years to keep Woolworths afloat under the weight of rising rents, shabby stores and an outdated business model.

This week the fight to save the much-loved but very under-shopped Woolworths chain finally drew to a close as the 800 stores and the wholesale distribution arm were placed into administration. ...

But how did it come to pass that the near 100-year-old chain, which in its heyday was opening a store a week and was still selling £1.7bn of goods a year through its stores at the time of its collapse, should end up in such a dire predicament?

Those close to Woolworths place this week's collapse firmly at the feet of those who demerged the retailer from Kingfisher in August 2001.

They argue that the decision to carry out a sale-and-leaseback deal for 182 Woolworths' stores in return for £641m of cash – paid back to Kingfisher share-holders – crippled the chain.

For in return for the princely price tag, Woolworths was saddled with oner-ous leases that guaranteed the landlords a rising income stream.

One person who knows Woolworths well says the rent bill rose from £70m a decade ago to £160m today.

'There is no doubt that back in 2001, with the demerger and the sale of these stores, the company was saddled with a huge amount of quasi debt in terms of these leases,' says one former adviser.

'I think probably that is really where this goes back to. If Woolworths had more financial flexibility they might have been able to do more of the stuff they needed to.

'To build a sustainable business requires investment but they were not in a position to incur more costs', the former adviser adds.

Tony Shiret, analyst at Credit Suisse, says Woolworths' lease-adjusted debt was the highest in the retail sector. 'They didn't really have enough cash flow to cover debt repayments.' ...

'It was already not a very strong format and it was suddenly coming under more competitive pressure and it didn't have the safety value of being backed by property,' says Mr Shiret. ...

'Given its onerous lease contracts and general cost inflation of 2–3 per cent, Woolworths needs to deliver at least 2 per cent underlying sales growth [a level not achieved in seven years] in order to avoid further margin dilution. To date, the management has not com-municated a convincing strategy that will result in a top-line turnaround.'

This week, Woolworths' fans were blaming its bankers for the variety chain store's demise. But while the credit crunch has proved the final catalyst, the seeds of Woolworths' failure were sown many years before.

EXHIBIT 16.9

Source: *Financial Times* 29 November 2008, p. 18.

On the other hand, one advantage of sale and leaseback is said to be that it makes managers more aware of the cost of holding property and can said to be lead to greater efficiency. This is because the managers are made to pay out rent on a regular basis for using the property.

Securitisation

In the strange world of modern finance you sometimes need to ask yourself who ends up with your money when you pay your monthly mortgage, or your credit card bill or the instalment payment on your car. In the old days you would have found that it was the organisation you originally borrowed from and whose name is at the top of the monthly statement. Today you cannot be so sure because there is now a thriving market in repackaged debt. In this market, a mortgage lender, for example, collects together a few thousand of its mortgage 'claims' (the right of the lender to receive regular interest and capital from the borrowers); it then sells those claims in a collective package to other institutions, or participants in the market generally. This permits the replacement of long-term assets with cash, improving liquidity and gearing, which can then be used to generate more mortgages. The borrower is often unaware that the mortgage is no longer owned by the original lender and everything appears as it did before, with the mortgage company acting as a collect- ing agent for the buyer of the mortgages. The mortgage company usually raises this cash by selling asset-backed securities to other institutions (the 'assets' are the claim on interest and capital) and so this form of finance is often called *asset securitization*. These asset-backed securities (ABS) may be bonds sold into a market with many players.

> This permits the replacement of long-term assets with cash, improving liquidity and gearing.

Usually a 'special purpose vehicle' (SPV) or 'special purpose entity' (SPE) is created separate from the originator of mortgages, etc. The bonds sold are secured against the assets of the SPV (e.g. mortgage claims). This separates the credit-worthiness of the assets involved from the general credit of the company.

> Asset backed securitisation involves the pooling and repackaging of a relatively small, homogeneous and illiquid financial assets into liquid securities.

The sale of the financial claims can be either 'non-recourse', in which case the buyer of the securities from the mortgage firm bears the risk of non-payment by the borrowers, or with recourse to the mortgage lender.

Securitization has even reached the world of rock. Iron Maiden issued a long-dated $30m asset-backed bond securitised on future earnings from royalties in 1999. It followed David Bowie's $55m bond securitised on the income from his earlier albums and Rod Stewart's $15.4m securitised loan from Nomura. Tussauds has securitised ticket and merchandise sales, Keele University has securitised the rental income from student accommodation and Newcastle United and Everton football clubs have securitised their future season ticket sales.

The innovation continues: the income from loans to Hong Kong taxi drivers worth HK$3 billion were securitised, as were the cash flows from 502 UK funeral homes and 21 crematoriums (raising £210m).

Securitisation is regarded as beneficial to the financial system because it permits banks and other financial institutions to focus on those aspects of the lending process where they have a competitive edge. Some, for example, have a greater competitive advantage in originating loans than in funding them, so they sell the loans they have created, raising cash to originate more loans.

Securitisation was at the heart of the financial turmoil in 2007 when US subprime (poor-quality) mortgage borrowers failed to repay in substantial numbers. Mortgage-backed bonds of SPVs plummeted in value, the asset-backed bond market froze and the business model of lending to households expecting to sell bonds backed with a bunch of mortgages (à la Northern Rock) became untenable as no one would buy the securitised bonds.

Exhibit 16.10 describes the securitisation of Dunkin' Donuts' royalties received from its hundreds of franchises around the world – a steady source of income.

It's all a question of the right packaging

Richard Beales

In a corporate securitisation, assets and related cash flows are carved out from a business into special purpose entities (SPEs) and repackaged. Debt is then raised against the SPEs alone.

'Securitisation isolates a cash flow and insulates it from extraneous events,' says Ted Yarbrough, head of global securitised products at Citigroup.

Depending on the credit quality and the quantum of borrowing, part or all the debt may be highly rated, and there is sometimes a low-rated or unrated subordinated slice of debt as well. This is not, however, an off-balance sheet financing method – the assets and debt within the SPEs are consolidated in the company's financial statements.

A financing structured this way can achieve higher credit ratings than the business on its own. This partly reflects the structural aspects – for example, the fact that the SPEs can survive a bankruptcy of the umbrella group – and partly the fact that the securities issued are often 'wrapped', or guaranteed, by highly-rated bond insurers such as Ambac, Figic or MBIA in return for a fee.

This is a complex and costly exercise, but can result in much cheaper debt. Once established, a securitisation can be tapped again later if a business grows.

Sometimes securitisation is best suited to part of a business rather than the whole. When applied to an entire business, as with Dunkin' Brands or Domino's, the new financing typically replaces all traditional debt.

While a securitisation does involve financial constraints, they can be fewer and less onerous than with traditional

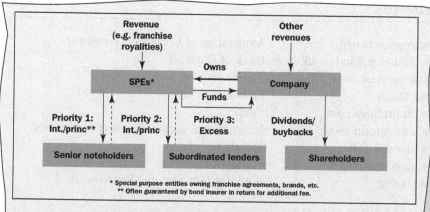

* Special purpose entities owning franchise agreements, brands, etc.
** Often guaranteed by bond insurer in return for additional fee.

bank and bond debt. Managers would, for example, have greater flexibility to pay dividends or buy back stock.

This reflects the fact that financiers in a securitisation look only to the specific assets and cash flows held within the SPEs. But Eric Hedman, analyst at Standard & Poor's in New York, notes there can be a trade-off in terms of operational flexibility. 'Prior to the securitisation, Dunkin' was an owner operator. Now, the company is no longer the franchisor, there's an SPE. Any new store agreement is for the benefit of the securitisation.' The company's manage-ment also does not have sole discretion over advertising spending, for example.

And the Dunkin' Donuts brand is no longer owned by the company. 'The sign on the wall says "Copyright DD IP Holder LLC". That's a bankruptcy-remote SPE set up for the benefit of noteholders [in the securitisation],' Mr Hedman says.

This kind of shift might not suit all managers. But for some executives – particularly those focused on maximis-ing cash returns to shareholders – such considerations can be outweighed by the financial benefits.

EXHIBIT 16.10

Source: *Financial Times* 25 July 2007, p. 2. Reprinted with permission.

Conclusion

We covered debt finance described as short- and medium-term available to almost any firm in the previous chapter. Long-term debt finance has been thor-oughly examined in this chapter together with financial market-based short- and medium-term finance. However the most important source of finance has only been touched on briefly so far, that is shareholders' ownership capital. The next chapter looks at the details of raising this type of capital from the stock market and in a variety of other ways.

Topics covered later in the book draw on the knowledge gained in this section of the book (Chapters 15, 16 and 17) to permit informed discussion of such cru-cial questions as: What is the appropriate mixture of debt and equity? How can the risk of certain forms of finance (for example a floating-interest-rate term loan) be reduced?

Websites

www.treasurers.org	Association of Corporate Treasurers
www.bankofengland.co.uk	Bank of England
www.economist.com	The Economist
www.FT.com	Financial Times
www.fitchratings.com	Fitch
www.icma-group.co.uk	International Capital Markets Association
www.moodys.com	Moody's
www.standardandpoors.com	Standard & Poor's
www.bis.org	Bank for International Settlements

Notes

1 If a trustee is not appointed the usual practice is to give each holder an independently exercisable right to take action against a deliquent borrower.

2 The term 'mandated lead arranger' or MLA is often used for the managing bank(s). Also 'bookrunner' or 'bookrunner group' indicates those who solicit interest in the loan from lenders and gather offers of support. They gradually 'build a book' – a list of confirmed buyers. They 'do the syndication'.

3 This example is designed to show the effect of leverage. It does lack realism in a number of respects; for example it is unlikely that profits will continue to rise at 25 percent per annum without further investment. This can be adjusted for – the time taken to pay off the debt lengthens but the principles behind the example do not alter.

4 Alternatively they may be convertible into preference shares.

5 This 7.25 percent is the nominal coupon rate. The actual rate of return Rank would have to pay in Decmber 2003 on the issue of a new five-year bond was 6 percent.

6 Just to confuse everyone, the traders in these markets often refer all types of eurocurrencies, from eurosterling to euroyen generically as 'eurodollars', failing to reserve that title for US dollars.

7 Although new EU rules mean that a prospectus is required if the bond is marketed at retail (non-professional) investors.

8 John Price, Director of Property, *Financial Times* 20 October 2000, p. 27.

17

RAISING EQUITY CAPITAL

To float or not to float? ...

Some firms are keen to float on the London Stock Exchange ...

Dunelm Mill, a very successful retailer of curtains and bedding, floated its shares in a new issue (or initial public offering, IPO) on the Main Market of the London Stock Exchange in 2006. 'The IPO represents the logical next step in the company's development,' said Will Adderley, Chief Executive. 'It will significantly raise Dunelm's profile and will help support the business in the next stage of our growth.'[1] It was also hoped that the float would bring some free advertising and 'the discipline of being listed will make us stronger'.[2] It was Will's mother, Jean, and his father Bill who started selling curtains on Leicester market in 1979. They opened their first shop in 1984 in the same city. They now have 82 stores, but plan to move to 150 which will require a considerable amount of capital. Jean, having retired in 2001, sold a 30 per cent stake in the business on flotation to institutional investors (pocketing £103m), retaining a 7.5 per cent stake, while Bill, a non-executive director, will keep his 50 per cent in a business worth £340m.

Some firms are desperate to leave the London Stock Exchange ...

Bernard Matthews, Richard Branson, Alan Sugar, Andrew Lloyd Webber and Anita and Gordon Roddick have demonstrated deep dissatisfaction with their companies' quotation. Sir Richard Branson floated the Virgin Group in 1986, then bought it back in 1988. Lord Lloyd Webber bought back his Really Useful Theatre Group in 1990 four years after floating. Lord Alan Sugar had made plain his dislike of the City and its ways, and was particularly annoyed when investors rejected his 1992 offer to buy the Amstrad group for £175m. Bernard Matthews concluded that his turkey business was paying too high a price for a quotation and so he bought back the company in 2000. Dame Anita Roddick, co-founder of Body Shop which floated in 1984, for many years made no secret of her desire to free herself of the misunderstanding and constraints imposed by City Folk, who she once described as 'pin-striped dinosaurs'.

And some firms are content to raise equity finance without being quoted on an exchange

Professor Steve Young, a specialist in information engineering at Cambridge University, became a millionaire by commercializing speech recognition software in the early 1990s. His project proceeded very nicely without a stock market quotation.

Initially his invention was licensed to a US company by Cambridge University. In 1995 the business was further developed by the creation of a UK company, half of which was owned by the US company. The other half was jointly held by the university, Professor Young and fellow academic Phil Woodland.

To grow further they needed 'venture money'. First, the US and UK companies combined and then the merged group took $3m from Amadeus Capital Partners (venture capitalists). By 1999, with 60 staff, the company, Entropic, was in need of more equity capital. Venture capitalists offered $20m, but here the story takes a strange twist. Young thought that it would be wise to have some of the shares bought by corporate investors. Microsoft was approached; they said they were not interested in making small corporate investments. A few weeks later, however, Microsoft telephoned and offered to buy the whole company instead. The deal is secret, but is thought to be worth tens of millions of pounds. Professor Young has returned to full-time academia a richer man and grateful for the existence of venture capital funds.

Sources: [1] *Financial Times* 22 September 2006, p. 22. 'Dunelm founders in £120m windfall' by Philip Stafford; [2] *The Independent* 22 September 2006, p. 52. 'Couple to cash in £120m from retail empire that grew out of market stall' by Susie Mesure; Bernard Matthews, etc.: based on *Financial Times* 1 November 1995 and 17 May 2000; Prof. Young: based on *Financial Times* 14 June 2001.

Introduction

There are many ways of raising money by selling shares. This chapter looks at the most important. It considers the processes that a firm would have to go through to gain a quotation on the Main Market of the London Stock Exchange and raise fresh equity finance. We will examine the tasks and responsibilities of the various advisers and other professionals who assist a company like Dunelm to present itself to investors in a suitable fashion.

A firm wishing to become quoted may, in preference to the Main Market (Official List), choose to raise finance on the Alternative Investment Market (AIM), also run by the London Stock Exchange, where the regulations and the costs are lower.

In addition to, or as an alternative to, a 'new issue' on a stock market (also called an initial public offering, IPO), which usually involves raising finance by selling shares to a new group of shareholders, a company may make a rights issue, in which existing shareholders are invited to pay for new shares in proportion to their present holdings. This chapter explains the mechanics and technicalities of rights issues as well as some other methods, such as placings and open offers.

It is necessary to broaden our perspective beyond stock markets, to consider the equity finance-raising possibilities for firms that are not quoted on an exchange. There are over one million limited liability companies in the UK and only 0.2 percent of them have shares traded on the recognized exchanges. For decades there has been a perceived financing gap for small and medium-sized firms which has to a large extent been filled by the rapidly growing venture capital/private equity capital industry. Venture capital firms have supplied share and debt capital to thousands of companies on fast-growth trajectories, such as the company established by Professor Young.

> There are over one million limited liability companies in the UK and only 0.2 percent of them have shares traded on the recognized exchanges.

Many, if not most, companies are content to grow without the aid of either stock markets or venture capital. For example, JC Bamford (JCB), which manufactures earth-moving machines, has built a large, export award winning company, without needing to bring in outside shareholders. This contentedness and absence of a burning desire to be quoted is reinforced by the stories that have emerged of companies which became disillusioned with being quoted. The pressures and strains of being quoted are considered by some (for example, Philip Green, owner of Arcadia (Burton, Top Shop, etc.) and BHS) to be an excessively high price to pay for access to equity finance. So to round off this chapter we examine some of the arguments advanced against gaining a quotation and contrast these with the arguments a growing company might make for joining a market.

What is equity capital?

Ordinary shares

Ordinary shares represent the equity share capital of the firm. The holders of these securities share in the rising prosperity of a company. These investors, as owners of the firm, have the right to exercise control over the company. They can vote at shareholder meetings to determine such crucial matters as the composition of the team of directors. They can also approve or disapprove of major strategic and policy issues such as the type of activities that the firm might engage in, or the decision to merge with another firm. These ordinary shareholders have a right to receive a share of dividends distributed as well as, if the worst came to the worst, a right to share in the proceeds of a liquidation sale of the firm's assets. To exercise effective control over the firm the shareholders will need information; and while management are reluctant to put large amounts of commercially sensitive information which might be useful to competitors into the public domain, they are required to make available to each shareholder a copy of the annual report.

> Ordinary shares represent the equity share capital of the firm.

There is no agreement between ordinary shareholders and the company that the investor will receive back the original capital invested. What ordinary shareholders receive depends on how well the company is managed. To regain invested funds an equity investor must either sell the shares to another investor (if the company is doing a share buy-back programme, it might be possible to sell shares to it, but this is rare) or force the company into liquidation, in which case all assets are sold and the proceeds distributed. Both courses of action may leave the investor with less than originally invested. There is a high degree of discretion left to the directors in proposing an annual or semi-annual dividend, and individual shareholders are often effectively powerless to influence the income from a share – not only because of the risk attached to the trading profits which generate the resources for a dividend, but also because of the relative power of directors in a firm with a disparate or divided shareholder body.

Ordinary shareholders are the last in the queue to have their claims met. When the income for the year is being distributed others, such as debenture holders and preference shareholders, get paid first. If there is a surplus after that, then ordinary shareholders may receive a dividend. Also when a company is wound up, employees, tax authorities, trade creditors and lenders all come before ordinary shareholders. Given these disadvantages there must be a very attractive feature to ordinary shares to induce individuals to purchase and keep them. The attraction is that if the company does well there are no limits to the size of the claim equity shareholders have on profit. There have been numerous instances of investors placing modest sums into the shares of young firms who find themselves millionaires. For example, if you had bought $1,000 shares in Google in 1999, your holding would now be worth millions.

From the company's point of view the issue of more shares has advantages, as discussed in Chapter 16, the most significant of which is their shock absorbing role. However, there are disadvantages compared with raising money by borrowing:

- **High cost** The cost of issuing shares is usually higher than the cost of raising the same amount of money by obtaining additional loans. There are two types of cost. First, there are the direct costs of issue such as the costs of advice from an investment bank and/or broker, and the legal, accounting and prospectus costs, etc. These costs can absorb up to 10 to 25 percent of the amount of money raised. Second, and by far the most important, there is the cost represented by the return required to satisfy shareholders, which is greater than that on safer securities such as bonds issued by the firm (*see* Chapter 10).

- **Loss of control** Entrepreneurs sometimes have a difficult choice to make – they need additional equity finance for the business but dislike the notion of inviting external equity investors to buy shares. The choice is sometimes between slow/no growth or dilution of the entrepreneurs' control. External equity providers may impose conditions such as veto rights over important business decisions and the right to appoint a number of directors. In many instances, founders take the decision to forgo expansion in order to retain control.

> Entrepreneurs dislike the notion of inviting external equity investors to buy shares.

- **Dividends cannot be used to reduce taxable profit** Dividends are paid out of after-tax earnings, whereas interest payments on loans are tax deductible. This affects the relative costs to the company of financing by issuing interest-based securities and financing through ordinary shares.

Authorised, issued and par values

When a firm is created the original shareholders will decide the number of shares to be *authorised* (the *authorised capital*).[1] This is the maximum amount of share capital that the company can issue (unless shareholders vote to change the limit). In many cases firms do not issue up to the amount specified. For example, Green plc has authorised capital of £5m, split between £1m of preference shares and £4m of ordinary shares. The company has issued all of the preference shares (at par) but the issued ordinary share capital is only £2.5m, leaving £1.5m as *authorised but unissued ordinary share capital*. This allows the directors to issue the remaining £1.5m of capital without the requirement of asking shareholders for further permission (subject to the rights issue or placing rules – *see* later in chapter).

> Authorized capital is the maximum amount of share capital that the company can issue.

Shares have a stated par value, say 25p or 5p. This nominal value usually bears no relation to the price at which the shares could be sold or their subsequent value on the stock market. So let us assume Green has ten million ordinary shares issued, each with a par value of 25p (£2.5m total nominal value divided by the nominal price per share, 25p = 10m shares); these were originally sold for £2 each, raising £20m, and the present market value is £3.80 per share.

The par value has no real significance[2] and for the most part can be ignored. However, a point of confusion can arise when one examines company accounts because issued share capital appears on the balance sheet at par value and so often seems pathetically small. This item has to be read in conjunction with the *share premium account*, which represents the difference between the price received by the company for the shares and the par value of those shares.

> Share premium account represents the difference between the price received by the company for the shares and the par value of those shares.

Thus, in the case of Green the premium on each share was 200p – 25p = 175p. The total share premium in the balance sheet will be £17.5m.

Limited companies, plcs and listed companies

Limited liability means that the ordinary shareholders are only liable up to the amount they have invested or have promised to invest in purchasing shares. Lenders and other creditors are not able to turn to the ordinary shareholder should they find on a liquidation that the company, as a separate legal 'person', has insufficient assets to repay them in full. This contrasts with the position for a partner in a partnership who will be liable for all the debts of the business to the point where personal assets such as houses and cars can be seized to be sold to pay creditors.

Private companies, with the suffix 'Limited' or 'Ltd', are the most common form of company (over 95 percent of all companies). The less numerous, but more influential, form of company is a public limited company (or just public companies). These firms must display the suffix 'plc'. The private company has no minimum amount of share capital and there are restrictions on the type of purchaser who can be offered shares in the enterprise, whereas the plc has to have a minimum share capital of £50,000 but is able to offer shares to a wide range of potential investors. Not all public companies are quoted on a stock market. This can be particularly confusing when the press talks about a firm 'going public' – it may have been a public limited company for years and has merely decided to 'come to the market' to obtain a quotation. Strictly speaking, the term 'listed' should only be applied to those firms on the Official List (i.e. those accepted by the UK Listing Authority – most of which are on the Main Market of the London Stock Exchange), but the term is used rather loosely and shares on the Alternative Investment Market are often referred to as being quoted or listed.

Preference shares

Preference shares usually offer their owners a fixed rate of dividend each year, unlike ordinary shares which offer no regular dividend. However if the firm has insufficient profits the amount paid would be reduced, sometimes to zero. Thus, there is no guarantee that an annual income will be received, unlike with debt capital. The dividend on preference shares is paid before anything is paid out to ordinary shareholders – indeed, after the preference dividend obligation has been met there may be nothing left for ordinary shareholders. Preference shares are attractive to some investors because they offer a regular income at a higher rate of return than that available on fixed interest securities, e.g. bonds. However this higher return also comes with higher risk, as the preference dividend ranks after bond interest, and upon liquidation preference holders are further back in the queue as recipients of the proceeds of asset sell-offs.

Preference shares are part of shareholders' funds but are not equity share capital. The holders are not usually able to benefit from any extraordinarily good performance of the firm – any profits above expectations go to the ordinary shareholders. Also preference shares usually carry no voting rights, except if the dividend is in arrears or in the case of liquidation.

Advantages to the firm of preference share capital

Preference share capital has the following advantages:

- **Dividend 'optional'** Preference dividends can be omitted for one or more years. This can give the directors more flexibility and a greater chance of surviving a downturn in trading. Although there may be no legal obligation to pay a dividend every year the financial community is likely to take a dim view of a firm that missed a dividend – this may have a deleterious effect on the ordinary share price as investors become nervous and sell. Dividends cannot be paid to ordinary shareholders until preference dividend arrears are cleared.

- **Influence over management** Preference shares are an additional source of capital which, because they do not (usually) confer voting rights, do not dilute the influence of the ordinary shareholders on the firm's direction. Thus, a family-run or small company wishing to raise shareholder capital may do so using preference shares, thereby retaining voting control.

- **Extraordinary profits** The limits placed on the return to preference shareholders means that the ordinary shareholders receive all the extraordinary profits when the firm is doing well (unless the preference shares are participating – *see* p 499).

- **Financial gearing considerations** There are limits to safe levels of borrowing. Preference shares are an alternative, if less effective, shock absorber to ordinary shares because of the possibility of avoiding the annual cash outflow due on dividends. In some circumstances a firm may be prevented from raising finance by borrowing as this increases the risk of financial distress, and the shareholders may be unwilling to provide more equity risk capital. If this firm is determined to grow by raising external finance, preference shares are one option.

Disadvantages to the firm of preference share capital

Preference share capital also has disadvantages:

- **High cost of capital** The higher risk attached to the annual returns and capital cause preference shareholders to demand a higher level of return than debt holders.

- **Dividends are not tax-deductible** Because preference shares are regarded as part of shareholders' funds the dividend is regarded as an appropriation of profits. Tax is payable on the firm's profit before the deduction of the preference dividend. In contrast, lenders are not regarded as having any ownership rights and interest has to be paid whether or not a profit is made. This cost is regarded as a legitimate expense reducing taxable profit. In recent years preference shares have become a relatively unpopular method of raising finance because bonds and bank loans, rival types of long-term finance, have this tax advantage. This is illustrated by the example of companies A and B. Both firms have raised £1m, but Company A sold bonds yielding 8 percent, Company B sold preference shares offering a dividend yield of 8 percent. (Here we assume the returns are identical for illustration purposes – in reality the return on preference shares might be a few percentage points higher than that on bonds.) *See* Figure 17.1.

Company A has a lower tax bill because its bond interest is used to reduce taxable profit, resulting in an extra £24,000 (£84,000 – £60,000) being available for the ordinary shareholders.

FIGURE 17.1
Preference shares versus bonds

	Company A	Company B
Profits before tax, dividends and interest	200,000	200,000
Interest payable on bonds	80,000	0
Taxable profit	120,000	200,000
Tax payable @ 30% of taxable profit	36,000	60,000
	84,000	140,000
Preference dividend	0	80,000
Available for ordinary shareholders	84,000	60,000

Types of preference share

There are a number of variations on the theme of preference share. Here are some features which can be added:

- **Cumulative** If dividends are missed in any year the right to eventually receive a dividend is carried forward. These prior-year dividends have to be paid before any payout to ordinary shareholders.

- **Participating** As well as the fixed payment, the dividend may be increased if the company has high profits. (Usually the additional payment is a proportion of any ordinary dividend declared.)

- **Redeemable** These have a finite life, at the end of which the initial capital investment will be repaid. Irredeemables have no fixed redemption date.

- **Convertibles** These can be converted into ordinary shares at specific dates and on pre-set terms (for example, one ordinary share for every two preference shares). These shares often carry a lower yield since there is the attraction of a potentially large capital gain.

- **Variable rate** A variable dividend is paid. The rate may be linked to general interest rates, e.g. LIBOR or to some other variable factor.

Floating on the Main Market (Official List)

To 'go public' and become a listed company is a major step for a firm. The substantial sums of money involved can lead to a new, accelerated phase of business growth. Obtaining a quotation is not a step to be taken lightly; it is a major legal undertaking. The United Kingdom Listing Authority, UKLA (part of the Financial Services Authority)[3] rigorously enforces a set of demanding rules and the directors will be put under the strain of new and greater responsibilities both at the time of flotation and in subsequent years. New issues can produce a greater availability of equity finance to fund expansion and development programmes. It may also allow existing shareholders to realize a proportion of their investment. Shareholders benefit from the availability of a speedy, cheap secondary market if they want to sell. Not only do shareholders like to know that they can sell when they want to, they may simply want to know the value of their holdings even if they have no intention of selling at present. By contrast, an unquoted firm's shareholders often find it difficult to assess the value of their holding. In addition it can raise the profile of a company both in the financial world and in its product markets, which may give it a competitive edge. A float may also make mergers easier. This is especially true if the payment for the target shares is shares in the acquirer; a quoted share has a value defined by the market, whereas shares in unquoted companies are less attractive because of the greater doubt about the value.

> Obtaining a quotation is not a step to be taken lightly; it is a major legal undertaking.

What managers need to consider

Prospectus

To create a stable market and encourage investors to place their money with companies the UKLA tries to minimise the risk of investing by ensuring that the firms which obtain a quotation abide by high standards and conform to strict rules. For example the directors are required to prepare a detailed prospectus ('Listing particulars') to inform potential shareholders about the company. This may contain far more information about the firm

> A successful flotation can depend on the prospectus acting as a marketing tool.

than it has previously dared to put into the public domain. Even without the stringent conditions laid down by the UKLA the firm has an interest in producing a stylish and informative prospectus. A successful flotation can depend on the prospectus acting as a marketing tool as the firm attempts to persuade investors to apply for shares.

The content and accuracy of this vital document is the responsibility of the directors. Contained within it must be three years of audited accounts, details of indebtedness and a statement as to the adequacy of working capital. Statements by experts are often required: valuers may be needed to confirm the current value of property, engineers may be needed to state the viability of processes or machinery and accountants may be needed to comment on the profit figures. All major contracts entered into in the past two years will have to be detailed. Any persons with a shareholding of more than 3 percent have to be named. A mass of operational data is required, ranging from an analysis of sales by geographic area and category of activity, to information on research and development and significant investments in other companies.

The Listing Rules state that the expected market value of the company's shares is to be at least £700,000 to allow for sufficient dealings to take place. However, this is an absurdly small number in this day and age. Given that the cost of advisers to the new issue will be at least £500,000, it is rarely worth floating on the Main Market unless the market capitalisation is at least £10m.

Conditions imposed and new responsibilities

All companies obtaining a full listing (i.e. on the Main Market rather than the AIM) must ensure that at least 25 percent of their share capital is in public hands, to ensure that the shares are capable of being traded actively on the market.[4] If a reasonably active secondary market is not established, trading may become stultified and the shares may become illiquid. 'Public' means people or organisations not associated with the directors or major shareholders.

Directors may find their room for discretion restricted when it comes to paying dividends. Stock market investors, particularly the major institutions, tend to demand regular dividends. Not only do they usually favour consistent cash flow, they also use dividend policy as a kind of barometer of corporate health (*see* Chapter 14). This can lead to pressure to maintain a growing dividend flow, which the unquoted firm may not experience.

There is also a loss of some privacy and autonomy, e.g. greater disclosure of directors' salaries and other remuneration, responding to the demands of a wider range of shareholders.

There are strict rules concerning the buying and selling of the company's shares by its own directors. The Criminal Justice Act 1993 and the Model Code for Directors' Dealings have to be followed. Directors are prevented from dealing for a minimum period (normally two months) prior to an announcement of regularly recurring information such as annual results. They are also forbidden to deal before the announcement of matters of an exceptional nature involving unpublished information that is potentially price sensitive. These rules apply to any employee in possession of such information. All dealings in the company's shares by directors have to be reported to the market.[5]

You might be rejected as unsuitable

The UKLA tries to ensure that the 'quality of the company' is sufficiently high to appeal to the investment community. The management team must have the necessary range and depth, and there must be a high degree of continuity and stability of management over recent years. Investors do not like to be over-reliant on the talents of one individual and so will expect a team of able directors, including some non-executives, and – preferably – a separation of the roles of chief executive and chair. They also expect to see an appropriately qualified finance director.

The UKLA usually insists that a company has a track record (in the form of accounting figures) stretching back at least three years. However this requirement has been relaxed for scientific research-based companies and companies undertaking major capital projects. In the case of scientific research-based companies there is the requirement that they have been conducting their activity for three years even if no revenue was produced. Some major project companies, for example Eurotunnel, have been allowed to join the market despite an absence of a trading activity or a profit record.

Technologically oriented companies can be admitted to the techMARK, part of the Official List, with only one year of accounts.

Another suitability factor is the timing of the flotation. Investors often desire stability, a reasonable spread of activities and evidence of potential growth in the core business. If the underlying product market served by the firm is going through a turbulent period it may be wise to delay the flotation until investors can be reassured about the long-term viability.

Other suitability factors are a healthy balance sheet, sufficient working capital, good financial control mechanisms and clear accounting policies.

The issuing process

The issuing process involves a number of specialist advisers (discussed below). The process is summarised in Figure 17.2.

FIGURE 17.2
The issuing process for the Official List

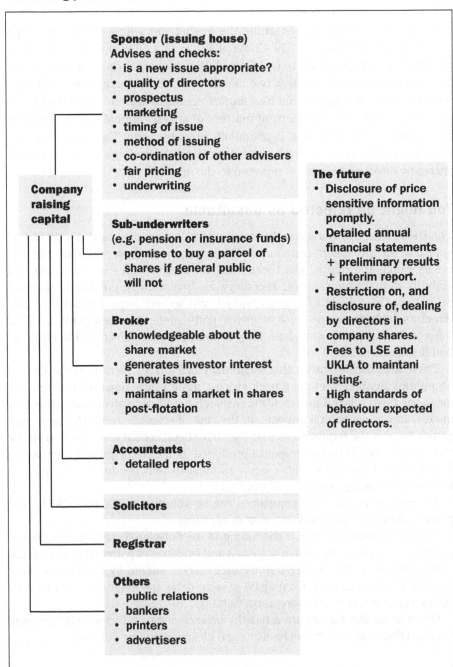

Hiring a sponsor

The UKLA is responsible for the approval of the prospectus and admission of a company to the Official List. In addition, the London Stock Exchange has to separately admit the company to its Main Market. Thus, a flotating company has to go through two parallel processes:

(a) to gain a 'listing' with the UKLA, and

(b) admission to trading on the Main Market.

Given the vast range of matters that directors have to consider to gain a place on the Official List (the 'Main Market') it is clear that experts are going to be required to guide firms through the complexities. The key adviser in a flotation is the sponsor. This may be an investment bank, stockbroker or other professional adviser. Directors, particularly of small companies, often first seek advice from their existing professional advisers, for example accountants and lawyers. These may have the necessary expertise (and approval of the UKLA – *see* www.fsa.gov.uk/ukla) themselves to act for the company in the flotation or may be able to recommend a more suitable sponsor. Sponsors have to be chosen with care as the relationship is likely to be one that continues long after the flotation. For large or particularly complex issues investment banks are employed, although experienced stockbrokers have been used.

Sponsors are required by the UKLA to certify that a company has complied with all the regulatory requirements, and to ensure that all necessary documentation is filed in time. The sponsor (sometimes called the issuing house) will first examine the company to assess whether flotation is an appropriate corporate objective by taking into account its structure and capital needs. The sponsor will also comment on the composition of the board and the calibre of the directors. The sponsor may even recommend supplementation with additional directors if the existing team does not come up to the quality expected. Sponsors can be quite forceful in this because they do not want to damage their reputation by bringing a poorly managed company to market. The sponsor will draw up a timetable, which can be lengthy – sometimes the planning period for a successful flotation may extend over two years. There are various methods of floating, ranging from a placing to an offer for sale (discussed later), and the sponsor will advise on the most appropriate. Another important function is to help draft the prospectus and provide input to the marketing strategy. Throughout the process of flotation there will be many other professional advisers involved and it is vital that their activities mesh into a coherent whole. It is the sponsor's responsibility to co-ordinate the activities of all the other professional advisers.

Paying underwriters

Shortly before the flotation the sponsor will have the task of advising on the best price to ask for the shares, and, at the time of flotation, the sponsor will underwrite the issue. Most new issues are underwritten, because the correct

> The underwriter guarantees to buy the proportion of the issue not taken up by the market.

pricing of a new issue of shares is extremely difficult. If the price is set too high, demand will be less than supply and not all the shares will be bought. The company is usually keen to have certainty that it will receive money from the issue so that it can plan ahead. To make sure it sells the shares it buys a kind of insurance called underwriting. In return for a fee the underwriter guarantees to buy the proportion of the issue not taken up by the market. An investment bank sponsoring the issue will usually charge a fee of 2–4 percent of the issue proceeds and then pays part of that fee, say 1.25–3.0 percent of the issue proceeds, to sub-underwriters (usually large financial institutions such as pension funds) who each agree to buy a certain number of shares if called on to do so. In most cases the underwriters do not have to purchase any shares because the general public are keen to take them up. However occasionally they receive a shock and have to buy large quantities.

Hiring a corporate broker

When a broker is employed as a sponsor the two roles can be combined. If the sponsor is, say, an investment bank the UKLA requires that a broker also be appointed. However, most investment banks also have corporate broking arms and so can take on both roles. Brokers play a vital role in advising on share market conditions and the likely demand from investors for the company's shares. They also represent the company to investors to try to generate interest. When debating issues such as the method to be employed, the marketing strategy, the size of the issue, the timing or the pricing of the shares the company may value the market knowledge the broker has to offer. Brokers can also organise sub-underwriting and in the years following the flotation may work with the company to maintain a liquid and properly informed market in its shares. They may also help raise additional money through rights issues, for example.

Accountants and lawyers

The reporting accountant in a flotation has to be different from the company's existing auditors, but can be a separate team in the same firm.

The accountant will be asked by the sponsor to prepare a detailed report on the firm's financial controls, track record, financing and forecasts (the 'long form' report). Not all of this information will be included in the prospectus but it does serve to reassure the sponsor that the company is suitable for flotation. Accountants may also have a role in tax planning both from the company's viewpoint and that of its shareholders. They also investigate working capital requirements. The UKLA insists that companies show that they have enough working capital for current needs and for at least the next 12 months.

All legal requirements in the flotation preparation and in the information displayed in the prospectus must be complied with. Examples of legal issues are directors' contracts, changes to the articles of association re-registering the company as a plc, underwriting agreements and share option schemes.

> Directors bear the ultimate responsibility for the truthfulness of the documents.

Lawyers also prepare the 'verification' questions that are used to confirm that every statement in the prospectus can be justified as fact. Directors bear the ultimate responsibility for the truthfulness of the documents.

Registrars

The records on the ownership of shares are maintained by registrars as shares are bought and sold. They keep the company's register and issue certificates. They are required to electronically adjust records of ownership of company shares within two hours of a trade.

Continuing obligations after flotation

The UKLA insists on listed companies having 'continuing obligations'. One of these obligations is that all price-sensitive information is given to the market as soon as possible and that there is 'full and accurate disclosure'. Information is price sensitive if it might influence the share price or the trading in the shares. Investors need to be sure that they are not disadvantaged by market distortions caused by some participants having the benefit of superior information. Public announcements will be required in a number of instances, for example: the development of major new products; the signing of major contracts; details of an acquisition; a sale of large assets; a change in directors; a decision to pay a dividend. The website www.investegate.co.uk shows all major announcements made by companies going back many years.

Listed companies are also required to provide detailed financial statements within six months of the year-end. Firms usually choose to make preliminary profit announcements based on unaudited results for the year a few weeks before the audited results are published. Interim reports for the first half of each accounting year are also required (within four months of the end of the half year). The penalty for non-compliance is suspension from the Exchange.

Other ongoing obligations include the need to inform the market about director dealings in the company's shares and the expectation that directors will conform to the standards of behaviour required by the UKLA and the Exchange, some of which are contained in the UK Corporate Governance Code (*see* Chapter 1). While these standards of behaviour are encouraged they are not required by the UKLA. However, if a company does not comply it must explain why not in its annual reports.

Methods of issue

The sponsor will look at the motives for wanting a quotation, at the amount of money that is to be raised, at the history and reputation of the firm and will then advise on the best method of issuing the shares. There are various methods, ranging from a full-scale offer for sale to a relatively simple introduction. The final choice often rests on the costs of the method of issue, which can vary considerably. Here are the main options.

Offer for sale

The company sponsor offers shares to the public by inviting subscriptions from institutional and individual investors. Sometimes newspapers carry a prospectus and an application form. However, most investors will need to contact the sponsor or the broker to obtain an application form. (Publications, such as *Investors Chronicle*, show the telephone numbers to call for each company floating. Details of forthcoming flotations are available at www.londonstockexchange.com, other useful websites are www.hemscott.com, www.iii.co.uk and www.proactiveinvestors.co.uk).

Normally the shares are offered at a fixed price determined by the company's directors and their financial advisers. A variation of this method is an *offer for sale by tender*. Here investors are invited to state a price at which they are willing to buy (above a minimum reserve price). The sponsor gathers the applications and then selects a price which will dispose of all the shares – the strike price. Investors who bid a price above this will be allocated shares at the strike price – not at the price of their bid. Those who bid below the strike price will not receive any shares. This method is useful in situations where it is very difficult to value a company, for instance, where there is no comparable company already listed or where the level of demand may be difficult to assess. Leaving the pricing to the public may result in a larger sum being raised. On the other hand it is more costly to administer and many investors will be put off by being handed the onerous task of estimating the share's value. This happened in the case of Google.com in 2004, which received fewer applications than expected in a type of auction system.

> The sponsor selects a price which will dispose of all the shares – the strike price.

Introduction

Introductions do not raise any new money for the company. If the company's shares are already quoted on another stock exchange or there is a wide spread of shareholders, with more than 25 percent of the shares in public hands, the Exchange permits a company to be 'introduced' to the market. This method may allow companies trading on AIM to move up to the Main Market or for foreign corporations to gain a London listing. This is the cheapest method of flotation since there are no underwriting costs and relatively small advertising expenditures. In 2004 ITV plc was introduced to the market. This company was created by merging Carlton with Granada, both of which had a wide spread of shareholdings and both were previously listed on the Exchange, so the company and its management were well known.

Offer for subscription

An offer for subscription is similar to an offer for sale, but it is only partially underwritten. This method is used by new companies that state at the outset that if the share issue does not raise a certain minimum the offer will be aborted. This is a particularly popular method for new investment trusts. If the fund managers do not raise enough to create a large investment company which will be able to pay them large ongoing management fees, then they abandon the whole idea.

Placing

In a placing, shares are offered to the public but the term 'public' is narrowly defined. Instead of engaging in advertising to the population at large, the sponsor or broker handling the issue sells the shares to institutions it is in contact with, such as pension and insurance funds. The costs of this method are considerably lower than those of an offer for sale. There are lower publicity costs and legal costs. A drawback of this method is that the spread of shareholders is going to be more limited. To alleviate this problem the Stock Exchange does insist on a large number of placees holding shares after the new issue.

In the 1980s the most frequently used method of new issue was the offer for sale. This ensured a wide spread of share ownership and thus a more liquid secondary market. It also permitted all investors to participate in new issues. Placings were only permitted for small offerings (< £15m) when the costs of an offer for sale would have been prohibitive. Today any size of new issue can be placed. As this method is much cheaper and easier than an offer for sale, the majority of companies have naturally switched to placings.

Intermediaries offer

Another method, which is often combined with a placing, is an intermediaries offer. Here the shares are offered for sale to financial institutions such as stockbrokers. Clients of these intermediaries can then apply to buy shares from them.

Reverse takeover

Sometimes a larger, unquoted company makes a deal with a smaller quoted company whereby the smaller company 'takes over' the larger firm by swapping newly created shares in itself for the shares in the unquoted firm currently held by its owners. Because the quoted firm creates and issues more new shares itself than it had to start with, the unquoted firm's shareholders end up with the majority of the shares in the newly merged entity. They therefore now control a quoted company. The only task remaining is to decide on a name for the company – frequently the name of the previously unquoted company is chosen. A reverse takeover is a way for a company to gain a listing/quotation without the hassle of an official new issue.

Eddie Stobart gained a quotation through a reverse takeover (*see* Exhibit 17.1).

Book-building

Selling new issues of shares through book-building is a popular technique in the USA and is starting to catch on in Europe. Under this method the financial advisers to an issue contact major institutional investors to get from them bids for the shares over a period of eight to ten working days. The investors' orders are sorted according to price, quantity and other factors such as 'firmness' of bid (e.g. a 'strike bid' means the investor will buy a given number of shares within the initial price range; leaving it to others to set the price; a 'limit bid' means the investor would buy a particular quantity at a particular price). These data may then be used to establish a price for the issue and the allocation of shares.

Eddie Stobart drives on to LSE

Chris Bryant

Eddie Stobart, the haulage group renowned for its distinctive green lorries, is planning to list on the London Stock Exchange through a reverse takeover to create a £250m transport and logistics business.

The group has agreed to be acquired by Westbury Property Fund, the listed commercial property, port and rail operator for £137.7m in cash and shares, continuing a trend towards consolidation and scale in the logistics industry.

The merged entity, called Stobart Group, will combine Eddie Stobart's 900-vehicle haulage fleet with Westbury's port and rail assets, to create a transport and logistics business with net assets of more than £250m. It also plans to acquire O'Connor, a rail freight handling business.

William Stobart, a son of the founder, who owns 27 per cent of the group and Andrew Tinker, who owns the other 73 per cent, together expect to hold 28.5 per cent of the enlarged group in the same proportions and would respectively become chief executive and chief operating officer.

They also intend to acquire Westbury's commercial property portfolio through WADI Properties, a separate wholly owned company, for £142m in cash and assumed debt, completing what is in effect an asset swap.

Exhibit 17.1

Source: *Financial Times* 16 August 2007, p. 16. Reprinted with permission

Timetable for a new issue (initial public offering, IPO)

The various stages of a new share issue will be explained using the example of the flotation of Sports Direct on the Main Market in 2007. This timetable is set out in Figure 17.3.

Sports Direct

Pre-launch

Mike Ashley started Sports Direct (Sports World and Lillywhites), the major sportswear retailer, by opening one shop at the age of 18. By the time he had reached 43 in 2007 the company had 465 shops and revenue of £1.2bn, and Mr Ashley decided to float it on the Main Market of the LSE. He floated because he thought by doing so he could achieve the company's ambitious goal of being 'the leading, most profitable retailer in the world'. It would raise its profile and allow acquisitions of other companies.

He intended to sell 43 percent of his shares to other investors on gaining a quotation, raising around £1bn to go into his bank account, while holding on to the other 57 percent of the company's shares. He appointed himself deputy executive chair. This is quite an unusual post given that chairs are usually independent and non-executive, who are there to make sure the executive directors are operating the company in the best interests of all shareholders.

Normally there would be a lot of publicity about a company a year or so before the actual float. But Mike Ashley is not someone who is very comfortable with publicity – he had shunned the spotlight for 25 years. Despite this, in February 2007 we started to read in the press about the company and the story of the remarkable growth of Mike Ashley's empire. Merrill Lynch did its best to talk up the company's prospects. We heard about Ashley's fearsome buying acumen and power, the company's record of consistent growth, and wisdom of the 'pile it high, sell it cheap' strategy.

Technicalities

Merrill Lynch was appointed global co-ordinator, bookrunner and sponsor of the float; Citigroup and Credit Suisse were co-lead managers.

To strengthen the management team Simon Bentley, former chairman and chief executive of Blacks Leisure, was appointed as a director, as was Chris Bulmer, former human resources director at Whitbread. David Richardson, finance director of Whitbread, was appointed non-executive chairman on the date of flotation. The executive management team was headed by Dave Forsey, who started as a Saturday boy when he was 18.

FIGURE 17.3

Timetable of an offer for sale and a placing

Time relative to impact day	1–2 years	Several weeks (usually 12–24 weeks)	A few days	Impact day		A few days	2 days to 2 weeks for offer for sale	2 weeks or so for an offer for sale
Stage	Pre-launch publicity	Sponsor and other advisers consider details such as drawing up accountant's report, price and method of issue. Also obtain underwriting, etc.	Pathfinder prospectus ■ to press; ■ to major investors No price	Prospectus published Price announced in a fixed-price sale offer or placing	Investors apply and send payments	Offer closes	Allotment	Admission to the Exchange and dealing begins
Dates for Sports Direct (placing)	January and February 2007	Late 2006 and early 2007	14 February: price range of 250p to 310p is announced		27 February: a price is given: 300p			2 March: first formal dealings

In February the directors went on a 'roadshow' – they made presentations to institutional investors at various locations. Roadshows are important not only for marketing the issue but also because they allow sponsors to gather information from investors, such as their opinions of the company and its valuation.

Pathfinder prospectus

On 14 February the pathfinder prospectus was published and the price range was set at 250p to 310p, valuing the group at £1.8bn to £2.2bn. This is not a firm expectation of the sale price, but a 'test the water' type of price announcement. As a result of the book-building period through late February, the book-builders (Merrill Lynch, etc.) built up a good picture of what demand was likely to be at different prices. In fact by 20 February the IPO had been 'more than covered', meaning that enough indicative offers had been received to sell the shares somewhere within the price range.

Impact day

The full prospectus is published on impact day, together with the price. For Sports Direct on 27 February the price was set at 300p, valuing the company at £2.16bn.

Offer closes

In an offer for sale, up to two weeks is needed for investors to consider the offer price and send in payments. There is a fixed cut-off date for applications. In the case of a placing/book-building, the time needed is much shorter as the share buyers have already indicated their interest to the sponsors and managers and transactions can be expedited between City institutions.

Allotment

Investors applied for more than twice the number of shares available. The shares are allocated by the sponsors in a placing/book-building depending on commitments made in the book-building process. In an offer for sale, allocation can be achieved in a number of different ways. A ballot means that only some investors receive shares (recipients are selected at random). In a scaledown applicants generally receive some shares, but fewer than they applied for. A cut-off point might be used in which applicants for large quantities are excluded.

Dealing begins

Formal dealing in the shares through the Stock Exchange started at 8 a.m. on 2 March. Formal dealing means on the Exchange after the shares have been allocated. However, deals had been made between investing institutions in an informal market from 27 February – buying and selling shares they believed they were to receive. The shares traded below the placing price, at 281p on 27 February, causing investors to lose 6.3 percent in the first day of (informal) trading. Mike Ashley sold his shares for £929m. In the following six months the shares tumbled to under 130p.

How does an alternative investment market (AIM) flotation differ from one on the Official List?

The driving philosophy behind AIM is to offer young and developing companies access to new sources of finance, while providing investors with the opportunity to buy and sell shares in a trading environment run, regulated and marketed by the LSE. Efforts were made to keep the costs down and make the rules as simple as possible. In contrast to the Main Market there is no requirement for AIM companies to be a minimum size, to have traded for a minimum period of three years or for a set proportion of their shares to be in public hands. If they wish to sell a mere 5 percent or 10 percent of the shares to outsiders, then that is acceptable. They do not have to ensure that 25 percent of the shares are in public hands.

> There is no requirement for AIM companies to be a minimum size, to have traded for a minimum period or for a set proportion of their shares to be in public hands.

Investors have some degree of reassurance about the quality of companies coming to the market by the requirement that the floating firms have to appoint, and retain at all times, a nominated adviser and nominated broker. The nominated adviser ('nomad') is selected by the corporation from a Stock Exchange approved register of firms. The nominated advisers are paid a fee by the company to act as an unofficial 'sponsor' in investigating and verifying its financial health. These advisers have demonstrated to the Exchange that they have sufficient experience and qualifications to act as a 'quality controller', confirming to the LSE that the company has complied with the rules. In contrast to Official List companies, there is no pre-vetting of admission documents by the UK Listing Authority (or the Exchange) as a lot of weight is placed on the nominated adviser's investigations and informed opinion about the company.

Nominated brokers have an important role to play in bringing buyers and sellers of shares together. Investors in the company are reassured that at least one broker is ready to trade or do its best to match up buyers and sellers. The adviser and broker are to be retained throughout the company's life in AIM. They have high reputations and it is regarded as a very bad sign if either of them abruptly refuses further association with a firm.

AIM companies are also expected to comply with strict rules regarding the publication of price-sensitive information and the quality of annual and interim reports. Upon flotation, an AIM admission document is required; this is similar to a prospectus required for companies floating on the Main Market, but it is less detailed. But it does go as so far as stating the directors' unspent convictions and all bankruptcies of companies where they were directors.

When the cost of the nominated advisers' time is added to those of the stock exchange fees, accountants, lawyers, printers and so on, the (administrative) cost of capital raising can be as much as 37 percent of the amount being raised. This, as a proportion, is comparable with the Main Market but the sums of money raised are usually much less on AIM and so the absolute cost is lower. AIM was designed so that the minimum cost of joining was in the region of £40,000–£50,000. But, as Exhibit 17.2 shows, it has now risen so that frequently more than £500,000 is paid. This sum is significantly higher than the originators of AIM planned. Most of the additional cost arises on raising funds rather than simply joining AIM, which is around £100,000–£200,000. The nominated advisers argue that they are forced to charge firms higher fees because they incur more investigatory costs due to the emphasis put on their policing role by the Stock Exchange.

> AIM was designed so that the minimum cost of joining was in the region of £40,000–£50,000. It has now risen so that frequently more than £500,000 is paid.

The prospectus (or AIM document) is less detailed than the prospectus for an OL quotation and therefore cheaper. The real cost savings come in the continuing annual expense of managing the quotation. For example AIM companies do not have to disclose as much information as companies on the Official List. Price-sensitive information has to be published but normally this will require only an electronic message from the adviser to the Exchange rather than a circular to shareholders. Having said this, the cost of maintaining a quote on AIM is too much for some companies – see Exhibit 17.3.

AIM companies are not bound by the Listing Rules administered by the UKLA but instead are subject to the AIM rules, written and administered by the LSE.

Note also that there are tax advantages for shareholders investing in AIM companies via venture capital trusts and the Enterprise Investment Scheme (see later in this chapter) or through the reduction in inheritance tax for some investors.

Offsetting the cost advantages AIM has over the Official List is the fact that the higher level of regulation and related enhanced image, prestige and security of Official List companies means that equity capital can usually be raised at a lower required rate of return (the shares can be sold for more per unit of projected profit).

AIM is not just a stepping-stone for companies planning to graduate to the Official List. It has many attractive features in its own right. Indeed, many Official List companies have moved to AIM in recent years. Over 300 new companies each year have joined the market in recent years, compared with fewer than 100 joining the Main Market, although new issues on both markets slowed considerably in 2009 and 2010.

Cost of Aim flotation rises, especially for the minnows

David Blackwell

The cost of raising money on Aim increased last year in spite of the reduction in the number of flotations from 519 to 462.

You might expect that competition among more than 80 nominated advisers (nomads) chasing fewer potential candidates would keep the lid on the cost of fees.

However, according to a survey by UHY Hacker Young, the accountancy firm, and Trowers & Hamlins, a City law firm, only the handful of companies raising more than £20m enjoyed a fall in the average costs as a percentage of funds raised.

The survey, which looked at the proportion of costs over funds raised in the last quarter of both 2005 and 2006, shows that an Aim flotation makes sense for the bigger companies. Costs accounted for 4.9 per cent of their total funds raised last year, a slight improvement on the 5.1 per cent in 2005.

However, the costs remain the same when smaller amounts are raised. So the survey shows that for amounts between £10m and £20m, the costs rose from 10.1 to 10.9 per cent of the total; for between £2m and £10m from 15.4 per cent to 18.1 per cent; and for anything than less than £2m from 23.6 per cent to a punitive 37.3 per cent.

Part of the reason for the increase in costs is the growing number of companies joining Aim from overseas.

Only recently, as last week's column pointed out, have nomads started to employ private investigation firms almost as a matter of course when dealing with clients from emerging markets.

The survey was also carried out well before the launch of the London Stock Exchange's first rule book for nomads.

The LSE might claim the rules are merely 'codification of best practice' – but nomads are well aware that part of the reason for their introduction is to enable the LSE to be more rigorous with disciplinary action. Due diligence practices will inevitably be more strictly applied, with a knock-on effect on fees.

It is therefore indicative of the growing importance of Aim that small companies are still prepared to bear the costs.

One of the latest is NetDimensions, a Hong Kong-based software publisher that is raising £3m through a placing and expects to have a market capitalisation of about £15m. The company provides the learning and performance management software used by global corporations to train their workforces.

Founded in 1999, the company has been profitable since 2003. Last year profits were $567,000 on sales of $3.5m (£1.8m). ...

Jay Shaw, NetDimensions founder and chief executive, cites as one of the main reasons for floating on Aim the ability to use 'the enhanced profile from being a public company to continue to increase our market share'. ...

'We had a bias towards floating in Hong Kong, but at the end of the day London won on everything,' said Mr Shaw.

He described the due diligence carried out as 'very thorough – they checked every single transacion over the past eight years. When I hear Aim described as a casino, I think – that's not the Aim we listed on.'

EXHIBIT 17.2

Source: *Financial Times* 27 April 2007, p. 21.

Roc Oil quits Aim in cost-cutting move

David Blackwell

Roc Oil is to cancel its quotation on Aim, reducing further the number of overseas companies traded on the junior market.

The company, which was already quoted on the Australian Stock Exchange, took a secondary listing on Aim in 2004 when the London Stock Exchange was wooing international companies. However, the share price has declined along with interest from UK investors, who hold just 6.5 per cent of the stock.

The board said: 'The costs incurred to administer the additional regulatory compliance requirements and to maintain the Aim quotation now exceed current and potential future benefits'. It expects the move to save more than A$200,000 (£104,000) a year.

The shares will be cancelled on Aim with effect from November 2. The company is retaining its Australian listing. ...

The latest statistics from Aim show that in August the total number of international companies quoted fell to 264, down 70 over the past 12 months. The total number of all companies was 1,365 at the end of last month, down from 1,626 a year ago. ...

EXHIBIT 17.3

Source: *Financial Times* 15 September 2009, p. 20.

The costs of new issues

There are three types of cost involved when a firm makes an issue of equity capital:

- administrative/transaction costs
- the equity cost of capital
- market pricing costs.

The first of these has already been discussed earlier in this chapter. For both the Main Market and AIM the costs as a proportion of the amount raised can be anywhere between 5 and 37 percent depending on the size of issue, and the method used (*see* Figure 17.4).

The second cost was discussed in more detail in Chapter 10. This relates to the investor's opportunity cost. By holding shares in one company shareholders give up the use of that money elsewhere. The firm therefore needs to produce a rate of return for those shareholders at least equal to the return they could obtain by investing in other shares of a similar risk class. Because ordinary shareholders face higher risks than debt or preference shareholders the rate of return demanded is higher. If the firm does not produce this return then shares will be sold and the firm will find raising capital difficult.

The market pricing cost is to do with the possibility of under-pricing new issues. It is a problem that particularly affects offers for sale at a fixed price and

FIGURE 17.4

Costs of new issues

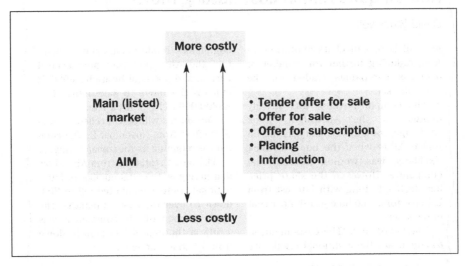

placings. The firm is usually keen to have the offer fully taken up by public investors. To have shares left with the underwriters gives the firm a bad image because it is perceived to have had an issue which 'flopped'. Furthermore, the underwriters, over the forthcoming months, will try to offload their shares and this action has the potential to depress the price for a long time. The sponsor also has an incentive to avoid leaving the underwriters with large blocks of shares. The sponsoring organisations consist of people who are professional analysts and dealmakers and an issue which flops can be very bad for their image. It might indicate that they are not reading the market signals correctly and that they have overestimated demand. They might have done a poor job in assessing the firm's riskiness or failed to communicate its virtues to investors. These bad images can stick, so both the firm and the sponsor have an incentive to err on the side of caution and price a little lower to make sure that the issue will be fully subscribed.[6] A major problem in establishing this discount is that in an offer for sale the firm has to decide the price two weeks before the close of the offer. In the period between Impact Day and first trading the market may decline dramatically. This makes potential investors nervous about committing themselves to a fixed price. To overcome this additional risk factor the issue price may have to be significantly less than the expected first day's trading price. Giving this discount to new shares deprives the firm of money which it might have received in the absence of these uncertainties, and can therefore be regarded as a cost.

> The sponsoring organizations consist of people who are professional analysts and dealmakers and an issue which flops can be very bad for their image.

In addition to the issue costs there are also high costs of maintaining a listing, running into hundreds of thousands or millions of pounds. Fees are paid to the corporate brokers, the stock exchange, lawyers, investment bankers, account-ants, PR companies and printers.

Recently the LSE has confused matters further for a company joining the Main Market. The company can either select a 'premium' listing (the full regula-tions that we are used to) or a less strict 'standard' listing – *see* Exhibit 17.4.

FSA grants 'light touch' to British LSE listings

Pan Kwan Yuk

British companies will be allowed to list on the London Stock Exchange using a 'light touch' set of rules previously available only to overseas companies as the UK seeks to bolster the City's posi-tion as a financial centre. ...

UK-based companies could formerly only list shares in London by a 'primary' listing that requires them to comply with more stringent rules including issues such as capital raising, disclosure of a record and board composition.

By contrast, overseas companies – which the LSE aggressively courted in the boom years – can list their shares through a 'secondary' listing that does not require them to respect pre-emption rights or to adhere to the combined code on corporate governance. [UK Corporate Governance Code]

Under the changes approved by the FSA's board late on Friday, UK compa-nies, beginning on October 6, can access this two-tier listing system and choose between a 'premium' or less onerous 'standard' listing. ...

Louise Wolfson, a partner at Allen & Overy, the law firm, said: 'I think you will probably end up with something that is slightly more regulated than Aim but not as regulated as a full listing is at the moment.'

She dismissed suggestions the changes were a sign the City was promoting lighter regulation. 'I see it as a positive development because there will be much more transparency about what standards apply to each type of listing,' she said.

'By having these two segments, investors should have a clearer under-standing what rules the companies they bought had to follow.'

The FSA said the effect of the amendments would be to 'simplify the process for companies with equity list-ings wishing to move from one segment to another by clarifying that a cancella-tion of their listings is not required'.

The LSE said it did not expect a deluge of UK companies to take advan-tage of the second-tier listing.

'The reality is that very few UK com-panies will want to go for the standard listing because it's seen as a lesser list-ing,' it said.

But the Exchange acknowledged the changes could make London a more attractive place.

EXHIBIT 17.4

Source: *Financial Times* 28 September 2009, p. 20.

Rights issues

A rights issue is an invitation to existing shareholders to purchase additional shares in the company. This is a very popular method of raising new funds. It is easy and relatively cheap (compared with new issues). Directors are not required to seek the prior consent of shareholders,[7] and the London Stock Exchange will only intervene in larger issues (to adjust the timing so that the market does not suffer from too many issues in one period). The UK has particularly strong traditions and laws concerning *pre-emption rights*. These require that a company raising new equity capital by selling shares first offers those shares to the existing shareholders. The owners of the company are entitled to subscribe for the new shares in proportion to their existing holding. This will enable them to maintain the existing percentage ownership of the company – the only difference is that each slice of the company cake is bigger because it has more financial resources under its control.

The shares are usually offered at a significantly discounted price from the trading price of the company's current shares – typically 10–40 percent. This gives the illusion that shareholders are getting a bargain. But, as we shall see, the benefit from the discount given is taken away by a decline in value of the old shares.

Shareholders can either buy these shares themselves or sell the 'right' to buy to another investor. For further reassurance that the firm will raise the anticipated finance, rights issues are usually underwritten by institutions.

An example

Take the case of the imaginary listed company Swell plc with 100 million shares in issue. It wants to raise £25m for expansion but does not want to borrow it. Given that its existing shares are quoted on the stock market at 120p, the new rights shares will have to be issued at a lower price to appeal to shareholders because there is a risk of the market share price falling in the period between the announcement and the purchasing of new shares. (The offer must remain open for at least two weeks (10 working days)). Swell has decided that the £25m will be obtained by issuing 25 million shares at 100p each. Thus the ratio of new shares to old is 25:100. In other words, this issue is a 'one-for-four' rights issue. Each shareholder will be offered one new share for every four already held.

If the market price before the rights issue is 120p valuing the entire company at £120m and another £25m is pumped into the company by selling 25 million shares at £1, it logically follows that the market price after the rights issue can not remain at 120p (assuming all else equal). A company that was previously valued at £120m which then adds £25m of value to itself (in form of cash) should be worth £145m. This company now has 125 million shares therefore each share is worth £1.16 (i.e. £145m divided by 125 million shares).

$$\frac{\text{Total market capitalization}}{\text{Total shares available}} = \frac{£145m}{125m} = £1.16$$

An alternative way of calculating the ex-rights price is as follows:

Four existing shares at a price of 120p	480p
One new share for cash at 100p	100p
Value of five shares	580p
Value of one share ex-rights 580p/5	116p

The shareholders have experienced a decline in the price of their old shares from 120p to 116p. A fall of this magnitude necessarily follows from the introduction of new shares at a discounted price. However the loss is exactly offset by the gain in share value on the new rights issue shares. They cost 100p but have a market price of 116p. This can be illustrated through the example of Sid, who owned 100 shares worth £120 prior to the rights announcement. Sid loses £4 on the old shares – their value is now £116. However he makes a gain of £4 on the new shares.

Cost of rights shares (25 × £1)	£25
Ex-rights value (25 × 1.16)	£29
Gain	£4

When the press talks glibly of a rights offer being 'very attractively priced for shareholders' they are generally talking nonsense. Whatever the size of the discount the same value will be removed from the old shares to leave the shareholder no worse or better off. Logically value cannot be handed over to the shareholders from the size of the discount decision. Shareholders own all the company's shares before and after the rights issue – they cannot hand value to themselves without also taking value from themselves. Of course, if the prospects for the company's profits rise because it can now make brilliant capital expenditures, which lead to dominant market positions, then the value of shares will rise – for both the old and the new shares. But this is value creation that has nothing to do with the level of the discount.

What if a shareholder does not want to take up the rights?

As owners of the firm all shareholders must be treated in the same way. To make sure that some shareholders do not lose out because they are unwilling or unable to buy more shares the law requires that shareholders have a third choice, other than to buy or not buy the new shares. This is to sell the rights on to someone else on the stock market (selling the rights nil paid). Take the case of impoverished Sid, who is unable to find the necessary £25. He could sell the rights to subscribe for the shares to another investor and not have to go through the process of taking up any of the shares himself. Indeed, so deeply enshrined are pre-emption rights that even if the shareholder does nothing the company will sell his rights to the new shares on his behalf and send the proceeds to him.[8] Thus, Sid would benefit to the extent of 16p per share or a total of £4 (if the market price stays constant) which adequately compensates for the loss on the 100 shares he holds. But the extent of his control over the company has been reduced – his percentage share of the votes has decreased.

The value of a right on one new share is:

$$\text{Theoretical market value of share ex-rights} - \text{Subscription price}$$
$$= 116p - 100p = 16p$$

The value of a right on one old share in Swell is:

$$\frac{\text{Theoretical market value of share ex-rights} - \text{Subscription price}}{\text{No. of old shares required to purchase one new share}}$$

$$= \frac{116 - 100}{4} = 4p$$

Exhibit 17.5 decribes Lloyds rights issue designed to rescue it from its disastrous purchase of HBOS.

Success expected for Lloyds rights issue

Sharlene Goff

The world's largest rights issue got off the ground as Lloyds Banking Group set the pricing for £13.5bn of new shares ahead of a crucial shareholder vote tomorrow at a meeting in Birmingham. ...

The capital raising is a milestone in the bank's convalescence since it was left seriously wounded by its hasty purchase of HBOS at the height of the financial crisis a year ago. ...

Investors, who are being offered 1.34 new shares for each existing one they own at 37p a share, are expected to vote in favour and, bar a small percentage of the bank's vast private shareholder base, are set to take up their rights over the next fortnight.

The price of the new shares works out at a 39 per cent discount to the so-called theoretical ex-rights price, which takes into account the dilutive effect of the issue on the bank's overall market capitalisation. ...

The rights issue is fully underwritten by an array of investment banks and

Lloyds has been sounding out its leading investors for weeks to be confident of their support.

Advisers believe that only about 5 per cent of the new shares will not be taken up, largely those belonging to some of Lloyds' 2.8m retail shareholders, including about 1m ex-HBOS investors. ...

Lloyds Banking

Rights issue

Issue price	37p
Discount to closing price on Nov 23 2009	59.5%
Discount to theoretical ex-rights price	38.6%
New shares for each existing share	1.34
Rights issue proceeds	£13.5bn

Since Lloyds announced the capital raising three weeks ago its shares have risen 10 per cent and yesterday closed up 2.34p at 93.8p. Providing that investors approve the fundraising tomorrow they will have two weeks in which they can trade their rights in the market before the new shares start trading on December 14. ...

Q&A

What's happening?

Lloyds is asking its 2.8m shareholders – the biggest investor base of any UK company – to pay 37p for new shares, a discount of about 60 per cent to the current market price.

Existing investors, including ex-HBOS holders, can buy just over four discounted shares for every three they already hold: a ratio of 1.34 per existing share. The offer will run until December 11.

What are the options?

To buy the new shares investors will need to find cash equivalent to just over half the value of their holdings. For the average private shareholder with 740 shares, taking up a full entitlement of 991 shares would cost £366.67.

Or they could sell their 'rights', with dealings in these entitlements to start on Friday. If investors do nothing, their rights will lapse and will be sold by the bank on their behalf.

Cashless take-up, or 'tail swallowing', is another option. This involves selling sufficient rights to fund a take-up of some new shares, without putting up extra cash.

EXHIBIT 17.5

Source: *Financial Times* 25 November 2009, p. 19.

Ex-rights and cum-rights

Shares bought in the stock market designated cum-rights carry with them to the new owner the right to subscribe for the new shares in the rights issue. After a cut-off date the shares go ex-rights, which means that any purchaser of old shares will not have the right to purchase the new shares; they remain with the former shareholder.

The price discount decision

It does not matter greatly whether Swell raises £25m on a one-for-four basis at 100p or on a one-for-three basis at 75p per share, or on some other basis (*see* Table 17.1).

TABLE 17.1

Comparison of different rights bases

Rights basis	Number of new shares (m)	Price of new shares (p)	Total raised (£m)
1 for 4	25	100	25
1 for 3	33.3	75	25
1 for 2	50	50	25
1 for 1	100	25	25

As Table 17.1 shows, whatever the basis of the rights issue, the company will receive £25m and the shareholders will see the price of their old shares decrease, but this will be exactly offset by the value of the rights on the new shares. However, the ex-rights price will change. For a one-for-three basis it will be £108.75:

Three shares at 120p	360p
One share at 75p	75p
Value of four shares	435p
Value of one share (435/4)	108.75p

If Swell chose the one-for-one basis this would be regarded as a *deep-discounted rights issue* (similar to Lloyds rights issue – *see* Exhibit 17.5). With an issue of this sort there is only a minute probability that the market price will fall below the rights offer price and therefore there is almost complete certainty that the offer will be taken up. It seems reasonable to suggest that the under-writing service provided by the institutions is largely redundant here and that the firm can make a significant saving. Yet 95 percent of all rights issues are underwritten, usually involving between 100 and 400 sub-underwriters. The underwriting fees used to be a flat 2 percent of the offer. Of this the issuing house received 0.5 per cent, the broker received 0.25 percent and the sub-underwriter 1.25 percent (the same distribution as in a new issue). However, fees have risen recently and are typically 4 per cent – *see* Exhibit 17.6.

Moves to cut cost of equity underwriting

Kate Burgess

Wanted: one small or mid-sized company urgently in need of money.

A group of influential investors is working on plans to cut out the investment banks that advise companies on raising fresh funds by issuing new shares.

All they need is a company willing to act as a guinea pig to practise on.

The investors involved in the embryonic scheme include M&G, Legal & General and Standard Life. They are being aided by Lazard, a mergers and acquisitions adviser.

The idea of the collaboration is to set up an informal club of well-capitalised institutional shareholders who could ensure that companies get the money they need but at a lower price than banks charge for providing the same assurances.

This group would promise executives that they would mop up all the unwanted new shares in a rights issue, thereby minimising the costs that are borne by companies and their investors.

The club is the latest initiative by investors angry at high fees charged by banks acting as intermediaries.

'It would only need one company keen to do a rights issue to push on the fault lines in the system,' says one company executive and former banker. Companies 'need a wider tool kit' for raising money.

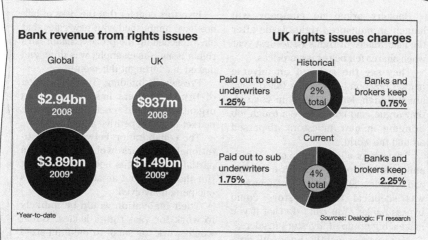

Bank revenue from rights issues

Global

$2.94bn
2008

$3.89bn
2009*

UK

$937m
2008

$1.49bn
2009*

*Year-to-date

UK rights issues charges

Historical

Paid out to sub underwriters
1.25%

2% total

Banks and brokers keep
0.75%

Current

Paid out to sub underwriters
1.75%

4% total

Banks and brokers keep
2.25%

Sources: Dealogic: FT research

The move may not go down well at the banks. UK rights issues have generated $1.5bn (£920m) in revenue for investment banks, according to Dealogic, compared with $84m (£51m) two years ago. Globally, banks have earned $4bn this year from rights issues, helping many to offset the write downs of 2008.

Nonetheless, disquiet over fees is growing alongside the ever-closer scrutiny by regulators and politicians of bankers' rewards.

Last month Lord Myners, UK city minister, highlighted equity underwriting as an area 'where market discipline doesn't appear to function at the heart of markets'.

He added: 'The primary responsibility for achieving rational outcomes lies with directors and shareholders. They need to explain why they are not pressing much harder, for instance, on fees at M&A or the costs of underwriting.' ...

'Investors want a different, fairer, system which doesn't gouge the company,' says one banker, pointing out that fees directly impact investor returns.

The UK's system of raising money through rights issues has evolved over centuries. Historically, companies would issue new shares at discounts of say, about 15 per cent to existing shares, giving holders tradeable rights to first refusal on new shares.

Prior to the launch of an issue, bankers would guarantee executives to make sure all new shares would be bought even if they had to buy the shares themselves. In exchange, the banks were paid a standard 'underwriting' fee of 2 per cent of the money raised. But they paid the bulk – 1.25 per cent – to investors who 'sub-underwrote' issues promising to take up all unwanted shares even if share prices fell over the next month while shareholders decided whether or not to take up their rights. Another 0.25 per cent went to brokers for arranging the sub-underwriting, leaving the banks 0.5 per cent.

But in the past couple of years the average price of underwriting has almost doubled. Banks charge on average 3.5 per cent to 4 per cent and they keep at least half for themselves, paying just 1.75 per cent to sub-underwriters. Big issue may cost loss.

'What sticks in the craw of the big investors is that banks take most of the fees by lay off most of the risk of a flop by establishing well in advance what investors will take,' says one would-be reformer.

In addition, he says, new shares are being issued at wide discounts of 40 per cent or more but companies still pay for issues to be underwritten.

Bankers argue no company will launch an uninsured rights issue after the near failure of rights issues last year when shares fell below issue prices.

They say the risks of an adverse market reaction leading to a failed issue are still high. Markets remain volatile, they argue, and banks have a tough job bringing in new investors dispersed around the world.

'Issuers put a lot of value on a bank's ability to secure a transaction quickly and confidentially,' says one banker who was sceptical that investors could bypass banks. 'You can't do that if you make a big group of investors insiders.'

Moreover, recently imposed constraints on shorting shares during rights issues make it harder for banks to offset risk.

Investors counter that the risks of failure have diminished with new rules that have speeded up the process. Ladbroke's rights issue, for example, was done and dusted in a fortnight this month.

Pressure is building. The Association of British Insurers has called for an urgent review of costs arguing the market is uncompetitive and opaque.

The collaboration between the institutional investors would only be a partial answer. 'It is not a replacement [for the banks] but an alternative,' says one person involved.

Their innovation would be unlikely to work for vast rights issues. But it would work for small to medium-sized companies with a core of well-capitalised shareholders. All investors need is the right company to put the idea into practice.

EXHIBIT 17.6

Source: *Financial Times* 26 October 2009, p. 23.

Other equity issues

Some companies argue that the lengthy procedures and expense associated with rights issues (e.g. the time and trouble it takes to get a prospectus prepared and approved by the UKLA) frustrate directors' efforts to take advantage of opportunities in a timely fashion. Firms in the USA have much more freedom to bypass pre-emption rights. They are able to sell blocks of shares to securities houses for distribution elsewhere in the market. This is fast. If this were permitted in the UK, there would be a concern for existing shareholders: they could experience a dilution of their voting power and/or the share could be sold at such a low price that a portion of the firm is handed over to new shareholders too cheaply.

The UK authorities have produced a compromise under which firms must obtain shareholders' approval through a special resolution (a majority of 75 percent of those voting) at the company's annual general meeting or at an extraordinary general meeting to waive the pre-emption right. Even then the shares must not be sold to outside investors at more than a 5 or 10 percent discount to the share price. While the maximum discount for Main Market companies under the listing rules is 10 percent, the Association of British Insurers' (as representatives of

> The shares must not be sold to outside investors at more than a 5 or 10 percent discount to the share price.

investors) guidelines are for a maximum of 5 percent. This is an important condition. It does not make any difference to existing shareholders if new shares are offered at a deep discount to the market price as long as they are offered to them. If external investors get a discount there is a transfer of value from the current shareholders to the new.

Placings and open offers

In placings, new shares are sold directly to a narrow group of external investors. Placings are usually structured so that a prospectus is not required, so this saves money. They can also be completed in a matter of days rather than weeks or months for a rights issue. The institutions, wearing their hat of existing shareholders, have produced guidelines to prevent abuse, which normally only allow a placing of a small proportion of the company's capital (a maximum of 5 percent in a single year and no more than 7.5 percent is to be added to the company's equity capital over a rolling three-year period)[9] in the absence of a *claw back*. Under claw back existing shareholders have the right to reclaim the shares as though they were entitled to them under a rights issue. They can

> With a claw back the issue becomes an 'open offer'.

buy them at the price they were offered to the external investors. With a claw back the issue becomes an 'open offer'. Under an open offer companies can increase their share capital by between 15 percent and 18 percent. Beyond that the investors (e.g. Association of British Insurers) prefer a rights issue. The major difference compared with a rights issue is that if they do not exercise this claw back right current shareholders receive no compensation for a reduction in the price of their existing shares – there are no nil-paid rights to sell.

The Association of British Insurers has indicated that they prefer for a company to select a rights issue rather than an open offer if the discount is greater than 7.5 percent. However, the regulations on the Main Market state a cut-off at 10 percent (this does not apply to AIM companies), but the investor groups encouraged AIM companies to apply the same restrictions. Exhibit 17.7 discusses the problems with clawback.

Acquisition for shares

Shares are often issued to purchase businesses or assets. This is usually subject to shareholder approval.

Vendor placing

If a company wishes to pay for an asset such as a subsidiary of another firm or an entire company with newly issued shares, but the vendor(s) does not want to hold the shares, the purchaser could arrange for the new shares to be bought by institutional investors for cash. In this way the buyer gets the asset, the vendors (for example shareholders in the target company in a merger or takeover)

Housebuilder succumbs to risk factor

Brooke Masters and Kate Burgess

Taylor Wimpey's failure to find investors willing to back its capital-raising plan points to the risks associated with an open offer of shares with a clawback.

As a method of raising equity capital, clawbacks are a bit of a 'Goldilocks solution', combining a placement of discounted shares with a few large investors and a 'clawback' right that allows existing investors to buy in at the same price.

As a result, clawbacks provide some of the speed and cost savings of a US-style private placement while preserving some of the 'pre-emption' rights against dilution that UK institutional investors hold clear.

In normal markets, clawbacks are usually shunted aside in favour of rights issues, which are even more protective of existing shareholders. But after the HBOS rights issue came under attack from short-sellers this spring, clawbacks started looking more attractive.

Clawbacks can be done more quickly than rights issues because the shareholder notice period can run simultaneously to the offer. This structure can also cost less in fees for the company involved if the strategic investors serve as the *de facto* underwriters.

Michael McKersie of the Association of British Insurers says an open offer with a clawback is less attractive for those shareholders unable or unwilling to participate, because, unlike in a rights issue, they do not receive compensation.

'But it might be the most efficient way to structure the issue from the perspective of a company and its shareholders in certain unusual circumstances,' he adds.

After Barclays raised money this way, Taylor Wimpey and one of the bidders for Bradford & Bingley talked about going down the same route. But clawbacks have turned out to be hard to pull off.

These deals can only work if the company in question can convince one or several large investors to back the offer and take all the shares that current shareholders decline to clawback.

Without these 'anchor tenants' the deal cannot go through and today's markets are making many big investors wary.

Unlike a rights issue, which can be deeply discounted, Financial Services Authority rules and ABI recommendations limit both the size and relative price of an open offer. That makes the deal even riskier for the strategic investors.

'The size has to be right and you have to be able to place with institutions subject to clawback,' says Andrew Ballheimer, managing partner of the corporate department at Allen & Overy, a law firm. 'A perfect storm has to be there,' he adds. ...

EXHIBIT 17.7

Source: *Financial Times* 3 July 2008, p. 4.

receive cash and the institutional investor makes an investment. There is usually a claw back arrangement for a vendor placing (if the issue is more than 10 percent of market capitalisation of the acquirer). Again the price discount can be no more than 5 or 10 percent of the current share price.

Bought deal

Instead of selling shares to investors companies are sometimes able to make an arrangement with a securities house whereby it buys all the shares being offered for cash. The securities house then sells the shares on to investors included in its distribution network, hoping to make a profit on the deal. Securities houses often compete to buy a package of shares from the company, with the highest bidder winning. The securities house takes the risk of being unable to sell the shares for at least the amount that they paid. Given that some of these bought deals are for over £100m, these securities houses need substantial capital backing. Bought deals are limited by the 5 or 10 percent pre-emption rules.

Scrip issues

Scrip issues do not raise new money: a company simply gives shareholders more shares in proportion to their existing holdings. The value of each shareholding does not change, because the share price drops in proportion to the additional shares. They are also known as capitalisation issues or bonus issues. The purpose is to make shares more attractive by bringing down the price. British investors are thought to consider a share price of £10 and above as less marketable than one in single figures. So a company with shares trading at £15 on the Exchange

> British investors are thought to consider a share price of £10 and above as less marketable than one in single figures.

might distribute two 'free' shares for every one held – a two-for-one scrip issue. Since the amount of money in the firm and its economic potential is constant the share price will theoretically fall to £5.[10]

A number of companies have an annual scrip issue while maintaining a constant dividend per share, effectively raising the level of profit distribution. For example, if a company pays a regular dividend of 20p per share but also has a one-for-ten scrip, the annual income will go up by 10 percent. (A holder of ten shares who previously received 200p now receives 220p on a holding of 11 shares.) Scrip issues are often regarded as indicating

> Scrip issues are often regarded as indicating confidence in future earnings increases.

confidence in future earnings increases. If this new optimism is expressed in the share price it may not fall as much as theory would suggest. However, many people are sceptical about there being any benefit from scrips and wary about the transaction costs.

Scrip dividends are slightly different: shareholders are offered a choice between receiving a cash dividend or receiving additional shares. This is more like a rights issue because the shareholders are making a cash sacrifice if they accept the scrip shares. With scrip dividends companies are able to raise additional equity capital (by not paying a cash dividend) without the expense of a rights issue; shareholders can add to their holding without paying a stockbroker's commission.

A *share split* (stock split) means that the nominal value of each share is reduced in proportion to the increase in the number of shares, so the total book value of shares remains the same. So, for example, a company may have one million shares in issue with a nominal value of 50p each. It issues a further one million shares to existing shareholders with the nominal value of each share reducing to 25p, but total nominal value remains at £500,000. Of course, the share price will halve – assuming all else is constant.

Warrants

Warrants give the holder the right to subscribe for a specified number of shares at a fixed price during or at the end of a specified time period. If a company has shares currently trading at £3 it might choose to sell warrants, each of which grants the holder the right to buy a share at, say, £4 in five years. If by the fifth year the share price has risen to £6 the warrant holders could exercise their rights and then sell the shares immediately, realizing £2 per share, which is likely to be a considerable return on the original warrant price of a few pence. Warrants are frequently attached to bonds, and make the bond more attractive because the investor benefits from a relatively safe (but low) income on the bond if the firm performs in a mediocre fashion, but if the firm does very well and the share price rises significantly the investor will participate in some of the extra returns through the 'sweetener' or 'equity kicker' provided by the warrant.

Equity finance for unquoted firms

We have looked at some of the details of raising money on the Stock Exchange. In the commercial world there are thousands of companies that do not have access to the Exchange. We now consider a few of the ways that unquoted firms can raise equity capital.

Business angels (informal venture capitalists)

Business angels are wealthy individuals, generally with substantial business and entrepreneurial experience, who usually invest between £10,000 and £250,000 primarily in start-up, early stage or expanding firms. About three-quarters of business angel investments are for sums of less than £100,000 with the average investment around £25,000–£30,000. The majority of investments are in the form of equity finance but angels do purchase debt instruments and preference shares. These companies will be years away from obtaining a market quotation for their shares or being advanced enough for a sale to other companies or investors, so in becoming a business angel the investor accepts that it

> Business angels are wealthy individuals, generally with substantial business and entrepreneurial experience.

may be difficult to dispose of their shares even if the company is progressing nicely. They also accept a relatively high degree of risk of complete failure – which happens in about one in three cases. But the upside, if all goes well, can be tremendous. Investors putting just a few thousand pounds in a small company have become very wealthy following the firm's flotation, or when it is sold to another company. The angels that put €2m into Skype multiplied their money by 350 times when the company was sold to eBay for €2.1 billion.

They usually do not have a controlling shareholding and they are willing to invest at an earlier stage than most formal venture capitalists. (They often dislike the term business angel, preferring the title informal venture capitalist).

> Business angels prefer the title informal venture capitalist.

They are generally looking for entrepreneurial companies with high aspirations and potential for growth. A typical business angel makes one or two investments in a three-year period, often in an investment syndicate (with an 'archangel' leading the group). They generally invest in companies within a reasonable travelling distance from their homes because most like to be 'hands-on' investors, playing a significant role in strategy and management – on average angels allocate ten hours a week to their investments. Most angels take a seat on the board.[11] Business angels are patient investors willing to hold their investment for at least a five-year period.

The main way in which firms and angels find each other is through friends and business associates, although there are a number of formal networks. *See* British Private Equity and Venture Capital Association at www.bvca.co.uk for a list of networks. Other useful contacts: Angel Bourse, www.angelbourse.com; Beer & Partners www.beerandpartners.com; Entrust, www.entrust.co.uk; Department for Business, Enterprise and Regulatory Reform, www.berr.gov.uk; and British Business Angels Association, www.bbaa.org.uk.

There are hundreds of groups of business angels throughout Europe.

Angel network events are organised where entrepreneurs can make a pitch to potential investors, who, if they like what they hear in response to their questions, may put in tens of thousands of pounds. Prior to the event the network organisers (or a member) generally screen the business opportunities to avoid time wasting by the no-hopers. To be a member of a network investors are expected to either earn at least £100,000 per year or have a net worth of at least £250,000 (excluding main residence). If you have a specialist skill to offer, for example you are an experienced company director or chartered accountant, you may be permitted membership despite a lower income or net worth.

Many business angel deals are structured to take advantage of tax breaks such as those through enterprise investment schemes, EIS, which offer tax relief – see later in this chapter. The economic downturn may have decreased the supply of business angel money to entrepreneurial businesses – *see* Exhibit 17.8.

Urgent call for more 'lead' angels

Jonathan Moules

Budding start-ups are being held back because the UK does not have enough of the right kind of business angel investor, an industry body has warned.

The British Business Angel Association (BBAA) this week launched a campaign to find wealthy individuals to invest in start-ups and support the founders through the development of these ventures.

These 'lead' investors are desperately needed as demand for angel funding is rising from start-ups but many existing angel investors find themselves less able to back new businesses because their personal fortunes have been hit by the recession, the BBAA claimed.

Anthony Clarke, BBAA chairman, said the downturn may increase the number of people willing to take a lead angel role because returns from property, equities and savings are so poor. 'We know there are people out there with both the wealth and industry knowledge to become effective angel investors,' he said, adding that accountants and private bankers would make ideal candidates.

A recent report by the National Endowment for Science, Technology and the Arts found that business angel investing was risky but on average generated returns of 2.2 times the capital invested in just under four years.

However, this return is not evenly spread, with 9 per cent of investments generating 80 per cent of the positive cash flows and the majority ending in failure.

Tom Flynn says he became a business angel by accident after being invited to an investor meeting by a friend two years ago. 'People are not really aware it's there,' he said.

But not everyone agrees with the BBAA's assessment. Angels Den, which brings together business founders and investors, receives up to 700 inquiries a month from people wishing to put money into start-ups.

Bill Morrow, Angels Den's co-founder, said: 'If you have got £400,000 in the bank, you need to do something with it. We are finding people coming to angel funding because what else are you going to do?'

He describes the new breed of business angel as the 'pinstripe brigade' of professional advisers from the City, who have suffered a sharp fall in their personal wealth from other investments because of the economic downturn.

Another trend is people investing in businesses and charging for their advice. Morrow said: 'They are putting in £200,000, the charging the company £2,000 a month for consultancy.'

Michelson Diagnostics is one of the fortunate start-ups that secured angel funding before the credit crunch. Its five founders began the business three years ago after being made redundant from the same engineering firm. They now have more than 50 investors, including venture capital (VC) firms, friends and business angels.

Martin Johns, operations director, said: 'Raising the money was nervewracking as we weren't sure how to do it, but it is easier to pitch to an angel than a VC.'

EXHIBIT 17.8

Source: *Financial Times* 30 May 2009, p. 32.

Private equity/venture capital

The distinction between venture capital and private equity is blurry. Some people use 'private equity' to define all unquoted company equity investment; others confine 'private equity' to management buy-outs and the like of companies already well established, leaving 'venture capital' for investment in companies at an early stage of development with high growth potential. Venture capital is a medium- to long-term investment and can consist of a package of debt and equity finance. Venture capitalists take high risks by investing in the equity of young companies often with a limited (or no) track record. Many of their investments are into little more than a management team with a good idea – which may not have started selling a product or even developed a prototype. It is believed, as a rule of thumb in the venture capital industry, that out of ten investments two will fail completely, two will perform excellently and the remaining six will range from poor to very good.

> Out of ten investments two will fail completely, two will perform excellently.

High risk goes with high return. Venture capitalists expect to get a return of between five and ten times their initial equity investment in about five to seven years. This means that the firms receiving the equity finance are expected to produce annual returns for investors of at least 26 percent. Alongside the usual drawbacks of equity capital from the investors' viewpoint (last in the queue for income and on liquidation, etc.), investors in small unquoted companies also suffer from a lack of liquidity because the shares are not quoted on a public exchange. There are a number of different types of venture capital (although these days the last three will often be separated from VC and grouped under the title 'private equity' – *see* private equity section later in this chapter):

- **Seedcorn** This is financing to allow the development of a business concept. Development may also involve expenditure on the production of prototypes and additional research.

- **Start-up** A product or idea is further developed, and/or initial marketing is carried out. Companies are very young and have not yet sold their product commercially.

- **Other early-stage** Funds for initial commercial manufacturing and sales. Many companies at this stage will remain unprofitable.

- **Expansion (development)** Companies at this stage are on to a fast-growth track and need capital to fund increased production capacity, working capital and for the further development of the product or market. Professor Steve Young's company Entropic (*see* Case study 17.1 at the beginning of the chapter) provides an example of this.

- **Management buyouts (MBO)** Here a team of managers make an offer to their employers to buy a whole business, a subsidiary or a section so that they own and run it for themselves. Large companies are often willing to sell to these teams, particularly if the business is under-performing and does not fit with the strategic core business. Usually the management team have limited funds of their own and so call on venture capitalists to provide the bulk of the finance.

■ **Management buy-ins (MBI)** A new team of managers from outside an existing business buy a stake, usually backed by a venture capital fund. A combination of an MBO and MBI is called a BIMBO – buy-in management buyout – where a new group of managers join forces with an existing team to acquire a business.

> A combination of an MBO and MBI is called a BIMBO – buy-in management buy-out.

■ **Public-to-private (PTP)** The management of a company currently quoted on a stock exchange may return it to unquoted status with the assistance of venture capital finance being used to buy the shares.

Private equity (PE) firms are less keen on financing seedcorn, start-ups and other early-stage companies than expansions, MBOs, MBIs and PTPs. This is largely due to the very high risk associated with early-stage ventures and the disproportionate time and costs of financing smaller deals. To make it worthwhile for a VC organization to consider a company the investment must be at least £250,000 – the average investment is about £5m – and it is difficult to find venture capitalists willing to invest less than £2m.

Because of the greater risks associated with the youngest companies, the VC funds may require returns of the order of 50–80 percent per annum. For well-established companies with a proven product and battle-hardened and respected management the returns required may drop to the high 20s. These returns may seem exorbitant, especially to the managers set the task of achieving them, but they have to be viewed in the light of the fact that many VC investments will turn out to be failures and so the overall performance of the VC funds is significantly less than these figures suggest.

There are a number of different types of PE/VC providers, although the boundaries are increasingly blurred as a number of funds now raise money from a variety of sources. The *independents* can be firms, funds or investment trusts, either quoted or private, which have raised their capital from more than one source. The main sources are pension and insurance funds, but banks, corporate investors and private individuals also put money into these PE/VC funds. *Captives* are funds managed on behalf of a parent institution (banks, pension funds, etc.). *Semi-captives* invest funds on behalf of parent and also manage independently raised funds.

For the larger investments, particularly MBOs and MBIs, the venture capitalist may provide only a fraction of the total funds required. Thus, in a £50m buyout the venture capitalist might supply (individually or in a syndicate with other PE funds), say, £15m in the form of share capital (ordinary and preference shares). Another £20m may come from a group of banks in the form of debt finance. The remainder may be supplied as mezzanine debt – high-return and high-risk debt which usually has some rights to share in the spoils should the company perform exceptionally well (*see* Chapter 16). In the case of the management buy out of the British company called UniPoly, of the £620m that was needed to buy the company and provide it with capital for expansion, 28 percent was equity, 64 percent bank debt (28 banks) and 8 percent mezzanine finance (eight lenders).

Private equity firms generally like to have a clear target set as the eventual 'exit' (or 'take-out') date. This is the point at which the private equity fund can recoup some or all of the investment. Many exits are achieved by a sale of the company to another firm ('trade sale' or 'corporate acquisition'), but a popular method is a flotation on a stock market. Alternative exit routes are for the company to repurchase its shares or for the venture capitalist to sell the holding to an institution such as an investment trust or another private equity group (a 'secondary buyout' or 'secondary sale').

Private equity funds are rarely looking for a controlling shareholding in a company and are often content with a 20 or 30 percent share.[12] They may also supply funds through the purchase of convertible preference (or preferred) shares which give them rights to convert to ordinary shares – which will boost their equity holding and increase the return if the firm performs well. They may also insist, in an initial investment agreement, on some widespread powers. For instance, the company may need to gain the private equity/venture capitalist's approval for the issue of further securities, and they may hold a veto over acquisition of other companies. Even though their equity holding is generally less than 50 percent, the private equity funds frequently have special rights to appoint a number of directors. If specific negative events happen, such as a poor performance, they may have the right to appoint most of the board of directors and therefore take effective control. More than once the founding entrepreneur has been aggrieved to find himself/herself removed from power. (Despite the loss of power, they often have a large shareholding in what has grown to be a multi-million pound company.) They are often sufficiently upset to refer to the fund which separated them from their creation as 'vulture capitalist'. But this is to focus on the dark side. When everything goes well, we have, as they say in the business jargon, 'a win-win-win situation': the company receives vital capital to grow fast, the venture capitalist receives a high return and society gains new products and economic progress.

> Private equity funds frequently have special rights to appoint a number of directors.

The private equity firm can help a company with more than money. They usually have a wealth of experience and talented people able to assist the budding entrepreneur. Many of the UK's most noteworthy companies were helped by the PE/VC industry, for example Waterstones bookshops, Oxford Instruments (and in America: Google, Apple computers, Sun Microsystems, Netscape, Lotus, Compaq and most of Silicon Valley).

Private equity categories

With the growth of share investment outside of stock markets private equity has become more differentiated. The main categories are shown in Figure 17.5. The title overarching all these activities is private equity. Private equity is defined as medium- to long-term finance provided in return for an equity stake in potentially high growth unquoted companies. In this more differentiated setting the term venture capital is generally confined to describing the building of companies from the ground floor, or at least from a very low base. Management buyouts and buy-ins of established businesses (already off the ground floor) have become specialist tasks, with a number of dedicated funds.

> The disadvantage of PEITs is the absence of tax benefits.

Many of these funds have been formed as private partnerships by wealthy individuals, a high proportion of which are American owned. However, funds still conduct traditional VC business and MBOs and MBIs. They are frequently classified as Private Equity Investment Trusts (PEITs), which means they are stock market quoted companies with the objective of investing their shareholders' money in unquoted developing companies. The disadvantage of PEITs is the absence of tax benefits. This is where the Venture Capital Trusts (VCTs) and the Enterprise Investment Scheme (EIS) come in. They both offer significant tax breaks to investors in small unquoted companies. Finally, some funds have specialised in providing financial and professional support to quoted companies that wish to leave the stock market – public-to-private deals.

Venture capital trusts (VCTs)

It is important to distinguish between venture capital trusts, investment vehicles designed to encourage investment in small and fast-growing companies which have important tax breaks, and two other types of venture capital organisation: Private Equity Investment Trusts (PEITs), which are standard investment trusts with a focus on more risky developing companies, and venture capital funds (described above).

FIGURE 17.5
Private equity and its component parts

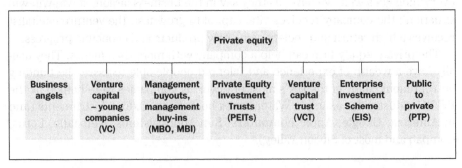

There are tax breaks for investors putting money into VCTs. There is an imme-diate relief on their current year's income at 30 percent (by putting £10,000 into a VCT an investor will pay £3,000 less tax, so the effective cost is only £7,000). The returns (income and capital gains) on a VCT are free of tax for investments. Investors can place up to £200,000 each per year in VCTs. These benefits are only available to investors buying new VCT shares (not VCT shares bought from other investors in the secondary market) who hold the investment for five years. The VCT managers can only invest in companies worth less than £7m and the maxi-mum amount a VCT is allowed to put into each unquoted company's shares is limited to £1m per year. ('Unquoted' for VCT is used rather loosely and includes AIM companies.) A maximum of 15 percent of the VCT fund can be invested in any one company. VCTs are quoted on the London Stock Exchange.

Enterprise Investment Scheme (EIS)

Another government initiative to encourage the flow of risk capital to smaller companies is the Enterprise Investment Scheme. Income tax relief is available for investments of up to £500,000 made directly into qualifying company shares. Capital gains tax relief is available as well. 'Direct investment' means investing when the company issues shares. It does not mean buying in the secondary market from other investors. The tax benefits are lost if the investments are held for less than three years. To raise money from this source the firm must have been carrying out a 'qualifying activity' for three years – this generally excludes financial investment and property companies. The company must not be quoted on the Official List and the most it can raise under the EIS in any one year is usually £2m. The company must not have gross assets worth more than £7m. Funds which invest in a range of EIS companies are springing up to help investors spread risk.

> 'Direct investment' means investing when the company issues shares.

Corporate venturing and incubators

Larger companies sometimes foster the development of smaller enterprises. This can take numerous forms, from joint product development work to an injec-tion of equity finance. The small firm can retain its independence and yet contribute to the large firm: perhaps its greater freedom to innovate will gener-ate new products which the larger firm can exploit to the benefit of both. Intel uses corporate venturing to increase demand for its technology by, for example, investing in start-up companies in China. Nokia Venture Partners invests in start-up companies in the wireless internet industry. BT set up Brightstar to harvest value from its 14,000 patents and 2,500 unique inventions in its laboratories.

> The small firm can retain its independence and yet contribute to the large firm.

Incubators are places where a start-up company not only will gain access to finance, but will be able to receive support in many forms. This may include all humdrum operational managerial tasks being taken care of (e.g. accounting, legal, human resources), business planning, the supply of managers for various stages of the company's development, property management, etc. As a result the entrepreneurial team can concentrate on innovation and grow the business, even if they have no prior managerial experience.

Government sources

Some local authorities have set up private equity-type funds to attract and encourage industry. Large organisations with similar aims include the Scottish Development Agency and the Welsh Development Agency. Equity, debt and grant finance may be available from these sources.

Disillusionment and dissatisfaction with quotation

There are many companies which either are dissatisfied with being quoted on a stock exchange or have never been quoted and feel no need to join. Many companies are able to expand and produce wealth without them. Some of the main points made by companies in many *Financial Times* articles are summarised in Table 17.2. The arguments are taken directly from the articles and do not necessarily represent reasoned scientific argument.

Conclusion

There are a number of alternative ways of raising finance by selling shares. The advantages and problems associated with each method and type mean that careful thought has to be given to establishing the wisest course of action for a firm, given its specific circumstances. Failure here could mean an unnecessary loss of control, an unbalanced capital structure, an excessive cost of raising funds or some other destructive outcome. Joining a stock market is merely one option; it has considerable drawbacks and so is not appropriate for many firms. Many of the UK's most well known entrepreneurs prefer to expand their businesses outside of the stock exchange with a mixture of bank finance, venture capital and ploughed-back profits.

TABLE 17.2

Arguments for and against joining a stock exchange

For	Against
■ Access to new capital for growth.	■ Dealing with 'City' folk is time-consuming and/or boring.
■ Liquidity for existing shareholders.	
■ Discipline on management to perform.	■ City is short-termist.
■ Able to use equity to buy businesses.	■ City does not understand entrepreneurs.
■ Allows founders to diversify.	■ Stifles creativity.
■ Borrow more easily or cheaply.	■ Focus excessively on return on capital.
■ Can attract better management.	■ Empire building through acquisitions on a stock exchange – growth for its own sake (or for directors) can be the result of a quote.
■ Forces managers to articulate strategy clearly and persuasively.	
■ Succession planning may be made easier – professional managers rather than family.	■ The stock market undervalues entrepreneur's shares in the entrepreneur's eyes.
■ Increased customer recognition.	■ Loss of control for founding shareholders.
■ Allow local people to buy shares.	■ Strong family-held companies in Germany, Italy and Asia where stock markets are used less.
■ Share incentive schemes are more meaningful.	
	■ Examples of good strong unquoted companies in UK: Bamford, Rothschilds.
	■ Press scrutiny is irritating.
	■ Market share building (and short-term low profit margins) are more possible off exchange.
	■ The temptation of over-rapid expansion is avoided off exchange.
	■ By remaining unquoted, the owners, if they do not wish to put shareholder wealth at the centre of the firm's purpose, don't have to (environment or ethical issues may dominate).
	■ Costs of maintaining a quote, e.g. SE fees, extra disclosure costs, management time.

Websites

www.bvca.co.uk	British Private Equity and Venture Capital Association
www.businesslinks.co.uk	BusinessLinks
www.theenterprisezone.org.uk	Enterprise zone
www.evca.com	European Private Equity and Venture Capital Association
www.fsa.gov.uk	Financial Services Authority
www.londonstockexchange.co.uk	London Stock Exchange
www.fsa.gov.uk/ukla	United Kingdom Listing Authority
www.hemscott.com	Hemscott
www.iii.co.uk	Interactive Investor
www.angelbourse.com	Angel Bourse
www.hotbed.uk.com	Hotbed
www.beerandpartners.com	Beer & Partners
www.entrust.co.uk	Entrust
www.berr.gov.uk	Department for Business, Enterprise and Regulatory Reform
www.investorschronicle.com	*Investors Chronicle*
www.ft.com	*Financial Times*

Notes

1 Note that not all businesses are incorporated, that is, set up as a separate legal 'person' with its own constitution (memorandum and articles of association), limited liability and ability to issue shares. Many businesses are set up in an unincorporated fashion, e.g. sole trader or partnership, in which one, two or more people share risks and profits. Each partner is liable for the debts and business actions of the others, to the full extent of his or her resources.

2 Except that it shows proportional voting and income rights.

3 Responsibility for governing admission to listing, the continuing obligations of issuers, the enforcement of those obligations and suspension and cancellation of listing was transferred from the LSE to the UKLA in 2000. However, companies also need to be admitted to trading by the Stock Exchange.

4 Occasionally a company is admitted with a free float of less than 25 percent. For example, Eurasian Natural Resources had a free float of only 21.3 percent when it joined the Main Market in 2008. The company successfully argued that it was large enough for its shares to be liquid in spite of the smaller free float.

5 This disclosure rule applies to the buying and selling of financial instruments that derive their value from share price movements such as contracts for difference. (For a description, *see The Financial Times Guide to Investing* by G. Arnold 2010.)

6 It has also been suggested that when sponsors are underwriters, they have an additional incentive to price the shares cheaply, as this reduces the risk of being required to buy the shares. If they do buy them, they then obtain them at a good price.

7 However, there may not be enough authorised share capital to permit the issue of more shares. In this case the company needs to convene an Extraordinary General Meeting (EGM) to increase the authorised share capital. Directors also need the authority to allot shares from the shareholders. The company will also need to publish a prospectus which must be vetted by the UKLA (time-consuming and expensive – it can take two or three months for planning, writing documents, verification and legal processes) whereas for placings (see below) the whole process is completed in about a week.

8 Another possibility is for the shareholder to sell some of the rights to provide finance to purchase the remainder ('tail swallowing'). Note that for companies whose shares are not quoted on a recognised stock exchange, it may be difficult to sell the rights to another investor.

9 Companies can ask to go beyond these limits if they give appropriate justification, but this is rare.

10 Scrip issues are achieved by taking reserves on the balance sheet and capitalising them – for example, taking £10m from the 'share premium account' or the 'profit and loss reserves' and transferring it to the 'ordinary share capital' account.

11 Having said this, many business angels (generally those with investments of £10,000–£20,000) have infrequent contact with the company.

12 However, MBO and MBI funds usually take most of the shares of a company because the investee company is so large that the management team can only afford a small proportion of the shares.

Section IV:

MANAGING RISK

18

THE FINANCIAL RISKS MANAGERS HAVE TO DEAL WITH

Introduction

Running a business naturally entails taking risks – it is what business activity is about. Satisfactory profits rarely emerge from a risk-eliminating strategy; some risk is therefore inevitable. However it is up to managers of firms to select those risks the business might take and those that it should avoid. Take a company like GlaxoSmithKline which accepts high risks in its research and development programme. Should it also take a risk with exchange rates when it receives money from sales around the world, or should it try to minimise that particular type of risk?

> Taking risks is what business activity is about.

Risk reduction is often costly. For example, insurance premiums may be payable or transaction costs may be incurred in the derivative markets. Given the additional cost burden managers have to think carefully about the benefits to be derived from reducing or eliminating risk. There are at least three reasons firms sacrifice some potential profits in order to reduce the impact of adverse events.

- **It helps financial planning** Being able to predict future cash flows, at least within certain boundaries, can be advantageous and can allow the firm to plan and invest with confidence. Imagine trying to organise a business if the future cash flows can vary widely depending on what happens to the currency, the interest rate or the price of a vital raw material input.

- **Reduce the fear of financial distress** Some events can disrupt and damage a business to the point of threatening its existence. For example, massive claims have been made against firms involved in the production of asbestos. If it had not been for the passing on of this risk to the insurance companies many of these firms would now be liquidated. A similar logic applies to the insurance of super tankers against an ocean oil spillage. By limiting the potential damage inflicted on firms, not only will the managers and shareholders benefit, but other finance providers, such as banks, will have greater confidence, which will lower the cost of capital.

- **Some risks are not rewarded** It is possible to reduce risk in situations where there are no financial rewards for accepting that extra risk. For example, if British Airways contracted to buy a dozen aircraft from Boeing for delivery over the next ten years and had to pay in dollars as each airplane was completed it would have to accept the risk of a recession in international flights and numerous other risks, but, in the sophisticated foreign exchange markets of today, at least it can eliminate one risk. It does not have to live with any uncertainty about the cost of the airplanes in terms of sterling because it could make an arrangement with a bank at the outset to purchase the required number of dollars for a specified number of pounds at set dates in the future. (These are forward agreements.) British Airways would then know precisely how many pounds will be needed to buy the dollars to pay Boeing in each year of the next decade (*see* Chapter 21 for more currency risk-hedging strategies).

Types of risk

A commercial organisation has to deal with many different types of risk and we will discuss the four most important: business risk, insurable risk, currency risk and interest-rate risk.

Business risk

Many of the risks of operating in a competitive business environment have to be accepted by management to a greater or lesser extent. Sales may fall because of, say, recession, or innovative breakthroughs by competitors. Costs may rise because of, say, strong union power or government-imposed tariffs. For some of these risk elements there is little that management can do. However in many areas management can take positive action to reduce risk. For example consider a bakery company heavily dependent on buying in wheat. The managers are likely to be worried that the price of wheat may rise over the forthcoming months, thereby making their operations unprofitable. On the other hand farmers may be worried by the possibility of wheat falling in price. Both would value certainty. One way of achieving this is for the baker and farmer to enter into a wheat futures agreement, in which the baker agrees to take delivery of wheat at a later date at a price that is agreed today. Both sides now know exactly how much the wheat will be sold for and so can plan ahead. Futures are discussed further in Chapter 20.

There are other ways of reducing business risk. For example, firms are often faced with a choice between two machines. The first is highly specialized to a particular task, for example, turning out a particular component. The second, slightly more expensive machine can turn out the same component, but can also be used in a more flexible fashion to switch production to other components. The option to use the machine in alternative ways can sometimes have a high value and so it is worthwhile paying the extra initial set-up costs and even higher production costs.

Consider also an electricity generator contemplating the construction of a power plant. The installation of a coal-fired station would be £100m. This would leave the generator dependent on coal price movements for future profitability. An alternative power plant can be switched from coal to gas but costs an additional £30m. The value of the option to switch is then for the management to evaluate and weigh against the extra cost of construction.

Likewise, a car production line may be more expensive if it is to be capable of being used for a number of different models. But the option to use the facility for more than one type of car reduces the firm's risk by making it less dependent on one model. These are examples of real options, which are considered further in Chapter 5 and Chapter 19.

Insurable risk

Many risks encountered by business can be transferred, through the payment of a premium, to insurance companies. These include factory fires, pollution damage and accidental damage to vehicles and machinery. Insurance companies are often better able to bear risk than ordinary commercial firms. The reasons for this are the following:

- experience in estimating probabilities of events and therefore 'pricing' risk more efficiently;

- knowledge of methods of reducing risk. They can pass on this knowledge to the commercial firms which may obtain lower premiums if they take precautionary measures;

- ability to *pool* risks, in other words, to diversify risk. The chance of an accident occurring in one firm is highly uncertain, but the probability of a particular proportion of a portfolio of insurance policies making a claim is fairly predictable.

Insurance can be an expensive option because of the tendency for insurance companies to charge for much more than the probability of having to pay out. For example, if there was a one in a hundred chance of your £10,000 car being stolen in a year and never recovered then for every 100 cars insured the insurance company will expect one £10,000 claim per year. The insurance premium to each owner to cover this specific type of risk would, justifiably, be slightly over £100 (£10,000/100), to allow for a modest profit. However, in reality, the premium may be much more than this. The insurance company is likely to have to bear significant administrative costs in setting up the policy in the first place and then dealing with subsequent claims. Anyone who has had to communicate with an insurance company quickly becomes aware of the mountain of paperwork they generate annually. Insurance companies also have to charge premiums sufficiently high to cover the problems of 'adverse selection'. Put it this way: you may be a sensible car owner, being cautious about where you park your car, never leave the doors unlocked and live in a good part of town, but many of the other purchasers of theft insurance may be less fastidious and fortunate. The grouping together of good and bad risks tends to increase the cost of insurance to relatively good policyholders. This is made worse for the good policyholders by the increased tendency of those in high-risk situations to buy insurance.

> The grouping together of good and bad risks tends to increase the cost of insurance.

The third boost to insurance premiums comes from 'moral hazard' (the encouragement of bad behaviour) which causes holders of insurance to be less careful than they might otherwise be – the 'It's all right, don't worry, it's insured' syndrome.[1] An extreme example of moral hazard has been created with the 'new-for-old' policies for electrical items in which a brand new TV, for example, is provided should the old one suffer accidental damage – some have been tempted to 'accidentally' drop the TV!

These three additional costs may push insurance premiums beyond acceptable levels for a firm. In some cases large corporations have taken the bold decision to bear many insurable risks. They may still pay insurance premiums to safeguard against major events which threaten the continuance of the firm but accept routine risks themselves such as machine breakdown, accidents at work, etc. There seems little point in paying premiums just to receive a regular, but lower, inflow in return – *see* Exhibit 18.1.

Fingers crossed

Paul J Davies

Is it wise to try and save money in the short term by cancelling the odd bit of insurance cover here and there? Insurance industry results in the coming weeks will tell us how much ordinary people are doing this, but in a piece of research from AM Best, the specialist rating agency, it appears that big companies are doing so.

Most big companies don't buy insurance – they write it themselves. The report says that 81 of the FTSE 100 self-insure, often through a special vehicle called a captive, while more than half of the FTSE 250 also self-insure. But the credit crunch has led increasing numbers of companies to start calling on their captives for increasing amounts of cash – through dividends or loans.

The biggest companies only tend to buy insurance directly when premiums are at their lowest – or for things such as Directors and Officers insurance where there may be a conflict of interests in self-cover. Insurers, meanwhile, are trying to push rates higher as their investment income drops with the markets and interest rates. . . .

EXHIBIT 18.1

Source: *Financial Times* 25 July 2009, p. 15.

Currency risk

Another major area of responsibility for the corporate treasurer is in the management of risk that arises because exchange rates move. Take the case of Acarus plc which has sold electrical goods to an Australian importer on six months' credit. The importer is sent an invoice requiring payment of A\$20m. The current exchange rate is two Australian dollars to one pound so if currency rates do not change in the subsequent six months Acarus will receive £10m. If the exchange moves to A\$1.80 : £1 then Acarus will receive £11.11m, and will be very pleased with the extra £1.11m of income. However matters might turn out worse than expected. Say the rate of exchange moved to A\$2.20 : £1. Then Acarus would receive only £9.09m. If the management team are risk averse they may say to themselves, 'While we like the possibility of making additional profit on the deal this is more than outweighed by the downside risk of making less than £10m'. There are various ways of ensuring that Acarus receives at least £10m and Chapter 21 is devoted to the subject of exchange-rate risk management. Here we will have just a taster. One of the possibilities is for Acarus to buy an option giving the firm the right but not the obligation to exchange A$20m for sterling at a rate of A$2 : £1 in six months. If the dollar appreciates against the pound to A$1.80 then Acarus would choose not to exercise the option – to let it lapse – and then exchange the A$20m for £11.11m in the spot market in six months' time. Alternatively, if the dollar falls against sterling Acarus would insist on exercising the option to receive £10m rather than exchanging at the spot rate of A$2.20 : £1 and therefore achieving a mere £9.09m. By purchasing the option Acarus ensures that the lowest amount it will receive is £10m and the upside potential is unrestrained. However it would need to pay a hefty premium to the option seller for passing on this risk – perhaps 2 to 4 percent of the amount covered. The difficult part is weighing the cost of risk-reducing action against the benefit.

Interest-rate risk

Future interest rates cannot be predicted with any degree of accuracy. If a company has large amounts of floating-rate debt it could be vulnerable to interest-rate rises. Alternatively, a company with large fixed-rate debt could have to face living with regret, and higher debt costs than necessary, if interest rates fall.

There is a wide variety of arrangements and financial products which enable a treasurer to reduce the firm's exposure to the vicissitudes of interest rates. Chapter 20 explores a number of them. Here we examine one of the weapons in the treasurer's armoury – the cap.

Ace plc wishes to borrow £20m to finance a major expansion. It does so at a floating rate of LIBOR plus 150 basis points. LIBOR is currently 8 percent and therefore Ace pays a rate of 9.5 percent. This loan is a large sum relative to Ace's capital base and profits, and the management are concerned that if LIBOR rises above 10 percent the firm will get into serious financial difficulty. To avoid this Ace purchases a cap agreement by which a bank promises to pay any interest charge above a LIBOR of 10 percent. Thus, if two years later LIBOR rises to 11 percent, without the cap Ace would pay 12.5 percent. However, Ace can call upon the bank that made the cap agreement to pay the extra 1 percent. Ace's interest charge cannot go beyond a total of (10 percent + 1.5 percent) = 11.5 percent. What is more, Ace can benefit if interest rates fall because rates are linked to a variable LIBOR at any rate below the cap. The premium charged by the bank for this form of interest-rate insurance can be quite substantial but there are ways of offsetting this cost, for example by simultaneously selling a floor, but consideration of these will have to wait until Chapter 20. Suffice to say, the judicious management of interest-rate risk can be an important managerial task.

Some other risks

We have briefly described the main categories of risk facing a corporation, and will discuss them further in subsequent chapters. However, it is important to note that there are a number of other risks that, while we cannot go into them in detail here, need to be considered:

- **Market value risk** The effect of financial prices or rates on corporate value. For example, commodity price rises on the international markets cause higher input costs and lower profits. Many airlines were caught out by the sudden rise in the price of aviation fuel in 2008. This particular form of market value risk might be termed *commodity risk*. When a company owns a portfolio of shares and bonds that trade in the financial markets, the value is subject to the risk of market prices changing.

- **Funding or financing risk** When borrowing facilities are renewed, the price, terms and conditions (or even availability) will be worse than the existing facilities. This includes the risk that the firm's credit rating is lowered, leading to more expensive debt. Other examples of funding risk: If the company's interest cover ratio or the debt–equity ratio becomes lower, the firm may also face higher interest rates. Alternatively, the appetite for lenders in certain debt markets changes, resulting in the company no longer being able to raise finance in its preferred market, or the cost of finance increases sharply. Financing risk may be made worse by a firm failing to diversify its funding sources or having a high proportion of debts maturing at one point in time.

- **Credit risk** Counterparties, e.g. customers, may not pay after being given credit. Likewise, a counterparty in a financial instrument, e.g. a derivative such as a swap, may default. The investment bank Lehman Brothers caused chaos when it was unable to fulfil its obligations to thousands of counterparties in 2008. This may also be called *counterparty risk*.

- **Liquid risk (Liquidity risk)** Cash is not available as and when needed, e.g. to pay salaries or tax. Many companies found themselves badly exposed to this risk during the 2009 recession. They had relied on a continuing volume of sales to produce cash; when those sales suddenly slowed or stopped they could not pay day-to-day bills – e.g. house-building companies had to go cap in hand to their bank to survive.

- **Legal risk** The actions of the firm, whether intentionally or unintentionally, lead to legal liabilities under tort or other laws, e.g. warranty claims, misleading advertising, hazards.

- **Reputational risks** The expectations of one or more stakeholders, e.g. customers or suppliers, regarding performance or behaviour of the firm are not met. It takes a lifetime to build a reputation; it can be lost in a heartbeat.

- **External risks** *(force majeure)* Examples include fire, accident, earthquake and terrorism.

- **Political risk** Changes in government or government policy impacting on returns and volatility of returns. For example, a government in a developing country fixes the price that can be charged for the firm's product. Another example would be expropriation of the firm's assets by a hostile government.

■ **Off balance-sheet risk** The potential of derivatives and other off-balance-sheet items to destabilise the company.

Risk in the financial structure

Obtaining the most appropriate mixture of finance is likely to be of great importance to most firms. The key issues are: whether your firm should be borrowing more through short-term lending agreements, by overdraft, say, or whether more long-term types of finance are more appropriate, (should you, for instance increase the proportion of long-term finance (debt plus equity) until it matches the value of all the firm's assets, or only to the point where long-term finance covers the long-term asset values and short-term finance is used for the purchase of short-term assets?); whether you should borrow only in your home currency or in a variety of currencies, perhaps to match the currencies in which the firm's assets and sources of revenue originate; whether fixed-rate interest rates are more appropriate than interest rates that go up and down with a benchmark rate, such as LIBOR. Finally, we need to work out what is an appropriate level of borrowing relative to the equity capital held in the company given the trade off between the lower rate of return demanded on debt capital and the dangers of taking on more borrowing.

Is it better to borrow long or short?

Once a company has decided to raise funds by borrowing, it then has to decide whether to raise the money through:

■ short-term debt – a loan which has to be repaid within, say, one year;

■ medium-term debt; or

■ long-term debt – where the loan is paid over a 7-, 25- or even 100-year period.

A number of factors need to be taken into consideration when making a decision of this nature:

■ **Maturity structure** A company will usually try to avoid having all of its debts maturing at or near the same date. It could be disastrous if the firm was required to repay loan capital on a number of different instruments all within, say, a six-month period. Even if the firm is profitable the sudden cash outflow could lead to insolvency. In the boom of 2004–2007, many companies financed themselves with debt due for repayment four to five years later. When the reccession hit, many analysts were worried that they had too much debt maturing in the 2009–2012 period – *see* Exhibit 18.2.

Debt woes rise for top 350

Anousha Sakoui

The UK's leading 350 listed companies have more than £210bn of debt that is due for repayment over the next five years.

As the availability of bank financing dwindles, concerns are rising that companies could struggle to have auditors sign off on their accounts over coming weeks as they prepare their full-year accounts.

Auditors will need to have confidence companies have enough liquidity to meet debt maturities over the next 12 months before they approve accounts on a 'going concern' basis.

David Winfield, head of law firm Freshfields Bruckhaus Deringer's banking practice, said: 'The economic environment means that company auditors are becoming increasingly conservative in their going concern sign-offs by scrutinising to an even greater degree head room against financial covenants.

'This is forcing some corporates to look urgently for ways to de-lever. Many companies have and will end up needing to ask banks to reset the covenants on their credit lines.'

Part of the problem is greater uncertainty about whether banks will support long-running clients, particularly where credit facilities are not committed. 'Many [debt] issuers are now seeing their traditional relationship banks being reluctant to anchor their facilities and are concerned only with reducing their exposures,' added Mr Winfield.

'In difficult refinancings, a bank might agree to extend but only if all the other lenders join the party – this can cause massive headaches for corporates who have a large number of lenders.'

**FTSE 350 companies – debt maturity schedule
By sector (£bn)**

	2009	2010	2011	2012
Mining & natural resources	5.6	14.4	11.0	11.8
Chemicals	0.0	0.0	0.3	0.0
Construction & materials	2.3	0.0	2.5	3.0
Food & beverage	1.7	3.7	1.3	2.9
Healthcare	0.4	0.0	0.1	2.7
Industrial goods & services	3.9	7.8	8.3	11.4
Insurance	3.4	5.9	1.7	0.3
Media	1.1	2.4	5.4	8.2
Oil & gas	1.0	2.3	0.9	1.1
Personal & household goods	1.2	5.0	0.0	4.9
Retail	2.9	1.6	4.9	2.1
Technology	0.1	1.3	0.8	0.1
Telecoms	0.0	0.5	7.2	3.6
Travel & leisure	3.4	4.7	3.1	7.5
Utilities	2.1	2.5	0.2	0.4
TOTAL	29.2	52.1	47.7	60.1

Source: Freshfields

EXHIBIT 18.2

Source: *Financial Times* 15 January 2009, p. 17.

■ **Costs of issue/arrangement** It is usually cheaper to arrange an overdraft and other one-off short-term finance than long-term debt facilities, but this advantage is sometimes outweighed by the fact that if funds are needed over a number of years short-term debt has to be renewed more often than long-term debt. So over, say, a 20-year period, the issuing and arrangement costs of short-term debt may be much greater than a 20-year bond.

■ **Flexibility** Short-term debt is more flexible than long-term debt. If a business has fluctuations in its needs for borrowed funds, for example it is a seasonal business, then for some months it does not need any borrowed funds, whereas at other times it needs large loans. A long-term loan may be inefficient because the firm will be paying interest even if it has surplus cash. True, the surplus cash could be invested but the proceeds are unlikely to be as great as the cost of the loan interest. It is cheaper to take out short-term loans or overdrafts when the need arises which can be paid back when the firm has high cash inflows.

■ **The uncertainty of getting future finance** If a firm is investing in a long-term project which requires borrowing for many years it would be risky to finance this project using one-year loans. At the end of each year the firm has to renegotiate the loan or issue a new bond. There may come a time when lenders will not supply the new money. There may, for example, be a change in the bank's policy or a reassessment of the borrower's creditworthiness, a crisis of confidence in the financial markets or an imposition of government restrictions on lending. Whatever the reason, the project is halted and the firm loses money. To some extent, the type of project or asset that is acquired determines the type of borrowing. If the project or asset is liquid and short term then short-term finance may be favoured. If it is long term then longer-term borrowing gives more certainty about the availability of finance, and (possibly) the interest rate. It became increasingly difficult for companies to roll over short-term bank loans in 2008 as banks took fright – *see* Exhibit 18.3.

■ **The term structure of interest rates** The term structure of interest rates describes how the same borrower (same risk class of borrower, at least) has to pay different interest rates depending on whether the loan is for 1, 2, 3, 4, 10 or 30 years. On a graph with number of years to maturity of the loan along the x-axis and interest rate on the y-axis we observe a rising or declining interest rate as the length of time to maturity of the loan increases. This is called a yield curve. It is usual to find interest rates on short-term borrowing are lower than on long-term debt.[2] This may encourage managers to borrow on a short-term basis. In many circumstances this makes sense. Take the case of Myosotis plc, which requires £10m of borrowed funds for a ten-year project. The corporate treasurer expects long-term interest rates to fall over the next year. It is therefore thought unwise to borrow for the full ten years at the outset. Instead the firm borrows one-year money at a low interest rate with the expectation of replacing the loan at the end of the year with a nine-year fixed-rate loan at the then reduced rate.

Financing problems increase as crunch spreads

John Willman and Jonathan Guthrie

Companies are reporting increased financing difficulties as the impact of the credit crunch spreads to the real economy.

Credit facilities are being scaled back, interest rates raised and businesses are under pressure to switch from unsecured lending such as overdrafts to secured loans.

Corporate advisers warn that even healthy businesses will find negotiations tricky as they seek to renew finance facilities for 2009. ...

Mark Lucas, head of corporate finance at accountancy firm Tenon, said banks were taking finance negotiations as an opportunity to raise lending margins by up to 150 basis points. 'The days of the unsecured overdraft are diminishing,' he said.

Mid-market companies had been unaffected by the credit crunch, said Rob Donaldson, head of M&A at Baker Tilley. '[But] as facilities come up for renewal, terms are tightening, the amount is coming down and the cost is definitely rising.'

Steve Sharratt, of the small and medium-sized enterprise council of the CBI employers' group, said banks' credit teams were taking a harsher approach to business lending.

'One company told me it was recently given three weeks' notice to reduce its overdraft facility by £25,000 a month until the end of the year,' he said. 'It won't be able to achieve that and will be a casualty.' ... manufacturing businesses in the north-east and Yorkshire are complaining about bankers' attitudes to requests for finance, according to Alan Hall, northern director of the EEF manufacturers' organisation.

'Members think they have an understanding with their bank manager and then find the goalposts have moved.' ...

With corporate bond markets hard to access and unsecured lending in short supply, finance directors will have to draw on their own cash resources, according to Alix Partners.

After years of cheap finance, many were ill prepared, said Eric Benedict, managing director.

EXHIBIT 18.3

Source: *Financial Times* 18 September 2008.

However there are circumstances where managers find short-term rates deceptively attractive. For example, they might follow a policy of borrowing at short-term rates while the yield curve is still upward sloping, only switching to long-term borrowing when short-term rates rise above long-term rates. Take the case of Rosa plc, which wishes to borrow money for five years and faces the term structure of interest rates shown in the lower line of Figure 18.1. If it issued one-year bonds the rate of return paid would be 7 percent. The returns required on four-year and five-year bonds are 8 percent and 8.3 percent respectively. The company opts for a one-year bond with the expectation of issuing a four-year bond one year later. However by the time the financing has to be replaced, 365 days after the initial borrowing, the entire yield curve has shifted

FIGURE 18.1

A shifting yield curve affects the relative cost of long- and short-term
borrowing – the example of Rosa plc

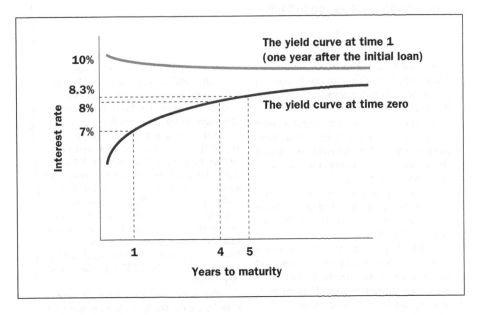

upwards due to general macroeconomic changes. Now Rosa has to pay an interest rate of 10 percent for the remaining four years. This is clearly more
expensive than arranging a five-year bond at the outset.

The case of Rosa shows that it can be cheaper to borrow long at low points in
the interest rate cycle despite the 'headline' interest charge on long-term debt
being greater than on short-term loans.

To 'match' or not to 'match'?

Firms usually come to the conclusion that there is a need for an appropriate mixture of debt finance with regard to length of time to maturity: some short-term
borrowing is desirable alongside some long-term borrowing. The major factors
which need to be taken into account in achieving the right balance are: (a) cost
(interest rate, arrangement fee, etc.) and (b) the risk (of not being able to renew
borrowings, of the yield curve shifting, of not being able to meet a sudden outflow if the maturity is bunched, etc.). Some firms follow the 'matching' principle,
in which the maturity structure of the finance matches the maturity of the project or asset. Here fixed assets and those current assets which are needed on a
permanent basis (for example cash, minimum inventory or debtor levels) are
financed through long-term sources, while current assets whose financing needs
vary throughout the year are financed by short-term borrowings. Examples of
the latter type of asset might be stocks of fireworks at certain times of the year,
or investment in inventories of Easter eggs in the spring.

Three types of asset need to be financed:

- fixed assets
- permanent current assets
- fluctuating current assets.

A firm taking the maturity matching approach is considered to be adopting a moderate stance. This is shown in Figure 18.2, where a rising level of total assets is financed principally through increases in long-term finance applied to fixed assets and permanent current assets. The fluctuating current assets, such as those related to seasonal variations, are financed with short-term funds.

A more aggressive approach is represented in Figure 18.3. This entails more risk because of the frequent need to refinance to support permanent current assets as well as fluctuating current assets. If the firm relied on an overdraft for this it will be vulnerable to a rapid withdrawal of that facility. If stocks and cash are reduced to pay back the overdraft the firm may experience severe disruption, loss of sales and output, and additional costs because of a failure to maintain the minimum required working capital to sustain optimum profitability.

The low-risk policy is to make sure that long-term financing covers the total investment in assets. If there are times of the year when surplus cash is available this will be invested in short-term instruments. This type of policy is shown in Figure 18.4.

Many managers would feel much happier under the conservative approach because of the lower risk of being unable to pay bills as they arise. However such a policy may not be in the best interests of the owners of the firm. The

FIGURE 18.2

Moderate financing policy stance – the matching principle

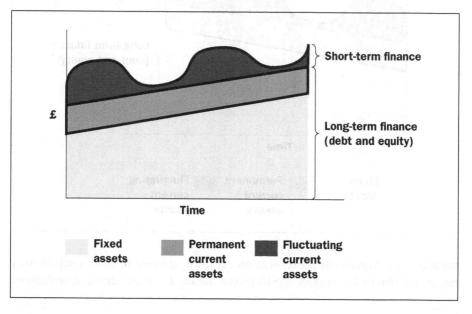

FIGURE 18.3

An aggressive financing policy

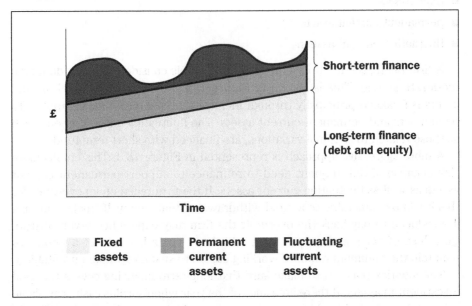

FIGURE 18.4

A conservative financing policy

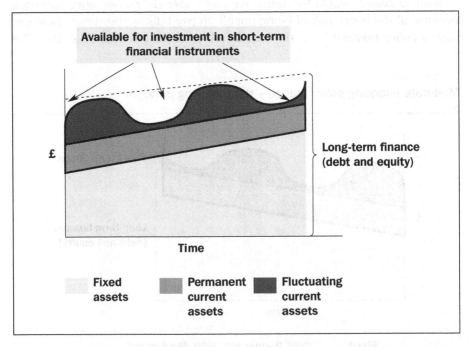

surplus cash invested in short-term securities is unlikely to earn a satisfactory return relative to the cost of the long-term funds. In all likelihood shareholders would be better off if the firm reduced its long-term financing, by returning cash to shareholders or paying off some long-term loans.

There is no sound theoretical formula to help decide the balance between long- and short-term finance. While many managers follow a policy of matching the maturity of their assets and liabilities, thereby accepting a modest level of risk while avoiding excessive amounts of surplus investible funds, this is far from universally accepted: for example, both Google and Microsoft have over $25bn of cash and short-term investments.

The currency of borrowing

Deciding on the maturity structure of the firm's debt is one aspect of the financing decision. Another is selecting the currency in which to borrow. For transnational firms it is common to find borrowing in the currency of the country where the funds are to be invested. This can reduce exposure to foreign exchange rate changes. For example, suppose that Union Jack plc borrows £100m to invest in the USA. It exchanges the £100m into $150m at the exchange rate of $1.5 to the pound. The net cash flows in subsequent years are expected to be $30m per annum. If the exchange rate remained constant Union Jack would therefore receive £20m per year to pay for the financing costs and produce a surplus. However if the rate of exchange moved to $2 for every pound the annual cash inflow in sterling terms would be merely £15m.[3] The project is producing £5m less than originally anticipated despite generating the same quantity of dollars, and this is insufficient as a rate of return for Union Jack. The risk attached to this project can be reduced by ensuring that the liabilities are in the same currency as the income flow. So if Union Jack borrows $150m to invest in the project, even though the exchange rate may move to $2 : £1 the project remains viable. Currency risk is considered in more detail in Chapter 21.

The interest rate choice

Another consideration for the debt portfolio is the balance to be struck between fixed and floating interest-rate borrowings. In many circumstances it is thought advisable to have a mixture of the two types of borrowing. If all the borrowings are floating rate then the firm is vulnerable to rising interest rates. This often happens at the most unfortunate times: for example, at the start of recessions interest rates are usually high at the same time as sales are in decline.

Industries with high fixed-cost elements, which need a large volume of sales to maintain profitability, may be particularly averse to floating-rate borrowing as this may add to their cost base and create an additional source of risk. Even if they have to pay more for fixed-rate borrowing initially, the directors may sleep better knowing that one element of risk has been eliminated.

On the other hand, if all borrowing is fixed rate the firm is unable to take advantage of a possible decline in interest rates. Other aspects of the debate about fixed or floating rates are considered in Chapter 15.

The dangers of gearing

Someone has to decide what is an appropriate level of borrowing for a firm given its equity capital base. This is a difficult decision given the range of positive and negative consequences of increased borrowing. As debt levels rise the firm's earnings attributable to shareholders become increasingly volatile due to the requirement to pay large amounts of interest prior to dividends. Eventually the burden of a large annual interest bill can lead the firm to become financially distressed and, in extreme circumstances, liquidated. If the gearing level is too low, shareholder value opportunities are forgone by not substituting 'cheap' debt for equity. Case study 18.1 provides some of the evidence that this is a key issue at the heart of senior managerial decision-making.

Case study 18.1

The balance between debt and ordinary share capital

Ennstone, the building materials company, found in 2008 that it had too much debt relative to the amount of equity capital in the firm. It needed to 'fix its balance sheet'. To regain the right mix of debt and equity it sold off assets and investigated the possibility of an issue of new shares to pay down some of its £200m debt. However, it was all to no avail; the company was placed in administration in March 2009. It had over–geared its balance sheet while on an acquisitions spree of similar firms in its industry – it paid a terrible price for not financing these acquisitions with a less risky mixture of equity and debt.

Whitbread (Beefeater, Costa Coffee, Premier Travel Inn, etc.) had already returned £400m to shareholders after disposing of Marriott UK when in 2005 it considered increasing its debt burden 'as part of a review of its capital structure'. According to the *FT* it was exploring ways of making its balance sheet more efficient: 'We've had a fairly conservative approach to the balance sheet', said Alan Parker, chief executive. 'We will be looking at a range of options to increase shareholder value'.[1] Similarly, David Finch, Chief Financial Officer of O_2, conceded that the company was 'not optimally financed at the moment' which could result in more cash being returned to shareholders.[2]

In the cases of Whitbread and O_2 the directors concluded that there was too much equity capital and too little debt and something had to be done about it. In the space of six years BT made first the decision that it had too much debt relative to its equity base and then that it had too little. In 2001 its management was in serious trouble. The company had accumulated debt of over £30bn following a worldwide acquisition spree and infrastructure investment (the 3G excitement). The net assets of the company were roughly half the debt level, at £14bn. City institutions were desperately concerned by the high level of debt. Sir Peter Bonfield, the chief executive, recognised that he had allowed the debt to rise too high. 'We identified the need to introduce new equity capital into the business to support the reduction in the unsustainable level of group debt.'[3] The company raised £5.9bn through a rights issue, sold off property, slashed investment and sold stakes in telecom businesses around the world. It also stopped paying a dividend. By mid-2007 the company had been so successful at reducing its debt (down to £8.1bn, or about one-third of the amount of equity capital in the business) that it pondered handing over £2bn to shareholders, financing this by raising its debt to £10bn 'to enhance returns to shareholders'.[4]

Bristol Water gave £51bn of cash to shareholders as part of a balance sheet restructuring in 2004. Then in 2005 it paid out a further £30m raising its borrowing levels again. 'Bristol Water was overcapitalised and it was time to do something for the shareholders',[5] said John Murray, representative of the largest shareholder. Moger Wooley, chairman, said, 'We concluded that shareholders' interests were best served by increasing the capital efficiency of the group.'[6]

[1] Quoted in Matthew Garrahan, 'Whitbread looks to extend debt', *Financial Times* 15 June 2005.
[2] Quoted in Mark Odell, 'O₂ review could return more cash to investors', *Financial Times* 21 July 2005, p. 21.
[3] BT Annual Report 2001.
[4] Andrew Parker, 'Resurgent BT planning £2bn share buy-back', *Financial Times* 5/6 May 2007, p. 15.
[5] Quoted in Rebecca Bream, 'Bristol Water plans to return £50m cash', *Financial Times* 22 July 2003.
[6] Quoted in Rebecca Bream, 'Bristol Water to deliver a £30m payback', *Financial Times* 21/22 May 2005, p. M5.

Debt finance is cheaper and riskier (for the company)

Financing a business through borrowing is cheaper than using equity. This is, first, because lenders require a lower rate of return than ordinary shareholders. Debt financial securities present a lower risk than shares for the finance providers because they have prior claims on annual income and in liquidation. In addition security is often provided and covenants imposed.

A profitable business effectively pays less for debt capital than equity for another reason: the debt interest can be offset against pre-tax profits before the calculation of the corporation tax bill, thus reducing the tax paid.

Third, issuing and transaction costs associated with raising and servicing debt are generally less than for ordinary shares.

There are some valuable benefits from financing a firm with debt. So why do firms tend to avoid very high gearing levels? One reason is financial distress risk. This could be induced by the requirement to pay interest regardless of the cash flow of the business. If the firm hits a rough patch in its business activities it may have trouble paying its bondholders, bankers and other creditors their entitlement. Figure 18.5 shows that, as gearing increases, the risk of financial failure grows.

Note the crucial assumption in Figure 18.5 – if the returns to equity are constant, or do not rise much, the overall cost of finance declines. This is obviously unrealistic because as the risk of financial distress rises ordinary shareholders are likely to demand higher returns. This is an important issue and we will return to it after a discussion of some basic concepts about gearing.

> If the returns to equity are constant, or do not rise much, the overall cost of finance declines.

What do we mean by gearing?

We need to avoid some confusion possible when using the word 'gearing'. First, we should make a distinction between operating gearing and financial gearing.

FIGURE 18.5

At low gearing levels the risk of financial distress is low, but the cost of capital is high; this reverses at high gearing levels

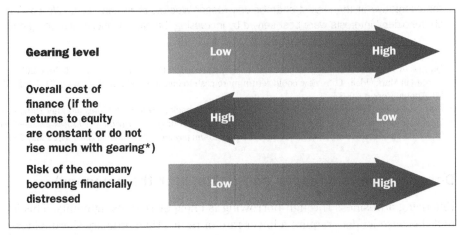

*This assumption is considered in the text.

Operating gearing refers to the extent to which the firm's total costs are fixed. The profits of firms with high operating gearing, such as car or steel manufacturers, are very sensitive to changes in the sales level. They have high break-even points (the turnover level at which profits are achieved) but when this level is breached a large proportion of any additional sales revenue turns into profit because of the relatively low variable costs.

Financial gearing is the focus for the remainder of this chapter and concerns the proportion of debt in the capital structure. Net income to shareholders in firms with high financial gearing is more sensitive to changes in operating profits.

Second, the terms gearing and leverage are used interchangeably by most practitioners, although leverage is used more in the USA.

Third, there are many different ways of calculating financial gearing (to be called simply 'gearing' throughout this chapter). Financial analysts, the press and corporate managers usually measure gearing by reference to balance sheet (book) figures, but it is important to recognise that much of finance theory concentrates on the market values of debt and equity. Both book and market approaches are useful, depending on the purpose of the analysis.

There are two ways of putting in perspective the levels of debt that a firm carries (Figure 18.6). *Capital gearing* focuses on the extent to which a firm's total capital is in the form of debt. *Income gearing* is concerned with the proportion of the annual income stream (that is, the pre-interest profits) which is devoted to the prior claims of debt holders, in other words, what proportion of profits is taken by interest charges.

FIGURE 18.6

A firm's financial gearing can be measured in two ways

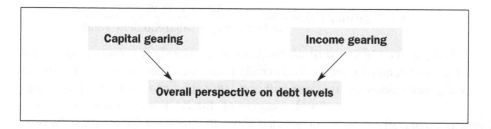

Capital gearing

There are alternative measures of the extent to which the capital structure consists of debt. One popular approach is the ratio of long-term debt to shareholders' funds (the debt to equity ratio). The long-term debt is usually taken as the balance sheet items 'amounts falling due after more than one year' and shareholders' funds is the net asset (or net worth) figure in the balance sheet.[4]

$$\text{Capital gearing (1)} = \frac{\text{Long-term debt}}{\text{Shareholders' fund}}$$

This ratio is of interest because it may give some indication of the firm's ability to sell assets to repay debts. For example, if the ratio stood at 0.3, or 30 percent, lenders and shareholders might feel relatively comfortable as there would be, apparently, over three times as many net (that is after paying off liabilities) assets as long-term debt. So, if the worst came to the worst, the company could sell assets to satisfy its long-term lenders.

There is a major problem with relying on this measure of gearing. The book value of assets can be quite different from the saleable value. This may be because the assets have been recorded at historical purchase value (perhaps less depreciation) and have not been revalued over time. It may also be due to the fact that companies forced to sell assets to satisfy creditors often have to do so at greatly reduced prices if they are in a hurry.[5]

Second, this measure of gearing can have a range of values from zero to infinity and this makes inter-firm comparisons difficult. The measure shown below puts gearing within a range of zero to 100 percent as debt is expressed as a fraction of all long-term capital.[6]

$$\text{Capital gearing (2)} = \frac{\text{Long-term debt}}{\text{Long-term debt + Shareholders' funds}}$$

These ratios could be further modified by the inclusion of 'provisions' and deferred taxation. Provisions are sums set aside in the accounts for anticipated loss or expenditure, for example a bad debt or costs of merger integration. Deferred tax likewise may be included as an expected future liability.

The third capital gearing measure, in addition to allowing for long-term debt, includes short-term borrowing.

$$\text{Capital gearing (3)} = \frac{\text{All borrowing}}{\text{All borrowing} + \text{Shareholders' funds}}$$

Many firms rely on overdraft facilities and other short-term borrowing, for example commercial paper. Technically these are classified as short term. In reality many firms use the overdraft and other short-term borrowing as a long-term source of funds. Furthermore, if we are concerned about the potential for financial distress, then we must recognise that an inability to repay an overdraft can be just as serious as an inability to service a long-term bond.

> An inability to repay an overdraft can be just as serious as an inability to service a long-term bond.

To add sophistication to capital gearing analysis it is often necessary to take into account any cash (or marketable securities) holdings in the firm. These can be used to offset the threat that debt poses.

A measure of gearing which is gaining prominence is the ratio of debt to the total market value of the firm's equity (also called the debt to equity ratio (market value)).

$$\text{Capital gearing (4)} = \frac{\text{Long-term debt}}{\text{Total market capitalisation}}$$

This has the advantage of being closer to the market-value-based gearing measures (assuming book long-term debt is similar to the market value of the debt). It gives some indication of the relative share of the company's total value belonging to debt holders and shareholders.

It is plain that there is a rich variety of capital gearing measures and it is important to know which measure people are using – it can be very easy to find yourself talking at cross-purposes.[7]

Income gearing

The capital gearing measures rely on the appropriate valuation of net assets either in the balance sheet or in a revaluation exercise. This is a notoriously difficult task to complete with any great certainty. Try valuing a machine on a factory floor, or a crate of raw material. Also the capital gearing measures focus on a worst case scenario: 'What could we sell the business assets for if we had to, in order to pay creditors?'

It may be erroneous to focus exclusively on assets when trying to judge a company's ability to repay debts. Take the example of a successful advertising agency. It may not have any saleable assets at all, apart from a few desks and chairs, and yet it may be able to borrow hundreds of millions of pounds because it has the ability to generate cash to make interest payments. Thus, quite often, a more appropriate measure of gearing is one concerned with the level of a firm's income relative to its interest commitments:

$$\text{Interest cover} = \frac{\text{Profit before interest and taxes}}{\text{Interest charges}} \quad \text{or} \quad \frac{\text{Operating cash flow}}{\text{Interest charges}}$$

The lower the interest cover ratio the greater the chance of interest payment default and liquidation. The inverse of interest cover measures the proportion of profits (or cash flow) paid out in interest – this is called income gearing.

Another popular income gearing ratio is the operating cash flow to total debt ratio. If a short-term focus on the company's ability to pay interest while stopping expenditure on capital items or increases in working capital is required, then the earnings before interest, tax, depreciation and amortisation divided by interest charges or total debt may be used.

The effect of gearing (leverage)

The introduction of interest-bearing debt 'gears up' the returns to shareholders. Compared with those of the ungeared firm the geared firm's returns to its owners are subject to greater variation than underlying earnings. If profits are high, the geared firm's shareholders will experience a more than proportional boost in their returns compared to the ungeared firm's shareholders. On the other hand, if profits turn out to be low the geared firm's shareholders will find their returns declining to an exaggerated extent.

The effect of gearing can best be explained through an example. Harby plc is shortly to be established. The prospective directors are considering three different capital structures which will all result in £10m of capital being raised.

1 All equity – 10 million shares sold at a nominal value of £1.

2 £3m debt (carrying 10 percent interest) and £7m equity.

3 £5m debt (carrying 10 percent interest) and £5m equity.

To simplify their analysis the directors have assigned probabilities to three potential future performance levels (*see* Table 18.1).

TABLE 18.1

Probabilities of performance levels

Customer response to firm's products	Income before interest*	Probability (%)
Modest success	£0.5m	20
Good response	£3.0m	60
Run-away success	£4.0m	20

* Taxes are to be ignored.

We can now examine what will happen to shareholder returns for each of the gearing levels.

Note, in Table 18.2, what happens as gearing increases: the changes in earnings attributable to shareholders is magnified. For example, when earnings before interest rise by 500 percent from £0.5m to £3.0m the returns on the 30 percent geared structure rises by 1,200 per cent from 3 percent to 39 percent. This magnification effect works in both positive and negative directions – if earnings before interest are only £0.5m the all-equity structure gives shareholders some return, but with the 50 percent geared firm they will receive nothing. Harby's shareholders would be taking a substantial risk that they would have no profits if they opted for a high level of gearing.

As the gearing levels rise for Harby, the expected return to shareholders (weighted average of the possible outcomes) also rises, but this is accompanied by a rising level of risk. Management need to weigh up the relative importance of the 'good' resulting from the increase in expected returns and the 'bad' from the wider dispersion of returns attributable to shareholders.

TABLE 18.2
The effect of gearing

Customer response	Modest	Good	Run-away
Earnings before interest	£0.5m	£3.0m	£4.0m
All-equity structure			
Debt interest at 10%	0.0	0.0	0.0
Earnings available for shareholders	£0.5m	£3.0m	£4.0m
Return on shares	$\dfrac{£0.5m}{£10m} = 5\%$	$\dfrac{£3.0m}{£10m} = 30\%$	$\dfrac{£4.0m}{£10m} = 40\%$
30% gearing (£3m debt, £7m equity)			
Debt interest at 10%	£0.3m	£0.3m	£0.3m
Earnings available for shareholders	£0.2m	£2.7m	£3.7m
Return on shares	$\dfrac{£0.2m}{£7m} = 3\%$	$\dfrac{£2.7m}{£7m} = 39\%$	$\dfrac{£3.7m}{£7m} = 53\%$
50% gearing (£5m debt, £5m equity)			
Debt interest at 10%	£0.5m	£0.5m	£0.5m
Earnings available for shareholders	0.0	£2.5m	£3.5m
Return on shares	$\dfrac{£0.0m}{£5m} = 0\%$	$\dfrac{£2.5m}{£5m} = 50\%$	$\dfrac{£3.5m}{£5m} = 70\%$

Business risk and financial risk

Business risk is the variability of the firm's operating income, that is, the income before interest. In the case of Harby this is found by examining the dispersion of returns for the all-equity capital structure. This dispersion is caused purely by business-related factors, such as the characteristics of the industry and the competitive advantage possessed by the firm within that industry. This risk will be influenced by factors such as the variability of sales volumes or prices over the business cycle, the variability of input costs, the degree of market power and the level of growth.

The business risk of a monopoly supplier of electricity, gas or water is likely to be significantly less than that for, say, an entrepreneurial company trying to gain a toehold in the internet optical switch market. The range of possible demand levels and prices is likely to be less for the utilities than for the hi-tech firm. Business risk is determined by general business and economic conditions and is not related to the firm's financial structure.

Financial risk is the additional variability in returns to shareholders and the increased probability of insolvency that arises because the financial structure contains debt.

Table 18.2 implies that firms with low business risk can take on relatively high levels of financial risk without exposing their shareholders to excessive total risk. The increased expected return more than compensates for the higher variability resulting in climbing share prices.

Financial distress

A major disadvantage for a firm taking on higher levels of debt is that it increases the risk of financial distress, and ultimately liquidation. This will have a detrimental effect on both the equity holders and the debt holders.

Financial distress: where obligations to creditors are not met or are met with difficulty.

The risk of incurring the costs of financial distress has a negative effect on a firm's value, which offsets the value of tax relief of increasing debt levels – *see* Chapter 10 for a discussion of the 'tax shield' effect of debt. These costs become considerable with very high gearing. Even if a firm manages to avoid liquidation its relationships with suppliers, customers, employees and creditors may be seriously damaged. Suppliers providing goods and services on credit are likely to reduce the generosity of their terms, or even stop supplying altogether, if they believe that there is an increased chance of the firm not being in existence in a few months' time. The situation may be similar with customers. Many customers expect to develop close relationships with their suppliers, and plan their own production on the assumption of a continuance of that relationship. If there is any doubt about the longevity of a firm it will not be able to secure high-quality contracts. For example, car assembly companies develop close relationships with component suppliers – the car producers will not make that effort if there is a doubt about the financial stability of a supplier. In the consumer markets customers often need assurance that firms are sufficiently stable to deliver on promises, for example package holiday companies taking bookings six months in advance. When NTL, the cable company, went through a financial reconstruction because it was heavily borrowed and unable to service its debts, it lost more than 800 customers a day. Not only were existing customers doubtful about the continuation of the company but the shortage of cash meant a cut in advertising and other expenditure on winning new customers.

Employees may become demotivated in a struggling firm as they sense increased job insecurity and few prospects for advancement. The best staff will start to move to posts in safer companies.

Bankers and other lenders will tend to look upon a request for further finance from a financially distressed company with a prejudiced eye – taking a safety-first approach – and this can continue for many years after the crisis has passed. They may also insist on restriction on managerial freedom of action. For example, Waterford Wedgewood was told by its bankers to reduce stock levels, to undertake no further capital expenditure other than what was already under way, to issue a high-yield bond to replace some of the bank debt, and to not pay an interim dividend.

Management find that much of their time is spent 'fire fighting' – dealing with day-to-day liquidity problems – and focusing on short-term cash flow rather than long-term shareholder wealth. Often companies are forced to sell off their most profitable operations in a desperate attempt to raise cash. For instance, in 2008 Premier Foods was forced to contemplate selling some of its most famous brands (Mr Kipling Cakes, Sharwood's Sauces, Branston Pickles) as it battled to cut its debt from £1.8bn.

The indirect costs associated with financial distress can be much more significant than the more obvious direct costs such as paying for lawyers and accountants and for refinancing programmes. Some of these indirect and direct costs are shown in Table 18.3.

In the 2008–09 recession, banks and other lenders were slow to jump to liquidation as a solution for a firm in financial distress. They preferred to restructure the debt, allowing the firms to continue – *see* Exhibit 18.4.

TABLE 18.3
Costs of financial distress

Indirect examples	Direct examples
Uncertainties in customers' minds about dealing with this firm – lost sales, lost profits, lost goodwill.	Lawyers' fees.
	Accountants' fees.
Uncertainties in suppliers' minds about dealing with this firm – lost inputs, more expensive trading terms.	Court fees.
	Management time.
If assets have to be sold quickly the price may be very low.	
Delays, legal impositions, and the tangles of financial reorganisation may place restrictions on management action, interfering with the efficient running of the business.	
Management may give excessive emphasis to short-term liquidity, e.g. cut R&D and training, reduce trade credit and stock levels.	
Temptation to sell healthy businesses as this will raise the most cash.	
Loss of staff morale, tendency to examine possible alternative employment.	
To conserve cash, lower credit terms are offered to customers, which impacts on the marketing effort.	

Debt for equity is the latest restructuring fashion

Anousha Sakoui

Gala Coral's board will today consider a restructuring proposal that will see its three shareholders cede overall control of the gaming company to a group of debtholders, including debt funds that are not traditional shareholders.

The move is a blow for Candover, Cinven and Permira, the three private equity companies that own Gala Coral's shares, but they can take comfort from the fact that they are not alone. Styles & Wood – which fits shops for Tesco and Marks and Spencer – saw Royal Bank of Scotland become its second-biggest shareholder earlier this year after it swapped debt for a 17 per cent stake. Jessops and Independent News & Media have also agreed debt-for-equity swaps with lenders.

Such deals are expected to become more common as the recession moves into a new phase. Although trading has started to pick up in some areas of the economy, many heavily leveraged companies face complex debt renegotiations as loans become due.

Henry Nicholson, partner at Deloitte, said: 'There have been 80–90 restructurings done this year or that are still in progress and I expect that level of activity to continue and increase as big debt maturities come due from 2012.'

The way debtholders are exercising their muscle contrasts with the last recession. In the early 1990s, banks dominated lending and would group together to decide how to restructure companies – the so-called London approach. Their options were limited and many companies were liquidated.

This time around work-out bankers – those specialising in problem loans – plan to use debt-for-equity swaps more often as a way to recover their money.

After the swap, the bank acts as a shareholder and runs the business as a private equity fund would, according to Derek Sach, head of RBS' global restructuring group. 'We can source management teams to put into companies and have been hiring corporate finance and private equity professionals to our restructuring group to be able to meet that need," he said.

Barclays has taken a similar stance. Kip Kapur, managing director of Barclays Ventures, the private equity group within the bank that manages the stakes it takes through debt-for-equity swaps, said that bankers from work-out teams had been transferred to his team to gain principal equity investor experience.

Such expertise can prove invaluable for the companies concerned, as well as for the banks.

'There is an argument that doing a debt-for-equity swap helps a company recover faster,' said Mr Sach.

'At the beginning of a restructuring, management teams are often concerned that a debt-equity swap will impair their ability to take decisive action,' said Joseph Swanson, co-head of European restructuring at Houlihan Lokey. His firm is advising INM's bondholders who are set to own 46 per cent of the company as a result of a debt-for-equity swap. "Most deals are structured with an eye to corporate governance best practices, where significant decision-making power is delegated to the new board and shareholder input is limited to board selection and approval of major strategic initiatives. The result is that management is empowered to create enterprise value.'

Styles & Wood has certainly benefited from restructuring. 'RBS was supportive and has no involvement in the running of the business day-to-day, but the restructuring itself has given us the ability to maintain our market share and we have the ability to invest in the business again,' said Ivan McKeever, chief executive.

But however desirable a debt-for-equity swap might be for companies and their lenders, restructurings are proving much harder to achieve than anyone expected. Negotiators have to contend with diverse and large creditor groups, a dearth in liquidity and complex debt structures. Banks and structured funds that invested heavily in riskier debt at the height of the credit boom have been accused of leaving too much debt on companies in restructurings.

'Coralling a diverse group of lenders into a deal is difficult,' said Andrew Grimstone, partner at Deloitte. 'Some are restricted in the debt writedowns they can take and others in their ability to swap debt for equity, which compounds the restructuring issues. In some cases, too much debt is being left on the company balance sheet and this will be a problem for lenders when they want to sell their equity stakes.'

EXHIBIT 18.4

Source: *Financial Times* 23 October 2009, p. 23.

As the risk of financial distress rises with the gearing ratio shareholders (and lenders) demand an increasing return in compensation. The important issue is at what point does the probability of financial distress so increase the cost of equity and debt that it outweighs the benefit of the tax relief on debt? Figure 18.7 shows that there is an optimal level of gearing. At low levels of debt the major influence on the overall cost of capital (the WACC – weighted average cost of capital) is the cheaper after-tax cost of debt. As gearing rises investors become more concerned about the risk of financial distress and therefore the required rates of return rise. The fear of loss factor becomes of overriding importance at high gearing levels. (There is more on this relationship in Chapter 10.)

Some factors influencing the risk of financial distress costs

The susceptibility to financial distress varies from company to company. Here are some influences:

- **The sensitivity of the company's revenues to the general level of economic activity** If a company is highly responsive to the ups and downs in the economy, shareholders and lenders may perceive a greater risk of liquidation and/or distress and demand a higher return in compensation for gearing compared with that demanded for a firm which is less sensitive to economic events.

- **The proportion of fixed to variable costs** A firm that is highly operationally geared, and which also takes on high borrowing, may find that equity and debt holders demand a high return for the increased risk.

- **The liquidity and marketability of the firm's assets** Some firms invest in a type of asset which can be easily sold at a reasonably high and certain value should they go into liquidation. This is of benefit to the financial security holders and so they may not demand such a high risk premium. A hotel chain, for example, should it suffer a decline in profitability, can usually sell hotels in a reasonably active property market. Investors in an advertising agency, with few saleable assets, would be less sanguine about rises in gearing.

- **The cash-generative ability of the business** Some firms produce a high regular flow of cash and so can reasonably accept a higher gearing level than a firm with lumpy and delayed cash inflows.

Table 18.4 illustrates that the optimal gearing level for firms shifts depending on key characteristics of the underlying business.

FIGURE 18.7

The cost of capital and the value of the firm with taxes and financial distress, as gearing increases

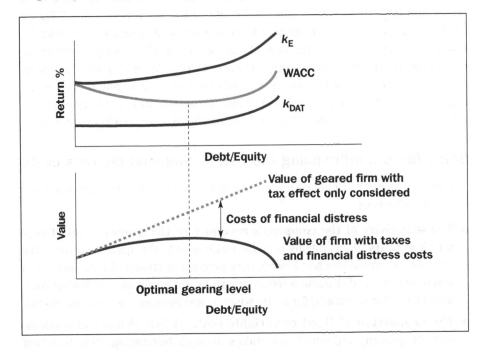

TABLE 18.4

The characteristics of the underlying business influences the risk of liquidation/distress, and therefore WACC, and the optimal gearing level

Characteristic	Food retailer	Steel producer
Sensitivity to economic activity	Relatively insensitive to economic fluctuations	Dependent on general economic prosperity
Operational gearing	Most costs are variable	Most costs are fixed
Asset liquidity	Shops, stock, etc., easily sold	Assets have few/no alternative uses. Thin secondhand market
Cash-generative ability	High or stable cash flow	Irregular cash flow
Likely acceptable gearing ratio	**HIGH**	**LOW**

Agency costs

Another restraining influence on the decision to take on high debt is the agency cost of doing so. Agency costs arise out of what is known as the 'principal–agent' problem. In most large firms the finance providers (principals) are not able to actively manage the firm. They employ 'agents' (managers) and it is possible for these agents to act in ways that are not always in the best interests of the equity or debt holders.

> Agency costs are the costs of preventing agents (e.g. managers) pursuing their own interests at the expense of their principals (e.g. shareholders). Examples include contracting costs and costs of monitoring. In addition, there is the agency cost of the loss of wealth caused by the extent to which prevention measures have not worked and managers continue to pursue non-shareholder wealth goals.

If management are acting for the maximisation of shareholder wealth debt holders may have reason to fear agency problems, because there may be actions that potentially benefit the owners at the expense of lenders. It is possible for lenders to be fooled or misled by managers. For example, management might raise money from bondholders saying that this is low-risk lending (and therefore paying a low interest rate) because the firm has low gearing and the funds will be used for a low-risk project. In the event the managers invest in high-risk ventures, and the firm becomes more highly geared by borrowing more. As a result the original lenders do not receive a return sufficient for the level of risk and the firm has the benefit of low-interest financing.

Alternatively, consider a firm already in financial distress. From the shareholders' point of view there is little to lose from taking an enormous gamble by accepting very high-risk projects. If the gamble pays off the shareholders will win but the debt holders will gain no more than the obligated fixed interest. If it fails, the shareholders are no worse off but the lenders experience default on their securities. Another temptation is for the shareholders to take large amounts out of a business through the payment of dividends when the managers become aware of a high chance of liquidation, leaving the debt holders with little to salvage.

The problem boils down to one of *information asymmetry* – that is, the managers are in possession of knowledge unavailable to the debt providers. One of the solutions is to spend money on monitoring. The lenders will require a premium on the debt interest to compensate for this additional cost. Also restrictions (covenants) are usually built into a lending agreement. For example, there may be limits on the level of dividends so that shareholders do not strip the company of cash. There may be limits placed on the overall level of indebtedness, with precise capital and income-gearing ratios. Managers may be restricted in the disposal of major assets or constrained in the type of activity they may engage in.

Extensive covenants imposed by lenders can be costly for shareholders because they reduce the firm's operating freedom and investment flexibility. Projects with a high NPV may be forgone because of the cautiousness of lenders. The opportunity costs can be especially frustrating for firms with high growth potential.

Thus agency costs include monitoring costs passed on as higher interest rates and the loss of value caused by the inhibition of managerial freedom to act. These increase with gearing, raising the implicit cost of debt and lowering the firm's value.

There may also be a psychological element related to agency costs; managers generally do not like restrictions placed on their freedom of action. They try to limit constraints by not raising a large proportion of capital from lenders. This may help to explain why, in practice, we find companies generally have modest gearing levels.

Borrowing capacity

Borrowing capacity has a close connection with agency costs. Lenders prefer secured lending, and this often sets an upper limit on gearing. They like to have the assurance that if the worst happened and the firm was unable to meet its interest obligations they could seize assets to sell off so that loans could be repaid. Thus, high levels of gearing are unusual because companies run out of suitable assets to offer as security against loans. So, the gearing level may not be determined by a theoretical, informed and considered management decision, but by the limits to total borrowing imposed by lenders.

Firms with assets which have an active secondhand market, and which do not tend to depreciate, such as property, are likely to have a higher borrowing capacity than firms that invest in assets with few alternative uses.

Managerial preferences

This is another agency cost. Liquidation affects not only shareholders but also managers and other employees. Indeed, the impact on these people can be far greater than the impact on well-diversified investors. It may be argued that managers have a natural tendency to be cautious about borrowing.

Pecking order

There is a 'pecking order' for financing. Firms prefer to finance with internally generated funds. If a firm has potentially profitable investments it will first of all try to finance the investments by using the store of previous years' profits, that is, retained earnings. If still more funds are needed, firms will go to the capital markets. However, the debt market is called on first, and only as a last resort will companies raise equity finance. The pecking order of financing is in sharp contrast to the model of trade-off between financial distress and the tax benefits of higher debt, in which an optimal capital structure is targeted (see chapter 10). Myers (1984, p. 581) puts it this way: 'In this story, there is no well-defined target debt–equity mix, because there are two kinds of equity, internal and external, one at the top of the pecking order and one at the bottom.'

One reason for placing new issues of equity at the bottom is supposedly that the stock markets perceive an equity issue as a sign of problems – an act of desperation. Myers and Majluf (1984) provide a theoretical explanation of why an equity issue might be bad news – managers will issue shares only when they believe the firm's shares are overpriced. In the capital structure literature, the term 'adverse selection problem' is used to convey the idea that managers are likely to act on their informational advantage over investors and so there is an extra degree of risk for equity investors because usually only those managers observing overpricing of their shares relative to the company's prospects would elect for a new share issue. Companies with underpriced shares would generally raise debt capital. This means that equity has an 'adverse selection premium' – a raised level of return required – making newly raised equity an expensive form of finance, thus only the desperate raise funds by selling shares. Bennett Stewart (1990, p. 391) puts it: 'Raising equity conveys doubt. Investors suspect that management is attempting to shore up the firm's financial resources for rough times ahead by selling over-valued shares.'[8]

There is an argument that firms do not try to reach the 'correct' capital structure as dictated by theory, because managers are following a line of least resistance. Internal funds are the first choice because using retained earnings does not involve contact with outside investors. This avoids the discipline involved in trying to extract investors' money. For example, the communication process required to raise equity finance is usually time consuming and onerous, with a formal prospectus, etc., and investors will scrutinize the detailed justifications advanced for the need to raise additional finance. It seems reasonable to suppose that managers will feel more comfortable using funds they already have in their hands. However, if they do have to obtain external financing then debt is next in the line of least resistance. This is because the degree of questioning and publicity associated with a bank loan or bond issue is usually significantly less than that associated with a share issue.

Another reason for a pecking order is that ordinary shares are more expensive to issue than debt capital, which in turn is more expensive than simply applying previously generated profits. The costs of new issues and rights issues of shares can be very expensive, whereas retained earnings are available without transaction costs.

The pecking order idea helps to explain why the most profitable companies often borrow very little. It is not that they have a low target debt ratio, but because they do not need outside finance. If they are highly profitable they will use these profits for growth opportunities and so end up with very little debt and no need to issue shares.

Less profitable firms with an extensive investment programme issue debt because they do not have internal funds sufficient for their capital investment programme and because debt is first in the pecking order of externally raised finance.

Market timing

A counter argument to the reluctance to issue equity under the pecking order theory is the **market timing theory** (*see* Baker and Wurgler, 2002). Here gearing decreases when firms have the opportunity to issue shares at a high price ('over-priced') and increases when share values are low as firms buy in their shares (remember that, in theory, gearing is measured by market values of debt and equity not balance sheet values). Thus gearing varies in response to opportunities to sell or buy shares, not according to a trade-off theory rationale; and movement away from optimal gearing levels persists into the long term. In Baker and Wurgler's view there is no attempt at an optimal capital structure; market timing decisions just accumulate into a capital structure.

However, Alti (2006) shows that despite advantage being taken of high share prices the gearing ratio effect of this completely vanishes within two years (this study examined 'hot' initial public offerings): 'the results are consistent with the modified version of the traditional trade-off view of capital structure, one that includes market timing as a short term factor' (Alti, p. 1684). Also, Leary and Roberts (2005) show that Baker and Wurgler's market timing effects of gearing are more likely to be due to the high cost of regularly changing debt or equity levels (issue or redemption costs). Firms do move back towards the target debt–equity range, but the high costs of issuance of debt and so on mean that this is gradual. Furthermore, Graham and Harvey's (2001) survey confirmed that the majority of firms have debt–equity ratio targets.

Some further key factors affecting the gearing level

Financial slack

Operating and strategic decisions are generally the prime determinants of company value, not the financing decision. Being able to respond to opportunities as they fleetingly appear in business is important. If a firm is already highly geared it may find it difficult to gain access to more funds quickly as the need arises. Financial slack means having cash (or near-cash) and/or spare debt capacity. This slack can be extremely valuable and firms may restrict debt levels below that of the 'optimal' gearing level in order that the risk of missing profitable investments is reduced.

> Financial slack means having cash (or near-cash) and/or spare debt capacity.

Graham and Harvey (2001) show that 59 percent of US companies deliberately restrict debt 'so we have enough internal funds available to pursue new projects when they come along'. This was the most important factor determining the debt levels of these firms, out-ranking tax deductibility of debt and risk of distress.

Financial slack is also valuable for meeting unforeseen circumstances. Managers may wish to be cautious and have a reserve of cash or spare borrowing capacity to cope with a 'rainy day'.

An interesting example of this is described by the treasurer of Pfizer, Richard Passov, who argued in a *Harvard Business Review* article (2003) that the reason Pfizer, Intel and other firms with high levels of investment in intangible assets have cash on their balance sheets and no borrowing is because they are subject to high business risk through their risky R&D programmes. This means that they cannot take the chance of having any financial risk at all. They have billions in cash as cushions to meet unforeseen shocks and allow the continuance of investment in potential winners, many of which may not be providing cash inflows for five years or more. They are concerned about the potential for financial distress either to halt promising investment or to force the hurried sale of expensive equity (i.e. selling a chunk of the company too cheaply) at a time of crisis.

Signalling

Managers and other employees often have a very powerful incentive to ensure the continuance of the business. They are usually the people who suffer most should it become insolvent. Because of this, it is argued, managers will generally increase the gearing level only if they are confident about the future. Shareholders are interested in obtaining information about the company's prospects, and changes in financing can become a signal representing management's assessment of future returns. It is thought that an increase in gearing should lead to a rise in share price as managers are signalling their increased optimism. Managers, therefore, need to consider the signal transmitted to the market concerning future income whenever it announces major gearing changes.

Control

The source of finance chosen may be determined by the effect on the control of the organisation. For example, if a shareholder with 50 percent of a company's shares is unable to pay for more shares in a rights issue, he or she may be reluctant to allow the company to raise funds in this way, especially if shares are sold to a rival. This limits the range of sources of finance and may lead to a rise in debt levels.

Tax exhaustion

Many companies do not have extremely high debt levels because their profits are not high enough to benefit from the tax shield.

Industry group gearing

Suppose you are a financial manager trying to decide on an appropriate gearing ratio and have absorbed all the above theories, ideas and models. You might have concluded that there is no precise formula which can be employed to establish the *best* debt–equity ratio for firms in all circumstances. It depends on so many specific, and often difficult-to-measure, factors. One must consider the tax position of the firm, the likelihood of financial distress, the type of business the firm is in, the saleability of its assets, the level of business risk and the 'psychology' of the market. (For example, are rights issues perceived as bad signals, and debt issues a sign of confidence, or not?)

Given all these difficulties about establishing the theoretically 'correct' gearing level that will maximise shareholder wealth, managers may be tempted simply to follow the crowd, to look at what similar firms are doing, to find out what the financial markets seem to regard as a reasonable level of gearing, and to follow suit.

Some further thoughts on debt finance

There are some intriguing ideas advanced to promote the greater use of debt in firms' capital structure. Three of them will be considered here.

Motivation

High debt will motivate managers to perform better and in the interests of shareholders. Consider this thought: if an entrepreneur (an owner-manager) wishes to raise finance for expansion purposes, debt finance is regarded as the better choice from the perspective of entrepreneurs and society. The logic works like this: if new shares are sold to outside investors, this will dilute the entrepreneur's control and thus the level of interest of the entrepreneur in the success of the business. The manager would now be more inclined to take rewards in the form of salary, perks and leisure rather than concentrating purely on returns to shareholders. The firm will be run less efficiently because of reduced effort by the key person.

Or consider this argument: Bennett Stewart argues that in firms without a dominant shareholder and with a diffuse shareholder base, a recapitalisation which substitutes debt for equity can result in the concentration of the shares in the hands of a smaller, more proactive group. These shareholders have a greater incentive to monitor the firm. (If managers are made part of this shareholder owning group there is likely to be a greater alignment of shareholder and managers' interests.) Large quoted firms often have tens of thousands of shareholders, any one of whom has little incentive to go to the expense of opposing managerial action detrimental to shareholders' interests – the costs of rallying and co-ordinating investors often outweigh the benefits to the individuals involved. However, if the shareholder base is shrunk through the substitution of debt for equity, the remaining shareholders would have greater incentive to act against mismanagement. An extreme form of this switch to concentration is when a management team purchases a company through a leveraged buyout or buy-in (*see* Chapter 17). Here a dispersed, divided and effectively powerless group of shareholders is replaced with a focused and knowledgeable small team, capable of rapid action and highly motivated to ensure the firm's success.

Reinvestment risk

High debt forces the firm to make regular payments to debt holders, thereby denying 'spare' cash to the managers. In this way the firm avoids placing a temptation in the manager's path, which might lead to investment in negative NPV projects and to making destructive acquisitions. Deliberately keeping managers short of cash avoids the problem that shareholders' funds may be applied to projects with little thought to returns. If funds are needed, instead of drawing on a large pot held within the firm, managers have to ask debt and equity finance providers. This will help to ensure that their plans are subject to the scrutiny and discipline of the market.

The problem of managers over-supplied with money, given the limited profitable investment opportunities open to them, seems to be widespread, but specific examples are only clearly seen with hindsight. For example, in the 1990s GEC was a cash rich company under Arnold Weinstock. New managers changed the name to Marconi and spent billions buying high technology communication infrastructure companies working at the cutting-edge, but with little in the way of certainty over the likely future demand for the services/goods they offered – hope of a glorious future was all that was needed for the spending of the large pot of money as well as additional borrowings. When demand projections were shown to be hopelessly optimistic the company barely survived – shareholder value was destroyed on a massive scale.

> Hope of a glorious future was all that was needed for the spending of the large pot of money.

The danger of poor investment decisions is at its worst in firms that are highly profitable but which have few growth opportunities. The annual surplus cash flow is often squandered on increasingly marginal projects within existing business units or wasted in a diversification effort looking to buy growth opportunities: unfortunately these often cost more than they are worth. It is far better, say Stewart (1990), Hart (1995), Jensen (1986) and others, that managers are forced to justify the use of funds by having to ask for it at regular intervals. This process can be assisted by having high debt levels which absorb surplus cash through interest and principal payments and deposit it out of the reach of empire-building, perk-promoting, lazy managers.

High debt can also bring with it covenants and monitoring that restricts managerial activities so as to reduce the risk of over-investment for both debt and equity holders. Evidence for this benefit was found in emerging financial markets by Harvey *et al.* (2004).

Operating and strategic efficiency

'Equity is soft; debt is hard. Equity is forgiving; debt is insistent. Equity is a pillow; debt is a dagger.' This statement by Bennett Stewart (1990, p. 580) emphasises that operating and strategic problems and inefficiencies are less likely to be attended to and corrected with a capital base that is primarily equity. However, the managers of a highly geared company are more likely to be attuned to the threat posed by falling efficiency and profitability. The failing is the same under both a high equity and a high debt structure: it just seems more of a crisis when there is a large interest bill each month. The geared firm, it is argued, simply cannot afford to have any value-destructive activities (business units or product lines). Managers are spurred on by the pressing need to make regular payments, to reform, dispose or close – and quickly.

> Equity is soft; debt is hard.

These are some of the arguments put forward, particularly during bouts of market confidence, when it is normal to see high levels of leveraged buyouts (LBOs), junk bonds and share repurchase programmes, in support of high debt.

They seem to make some sense, but the downside of excessive debt must be balanced against these forcefully advanced ideas. Turning back to Table 18.3, which shows the costs of financial distress, can help to give some perspective. In addition, many firms have found themselves crippled and at a competitive disadvantage because of the burden of high debt – e.g. Marconi is a shadow of its former self, as are many house-building companies following their over-borrowing in 2008.

Rounding up the capital structure arguments

The proportion of debt in the total capital of a firm can influence the overall cost of capital and therefore the value of the firm and the wealth of shareholders. If, as a result of increasing the gearing ratio, it is possible to lower the weighted average cost of capital, then all the future net cash flows will be discounted at a lower rate. It is generally observed that as gearing increases, the WACC declines because of the lower cost of debt. This is further enhanced by the tax relief available on debt capital.

But as gearing rises the risk of financial distress causes shareholders (and eventually debt holders) to demand a greater return. This eventually rises to such an extent that it outweighs the benefit of the lower cost of debt, and the WACC starts to rise. This risk factor is difficult, if not impossible, to quantify and therefore the exact position and shape of the WACC curve for each firm remains largely unknown. Nevertheless, it seems reasonable to postulate there is a U-shaped relationship like that shown in Figure 18.8.

We cannot scientifically establish a best debt–equity ratio. There are many complicating factors that determine the actual gearing levels adopted by firms. These cloud the picture sufficiently for us to say that while we accept that the WACC is probably U-shaped for firms generally, we cannot precisely calculate a best gearing level.

This explains why there is such a variation in gearing levels. Some firms are under the influence of particular factors to a greater extent than other firms: some may have very low borrowing capacity, and others may have management keen on signalling confidence in the future; some may have very cautious management unwilling to borrow and a diffuse unco-ordinated shareholder body; some may be in very volatile product markets with high liquidation probabilities and others in stable industries with marketable tangible assets; other companies may be dominated by leaders steeped in the high gearing thinking of the late 1980s and early 1990s, believing that managers are better motivated and less likely to waste resources if the firm is highly indebted.

So, to the question of whether a firm can obtain a level of gearing which will maximise shareholder wealth the answer is 'yes'. The problem is finding this level in such a multifaceted analysis.

FIGURE 18.8

The weighted average cost of capital is U-shaped and value can be altered by changing the gearing level

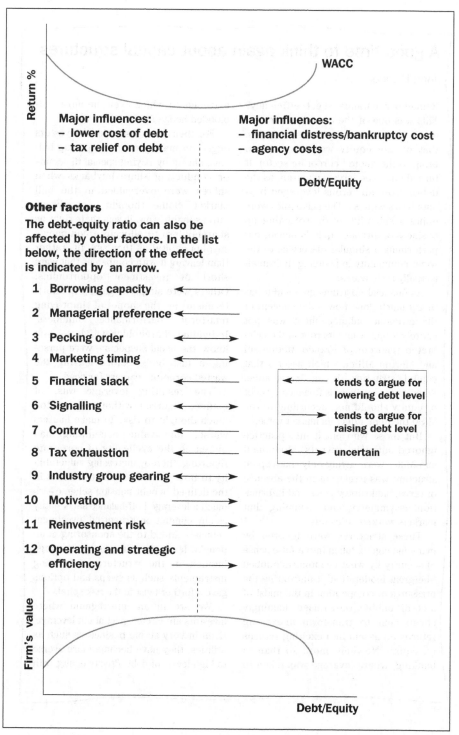

Exhibit 18.5 attacks the view that very high borrowing leads to an 'efficient balance sheet'.

A good time to think again about capital structures

John Plender

Remember balance sheet efficiency? This was one of the countless virtues, much trumpeted in business schools, that private equity was supposed to bring to the quoted corporate sector. It turned out to be largely claptrap, as the debris from numerous leveraged buyouts bears witness. The academics were doing a splendid job in softening up business on private equity's behalf, but performing a singular disservice to the wider community in peddling their intellectually toxic wares.

As financial nostrums go – and it has pretty much gone now – the concept of the efficient balance sheet was not entirely loopy. It had its root in the celebrated theorem of Franco Modigliani and Merton Miller, which asserts that capital structure is an irrelevance. Whether the business is financed by debt or equity should not, according to the M&M theorem, affect its market value.

But those who put it into practice ignored authorial caveats. Modigliani and Miller were saying only that capital structure was irrelevant in the absence of taxes, bankruptcy costs and information assymmetry, and assuming that markets worked efficiently.

These strictures were ignored by many managers, lulled into a false sense of security by what economists dubbed 'the great moderation'. Confronting the pressures of competition in the midst of a credit bubble, they raised seemingly cheap debt to transform unexciting returns on assets into exciting returns on equity. Nowhere more so than in banking, where leverage was taken to

extremes to which even the most red-blooded hedge funds did not aspire.

For their part, institutional investors egged on management to gear up balance sheets by paying special dividends or conducting share buybacks when shares were overvalued in the bull market. Some thought, not always unreasonably, that it was their right as shareholders to allocate a company's surplus capital as they saw fit, rather than leaving it with companies that were short of investment opportunites. Others were simply engaging in short-termism in the hope of improving quarterly performance numbers. Individual shareholder activists – you know, the usual suspects – were pursuing a fast buck before leaving the wasted corporate carcass for dead.

The resulting leverage was, of course, incurred without giving too much thought to risk. To make matters worse, fair value accounting had increased the cyclicality of corporate reporting, thereby increasing vulnerability to breaches of covenant. Deficits in the defined benefit pension scheme – as much a leveraged off-balance sheet entity as any conduit or structured investment vehicle – added to the sponsoring company's leverage. Embedded leverage implicit in the structure of hedging instruments such as swaps and options gave a further twist to the risk spiral.

We are in an interregnum where investors are circumspect about leverage. Even in very stable businesses such as utilities, they have become more averse to high levels of debt. Private equity, with little access to leverage, no longer poses a predatory threat to quoted companies that run 'inefficient' balance sheets. There is time for companies to think again about capital structures.

Clearly bankers and other creditors will do some of the thinking for them. As banks deleverage their balance sheets, the corporate sector has to deleverage too. But when the cycle turns up, managers will need to avoid simplistically equating leverage with a reduced cost of capital. They should remember, too, that the effect of changes in credit are assymmetric. The cost of a ratings downgrade, especially to below investment grade,

may exceed the cost of going above the optimal rating, so it may make sense to overshoot upwards. There may also be a case, says Markus Pertl, managing partner of consultants SCCO International, for adjusting leverage counter-cyclically. This would complement the probable shift to counter-cyclical provisioning in banking.

Policymakers should, in turn, think about the tax treatment of debt. It beggars belief, after such a monumental debt binge, that this fundamental spur to leverage scarcely features on the policy agenda.

Exhibit 18.5

Source: *Financial Times* 28 October 2009, p. 34.

Conclusion

The main focus of this chapter has been on the proportion of debt to equity and the type of debt finance that is most suitable for the company. These ideas and principles must be read with the knowledge of the characteristics of different types of finance in Chapters 15, 16 and 17, and with an understanding of the calculation of the cost of capital (Chapter 10). Each company faces different circumstances and so the most appropriate mixture of finance, with its concomitant risks, is likely to be different from other companies, even those in the same industry. The tools provided in this chapter will hopefully allow a thoughtful discussion when contemplating the best debt level and mixture of debt-types for your firm.

Websites

www.treasurers.org   Association of Corporate Treasurers
www.ft.com   Financial Times

Notes

1 Moral hazard was one of the causes of the financial crisis of 2008–09. Bankers could say to themselves: 'It's alright if we take great risks. If it works out, we get large bonuses. If it doesn't, the taxpayer has provided a kind of backstop insurance to bail us out.'

2 However there are long periods (years) when yield curves show interest rates lower 'at the long end' than 'at the short end'.

3 Assume no hedging in the derivative or money markets.

4 Some analysts might substitute total liabilities for long-term debt.

5 These problems also apply to capital gearing measures (2) and (3).

6 To make this discussion easier to follow it will be assumed that there are only two types of finance, debt and ordinary shares. However, the introduction of other types of finance does not fundamentally alter the analysis.

7 Net worth (or shareholders' equity) divided by debt plus equity is another popular capital gearing ratio.

8 Some theorists have taken the argument a step further: managers will want to issue debt even if their shares are currently over-valued. The logic is as follows: investors are aware that managers have an incentive to sell shares when they are over-priced and therefore take an equity issue as a bad signal. So, if management go ahead with the share sale, the equity price will fall. To avoid this, managers choose to issue debt.

19

OPTIONS

Introduction

Derivatives – options, futures, forwards, etc. – are the subject of this and the next two chapters. Derivative instruments have become increasingly important for companies over the past 30 years. Managers can exploit these powerful tools to either reduce risk or to go in search of high returns. Naturally, exceptionally high returns come with exceptionally high risk. So managers using derivatives for this purpose need to understand the risk they are exposing their company to. Many companies have lost fortunes by allowing managers to be mesmerised by the potential for riches while failing to take time to fully understand the instruments they were buying. They jumped in, unaware of, or ignoring, the potential for enormous loss. These three chapters describe the main types of derivative and show how they can be used for controlling risk (hedging) and for revving-up returns (speculation).

> Exceptionally high returns come with exceptionally high risk.

What is a derivative?

A derivative instrument is an asset whose performance is based on (derived from) the behaviour of the value of an underlying asset (usually referred to simply as the 'underlying'). The most common underlyings include commodities (for example tea or pork bellies), shares, bonds, share indices, currencies and interest rates. Derivatives are contracts that give the *right*, and sometimes the obligation, to buy or sell a quantity of the underlying, or benefit in another way from a rise or fall in the value of the underlying. It is the legal right that becomes an asset, with its own value, and it is the right that is purchased or sold.

The derivatives markets have received an enormous amount of attention from the press in recent years. This is hardly surprising as spectacular losses have been made and a number of companies have been brought to the point of collapse using derivatives. Some examples of the unfortunate use of derivatives include:

- Procter & Gamble, which lost $102m speculating on the movements of future interest rates in 1994;

- Barings, Britain's oldest merchant bank, which lost over £800m on the Nikkei Index (the Japanese share index) contracts on the Singapore and Osaka derivatives exchanges, leading to the bank's demise in 1995;

- Long-Term Capital Management, which attempted to exploit the 'mispricing' of financial instruments, by making use of option pricing theory. In 1998 the firm collapsed and the Federal Reserve Bank of New York cajoled 14 banks and brokerage houses to put up $3.6bn to save it, thereby preventing a financial system breakdown;

- Financial institutions that were destroyed in 2008 because they bought derivatives whose value depended on US mortgage borrowers continuing to pay their mortgages. When a proportion could not pay their debts, the derivatives (of asset-backed securitised bonds) became either very difficult/impossible to value. The uncertainty surrounding the value of these derivatives was a trigger for the financial crisis and the subsequent recession. There was financial distress for hundreds of financial institutions that had no connection with the US mortgage market or the related derivatives, e.g. Northern Rock;

- Société Générale, which lost €49 billion in 2008 when a trader placed bets on the future movements of equity markets using derivatives (up to €50 billion was gambled at one time).

In many of the financial scandals derivatives have been used (or misused) to speculate rather than to reduce risk. These chapters examine both of these applications of derivatives but places particular emphasis on the hedging (risk-mitigating) facility they provide. These are powerful tools and managers can abuse that power either through ignorance or through deliberate acceptance of greater risk in the anticipation of greater reward. However there is nothing inherently wrong with the tools themselves. If employed properly they can be remarkably effective at limiting risk.

A long history

Derivative instruments have been employed for more than two thousand years. Olive growers in ancient Greece unwilling to accept the risk of a low price for their crop when harvested months later would enter into forward agreements whereby a price was agreed for delivery at a specific time. This reduced uncertainty for both the grower and the purchaser of the olives. In the Middle Ages forward contracts were traded in a kind of secondary market, particularly for wheat in Europe. A futures market was established in Osaka's rice market in Japan in the seventeenth century. Tulip bulb options were traded in seventeenth-century Amsterdam.

Commodity futures trading really began to take off in the nineteenth century with the Chicago Board of Trade regulating the trading of grains and other futures and options, and the London Metal Exchange dominating metal trading.

So derivatives are not new. What is different today is the size and importance of the derivatives markets. The past 30 years have witnessed an explosive growth of volumes of trade, variety of derivatives products, and the number and range of users and uses. In the 20 years to 2009 the face value of outstanding derivatives contracts rose dramatically to stand at over US$600 trillion (US$600,000,000,000,000,000). Compare that with the total production of all the goods and services in the UK in a year of around £1.3 trillion.

> Derivatives are not new. What is different today is the size and importance of the markets.

What is an option?

An option is a contract giving one party the right, but not the obligation, to buy or sell a financial instrument, commodity or some other underlying asset at a given price, at or before a specified date. The purchaser of the option can either exercise the right or let it lapse – the choice is theirs.

A very simple option would be where a firm pays the owner of land a non-returnable *premium* (say £10,000) for an option to buy the land at an agreed price (say, £1m) because the firm is considering the development of a retail park within the next five years. The property developer may pay a number of option premiums to owners of land in different parts of the country. If planning permission is eventually granted on a particular plot the option to purchase may be *exercised*. In other words the developer pays the price agreed at the time that the option contract was arranged to purchase the land (say, £1m). Options on other plots will be *allowed to lapse* and will have no value. By using an option the property developer has 'kept the options open' with regard to which site to buy and develop and, indeed whether to enter the retail park business at all.

Options can also be *traded*. Perhaps the option to buy could be sold to another company keener to develop a particular site than the original option purchaser. It may be sold for much more than the original £10,000 option premium, even before planning permission has been granted.

Once planning permission has been granted the greenfield site may be worth £1.5m. If there is an option to buy at £1m the option right has an *intrinsic value* of £500,000, representing a 4,900 percent return on £10,000. From this we can see the gearing effect of options: very large sums can be gained in a short period of time for a small initial cash outlay.

Share options

Share options have been traded for centuries but their use expanded dramatically with the creation of traded option markets in Chicago, Amsterdam and, in 1978, the London Traded Options Market. In 1992 this became part of the London International Financial Futures and Options Exchange, LIFFE (pronounced 'life'). Euronext bought LIFFE in 2002, which later combined with the New York Stock Exchange, so LIFFE is now called NYSE Liffe.

A share call option gives the purchaser a right, but not the obligation, to *buy* a fixed number of shares at a specified price at some time in the future. In the case of traded options on NYSE Liffe, one option contract relates to a quantity of 1,000 shares. The seller of the option, who receives the premium, is referred to as the *writer*. The writer of a call option is obligated to sell the agreed quantity of shares at the agreed price some time in the future. American-style options can be exercised by the buyer at any time up to the expiry date, whereas European-style options can only be exercised on a predetermined future date. Just to confuse everybody, the distinction has nothing to do with geography: most options traded in Europe are US-style options.

Call option holder (call option buyers)

Now let us examine the call options available on an underlying share – Land Securities, on Friday 5 December 2009. There are a number of different options available for this share, many of which are not reported in the table presented in the *Financial Times*,[1] part of which is reproduced as Table 19.1.

TABLE 19.1
Call options on Land Securities shares, 5 December 2009

	Call option prices (premiums) pence		
Exercise price	Dec	Jan	Feb
680p	16.5	26.5	38
700p	8	17.5	29
Share price on 5.12.09 = 685p			

Source: *Financial Times* 7 December 2009. Reprinted with permission.

So, what do the figures mean? If you wished to obtain the right to buy 1,000 shares on or before late January 2010, at an exercise price of 700p, you would pay a premium of £175 (1,000 × 17.5p). If you wished to keep your option to purchase open for another month you could select the February call. But this right to insist that the writer sells the shares at the fixed price of 700p on or before a date in late February[2] will cost another £115 (the total premium payable on one option contract is £290 rather than £175). This extra £115 represents additional *time value*. Time value arises because of the potential for the market price of the underlying to change in a way that creates intrinsic value. The intrinsic value of an option is the pay-off that would be received if the underlying were at its current level when the option expires. In this case, there is currently (5 December) no intrinsic value because the right to buy is at 700p whereas the share price is 685p. However if you look at the call option with an exercise price of 680p then the right to buy at 680p has intrinsic value because if you purchased at 680p by exercising the option, thereby obtaining 1,000 shares, you could immediately sell at 685p in the share market: intrinsic value = 5p per share, or £50 for 1,000 shares. The longer the time over which the option is exercisable the greater the chance that the price will move to give intrinsic value – this explains the higher premiums on more distant expiry options. Time value is the amount by which the option premium exceeds the intrinsic value.

The two exercise price (also called strike price) levels presented in Table 19.1 illustrate an *in-the-money-option* (the 680p call option) and an *out-of-the-money-option* (the 700p call option). The underlying share price is above the strike price of 680p and so this call option has an intrinsic value of 5p and is therefore in-the-money. The right to buy at 700p is out-of-the-money because the share price is below the option exercise price and therefore has no intrinsic value. The holder of a 700p option would not exercise this right to buy at 700p because the shares can be bought on the Stock Exchange for 685p. (It is sometimes possible to buy an *at-the-money option*, which is one where the market share price is equal to the option exercise price.)

To emphasise the key points: The option premiums vary in proportion to the length of time over which the option is exercisable (e.g. they are higher for a February option than for a January option). Also, call options with a lower exercise prices will have higher premiums.

Illustration

Suppose that you are confident that Land Securities shares are going to rise significantly over the next month and a half to 900p and you purchase a January 680 call at 26.5 pence.[3] The cost of this right to purchase 1,000 shares is £265 (26.5p × 1,000 shares). If the share rises as expected then you could exercise the right to purchase the shares for a total of £6,800 and then sell these in the market for £9,000. A profit of £2,200 less £265 = £1,935 is made before transaction costs (the brokers' fees, etc. would be in the region of £20–£50). This represents a massive 730 percent rise before costs (£1,935/£265).

However the future is uncertain and the share price may not rise as expected. Let us consider two other possibilities. First, the share price may remain at 685p throughout the life of the option. Second, the stock market may have a severe downturn and Land Securities shares may fall to 500p. These possibilities are shown in Table 19.2.

TABLE 19.2

Profits and losses on the January 680 call option following purchase on 5 December 2009

	Assumptions on share price in January at expiry		
	900p	685p	500p
Cost of purchasing shares by exercising the option	£6,800	£6,800	£6,800
Value of shares bought	£9,000	£6,850	£5,000
Profit from exercise of option and sale of shares in the market	£2,200	£50	Not exercised
Less option premium paid	£265	£265	£265
Profit (loss) before transaction costs	£1,935	−£215	−£265
Percentage return over $1\frac{1}{2}$ months	730%	−81%	−100%

In the case of a standstill in the share price the option gradually loses its time value over the one and a half months until, at expiry, only the intrinsic value of 5p per share remains. The fall in the share price to 500p illustrates one of the advantages of purchasing options over some other derivatives: the holder has a right to abandon the option and is not forced to buy the underlying share at the option exercise price – this saves £1,800. It would have added insult to injury to have to buy at £6,800 and sell at £5,000 after having already lost £265 on the premium for the purchase of the option.

A comparison of Figures 19.1 and 19.2 shows the extent to which the purchase of an option gears up the return from share price movements: a wider dispersion of returns is experienced. On 5 December 2009, 1,000 shares could be bought for £6,850. If the value rose to £9,000, a 31 percent return would be made, compared with a 730 percent return if options are bought. We would all like the higher positive return on the option than the lower one available on the underlying – but would we all accept the downside risk associated with this option? Consider the following possibilities:

- If share price remains at 685p:
  - Return if shares are bought: 0%
  - Return if one 680 January call option is bought: –81% (paid £265 for the option which declines to its intrinsic value of only £50*)

* £50 is the intrinsic value at expiry (685p – 680p) × 1,000 = £50

- If share price falls to 500p:
  - Return if shares are bought: –27%
  - Return if one 680 January call option is bought: –100% (the option is worth nothing).

FIGURE 19.1

Profit if 1,000 shares are bought in Land Securities on 5 December 2009 at 685p

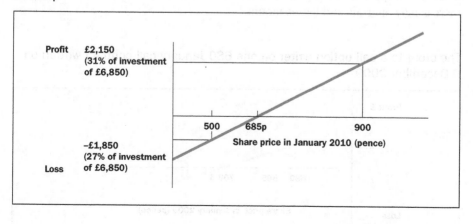

FIGURE 19.2

Profit if one 680 January call option contract (for 1,000 shares) in Land Securities is purchased on 5 December 2009 and held to maturity

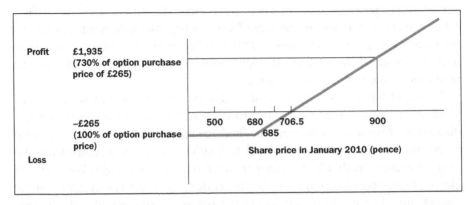

The holder of the call option will not exercise unless the share price is at least 680p. At a lower price it will be cheaper to buy the 1,000 shares on the stock market. Break-even does not occur until a price of 706.5p because of the need to cover the cost of the premium (680p + 26.5p). However at higher prices the option value increases, pence for pence, with the share price. Also the downside risk is limited to the size of the option premium.

Call option writers

The returns position for the writer of a call option in Land Securities can also be presented in a diagram (*see* Figure 19.3). With all these examples note that there is an assumption that the position is held to expiry.

If the market price is less than the exercise price (680p) in January the option will not be exercised and the call writer profits to the extent of the option premium (26.5p per share). A market price greater than the exercise price will result in the option being exercised and the writer will be forced to deliver 1,000 shares for a price of 680p. This may mean buying shares on the stock market to supply to the option holder. As the share price rises this becomes increasingly onerous and losses mount.

FIGURE 19.3

The profit to a call option writer on one 680 January call contract written on 5 December 2009

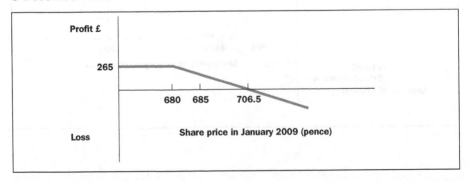

Note that in the sophisticated traded option markets of today very few option positions are held to expiry. In most cases the option holder sells the option in the market to make a cash profit or loss. Option writers often cancel out their exposure before expiry – for example they could purchase an option to buy the same quantity of shares at the same price and expiry date.

An example of an option writing strategy

Joe has a portfolio of shares worth £100,000 and is confident that while the market will go up steadily over time it will not rise over the next few months. He has a strategy of writing out-of-the-money (i.e. no intrinsic value) call options and pocketing premiums on a regular basis. Today (5 December 2009) Joe has written one option on February calls in Land Securities for an exercise price of 700p (current share price 685p). In other words, Joe is committed to delivering (selling) 1,000 shares at any time between 5 December 2009 and near the end of February 2010 for a price of 700p at the insistence of the person that bought the call. This could be very unpleasant for Joe if the market price rises to say 800p. Then the option holder will require Joe to sell shares worth £8,000 to him/her for only £7,000. However, Joe is prepared to take this risk for two reasons. First he receives the premium of 29p per share up front – this is 4.2% of each share's value, roughly equivalent to the annual dividend. This £290 will cushion any feeling of future regret at his actions. Second, Joe holds 1,000 Land Securities shares in his portfolio and so would not need to go into the market to buy the shares to then sell them to the option holder if the price did rise significantly. Joe has written a *covered* call option – so-called because he has backing in the form of the underlying shares. Joe only loses out if the share price on the day the option is exercised is greater than the strike price (700p) plus the premium (29p). He is prepared to risk losing some of the potential up side (above 700p + 29p = 729p) to gain the premium. He also reduces his loss on the downside: if the shares in his portfolio fall he has the premium as a cushion.

Some speculators engage in *uncovered (naked)* option writing. It is possible to lose a multiple of your current resources if you write a lot of option contracts and the price moves against you. Imagine if Joe had only £10,000 in savings and entered the options market by writing 30 Land Securities February 2010 700 calls receiving a premium of 29p × 30 × 1,000 = £8,700.* If the price moves to £8 Joe has to buy shares for £8 and then sell them to the option holders for £7.00, a loss of £1 per share: £1 × 30 × 1,000 = £30,000. Despite receiving the premiums Joe has wiped out his savings.

---

* This is simplified. In reality Joe would have to provide margin of cash or shares to reassure the clearing house that he could pay up if the market moved against him. So it could be that all of the premium received would be tied up in margin held by the clearing house (the role of a clearing house is explained in the next chapter).

Liffe share options

The *Financial Times* lists over eighty companies' shares in which options are traded (*see* Exhibit 19.1).

EQUITY OPTIONS

Option	Calls Dec	Calls Jan	Calls Feb	Puts Dec	Puts Jan	Puts Feb
AstraZeneca (*2843) 2800	68.5	100.5	127	26	55.5	144
2900	22	50	78.5	77.5	105.5	208.5
Aviva (*379.400) 370	15.75	23.25	32	5.75	13.75	22
380	9.5	17.75	26.75	10	17.75	26.25
Barclays (*303.5) 300	13.25	20	26.75	9.25	16.25	23.25
312	6.75	–	–	15.75	–	–
BG Group (*1099.5) 1050	59.5	72.5	95	6.5	21.5	44.5
1100	25.5	42.5	67.5	23	41	66.5
BHP Billiton (*1890.5) 1850	80	113	156.5	38.5	71	114.5
1900	52.5	85	131	60	94.5	138.5
BP 584.700) 580	12.5	19.5	27	8	14.5	25.75
600	4	9.75	16.75	19.5	24.75	37.25
Br Airways (*212) 210	8	12.25	16.75	6.75	11.5	17.75
215	5.5	9.75	–	9.5	14.25	–
BAT (*1938) 1900	52	67	88.5	12	28.5	49.5
1950	22.5	38.5	61.5	33.5	51	71.5
BSkyB (*543.5) 540	11.75	18	26	8	14.75	22.5
550	6.75	–	–	12.75	–	–
BT Group (*142.300) 140	4.5	5	7.5	2	4.75	7.5
145	1.75	2.75	5.25	4.25	7.5	10.25
Cable & Wire (*143) 140	5.25	7	9	2.25	3.75	5.75
145	2.5	4.5	6.25	4.5	6.25	8.25
Diageo (*1055) 1050	19.5	29.5	43.5	14.5	24.5	38
1100	3.5	11	22.5	49	56	66
GlaxoSmKl (*1311.5) 1300	25.5	39	52.5	13.5	27	50
1350	6	16	29.5	44	55.5	80
HSBC (*723.600) 720	20.5	32.5	44	17.5	28.5	40.5
741	11	–	–	29	–	–
Kingfisher (*238.800) 235	7.75	11.25	15.5	3.75	7	11.5
240	4.75	8.25	13	6	9.25	14
Land Secur (*685) 680	16.5	26.5	38	18	28.5	39.5
700	8	17.5	29	29.5	39.5	50

Option	Calls Dec	Calls Jan	Calls Feb	Puts Dec	Puts Jan	Puts Feb
Lloyds Bkg (*56) 51	6	7.25	–	1	2	–
56	2.75	3.75	5.75	2.5	4	5.5
Marks & S (*402.200) 400	8.75	15	21.25	6.25	13	18.75
410	4.25	10	16.25	11.5	18.	23.75
Morrison (Wm) (*279.700) 270	11	13.25	16	1.25	3	5.75
280	4	6.75	10.25	4.75	7	10.25
Rio Tinto (*3125) 3100	122.5	189	261.5	102	164.5	249.5
3200	75.5	143	212.5	151.5	217	304
Royal Bk Scot (*34.630) 32	3.75	4.5	5.75	1.25	1.75	3
34	2.25	3.25	4.25	1.5	2.75	3.75
Royal Dutch Shell 'B' (*1782.5) 1750	54	72.5	92	20	39.5	74
1800	25	44	64.5	42	63	99.5
RSA Ins Gp (*118) 115	4.25	5.75	7	1.25	2.75	4.25
120	1.75	3.25	4.75	3.75	5	6.75
Sainsbury (*323.800) 320	9	13.5	17.5	4.25	9	13
330	4.25	8.5	12.5	10.25	14.5	18.75
Std Chartd (*1513) 1500	57	83	111	45.5	69	95.5
1550	33	58	85	69.5	92.5	120
Tesco (*433.400) 430	9.5	13.75	18.25	6.25	10.25	14.75
440	4.75	8.5	13	11.25	15.25	19.75
Vodafone (*142.400) 140	3.75	5.5	7.5	1.5	3	5
145	1.25	2.75	5	3.75	5.5	7.5
Xstrata (*1066) 1050	52	79.5	112.5	36.5	62.5	94
1100	29	56	89	62.5	89	121

Option	Calls Dec	Calls Mar	Puts Dec	Puts Mar
Thomson Reuters xe (*1961.160) 1900	88	–	26.5	–
2000	34.5	111	73	160.5

Option	Calls Dec	Calls Mar	Calls Jun	Puts Dec	Puts Mar	Puts June
3i Group (*276.600) 274	8.25	19.5	–	6.5	23.5	–
280	5.25	–	28	9.75	–	32.75
BAE Systems (*336) 330	10	22.5	–	3.5	15.75	–
340	4.5	17.25	22.75	8.25	20.5	32.75
Capita (*728.5) 720	17	36	44	8.5	25.5	42.5
740	7	–	–	18.5	–	–
Carnival (*2097) 2000	118	193	239.5	20	105	166.5
2100	50.5	–	–	53.5	–	–
Compass (*438.300) 430	13.25	18.5	–	4.75	27.25	–
440	7.5	–	28.5	9	–	37.5
Experian (*602) 600	12.5	32.75	48	10.25	34	48.5
620	4.5	–	–	22.25	–	–
Impl Tobacco (*1884) 1850	48	53.5	84	13	112.5	144
1900	18.5	–	–	34.5	–	–
IntCont Hotels (*870.5) 860	25.5	58.5	78	15	67	101.5
880	15.5	–	–	25	–	–
Intl Power (*286.100) 280	14	30.25	35.75	8.5	23.75	34.5
290	9.25	–	–	13.75	–	–
ITV (*51.900) 48	4.5	7.25	9.25	0.75	3.75	5.5
52	2	–	–	2	–	–
Legal & Gen (*78.400) 76	4	9	11.75	1.75	6.75	10.75
80	2	7.25	9.75	3.5	8.75	13
Lon Stk Exchg (*752.5) 740	28.75	51.5	70	13	53.75	68
760	16.25	–	–	21.75	–	–
Man Group (*328.600) 320	13.75	33.5	44.5	5.5	24.75	35.25
330	8.25	–	–	9.5	–	–
Natl Grid (*648) 640	15	31.5	42	7	23	45.5
660	5	–	–	17.5	–	–
Next (*2059) 2000	78.5	155.5	195	17	94	158.5
2100	24.5	–	–	63	–	–
Pearson (*846) 840	18.5	47	56	12.5	40.5	67.5
850	13.5	–	–	17.5	–	–

Call option premium payable – in this case, with a March 2010 exercise date

Option	Calls Dec	Calls Mar	Calls Jun	Puts Dec	Puts Mar	Puts Jun
Reckitt Bnckisr Gp (*3194) 3100	111	–	–	16	171	219.5
3200	46	129.5	179	52	–	–
Reed Elsevier (*468.400) 460	12.5	31.5	37	4	21.5	35
470	7	–	–	8	–	–
Rentokil Init (*101.800) 100	3.25	8	11.25	1.25	6	9
110	0.25	–	–	8.25	–	–
Rolls-Royce (*500) 490	17	–	–	6.5	–	–
500	11	–	–	10.25	–	–
SAB Miller (*1830) 1800	48	108	143.5	19	76.5	111.5
1850	21	–	–	39	–	–
Sage (*230.800) 225	7.75	–	–	2.75	–	–
230	4.5	11.25	15	4.75	14.25	20
Scot & Sthn Energy (*1125) 1100	33.5	56	73	6.5	44	64
1150	7.5	–	–	31.5	–	–
Shire (*1196) 1150	54.5	–	–	8.5	77.5	103
1200	23.5	70.5	99	26	–	–
Sm & Nephew (*602) 600	13.5	34.5	46	11	31.5	45.5
620	6	–	–	23	–	–
Standard Life (*213.100) 210	6.5	16	19.75	3.5	17	22.75
215	4	–	–	6	–	–
Unilever (*1860) 1850	38	72	103	26.5	123.5	167
1900	17	–	–	56.5	–	–
Utd Utilities (*495.300) 490	10.5	–	–	13	–	–
500	6	–	–	20	–	–
Whitbread (*1306) 1300	33.5	87.5	114.5	30	79.5	126
1350	12.5	–	–	59	–	–
Wolseley (*1250) 1200	76.25	139.75	178.5	26.75	87	123.75
1250	47	–	–	46.25	–	–
WPP (*586) 580	15.5	–	–	8.25	–	–
600	6.5	29	42.75	18.75	41.5	61.75

Put option premium payable – in this case, with a June exercise date

Call option premium payable – in this case, with a June exercise date

* Underlying security price. Premiums shown are based on settlement prices. **Source: Euronext.liffe**
December 4 Total contracts, Equity & Index options: 319,756 Calls: 102,006 Puts 61,557

EXHIBIT 19.1

Source: *Financial Times* 7 December 2009.

Put options

A put option gives the holder the right, but not the obligation, to sell a specific quantity of shares on or before a specified date at a fixed exercise price.

Imagine you are pessimistic about the prospects for Land Securities on 5 December 2009. You could purchase, for a premium of 39.5 per share (£395 in total), the right to sell 1,000 shares in or before late February 2010 at 680p (*see* Exhibit 19.1). If a fall in price subsequently takes place, to, say, 550p, you can insist on exercising the right to sell at 680p. The writer of the put option is obliged to purchase shares at 680p while being aware that the put holder is able to buy shares at 550p on the Stock Exchange. The option holder makes a profit of 680 – 550 – 39.5 = 90.5p per share, a 229 percent return (before costs).

For the put option holder, if the market price exceeds the exercise price, it will not be wise to exercise as shares can be sold for a higher price on the Stock Exchange. Therefore the maximum loss, equal to the premium paid, is incurred. The option writer gains the premium if the share price remains above the exercise price, but may incur a large loss if the market price falls significantly (*see* Figures 19.4 and 19.5).

As with calls, in most cases the option holder would take profits by selling the option on to another investor via LIFFE rather than waiting to exercise at expiry.

Using share options to reduce risk: hedging

Hedging with options is especially attractive because they can give protection against unfavourable movements in the underlying while permitting the possibility of benefiting from favourable movements. Suppose you hold 1,000 shares in Land Securities on 5 December 2009. Your shareholding is worth £6,850. There are rumours flying around the market that the company may become the target

FIGURE 19.4

Put option holder profit profile (Land Securities 680 February put, purchased 5 December 2009)

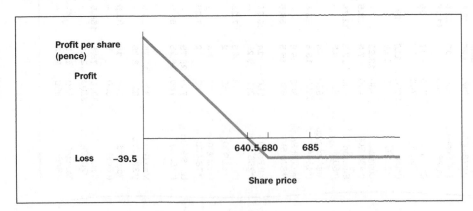

FIGURE 19.5

Put option writer profit profile (Land Securities 680 February put, sold 5 December 2009)

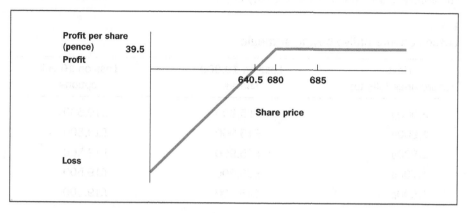

of a takeover bid. If this materialises the share price will rocket; if it does not the market will be disappointed and the price will fall dramatically. What are you to do? One way to avoid the downside risk is to sell the shares. The problem is that you may regret this action if the bid does subsequently occur and you have forgone the opportunity of a large profit. An alternative approach is to retain the shares and buy a put option. This will rise in value as the share price falls. If the share price rises you gain from your underlying share holding.

Assume a 700 February put is purchased for a premium of £500 (*see* Exhibit 19.1). If the share price falls to 550p in late February you lose on your underlying shares by £1,350 ((685p – 550p) × 1,000). However the put option will have an intrinsic value of £1,500 ((700p – 550p) × 1,000), thus reducing the loss and limiting the downside risk. Below 700p, for every 1p lost in a share price, 1p is gained on the put option, so the maximum loss is £500 (the option premium).

This hedging reduces the dispersion of possible outcomes. There is a floor below which losses cannot be increased, while on the upside the benefit from any rise in share price is reduced due to the premium paid. If the share price stands still at 685p, however, you may feel that the premium you paid to insure against an adverse movement at 50p, or 7.3 percent of the share price, was excessive. If you keep buying this type of 'insurance' through the year, it can reduce your portfolio returns substantially.

A simpler example of risk reduction occurs when an investor is fairly sure that a share will rise in price but is not so confident as to discount the possibility of a fall. Suppose that the investor wished to buy 10,000 shares in Next, currently priced at £20.59 (on 5 December 2009) – *see* Exhibit 19.1. This can be achieved either by a direct purchase of shares in the market or through the purchase of an option. If the share price does fall significantly, the size of the loss is greater with the share purchase – the option loss is limited to the premium paid.

Suppose that ten June 2010 call options are purchased at a cost of £19,500 (195p × 1,000 × 10). Table 19.3 shows that the option is less risky because of the ability to abandon the right to buy at £20.

TABLE 19.3
Losses on alternative buying strategies

Next share price falls to:	Loss on 10,000 shares	Loss on 10 call options
2,000p	£5,900	£19,500
1,900p	£15,900	£19,500
1,800p	£25,900	£19,500
1,700p	£35,900	£19,500
1,600p	£45,900	£19,500

Writing a put option can be a very risky thing to do, as General Motors found out to its cost – see Exhibit 19.2.

GM pays Fiat €1.55bn to end joint ventures

Adrian Michaels and Bernard Simon

General Motors and Fiat ended threats of legal action yesterday when the US industrial group agreed to pay €1.55bn (£1.07bn) to terminate the companies joint venture agreements and forestall attempts to force it to take over the Italian company's lossmaking car division. ...

GM is paying a heavy price to cancel an agreement it signed with Fiat in headier days for both companies five years ago. In 2000 GM took a 20 per cent stake in Fiat Auto, subsequently reduced to 10 per cent, and agreed to a 'put' arrangement that gave Fiat the option to sell the rest of its car unit to GM.

Neither company dreamed the put would become an issue but both have stumbled badly. GM was keen to avoid taking over Fiat Auto and argued that the Italian company invalidated the put by restructuring. ...

About two-thirds of GM's €1.55bn payment will go towards settling the put option. The remaining third will pay for GM's stake in the Polish diesel engine plant and for technology currently held by Fiat on two diesel engines installed in GM vehicles.

Fiat will still be part of GM's worldwide purchasing operation and will benefit from a GM commitment to use a Fiat plant in Italy for some of its European engine requirements.

EXHIBIT 19.2

Source: *Financial Times* 14 February 2005, p. 1.

Index options

Options on whole share indices can be purchased, for example, Standard and Poor's 500 (USA), FTSE 100 (UK), CAC 40 (France), DAX (Germany) and so on. Large investors usually have a varied portfolio of shares so, rather than hedging individual shareholdings with options, they may hedge through options on the entire index of shares. Also speculators can take a position on the future movement of the market as a whole.

> Large investors may hedge through options on the entire index of shares.

A major difference between index options and share options is that the former are 'cash settled' – so for the FTSE 100 option, 100 different shares are not delivered on the expiry day. Rather, a cash difference representing the price change passes hands.

If you examine the table in Exhibit 19.3, you will see that the index is regarded as a price and each one-point movement on the index represents £10. Only the February expiry index options are shown (there are many others). The date this was downloaded was 8 December 2009 and the FTSE 100 index that day was at 5229. So if you purchased one contract in February expiry 5350 calls (C) you would pay an option premium of 142.5 index points × £10 = £1,425. Imagine that the following day, i.e. 9 December, the FTSE 100 Index moved from its closing level on 8 December of 5229 to 5400 and the option price on the 5,350 call moved to 300 index points (50 points of intrinsic value and 250 points of time value). To convert this into money you could sell the option at £10 per point per contract (300 × £10 = £3,000). In 24 hours your £1,425 has gone up to £3,000, a 111 percent rise. This sort of gain is great when the market moves in your favour. If it moves against you large percentage losses will occur in just a few hours.

Note that there are many additional option expiry dates stretching months into the future – go to www.euronext.com to find them.

FTSE 100 Index Option (European-style)

Codes and classification

Code	ESX	Market	NYSE Liffe London	Vol.	38,196	08/12/09
Exercise type	European	Currency €		O.I	4,528,238	07/12/09

Underlying

Name	London FTSE 100	ISBN	GB0001383545		Market		LSE
Currency	GBX						
Time	CET	Last	522,906.00	08/12/09 16:30:34	Last change %		−1.54
		High	532,336.00		Low		520,638.00

February 2010 Prices – 08/12/09

			Calls													Puts			
Settl.	Day volume	Vol Time (CET)	Last	Bid	Ask	AQ Bid	AQ Ask	Strike C	AQ P Bid	AQ Ask	Bid	Ask	Last	Time (CET)	Vol	Day volume	Settl.
261.00	7	3 15:29	224.00	214.50	216.50	214.50	219.50	C 5,200 P	210.00	215.00	210.50	214.00	200.00	12:31	4	4	179.00
230.50	19	19 15:33	191.00	187.50	191.50	187.50	191.50	C 5,250 P	232.00	237.00	233.00	237.00	220.50	12:31	2	10	198.50
201.50	–	–	–	–	162.00	165.50	161.50	165.50	C 5,300 P	256.50	261.50	257.50	261.00	265.00	13:33	3	33	219.50
175.00	74	24 12:43	146.50	139.00	142.50	138.50	142.50	C 5,350 P	283.50	268.50	284.00	288.50	–	–	–	–	243.00
151.00	135	5 18:27	119.00	118.00	121.00	117.50	121.50	C 5,400 P	312.00	318.00	312.50	318.00	–	–	–	–	269.00

Note: Settlement price is for the trading day 07/12/09

Vol – (Volume) is the number of contracts traded in the most recent transaction.

Day's Volume – Number of trades that have taken place so far in the trading day. This figure updates as the day progresses and more trades take place.

%+ – Percentage price of last trade compared to yesterday's settlement price.

Settl. – The previous day's settlement price.

O.I. – (Open Interest) is the outstanding long and short positions of the previous trading day updated in the morning each day.

EXHIBIT 19.3 FTSE 100 index option for February delivery options, £10 per index point

Source: http://www.euronext.com/

Hedging against a decline in the market

A fund manager controlling a £30m portfolio of shares on behalf of a group of pensioners is concerned that the market may fall over the next two months. One strategy to lower risk is to purchase put options on the share index. If the market does fall, losses on the portfolio will be offset by gains on the value of the index put option.

First the manager has to calculate the number of option contracts needed to hedge the underlying. With the index at 5229 on 8 December 2009 and each point of that index settled at £10, one contract has a value of 5229 × £10 = £52,290. To cover a £30m portfolio:

$$\frac{£30m}{£52,290} = 574 \text{ contracts}$$

The manager opts to buy 574 February 5200 puts for 215 points per contract.[4] (see Exhibit 19.3) The premium payable is:

$$215 \text{ points} \times £10 \times 574 = £1,234,100$$

This amounts to a 4.1 percent 'insurance premium' (1.234m/30m) against a downturn in the market.

Consider what happens if the market does fall by a large amount, say, 15 percent, between December and February. The index falls to 4445, and the loss on the portfolio is:

$$£30m \times 0.15 = £4,500,000$$

If the portfolio was unhedged the pensioners suffer from a market fall. However in this case the put options gain in value as the index falls because they carry the right to sell at 5200. If the manager closed the option position by buying at a level of 4445, with the right to sell at 5200, a 755-point difference, a gain is made:

Gain on options $(5200 - 4445) \times 574 \times £10$ = £4,333,700

Less option premium paid   – £1,234,100

                              £3,099,600

A substantial proportion of the fall in portfolio value is compensated for through the use of the put derivative.

Aunt Agathas and derivatives

Millions of ordinary small investors (Aunt Agathas in the City jargon) have their money applied to the derivatives markets even though they may remain blissfully unaware that such 'exotic' transactions are being conducted on their behalf. Take the case of equity-linked bonds. Investors nervous of investing in the stock market for fear of downward swings are promised a guarantee that they will receive at least the return of their original capital, even if the stock market falls. If it rises they will receive a return linked to the rise (say the capital gain element – excluding dividends). The bulk of the capital invested may be placed in safe fixed-interest investments, with the stock market linked return created through the use of options and other derivatives. There has been some discussion over the wisdom of using such highly geared instruments. However the financial services industry easily defended itself by pointing out the risk-reducing possibilities of these products if properly managed.

EXHIBIT 19.4

Corporate uses of options

There are a number of corporate uses of options.

- **Share option schemes** Many companies now grant (or sell to) employees share options (calls) as a means of achieving commitment and greater goal congruence between agents and principals. Employees are offered the right to buy shares at a fixed price some time in the future. They then have the incentive over the intervening years to perform well and push up the share price so as to realize a large gain when the options may be exercised.

- **Warrants** A share warrant is an option issued by a company which gives the owner the right, but not the obligation, to purchase a specified number of shares at a specified price over a given period of time. Note that it is the company that writes the option rather than speculators or hedgers.

- **Convertible bonds** A convertible bond can be viewed as a bundle of two sets of rights. First, there are the usual rights associated with a bond, for example interest and principal payments, and second, there is the right, but not the obligation, to exercise a call option and purchase shares using the bond itself as the payment for those shares.

- **Rights issues** In a rights issue shareholders are granted the right, but not the obligation, to purchase additional shares in the company. This right has value and can be sold to other investors.

- **Share underwriting** Effectively when an underwriter agrees to purchase securities if investors do not purchase the whole issue, a put option has been bought with the underwriting fee, and the company has the right to insist that the underwriter buys at the price agreed.

- **Commodities** Many firms are exposed to commodity risk. Firms selling commodities, or buying for production purposes, may be interested in hedging against price fluctuations in these markets. Examples of such firms are airlines, food processors, car manufacturers, chocolate manufacturers. Some of the commodity options available are:
  - crude oil
  - aluminum
  - copper
  - coffee
  - cocoa.

- **Taking control of a company** A novel use of options occurred in 2003 when the family that founded the retail chain Monsoon sold put options to shareholders owning 19.5 percent of Monsoon's shares. The holders of the puts bought a right to sell their shares at 140p. If the share price on the stock market remains below 140p many holders will exercise the option. The founding family controlled 72.5 percent of the company and saw the use of put options as a cheap way of raising their stake to over 90 percent (cheaper than a full takeover bid).

- **Protecting the company from foreign exchange rate losses** This topic is covered in Chapter 21.

Real options

Managers often encounter decisions with call or put options embedded within them. An example is the option to expand an investment project, say a project to open 50 retail stores can be expanded to a 100-store programme. The option to abandon an investment project once it is under way can be valuable, as can the option to delay the start of a project until more information comes in, say about likely customer demand. Real options are discussed in Chapter 5.

Illustration of a real option

Suppose your company owns an oil field that is largely played out. You estimate that the net (after costs) cash flows from the oil still remaining have a
discounted present value of £100m. It would cost £105m now to revive the
oil field. On a simple NPV analysis the project is not worthwhile with a negative NPV of £5m.

Taking a real options approach we see the oil reserves as having option
value. This value arises because conditions may change in the future in such
a way as to make the right to develop the field very valuable. For example,
the price of oil could rise significantly. So, how do we derive the numbers
showing the likelihood of oil prices moving to various elevated levels?
Analysts generally look to the volatility of the oil price in the past. From this
it is possible (with a leap of faith that the past volatility of oil prices represents future volatility) to come up with some numbers for the volatility of
the developed reserve value.

Currently the call option to develop the field has no intrinsic value.
However it might have time value – that is, there might be a reasonable
expectation, judging from historic price movements that the oil price will
move to a level that gives the oil field intrinsic value – i.e. a positive NPV.

Of course the value of the oil in the ground is subject to many uncertainties other than the oil price. For example, the difficulty of extraction has to
be estimated by specialists. Thus, any model developed to assist this decision has to be both sophisticated in its breadth of input variables and
sufficiently transparent so that managers realise the subjective nature of
many of the figures and evaluate the numerical results accordingly.

Also consider whether the managers have to make the decision to spend
£105m now? There is option value in waiting to see what happens to the oil
price – keep open a variety of possible dates of implementation.

Conclusion

From a small base in the 1970s derivatives have grown to be of enormous importance. Almost all medium and large industrial and commercial firms use derivatives,
usually to manage risk, but occasionally to speculate and arbitrage (discussed in the
next chapter). Banks are usually at the centre of derivatives trading, dealing on
behalf of clients, as market makers or trading on their own account. Other financial
institutions are increasingly employing these instruments to lay off risk or to speculate. They can be used across the globe, and traded night and day.

The trend suggests that derivatives will continue their relentless rise in significance. They can no longer be dismissed as peripheral to the workings of the
financial and economic systems. The implications for investors, corporate institutions, financial institutions, regulators and governments are going to be

> Derivatives can no longer be dismissed as peripheral to the workings of the financial and economic systems.

profound. (This was written in the first edition. Since then, everyone has become aware of the detrimental role played by derivative creators in helping to bring about the financial crisis. Derivatives based on mortgage-backed securities became worthless.) These are incredibly powerful tools, and, like all powerful tools, they can be used for good or ill. Ignorance of the nature of the risks being transferred, combined with greed, will continue to lead to some very unfortunate consequences. However, on a day-to-day basis, and away from the newspaper headlines, the ability of firms to quietly tap the markets and hedge risk encourages wealth creation and promotes general economic well-being.

The next chapter examines derivative tools in the form of futures, forwards and swaps among others.

Websites

www.advfn.com	ADVFN
www.bloomberg.com	Bloomberg
www.reuters.com	Reuters
www.money.cnn.com	CNN Financial News
www.wsj.com	Wall Street Journal
www.ft.com	Financial Times
www.fow.com	Futures and Options World
www.euronext.com	London International Financial Futures and Options Exchange
www.cbot.com	Chicago Board of Trade
www.cboe.com	Chicago Board Options Exchange
www.nyse.com	New York Stock Exchange
www.eurexchange.com	Eurex, the European Derivative Exchange
www.isda.org	International Swaps and Derivatives Association

Notes

1 The table taken from the *FT* for Monday 7 December – this is only shown on Monday in the paper. www.euronext.com and www.advfn.com provide a wider range of option prices (more companies and more exercise prices for each company).

2 Expiry date is third Wednesday in expiry month.

3 For this exercise we will assume that the option is held to expiry and not traded before then. However in many cases this option will be sold on to another trader long before expiry date approaches (probably at a profit or loss).

4 This is not a perfect hedge as there is an element of the underlying risk without offsetting derivative cover.

20

USING FUTURES, FORWARDS AND SWAPS TO MANAGE RISK

Introduction

There are two main classes of derivative contracts. First there are those where you have a right but not the obligation to go ahead with a transaction – options. Given that the future is uncertain and that the right to abandon may turn out to be valuable you are obliged to pay the option writer a premium. Option writers expose themselves to unfavourable outcomes because they grant you the right to go ahead with the deal if it is favourable to you; or to abandon it, if that is your most profitable course of action.

The second class of derivative, the subject of this chapter, commit you to going ahead with the agreed transaction at some point(s) in the future regardless of the change in underlying conditions – you have no right to abandon the bargain.[1]

Futures

Futures are contracts between two parties to undertake a transaction at an agreed price on a specified future date. In contrast to buying options, which give you the choice to walk away from the deal, with futures you are committed and are unable to back away. This is a very important difference. In purchasing an option the maximum you can lose is the premium paid whereas you can lose multiples of the amount you employ in taking a futures position.

> In contrast to buying options, with futures you are committed and are unable to back away.

A simple example will demonstrate this. Imagine a farmer wishes to lock-in a price for his wheat, which will be harvested in six months. You agree to purchase the wheat from the farmer six months hence at a price of £60 per tonne. You are hoping that by the time the wheat is delivered the price has risen and you can sell at a profit. The farmer is worried that all he has from you is the promise to pay £60 per tonne in six months, and if the market price falls you will walk away from the deal. To reassure him you are asked to put money into what the farmer calls a *margin account*. He asks, and you agree, to deposit £6 for each tonne you have agreed to buy. If you fail to complete the bargain the farmer will be able to draw on the money from the margin account and then sell the wheat as it is harvested at the going rate for immediate ('spot') delivery. So as far as the farmer is concerned the price of wheat for delivery at harvest time could fall to £54 and he is still going to get £60 for each tonne: £6 from what you paid into the margin account and £54 from selling at the spot price.

But what if the price falls below £54? The farmer is exposed to risk – something he had tried to avoid by entering a futures deal. It is for this reason that the farmer asks you to top up your margin account on a daily basis so that there is always a buffer. He sets a *maintenance margin* level of £6 per tonne.

You have to maintain at least £6 per tonne in the margin account. So, if the day after buying the future, the harvest time price in the futures market falls to £57 you have only £3 per tonne left in the margin account as a buffer for the farmer. You agreed to buy at £60 but the going rate is only £57. To bring the margin account up to a £6 buffer you will be required to put in another £3 per tonne. If the price the next day falls to £50 you will be required to put up another £7 per tonne. You agreed to buy at £60: with the market price at £50 you have put a total of £6 + £3 + £7 = £16 into the margin account. By providing top ups as the price moves against you there will always be at least £6 per tonne providing security for the farmer. Even if you go bankrupt or simply renege on the deal he will receive at least £60 per tonne, either from the spot market or from a combination of a lower market price plus money from the margin account. As the price fell to £50 you have a £10 per tonne incentive to walk away from the deal except for the fact that you have put £16 into an account that the farmer can draw on should you be so stupid or unfortunate. If the price is £50 per tonne at expiry of the contract and you have put £16 in the margin account you are entitled to the spare £6 of margin.

It is in the margin account that we have the source of multiple losses in the future markets. Say your life savings amount to £10 and you are convinced there will be a drought and shortage of wheat following the next harvest. In your view the price will rise to £95 per tonne. So, to cash-in on your forecast you agree to buy a future for one tonne of wheat. You have agreed with the farmer that in six months you will pay £60 for the wheat, which you expect to then sell for £95. (The farmer is obviously less convinced that prices are destined to rise than you.)

To gain this right to buy at £60 you need only have £6 for the *initial margin*. The other £4 might be useful to meet day-to-day *margin calls* should the wheat price fall from £60 (temporarily in your view). If the price does rise to £95 you will make a £35 profit having laid out only £6 (plus some other cash temporarily). This is a very high return of 583 percent over six months. But what if the price at harvest time is £40. You have agreed to pay £60 therefore the loss of £20 wipes out your savings and you are made bankrupt. You lose three times your initial margin. That is the downside to the gearing effect of futures.

The above example demonstrates the essential features of futures market trading but in reality, participants in the market do not transact directly with each other but go through a regulated exchange. Your opposite number, called a *counterparty*, is not a farmer but an organisation that acts as counterparty to all futures traders, buyers or sellers, called the *clearing house*. This reduces the risk of non-compliance with the contract significantly for the buyer or seller of a future, as it is highly unlikely that the clearing house will be unable to fulfil its obligation.

In the example we have assumed that the maintenance margin level is set at the same level as the initial. In reality it is often set at 70 to 80 percent of the initial margin level.

The exchange provides standardised legal agreements traded in highly liquid markets. The contracts cannot be tailor-made, e.g. for 77 tonnes of wheat or coffee delivered in 37 days from now. The fact that the agreements are standardised allows a wide market appeal because buyers and sellers know what is being traded: the contracts are for a specific quality of the underlying, in specific amounts with specific delivery dates. For example, for sugar traded on Euronext.liffe (*see* Exhibit 20.1) one contract is for a specified grade of sugar and each contract is for a standard 50 tonnes with fixed delivery days in late August, October, December, March and May.

In examining the table in Exhibit 20.1, it is important to remember that it is the contracts themselves that are a form of security bought and sold in the market. Thus the March future priced at $610.30 per tonne is a derivative of sugar and is not the same thing as sugar. To buy this future is to enter into an agreement with rights. The rights are being bought and sold and not the commodity. When exercise takes place *then* sugar is bought. However, as with most derivatives, usually future positions are cancelled by an offsetting transaction before exercise.

Exhibit 20.2 describes the importance of commodity hedging to a number of companies.

Marking to market and margins

With the clearing house being the formal counterparty for every buyer or seller of a futures contract, an enormous potential for credit risk is imposed on the organization given the volume of futures traded and the size of the underlying they represent (NYSE Liffe has an average daily volume of around £1,500bn). If only a small fraction of market participants fail to deliver this could run into hundreds of millions of pounds. To protect itself the clearing house operates a margining system. The futures buyer or seller has to provide, usually in cash, an initial margin. The amount required depends on the futures market, the level of volatility of the underlying and the potential for default; however it is likely to be in the region of 0.1 percent to 15 percent of the value of the underlying. The initial margin is not a 'down-payment' for the underlying; the funds do not flow to a buyer or seller of the underlying, but stay with the clearing house. It is merely a way of guaranteeing that the buyer or seller will pay up should the price of the underlying move against them. It is refunded when the futures position is closed – if the market has not moved adversely.

The clearing house also operates a system of daily marking to market. At the end of every trading day each counterparty's profits or losses created as a result of that day's price change are calculated. Any counterparty that made a loss has their member's margin account debited. The following morning, the losing counterparty must inject more cash to cover the loss if the amount in the account has fallen below a threshold level (the maintenance margin). An inability to pay a daily loss causes default and the contract is closed, thus protecting the clearing house from the possibility that the counterparty might accumulate further daily losses without providing cash to cover them. The margin account of the counterparty that makes a daily gain is credited. This may be withdrawn the next day. The daily credits and debits to members' margin accounts are known as variation margin.

COMMODITY PRICES

Energy		Price*	Change
WTI Crude Oil †	Jan	77.28	1.23
Brent Crude Oil ‡	Jan	78.47	1.29
RBOB Gasoline †	Dec	2.0008	+0.0746
Heating Oil †	Dec	2.0181	+0.0559
Natural Gas †	Jan	4.848	–0.344
Ethanol ◆	Dec	2.135	+0.014
Uranium		43.00	nc
Carbon Emissions ‡	Dec	€13.14	–0.04
Diesel (French)		633.75	+11.75
Unleaded (95R)		684.00	nc
globalCOAL RB Index		68.85	–0.03
Base Metals (♠ LME 3 Month)			
Aluminium		2034.00	+47.00
Aluminium Alloy		1830.00	+20.00
Copper		6831.00	+60.50
Lead		2315.00	+10.00
Nickel		16075.00	–150.00
Tin		14750.00	–50.00
Zinc		2250.00	+25.00
Precious Metals (PM London Fix)			
Gold		1175.75	+9.25
Silver		1814.00	+16.00
Platinum		1442.00	+16.00
Palladium		360.50	+2.50
Agricultural & Cattle Futures			
Corn ◆	Dec	402.75	+5.50
Wheat ◆	Dec	567.50	+18.75
Soyabeans ◆	Jan	1060.50	+7.50
Soyabeans Meal ◆	Dec	326.80	+0.30
Cocoa ❖	Dec	£2140	–14
Cocoa ♥	Dec	3.214	0
Coffee (Robusta) ❖	Nov	1318	nc
Coffee (Arabica) ♥	Dec	141.75	+3.80
White Sugar ❖	Mar	610.30	–8.10
Sugar 11 ♥	Jan	22.07	–0.13
Cotton ♥	Dec	70.75	+1.01
Orange Juice ♥	Jan	119.30	+1.40
Palm Oil	Dec	765.00	+15.00
Live Cattle ♣	Dec	83.200	nc
Feeder Cattle ♣	Jan	92.950	+0.450
Lean Hogs ♣	Dec	58.600	–0.425
Frozen Pork Bellies ♣	Feb	86.050	–0.700
Baltic Dry Index		3887	–87

Sources: † NYMEX, ‡ ECX/ICE, ◆ CBOT, ❖ NYSE Liffe, ♥ NYBOT, ♣ CME, ♠ LME/London Metal Exchange, *$ unless otherwise stated. London Closing prices.

EXHIBIT 20.1

Source: *Financial Times* 1 December 2009.

Hedging now second nature for food groups

Jenny Wiggins and Javier Blas

Food companies were once a little blasé about the price they paid for the ingredients that went into their corn flakes, chocolate bars and yoghurts because in the 1980s and 1990s, prices of agricultural commodities were falling.

While many food companies took the precaution of hedging some of their key ingredients – Mars, the owner of Snickers bars, has been hedging cocoa since the 1960s – they did not have to worry too much about being caught out by unexpectedly big price jumps.

Today, that luxury has vanished. Soaring global demand for commodities has driven prices of all kinds of food ingredients, from corn to cocoa to coffee, to new highs, and more than a few good companies have been unpleasantly suprised.

On Friday Hershey, the US chocolate group, became the lastest in a long line of food companies to warn that its commodity costs – which include sugar and peanuts as well as cocoa and are up as much as 45 per cent since the start of the year – were rising faster than expected.

The company said it would spend up to $12m hedging its 2009 costs – it expects cost increases next year to be double this year's – and take a hit to third-quarter profits.

Other companies caught out by soaring commodity prices include Hershey's competitor Cadbury, which recently said it was proceeding with a new round of restructuring after finding rising raw material prices 'a stronger challenge' than it had previously anticipated.

Meanwhile, Unilever, the multinational food and household products group, which estimates its commodity costs rose by €1bn ($1.47bn) in the first half of the year, has warned it will face its biggest ever annual rise. Analysis estimate this will amount to €2bn.

Companies have been trying to counter higher costs by raising the whole-sale prices for their products. On Friday, Hershey said it was putting through another round of price increases (it raised them 13 per cent in January) on its chocolate bars and other confectionary, lifting them by a further 11 per cent.

But companies are starting to find that consumers are reluctant to pay more for groceries as inflation rises and disposable incomes fall, and many price increases are being followed by drops in sales volumes.

Good commodity risk management is consequently becoming an essential part of remaining profitable.

Michael Steib, consumer goods analyst at Morgan Stanley, says: 'Companies are more focused on hedging, particularly the ones that got burned.'

Although food companies have long employed 'procurement' people wth logistical skills in sourcing commodities, they are now looking for people with experience in trading commodities.

'Consumer industry companies are turning into agriculture commodities trading houses,' said one senior commodities banker in London.

Meanwhile, consumer industry bankers say investment banks are putting money in commodities teams that give food and consumer goods companies advice on how to hedge their risk exposure.

When corn prices rose or fell 5 cents per bushel per day, companies could afford not to be hedged because the price movements were not big enough to lower profits.

But now that they are swinging by 30–40 cents a day, and prices have soared – which means they account for a bigger proportion of total sales – companies are being hit with considerably higher additional costs.

Pilgrim's Pride, the US group that claims to be the world's biggest producer of processed chickens, has hired a

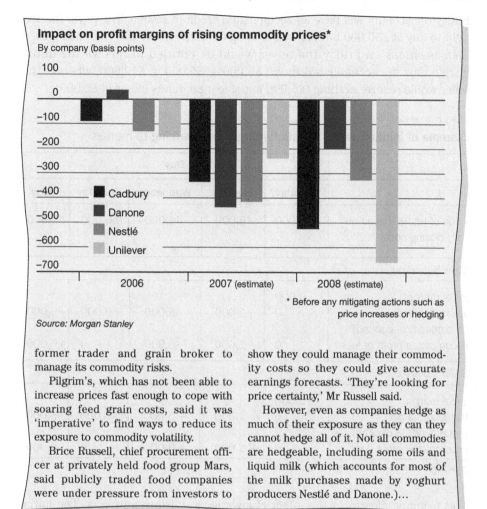

Impact on profit margins of rising commodity prices*
By company (basis points)

Legend:
- Cadbury
- Danone
- Nestlé
- Unilever

* Before any mitigating actions such as price increases or hedging

Source: Morgan Stanley

former trader and grain broker to manage its commodity risks.

Pilgrim's, which has not been able to increase prices fast enough to cope with soaring feed grain costs, said it was 'imperative' to find ways to reduce its exposure to commodity volatility.

Brice Russell, chief procurement officer at privately held food group Mars, said publicly traded food companies were under pressure from investors to show they could manage their commodity costs so they could give accurate earnings forecasts. 'They're looking for price certainty,' Mr Russell said.

However, even as companies hedge as much of their exposure as they can they cannot hedge all of it. Not all commodities are hedgeable, including some oils and liquid milk (which accounts for most of the milk purchases made by yoghurt producers Nestlé and Danone.)...

Exhibit 20.2

Source: *Financial Times* 18 August 2008, p. 19.

Worked example showing margins

Imagine a buyer and seller of a future on Monday with an underlying value of £50,000 are each required to provide an initial margin of 10 percent, or £5,000. The buyer will make profits if the price rises while the seller will make profits if the price falls. In Table 20.1 it is assumed that counterparties have to keep the entire initial margin permanently as a buffer. (In reality this may be relaxed by an exchange.)

At the end of Tuesday the buyer of the contract has £1,000 debited from their member's account. This will have to be handed over the following day or the exchange will automatically close the member's position and crystallise the loss. If the buyer does provide the variation margin and the position is kept open until

Friday the account will have an accumulated credit of £5,000. The buyer has the right to buy at £50,000 but can sell at £55,000. If the buyer and the seller closed their positions on Friday the buyer would be entitled to receive the initial margin plus the accumulated profit, £5,000 + £5,000 = £10,000, whereas the seller would receive nothing (£5,000 initial margin minus losses of £5,000).

TABLE 20.1

Example of initial margin, variation margin and marking to market

			Day		
£	Monday	Tuesday	Wednesday	Thursday	Friday
Value of future (based on daily closing price)	50,000	49,000	44,000	50,000	55,000
Buyer's position					
Initial margin*	5,000				
Variation margin (+ credited) (– debited)	0	–1,000	–5,000	+6,000	+5,000
Accumulated profit or loss	0	–1,000	–6,000	0	+5,000
Seller's position					
Initial margin	5,000				
Variation margin (+ credited) (– debited)	0	+ 1,000	+ 5,000	–6,000	–5,000
Accumulated profit (loss)	0	+ 1,000	+ 6,000	0	–5,000

*Initial margin is the same as maintenance margin in this case.

This example illustrates the effect of leverage in futures contracts. The initial margin payments are small relative to the value of the underlying. When the underlying changes by a small percentage the effect is magnified for the future, and large percentage gains and losses are made on the amount committed to the transaction:

$$\text{Underlying change (Monday–Friday)} \quad \frac{£55,000 - 50,000}{£50,000} \times 100 = 10\%$$

$$\text{Percentage return to buyer of future} \quad \frac{£5,000}{£5,000} \times 100 = 100\%$$

$$\text{Percentage return to seller of future} \quad \frac{-£5,000}{£5,000} \times 100 = -100\%$$

To lose all the money committed to a financial transaction may seem disappointing but it is nothing compared with the losses that can be made on futures. It is possible to lose a multiple of the amount set down as an initial margin. For example, if the future rose to £70,000 the seller would have to provide a £20,000 variation margin – four times the amount committed in the first place.

Clearly, playing the futures market can seriously damage your wealth. This was proved with a vengeance by Nick Leeson of Barings Bank. He bought futures in the Nikkei 225 Index – the main Japanese share index – in both the Osaka and the Singapore derivative exchanges. He was betting that the market would rise as he committed the bank to buying the index at a particular price. When the index fell margin payments had to be made. Leeson took a double-or-quits attitude, 'I mean a lot of futures traders when the market is against them will double up.'[2] He continued to buy futures. To generate some cash, to make variation margin payments, he wrote combinations of call and put options ('straddles'). This compounded the problem when the Nikkei 225 Index continued to fall in 1994. The put options became an increasingly expensive commitment to bear – counterparties had the right to sell the index to Barings at a price much higher than the prevailing price. Over £800m was lost.

> Clearly, playing the futures market can seriously damage your wealth.

Settlement

Historically the futures markets developed on the basis of the *physical delivery* of the underlying. So if you had contracted to buy 40,000 lb. of lean hogs you would receive the meat as settlement. However in most futures markets today (including that for lean hogs) only a small proportion of contracts result in physical delivery. The majority are *closed out* before the expiry of the contract and all that changes hands is cash, either as a profit or a loss. Speculators certainly do not want to end up with five tonnes of coffee or 15,000 lb. of orange juice and so will *reverse their trade* before the contract expires; for example, if they originally bought 50 tonnes of white sugar they later sell 50 tonnes of white sugar for the same future delivery date.

Hedgers, say a confectionery manufacturer, may sometimes take delivery from the exchange but in most cases will have established purchasing channels for sugar, cocoa, etc. In these cases they may use the futures markets not as a way of obtaining goods but as a way of offsetting the risk of the prices of goods moving adversely. So a confectionery manufacturer may still plan to buy, say, sugar, at the spot price from its longstanding supplier in six months and simultaneously, to hedge the risk of the price rising, will buy six-month futures in sugar. The position will then be closed before expiry. If the price of the underlying has risen the manufacturer pays more to the supplier but has a compensating gain on the future. If the price falls the supplier is paid less and so the confectioner makes a gain here, but, under a perfect hedge, the future has lost an equal value.

> They may use the futures markets not as a way of obtaining goods but as a way of offsetting the risk of the prices of goods moving adversely.

As the futures markets developed it became clear that most participants did not want the complications of physical delivery and this led to the development of futures contracts where cash settlement takes place. This permitted a wider range of futures contracts to be created. Futures contracts based on intangible commodities such as a share index or a rate of interest are now important financial instruments. With these, even if the contract is held to the maturity date one party will hand over cash to the other (via the clearing house system).

Equity index futures are an example of a cash settlement market. The underlyings here are collections of shares, for example 225 Japanese shares for the Nikkei 225. Hedgers and speculators do not want 225 different shares to be delivered say one month from now. They are quite content to receive or hand over the profit or loss made by buying and then selling (or the other way around) a future of the index. The FTSE 100 futures (*see* Exhibit 20.3) are notional futures contracts. If not closed out before expiry they are settled in cash based on the average level of the FTSE 100 Index between stated times on the last trading day of the contract. Each index point is valued at £10.

The equity index futures table (Exhibit 20.3) in the *Financial Times* shows futures in indices from stock markets around the world for 21 October 2009. We will focus on the line for the FTSE 100 index future. This is very much a cut

Worked example 20.1
HEDGING WITH A SHARE INDEX FUTURE

It is 21 October 2009 and the FT 100 is at 5290. A fund manager wishes to hedge a £13m fund against a decline in the market. A December FTSE 100 future is available at 5227.50 – *see* Exhibit 20.3. The investor retains the shares in the portfolio and *sells* 249 index futures contracts. Each futures contract is worth £52,275 (5227.5 points × £10). So 249 contracts are needed to cover £13m (£13m/(£10 × 5227.5) = 249).

Outcome in December
For the sake of argument assume that the index falls by 10 percent to 4761, leaving the portfolio value at £11,700,000. The closing of the future position offsets this £1,300,000 loss by buying 249 futures at 4761 producing a profit of*:

Able to sell at	5227.5 × 249 × £10	= £13,016,475
Able to buy at	4761 × 249 × £10 =	£11,854,890
		£ 1,161,585

These contracts are cash settled so £1,161,585 will be paid, plus the investor gets back margin, less broker's fees.

* Assuming that the futures price is equal to the spot price of the FTSE 100. This would occur close to the expiry date of the future.

Equity Index Futures

Oct 21		Open	Sett	Change	High	Low	Est. vol.	Open int.
DJIA	Dec	9965.00	9901.00	-99.00	10070.00	9850.00	1	12,741
DJ Euro Stoxx ‡	Dec	2919.00	2929.00	+12.00	2940.00	2873.00	1,348,581	2,320,549
S&P 500	Dec	1076.60	1078.10	-11.30	1076.80	1076.10	92	385,655
Mini S&P 500	Dec	1076.50	1078.00	-11.50	1077.00	1076.25	6,795	2,372,653
Nasdaq 100	Dec	1749.25	1753.25	-5.00	1749.50	1749.00	16	20,299
Mini Nasdaq	Dec	1749.50	1753.25	-5.00	1750.00	1748.75	1,073	318,093
CAC 40	Nov	3859.50	3860.00	+2.50	3876.50	3791.00	136,968	385,207
DAX	Dec	5828.00	5840.00	+21.00	5862.50	5739.50	185,514	173,055
AEX	Nov	325.10	324.35	+0.30	326.25	319.70	40,754	48,225
MIB 30	Dec	24240.00	24102.00	-71.00	24265.00	23685.00	19,083	24,275
IBEX 35	Nov	11710.00	11810.50	+94.50	11846.00	11570.00	15,612	56,574
SMI	Dec	6422.00	6434.00	+6.00	6457.00	6348.00	30,639	167,223
FTSE 100	Dec	5243.50	5227.50	+6.00	5243.50	5146.00	109,747	612,490
Hang Seng	Oct	22300.00	22289.00	-46.00	22420.00	22206.00	57,637	85,618
Nikkei 225 †	Dec	10330.00	10330.00	–	10350.00	10260.00	9,918	333,017
Topix	Dec	913.50	914.50	+2.50	914.50	907.00	606	371,235
KOSPI 200	Dec	216.60	217.10	-1.15	218.45	215.85	284,359	110,193

North American Latest. Contracts shown are among the 25 most traded based on estimates of average volumes in 2004. CBOT volume, high & low for pit & electronic trading at settlement. Previous day's Open Interest. † Osaka contract. ‡ Eurex contract.

Exhibit 20.3

Source: *Financial Times*, www.ft.com, 22 October 2009 (no longer shown in the paper version of *FT*).

down version of the futures available to traders. As well as the December delivery future shown Liffe also offers traders the possibility of buying or selling futures that 'deliver' in March, June and September.

The table shows the first price traded at the beginning of the day (Open), the settlement price used to mark to market (usually the last traded price), the change from the previous day, highest and lowest prices during the day, the number of contracts traded that day (Est. vol.) and the total number of open contracts (these are trading contracts opened over the last few months that have not yet been closed by an equal and opposite futures transaction).

With each point on the FTSE 100 share index future being worth £10 if the future 100 index rises from 5,000 to 5050 and you had bought a future at 5,000, you have made 50 × £10 = £500 if you were to now sell at 5050.

Buying and selling futures

A trader in futures must deal through a registered broker. NYSE Liffe provide a list of designated brokers (these follow rules and codes of conduct imposed by the regulators and the exchange).

Gone are the days of open pit trading and those brightly colored jackets in the UK. Trades are now conducted over a computer system on LIFFE (LIFFE CONNECT™). You can place a price limit for your trade – a maximum you are willing to pay if you are buying or a minimum if you are selling. Alternatively you can make an 'at-the-market order', that is, to be executed immediately at the price determined by current supply and demand conditions. The buyer of a contract is said to be in a long position – he/she agrees to receive the underlying. The seller who agrees to deliver the underlying is said to be in a short position.

> Gone are the days of open pit trading and those brightly coloured jackets in the UK.

If the amount in the trader's account falls below the maintenance margin the trader will receive a demand to inject additional money. This may happen every day so the trader cannot buy/sell a future and then ignore the markets (unless he/she leaves plenty of cash with the broker to meet margin calls). Prices are set by competing market makers on LIFFE CONNECT™. Real time market prices are available on the internet, as well as historical prices (e.g. liffe-data.com).

> The trader cannot buy/sell a future and then ignore the markets (unless he/she leaves plenty of cash with the broker to meet margin calls).

Short-term interest rate futures

Trillions of pounds worth of trading takes place every year in the short-term interest rate futures markets. These are notional fixed-term deposits, usually for three-month periods starting at a specific time in the future. The buyer of one contract is buying the (theoretical) right to deposit money at a particular rate of interest for three months. So if the current time is November you could arrange a futures contract for you to 'deposit' and 'receive interest' on say £1m with the deposit starting in June and ending in September. The rate of interest you will 'receive' over the three summer months is agreed in November. (This is a notional receipt of interest, as these contracts are cash settled rather than actual deposits made and interest received – see below for an example.) So you now own the right to deposit £1m and receive x% interest for three months (at least in notional terms).

Short-term interest rate futures will be illustrated using the three-month sterling market. That is, deposits of pounds receiving notional interest for three months starting some point in the future. Note, however, that there are many other three-month deposits you could make. For example, you could deposit euros for three months, the interest rate on which is calculated with reference to 'Euribor 3m', which is the interest rate highly rated banks pay to other banks for three month deposits of the currency for the Eurozone countries, the euro. Other three-month deposits are often for money held outside of the jurisdiction of the currency's country of origin (i.e. 'Euro' currencies, in the sense of being international money and *not* the currency in the Eurozone) include Swiss francs deposited in London (Euroswiss), Eurodollars and Euroyens (*see* Exhibit 20.4). (Eurocurrency is discussed in Chapter 16.)

The unit of trading for a three-month sterling time deposit is £500,000. Cash delivery by closing out the futures position is the means of settlement, so the buyer would not actually require the seller of the future to place the £500,000 on deposit for three months at the interest rate indicated by the futures price. Although the term 'delivery' no longer has significance for the underlying it does define the date and time of the expiry of the contract. This occurs in late September, December, March and June (see www.euronext.com for precise definitions and delivery dates).

Short-term interest contracts are quoted on an index basis rather than on the basis of the interest rate itself. The price is defined as:

$$P = 100 - i$$

where:

P = price index;
i = the future interest rate in percentage terms.

Thus, on 30 November 2009 the settlement price for a June three-month sterling future was 99.05, which implies an interest rate of 100 – 99.05 = 0.95 percent for the period June to September – *see* Exhibit 20.4. Similarly the September quote would imply an interest rate of 100 – 98.67 = 1.33 percent for the three months September to December 2010.

Interest rates – Futures

Nov 30		Open	Sett	Change	High	Low	Est. vol.	Open int.
Euribor 3m*	Jan	99.18	99.21	+0.01	99.19	99.18	190	5,836
Euribor 3m*	Apr	0.00	98.97	-0.01	0.00	0.00	–	–
Euribor 3m*	Jun	98.83	98.81	-0.02	98.83	98.78	159,549	744,048
Euribor 3m*	Sep	98.53	98.53	–	98.55	98.50	118,198	415,086
Euroswiss 3m*	Dec	99.74	99.74	–	99.75	99.74	1,311	32,343
Euroswiss 3m*	Mar	99.70	99.69	–	99.71	99.69	7,638	51,756
Euroswiss 3m*	Jun	99.60	99.62	+0.01	99.62	99.60	4,128	39,777
Sterling 3m*	Jan	0.00	99.32	+0.02	0.00	0.00	–	–
Sterling 3m*	Mar	99.22	99.26	+0.03	99.26	99.22	37,321	362,054
Sterling 3m*	Jun	98.99	99.05	+0.04	99.05	98.99	37,320	423,217
Sterling 3m*	Sep	98.61	98.67	+0.04	98.68	98.61	36,512	305,190
Eurodollar 3m†	Jan	99.685	99.67	–	99.685	99.670	4,985	23,075
Eurodollar 3m†	Apr	0.000	99.55	–	0.000	0.000	–	265
Eurodollar 3m†	Jun	99.450	99.48	+0.020	99.485	99.450	191,351	1,013,560
Eurodollar 3m†	Sep	99.195	99.23	+0.025	99.240	99.190	168,073	759,757
Fed Fnds 30d‡	Nov	0.000	99.88	–	0.000	0.000	–	69,245
Fed Fnds 30d‡	Dec	0.000	99.87	-0.01	0.000	0.000	–	71,720
Fed Fnds 30d‡	Jan	0.000	99.86	-0.01	0.000	0.000	–	63,403
Euroyen 3m‡‡	Jan	0.000	99.500	–	0.000	0.000	–	–
Euroyen 3m‡‡	Mar	99.540	99.560	+0.025	99.560	99.540	26,315	241,873
Euroyen 3m‡‡	Jun	99.560	99.580	+0.025	99.585	99.560	23,913	246,879
Euroyen 3m‡‡	Sep	99.565	99.580	+0.020	99.585	99.555	16,689	155,205

Contracts are based on volumes traded in 2004   Sources: *NYSE LIFFE † CME. ‡ TIFFE
Notes: Euribor 3m: a benchmark interest rate in Euros for three-month deposits.
Euroswiss 3m: three-month interest rate in Euro-Swiss francs.
Sterling 3m: sterling three-month interest rate.
Eurodollar 3m: three-month notional deposit rate for Eurodollars.
Fed Fnds 30d: federal funds 30-day interest – a US benchmark rate.
Euroyen 3m: three-month interest rate for Euroyen deposits.

Exhibit 20.4

Source: *Financial Times* 1 December 2009.

In both cases the implied interest rate refers to a rate applicable for a notional deposit of £500,000 for three months on expiry of the contract – the June futures contract expires in June and the September future expires in September. The 0.95 percent rate for three-month money starting from June 2010 is the *annual* rate of interest even though the deal is for a deposit of only one-quarter of a year.

The price of 99.05 is not a price in the usual sense – it does not mean £99.05. It is used to maintain the standard inverse relationship between prices and interest rates. For example, if traders in this market one week later, on 6 December 2009, adjusted supply and demand conditions because they expect generally raised inflation and raised interest rates by the middle of 2010, they would push up the interest rates for three-month deposits starting in June 2010 to, say, 2.0 percent. Then the price of the future would fall to 98.00. Thus, a rise in interest rates for a three-month deposit of money results in a fall in the price of the contract – analogous to the inverse relationship between interest rates offered on long-term bonds and the price of those bonds.

It is this inverse change in capital value when interest rates change which is of crucial importance to grasp about short-term interest rate futures. This is more important than trying to envisage deposits of £500,000 being placed some time in the future.

Worked example 20.2
HEDGING THREE-MONTH DEPOSITS

An example of these derivatives in use may help with gaining an understanding of their hedging qualities. Imagine the treasurer of a large company anticipates the receipt of £100m in September 2010, ten months hence. She expects that the money will be needed for production purposes in the Winter of 2010–11 but for the three months following late September it can be placed on deposit. There is a risk that interest rates will fall between now (30 November 2009) and September 2010 from their present level of 1.33% per annum for three-month deposits starting in late September. (The Sterling 3m September future in Exhibit 20.3 shows a price of 98.67, indicating an interest rate of 1.33.)

The treasurer does not want to take a passive approach and simply wait for the inflow of money and deposit it at whatever rate is then prevailing without taking some steps to ensure a good return.

To achieve certainty in September 2010 the treasurer buys, on 30 November 2009, September expiry three-month sterling interest rate futures at a price of 98.67. Each future has a notional value of £500,000 and therefore she has to buy 200 to hedge the £100m inflow.

Suppose in September that three-month interest rates have fallen to 1%. Following the actual receipt of the £100m the treasurer can place it on deposit and receive a return over the next three months of £100m × 0.01 × 3/12 = £250,000. This is significantly less than if September 2010 three-month deposit interest rates had remained at 1.33% throughout the 10 month waiting period.

Return at 1.33% (£100m × 0.0133 × $\frac{3}{12}$)	= £332,500
Return at 1.00% (£100m × 0.010 × $\frac{3}{12}$)	= £250,000
Loss	£82,500

However the cautiousness of the treasurer pays off because the futures have risen in value as the interest rates have fallen.

The 200 futures contracts were bought at 98.67. With interest rates at 1% for three-month deposits starting in September the futures in September have a value of 100 – 1 = 99.00. The treasurer in September can close the futures position by selling the futures for 99.00. Thus, a purchase was made in November at 98.67 and a sale in September at 99, therefore the gain that is made amounts to 99.00 – 98.67 = 0.33.

This is where a *tick* needs to be introduced. A tick is the minimum price movement on a future. On a three-month sterling interest rate contract a tick is a movement of 0.01% on a trading unit of £500,000.

One-hundredth of 1% of £500,000 is equal to £50, but this is not the value of one tick. A further complication is that the price of a future is based on annual interest rates whereas the contract is for three months. Therefore £50/4 = £12.50 is the value of a tick movement in a three-month sterling interest rate futures contract. In this case we have a gain of 33 ticks with an overall value of 33 × £12.50 = £412.50 per contract, or £82,500 for 200 contracts. The profit on the futures exactly offsets the loss of anticipated interest when the £100m is put on deposit for three months in September.

Note that the deal struck in November was not to enter into a contract to actually deposit £100m with the counterparty on the NYSE Liffe market. The £100m is deposited in September with any one of hundreds of banks with no connection to the futures contract that the treasurer entered into. The actual deposit and the notional deposit (on NYSE Liffe) are two separate transactions. However, the transactions are cleverly arranged so that the value movement on these two exactly offset each other. All that is received from NYSE Liffe is the tick difference, based on the price change between buying and selling prices of the futures contracts – no interest is received.

Worked example 20.3
HEDGING A LOAN

On 30 November 2009, Holwell plc makes plans to borrow £5m for three months at a later date. This will begin in March 2010. Worried that short-term interest rates will rise Holwell hedges by *selling* ten three-month sterling interest rate futures contracts with March expiry. The price of each futures contract is 99.26, so Holwell has locked into an annual interest rate of 0.74% or 0.185% for three months. The cost of borrowing is therefore:

$$£5m \times 0.00185 = £9,250$$

Suppose that interest rates rise to annual rates of 1.6%, or 0.4% per quarter. The cost of borrowing for Holwell will be:

$$£5m \times 0.004 = £20,000$$

However, Holwell is able to *buy* ten futures contracts to close the position on the exchange. Each contract has fallen in value from 99.26 to 98.4; this is 86 ticks. The profit credited to Holwell's margin account of NYSE Liffe will now stand at:

Bought at 98.4, sold at 99.26:

$$86 \text{ ticks} \times £12.50 \times 10 \text{ contracts} = £10,750$$

Holwell pays interest to its lender for the three months March to May at 1.6% annual rate. The extra interest is £20,000 – £9,250 = £10,750. However, the derivative profit offsets the extra interest cost on the loan Holwell takes out in March.

Note that if interest rates fall Holwell will gain by being charged lower interest on the actual loan, but this will be offset by the loss of the futures. Holwell sacrifices the benefits of potential favourable movements in rates to reduce risk.

As Exhibit 20.5 shows, the price of short-term interest rate futures are followed closely as they give an indication of the market view on the level of short-term interest rates a few months hence.

Betting on interest rates

Graham Bowley

As the Chancellor and the Governor of the Bank of England sit down to ponder interest rate policy at their monthly monetary meeting today, a £40bn-a-day industry will be pronouncing its own judgment on where rates are going next.

The betting in the so-called 'short sterling' futures market is that policymakers will leave rates unchanged until well into next year. Banks and companies use this market to protect themselves against adverse changes in rates, while speculators use it to gamble on how rates might move.

Short sterling futures are traded on the London International Financial Futures and Options Exchange. Their current price implies a prediction that base rates will still be at $6\frac{3}{4}$ per cent by the end of this year, rising to 7 per cent by the end of next year. With more than £10,000bn each year backing these bets, this is a forecast that policymakers ignore at their peril.

'Short sterling takes in all the latest economic and political news to give an indication of where the money market thinks short-term interest rates will be going in the future,' said Mr Nigel Richardson, an economist at Yamaichi International, a Japanese bank.

The companies and banks buying short sterling futures are making a simple bet. The price of the short sterling contract is equal to 100 minus whatever interest rate is expected when the three month contract expires, so the price of the contract rises when interest rates fall.

If a company thought interest rates would be $6\frac{3}{4}$ per cent by December it would expect the price of the December contract to be 93.25. If the current price of the December contract was below 93.25 – in other words the market expected interest rates to be higher than $6\frac{3}{4}$ per cent at the end of the year – then the company could buy the contract and expect to profit when it expired in December.

This allows a short sterling trader to protect itself against a possible interest rate movement, effectively fixing the interest rate at which it borrows or lends. A more aggressive investor can use short sterling to gamble on an interest rate change.

Imagine a company has a sum of money to invest in a bank, but fears interest rates will fall. The company could buy a short sterling contract expiring in three months. If, by then, interest rates had not fallen, the company would have lost nothing. If rates did fall the company would get a lower return on its investment, but

this would have been offset by a rise in the price of the futures contract.

Another company might want to borrow money, but fear that interest rates are set to rise. It could hedge against this risk by selling short sterling futures. If rates did rise the company's borrowing costs would be higher, but it would be able to buy the contract back at a lower price and use the profit to offset the cost.

This is useful for banks providing fixed-rate mortgages. They use the short sterling market to fix the interest rates at which they borrow, which they can then pass on to customers.

Economists in the City use the forecast provided by the short sterling market as a basis for their own projections. 'It is very useful. It tells you what the market is predicting and you then take the market into account when making your own forecast,' said Mr Stuart Thomson, economist at Nikko, a Japanese bank.

But there have been times when the forecasts have been very different – and short sterling has not always been right. This year the short sterling market was expecting interest rates to be close to 9 per cent by December. Economists were expecting a more modest increase, and in the event they were proved more accurate.

Similarly, after the pound's exit from the European exchange rate mechanism in 1992, short sterling predicted that interest rates would have to remain high. In event they were cut aggressively.

'If you just want an average of the views of everybody acting in the market, then short sterling is fine,' said Mr Ian Shepherdson, an economist at HSBC Markets. 'But if you want an opinion, you need an economist. Short sterling gives the consensus, but the consensus is not always right.'

Policymakers will no doubt draw solace from the fact that markets can be wrong sometimes too.

EXHIBIT 20.5

Source: *Financial Times* 1 November 1995.

Forwards

Imagine you are responsible for purchasing potatoes to make crisps for your firm, a snack food producer. In the free market for potatoes the price rises or falls depending on the balance between buyers and sellers. These movements can be dramatic. Obviously you would like to acquire potatoes at a price that was as low as possible, while the potato producer wishes to sell for a price that is as high as possible. However both parties may have a similar interest in reducing the uncertainty of price. This will assist both to plan production and budget effectively. One way in which this could be done is to reach an agreement with the producer(s) to purchase a quantity of potatoes at a price agreed today to be delivered at a specified time in the future. Bensons, the UK crisp producer, buys 80 percent of its potatoes up to 19 months forward. Once the forward agreements have been signed and sealed Bensons may later be somewhat regretful if the spot price (price for immediate delivery) subsequently falls below the price agreed months earlier. Unlike option contracts, forwards commit both parties to complete the deal. However Bensons is obviously content to live with this potential for regret in order to remove the risk associated with such an important raw material.

> **Unlike option contracts, forwards commit both parties to complete the deal.**

> A forward contract is an agreement between two parties to undertake an exchange at an agreed future date at a price agreed now.

The party agreeing to buy at the future date is said to be taking a long position. The counterparty which will deliver at the future date is said to be taking a short position.

There are forward markets in a wide range of commodities but the most important forward markets today are for foreign exchange, in which hundreds of billions of dollars worth of currency are traded every working day – this is considered in Chapter 21.

Forward contracts are tailor-made to meet the requirements of the parties. This gives flexibility on the amounts and delivery dates. Forwards are not traded on an exchange but are 'over-the-counter' instruments – private agreements outside the regulation of an exchange. This makes them different to futures, which are standardised contracts traded on exchanges. Such an agreement exposes the counterparties to the risk of default – the failure by the other to deliver on the agreement. The risk grows in proportion to the extent to which the spot price diverges from the forward price as the incentive to renege increases.

Forward contracts are difficult to cancel, as agreement from each counterparty is needed. Also to close the contract early may result in a penalty being charged. Despite these drawbacks forward markets continue to flourish – as you can see in Exhibit 20.6.

Northern Foods passes price rises to customers

Lucy Warwick-Ching and Ed Crooks

Consumers will be hit by higher food prices as Northern Foods, maker of Fox's biscuits and Goodfella's pizza, prepares to pass on £40m of rising commodity costs to customers, including the big supermarkets.

Stefan Barden, chief excutive, said that in the last three months short supplies and high demand had pushed up the prices of cereals, dairy products, cocoa and fats. Poor harvests have also hit vegetable prices.

These cost increases are expected to add £32m–£40m to Northern Foods' £400m raw material bill, an increase of 8–10 per cent. However, Mr Barden said that, thanks to long-term contracts, forward buying and hedging, the increase this year would only be between 4–5 per cent, resulting in an extra £16m–£20m....

Exhibit 20.6

Source: Financial Times 10 October 2007, p. 25.

Forward rate agreements (FRAs)

FRAs are useful devices for hedging future interest rate risk. They are agreements about the future level of interest rates. The rate of interest at some point in the future is compared with the level agreed when the FRA was established and compensation is paid by one party to the other based on the difference.

For example, a company needs to borrow £6m in six months' time for a period of a year. It arranges this with bank X at a variable rate of interest. The current rate of interest for borrowing starting in six months is 7 percent. (For the sake of argument assume that this is Libor rate for borrowing starting in six months and this company can borrow at Libor). The company is concerned that by the time the loan is drawn down interest rates will be higher than 7 percent, increasing the cost of borrowing.

The company enters into a separate agreement with another bank (Y) – an FRA. It 'purchases' an FRA at an interest rate of 7 percent. This is to take effect six months from now and relate to a 12-month loan. Bank Y will never lend any money to the company but it has committed itself to paying compensation should interest rates (Libor) rise above 7 percent.

Suppose that in six months spot one-year interest rates are 8.5 percent. The company will be obliged to pay Bank X this rate: £6m × 0.085 = £510,000; this is £90,000 more than if the interest rates were 7 percent.[3] However, the FRA with Bank Y entitles the company to claim compensation equal to the difference between the rate agreed in the FRA and the spot rate. This is (0.085 – 0.07) × £6m = £90,000. So any increase in interest cost above 7 percent is exactly matched by a compensating payment provided by the counterparty to the FRA. However, if rates fall below 7 percent the company makes payments to Bank Y. For example, if the spot rate in six months is 5 percent the company benefits because of the lower rate charged by Bank X, but suffers an equal offsetting compensation payment to Bank Y of $(0.07 - 0.05) \times £6m = £120,000$. The company has generated certainty over the effective interest cost of borrowing in the future. Whichever way the interest rates move it will pay £420,000.

This example is a gross simplification. In reality FRAs are generally agreed for three-month periods. So this company could have four separate FRAs for the year. It would agree different interest rates for each three-month period. If three-month Libor turns out to be higher than the agreed interest rate, Bank Y will pay the difference to the company. If it is lower the company pays Bank Y the difference. The 'sale' of an FRA by a company protects against a fall in interest rates. For example, if £10m is expected to be available for putting into a one-year bank deposit in three months the company could lock into a rate now by selling an FRA to a bank. Suppose the agreed rate is 6.5 percent and the spot rate in three months is 6 percent, then the depositor will receive 6 percent from the bank into which the money is placed plus $\frac{1}{2}$ percent from the FRA counterparty bank.

The examples above are described as 6 against 18 (or 6 × 18) and 3 against 15 (or 3 × 15). The first is a 12-month contract starting in six months, the second is a 12-month contract starting in three months. More common FRA periods are 3 against 6 and 6 against 12. Typically sums of £5m–£100m are hedged in single deals in this market. Companies do not need to have an underlying lending or borrowing transaction – they could enter into an FRA in isolation and make or receive compensating payments only.

A comparison of options, futures and FRAs

We have covered a lot of ground in field of derivatives. It is time to summarise the main advantages and disadvantages of the derivatives covered so far – *see* Table 20.2.

Caps

An interest rate cap is a contract that gives the purchaser the right to effectively set a maximum level for interest rates payable. Compensation is paid to the purchaser of a cap if interest rates rise above an agreed level. This is a hedging technique used to cover interest rate risk on longer-term borrowing (usually two to five years). Under these arrangements a company borrowing money can benefit from interest rate falls but can place a limit to the amount paid in interest should interest rates rise.

The size of the cap premium depends on the difference between current interest rates and the level at which the cap becomes effective; the length of time covered; and the expected volatility of interest rates. The cap seller does not need to assess the creditworthiness of the purchaser because it receives payment of the premium in advance. Thus a cap is particularly suitable for highly geared firms, such as leveraged buyouts. See Worked example 20.4.

TABLE 20.2

A comparison of options, futures, forwards and forward rate agreements

Options	Futures	Forwards and FRAs
Advantages		
Downside risk is limited but the buyer is able to participate in favourable movements in the underlying.	Can create certainty: Specific rates are locked in.	Can create certainty: Specific rates are locked in.
Available on or off exchanges. Exchange regulation and clearing house reduce counterparty default risk for those options traded on exchanges.	Exchange trading only. Exchange regulation and clearing house reduce counterparty default risk.	Tailor-made, off-exchange. Not standardised as to size, duration and terms. Good for companies with non-standard risk exposures.
	No premium is payable. (However margin payments are required.)	No margins or premiums payable.* (Occasionally a good faith performance margin is required by one or more parties in a forward. Also credit limits may be imposed.)
For many options there are highly liquid markets resulting in keen option premium pricing and ability to reverse a position quickly at low cost. For others trading is thin and so premiums payable may become distorted and offsetting transactions costly and difficult.	Very liquid markets. Able to reverse transactions quickly and cheaply.	
Disadvantages		
Premium payable reduces returns when market movements are advantageous.	No right to let the contract lapse. Benefits from favourable movements in underlying are forgone.	No right to let the contract lapse. Benefits from favourable movements in underlying are forgone.
	In a hedge position if the underlying transaction does not materialise, the future position owner can experience a switch from a covered to an uncovered position, the potential loss is unlimited.	In a hedge position if the underlying transaction does not materialise, the forward/FRA position owner can experience a switch from a covered to an uncovered position, the potential loss is unlimited.
Margin required when writing options.	Many exchange restrictions – on size of contract, duration (e.g. only certain months of the year), trading times (e.g. when NYSE Liffe is open).	Greater risk of counterparty default – not exchange traded therefore counterparty is not the clearing house.*
	Margin calls require daily work for 'back office'.	More difficult to liquidate position (than with exchange-traded instruments) by creating offsetting transaction that cancels position.

---

* In 2009 governments around the world talked about insisting that over-the-counter derviatives be cleared through a formal system with a central counterparty (a clearing house) reducing risk for each participant. This is likely to mean margin payments will be required.

Worked example 20.4
INTEREST RATE CAP

Oakham plc wishes to borrow £20m for five years. It arranges this with bank A at a variable rate based on Libor plus 1.5%. The interest rate is reset every quarter based on three-month Libor. Currently this stands at an annual rate of 7%. The firm is concerned that over a five-year period the interest rate could rise to a dangerous extent.

Oakham buys an interest rate cap set at Libor of 8.5%. For the sake of argument we will assume that this costs 2.3% of the principal amount, or £20m × 0.023 = £460,000 payable immediately to the cap seller. If over the subsequent five years Libor rises above 8.5% in any three-month period Oakham will receive sufficient compensation from the cap seller to exactly offset any extra interest above 8.5%. So if for the whole of the third year Libor rose to 9.5% Oakham would pay interest at 9.5% plus 1.5% to bank A but would also receive 1% compensation from the cap seller (a quarter every three months), thus capping the interest payable. If interest rates fall Oakham benefits by paying bank A less.

The premium (£460,000) payable up front covers the buyer for the entire five years with no further payment due.

Floors and collars

Buyers of interest rate caps are sometimes keen to reduce the large cash payment at the outset. They can do this by simultaneously selling a floor, which results in a counterparty paying a premium. With a floor, if the interest rate falls below an agreed level, the seller (the floor writer) makes compensatory payments to the floor buyer. These payments are determined by the difference between the prevailing rates and the floor rate.

Returning to Oakham, the treasurer could buy a cap set at 8.5 percent Libor for a premium of £460,000 and sell a floor at 6 percent Libor receiving, say, £200,000. In any three-month period over the five-year life of the loan, if Libor rose above 8.5 percent the cap seller would pay compensation to Oakham; if Libor fell below 6 percent Oakham would save on the amount paid to bank A but will have to make payments to the floor buyer, thus restricting the benefits from falls in Libor. Oakham, for a net premium of £260,000, has ensured that its effective interest payments will not diverge from the range 6 percent + 1.5 percent = 7.5 percent at the lower end, to 8.5 percent + 1.5 percent = 10 percent at the upper end.

Selling a floor at a low strike rate and buying a cap at a higher strike rate is called a collar or a cylinder.

The combination of selling a floor at a low strike rate and buying a cap at a higher strike rate is called a collar or a cylinder.

Swaps

A swap is an exchange of cash payment obligations. An interest-rate swap is where one company arranges with a counterparty to exchange interest-rate payments. For example, the first company may be paying fixed-rate interest but prefers to pay floating rates. The second company may be paying floating rates of interest, which go up and down with Libor, but would benefit from a switch to a fixed obligation. Imagine that firm S has a £200m ten-year loan paying a fixed rate of interest of 8 percent, and firm T has a £200m ten-year loan on which interest is reset every six months with reference to Libor, at Libor plus 2 percent. Under a swap arrangement S would agree to pay T's floating-rate interest on each due date over the next ten years, and T would be obligated to pay S's 8 percent interest.

> A swap is an exchange of cash payment obligations.

One motive for entering into a swap arrangement is to reduce or eliminate exposure to rises in interest rates. Over the short run, futures, options and FRAs could be used to hedge interest-rate exposure. However for longer-term loans (more than two years) swaps are usually more suitable because they can run the entire lifetime of the loan. So if a treasurer of a company with a large floating-rate loan forecasts that interest rates will rise over the next four years, he/she could arrange to swap interest payments with a fixed-rate interest payer for those four years.

Another reason for using swaps is to take advantage of market imperfections. Sometimes the interest-rate risk premium charged in the fixed-rate borrowing market differs from that in the floating-rate market for a particular borrower – see worked example 20.5.

Worked example 20.5
SWAPS

Take the two companies, Cat plc and Dog plc, both of which want to borrow £150m for eight years. Cat would like to borrow on a fixed-rate basis because this would better match its asset position. Dog prefers to borrow at floating rates because of optimism about future interest-rate falls. The treasurers of each firm have obtained quotes from banks operating in the markets for both fixed- and floating-rate eight-year debt. Cat could obtain fixed-rate borrowing at 10% and floating rate at Libor +2%. Dog is able to borrow at 8% fixed and Libor +1% floating:

	Fixed	*Floating*
Cat can borrow at	10%	Libor +2%
Dog can borrow at	8%	Libor +1%

In the absence of a swap market Cat would probably borrow at 10% and Dog would pay Libor +1%. However with a swap arrangement both firms can achieve lower interest rates.

Notice that because of Dog's higher credit rating it can borrow at a lower rate than Cat in both the fixed and the floating-rate market – it has an absolute advantage in both. However the risk premium charged in the two markets is not consistent. Cat has to pay an extra 1% in the floating-rate market, but an extra 2% in the fixed-rate market. Cat has an absolute disadvantage for both, but has a comparative advantage in the floating-rate market.

To achieve lower interest rates each firm should borrow in the market where it has comparative advantage and then swap interest obligations. So Cat borrows floating-rate funds, paying Libor +2%, and Dog borrows fixed-rate debt, paying 8%.

Then they agree to swap interest payments at rates which lead to benefits for both firms in terms of (a) achieving the most appropriate interest pattern (fixed or floating), and (b) the interest rate that is payable is lower than if Cat had borrowed at fixed and Dog had borrowed at floating rates. *One* way of achieving this is to arrange the swap on the following basis:

- Cat pays to Dog fixed interest of 9.5%;
- Dog pays to Cat Libor +2%.

This is illustrated in Figure 20.1.

FIGURE 20.1
An interest rate swap

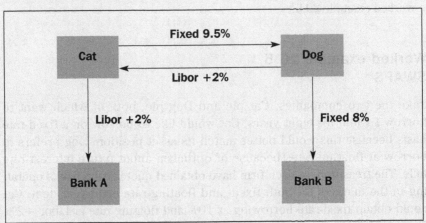

Now let us examine the position for each firm.

Cat pays Libor +2% to a bank but also receives Libor +2% from Dog and so these two cancel out. Cat also pays 9.5% fixed to Dog. This is 50 basis points (0.5%) lower than if Cat had borrowed at fixed rate directly from the bank. On £150m this is worth £750,000 per year.

Cat:

Pays	Libor +2%
Receives	Libor +2%
Pays	Fixed 9.5%
Net payment	Fixed 9.5%

Dog takes on the obligation of paying a bank fixed interest at 8% while receiving 9.5% fixed from Cat on the regular payment days. The net effect is 1.5% receivable less the Libor +2% payment to Cat – a floating-rate liability of Libor +0.5%.

Dog:

Pays	Fixed 8%
Receives	Fixed 9.5%
Pays	Libor +2%
Net payment	Libor +0.5%

Again there is a saving of 50 basis points or £750,000 per year.[4] The net annual £1.5m saving is before transaction costs.

Prior to the widespread development of a highly liquid swap market each counterparty incurred considerable expense in making the contracts watertight. Even then, the risk of one of the counterparties failing to fulfil its obligations was a potential problem. Today intermediaries (for example banks) take counterparty positions in swaps and this reduces risk and avoids the necessity for one corporation to search for another with a corresponding swap preference. The intermediary generally finds an opposite counterparty for the swap at a later date. Furthermore, standardised contracts reduce the time and effort to arrange a swap and have permitted the development of a thriving secondary market, and this has assisted liquidity.

A practical use of a swap arrangment is shown in Exhibit 20.7. The mortgage holder starts by paying base rate plus 1 percent to the mortgage company (5.5% + 1%) but agrees a swap, whereby he pays 6.2 percent fixed and receives base rate.

There are many variations on the swaps theme. For example, a 'swaption' is an option to have a swap at a later date. In a currency swap the two parties exchange interest obligations (or receipts) and the principal amount for an agreed period, between two different currencies. On reaching the maturity date of the swap the principal amounts will be re-exchanged at a pre-agreed exchange rate. An example of such an arrangement is shown in Exhibit 20.8.

Rate rise is music to the ears of 'swappers'

Unlike many home owners, those who have taken out interest rate swaps will be hoping that the Bank of England raises interest rates sooner rather than later.

One client of Stonehage, which advises wealthy families, recently arranged an interest rate swap on his £5m mortgage for three years. Due to the size of the loan he had to take out a variable mortgage at a rate of 6.5 per cent. Convinced that interest rates will increase significantly over the next three years he was concerned that this variable rate left him vulnerable to the possibility of large and changeable repayments.

He decided to take out a swap, which effectively takes the cost of his mortgage to 7.2 per cent. This meant taking out a 3 year swap priced at 6.2 per cent. 0.7 of a percentage point above base rates of current base rates of 5.5 per cent.

If base rates go above his swap rate of 6.2 per cent, the bank will pay him the difference between his fixed rate and the interest rate, effectively insuring him against further interest rate hikes. If base rates stay below this level he pays out the difference.

The benefits come if the Bank of England raises rates higher. If rates rise to 6.5 per cent, say, his variable mortgage would jump to 7.5 per cent and each year he would need to pay £375,000. While rising interest rates will push up his variable rate, they will also push up the amount he receives back from his bank on his swap.

In this case he would get back the difference between his swap rate of 6.2 per cent and the interest rate of 6.5 per cent. He can then use this 0.3 percent payment to offset his variable rate of 7.5 per cent, keeping his payments at a fixed rate of 7.2 per cent.

But by using an interest rate swap, he has ensured that his payments never exceed 7.2 per cent – or £360,000 per year.

EXHIBIT 20.7

Source: *Financial Times* 30 June 2007, p. 2.

TVA, EIB find winning formula

Richard Lapper

The back-to-back swap deal priced yesterday for the Tennessee Valley Authority and the European Investment Bank will give both cheaper funding than they could obtain through conventional bond issuance.

TVA, the US government-owned power utility, is issuing a 10-year DM1.5bn eurobond with a Frankfurt listing, while EIB is raising $1bn with a 10-year issue in the US market. The issuers will swap the proceeds.

Speaking in London yesterday, the treasurers of both organisations said the arrangement – now relatively unusual in the swaps market – had allowed them to reduce borrowing costs, although they did not specify by what amount.

Two elements of the deal were important in this respect. First, the EIB has a much stronger comparative advantage over TVA in funding in dollars than it does in D-Marks. Lehman Brothers, co-bookrunner on both deals, said the EIB priced its 10-year dollar paper at 17 basis points over Treasuries, about 6 to 7 points lower than TVA could have done.

In the German market EIB enjoys a smaller advantage; it could raise funds at about 4 basis points less than the 17 points over bonds achieved by TVA.

Second, by swapping the proceeds on a back-to-back basis rather than through counter-parties, bid/offer spreads were eliminated and transaction costs reduced.

Resulting savings were pooled, providing benefits for both borrowers.

Both also diversified their funding sources. Lehman said some 65 per cent of the TVA bonds were placed in Europe, 20 per cent in Asia, and 15 per cent in the US. About half the EIB issue was placed in the US, 35 per cent in Europe, and 15 per cent in Asia.

EXHIBIT 20.8

Source: *Financial Times* 12 September 1996.

Derivatives users

There are three types of user of the derivatives markets: hedgers, speculators and arbitrageurs.

Hedgers

To hedge is to enter into a transaction(s) that protects a business or assets against changes in some underlying. The instruments bought as a hedge tend to have the opposite-value movements to the underlying. Financial and commodity markets are used to transfer risk from an individual or corporation to another more willing and/or able to bear that risk.

> To hedge is to enter into a transaction(s) that protects a business or assets against changes in some underlying.

Consider a firm that discovers a rich deposit of platinum in Kenya. The management is afraid to develop the site because they are uncertain about the revenues that will actually be realised. Some of the sources of uncertainty are that: (a) the price of platinum could fall; (b) the floating-rate loan taken out to develop the site could become expensive if interest rates rise; and (c) the value of the currencies could move adversely. The senior managers have more or less decided that they will apply the firm's funds to a less risky venture. A young executive steps forward and suggests that this would be a pity, saying: 'The company is passing up a great opportunity, and Kenya and the world economy will be poorer as a result. Besides, the company does not have to bear all of these risks given the sophistication of modern financial markets. The risks can be hedged, to limit the downside. For example, the platinum could be sold on the futures market, which will provide a firm price. The interest-rate liability can be capped or swapped into a fixed-rate loan. Other possibilities include using the FRA and the interest futures markets. The currency risk can be controlled by using currency forwards or options.' The Board decides to press ahead with development of the mine and thus show that derivatives can be used to promote economic well-being by transferring risk.

Speculators

Speculators take a position in financial instruments and other assets with a view to obtaining a profit on changes in price. Speculators accept high risk in anticipation of high reward. The gearing effect of derivatives makes speculations in these instruments particularly profitable, or particularly ruinous. Speculators are also attracted to derivatives markets because they are often more liquid than the underlying markets. In addition the speculator is able to sell before buying (to 'short' the market) to profit from a fall. More complex trading strategies are also possible.

> Speculators take a position in financial instruments and other assets with a view to obtaining a profit on changes in price.

The term speculator in popular parlance is often used in a somewhat critical fashion. This is generally unwarranted. Speculators are needed by financial markets to help create trading liquidity. Many people argue that prices are more, not less, likely to be stable as a result of speculative activity. Usually speculators have dissimilar views regarding future market movements and this provides two-way liquidity that allows other market participants, such as hedgers, to carry out a transaction quickly without moving the price. Imagine if only hedgers with an underlying were permitted to buy or sell derivatives. Very few trades would take place each day. If a firm wished to make a large hedge this would be noticed in the market and the price of the derivative would be greatly affected – moving against the trader. Speculators also provide a kind of insurance for hedgers – they accept risk in return for a premium.

Arbitrageurs

The act of arbitrage is to exploit price differences on the same instrument or similar assets. The arbitrageur buys at the lower price and immediately resells at the higher price. So, for example, Nick Leeson claimed that he was arbitraging Nikkei 225 Index futures. The same future is traded in both Osaka and Singapore. Theoretically the price should be identical on both markets, but in reality this is not always the case, and it is possible simultaneously to buy the future in one market and sell the future in the other and thereby make a risk-free profit. An arbitrageur waits for these opportunities to exploit market inefficiency. The problem for Barings Bank was that Nick Leeson obtained funds to put down as margin payments on arbitrage trades but then bought futures in both markets – surreptitiously switching from an arbitrage activity to a highly risky, speculative activity. True arbitrageurs help to ensure pricing efficiency – their acts of buying or selling tend to reduce pricing anomalies.

> The act of arbitrage is to exploit price differences on the same instrument or similar assets.

Over-the-counter (OTC) and exchange-traded derivatives

An OTC derivative is a tailor-made, individual arrangement between counterparties, usually a company and its bank. Standardised contracts (exchange-traded derivatives) are available on dozens of derivatives around the world, for example the Chicago Board of Trade (CBOT), Chicago Board Options Exchange (CBOE), the Chicago Mercantile Exchange (CME), NYSE.Liffe and the Eurex in Germany and Switzerland. Roughly one-half of outstanding derivatives contracts are traded on exchanges.

> An OTC derivative is a tailor-made, individual arrangement between counterparties, usually a company and its bank.

Many derivatives markets are predominantly, if not exclusively, OTC: interest-rate FRAs, swaps, caps, collars, floors, currency forwards and currency swaps. Figure 20.2 compares OTC and exchange-traded derivatives.

FIGURE 20.2

OTC and exchange-traded derivatives

OTC derivative

Advantages

- Contracts can be tailor-made, which allows perfect hedging and permits hedges of more unusual underlyings.
- Companies which have a longstanding relationship with a bank can often arrange derivative deals with it, without the need to find any specific margin or deposit. The bank is willing to accept the counterparty risk of its customer reneging on the deal because it regards this possibility as very low risk, given its longstanding knowledge of the firm.

Disadvantages

- There is a risk (credit risk) that the counterparty will fail to honour the transaction.
- Low level of market regulation with resultant loss of transparency and price dissemination.
- Often difficult to reverse a hedge once the agreement has been made.
- Higher transaction costs.

Exchange-traded derivative

Advantages

- Credit risk is reduced because the clearing house is counterparty.
- High regulation encourages transparency and openness on the price of recent trades.
- Liquidity is usually much higher than for OTC – large orders can be cleared quickly due to high daily volume of trade.
- Positions can be reversed by closing quickly – an equal and opposite transaction is completed in minutes.

Disadvantages

- Standardisation may be restrictive, e.g. standardised terms for quality of underlying, quantity, delivery dates.
- The limited trading hours and margin requirements may be inconvenient.

The political pressure to move much of the OTC derivatives so that it is cleared by a central counterparty (which is likely to increase the role of exchanges) is enormous – see Exhibit 20.9.

Clearing up the system

Jeremy Grant

Out of the ashes of the credit crisis, one financial process has emerged that could not be further removed from the high-profile drama of the global banking meltdown: clearing.

Long consigned to the back office, clearing is now on the lips of regulators as they push sweeping plans to clean up the financial system

Clearing is the process by which a trade between two counterparties is guaranteed by a clearing house, which holds margin collateral paid in by market participants for this purpose. Should one party default, the clearing house steps in to ensure the deal goes ahead.

This safeguard was not a feature of most of the over-the-counter derivatives that were traded routinely between banks and other counterparties before the Lehman Brothers bankruptcy last year. When Lehman defaulted, hundreds of banks and other institutions were left with large exposures, triggering a wave of fear over 'counterparty risk' in the broader markets – and the resulting meltdown.

Since then, governments and regulators in the US and Europe have made wider use of clearing – particularly in the over-the-counter markets – a pillar of reform of financial markets.

Even before any legislation is written that would prescribe how this will happen, exchanges and clearing houses have been jostling for a piece of the action, pressing ahead with initiatives they believe will provide a source of new revenues. ...

Nasdaq OMX is preparing to launch interest rate swaps clearing through a new majority-owned clearing company called the International Derivatives Clearing Group.

In London, LCH.Clearnet's SwapClear interest rate clearing division has added new members and now clears almost 64 per cent of all such products dealt in the inter-bank market.

While most market participants accept that clearing will have a bigger role in the financial system in coming years, questions remain over the extent to which clearing should – and could – be used to make the financial system safer. In particular, there is increasing debate over how far to force OTC derivatives into a cleared environment. Corporate users of such products argue that the current proposals go too far and would cause a huge drain on corporate cash because clearing would require the posting of margin collateral. This is not a feature of the way in which companies currently buy their bespoke OTC derivatives from banks.

Inter-dealer brokers active as intermediaries in OTC derivatives say that many transactions are too bespoke to be processed through the clearing houses, adding that financial innovation would be hampered.

Recent legislation produced by the US House of Representatives' Financial Services Committee appeared to take some of those concerns on board by offering concessions to certain users of OTC derivatives on the clearing issue.

Clearing houses have cautioned that regulators should be careful before mandating the shifting of too many OTC products into a cleared environment, because some products may actually add to a clearing house's risks, especially if they are thinly traded or in cases where it is hard to value certain derivatives.

Chris Wilcox, global head of rates trading at JP Morgan, says: 'Even the clearing houses themselves agree on the need to ensure only products with sufficient liquidity and price transparency in the market are deemed suitable for clearing.'

Others worry that as clearing initiatives proliferate, some could be tempted to lower margin requirements to win business, possibly to levels that could be considered imprudent for the safety of the financial system. ...

Exhibit 20.9

Source: *Financial Times* 2 November 2009, p. 11.

Conclusion

As derivatives become increasingly important we need to be aware of the potential for harm that can arise from their misuse. However, the danger must not lead us to reject their use entirely. For some firms in some circumstance they can help create value. In others they can be, as Warren Buffett has called them, financial weapons of mass destruction. Given the wide-ranging nature of this book we can only touch on the main characteristics of derivatives here. But hopefully, even this limited discussion has given you some insight into their power for both wealth creation and wealth destruction. The next chapter builds on knowledge of the main types of derivatives to show how they can be used to reduce the risk of companies that operate across international borders.

Websites

www.bloomberg.com	Bloomberg
www.reuters.com	Reuters
www.money.cnn.com	CNN Financial News
www.wsj.com	Wall Street Journal
www.ft.com	Financial Times
www.fow.com	Futures and Options World
www.euronext.com	NYSE Liffe Futures and Options
www.cbot.com	Chicago Board of Trade
www.cboe.com	Chicago Board Options Exchange
www.amex.com	American Stock Exchange
www.nyse.com	New York Stock Exchange
www.eurexchange.com	Eurex, the European Derivative Exchange
www.isda.org	International Swaps and Derivatives Association
www.ukcitymedia.co.uk	UK City Media

Notes

1 Caps, floors and collars are usually constructed from options on interest rates and so, in truth, belong in the option category. However, they are included in this chapter because they are another tool for managing interest rate risk, a major theme of this chapter.

2 Nick Leeson in an interview with David Frost, reported in *Financial Times* 11 September 1995.

3 All figures are slightly simplified because we are ignoring the fact that the compensation is received in six months whereas interest to Bank X is payable in 18 months.

4 Under a swap arrangement the principal amount (in this case £150m) may never be swapped and Cat retains the obligation to pay the principal to bank A. Neither of the banks is involved in the swap and may not be aware that it has taken place. The swap focuses entirely on the three-monthly or six-monthly interest payments.

21

MANAGING EXCHANGE-RATE RISK

Introduction

This chapter discusses how changes in exchange rates can lead to an increase in uncertainty about income from operations in foreign countries or from trading with foreign firms. Shifts in foreign exchange rates have the potential to undermine the competitive position of the firm and destroy profits. This chapter describes some of the techniques used to reduce the risk associated with business dealings outside the home base.

The message from the ups and downs of sterling and other currencies in the last two decades is that foreign exchange shifts and the management of the associated risk are not issues to be separated and put into a box marked 'for the attention of the finance specialists only'. The profound implications for jobs, competitiveness, national economic growth and firms' survival mean that all managers need to be aware of the consequences of foreign exchange rate movements and of how to prepare the firm to cope with them. See Case study 21.1.

Case study 21.1

What a difference a few percentage point moves on the exchange rate make

Until autumn 1992 sterling was a member of the European exchange rate mechanism (ERM), which meant the extent it could move in value vis-à-vis the other currencies in the ERM was severely limited. Then came 'Black Wednesday' when the pound fell out of the ERM, the government gave up the fight to retain the high level of sterling and the pound fell by around 20%.

George Soros was one of the speculators who recognised economic gravity when he saw it, and bet the equivalent of $10bn against sterling by buying other currencies. After the fall the money held in other currencies could be converted back to make $1bn in just a few days. When sterling was highly valued against other currencies exporters found life very difficult because, to the foreign buyer, British goods appeared expensive – every unit of their currency bought few pounds.

However, in the four years following 'Black Wednesday' UK exporters had a terrific boost and helped pull the economy out of recession as overseas customers bought more goods. Other European companies, on the other hand, complained bitterly. The French government was prompted by its hard-pressed importers to ask for compensation from the European Commission for the 'competitive devaluations by their neighbours'.

Then things turned around. Between 1996 and 2001 the pound rose against most currencies. Looked at from the German importers' viewpoint UK goods relative to domestic goods rose in price by something of the order of 30–40 percent. UK firms lined up to speak of the enormous impact the high pound was having on profits. British Steel (Corus) cut thousands of jobs in response to sterling's rise and started losing money at an alarming rate. It also passed on the pain by telling 700 of its UK suppliers to cut prices.

James Dyson, the vacuum cleaner entrepreneur, announced that he was planning to build a factory in East Asia rather than Britain because of the strength of the pound. The Japanese car makers Toyota, Honda and Nissan, which had established plants in Britain, complained bitterly about the high level of the pound. Their factories were set up to export cars. They were hurt by having to reduce prices and also by their commitment to buy 70 percent of components from UK suppliers (continental European suppliers benefited from a 30–40 percent price advantage because of the high pound).

Then things turned around again. European companies had an increasingly hard time trying to export, particularly into the US and UK markets, because between 2002 and 2010 the euro rose by around 50 percent, making European goods 50 percent more expensive in the eyes of US and UK consumers. Worse, US exporters could compete against their European rivals more effectively when selling to countries in Asia and elsewhere because of the rise in the euro. Heineken, exporting beer to the USA, to maintain profits *should* have raised its export prices by 50 percent but found that competition meant it could only raise them 2–3 percent per year. Operating profit from its USA unit alone fell by an estimated two-thirds. Similar difficulties were experienced by a whole range of European exporters, from German car makers to Scotch whisky distillers.

Also complaining were the UK companies that buy goods and services and borrow money abroad, because their margins were being squeezed. Next and JJB Sports source most of their goods from overseas manufacturers; the low pound against the dollar as well as the euro meant that they had to pay more in pound terms for the same items. The housebuilder Taylor Wimpey suffered because most of their debt was in dollars, which now needed more pounds for each unit of dollar interest. Branston Pickle (Premier Foods) prices rose in part because the falling pound pushed up the cost of many of its (imported) raw materials.

Those benefiting from the weak pound included pharmaceutical companies, which make a large share of their revenues overseas but report their results in pounds. And, of course, exporters, from engineers to English hoteliers, received a boost when their products or services became more competitive in the eyes of the overseas buyer.

The impact of currency rate changes on the firm

Shifts in the value of foreign exchange, from now on to be referred to as simply 'forex' (FOReign EXchange),[1] can impact on various aspects of a firm's activities:

- **Income to be received from abroad** For example, if a UK firm has exported goods to Canada on six months' credit terms, payable in Canadian dollars (C$), it is uncertain as to the number of pounds it will actually receive because the dollar could move against the pound in the intervening period.

- **The amount actually paid for imports at some future date** For example, a Japanese firm importing wood from the USA may have a liability to pay dollars a few months later. The quantity of yen (¥) it will have to use to exchange for the dollars at that point in the future is uncertain at the time the deal is struck.

- **The valuation of foreign assets and liabilities** In today's globalised marketplace many firms own assets abroad and incur liabilities in foreign currencies. The value of these in home-currency terms can change simply because of forex movements. For example, Sage's debt rose over £100m in a three-month period because of exchange rate change – *see* Exhibit 21.1.

Sterling's plunge adds to debt burden at Sage

Lucy Killgren

Debt levels at Sage rose in the final three months of last year, the software group said, because of the pound's weakness.

Net debt, a substantial proportion of which is denominated in dollars and euros, rose from £541m in September to £649m by December 31, as a result of currency translation. ...

It said the weakness of sterling had also lifted profits in the three months to December 31. ...

Exhibit 21.1

Source: *Financial Times* 5 February 2009, p. 18.

- **The long-term viability of foreign operations** The long-term future returns of subsidiaries located in some countries can be enhanced by a favourable forex change. On the other hand firms can be destroyed if they are operating in the wrong currency at the wrong time.

- **The acceptability, or otherwise, of an overseas investment project** When evaluating the value-creating potential of major new investments a firm must be aware that the likely future currency changes can have a significant effect on estimated NPV.

In summary, fluctuating exchange rates create risk, and badly managed risk can lead to a loss of shareholder wealth.

Volatility in foreign exchange

Figures 21.1 and 21.2 show the extent to which forex rates can move even over a period as short as a few weeks – 5 or 10 percent point shifts are fairly common.

In the mid-1970s a regime of (generally) floating exchange rates replaced the fixed exchange-rate system that had been in place since the 1940s. Today most currencies fluctuate against each other, at least to some extent.

If a UK firm holds dollars or assets denominated in dollars and the value of the dollar rises against the pound a forex profit is made. Conversely, should the pound rise relative to the dollar, a forex loss will be incurred. These potential gains or losses can be very large. For example, between July 2008 and February 2009 the dollar appreciated by 28 percent against the pound so you could have made a large gain by holding dollars even before the money was put to use, say, earning interest. In other periods fluctuating forex rates may wipe out profits from a project, an export deal or a portfolio investment (for example, a pension fund buying foreign shares).

FIGURE 21.1

Exchange-rate movements, US$ to UK£, November 1989–November 2009 (monthly)

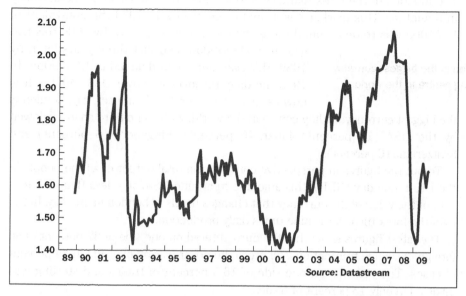

Source: Datastream

FIGURE 21.2

Exchange-rate movements, UK pound to euro, November 2009 (weekly)

Source: Datastream

The currency markets

The function of the forex markets is to facilitate the exchange of one currency into another. This market has grown dramatically. In 1973 the equivalent of US$10bn was traded around the globe on average each day. By 1986 this had grown to US$300bn, and just three years later, by 1989, this had more than doubled to US$590bn. In 1998 the daily turnover was over US$1,490bn. It is now estimated at over $3,000bn each day. London is the biggest currency trading centre in the world, with a one-third share, followed by the USA (17 percent) Japan (6 percent), Singapore (6 percent) and Switzerland (6 percent).

> London is the biggest currency trading centre in the world.

To put the figures in perspective consider the total output of all the people in the UK in one day (GDP): this amounts to around US$7bn – less than one percent of the value of the currency that changes hands in London in one day. In the USA the forex turnover is nine times daily production.

The latest figures show that the euro entered on one side of 37 percent of all foreign exchange transactions, whereas the dollar was on one side in 86 percent of cases. The yen was on one side of 16.5 percent of trades and sterling was involved in only 15 percent of trades.

Who is trading?

The buyers and sellers of foreign currencies are:

- exporters/importers
- tourists
- fund managers (pensions, insurance companies, etc.)
- governments (for example, to pay for activities abroad)
- central banks (smoothing out fluctuations)
- speculators
- banks.

The first five groups account for only a small fraction of the transactions. The big players are the large commercial banks. In addition to dealing on behalf of customers, or acting as market makers, they carry out 'proprietary' transactions of their own in an attempt to make a profit by taking a position in the market – that is, speculating on future movements. Companies and individuals usually obtain their foreign currencies from the banks.

> The big players are the large commercial banks.

Foreign exchange interbank brokers often act as intermediaries between large buyers and sellers. They allow banks to trade anonymously, thus avoiding having the price move simply because of the revelation of the name of a bank in a transaction.

Most deals are still made over the telephone and later confirmed in writing. However the new electronic trading systems in which computers match deals automatically have taken a rapidly increasing share of deals.

Twenty-four hour trading

Dealing takes place on a 24-hour basis, with trading moving from one major financial centre to another. Most trading occurs when both the European and New York markets are open – this is when it is afternoon in Frankfurt, Zurich and London and morning on the east coast of the Americas. Later the bulk of the trade passes to San Francisco and Los Angeles, followed by Wellington, Sydney, Tokyo, Hong Kong, Singapore and Bahrain. There are at least 40 other trading centres around the world.

Most banks are in the process of concentrating their dealers in three or four regional hubs. These typically include London as well as New York and two sites in Asia, where Tokyo, Hong Kong and Singapore are keen to establish their dominance.

The vast sums of money traded every working day across the world means that banks are exposed to the risk that they may irrevocably pay over currency to a counterparty before they receive another currency in return because settlement systems are operating in different time zones. A bank could fail after receiving one leg of its foreign exchange trades but before paying the other leg – this is called Herstatt risk after a German bank that failed in 1974 leaving the dollars that it owed on its foreign exchange deals unpaid. Its failure caused panic and gridlock in the forex market, which took weeks to unravel. An organisation set up in 2002, the CLS Bank, allows both legs of the trade to be paid simultaneously,

> Under CLS, payments will be made by banks to an orderly schedule in a five-hour slot the day after the deal.

eliminating the risk that one bank might fail in midstream. Under CLS (Continuous Limited Settlement), payments are made by banks to an orderly schedule in a five-hour slot the day after the deal. A second major advantage of this system is that the net value of the trades are settled rather than the gross amounts of trades. So if a bank sold $1bn, but also bought $900m, the settlement is for only $100m.[2]

Exchange rates

We now look more closely at exchange rates, starting with some terms used in forex markets. First, we provide a definition of an exchange rate:

> An exchange rate is the price of one currency expressed in terms of another.

Therefore if the exchange rate between the US dollar and the pound is US$1.89 = £1.00 this means that £1.00 will cost US$1.89. Taking the reciprocal, US$1.00 will cost 52.91 pence. The standardized forms of expression are:

US$1.89/£

or

US$/£ : 1.89

Exchange rates are expressed in terms of the number of units of the first currency per single unit of the second currency. Also forex rates are normally given to five or six significant figures. So for the US$/£ exchange rate the more accurate rate is:

US$1.8895/£

However this is still not accurate enough because currency exchange rates are not generally expressed in terms of a single 'middle rate', but are given as a rate at which you can buy the first currency (bid rate) and a rate at which you can sell the first currency (offer rate). In the case of the US$/£ exchange rate the market rates are:

US$1.8895/£ 'middle rate'

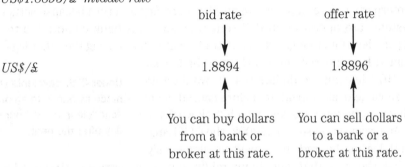

So if you wished to purchase US$1m the cost would be:

$$\frac{\$1,000,000}{1.8894} = £529,269$$

However if you wished to sell US$1m you would receive:

$$\frac{\$1,000,000}{1.8896} = £529,213$$

The foreign exchange dealers make profit in two ways. First, they may charge commission on a deal. Depending on the size of the transaction this can vary, but it is generally well below 1 percent. Second, these institutions are dealing with numerous buyers and sellers every day and they make a profit on the difference between the bid price and offer price (the bid/offer spread). In the above example if a dealer sold US$1m and bought US$1m with a bid/offer spread of 0.02 of a cent, a profit of £529,269 – £529,213 = £56 is made.

The spot and forward exchange markets

There are two main forex markets.

- **The 'spot' market** In the spot market transactions take place which are to be settled quickly. Officially this is described as immediate delivery, but this usually takes place two business days after the deal is struck. However, this is reduced to the next morning (Greenwich mean time) for those trades going through CLS.

- **The 'forward' market** In the forward market a deal is arranged to exchange currencies at some future date at a price agreed now. The periods of time are generally one, three or six months, but it is possible to arrange an exchange of currencies at a pre-determined rate many years from now.

Forward transactions represent about one-third to one-half of all forex deals. There are many currencies, however, for which forward quotes are difficult to obtain. The so-called exotic currencies generally do not have forward rates quoted by dealers. These are currencies for which there is little trading demand to support international business, etc. On the other hand, spot markets exist for most of the world's currencies.

> **Spot markets exist for most of the world's currencies.**

The *Financial Times* reports the previous day's trading in the forex market. The figures shown in Exhibit 21.2 relate to dealing on 10 December 2009. Of course by the time a newspaper reader receives the information in this table the rates have changed as the 24-hour markets follow the sun around the world. However, FT.com and other websites provide much more up-to-the-minute and detailed information.

The prices shown under the pound columns in Exhibit 21.2 are the middle price of the foreign currency in terms of £1 in London the previous afternoon.[3] So, for instance, the mid price of £1 for immediate delivery is 1.7733 Australian dollars. For the US dollar columns the prices for the pound and euro are the number of dollars per currency unit, either per pound or per one euro. However for other currencies the rate shown is the number of units of the other currency per US$1 – for example, 1.0521 Canadian dollars per US dollar. For the euro columns the rate shown is the number of units of the other currency per euro – for example the spot mid-rate against the pound is 90.58 pence per euro.

The first forward price (middle price) is given as the 'one month' rate. So you could commit yourself to the sale of a quantity of dollars for delivery in one month at a rate that is fixed at about US$1.6249 per pound. In this case you will need fewer US dollars to buy £1 in one month's time compared with the spot rate of exchange, therefore the dollar is at a *premium* on the one-month forward rate.

If the forward rate was such that you needed more dollars in one month's time compared with the spot rate, we would say that the one-month forward rate was at a discount.

Currency rates

www.ft.com/currency data

Dec 10	Currency	DOLLAR Closing mid	DOLLAR Day's change	EURO Closing mid	EURO Day's change	POUND Closing mid	POUND Day's change
Argentina	(Peso)	3.8013	-0.0007	5.5955	-0.0008	6.1779	0.0116
Australia	(A$)	1.0911	-0.0102	1.6061	-0.0178	1.7733	-0.0128
Bahrain	(Dinar)	0.3771	0.0000	0.5551	-0.0009	0.6128	0.0013
Bolivia	(Boliviano)	7.0200	0.0000	10.3335	-0.0179	11.4090	0.0235
Brazil	(R$)	1.7660	0.0055	2.5996	0.0036	2.8701	0.0149
Canada	(C$)	1.0521	-0.0027	1.5486	-0.0067	1.7098	-0.0009
Chile	(Peso)	496.750	-2.9000	731.216	-5.5429	807.318	-3.3392
China	(Yuan)	6.8266	-0.0010	10.0488	-0.0189	11.0946	0.0213
Colombia	(Peso)	2022.00	8.8250	2976.38	7.8569	3286.15	21.0865
Costa Rica	(Colon)	573.865	1.1750	844.730	0.2695	932.646	3.8279
Czech Rep.	(Koruna)	17.5136	0.0133	25.7800	-0.0250	28.4631	0.0803
Denmark	(DKr)	5.0555	0.0088	7.4417	0.0002	8.2163	0.0313
Egypt	(Egypt £)	5.4838	0.0038	8.0721	-0.0084	8.9122	0.0245
Estonia	(Kroon)	10.6294	0.0184	15.6465	-0.0194	17.2750	0.0655
Hong Kong	(HK$)	7.7508	0.0003	11.4091	-0.0194	12.5966	0.0264
Hungary	(Forint)	185.177	-1.1005	272.580	-2.0950	300.949	-1.1646
India	(Rs)	46.6438	0.1088	68.6596	0.0414	75.8054	0.3327
Indonesia	(Rupiah)	9437.00	4.0000	13891.3	-18.1667	15337.0	38.0999
Iran	(Rial)	9901.00		14574.3	-23.7730	16091.1	34.7902
Israel	(Shk)	3.7728	-0.0158	5.5535	-0.0329	6.1315	-0.0129
Japan	(Y)	88.3200	0.3850	130.007	0.3425	143.538	0.9202
One Month		88.2994	0.0001	129.966	-0.0010	143.475	0.0004
Three Month		88.2685	-0.0028	129.889	-0.0061	143.368	-0.0040
One Year		87.8680	-0.0140	128.970	-0.0374	142.452	-0.0017
Kenya	(Shilling)	75.8000	-0.1500	111.578	-0.4145	123.190	0.0107
Kuwait	(Dinar)	0.2852	0.0000	0.4199	-0.0008	0.4635	0.0009
Malaysia	(M$)	3.3975	-0.0010	5.0012	-0.0102	5.5217	0.0098
Mexico	(New Peso)	12.9733	0.0099	19.0967	-0.0184	21.0843	0.0597
New Zealand	(NZ$)	1.3701	-0.0329	2.0167	-0.0520	2.2266	-0.0487
Nigeria	(Naira)	150.350	0.9000	221.315	0.9437	244.349	1.9633
Norway	(NKr)	5.7594	-0.0001	8.4779	-0.0149	9.3602	0.0191
Pakistan	(Rupee)	84.2250	0.0050	123.979	-0.2073	136.883	0.2903
Peru	(New Sol)	2.8715	-0.0020	4.2269	-0.0103	4.6668	0.0064
Philippines	(Peso)	46.2000	-0.1750	68.0064	-0.3759	75.0843	-0.1290

	Currency	DOLLAR Closing mid	DOLLAR Day's change	EURO Closing mid	EURO Day's change	POUND Closing mid	POUND Day's change
Poland	(Zloty)	2.8178	0.0058	4.4178	0.0012	4.5795	0.0188
Romania	(New Leu)	2.8837	0.0029	4.2448	-0.0031	4.6865	0.0142
Russia	(Rouble)	30.3960	-0.0075	44.7429	-0.0886	49.3996	0.0897
Saudi Arabia	(SR)	3.7504	-0.0002	5.5206	-0.0098	6.0952	0.0123
Singapore	(S$)	1.3896	0.0001	2.0454	-0.0034	2.2583	0.0048
South Africa	(R)	7.5330	-0.0532	11.0886	-0.0976	12.2427	-0.0611
South Korea	(Won)	1165.50	4.0000	1715.62	2.9262	1894.17	10.3917
Sweden	(SKr)	7.0931	-0.0098	10.4410	-0.0326	11.5276	0.0078
Switzerland	(SFr)	1.0267	0.0018	1.5113	-0.0846	1.6685	0.0063
Taiwan	(T$)	32.2950	-0.0015	47.5382	-0.0699	52.4859	0.1058
Thailand	(Bt)	33.1950	0.0100	48.8631	0.0015	53.9485	0.1274
Tunisia	(Dinar)	1.3003	0.0032	1.9141	0.0015	2.1133	0.0095
Turkey	(Lira)	1.4956	-0.0110	2.2015	-0.0200	2.4306	-0.0129
UAE	(Dirham)	3.6730		5.4067	-0.0093	5.9694	0.0123
UK (0.6153)*	(£)	1.6252	0.0033	0.9058	-0.0034	–	–
One Month		1.6249		0.9059		–	–
Three Month		1.6242	0.0000	0.9060	0.0000	–	–
One Year		1.6212	0.0003	0.9054	-0.0003	–	–
Ukraine	(Hryvnia)	7.9940	-0.0060	11.7672	11.7672	12.9919	0.0170
Uruguay	(Peso)	19.6500		28.9249	28.9249	31.9353	0.0659
USA	($)	–		1.4720	-0.0026	1.6252	0.0033
One Month				1.4719		1.6249	
Three Month				1.4715	0.0000	1.6242	0.0000
One Year				1.4678	-0.0002	1.6212	0.0072
Venezuela †(Bolivar Fuerte)		2.1473		3.1608	-0.0055	3.4898	0.0072
Vietnam	(Dong)	18474.0		27193.7	-45.6339	30023.9	63.5095
Euro (0.6793)*	(Euro)	1.4720	-0.0026	–		1.1041	0.0042
One Month		1.4719		–		1.1040	0.0000
Three Month		1.4715	0.0000	–		1.1038	0.0000
One Year		1.4678	-0.0002	–		1.1046	0.0003
SDR	–	0.6287	0.0006	0.9254	-0.0007	1.0218	0.0032

Rates are derived from WM/Reuters at 4pm (London time). *The closing mid-point rates for the Euro and £ against the $ are shown in brackets. The other figures in the dollar column of both the Euro and Sterling rows are in the reciprocal form in line with market convention. † New Venezuelan Bolivar Fuerte introduced on Jan 1st, 2008. Currency redenominated by 1000. Some values are rounded by the F.T. The exchange rates printed in this table are also available on the internet at **http://www.FT.com/marketsdata**

Euro Locking Rates: Austrian Schilling 13.7603, Belgium/Luxembourg Franc 40.3399, Cyprus 0.585274, Finnish Markka 5.94572, French Franc 6.55957, German Mark 1.95583, Greek Drachma 340.75, Irish Punt 0.787564, Italian Lira 1936.27, Malta 0.4293, Netherlands Guilder 2.20371, Portuguese Escudo 200.482, Slovenia Tolar 239.64, Spanish Peseta 166.386

EXHIBIT 21.2

Source: *Financial Times*, 11 December 2009.

The *Financial Times* table lists quotations up to one year, but, as this is an over-the-counter market (*see* Chapter 20), you are able to go as far forward in time as you wish – provided you can find a counterparty. For some currencies trading in three-month and one-year forwards is so thin as to not warrant a quotation in the table. However for the major currencies such as the US dollar, sterling, the euro, the Swiss franc and the Japanese yen, forward markets can stretch up to ten years. Airline companies expecting to purchase planes many years hence may use this distant forward market to purchase the foreign currency they need to pay the manufacturer so that they know with certainty how much home currency they have to find when the planes are delivered.

The table in Exhibit 21.2 displays standard periods of time for forward rates. These are instantly available and are frequently traded. However forward rates are not confined to these particular days in the future. It is possible to obtain rates for any day in the future, say, 74 or 36 days hence. But this would require a specific quotation from a bank.

(The Special Drawing Rights (SDRs) of the International Monetary Fund (IMF) shown at the bottom of the table are artificial currencies made up from baskets of other currencies.)

Covering in the forward market

Suppose that on 10 December 2009 a UK exporter sells goods to a customer in Norway invoiced at NKr5,000,000. Payment is due three months later. With the spot rate of exchange at NKr9.3602/£ (*see* Exhibit 21.2) the exporter, in deciding to sell the goods, has in mind a sales price of:

$$\frac{5,000,000}{9.3602} = £534,177$$

The UK firm bases its decision on the profitability of the deal on this amount expressed in pounds.

However the rate of exchange may vary between December and March: the size and direction of the move is uncertain. If sterling strengthens against the Norwegian Krone the UK exporter makes a currency loss by waiting three months and exchanging the Krone received into sterling at spot rates in March. If, say, one pound is worth NKr12 in March the exporter will receive only £416,667:

$$\frac{5,000,000}{12} = £416,667$$

The loss due to currency movement is:

$$
\begin{array}{r}
£534,177 \\
£416,667 \\
\hline
£117,510
\end{array}
$$

If sterling weakens to, say, NKr8/£ a currency gain is made. The pounds received in March if Krone are exchanged at the spot rate are:

$$\frac{5,000,000}{8} = £625,000$$

The currency gain is:

$$\begin{array}{r} £625,000 \\ £534,177 \\ \hline £90,823 \end{array}$$

Rather than run the risk of a possible loss on the currency side of the deal the exporter may decide to cover in the forward market at the time of the export (10 December). Under this arrangement the exporter promises to sell NKr5,000,000 against sterling in three months (the agreement is made on 10 December for delivery of currency in March). The *Finanical Times* website shows forward rates for a number of currencies – *see* Exhibit 21.3. The 3-month forward rate available[4] on 10 December is NKr9.3906/£ (*see* Exhibit 21.3). This forward contract means that the exporter is assured of the receipt of £532,447 in March regardless of the way in which spot exchange rate change over the three months:

$$\frac{5,000,000}{9.3906} = £532,447$$

In March the transactions shown in Figure 21.3 take place.

FIGURE 21.3
Forward market transaction

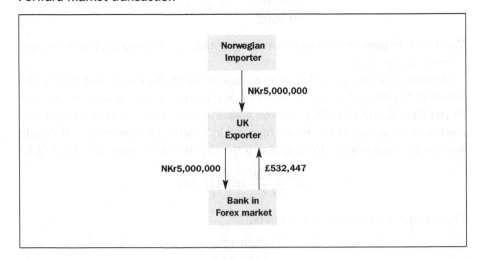

Pound spot forward against the pound

Dec 10		Closing mid-point	Change on day	Bid/offer spread	Day's mid High	Day's mid Low	One month Rate	One month %PA	Three month Rate	Three month %PA	One year Rate	One year %PA	Bank of Eng.Index
Europe													
Czech Rep.	(Koruna)	28.4631	0.0803	392 – 870	28.5510	28.3120	28.4767	-0.6	28.5035	-0.6	28.5779	-0.4	–
Denmark	(Danish Krone)	8.2163	0.0314	139 – 186	8.2488	8.2047	8.2185	-0.3	8.2228	-0.3	8.2503	-0.4	–
Hungary	(Forint)	300.949	-1.1646	706 – 193	304.620	298.920	302.286	-5.3	304.455	-4.6	312.903	-3.8	–
Norway	(Nor. Krone)	9.3602	0.0191	555 – 649	9.3956	9.3012	9.3700	-1.3	9.3906	-1.3	9.5090	-1.6	102.3
Poland	(Zloty)	4.5795	0.0188	771 – 818	4.6099	4.5600	4.5869	-1.9	4.6035	-2.1	4.6780	-2.1	–
Russia	(Rouble)	49.3996	0.0897	878 – 113	49.9701	49.3171	49.6229	-5.4	50.1635	-6.1	52.4896	-5.9	–
Sweden	(Krona)	11.5276	0.0079	229 – 323	11.5902	11.4851	11.5236	0.4	11.5158	0.4	11.4974	0.3	75.0
Switzerland	(Fr)	1.6685	0.0063	678 – 692	1.6753	1.6669	1.6678	0.5	1.6664	0.5	1.6577	0.7	119.9
Turkey	(New Lira)	2.4306	-0.0129	295 – 316	2.4538	2.4302	2.4445	-6.9	2.4700	-6.4	2.6143	-7.0	–
UK	(£)	1.0000											79.7
Euro	(Euro)	1.1041	0.0042	038 – 044	1.1085	1.1025	1.1040	0.1	1.1038	0.1	1.1046	0.0	104.4
SDR		1.0218	0.0032										–
Americas													
Argentina	(Peso)	6.1179	0.0116	747 – 811	6.2095	6.1641	6.2153	-7.2	6.3062	-8.1	6.9004	-10.5	–
Brazil	(Real)	2.8701	0.0149	689 – 713	2.8769	2.8541	2.8868	-7.0	2.9187	-6.7	3.0921	-7.2	–
Canada	(Canadian $)	1.7098	-0.0009	092 – 104	1.7212	1.7067	1.7095	0.2	1.7088	0.2	1.7073	0.1	106.8
Mexico	(Mexican Peso)	21.0843	0.0597	797 – 888	21.1245	20.9186	21.1556	-4.0	21.2978	-4.0	22.0951	-4.6	–
Peru	(New Sol)	4.6668	0.0064	638 – 698			4.6677	-0.2	4.6686	0.2	4.6671	0.0	–
USA	(US $)	1.6252	0.0034	250 – 254	1.6345	1.6217	1.6249	0.2	1.6242	0.2	1.6242	0.2	81.0
Pacific/Middle East/Africa													
Australia	(A$)	1.7733	-0.0128	727 – 739	1.7923	1.7707	1.7784	-3.5	1.7890	-3.5	1.8454	-3.9	97.1
Hong Kong	(HK $)	12.5966	0.0264	946 – 985	12.6682	12.5698	12.5906	0.6	12.5794	0.5	12.5236	0.6	–
India	(Indian Rupee)	75.8054	0.3327	900 – 208	76.2450	75.5090	75.9466	-2.2	76.1966	-2.1	77.4771	-2.2	–
Indonesia	(Rupiah)	15337.0	38.0999	700 – 703	15416.6	15312.1	15423.3	-6.7	15599.9	-6.7	16417.9	-6.6	–
Iran	(Rial)	16091.1	34.7902	505 – 317	16140.7	16050.5							–
Israel	(Shekel)	6.1315	-0.0130	254 – 375	6.1946	6.1264	6.1299	0.3	6.1271	0.3	6.1245	0.1	–
Japan	(Yen)	143.538	0.9203	488 – 588	144.400	142.510	143.475	0.5	143.368	0.5	142.452	0.8	155.8
Kuwait	(Kuwaiti Dinar)	0.4635	0.0009	631 – 639	0.4653	0.4598	0.4637	-0.5	0.4640	-0.5	0.4646	-0.2	–
Malaysia	(Ringgit)	5.5217	0.0098	169 – 264	5.5491	5.5146	5.5280	-1.4	5.5394	-1.3	5.5737	-0.9	–
New Zealand	(NZ $)	2.2266	-0.0487	257 – 275	2.2627	2.2216	2.2311	-2.4	2.2397	-2.3	2.2940	-2.9	101.6
Philippines	(Peso)	75.0843	-0.1291	588 – 097	75.4976	74.8205	75.3503	-4.2	75.8596	-4.1	77.4278	-3.0	–
Saudi Arabia	(Riyal)	6.0952	0.0124	939 – 964	6.1299	6.0753	6.0930	0.4	6.0874	0.5	6.6609	0.6	–
Singapore	($)	2.2583	0.0048	575 – 591	2.2699	2.2556	2.2583	0.0	2.2584	0.0	2.2561	0.1	–
South Africa	(Rand)	12.2427	-0.0611	330 – 523	12.3457	12.1882	12.3166	-7.2	12.4532	-6.8	13.0797	-6.4	–
Korea South	(Won)	1894.17	10.3918	378 – 457	1904.85	1887.79	1895.09	-0.6	1897.43	-0.7	1907.35	-0.7	–
Taiwan	(T$)	52.4859	0.1058	583 – 134	52.7649	52.3647	52.2723	4.9	51.8210	5.1	50.5085	3.9	–
Thailand	(Baht)	53.9485	0.1274	175 – 795	54.1020	53.7430	53.9475	0.0	53.9731	-0.2	54.0103	0.0	–
UAE	(Dirham)	5.9694	0.0123	678 – 709	5.9941	5.9556	5.9706	-0.2	5.9715	-0.1	5.9701	-0.1	–

Euro Locking Rates: Austrian Schilling 13.7603, Belgium/Luxembourg Franc 40.3399, Cyprus 0.585274, Finnish Markka 5.94572, French Franc 6.55957, German Mark 1.95583, Greek Drachma 340.75, Irish Punt 0.787564, Italian Lira 1936.27, Malta 0.4293, Netherlands Guilder 2.20371, Portuguese Escudo 200.482, Slovakian Koruna 30.1260, Slovenia Tolar 239.64, Spanish Peseta 166.386. Bid/offer spreads in the PoundSpot table show only the last three decimal places Bid, offer, Mid spot rates and forward rates are derived from the WM/REUTERS CLOSING SPOT and FORWARD RATE services. Some values are rounded by the F.T.

Exhibit 21.3

Source: Financial Times 10 December 2009. www.markets.ft.com

From the outset the exporter knew the amount to be received in March (assuming away credit risk). It might, with hindsight, have been better not to use the forward market but to exchange the dollars at a spot rate of, say, NKr8/£. This would have resulted in a larger income for the firm. But there was uncertainty about the spot rate in March when the export took place in December. If the spot rate in March had turned out to be NKr12/£ the exporter would have made much less. Covering in the forward market is a form of insurance, which leads to greater certainty – and certainty has a value.

Types of foreign-exchange risk

There are three types of risk for firms that operate in an international market-place:

- transaction risk
- translation risk
- economic risk.

Transaction risk

Transaction risk is the risk that transactions already entered into, or for which the firm is likely to have a commitment in a foreign currency, will have a variable value in the home currency because of exchange-rate movements.

This type of risk is primarily associated with imports or exports. If a company exports goods on credit then it carries a figure for debtors in its accounts. The amount it will receive in home-currency terms is subject to uncertainty if the customer pays in a foreign currency.

Likewise a company that imports on credit will have a creditor figure in its accounts. The amount that is finally paid in terms of the home currency depends on forex movements, if the invoice is in a foreign currency. Transaction risk also arises when firms invest abroad, say, opening a new office or manufacturing plant. If the costs of construction are paid for over a period the firm may be exchanging the home currency for the foreign currency to make the payments. The amounts of the home currency required are uncertain if the exchange rate is subject to rate shifts. Also the cash inflows back to the parent are subject to exchange-rate risk.

In addition, when companies borrow in a foreign currency, committing themselves to regular interest and principal payments in that currency, they are exposed to forex risk. This is a problem that beset a number of Brazilian companies in 2002. They had committed themselves to paying off borrowings in a hard currency (e.g. US dollars, sterling). This became a serious problem when the debt rose by 40 percent simply because of the decline in their currency against the hard currency.

Translation risk

Translation risk arises because financial data denominated in one currency are then expressed in terms of another currency. Between two accounting dates the figures can be affected by exchange-rate movements, greatly distorting comparability. The financial statements of overseas business units are usually translated into the home currency so that they might be consolidated with the group's financial statements. Income, expenses, assets and liabilities have to be re-expressed in terms of the home currency. Note that this is purely a paper-based exercise; it is translation and not the conversion of real money from one currency to another. If exchange rates were stable, comparing subsidiary performance and asset position would be straightforward. However, if exchange rates move significantly the results can be severely distorted. For example, GlaxoSmithKline, the UK-based pharmaceutical company, found that even though overseas earnings rose in local currency terms, when the figures were translated into sterling a fall in profits was reported. This was mainly because sterling rose against the dollar (Exhibit 21.4).

> This is purely a paper-based exercise; it is translation and not the conversion of real money from one currency to another.

There are two elements to translation risk.

- **The balance sheet effect** Assets and liabilities denominated in a foreign currency can fluctuate in value in home-currency terms with forex-market changes. For example, if a UK company acquires A$1,000,000 of assets in Australia when the rate of exchange is A$2.2/£ this can go into the UK group's accounts at a value of £454,545. If, over the course of the next year, the Australian dollar falls against sterling to A$2.7/£, when the consolidated accounts are drawn up and the asset is translated at the current exchange rate at the end of the year it is valued at only £370,370 (1,000,000/2.7) a 'loss' of £84,175. And yet the asset has not changed in value in A$ terms one jot.

- **The profit and loss account effect** Currency changes can have an adverse impact on the group's profits because of the translation of foreign subsidiaries' profits. This often occurs even though the subsidiaries' managers are performing well and increasing profit in terms of the currency in which they operate, as the case of GSK (*see* Exhibit 21.4) indicates.

Economic risk

A company's economic value may decline as a result of forex movements causing a loss in competitive strength. The worth of a company is the discounted cash flows payable to the owners. It is possible that a shift in exchange rates can reduce the cash flows of foreign subsidiaries and home-based production far into the future (and not just affect the near future cash flows as in transaction exposure). There are two ways in which competitive position can be undermined by forex changes:

Exchange rate woes hit GSK

Andrew Jack

The strengthening pound pegged back first-quarter earnings per share at GlaxoSmithKline, the UK-based pharmaceutical group to 27p – a modest 2 per cent. Pre-tax profit in cash terms fell 1 per cent to £2.1bn for the quarter.

At constant exchange rates, earnings per share rose 14 per cent and the company said its guidance for the year on the same terms remained unchanged at 8–10 per cent.

The weakening dollar reduced sales in cash terms to £5.6bn (£5.8bn), though adjusted pharmaceutical sales in the key US market rose 3 per cent to £2.4bn and 3 per cent to $4.8bn worldwide, in spite of challenges from generic drugs.

But Jean-Pierre Garnier, chief executive said: 'This was a great quarter for the pipeline.' He added the underlying business was 'strong and a bit ahead of expectations.'

He dismissed the short-term headline exchange rate effect, arguing that the market had seen through the figures to the underlying performance.

'There is nothing we can do about [the weakening dollar]. What comes up must come down.' he said. 'It's a bit like the weather: you have to live with it.'

He added that consultation with the group's investor base, which remains 60 per cent UK-based in spite of an increasing US share, currently indicated no desire to switch to dollar reporting.

EXHIBIT 21.4

Source: *Financial Times* 26 April 2007, p. 22.

- **Directly** If your firm's home currency strengthens then foreign competitors are able to gain sales and profits at your expense because your products are more expensive (or you have reduced margins) in the eyes of customers both abroad and at home.

- **Indirectly** Even if your home currency does not move adversely *vis-à-vis* your customer's currency you can lose competitive position. For example suppose a South African firm is selling into Hong Kong and its main competitor is a New Zealand firm. If the New Zealand dollar weakens against the Hong Kong dollar the South African firm has lost some competitive position.

Economic risk can badly damage a business – *see* Exhibit 21.5.

Transaction risk strategies

This section illustrates a number of strategies available to deal with transaction risk by focusing on the alternatives open to an exporter selling goods on credit.

Suppose a UK company exports £1m of goods to a Canadian firm when the spot rate of exchange is C$2.20/£. The Canadian firm is given three months to

Small fry flounder in wake of surge

Raphael Minder

Hank Morrison, whose Philippine company makes model aircraft, says he could be out of business within six months if the Filipino peso continues to rally against the US dollar.

'With the way the peso is going, it's become almost impossible,' he says, 'I'm not only operating at a loss but in effect the more I make, the more I lose.'

As an emergency step, Mr Morrison has decided to halve his production of model aircraft, 95 per cent of which end up in America on the shelves of collectors or industry buyers such as Boeing. This is bad news both for Mr Morrison's 60 Filipino employees and for Philippine exports. ...

EXHIBIT 21.5

Source: *Financial Times* 10 October 2007, p. 15.

pay, and naturally the spot rate in three months is unknown at the time of the shipment of goods. What can the firm do?

Invoice the customer in the home currency

One easy way to bypass exchange-rate risk is to insist that all foreign customers pay in your currency and your firm pays for all imports in your home currency. In the case of this example the Canadian importer will be required to send £1m in three months.

However the exchange-rate risk has not gone away, it has just been passed on to the customer. This policy has an obvious drawback: your customer may dislike it, the marketability of your products is reduced and your customers look elsewhere for supplies. If you are a monopoly supplier you might get away with the policy but for most firms this is a non-starter. EADS passed on forex risk to its suppliers – *see* Exhibit 21.6.

Do nothing

Under this policy the UK firm invoices the Canadian firm for C$2.2m, waits three months and then exchanges into sterling at whatever spot rate is available then. Perhaps an exchange-rate gain will be made, perhaps a loss will be made. Many firms adopt this policy and take a 'win some, lose some' attitude. Given the fees and other transaction costs of some hedging strategies this can make sense.

There are two considerations for managers here. The first is their degree of risk aversion to higher cash flow variability, coupled with the sensitivity of shareholders to reported fluctuations of earnings due to foreign exchange gains and

EADS to insist on paying its suppliers in dollars

Kevin Done and Peggy Hollinger

EADS, the Franco-German aerospace group, is preparing to adjust to a 'weaker and weaker US dollar' by demanding that its big European suppliers bid for new contracts in the US currency, according to Louis Gallois, chief exceecutive.

Announcing bigger than expected annual net losses of €499m ($765m) yesterday, Mr Gallois told the Financial Times that the Airbus aircraft subsidiary would seek to shift the punishing burden of dollar risk on to suppliers in

its next aircraft project, the A350 XWB midsized jet.

'We will pay them in dollars. That is clear,' he said. 'We must prepare ourselves to be competitive with a weaker and weaker dollar.'

The EADS boss was confident that the group would rise to the challenge, in spite of the fact that exchange rate movements had cost the group €1bn in 2007, a year also hit by heavy provisions for troubled aircraft projects. ...

EXHIBIT 21.6

Source: *Financial Times* 12 March 2008, p. 27.

losses. The second, which is related to the first point, is the size of the transaction. If £1m is a large proportion of annual turnover, and greater than profit, then the managers may be more worried about forex risk. If, however, £1m is a small fraction of turnover and profit, and the firm has numerous forex transactions, it may choose to save on hedging costs.

There is an argument that it would be acceptable to do nothing if it was anticipated that the Canadian dollar will appreciate over the three months. Be careful. Predicting exchange rates is a dangerous game and more than one 'expert' has made serious errors of judgment.

> Predicting exchange rates is a dangerous game.

Netting

Multinational companies often have subsidiaries in different countries selling to other members of the group. Netting is where the subsidiaries settle intra-organisational currency debts for the *net* amount owed in a currency rather than the *gross* amount. For example, if a UK parent owned a subsidiary in Canada and sold C$2.2m of goods to the subsidiary on credit while the Canadian subsidiary is owed C$1.5m by the UK company, instead of transferring a total of C$3.7m the intra-group transfer is the net amount of C$700,000 (*see* Figure 21.4).

The reduction in the size of the currency flows by offsetting inflows and outflows in the same currency diminishes the net exposure that may have to be hedged. It also reduces the transaction costs of currency transfers in terms of fees and commissions.

FIGURE 21.4
Netting

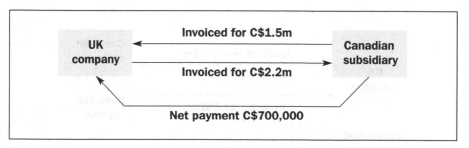

This type of netting, involving two companies within a group, is referred to as bilateral netting, and is simple to operate without the intervention of a central treasury. However for organisations with a matrix of currency liabilities between numerous subsidiaries in different parts of the world, multilateral netting is required. A central treasury is usually needed so that there is knowledge at any point in time of the overall exposure of the firm and its component parts. Subsidiaries will be required to inform the group treasury about their overseas dealings, which can then co-ordinate payments after netting out intra-company debts. The savings on transfer costs levied by banks can be considerable.

Matching

Netting only applies to transfers within a group of companies. Matching can be used for both intra-group transactions and those involving third parties. The company matches the inflows and outflows in different currencies caused by trade, etc., so that it is only necessary to deal on the forex markets for the unmatched portion of the total transactions.

So if, say, the Canadian importer is not a group company and the UK firm also imported a raw material from another Canadian company to the value of C$2m it is necessary only to hedge the balance of C$200,000 (*see* Figure 21.5).

Naturally, to net and match properly, the timing of the expected receipts and payments would have to be the same.

Leading and lagging

Leading is the bringing forward from the original due date the payment of a debt. Lagging is the postponement of a payment beyond the due date. This speeding up or delaying of payments is particularly useful if you are convinced exchange rates will shift significantly between now and the due date.

So, if the UK exporter who invoiced a Canadian company for C$2.2m on three months' credit expects that the Canadian dollar will fall over the

FIGURE 21.5
Matching

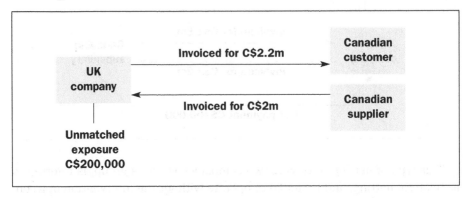

forthcoming three months it may try to obtain payment immediately and then exchange for sterling at the spot rate. Naturally the Canadian firm will need an incentive to pay early and this may be achieved by offering a discount for immediate settlement.

An importer of goods in a currency that is anticipated to fall in value may attempt to delay payment as long as possible. This may be achieved either by agreement or by exceeding credit terms.

Forward market hedge

Although other forms of exchange-risk management are available, forward cover represents the most frequently employed method of hedging. A contract is agreed to exchange two currencies at a fixed time in the future at a predetermined rate. The risk of forex variation is removed.

So if the three-month forward rate is C$2.25/£ the UK exporter could lock in the receipt of £977,778 in three months by selling forward C$2.2m.

$$\frac{C\$2.2m}{2.25} = £977,778$$

No foreign exchange-rate risk now exists because the dollars to be received from the importer are matched by the funds to be exchanged for sterling. (There does remain the risk of the importer not paying, at all or on time, and the risk of the counterparty in the forex market not fulfilling its obligations.)

Rolls Royce has a policy of using forward markets to hedge – *see* Exhibit 21.7.

Extensive hedging mitigates exchange-rate windfalls for jet engine maker

Sylvia Pfeifer

Rolls-Royce should be an obvious beneficiary of the rising dollar. The world's second-biggest jet engine maker bears most if its costs in sterling – Derby is still its largest manufacturing site in spite of moves to 'dollarise' its production to lower-cost, dollar-denominated markets – but it books the majority of its sales in dollars.

The recent rise in the dollar should therefore be good news for Rolls-Royce.

But any immediate, positive impact will be delayed by the company's extensive hedging policy – and it could even hurt its profits in the short term.

Rolls-Royce has had the same approach to hedging for more than 20 years, continuously selling dollars forward in order to ensure visibility for the future.

Each year it will use part of its hedge book and take more cover for future years. At its interim results in July, the company had $9.1bn ($5.1bn) of hedges in place at an average sterling exchange rate of $1.87, equivalent to about three years' cover.

The company has told investors that, given the recent rise in the dollar, it expects the average annual exchange rate it achieves to deteriorate by between 7 and 8 cents, costing it £100m more than it did last year.

But, as it burns through its current hedge book over the next few years, Rolls-Royce will reap some benefit from the rising dollar at some point.

Nick Cunningham, aerospace and defence analyst at Evolution Securities, says he expects the company to see 'some real benefit' from an improved exchange rate from 2011 onwards.

'Rolls-Royce should absolutely manage risk and should continue to stick to their hedging policy,' says Mr Cunningham. 'The best thing you can do is smooth out any sharp fluctuations in the currencies in which you operate. By smoothing out that risk, even if it costs you a bit of money, it will help reduce your cost of capital.' …

EXHIBIT 21.7

Source: *Financial Times* 5 September 2008, p. 21.

Money market hedge

Money market hedging involves borrowing in the money markets. For example, the exporter could, at the time of the export, borrow in Canadian dollars on the money markets for a three-month period. The

> Money market hedging involves borrowing in the money markets.

amount borrowed, plus three months' interest, will be designed to be equal to the amount to be received from the importer (C$2.2m).

If the interest rate charged over three months is 2 percent then the appropriate size of the loan is:

$$C\$2.2m = C\$?(1+0.02)$$

$$C\$? = \frac{C\$2.2m}{1.02} = C\$2,156,863$$

Thus the exporter has created a liability (borrowed funds) that matches the asset (debt owed by Canadian firm).

The borrowed dollars are then converted to sterling on the spot market for the exporter to receive £980,392 immediately:

$$\frac{C\$2,156,863}{2.2} = £980,392$$

The exporter has removed forex risk because it now holds cash in sterling.

Three months later C$2.2m is received from the importer and this exactly matches the outstanding debt:

Amount borrowed + interest = debt owed at end of period

$$C\$2,156,863 + C\$2,156,863 \times 0.02 = C\$2.2m$$

The receipt of £980,392 is £19,608 less than the £1m originally anticipated. However it is received three months earlier and can earn interest.

The steps in the money market hedge are as follows.

1 Invoice customer for C$2.2m.

2 Borrow C$2,156,863.

3 Sell C$2,156,863 at spot to receive pounds now.

4 In three months receive C$2.2m from customer.

5 Pay lender C$2.2m.

An importer could also use a money market hedge. So a Swiss company importing Japanese cars for payment in yen in three months could borrow in Swiss francs now and convert the funds at the spot rate into yen. This money is deposited to earn interest, with the result that after three months the principal plus interest equals the invoice amount.

Futures hedge

A foreign currency futures contract is an agreement to exchange a specific amount of a currency for another at a fixed future date for a predetermined price. Futures are similar to forwards in many ways. They are, however, standardised contracts traded on regulated exchanges. Forwards can be tailor-made in a wide range of currencies as to quantity of currency and delivery date, whereas futures are only available in a limited range of currencies and for a few specific forward time periods.

The Chicago Mercantile Exchange (CME) and Intercontinental Exchange (ICE) operate futures markets in currencies.[5] The CME includes the following currency pairs: US$/£, US$/¥, US$/SFr (Swiss franc), US$/€, US$/Mex. Peso, US$/C$ and US$/A$. A single futures contract is for a fixed amount of currency. For example, a sterling contract on CME is for £62,500. It is not possible to buy or sell a smaller amount than this, nor to transact in quantities other than whole-number multiples of this. To buy a sterling futures contract is to make a commitment to deliver a quantity of US dollars and receive in return £62,500. On 10 December 2009 the CME quoted contracts for delivery of dollars in late March 'MARO' (and for no months in between)[6] – see Exhibit 21.8. The contract was priced at 1.6254 (the 'open' column indicates the rate at the start of trading on 10 December; the 'Sett' column indicates closing prices). This means that if you *buy* one contract you are committed to deliver US$1.6254 for every pound of the £62,500 you will receive in late March, that is US$101,588. If you *sold* one contract at 1.6254 you would deliver £62,500 and receive US$101,588.

A firm hedging with currency futures will usually attempt to have a futures position which has an equal and opposite profit profile to the underlying trans-action. Frequently the futures position will be closed before delivery is due, to give a cash profit or loss to offset the spot market profit or loss (for more details on futures *see* Chapter 20) – although physical delivery of the currency is possi-ble. For example, if a US firm exports £62,500 worth of goods to a UK firm in December on three months' credit for payment in late March and the current spot exchange rate is US$1.6252/£ there is a foreign exchange risk. If the March future is trading at a price of US$1.6254 per £ the exporter's position could be hedged by selling one sterling futures contract on CME.

Currency futures on the Chicago Mercantile Exchange and ICE

Dec 10		Open	Sett	Change	High	Low	Est. vol.	Open int.
£-Sterling*	Dec	–	0.9050	-0.0009	–	–	36	2,801
£-Yen*	Dec	129.8500	129.8350	0.6950	129.85	129.85	33	4,249
$-Can $ †	Dec	0.9481	0.9522	0.0033	0.9543	0.9448	36,929	67,465
$-Euro € †	Dec	1.4737	1.4719	0.0004	1.4760	1.4684	125,505	119,417
$-Euro € †	MARO	1.4731	1.4714	0.0003	1.4755	1.4680	101,474	67,286
$-Sw Franc †	Dec	0.9748	0.9739	0.0003	0.9768	0.9706	26,523	29,792
$-Yen †	Dec	1.1361	1.1332	-0.0067	1.1399	1.1306	53,568	81,417
$-Yen †	MARO	1.1374	1.1339	-0.0067	1.1405	1.1312	37,479	54,284
$-Sterling †	MARO	1.6273	1.6254	0.0019	1.6337	1.6206	52,433	43,958
$-Aust $ †	Dec	0.9096	0.9167	0.0107	0.9189	0.9088	49,635	66,888
$-Mex. Peso † FEBO		–	76800	-225.00	–	–	–	–

Sources: *NYBOT [ICE]; Sterling €100,000 and Yen: €100,000. †CME: Australian $: A$100,000, †CME: Canadian $: C$100,000, Euro: €125,000; Mexican Peso: 500.000; Swiss Franc: SFr125,000; Yen: ¥12,5m ($ per ¥100); Sterling: £62,500. CME volume, high & low for pit & electronic trading at settlement. Contracts shown are based on the volumes traded in 2004.

EXHIBIT 21.8

Source: *Financial Times* 10 December 2009. www.ft.com

If in March sterling falls against the dollar to US$1.40/£ the calculation is:

Value of £62,500 received from customer when converted to dollars at spot in June (£62,500 × 1.40)	US$87,500
Amount if exchange rate was constant at US$1.6252/£	US$101,575
Forex loss	US$14,075

However an offsetting gain is made on the futures contract:	
Sold at US$1.6254/£ (£62,500 × 1.6254)	US$101,588
Bought in March to close position at US$1.40/£ (£62,500 × 1.40)	US$87,500
Futures gain	US$14,088

Alternatively the exporter could simply deliver the £62,500 received from the importer to CME in return for US$101,588. (Note that the futures contract rate of exchange in March converges with the spot rate at the date of expiry, in late June, i.e. US$1.40/£.)

In the above example a perfect hedge was not achieved because the gain on the futures contract did not exactly offset the loss on the underlying position (i.e. the pounds to be received from the UK customer). Perfect hedging is frequently unobtainable with futures because of their standardised nature. Perhaps the amount needed to be hedged is not equal to a whole number of contracts, for example £100,000, or the underlying transaction takes place in November (when no future is available).

> Perfect hedging is frequently unobtainable with futures because of their standardised nature.

Currency options

The final possible course of action to reduce forex transaction risk to be discussed in this chapter is to make use of the currency option market.

A currency option is a contract giving the buyer (that is, the holder) the right, but not the obligation, to buy or sell a specific amount of currency at a specific exchange rate (the strike price), on a specified future date.[7]

> A call option gives the right to buy a particular currency.
> A put option gives the right to sell a particular currency.

The option writer (usually a bank) guarantees, if the option buyer chooses to exercise the right, to exchange the currency at the predetermined rate. Because the writer is accepting risk the buyer must pay a premium to the writer – normally within two business days of the option purchase. (For more details on options *see* Chapter 20.)

Currency options premiums are shown for the currency rates between the US$ and various currencies on the website of the Chicago Mercantile Exchange (CME). For the US$/UK£ call options the purchaser has the right but not the obligation to purchase pounds for dollars – *see* Exhibit 21.9. The call holder has a number of possible rates of exchange open to himself/herself. The ones shown in the exhibit ($1.61/£ to $1.65/£) represent just a few of the possibilities. Only the March expiry options are shown here for the date of download, which was 11.12.09. Other expiry dates are available on other webpages. The premiums payable, shown in the body of the table (under 'Last'), are quoted as US cents per pound (thus, 0.0456 means 4.56 cents per pound). One contract is for £62,500, and you are only able to purchase whole numbers of contracts on the exchange. If you purchased a 1640 call option for expiry in March you would pay a premium of 3.04 US cents per UK pound (the total premium payable would be $0.0304 × 62,500 = $1,900) giving you the right to buy pounds with dollars in March at a rate of $1.64/£. Note that a less favourable exchange rate, e.g. 1650 commands a lower premium, only 2.63 cents per pound under the contract.

Currency options US$/UK£ on the Chicago Mercantile Exchange

Strike Price	Type	Last	Change	Prior Settle	High	Low	Volume	Updated
16100	CALL	0.0456 a	–0.0043	0.0499	–	0.456 a	–	9:48:58 AM CST 12/11/2009
16100	PUT	0.0356 b	+0.0011	0.0345	0.0356 b	0.0314	37	9:49:56 AM CST 12/11/2009
16200	CALL	0.0400 a	–0.0042	0.0442	0.0474 b	0.0400 a	–	9:49:27 AM CST 12/11/2009
16200	PUT	0.0401 b	+0.0013	0.0388	0.0401 b	0.0355	50	9:49:28 AM CST 12/11/2009
16300	CALL	0.0350 a	–0.0040	0.0390	0.0395	0.0350 a	50	9:49:28 AM CST 12/11/2009
16300	PUT	0.0452 b	+0.0016	0.0436	0.0452 b	0.0401 a	–	9:49:56 AM CST 12/11/2009
16400	CALL	0.0304 a	–0.0038	0.0342	0.0367 b	0.0304 a	–	9:49:28 AM CST 12/11/2009
16400	PUT	0.0507 b	+0.0019	0.0488	0.0507 b	0.0450 a	–	9:49:56 AM CST 12/11/2009
16500	CALL	0.0263 a	–0.0035	0.0298	0.0300	0.0263 a	50	9:49:29 AM CST 12/11/2009
16500	PUT	0.0559 b	+0.0016	0.0543	0.0559 b	0.0502 a	–	9:49:56 AM CST 12/11/2009

EXHIBIT 21.9

Source: www.cmegroup.com

The purchase of a put option gives you the right but not the obligation to *sell* pounds and receive dollars. Again the quantity of a contract is for £62,500.

On CME the $/€ call and put premiums are quoted as US cents per euro under the contract. One contract is for €125,000. The yen contracts are different in that the quoted premiums are US cents per 100 yen. Each contract is for 12.5m yen.

The crucial advantage an option has over a forward is the absence of an obligation to buy or sell. It is the option buyer's decision whether to exercise the option and insist on exchange at the strike rate or to let the option lapse.

With a forward there is a hedge against both a favourable and an unfavourable movement in forex rates. This means that if the exchange rate happens to move in your favour after you are committed to a forward contract you cannot take any advantage of that movement. We saw above that if the forward rate was C$2.25/£ the exporter will receive £977,778 in three months. If the spot exchange rate had moved to, say, C$1.9/£ over the three months the exporter would have liked to abandon the agreement to sell the dollars at C$2.25/£, but is unable to do so because of the legal commitment. By abandoning the deal and exchanging at spot when the Canadian firm pays the exporter will receive an income of:

$$\frac{C\$2.2m}{1.9} = £1,157,895$$

This is an extra £180,117.

An option permits both:

- hedging against unfavourable currency movement; and
- profit from favourable currency movement.

Worked example 21.1
CURRENCY OPTION CONTRACT

Now, imagine that the treasurer of the UK firm hedges by buying a three-month sterling call option giving the right but not the obligation to deliver Canadian dollars in exchange for pounds with a strike price of C$2.25/£ when the goods are delivered to the Canadian firm.

To induce a bank to make the commitment to exchange at the option holder's behest a premium will need to be paid up front. Assume this is 2% of the amount covered, that is a non-refundable $0.02 \times C\$2,200,000 = C\$44,000$ is payable two business days after the option deal is struck. We are assuming in this example that over-the-counter options are written by a bank rather than exchange-based options on, say, the CME.

Three months later
The dollars are delivered by the importer on the due date. The treasurer now has to decide whether or not to exercise the right to exchange those dollars for sterling at C$2.25/£. Let us consider two scenarios:

Scenario 1
The dollar has strengthened against the pound to C$1.9/£. If the treasurer exercises the right to exchange at C$2.25/£ the UK firm will receive:

$$\frac{C\$2,200,000}{2.25} = £977,778$$

If the treasurer takes the alternative and lets the option lapse – 'abandons it' – and exchanges the dollars in the spot market, the amount received will be:

$$\frac{C\$2,200,000}{1.9} = £1,157,895$$

Clearly in this case the best course of action would be not to exercise the option, but to exchange at spot rate. Note that the benefit of this action is somewhat reduced by the earlier payment of C$44,000 for the premium.

Scenario 2
Now assume that the dollar has weakened against sterling to C$2.5/£. If the treasurer contacts the bank (the option writer) to confirm that the exporter wishes to exercise the option the treasurer will arrange delivery of C$2,200,000 to the bank and will receive £977,778 in return:

$$\frac{C\$2,200,000}{2.25} = £977,778$$

The alternative, to abandon the option and sell the C$2.2m in the spot forex market, is unattractive:

$$\frac{C\$2,200,000}{2.5} = £880,000$$

Again, the option premium needs to be deducted to give a more complete picture.

With the option, the worst that could happen is that the exporter receives £977,778, less the premium. However the upside potential is unconstrained.

(Note: It is possible to elect for cash settlement (i.e. profit made if the market value is greater than exercise value) on the option rather than the physical exchange of the currencies.)

Option contracts are generally for sums greater than US$1m on the OTC (over-the-counter) market (direct deals with banks) whereas one contract on CME is, for example, for £62,500. The drawback with exchange-based derivatives is the smaller range of currencies available and the inability to tailor-make a hedging position.

It can be very difficult to determine the correct hedging strategy – as the case of Air Products illustrates in Exhibit 21.10.

Choose the correct path for a viable deal

James Politi

In May 2000, Air Products & Chemicals came out with a sobering announcement. Because of opposition from regulators at the US Federal Trade Commission, the Pennsylvania-based industrials group would drop an $11.2bn deal to buy British rival BOC that it had sealed with France's Air Liquide a year earlier.

In addition to being forced to abandon a crucial strategic move, there was another reason for Air Products and its investors to be gloomy. A strong fluctuation in the dollar/pound exchange rate in previous months meant Air Products would have to take a charge of nearly $300m, mostly from losses on the currency hedge that the company had put in place for the BOC deal in January 2000.

The Air Products case illustrates the challenges facing corporate chiefs and investment banks as they study ways to manage foreign exchange risk during M&A deals. A tricky balance has to be struck between properly managing currency exposure, and not hedging so much that it undermines the economics of a deal.

Paul Huck, chief financial officer of Air Products, grappled with these issues. Speaking to the FT today, he believes his company had little choice but to put a hedge in place once it expected the BOC takeover to be approved. Air Products was paying for a collection of assets outside the UK in sterling – Air Liquide was slated to take over the British BOC business – and as such was heavily exposed to any movements in the UK currency between announcement and closing.

'We still feel we did the right thing in hedging the transaction,' says Mr Huck. 'When you do M&A you worry about having the economics of a deal change because of currency movements, and we're not in the business of making currency bets'.

The trouble with the hedge put in place by Air Products – a mix of options and forward contracts – is that its structure may have been too optimistic. While forwards are less expensive than options because they carry no fee, they leave the company heavily exposed to a currency shift in the wrong direction if the deal does not close. Options, on the other hand, can be expensive, carrying hefty up-front fees.

However, if the currency moves in the wrong direction and the deal does not close, the company can simply let the options expire.

'If I had been willing to do this [use more options and less forwards] and pay higher premiums, it would have been very expensive, and might have hurt the deal [if the FTC had approved it],' says Mr Huck.

Hedging currency risk in M&A deals has become an increasingly popular product in the universe of risk management.

As global M&A volumes have grown, and the markets for derivatives – the primary hedging instruments – have become increasingly liquid, banks have been able to match supply and demand on foreign exchange risk with a series of customised hedging packages (see over).

FX option

A foreign exchange option gives the buyer of the option the right to purchase the currency at a specific price. The client would buy a call option to protect itself against a rising currency and would pay a premium for the option – typically in the range of 50–200 basis points (depending on the maturity and price of the strike). The most money one can lose on an option is the premium that one pays for it, which makes it a particularly good strategy for cross-border M&A. With an option you will always know how much you will spend on your hedge, which makes budgeting for the hedge relatively easy. An option is also a marketable asset and could be sold in the free market in the event the hedge needs to be liquidated. The only disadvantage of an option is its upfront cost.

Do nothing

'Clients may adopt this strategy, particularly early in the M&A process, as the uncertainty surrounding deal completion can be significant,' says Leo Civitillo and Steve Zannetos at Morgan Stanley.

'When the deal progresses and the probability of completion increases, execution of a currency hedge is typically warranted. However, there may also be other considerations that drive a decision not to hedge, including a view on the market, the implied costs of hedging, and accounting considerations.

'The risk of remaining unhedged is that the currency could significantly move against the company and adversely affect the economics of the acquisition.'

Natural hedge

'A natural hedge would essentially be issuing the debt for the acquisition in the target's local currency, which would negate the need for foreign exchange hedge,' says Courtney McLaughlin, head of the foreign exchange capital markets group in the investment banking division at Credit Suisse, the Swiss bank.

'If the deal is signed and the currency appreciates, the acquirer will pay more for the business in dollar terms, but because they are issuing debt in the local currency market they are getting more (in dollar terms) for the debt they are issuing, thereby creating the natural hedge.'

FX forward

'FX forwards are simply an obligation to exchange one currency for another at a specified rate on a future date,' says Mr Civitillo and Mr Zannetos at Morgan Stanley.

'We typically do not recommend that clients employ vanilla FX forwards to hedge the currency risk embedded in a cross-border transaction until we are absolutely certain that the deal will close. The reason is that the potential breakage or unwind cost of an FX forward can be significant, if the underlying transaction does not close as expected. However, assuming that all of the deal risks have passed, forward contracts can be a very efficient and cost effective way to lock-in the price of a foreign asset.'

Deal-contingent FWD

A deal-contingent forward is similar to a vanilla forward with two key differences: the ability of the client to walk away from the contract if the deal is not consummated, and its price. A deal-contingent forward allows a client to exchange one currency for another at a specified rate on a future date. The client would define contingencies that, if met, would allow the client to walk away from the forward with no cost or obligation. Typical contingencies are: material adverse change clauses, shareholder approvals and regulatory approvals. A deal-contingent forward has an implicit cost that is paid for by striking the forward rate slightly off market. It allows the client to enjoy the efficiency of a forward without the out-of-pocket cost of an option.

Exhibit 21.10

Source: *Financial Times* 25 January 2007, p. 2.

Managing translation risk

The effect of translation risk on the balance sheet can be lessened by matching the currency of assets and liabilities. For example, Graft plc has decided to go ahead with a US$190m project in the USA. One way of financing this is to borrow £100m and exchange this for dollars at the current exchange rate of US$1.9/£. Thus at the beginning of the year the additional entries into the consolidated accounts are as shown in Worked example 21.2.

Worked example 21.2
TRANSLATION RISK

Opening balance sheet

Liabilities		Assets	
Loan	£100m	US assets	£100m

The US$190m of US assets are translated at US$1.9/£ so all figures are expressed in the parent company's currency.

Now imagine that over the course of the next year the dollar depreciates against sterling to US$2.30/£. In the consolidated group accounts there is still a £100m loan but the asset bought with that loan, while still worth US$190m,[8] is valued at only £82.61m when translated into sterling. In the parent company's currency terms, £17.39m needs to be written off:

Year-end balance sheet

Liabilities		Assets	
Loan	£100m	US assets	£100m
	£100m		£82.61m
Forex loss	−£17.39m		

Alternatively Graft plc could finance its dollar assets by obtaining a dollar loan. Thus, when the dollar depreciates, both the asset value and the liability value in translated sterling terms becomes less.

Opening balance sheet

Liabilities		Assets	
Loan	£100m	US assets	£100m

If forex rates move to US$2.30/£:

Year-end balance sheet

Liabilities		Assets	
Loan	£82.61m	US assets	£82.61m

There is no currency loss to deal with.

One constraint on the solution set out in Worked example 21.2 is that some governments insist that a proportion of assets acquired within their countries is financed by the parent firm. Another constraint is that the financial markets in some countries are insufficiently developed to permit large-scale borrowing.

Many economists and corporate managers believe that translation hedging is unnecessary because, on average over a period of time, gains and losses from forex movements will even out to be zero.

Managing economic risk

Economic exposure is concerned with the long-term effects of forex movements on the firm's ability to compete, and add value. These effects are very difficult to estimate in advance, given their long-term nature, and therefore the hedging techniques described for transaction risk are of limited use. The forwards markets may be used to a certain extent, but these only extend for a short period for most currencies. Also the matching principle could be employed, whereby overseas assets are matched as far as possible by overseas liabilities.

The main method of insulating the firm from economic risk is to position the company in such a way as to maintain maximum flexibility – to be able to react to changes in forex rates which may be causing damage to the firm. Internationally diversified firms may have a greater degree of flexibility than those based in one or two markets. For example, a company with production facilities in numerous countries can shift output to those plants where the exchange rate change has been favourable. The international car assemblers have an advantage here over the purely domestic producer.

Forex changes can impact on the costs of raw materials and other inputs. By maintaining flexibility in sourcing supplies a firm could achieve a competitive advantage by deliberately planning its affairs so that it can switch suppliers quickly and cheaply.

> Forex changes can impact on the costs of raw materials and other inputs.

An aware multinational could allow for forex changes when deciding in which countries to launch an advertising campaign. For example, it may be pointless increasing marketing spend in a country whose currency has depreciated rapidly recently, making the domestically produced competing product relatively cheap. It might also be sensible to plan in advance the company's response to a forex movement with regard to the pricing of goods so that action can be rapid. For example, a UK company exporting to Norway at a time when sterling is on a rising trend can either keep the product at the same price in sterling terms to maintain profits per unit sold and face the consequential potential loss of market share, or reduce the sterling price to maintain a constant price in krone and thereby keep its market share. Being prepared may avert an erroneous knee-jerk decision.

> Being prepared may avert an erroneous knee-jerk decision.

The principle of contingency planning to permit quick reaction to forex changes applies to many areas of marketing and production strategies. This idea links with the notion of the real option described in Chapter 5. The option to switch sources of supply and output, or to change marketing focus, may have a high value. Despite the cost of creating an adaptable organisation, rather than a dedicated fixed one, the option to switch may be worth far more in an uncertain world.

Conclusion

> Managers need to be aware of, and to assess, the risk to which their firms are exposed.

Managers need to be aware of, and to assess, the risk to which their firms are exposed. The risk that arises because exchange rates move over time is one of the most important for managers to consider. Once the extent of the exposure is known managers then need to judge what, if anything, is to be done about it. Sometimes the threat to the firm and the returns to shareholders are so great as to call for robust risk-reducing action. In other circumstances the cost of hedging outweighs the benefit. Analysing and appraising the extent of the problem and weighing up alternative responses are where managerial judgment comes to the fore. Knowledge of derivatives markets and money markets, and of the need for flexible manufacturing, marketing and financing structures, is useful background, but the key managerial skill required is discernment in positioning the company to cope with forex risk. The ability sometimes to stand back from the fray, objectively assess the cost of each risk-reducing option and say, 'No, this risk is to be taken on the chin because in my judgment the costs of managing the risk reduce shareholder wealth with little to show for it,' is sometimes required.

Websites

www.bis.org	Bank for International Settlements
www.bloomberg.co.uk	Bloomberg
www.reuters.co.uk	Reuters
www.ft.com	*Financial Times*
www.bankofengland.co.uk	Bank of England
www.ecb.int	European Central Bank
www.theice.com	Intercontinental Exchange (ICE)
www.cmegroup.com	Chicago Mercantile Exchange
www.euronext.com	NYSE Liffe

Notes

1 It is also shortened to FX.

2 Not all banks trading in forex markets are signed up to using CLS, so there is still a substantial Herstatt risk remaining.

3 The *Financial Times* (or, rather, WM/Reuters) takes a representative sample of rates from major dealers in London at 4 p.m.

4 If we ignore the marketmakers' bid/offer spread and transaction costs.

5 NYSE Liffe also trades currency futures.

6 The CME and ICE trade later months than those shown by the FT, but these, again, are usually at three-month intervals.

7 With some currency option contracts the exercise can take place any time up to the expiry date, rather than only on the expiry date.

8 Assuming, for the sake of simplicity, no diminution of asset value in dollar terms.

FUTURE VALUE OF £1 AT COMPOUND INTEREST

Interest rates (%)

Periods	1	2	3	4	5	6	7	8	9	10	11	12	13	14	15
1	1.0100	1.0200	1.0300	1.0400	1.0500	1.0600	1.0700	1.0800	1.0900	1.1000	1.1100	1.1200	1.1300	1.1400	1.1500
2	1.0201	1.0404	1.0609	1.0816	1.1025	1.1236	1.1449	1.1664	1.1881	1.2100	1.2321	1.2544	1.2769	1.2996	1.3225
3	1.0303	1.0612	1.0927	1.1249	1.1576	1.1910	1.2250	1.2597	1.2950	1.3310	1.3676	1.4049	1.4429	1.4815	1.5209
4	1.0406	1.0824	1.1255	1.1699	1.2155	1.2625	1.3108	1.3605	1.4116	1.4641	1.5181	1.5735	1.6305	1.6890	1.7490
5	1.0510	1.1041	1.1593	1.2167	1.2763	1.3382	1.4026	1.4693	1.5386	1.6105	1.6851	1.7623	1.8424	1.9254	2.0114
6	1.0615	1.1262	1.1941	1.2653	1.3401	1.4185	1.5007	1.5869	1.6771	1.7716	1.8704	1.9738	2.0820	2.1950	2.3131
7	1.0721	1.1487	1.2299	1.3159	1.4071	1.5036	1.6058	1.7138	1.8280	1.9487	2.0762	2.2107	2.3526	2.5023	2.6600
8	1.0829	1.1717	1.2668	1.3686	1.4775	1.5938	1.7182	1.8509	1.9926	2.1436	2.3045	2.4760	2.6584	2.8526	3.0590
9	1.0937	1.1951	1.3048	1.4233	1.5513	1.6895	1.8385	1.9990	2.1719	2.3579	2.5580	2.7731	3.0040	3.2519	3.5179
10	1.1046	1.2190	1.3439	1.4802	1.6289	1.7908	1.9672	2.1589	2.3674	2.5937	2.8394	3.1058	3.3946	3.7072	4.0456
11	1.1157	1.2434	1.3842	1.5395	1.7103	1.8983	2.1049	2.3316	2.5804	2.8531	3.1518	3.4785	3.8359	4.2262	4.6524
12	1.1268	1.2682	1.4258	1.6010	1.7959	2.0122	2.2522	2.5182	2.8127	3.1384	3.4985	3.8960	4.3345	4.8179	5.3503
13	1.1381	1.2936	1.4685	1.6651	1.8856	2.1329	2.4098	2.7196	3.0658	3.4523	3.8833	4.3635	4.8980	5.4924	6.1528
14	1.1495	1.3195	1.5126	1.7317	1.9799	2.2609	2.5785	2.9372	3.3417	3.7975	4.3104	4.8871	5.5348	6.2613	7.0757
15	1.1610	1.3459	1.5580	1.8009	2.0789	2.3966	2.7590	3.1722	3.6425	4.1772	4.7846	5.4736	6.2543	7.1379	8.1371
16	1.1726	1.3728	1.6047	1.8730	2.1829	2.5404	2.9522	3.4259	3.9703	4.5950	5.3109	6.1304	7.0673	8.1372	9.3576
17	1.1843	1.4002	1.6528	1.9479	2.2920	2.6928	3.1588	3.7000	4.3276	5.0545	5.8951	6.8660	7.9861	9.2765	10.7613
18	1.1961	1.4282	1.7024	2.0258	2.4066	2.8543	3.3799	3.9960	4.7171	5.5599	6.5436	7.6900	9.0243	10.5752	12.3755
19	1.2081	1.4568	1.7535	2.1068	2.5270	3.0256	3.6165	4.3157	5.1417	6.1159	7.2633	8.6128	10.1974	12.0557	14.2318
20	1.2202	1.4859	1.8061	2.1911	2.6533	3.2071	3.8697	4.6610	5.6044	6.7275	8.0623	9.6463	11.5231	13.7435	16.3665
25	1.2824	1.6406	2.0938	2.6658	3.3864	4.2919	5.4274	6.8485	8.6231	10.8347	13.5855	17.0001	21.2305	26.4619	32.9190

Periods	16	17	18	19	20	21	22	23	24	25	26	27	28	29	30
1	1.1600	1.1700	1.1800	1.1900	1.2000	1.2100	1.2200	1.2300	1.2400	1.2500	1.2600	1.2700	1.2800	1.2900	1.3000
2	1.3456	1.3689	1.3924	1.4161	1.4400	1.4641	1.4884	1.5129	1.5376	1.5625	1.5876	1.6129	1.6384	1.6641	1.6900
3	1.5609	1.6016	1.6430	1.6852	1.7280	1.7716	1.8158	1.8609	1.9066	1.9531	2.0004	2.0484	2.0972	2.1467	2.1970
4	1.8106	1.8739	1.9388	2.0053	2.0736	2.1436	2.2153	2.2889	2.3642	2.4414	2.5205	2.6014	2.6844	2.7692	2.8561
5	2.1003	2.1924	2.2878	2.3864	2.4883	2.5937	2.7027	2.8153	2.9316	3.0518	3.1758	3.3038	3.4360	3.5723	3.7129
6	2.4364	2.5652	2.6996	2.8398	2.9860	3.1384	3.2973	3.4628	3.6352	3.8147	4.0015	4.1959	4.3980	4.6083	4.8268
7	2.8262	3.0012	3.1855	3.3793	3.5832	3.7975	4.0227	4.2593	4.5077	4.7684	5.0419	5.3288	5.6295	5.9447	6.2749
8	3.2784	3.5115	3.7589	4.0214	4.2998	4.5950	4.9077	5.2389	5.5895	5.9605	6.3528	6.7675	7.2058	7.6686	8.1573
9	3.8030	4.1084	4.4355	4.7854	5.1598	5.5599	5.9874	6.4439	6.9310	7.4506	8.0045	8.5948	9.2234	9.8925	10.6045
10	4.4114	4.8068	5.2338	5.6947	6.1917	6.7275	7.3046	7.9259	8.5944	9.3132	10.0857	10.9153	11.8059	12.7614	13.7858
11	5.1173	5.6240	6.1759	6.7767	7.4301	8.1403	8.9117	9.7489	10.6571	11.6415	12.7080	13.8625	15.1116	16.4622	17.9216
12	5.9360	6.5801	7.2876	8.0642	8.9161	9.8497	10.8722	11.9912	13.2148	14.5519	16.0120	17.6053	19.3428	21.2362	23.2981
13	6.8858	7.6987	8.5994	9.5964	10.6993	11.9182	13.2641	14.7491	16.3863	18.1899	20.1752	22.3588	24.7588	27.3947	30.2875
14	7.9875	9.0075	10.1472	11.4198	12.8392	14.4210	16.1822	18.1414	20.3191	22.7374	25.4207	28.3957	31.6913	35.3391	39.3738
15	9.2655	10.5387	11.9737	13.5895	15.4070	17.4494	19.7423	22.3140	25.1956	28.4217	32.0301	36.0625	40.5648	45.5875	51.1859
16	10.7480	12.3303	14.1290	16.1715	18.4884	21.1138	24.0856	27.4462	31.2426	35.5271	40.3579	45.7994	51.9230	58.8079	66.5417
17	12.4677	14.4265	16.6722	19.2441	22.1861	25.5477	29.3844	33.7588	38.7408	44.4089	50.8510	58.1652	66.4614	75.8621	86.5042
18	14.4625	16.8790	19.6733	22.9005	26.6233	30.9127	35.8490	41.5233	48.0386	55.5112	64.0722	73.8698	85.0706	97.8622	112.4554
19	16.7765	19.7484	23.2144	27.2516	31.9480	37.4043	43.7358	51.0737	59.5679	69.3889	80.7310	93.8147	108.8904	126.2422	146.1920
20	19.4608	23.1056	27.3930	32.4294	38.3376	45.2593	53.3576	62.8206	73.8641	86.7362	101.7211	119.1446	139.3797	162.8524	190.0496
25	40.8742	50.6578	62.6686	77.3881	95.3962	117.3909	144.2101	176.8593	216.5420	264.6978	323.0454	393.6344	478.9049	581.7585	705.6410

PRESENT VALUE OF £1 AT COMPOUND INTEREST

Interest rates (%)

Periods	1	2	3	4	5	6	7	8	9	10	11	12	13	14	15
1	0.9901	0.9804	0.9709	0.9615	0.9524	0.9434	0.9346	0.9259	0.9174	0.9091	0.9009	0.8929	0.8850	0.8772	0.8696
2	0.9803	0.9612	0.9426	0.9246	0.9070	0.8900	0.8734	0.8573	0.8417	0.8264	0.8116	0.7972	0.7831	0.7695	0.7561
3	0.9706	0.9423	0.9151	0.8890	0.8638	0.8396	0.8163	0.7938	0.7722	0.7513	0.7312	0.7118	0.6931	0.6750	0.6575
4	0.9610	0.9238	0.8885	0.8548	0.8227	0.7921	0.7629	0.7350	0.7084	0.6830	0.6587	0.6355	0.6133	0.5921	0.5718
5	0.9515	0.9057	0.8626	0.8219	0.7835	0.7473	0.7130	0.6806	0.6499	0.6209	0.5935	0.5674	0.5428	0.5194	0.4972
6	0.9420	0.8880	0.8375	0.7903	0.7462	0.7050	0.6663	0.6302	0.5963	0.5645	0.5346	0.5066	0.4803	0.4556	0.4323
7	0.9327	0.8706	0.8131	0.7599	0.7107	0.6651	0.6227	0.5835	0.5470	0.5132	0.4817	0.4523	0.4251	0.3996	0.3759
8	0.9235	0.8535	0.7894	0.7307	0.6768	0.6274	0.5820	0.5403	0.5019	0.4665	0.4339	0.4039	0.3762	0.3506	0.3269
9	0.9143	0.8368	0.7664	0.7026	0.6446	0.5919	0.5439	0.5002	0.4604	0.4241	0.3909	0.3606	0.3329	0.3075	0.2843
10	0.9053	0.8203	0.7441	0.6756	0.6139	0.5584	0.5083	0.4632	0.4224	0.3855	0.3522	0.3220	0.2946	0.2697	0.2472
11	0.8963	0.8043	0.7224	0.6496	0.5847	0.5268	0.4751	0.4289	0.3875	0.3505	0.3173	0.2875	0.2607	0.2366	0.2149
12	0.8874	0.7885	0.7014	0.6246	0.5568	0.4970	0.4440	0.3971	0.3555	0.3186	0.2858	0.2567	0.2307	0.2076	0.1869
13	0.8787	0.7730	0.6810	0.6006	0.5303	0.4688	0.4150	0.3677	0.3262	0.2897	0.2575	0.2292	0.2042	0.1821	0.1625
14	0.8700	0.7579	0.6611	0.5775	0.5051	0.4423	0.3878	0.3405	0.2992	0.2633	0.2320	0.2046	0.1807	0.1597	0.1413
15	0.8613	0.7430	0.6419	0.5553	0.4810	0.4173	0.3624	0.3152	0.2745	0.2394	0.2090	0.1827	0.1599	0.1401	0.1229
16	0.8528	0.7284	0.6232	0.5339	0.4581	0.3936	0.3387	0.2919	0.2519	0.2176	0.1883	0.1631	0.1415	0.1229	0.1069
17	0.8444	0.7142	0.6050	0.5134	0.4363	0.3714	0.3166	0.2703	0.2311	0.1978	0.1696	0.1456	0.1252	0.1078	0.0929
18	0.8360	0.7002	0.5874	0.4936	0.4155	0.3503	0.2959	0.2502	0.2120	0.1799	0.1528	0.1300	0.1108	0.0946	0.0808
19	0.8277	0.6864	0.5703	0.4746	0.3957	0.3305	0.2765	0.2317	0.1945	0.1635	0.1377	0.1161	0.0981	0.0829	0.0703
20	0.8195	0.6730	0.5537	0.4564	0.3769	0.3118	0.2584	0.2145	0.1784	0.1486	0.1240	0.1037	0.0868	0.0728	0.0611
25	0.7795	0.6095	0.4776	0.3751	0.2953	0.2330	0.1842	0.1460	0.1160	0.0923	0.0736	0.0588	0.0471	0.0378	0.0304
30	0.7419	0.5521	0.4120	0.3083	0.2314	0.1741	0.1314	0.0994	0.0754	0.0573	0.0437	0.0334	0.0256	0.0196	0.0151
35	0.7059	0.5000	0.3554	0.2534	0.1813	0.1301	0.0937	0.0676	0.0490	0.0356	0.0259	0.0189	0.0139	0.0102	0.0075
40	0.6717	0.4529	0.3066	0.2083	0.1420	0.0972	0.0668	0.0460	0.0318	0.0221	0.0154	0.0107	0.0075	0.0053	0.0037
45	0.6391	0.4102	0.2644	0.1712	0.1113	0.0727	0.0476	0.0313	0.0207	0.0137	0.0091	0.0061	0.0041	0.0027	0.0019
50	0.6080	0.3715	0.2281	0.1407	0.0872	0.0543	0.0339	0.0213	0.0134	0.0085	0.0054	0.0035	0.0022	0.0014	0.0009

Periods	16	17	18	19	20	21	22	23	24	25	26	27	28	29	30
1	0.8621	0.8547	0.8475	0.8403	0.8333	0.8264	0.8197	0.8130	0.8065	0.8000	0.7937	0.7874	0.7812	0.7752	0.7692
2	0.7432	0.7305	0.7182	0.7062	0.6944	0.6830	0.6719	0.6610	0.6504	0.6400	0.6299	0.6200	0.6104	0.6009	0.5917
3	0.6407	0.6244	0.6086	0.5934	0.5787	0.5645	0.5507	0.5374	0.5245	0.5120	0.4999	0.4882	0.4768	0.4658	0.4552
4	0.5523	0.5337	0.5158	0.4987	0.4823	0.4665	0.4514	0.4369	0.4230	0.4096	0.3968	0.3844	0.3725	0.3611	0.3501
5	0.4761	0.4561	0.4371	0.4190	0.4019	0.3855	0.3700	0.3552	0.3411	0.3277	0.3149	0.3027	0.2910	0.2799	0.2693
6	0.4104	0.3898	0.3704	0.3521	0.3349	0.3186	0.3033	0.2888	0.2751	0.2621	0.2499	0.2383	0.2274	0.2170	0.2072
7	0.3538	0.3332	0.3139	0.2959	0.2791	0.2633	0.2486	0.2348	0.2218	0.2097	0.1983	0.1877	0.1776	0.1682	0.1594
8	0.3050	0.2848	0.2660	0.2487	0.2326	0.2176	0.2038	0.1909	0.1789	0.1678	0.1574	0.1478	0.1388	0.1304	0.1226
9	0.2630	0.2434	0.2255	0.2090	0.1938	0.1799	0.1670	0.1552	0.1443	0.1342	0.1249	0.1164	0.1084	0.1011	0.0943
10	0.2267	0.2080	0.1911	0.1756	0.1615	0.1486	0.1369	0.1262	0.1164	0.1074	0.0992	0.0916	0.0847	0.0784	0.0725
11	0.1954	0.1778	0.1619	0.1476	0.1346	0.1228	0.1122	0.1026	0.0938	0.0859	0.0787	0.0721	0.0662	0.0607	0.0558
12	0.1685	0.1520	0.1372	0.1240	0.1122	0.1015	0.0920	0.0834	0.0757	0.0687	0.0625	0.0568	0.0517	0.0471	0.0429
13	0.1452	0.1299	0.1163	0.1042	0.0935	0.0839	0.0754	0.0678	0.0610	0.0550	0.0496	0.0447	0.0404	0.0365	0.0330
14	0.1252	0.1110	0.0985	0.0876	0.0779	0.0693	0.0618	0.0551	0.0492	0.0440	0.0393	0.0352	0.0316	0.0283	0.0254
15	0.1079	0.0949	0.0835	0.0736	0.0649	0.0573	0.0507	0.0448	0.0397	0.0352	0.0312	0.0277	0.0247	0.0219	0.0195
16	0.0930	0.0811	0.0708	0.0618	0.0541	0.0474	0.0415	0.0364	0.0320	0.0281	0.0248	0.0218	0.0193	0.0170	0.0150
17	0.0802	0.0693	0.0600	0.0520	0.0451	0.0391	0.0340	0.0296	0.0258	0.0225	0.0197	0.0172	0.0150	0.0132	0.0116
18	0.0691	0.0592	0.0508	0.0437	0.0376	0.0323	0.0279	0.0241	0.0208	0.0180	0.0156	0.0135	0.0118	0.0102	0.0089
19	0.0596	0.0506	0.0431	0.0367	0.0313	0.0267	0.0229	0.0196	0.0168	0.0144	0.0124	0.0107	0.0092	0.0079	0.0068
20	0.0514	0.0433	0.0365	0.0308	0.0261	0.0221	0.0187	0.0159	0.0135	0.0115	0.0098	0.0084	0.0072	0.0061	0.0053
25	0.0245	0.0197	0.0160	0.0129	0.0105	0.0085	0.0069	0.0057	0.0046	0.0038	0.0031	0.0025	0.0021	0.0017	0.0014
30	0.0116	0.0090	0.0070	0.0054	0.0042	0.0033	0.0026	0.0020	0.0016	0.0012	0.0010	0.0008	0.0006	0.0005	0.0004
35	0.0055	0.0041	0.0030	0.0023	0.0017	0.0013	0.0009	0.0007	0.0005	0.0004	0.0003	0.0002	0.0002	0.0001	0.0001
40	0.0026	0.0019	0.0013	0.0010	0.0007	0.0005	0.0004	0.0003	0.0002	0.0001	0.0001	0.0001	0.0000	0.0000	0.0000
45	0.0013	0.0009	0.0006	0.0004	0.0003	0.0002	0.0001	0.0001	0.0001	0.0001	0.0000	0.0000	0.0000	0.0000	0.0000
50	0.0006	0.0004	0.0003	0.0002	0.0001	0.0001	0.0000	0.0000	0.0000	0.0000	0.0000	0.0000	0.0000	0.0000	0.0000

PRESENT VALUE OF AN ANNUITY OF £1 AT COMPOUND INTEREST

Interest rate (%)

Periods	1	2	3	4	5	6	7	8	9	10	11	12	13	14	15
1	0.9901	0.9804	0.9709	0.9615	0.9524	0.9434	0.9346	0.9259	0.9174	0.9091	0.9009	0.8929	0.8850	0.8772	0.8696
2	1.9704	1.9416	1.9135	1.8861	1.8594	1.8334	1.8080	1.7833	1.7591	1.7355	1.7125	1.6901	1.6681	1.6467	1.6257
3	2.9410	2.8839	2.8286	2.7751	2.7232	2.6730	2.6243	2.5771	2.5313	2.4869	2.4437	2.4018	2.3612	2.3216	2.2832
4	3.9020	3.8077	3.7171	3.6299	3.5460	3.4651	3.3872	3.3121	3.2397	3.1699	3.1024	3.0373	2.9745	2.9137	2.8550
5	4.8534	4.7135	4.5797	4.4518	4.3295	4.2124	4.1002	3.9927	3.8897	3.7908	3.6959	3.6048	3.5172	3.4331	3.3522
6	5.7955	5.6014	5.4172	5.2421	5.0757	4.9173	4.7665	4.6229	4.4859	4.3553	4.2305	4.1114	3.9975	3.8887	3.7845
7	6.7282	6.4720	6.2303	6.0021	5.7864	5.5824	5.3893	5.2064	5.0330	4.8684	4.7122	4.5638	4.4226	4.2883	4.1604
8	7.6517	7.3255	7.0197	6.7327	6.4632	6.2098	5.9713	5.7466	5.5348	5.3349	5.1461	4.9676	4.7988	4.6389	4.4873
9	8.5660	8.1622	7.7861	7.4353	7.1078	6.8017	6.5152	6.2469	5.9952	5.7590	5.5370	5.3282	5.1317	4.9464	4.7716
10	9.4713	8.9826	8.5302	8.1109	7.7217	7.3601	7.0236	6.7101	6.4177	6.1446	5.8892	5.6502	5.4262	5.2161	5.0188
11	10.3676	9.7868	9.2526	8.7605	8.3064	7.8869	7.4987	7.1390	6.8052	6.4951	6.2065	5.9377	5.6869	5.4527	5.2337
12	11.2551	10.5753	9.9540	9.3851	8.8633	8.3838	7.9427	7.5361	7.1607	6.8137	6.4924	6.1944	5.9176	5.6603	5.4206
13	12.1337	11.3484	10.6350	9.9856	9.3936	8.8527	8.3577	7.9038	7.4869	7.1034	6.7499	6.4235	6.1218	5.8424	5.5831
14	13.0037	12.1062	11.2961	10.5631	9.8986	9.2950	8.7455	8.2442	7.7862	7.3667	6.9819	6.6282	6.3025	6.0021	5.7245
15	13.8651	12.8493	11.9379	11.1184	10.3797	9.7122	9.1079	8.5595	8.0607	7.6061	7.1909	6.8109	6.4624	6.1422	5.8474
16	14.7179	13.5777	12.5611	11.6523	10.8378	10.1059	9.4466	8.8514	8.3126	7.8237	7.3792	6.9740	6.6039	6.2651	5.9542
17	15.5623	14.2919	13.1661	12.1657	11.2741	10.4773	9.7632	9.1216	8.5436	8.0216	7.5488	7.1196	6.7291	6.3729	6.0472
18	16.3983	14.9920	13.7535	12.6593	11.6896	10.8276	10.0591	9.3719	8.7556	8.2014	7.7016	7.2497	6.8399	6.4674	6.1280
19	17.2260	15.6785	14.3238	13.1339	12.0853	11.1581	10.3356	9.6036	8.9501	8.3649	7.8393	7.3658	6.9380	6.5504	6.1982
20	18.0456	16.3514	14.8775	13.5903	12.4622	11.4699	10.5940	9.8181	9.1285	8.5136	7.9633	7.4694	7.0248	6.6231	6.2593
25	22.0232	19.5235	17.4131	15.6221	14.0939	12.7834	11.6536	10.6748	9.8226	9.0770	8.4217	7.8431	7.3300	6.8729	6.4641
30	25.8077	22.3965	19.6004	17.2920	15.3725	13.7648	12.4090	11.2578	10.2737	9.4269	8.6938	8.0552	7.4957	7.0027	6.5660
35	29.4086	24.9986	21.4872	18.6646	16.3742	14.4982	12.9477	11.6546	10.5668	9.6442	8.8552	8.1755	7.5856	7.0700	6.6166
40	32.8347	27.3555	23.1148	19.7928	17.1591	15.0463	13.3317	11.9246	10.7574	9.7791	8.9511	8.2438	7.6344	7.1050	6.6418
45	36.0945	29.4902	24.5187	20.7200	17.7741	15.4558	13.6055	12.1084	10.8812	9.8628	9.0079	8.2825	7.6609	7.1232	6.6543
50	39.1961	31.4236	25.7298	21.4822	18.2559	15.7619	13.8007	12.2335	10.9617	9.9148	9.0417	8.3045	7.6752	7.1327	6.6605

Periods	16	17	18	19	20	21	22	23	24	25	26	27	28	29	30
1	0.8621	0.8547	0.8475	0.8403	0.8333	0.8264	0.8197	0.8130	0.8065	0.8000	0.7937	0.7874	0.7812	0.7752	0.7692
2	1.6052	1.5852	1.5656	1.5465	1.5278	1.5095	1.4915	1.4740	1.4568	1.4400	1.4235	1.4074	1.3916	1.3761	1.3609
3	2.2459	2.2096	2.1743	2.1399	2.1065	2.0739	2.0422	2.0114	1.9813	1.9520	1.9234	1.8956	1.8684	1.8420	1.8161
4	2.7982	2.7432	2.6901	2.6386	2.5887	2.5404	2.4936	2.4483	2.4043	2.3616	2.3202	2.2800	2.2410	2.2031	2.1662
5	3.2743	3.1993	3.1272	3.0576	2.9906	2.9260	2.8636	2.8035	2.7454	2.6893	2.6351	2.5827	2.5320	2.4830	2.4356
6	3.6847	3.5892	3.4976	3.4098	3.3255	3.2446	3.1669	3.0923	3.0205	2.9514	2.8850	2.8210	2.7594	2.7000	2.6427
7	4.0386	3.9224	3.8115	3.7057	3.6046	3.5079	3.4155	3.3270	3.2423	3.1611	3.0833	3.0087	2.9370	2.8682	2.8021
8	4.3436	4.2072	4.0776	3.9544	3.8372	3.7256	3.6193	3.5179	3.4212	3.3289	3.2407	3.1564	3.0758	2.9986	2.9247
9	4.6065	4.4506	4.3030	4.1633	4.0310	3.9054	3.7863	3.6731	3.5655	3.4631	3.3657	3.2728	3.1842	3.0997	3.0190
10	4.8332	4.6586	4.4941	4.3389	4.1925	4.0541	3.9232	3.7993	3.6819	3.5705	3.4648	3.3644	3.2689	3.1781	3.0915
11	5.0286	4.8364	4.6560	4.4865	4.3271	4.1769	4.0354	3.9018	3.7757	3.6564	3.5435	3.4365	3.3351	3.2388	3.1473
12	5.1971	4.9884	4.7932	4.6105	4.4392	4.2784	4.1274	3.9852	3.8514	3.7251	3.6059	3.4933	3.3868	3.2859	3.1903
13	5.3423	5.1183	4.9095	4.7147	4.5327	4.3624	4.2028	4.0530	3.9124	3.7801	3.6555	3.5381	3.4272	3.3224	3.2233
14	5.4675	5.2293	5.0081	4.8023	4.6106	4.4317	4.2646	4.1082	3.9616	3.8241	3.6949	3.5733	3.4587	3.3507	3.2487
15	5.5755	5.3242	5.0916	4.8759	4.6755	4.4890	4.3152	4.1530	4.0013	3.8593	3.7261	3.6010	3.4834	3.3726	3.2682
16	5.6685	5.4053	5.1624	4.9377	4.7296	4.5364	4.3567	4.1894	4.0333	3.8874	3.7509	3.6228	3.5026	3.3896	3.2832
17	5.7487	5.4746	5.2223	4.9897	4.7746	4.5755	4.3908	4.2190	4.0591	3.9099	3.7705	3.6400	3.5177	3.4028	3.2948
18	5.8178	5.5339	5.2732	5.0333	4.8122	4.6079	4.4187	4.2431	4.0799	3.9279	3.7861	3.6536	3.5294	3.4130	3.3037
19	5.8775	5.5845	5.3162	5.0700	4.8435	4.6346	4.4415	4.2627	4.0967	3.9424	3.7985	3.6642	3.5386	3.4210	3.3105
20	5.9288	5.6278	5.3527	5.1009	4.8696	4.6567	4.4603	4.2786	4.1103	3.9539	3.8083	3.6726	3.5458	3.4271	3.3158
25	6.0971	5.7662	5.4669	5.1951	4.9476	4.7213	4.5139	4.3232	4.1474	3.9849	3.8342	3.6943	3.5640	3.4423	3.3286
30	6.1772	5.8294	5.5168	5.2347	4.9789	4.7463	4.5338	4.3391	4.1601	3.9950	3.8424	3.7009	3.5693	3.4466	3.3321
35	6.2153	5.8582	5.5386	5.2512	4.9915	4.7559	4.5411	4.3447	4.1644	3.9984	3.8450	3.7028	3.5708	3.4478	3.3330
40	6.2335	5.8713	5.5482	5.2582	4.9966	4.7596	4.5439	4.3467	4.1659	3.9995	3.8458	3.7034	3.5712	3.4481	3.3332
45	6.2421	5.8773	5.5523	5.2611	4.9986	4.7610	4.5449	4.3474	4.1664	3.9998	3.8460	3.7036	3.5714	3.4482	3.3333
50	6.2463	5.8801	5.5541	5.2623	4.9995	4.7616	4.5452	4.3477	4.1666	3.9999	3.8461	3.7037	3.5714	3.4483	3.3333

FUTURE VALUE OF AN ANNUITY OF £1 AT COMPOUND INTEREST

Interest rate

Periods	1	2	3	4	5	6	7	8	9	10	12	14	16	18	20	25	30	35	40	45	50
1	1.0000	1.0000	1.0000	1.0000	1.0000	1.0000	1.0000	1.0000	1.0000	1.0000	1.0000	1.0000	1.0000	1.0000	1.0000	1.0000	1.0000	1.0000	1.0000	1.0000	1.0000
2	2.0100	2.0200	2.0300	2.0400	2.0500	2.0600	2.0700	2.0800	2.0900	2.1000	2.1200	2.1400	2.1600	2.1800	2.2000	2.2500	2.3000	2.3500	2.4000	2.4500	2.5000
3	3.0301	3.0604	3.0909	3.1216	3.1525	3.1836	3.2149	3.2464	3.2781	3.3100	3.3744	3.4396	3.5056	3.5724	3.6400	3.8125	3.9900	4.1725	4.3600	4.5525	4.7500
4	4.0604	4.1216	4.1836	4.2465	4.3101	4.3746	4.4399	4.5061	4.5731	4.6410	4.7793	4.9211	5.0665	5.1254	5.3680	5.7656	6.1870	6.6329	7.1040	7.6011	8.1250
5	5.1010	5.2040	5.3091	5.4163	5.5256	5.6371	5.7507	5.8666	5.9847	6.1051	6.3528	6.6101	6.8771	7.1542	7.4416	8.2070	9.0431	9.9544	10.9456	12.0216	13.1875
6	6.1520	6.3081	6.4684	6.6330	6.8019	6.9753	7.1533	7.3359	7.5233	7.7156	8.1152	8.5355	8.9775	9.4420	9.9299	11.2588	12.7560	14.4834	16.3238	18.4314	20.7813
7	7.2135	7.4343	7.6625	7.8983	8.1420	8.3938	8.6540	8.9228	9.2004	9.4872	10.0890	10.7305	11.4139	12.1415	12.9159	15.0735	17.5828	20.4919	23.8534	27.7255	32.1719
8	8.2857	8.5830	8.8923	9.2142	9.5491	9.8975	10.2598	10.6366	11.0285	11.4359	12.2997	13.2328	14.2401	15.3270	16.4991	19.8419	23.8577	28.6640	34.3947	41.2019	49.2578
9	9.3685	9.7546	10.1591	10.5828	11.0266	11.4913	11.9780	12.4876	13.0210	13.5795	14.7757	16.0853	17.5185	19.0859	20.7989	25.8023	32.0150	39.6964	49.1526	60.7428	74.8867
10	10.4622	10.9497	11.4639	12.0061	12.5779	13.1808	13.8164	14.4866	15.1929	15.9374	17.5487	19.3373	21.3215	23.5213	25.9587	33.2529	42.6195	54.5902	69.8137	89.0771	113.330
11	11.5668	12.1687	12.8078	13.4864	14.2068	14.9716	15.7836	16.6455	17.5603	18.5312	20.6546	23.0445	25.7329	28.7551	32.1504	42.5661	56.4053	74.6967	98.7391	130.162	170.995
12	12.6825	13.4121	14.1920	15.0258	15.9171	16.8699	17.8885	18.9771	20.1407	21.3843	24.1331	27.2707	30.8502	34.9311	39.5805	54.2077	74.3270	101.841	139.235	189.735	257.493
13	13.8093	14.6803	15.6178	16.6268	17.7130	18.8821	20.1406	21.4953	22.9534	24.5227	28.0291	32.0887	36.7862	42.2187	48.4966	68.7596	97.6250	138.485	195.929	276.115	387.239
14	14.9474	15.9739	17.0863	18.2919	19.5986	21.0151	22.5505	24.2149	26.0192	27.9750	32.3926	37.5811	43.6720	50.8180	59.1959	86.9495	127.913	187.954	275.300	401.367	581.859
15	16.0969	17.2934	18.5989	20.0236	21.5786	23.2760	25.1290	27.1521	29.3609	31.7725	37.2797	43.8424	51.6595	60.9653	72.0351	109.687	167.286	254.738	386.420	582.982	873.788
16	17.2579	18.6393	20.1569	21.8245	23.6575	25.6725	27.8881	30.3243	33.0034	35.9497	42.7533	50.9804	60.9250	72.9390	87.4421	138.109	218.472	344.897	541.988	846.324	1311.68
17	18.4304	20.0121	21.7616	23.6975	25.8404	28.2129	30.8402	33.7502	36.9737	40.5447	48.8837	59.1176	71.6730	87.0680	105.931	173.636	285.014	466.611	759.784	1228.17	1968.52
18	19.6147	21.4123	23.4144	25.6454	28.1324	30.9057	33.9990	37.4502	41.3013	45.5992	55.7497	68.3941	84.1407	103.740	128.117	218.045	371.518	630.925	1064.70	1781.85	2953.78
19	20.8109	22.8406	25.1169	27.6712	30.5390	33.7600	37.3790	41.4463	46.0185	51.1591	63.4397	78.9692	98.6032	123.414	154.740	273.556	483.973	852.748	1491.58	2584.68	4431.68
20	22.0190	24.2974	26.8704	29.7781	33.0660	36.7856	40.9955	45.7620	51.1601	57.2750	72.0524	91.0249	115.380	146.628	186.688	342.945	630.165	1152.21	2089.21	3748.78	6648.51
25	28.2432	32.0303	36.4593	41.6459	47.7271	54.8645	63.2490	73.1059	84.7009	98.3471	133.334	181.871	249.214	342.603	471.981	1054.79	2348.80	5176.50	11247.2	24040.7	50500.3
30	34.7849	40.5681	47.5754	56.0849	66.4388	79.0582	94.4608	113.283	136.308	164.494	241.333	356.787	530.312	790.948	1181.88	3227.17	8729.99	23221.6	60501.1	154107	383500
35	41.6603	49.9945	60.4621	73.6522	90.3203	111.435	138.237	172.317	215.711	271.024	431.663	693.573	1120.71	1816.65	2948.34	9856.76	32422.9	104136	325400	987794	2912217
40	48.8864	60.4020	75.4013	95.0255	120.800	154.762	199.635	259.057	337.882	442.593	767.091	1342.03	2360.76	4163.21	7343.86	30088.7	120393	466960	1750092	6331512	22114663
45	56.4811	71.8927	92.7199	121.029	159.700	212.744	285.749	368.506	525.859	718.905	1358.23	2590.56	4965.27	9531.58	18281.3	91831.5	447019	2093876	9412424	40583319	167933233
50	64.4632	84.5794	112.797	152.667	209.348	290.336	406.529	573.770	815.084	1163.91	2400.02	4994.52	10435.6	21813.1	45497.2	280256	1659761	9389020	50622288	260128295	1275242998

GLOSSARY

'A' shares Sometimes the 'A' shares are the ordinary shares that carry fewer or no votes. However, in many companies 'A' shares carry more votes than the 'B' shares. The shares may also differ with regard to the size of dividend.

Abandon The choice made by a holder of a warrant or option to allow it to expire without exercise.

Abnormal return (residual return) A return greater than the market return after adjusting for differences in risk.

Absolute advantage A firm, person, organization or country has an absolute advantage if it can obtain a benefit at a lower cost than other firms, people, organizations or countries. For example, Costa Rica has an absolute advantage in growing bananas *vis-à-vis* Europe.

Acceptance credit (bank bill) An institution (e.g. bank) commits itself to the payment of a sum of money in the future as stated in the acceptance credit document. The borrower is given this document (which can be passed on to a supplier) in return for a promise to pay a sum on the maturity date to the institution. The acceptance credit can be sold in the discount market to obtain funds for the borrower (or to pass on to a supplier).

Accounting rate of return (ARR) A measure of profitability based on accounting numbers. Profit divided by assets devoted to the activity (e.g. project, entire business) as a percentage.

Accounting standards A set of formal rules and conventions set by the accounting profession to calculate accounting numbers.

Accounts payable Short-term debts owed by a firm to its creditors for goods and services received. A term used more in the USA; in the UK the term 'creditors' is usually used.

Accounts receivable Customer debts to this company. A term used more in the USA; in the UK the term 'debtors' is usually used.

Acid test *See* Quick ratio.

Additivity Ability to add up.

Administration An administrator ('administrative receiver') takes over the running of a distressed company following the failure to abide by loan agreements to recover debt due to the creditor(s). Administrators often keep the business running as a going concern but may have no alternative to liquidation to release money for the creditor(s).

Adverse selection problem When there is an opportunity or incentive for some firms/individuals to act to take advantage of their informational edge over others, then the firm/individual doing that activity will be disproportionately those taking advantage rather than being truly representative of the population as a whole, e.g. the tendency for poorer-than-average risks to continue with insurance. This will raise the cost of insurance for the whole group, including those of less-than-average risk. This is caused by asymmetric information in which the poorer-than-average risk policy holder knows more about their risk level than the insurer does.

Affirmative covenants Loan agreement conditions that require positive action on the part of the borrower, e.g. a statement that a bond will pay regular dividends, or that the borrower will distribute information regularly.

Ageing schedule The total debtor figure is broken down to show how long invoices have been outstanding (i.e. have remained unpaid).

Agency Acting for or in the place of another with their authority.

Agency costs Costs of preventing agents (e.g. managers) pursuing their own interests at the expense of their principals (e.g. shareholders). Examples include contracting costs and costs of monitoring. In addition there is the agency cost of the loss of wealth caused by the extent to which prevention measures have not worked and managers continue to pursue non-shareholder wealth goals.

Agent A person who acts for or in the place of another with that other person's authority (the 'principal').

Aggressive shares Shares having a beta value greater than 1.

AGM *See* Annual general meeting.

AIM admission document The document needed for a company to be quoted on the Alternative Investment Market in the first instance. It is similar to a prospectus.

Allocation of capital The mechanism for selecting competing investment projects leading to the production of a mixture of goods and services by a society. This can be influenced by the forces of supply and demand, and by central authority direction. The term may also be used for selection of securities (e.g. shares) by investors or business units and activities by managers.

Allocational efficiency of markets Efficiency in the process of allocating society's scarce resources between competing real investments.

Allotment In a new issue of shares, if more shares are demanded at the price than are available, they may be apportioned (allotted) between the applicants.

All-paper deal When a bidder offers to buy shares in a target, the payment is entirely in the form of shares in the bidder.

Alpha (Alpha coefficient, α) A measure of performance greater than or less than the market as a whole after allowing for beta in the capital asset pricing model (q.v.). That portion of a share's return that cannot be explained by its responsiveness to moves in the market as a whole. Sometimes called stock-specific return.

Alternative Investment Market (AIM) The lightly regulated share market operated by the London Stock Exchange, focused particularly on smaller, less well-established companies.

Alternative investments Outside the mainstream, e.g. art, stamps, coins, wine.

American depositary receipts (ADRs) Depositary receipts issued in the USA.

American-style option (American option) An option that can be exercised by the purchaser at any time up to the expiry date.

AMEX The American Stock Exchange. Trades equities, options and exchange-traded funds.

Amortisation The repayment of a debt by a series of instalments.

Amortisation of assets The reduction in book value of an intangible asset such as goodwill.

Analyst A researcher of companies' prospects and predictor of their share price performance. Also analyses other securities.

Angel *See* Business angels.

Annual equivalent annuity (AEA) A regular annual amount that is equivalent, in present value terms, to another set of cash flows.

Annual equivalent rate (AER) *See* Annual percentage rate.

Annual general meeting (AGM) A limited company must hold in each calendar year an annual general meeting. It is an opportunity for shareholders to meet and talk with each other and with those who run the company on their behalf.
The managers give an account of their stewardship. All shareholders are entitled to attend and vote. Election of directors may take place.

Annual percentage rate (APR) The true annual interest rate charged by a lender. It takes full account of the timing of payments of interest and principal.

Annual results Annual company accounts. This term is often used for the preliminary results.

Annuity An even stream of payments (the same amount each time) over a given period of time with a fixed frequency of payments.

Annuity due An annuity where the cash flows occur at the start of each period rather than at the end – the first payment is due now, not in one year's time.

Arbitrage The act of exploiting price differences on the same instrument or similar securities by simultaneously selling the overpriced security and buying the underpriced security.

Arbitrage pricing theory (APT) A type of multifactor model that relates return on securities to various non-diversifiable risk factors. The expected return on any risky security is a linear combination of these factors.

Arithmetic mean or average The average of a set of numbers equals the sum of the observations divided by the number of observations.

Arrangement fee A fee for agreeing and setting up a financial transaction such as a bank loan.

Articles of association Internal rules governing a company. Can be unique to a company.

Asset In the financial markets an asset is anything that can be traded as a security, e.g. share, option, commodity, bond.

Asset allocation An investment methodology that specifies the proportion of funds to be invested in different asset classes, e.g. property, shares, bonds.

Asset-backed securities (ABS) *See* Securitisation.

Asset backing The value of the assets held in the business – often measured on a per share basis.

Asset class Asset types, e.g. bonds, shares.

Asset liquidity The extent to which assets can be converted to cash quickly and at a low transaction cost.

Asset lock-up In a hostile takeover situation, the target sells to a friendly firm those parts of the business most attractive to the bidder.

Asset securitization *See* Securitization.

Asset transformers Intermediaries who, by creating a completely new security – the intermediate security – mobilize savings and encourage investment. The primary security is issued by the ultimate borrower to the intermediary, who offers intermediate securities to the primary investors.

Associated company A company in which an investor (usually a holding company) holds a participating interest and exercises significant influence over the entity. 'Interest' includes shares, options and convertible securities. 'Participating' means the interest is held on a long-term basis and there is significant influence. Usually a 20 percent or more holding of the shares is presumed to be participating.

Asymmetric information One party in a negotiation or relationship is not in the same position as other parties, being ignorant of, or unable to observe, some information which is essential to the contracting and decision-making process.

At-the-money option The current underlying price is equal to the option exercise price.

Audit committee A group of independent non-executive directors responsible for validating financial figures.

Auditor Auditors determine whether the company's financial statements are misleading and whether the accounts show a true and fair view.

Authorized but unissued ordinary share capital Shares that have not yet been sold by the company to investors. However, they have been created (authorized by shareholders) and may be sold or given to existing shareholders or sold to new shareholders.

Authorized share capital The maximum amount of share capital that a company can issue. The limit can be changed by a shareholder vote.

Average collection period (ACP) The average number of days it takes to collect debts from customers. The total debtors outstanding divided by the average daily sales.

Back office That part of a financial institution that deals with the settlement of contracts, accounting, regulatory matters and management information processes.

Back-to-back loan Company A and Company B lend to each other the same amount with the same maturity but in different currencies. The purpose is to hedge against currency fluctuations.

Bad debts Debts that are unlikely to be paid.

Bad growth When a company increases investment in an area of business that generates returns less than the opportunity cost of capital.

Balance of payments A record of the payment for goods and services obtained by a country and other transfers of currency from abroad and the receipts for goods and services sold and other transfers of currency abroad. The balance on the current account (visible trade and invisible trade) is the difference between national income and national expenditure in the period. The capital account is made up of such items as the inward and outward flow of money for investment and international grants and loans.

Balance sheet Provides a picture of what a company owned, what it owes and what is owed to it on a particular day in the past. It summarizes assets, liabilities and net worth (capital).

Balance sheet hedge To counter the risk of forex (q.v.) translation or economic exposure a company may hedge (q.v.) by borrowing in the same currency as the denomination of the assets.

Balloon repayment on a loan The majority of the repayment of a loan is made at or near the maturity date, with the final payment substantially larger than the earlier payments.

Ballot In a new issue of shares when a company floats on a stock exchange if the demand is greater than the supply, the shares are allocated to some applicants but not others, selected at random.

Bancassurance Companies offering both banking and insurance.

Bank bill *See* Acceptance credit.

Bank covenants *See* Covenant.

Bank for International Settlements (BIS) Controlled by central banks, the BIS was established to assist international financial co-ordination. It promotes international monetary co-ordination, provides research and statistical data, co-ordination and trusteeship for intergovernmental loans and acts as a central bank for national central banks, accepting deposits and making loans.

Bank of England The central bank of the United Kingdom, responsible for monetary policy. It oversees the affairs of other financial institutions, issues banknotes and coins, manages the national debt and exchange rate, and is lender of last resort.

Banker's draft A payment drawn upon the bank itself rather than the customer. It is therefore very reassuring to the supplier, because of the higher probability of being paid compared with a standard cheque.

Bankruptcy Commonly used to describe an individual or company that cannot meet its fixed commitments on borrowing which leads to legal action. However, technically, in the UK individuals become bankrupt whereas firms become insolvent.

Barriers to entry The obstacles that a company entering a market for the first time has to overcome to do well in that market.

Base-case strategy A continuation of current strategy.

Base rate The reference rate of interest that forms the basis for interest rates on bank loans, overdrafts and deposit rates.

Basic (FRS 3) earnings per share Includes deductions from profit of one-off exceptional items and goodwill amortization.

Basis point (bp) One-hundredth of 1 percent, usually applied to interest rates.

Bear An investor who takes the view that prices are likely to fall.

Bear fund Designed to do well when shares are falling in price.

Bearer bond The ownership of a bond is not recorded on a register. Possession of the bond is sufficient to receive interest, etc.

Bells and whistles Additional features placed on derivatives or securities, such as bonds, that are designed to attract investors or reduce issue costs.

Benchmark index An index of shares or other securities that sets a standard for fund manager performance, e.g. a fund manager controlling a portfolio of pharmaceutical shares would measure performance against a pharmaceutical index. This is calculated by an independent person to be representative of the sector.

Benefit–cost ratio A measure of present value per £ invested. Benefit–cost ratio = net present value (NPV) (q.v.) divided by initial outlay.

Beta A measure of the systematic risk of a financial security. In the capital asset pricing model (q.v.) it is a measure of the sensitivity to market movements of a financial security's return, as measured by the covariance between returns on the asset and returns on the market portfolio divided by the variance of the market portfolio. In practice a proxy (e.g. FTSE 100 index) is used for the market portfolio.

Bid premium The additional amount an acquirer has to offer above the pre-bid share price in order to succeed in a takeover offer.

Bid price The price at which a market maker will buy shares or a dealer in other markets will buy a security or commodity.

Bid–offer spread ('Bid–ask spread' in USA) The difference between the market maker's buy and sell prices.

Bid yield The yield to maturity on a bond given the market price at which the market makers will buy from investors.

Bill A legal document with a promise to pay or a demand for payment.

Bill of exchange A document setting out a commitment to pay a sum of money at a specified point in time, e.g. an importer commits itself to paying a supplier. Bills of exchange may be discounted – sold before maturity for less than face value.

BIMBO A buy-in management buyout. A combination of a management buyout and a buy-in. Outside managers join forces with existing managers to take over a company, subsidiary or unit.

Bird-in-the-hand fallacy The belief that dividends received earlier are discounted at a lower annual rate than those received in more distant years.

Black Monday 19 October 1987, the date of a large fall in stock market prices (also Monday 28 October 1929 in USA).

Black Wednesday 16 September 1992, a day of severe currency turbulence when sterling and the Italian lira devalued significantly and were forced to leave the Exchange Rate Mechanism.

Blue chip A company regarded as of the highest quality – little risk of a sharp decline in profits or market value.

Board of Directors People elected by shareholders to run a company.

Bond A debt obligation with a long-term maturity (more than one year), usually issued by firms and governments.

Bond covenant *See* Covenant.

Bonus issue *See* Scrip issue.

Book-building A book runner (lead manager) invites major institutional investors to suggest how many shares (or other financial securities) they would be interested in purchasing and at what price in a new issue or secondary issue of shares (or other financial securities). This helps to establish the price and allocate shares.

Book-to-market equity ratio The ratio of a firm's balance sheet net asset value to the total market value of its shares.

Bookrunner *See* Book-building

Book value Balance sheet value. Can be expressed on a per share basis.

Bootstrapping game *See* Price–earnings ratio game.

Borrowing capacity Limits to total borrowing levels imposed by lenders, often determined by available collateral.

Bottom line Profit attributable to the shareholders.

Bought deal An investment bank (the 'lead manager', perhaps together with co-managers of the issue) buys an entire security issue (e.g. shares) from a client corporation raising finance. The investment bank usually intends to then sell it out to institutional clients within hours.

Bourse Alternative name for a stock exchange. A French word, but used in other countries, particularly in Continental Europe.

Break-even analysis Analyzing the level of sales at which a project, division or business produces a zero profit (accounting emphasis).

Break-even NPV The point at which when a single variable is changed, the net present value (NPV) (q.v.) of a proposed project switches from positive to negative (or vice versa).

Break-up value The total value of separate parts of the company if the parts are sold off to the highest bidder.

British Bankers Association (BBA) Trade association of British banks. Sets model contracts, publishes interest rates, e.g. interbank rates, advocates on behalf of banks.

Broker Assists in the buying and selling of financial securities by acting as a 'go-between', helping to reduce search and information costs.

Broker-dealer An individual acting as agent for buyers and sellers, but who, at the same time, trades for his or her own account and may also be a market maker.

Bubble An explosive upward movement in financial security or other asset prices not based on fundamentally rational factors, followed by a crash.

Budget (national) Sets out government expenditure and revenue for the financial year. In the UK it is presented by the Chancellor of the Exchequer to the British Parliament.

Buffer stock Stock (raw material, work-in-progress or finished goods) held to reduce the negative effects (stock-out costs) of an unusually large usage of stock.

Building society A UK financial institution, the primary role of which is the provision of mortgages. Building societies are non-profit-making mutual organizations. Funding is mostly through small deposits by individuals.

Bulge bracket A leading investment bank.

Bull An investor taking the view that prices will rise.

Bulldog A foreign bond issued in the UK.

Bullet bond A bond where all the principal on a loan is repaid at maturity.

Bulletin board A computer-based site for infrequently traded shares on which investors (via brokers) can display their unfilled orders in the hope of finding a match.

Business angels Wealthy individuals prepared to invest between £10,000 and £250,000 in a start-up, early-stage or developing firm. They often have managerial and/or technical experience to offer the management team as well as equity and debt finance. Medium- to long-term investment in high-risk situation.

Business risk The risk associated with the underlying operations of a business. The variability of the firm's operating income, before interest income: this dispersion is caused purely by business-related factors and not by the debt burden.

Buy-back *See* Share repurchase.

BVCA British Private Equity and Venture Capital Association.

CAC 40 (Compagnie des Agents de Change 40 Index) A stock market index of French shares quoted in Paris.

Cadbury report The Committee on the Financial Aspects of Corporate Governance chaired by Sir Adrian Cadbury made recommendations on the role of directors and auditors, published in 1992.

Call option This gives the purchaser the right, but not the obligation, to buy a fixed quantity of a commodity, financial instrument or some other underlying asset at a given price, at or before a specified date.

Call-back features *See* Call option.

Called-up (issued) share capital The total value of shares sold by a company when expressed at par or nominal value.

Cap (1) An interest rate cap is a contract that effectively gives the purchaser the right to set a maximum level for interest rates payable. Compensation is paid to the purchaser of a cap if interest rates rise above an agreed level. (2) (Derivatives) Any feature that sets a maximum return, payout or cost.

Capex *See* Capital expenditure

Capital (1) Funding for a business – can be equity only or equity plus debt. (2) Another term for net worth – total assets minus total liabilities.

Capital Asset Pricing Model (CAPM) An asset (e.g. share) pricing theory that assumes that financial assets, in equilibrium, will be priced to produce rates of return that compensate investors for systematic risk as measured by the covariance of the assets' return with the market portfolio return (i.e. beta).

Capital budgeting The process of analyzing and selecting long-term capital investments.

Capital expenditure (Capex) The purchase of long-lived (more than one year) assets (i.e. fixed assets).

Capital gearing The extent to which the firm's total capital is in the form of debt.

Capital lease *See* Finance lease and Leasing.

Capital market Where those raising finance can do so by selling financial investments to investors, e.g. bonds, shares.

Capital rationing When funds are not available to finance all wealth-enhancing (positive NPV) projects.

Capital reconstruction (restructuring) Altering the shape of the firm's liabilities, e.g. increases/decreases in the amount of equity, increases/decreases in debt, and lengthening/shortening debt maturities.

Capital structure The proportion of the firm's capital that is equity or debt.

Capitalisation (1) An item of expenditure is taken on to the balance sheet and capitalized as an asset rather than written off against profits. (2) Short for market capitalization (q.v.).

Capitalisation factor A discount rate.

Capitalisation issue *See* Scrip issue.

Capitalisation rate Required rate of return for the class of risk.

Capped bonds The floating interest rate charged cannot rise above a specified level.

Captives A venture capital organisation that raises its capital from one institution (or a small group of institutions).

Cartel A group of otherwise competing firms entering into an agreement to set mutually acceptable prices, output levels and market shares for their products.

Cash-conversion cycle The stock-conversion period plus the debtor-conversion period minus the credit period granted by suppliers. It focuses on the length of time between the company's outlay on inputs and the receipt of money from the sale of goods.

Cash cow A company with low growth and stable market conditions with low investment needs. The company's competitive strength enables it to produce surplus cash.

Cash dividend A normal dividend by a company, paid in cash rather than a scrip dividend.

Cash settled In the derivatives market some contracts are physically settled at expiry date (e.g. pork bellies are delivered in return for cash under the derivative contract). However, many derivatives are not physically delivered; rather, a cash difference representing a gain or loss on the closed derivative position changes hands.

Causal ambiguity A potential imitator is unable to see clearly which resource is giving the sustainable competitive advantage to a firm, or it is difficult to identify the way in which the extraordinary resource was created in the first place.

CBOT *See* Chicago Board of Trade.

Central bank A bankers' bank and lender of last resort, which controls the credit system of an economy, e.g. controls note issue, acts as the government's bank, controls interest rates and regulates the country's banking system.

Central Counter-party (CCP) clearing house *See* Clearing house.

CEO (chief executive officer) The director with the highest power over the actions of the firm.

Certainty equivalent The value of a risk-free cash flow that would make the investor indifferent as to the choice between this safe cash flow or an alternative risky cash flow.

Certificate of deposit (CD) A deposit is made at a bank. A certificate confirming that a deposit has been made is given by the bank to the lender. This is normally a bearer security. Most CDs can then be sold in the secondary market whenever the depositor (firm or investor) needs cash.

CHAPS (Clearing House Automated Payment System) The UK same-day interbank clearing system for sterling payments (computer-based).

Characteristic line The line that best relates the return on a share to the return on a broad market index.

Chartist Security analyst who relies on historical price charts (and/or trading volumes) to predict future movements.

Chicago Board Options Exchange (CBOE) The largest options exchange in the world, trading options on shares, indices and interest rates.

Chicago Board of Trade (CBOT) A futures and options exchange in Chicago, USA – the world's oldest (established 1848).

Chicago Mercantile Exchange (CME) An exchange that trades a wide range of currency futures and options, interest rate futures and options, commodity futures and options and share index futures and options.

Chief executive officer (CEO) The manager/director in overall charge of the running of the business.

Chief executive's review (operational review) A comment, contained in a company's annual report and accounts, on performance, strategy and managerial intentions.

Chinese walls Barriers within a financial service company designed to prevent sensitive information being passed on to another branch of the organization.

CHIPS (Clearing House Interbank Payment System) The US system for settling US dollar payment the same day between banks.

Circle of competence The business areas that an individual thoroughly understands and is equipped to analyze.

City Code on Takeovers and Mergers Provides the main governing rules for UK-based companies engaged in merger activity. Self-regulated and administered by the Takeover Panel.

City of London A collective term for the financial institutions located in the financial district to the east of St Paul's Cathedral in London (also called the Square Mile). However, the term is also used to refer to all UK-based financial institutions, wherever they are located.

Clawback Existing shareholders often have the right to reclaim shares sold under a placing as though they were entitled to them under a rights issue.

Clean price On a bond the prices are generally quoted 'clean', i.e. without taking account of the accrued interest since the last coupon payment.

Clearing bank Member of the London Bankers' Clearing House, which clears cheques, settling indebtedness between two parties.

Clearing house An institution that registers, monitors, matches and settles mutual indebtedness between a number of individuals or organizations. The clearing house may also act as a counterparty to all participants in the market, providing reassurance to both buyer and seller.

Clearing a trade The stock exchange ensures that (1) all reports of a trade are reconciled to make sure all parties are in agreement as to the number of shares traded and the price; and (2) the buyer and seller have the cash and securities to do the deal.

Clientele effect In dividend theory the level of dividend may be influenced by shareholders preferring a dividend pattern which matches their consumption pattern and/or tax position.

Closed-end funds Collective investment vehicles (e.g. investment trusts) that do not create or redeem shares on a daily basis in response to increases and decreases in demand. They have a fixed number of shares for lengthy periods.

Closing out a futures position The act of taking a second action in the futures market (say, selling the future), which is exactly opposite to the first action (say, buying the future). Also called reversing the trade.

CLS bank *See* Continuous linked settlement.

Coefficient of determination, R-squared For single linear regression, this is the proportion of variation in the dependant variable that is related to the variation in the independent variable. A measure of the 'goodness of fit' in a regression equation.

Co-lead manager The title given to an underwriter (e.g. for a bond sale) who has joint lead manager status and may sometimes be engaged in structuring the transaction. Usually part of the selling group. Usually does not act as a bookrunner.

Collar A ceiling and floor interest rate placed on the variability of interest payable on a debt, often achieved by the simultaneous purchase of an interest rate cap and sale of an interest rate floor.

Collateral Property pledged by a borrower to protect the interests of the lender.

Collective funds *See* Pooled funds.

UK Corporate Governance Code A set of guidelines for best practice corporate governance. Oversight of the guidelines is by the Financial Reporting Council. The United Kingdom Listing Authority (q.v.) requires compliance or an explanation.

Commercial banking A range of banking services undertaken, including taking deposits and making loans, chequing facilities, trustee services and securities advisory services.

Commercial bill (bank bill or trade bill) A document expressing the commitment of a borrowing firm to repay a short-term debt at a fixed date in the future.

Commercial paper (CP) An unsecured note promising the holder (lender) a sum of money to be paid in a few days – average maturity of 40 days. If they are denominated in a foreign currency and placed outside the jurisdiction of the authorities of that currency, then the notes are Eurocommercial paper.

Commitment fee A fee payable in return for a commitment by a bank to lend money at some future date. In some cases the fee is payable only on the undrawn portion of the loan; in others the fee also applies to funds already drawn down under the arrangement.

Commodity product (1) Undifferentiated compared with competitor offerings in any customer-important way by factors such as performance, appearance, service support, and so on. For example, many personal computers are said to be commodity products. (2) Raw materials and foodstuffs.

Common stock The term used in the USA to describe ordinary shares in a company.

Companies Acts The series of laws enacted by Parliament governing the establishment and conduct of incorporated business enterprises. The Companies Act 2006 consolidated the Acts that preceded it.

Companies House The place where records are kept of every UK company. These accounts and so on are then made available to the general public.

Company registrar *See* Registrar.

Comparative advantage A firm or a country has a comparative advantage in the production of good X if the opportunity cost of producing a unit of X, in terms of other goods forgone, is lower, in that country compared with another country, or in that firm compared with another firm.

Competition Commission The Commission may obtain any information needed to investigate possible monopoly anti-competitive situations referred to it. It may then block anti-competitive action.

Competitive advantage (edge) The possession of extraordinary resources that allow a firm to rise above the others in its industry to generate exceptional long-run rates of return on capital employed.

Competitive floor Where shareholders receive a rate of return that only just induces them to put money into the firm and hold it there. This minimal rate of return occurs because of the high level of competition in the market for the firm's product.

Competitive position The competitive strength of the firm *vis-à-vis* rivals, suppliers, customer and substitutes in a product market.

Complementary product One that is generally bought alongside the product in question.

Compliance Methods of ensuring that financial market operators meet any legal and supervisory requirements.

Compound interest Interest is paid on the sum that accumulates, whether or not that sum comes from principal or from interest received at intermediate dates.

Compound return The income received on an investment is reinvested in the investment and future returns are gained on both the original capital and the ploughed-back income.

Concert party A group of investors, acting together or under the control of one person, that buys shares in a company.

Conflict of preferences There is a conflict of preferences between the primary investors wanting low-cost liquidity and low risk on invested funds, and the ultimate borrowers wanting long-term risk-bearing capital.

Conglomerate A holding company with subsidiaries with operations in different business areas.

Conglomerate bank A bank with a wide range of activities, products and markets.

Conglomerate merger The combining of two firms that operate in unrelated business areas.

Consideration The price paid for something.

Consolidated accounts All the income, costs, assets and liabilities of all group companies, whether wholly or partially owned, are brought together in the consolidated accounts. Consolidation must take place if 50 percent or more of a subsidiary's shares are held by the parent. If less than 50 percent of the shares are held, consolidation may still be required.

Consolidation of shares The number of shares is reduced and the nominal value of each remaining share rises.

Consumer Price Index (CPI) A measure of general inflation.

Continuing obligations Standards of behaviour and actions required of firms listed on the London Stock Exchange, enforced by the United Kingdom Listing Authority (q.v.).

Continuous Linked Settlement (CLS) A system designed to reduce the risk of failure of one counterparty to a foreign exchange transaction to fulfil an obligation. Payment of the two sides of the currency deal is made the day after the deal, organized by the CLS Bank.

Continuous order book Throughout the trading day orders are automatically matched and executed against one another.

Contract for differences (CFD) The buyer and seller agree to pay, in cash, at the closing of the contract, the difference between the opening and closing price of the underlying shares, multiplied by the number of shares in the contract. *See* Arnold, G.C. (2010) *The Financial Times Guide to Investing* 2nd Edition (Harlow: FT Prentice Hall) for more details.

Contractual theory Views the firm as a network of contracts, actual and implicit, which specify the roles to be played by various participants. Most participants bargain for low risk and a satisfactory return. Shareholders accept high risk in anticipation of any surplus returns after all other parties have been satisfied.

Contrarian Taking the opposite position to the generality of investors.

Controlling shareholder Any shareholder able to control the composition of the board of directors and therefore the direction of the company. Strictly speaking this is 50 percent, but even a 30 percent shareholder can exercise this degree of power, and therefore 30 percent is used as the cut-off point for some purposes.

Conventional cash flows Where an outflow is followed by a series of inflows, or a cash inflow is followed by a series of cash outflows.

Convergence The coming together of the futures price and the underlying share price as the final trading day of a futures contract approaches.

Conversion premium The difference between the current share price and the conversion price, expressed as a percentage of the current share price for convertible bonds.

Conversion price The share price at which convertible bonds may be converted.

Conversion ratio The nominal (par) value of a convertible bond divided by the conversion price. The number of shares available per bond.

Conversion value The value of a convertible bond if it were converted into ordinary shares at the current share price.

Convertible bonds Bonds that carry a rate of interest and give the owner the right to exchange the bonds at some stage in the future into ordinary shares according to a prearranged formula.

Convertible currency A currency that may be exchanged into another with no or few restrictions on individuals, companies or institutions, such as government prohibitions.

Convertible loan stock *See* Convertible bond.

Convertible preferred stock A preferred share that can be changed into another type of security, e.g. an ordinary share, at the holder's option.

Coredeal An international exchange for international debt-related securities, owned by the International Securities Markets Association (ISMA).

Corporate acquisition *See* Takeover (acquisition).

Corporate bond A bond issued by a company.

Corporate broker Stockbrokers that act on behalf of companies quoted on an exchange. For example, they may provide advice on market conditions or may represent the company to the market. Corporate brokers are knowledgeable about the share and other financial markets. They advise companies on fund raising (e.g. new issues). They try to generate interest among investors for the company's securities. They stand prepared to buy and sell companies' shares.

Corporate finance department of investment banks The department assisting firms in raising funds (e.g. rights issues, bond issues) and managing their finances.

Corporate governance The system of management and control of the corporation.

Corporate raider An organization that makes hostile takeover approaches for quoted companies.

Corporate value The present value of cash flows for the entire corporation within the planning horizon plus the present value of cash flows after the planning horizon plus the saleable value of assets not required for cash flow generation. Includes cash flows attributable to equity and debt holders.

Corporate venturing Large companies fostering the development of smaller enterprises through, say, joint capital development or equity capital provision.

Corporation tax A tax levied on the profits of companies.

Correlation coefficient A measure of the extent to which two variables show a relationship, expressed on a scale of -1 to $+1$.

Correlation scale A scale between −1 and +1 showing the degree of co-movement of two variables, e.g. the return on two shares. A value of −1 indicates exact opposite movement, while a value of +1 indicates perfect movement in the same direction.

Cost of capital The rate of return that a company has to offer finance providers to induce them to buy and hold a financial security.

Cost leadership strategy Standard no-frills product. Emphasis on scale economies and other cost advantages.

Counterparty The buyer for a seller or the seller for a buyer.

Counterparty risk The risk that a counterparty to a contract defaults and does not fulfil its obligations.

Country risk Risk to transactions overseas or assets held abroad due to political, legal, regulatory or settlement changes or difficulties, e.g. nationalization or law forbidding repatriation of profits.

Coupons An attachment to bond or loan note documents that may be separated and serve as evidence of entitlement to interest. Nowadays it refers to the interest itself: the nominal annual rate of interest expressed as a percentage of the principal value.

Covariance The extent to which two variables move together.

Covenant A solemn agreement.

Cover Offsetting one position in a financial security with an equal and opposite transaction in the same or linked (e.g. derivative) security.

Covered call option writing Writing a call option on an underlying when the writer owns at least the number of underlying securities included in the option.

Covered warrants The same as warrants except that financial institutions issue them, selling the right to buy or sell shares in industrial and commercial companies.

Creative accounting The drawing up of accounts that obey the letter of the law and accounting body rules but that involve the manipulation of accounts to show the most favourable profit and balance sheet.

Credit derivative An instrument for which the payoff is linked to changes in the underlying's credit standing, e.g. if the credit rating changes on a bond issued by a company from BBB− to D the holder will receive a payout on a credit derivative (sold by a financial institution) which takes as its underlying that particular company's bond.

Credit facility or credit line A borrowing arrangement with a bank or other lender under which borrowing may fluctuate at the behest of the borrower up to a fixed total amount, e.g. overdraft, revolving facility.

Credit insurance An insurance policy that pays out on trade debts held by the firm when customers fail to meet their obligations.

Credit period The average length of time between the purchase of inputs and the payment for them. Equal to the average level of creditors divided by the purchases on credit per day.

Credit rating An estimate of the quality of a debt from the lender's viewpoint in terms of the likelihood of interest and capital not being paid and of the extent to which the lender is protected in the event of default. Credit-rating agencies are paid fees by companies, governments, etc. wishing to attract lenders.

Credit risk The risk that a counterparty to a financial transaction will fail to fulfil its obligation.

Credit risk premium or credit spread The additional yield (over, say, reputable government bonds) on a debt instrument due to the borrower's additional perceived probability of default.

Credit union A non-profit organization accepting deposits and making loans, operated as a co-operative.

Creditor One to whom a debt is owed.

Crest or CREST An electronic means of settlement and registration of shares and other securities following a sale on the London Stock Exchange, operated by CRESTCo.

Crown jewels defence In a hostile merger situation, the target sells off the most attractive parts of the business.

Cum-dividend (1) When an investor buys a bond (q.v.) when it is still designated cum-dividend or cum-coupon the investor is entitled to the accrued interest since the last coupon was paid. (2) A share (q.v.) designated cum-dividend indicates that the buyer will be entitled to a dividend recently announced by the company.

Cum-rights Shares bought on the stock market prior to the ex-rights day are designated cum-rights and carry to the new owner the right to subscribe for the new shares in the rights issue.

Cumulative If a payment (interest or dividend) on a bond (q.v.) or share (q.v.) is missed in one period those securities are given priority when the next payment is made. These arrears must be cleared up before shareholders received dividends.

Currency swap *See* Swap.

Current account deficit *See* Balance of payment.

Current asset value (net) Current assets (cash, accounts receivable, inventory) minus current liabilities (also called working capital).

Current assets Cash and other assets that can be rapidly turned into cash. Includes stocks of raw materials, partially finished goods and finished goods, debtors and investments expected to be sold within one year.

Current liabilities Amounts owed that the company expects to have to pay within the next year.

Current ratio The ratio of current liabilities to the current assets of a business.

Current yield (flat yield, income yield or running yield) The ratio of the coupon (q.v.) on a bond (q.v.) to its current market price.

Cyclical companies (industries, shares) Those companies in which profits are particularly sensitive to the growth level in the economy, which may be cyclical.

Daily Official List (DOL) The daily record setting out the prices of all trades in securities conducted on the London Stock Exchange.

Darling A stock market darling is one that receives a lot of attention and is regarded as very attractive.

Dawn raid An acquirer acts with such speed in buying the shares of the target company that the raider achieves the objective of a substantial stake in the target before its management has time to react.

DAX 30 (Deutsche Aktienindex) A stock market index of German shares quoted on Deutsche Börse (q.v.).

Debentures Bonds issued with redemption dates a number of years into the future or irredeemable. Usually secured against specific assets (mortgage debentures) or through a floating charge on the firm's assets (floating debentures). In the USA debenture means an unsecured debt with a fixed coupon.

Debt An obligation to pay.

Debt capital Capital raised with (usually) a fixed obligation in terms of interest and principal payments.

Debt maturity The length of time left until the repayment on a debt becomes due.

Debt-to-equity ratio The ratio of a company's long-term debt to shareholders' funds.

Debtor conversion period The average number of days to convert customer debts into cash. Equal to the average value of debtors divided by the average value of sales per day.

Debtors Those who owe a debt.

Declining (reducing) balance method of depreciation The amount by which an asset is depreciated declines from one year to the next as it is determined by a constant percentage of the asset's depreciated value at the start of each year.

Deep discounted bonds Bonds sold well below par value, usually because they have little or no coupon.

Deep discounted rights issue A rights issue price is much less than the present market price of the old shares.

Default A failure to make agreed payments of interest or principal, or failure to comply with some other provision.

Defensive industries Those industries where profits are not particularly sensitive to the growth level in the economy.

Defensive shares Having a beta value of less than 1.

Deferred ordinary shares (1) Rank below preferred ordinary shares for dividends. So, if profits are low deferred ordinary holders may not receive a dividend. However, if the company achieves a predetermined level of profit or other performance target the deferred ordinary shares often entitle the owner to a higher-than-normal dividend. (2) The right to the dividend is deferred for a set period, after which the holders rank equal with ordinary shareholders.

Deferred tax With a fixed asset the writing down allowance, which can be used to reduce current tax payable, is often greater than the depreciation charge as determined by the company's accounting policy. The difference is called a timing difference. A deferred tax provision is the difference between (i) the corporation tax actually payable on the taxable trading profit and (ii) the tax that would have been payable if the taxable trading profit is the same as the accounting profit (using normal depreciation not writing down allowance).

Dematerialization Traditionally the evidence of financial security ownership is by written statements on paper (e.g. share certificates). Increasingly such information is being placed on electronic records and paper evidence is being abandoned.

Demerger The separation of companies or business units that are currently under one corporate umbrella. It applies particularly to the unravelling of a merger.

Depletion A reduction in the value of a natural resource, e.g. oil in the ground, owned by a company.

Depositary receipts Certificates, representing evidence of ownership of a company's shares (or other securities) held by a depository. Depositary receipts (DRs) are negotiable (can be traded) certificates that represent ownership of a given number of a company's shares and that can be listed and traded independently from the underlying shares. There are a number of forms of DRs, including American depositary receipts (ADRs), global depositary receipts (GDRs), euro depositary receipts (EDRs) and retail depositary receipts (RDRs).

Derivative A financial asset (instrument), the performance of which is based on (derived from) the behaviour of the value of an underlying asset.

Deutsche Börse AG The German Stock Exchange based in Frankfurt.

Development capital Second-stage finance (following seed finance – *see* Seedcorn capital or money *and* Early-stage capital) to permit business expansion.

Differentiated product One that is slightly different in significant ways from those supplied by other companies. The unique nature of the product/service offered allows for a premium price to be charged.

Diluted earnings per share Takes into account any additional shares that may be issued in the future under executive share option schemes and other commitments.

Dilution The effect on the earnings and voting power per ordinary share from an increase in the number of shares issued without a corresponding increase in the firm's earnings.

Diminishing marginal utility Successive equal increments in quantity of a good (or money) yield smaller and smaller increases in utility.

Direct foreign investment The cross-border purchase of commercial assets such as factories and industrial plant for productive purposes.

Directors' dealings The purchase or sale of shares in their own company. This is legal (except at certain times of the company's year). Some investors examine directors' dealings to decide whether to buy or sell.

Directors' report Information and commentary on company performance and other matters contained in a company's annual report and accounts.

Dirty price On a bond a buyer pays a total of the clean price and the accrued interest since the last coupon payment.

Disclosure of shareholdings If a stake of 3 percent or more is held by one shareholder in a UK public company, then this has to be declared to the company.

Discount (1) The amount below face value at which a financial claim sells, e.g. bill of exchange or zero coupon bond. (2) The extent to which an investment trust's shares sell below the net asset value. (3) The amount by which a future value of a currency is less than its spot value. (4) The action of purchasing financial instruments, e.g. bills, at a discount. (5) The degree to which a security sells below its issue price in the secondary market. (6) The process of equating a cash flow at some future date with today's value using the time value of money.

Discount house An institution that purchases promissory notes and resells them or holds them until maturity.

Discount market deposit Originally it was money deposited with a London discount house. However, there is now a collection of UK institutions and dealers in money market instruments such as trade bills. These are normally repayable at call or very short term. Clearing banks are the usual depositors.

Discount rate (1) The rate of return used to discount cash flows received in future years. It is the opportunity cost of capital given the risk class of the future cash flows. (2) The rate of interest at which some central banks lend money to the banking system.

Discounted cash flow Future cash flows are converted into the common denominator of time zero money by adjusting for the time value of money.

Discounted payback The period of time required to recover initial cash outflow when the cash inflows are discounted at the opportunity cost of capital.

Discounting The process of reducing future cash flows to a present value using an appropriate discount rate.

Disintermediation Borrowing firms bypassing financial institutions and obtaining debt finance directly from the market.

Disinvest To sell an investment.

Diversifiable risk *See* Unsystematic risk.

Diversification To invest in varied projects, enterprises, financial securities, products, markets, etc.

Divestiture (divestment) The selling off of assets or subsidiary businesses by a company or individual.

Dividend That part of profit paid to ordinary shareholders, usually on a regular basis.

Dividend cover The number of times net profits available for distribution exceed the dividend actually paid or declared. Earnings per share divided by gross dividend per share, *or* total post-tax profits divided by total dividend payout.

Dividend discount model – *See* Dividend valuation models.

Dividend payout ratio The percentage of a company's earnings paid out as dividends.

Dividend per share The total amount paid or due to be paid in dividends for the year (interim and final) divided by the number of shares in issue.

Dividend policy The determination of the proportion of profits paid out to shareholders over the longer term.

Dividend reinvestment plan (DRIP) A shareholder receives shares from a company in lieu of a cash dividend. This avoids the cost and trouble of receiving cash and then reinvesting.

Dividend valuation models (DVM) These methods of share valuation are based on the premise that the market value of ordinary shares represents the sum of the expected future dividend flows, to infinity, discounted to present value.

Dividend yield The amount of dividend paid on each share as a percentage of the share price.

Divisible projects It is possible to undertake a fraction of a project.

Divorce of ownership and control In large corporations shareholders own the firm but may not be able to exercise control. Managers often have control because of a diffuse and divided shareholder body, proxy votes and apathy.

Dominance When one (investment) possibility is clearly preferable to a risk-averse investor because it possesses a better expected return than another possibility for the same level of risk.

Dow or Dow Jones Industrial Average The best-known index of movements in the price of US stocks and shares. There are 30 shares in the index.

Drawdown arrangement A loan facility is established and the borrower uses it (takes the money available) in stages as the funds are required.

Due diligence When a transaction is contemplated, such as a merger or a loan, a detailed investigation of the company is carried out, usually by specialists, to ensure that its condition is suitable for the transaction.

Early-settlement discount The reduction of a debt owed if it is paid at an early date.

Early-stage capital Funds for initial manufacturing and sales for a newly formed company. High-risk capital available from entrepreneurs, business angels and venture capital funds.

Earning power The earning (profit) capacity of a business in a normal year. What the company might be expected to earn year after year if the business conditions continue unchanged.

Earnings Profits, usually after deduction of tax.

Earnings guidance A company guiding analysts to estimates of profits for the current period.

Earnings multiple Price–earnings ratio.

Earnings per share (EPS) Profit after tax and interest divided by number of shares in issue.

Earnings yield Earnings per share divided by current market price of share.

Earn-out The purchase price of a company is linked to the future profits performance. Future instalments of the purchase price may be adjusted if the company performs better or worse than expected.

EBIT A company's earnings (profits) before interest and taxes are deducted.

EBITDA Earnings before interest, taxation, depreciation and amortization. Or as cynics have it: Earnings Before I Tricked The Dumb Auditor.

Economic Book Value A term used by Stern Stewart & Co. It is based on the balance sheet capital employed figure subject to a number of adjustments.

Economic exposure *See* Economic risk.

Economic franchise Pricing power combined with strong barriers to entry. The strength and durability of an economic franchise are determined by (1) the structure of the industry; and (2) the ability of the firm to rise above its rivals in its industry and generate exceptional long-run rates of return on capital employed.

Economic order quantity (EOQ) The quantity of inventory items (e.g. raw materials) to order on each occasion which minimizes the combined costs of ordering and holding stock.

Economic profit (EP) For a period the economic profit is the amount earned by a business after deducting all operating expenses and a charge for the opportunity cost of the capital employed.

Economic risk The risk that a company's economic value may decline as a result of currency movements causing a loss in competitive strength.

Economic Value Added (EVA) Developed by Stern Stewart & Co. A value-based metric of corporate performance that multiplies the invested capital (after adjustments) by the spread between the (adjusted) actual return on capital and the weighted average cost of capital (q.v.). The adjustments are to the profit figures to obtain the actual return and to the balance sheet to obtain the invested capital figure.

Economies of scale Larger size of output often leads to lower cost per unit of output.

Economies of scope The ability to reduce the unit costs of an item by sharing some costs between a number of product lines, e.g. using the same truck to deliver both ketchup and beans to a store.

Effective annual rate *See* Annual percentage rate.

Efficient market hypothesis (EMH) The EMH implies that new information is incorporated into a share price (1) rapidly and (2) rationally. *See also* Efficient stock market.

Efficient portfolio A portfolio that offers the highest expected return for a given level of risk (standard deviation) and the lowest risk for its expected return.

Efficient stock market Share prices rationally reflect available information. In an efficient market no trader will be presented with an opportunity for making an abnormal return, except by chance. *See also* Efficient market hypothesis.

EGM *See* Extraordinary general meeting.

Electronic funds transfer at a point of sale (EFTPOS) A computerized system allowing the automatic transfer of money from a buyer to a seller of goods or services at the time of sale.

Electronic settlement Transferring shares from sellers to buyers without certificates – it is a computer entry only.

Emerging markets Security markets in newly industrializing countries and/or capital markets at an early stage of development.

Employee share ownership plans (ESOP) Schemes designed to encourage employees to build up a share-holding in their company.

Endowment policies (savings schemes) Insurance policies in which a lump sum is payable, either at the end of the term of the policy or on death during the term of the policy.

Enfranchisement Granting voting rights to holders of non-voting shares.

Enterprise investment scheme (EIS) Tax relief is available to investors in qualifying company shares (unquoted firms not involved in financial investment and property).

Enterprise value The sum of a company's total equity market capitalization and borrowings.

Entrepreneur Defined by economists as the owner-manager of a firm. Usually supplies capital, organizes production, decides on strategic direction and bears risk.

Equilibrium in markets When the forces of supply and demand are evenly balanced.

Equities An ownership share of a business, each equity share representing an equal stake in the business. The risk capital of a business.

Equitization An increasing emphasis placed on share (equity) finance and stock exchanges in economies around the world. A growing equity culture.

Equity approach An economic profit approach to value measurement that deducts interest from operating profit as well as tax. From this is deducted the required return on equity funds devoted to the activity only (i.e. does not include required return for debt capital).

Equity indices Baskets of shares indicating the movement of the equity market as a whole or subsets of the markets.

Equity kicker (sweetener) The attachment to a bond or other debt finance of some rights to participate in and benefit from a good performance (e.g. to exercise an option to purchase shares). Often used with mezzanine finance (q.v.) and high-yield bonds.

Equity-linked bonds Bonds that also carry the right to either convert to ordinary shares (convertibles) or to purchase ordinary shares while retaining ownership of the bond (warrants) – *see* equity warrants.

Equity shareholders' funds *See* Shareholders' funds.

Equity warrants A security issued by a company that gives to the owners the right but not the obligation to purchase shares in the company from the company at a fixed price during or at the end of a specified time period.

Euribor Short-term interest rates in the interbank market (very stable and safe banks lending to each other) in the currency of euros.

Euro The name of the single European currency in use since 1999 in the eurozone.

Euro medium-term notes (EMTN) *See* Medium-term note.

Euro Swiss francs Swiss francs traded in the eurocurrency market.

Eurobond Bond sold outside the jurisdiction of the country in whose currency the bond is denominated. For example, a bond issued in yen outside Japan.

Eurocommercial paper *See* Commercial paper.

Eurocredit A market in credit outside the jurisdiction of the country in whose currency the loan is denominated. (Borrowers can gain access to medium-term bank lending, for 1–15 years.)

Eurocurrency Currency held outside its country of origin, for example, Australian dollars held outside Australia. Note: this market existed long before the creation of the currency in the eurozone. It has no connection with the euro.

Eurocurrency banking Transactions in a currency other than the host country's currency. For example, transactions in Canadian dollars in London. No connection with the currency in the eurozone.

Eurocurrency deposits Short-term wholesale money market deposits made in the eurocurrency market.

Eurodeposit account Short-term wholesale money market deposits are made into an account set up for that purpose made in the eurocurrency market.

Eurodollar A deposit or credit of dollars held outside the regulation of the US authorities, say in Tokyo, London or Paris. No connection with the currency in the eurozone.

Euromarkets Informal (unregulated) markets in money held outside the jurisdiction of the country of origin, e.g. Swiss francs lending outside the control of the Swiss authorities – perhaps the francs are in London. No connection with the euro, the currency in use in the eurozone. Euromarkets began in the late 1950s and now encompass the eurocurrency, eurocredit and eurobond markets as well as over-the-counter derivatives and commodity markets.

Euronext The combined financial stock market comprising the French, Dutch, Belgian and Portuguese bourses. It is now merged with the New York Stock Exchange to form NYSE.Euronext.

Euronext.liffe Euronext, the organization combining the French, Dutch, Belgian and Portuguese stock markets, bought LIFFE (q.v.) and renamed it Euronext.liffe.

Euronotes A short-term debt security. These are normally issued at a discount to face value for periods of one, three and six months' maturity. They are tradeable once issued and are bearer securities. They are issued outside the jurisdiction of the currency stated on the note. They are backed up by a revolving underwriting facility, which ensures that the issuer will be able to raise funds.

European Monetary Union (EMU) A single currency with a single central bank having control over interest rates being created for those EU member states that join. The process of moving towards a monetary union began in 1999.

European-style options Options that can be exercised only by the purchaser on a predetermined future date.

Eurosecurities Financial securities such as bonds, commercial paper, ordinary shares, convertibles, floating rate notes, medium-term notes and promissory notes offered on or traded in the euromarkets.

Eurosterling Sterling deposit and loans in the eurocurrency market.

Euroyen Japanese yen deposits and loans in the eurocurrency market.

Eurozone Those countries that joined together in adopting the euro as their currency in 1999 and those that joined them later.

Event risk The risk that some future event may increase the risk on a financial investment, e.g. an earthquake event affects returns on Japanese bonds.

Ex-ante Intended, desired or expected before the event.

Ex-coupon A bond sold without the right to the next interest payment – *see* ex-dividend.

Ex-dividend When a share or bond is designated ex-dividend a purchaser will not be entitled to a recently announced dividend or the accrued interest on the bond since the last coupon – the old owner will receive the dividend (coupon).

Ex-post The value of some variable after the event.

Ex-rights When a share goes 'ex-rights' any purchaser of a share after that date will not have a right to subscribe for new shares in the rights issue.

Ex-rights price of a share The theoretical market price following a rights issue.

Exceptional items Gains or costs that are part of the company's ordinary activities but either are unusual in themselves or have an exceptionally large impact on profits that year.

Excess return (ER) (1) The return above the level expected given the level of risk taken. (2) A value metric that examines the amount of capital invested in previous years and then charges the company for its use over the years. It also credits companies for the returns shareholders can make from the money paid to them (e.g. as dividends) when reinvested in the market. Excess return expressed in present value terms equals actual wealth expressed in present value terms minus expected wealth expressed in present value terms.

Exchange controls The state controls the purchase and sale of currencies by its residents.

Exchange rate The price of one currency expressed in terms of another.

Exchangeable bond A bond that entitles the owner to choose at a later date whether to exchange the bond for shares in a company. The shares are in a company other than the one that issued the bond.

Exclusive franchise *See* Economic franchise.

Execution-only brokers A stockbroker who will buy or sell shares cheaply but will not give advice or other services.

Executive directors Manage day-to-day activities of the firms as well as contributing to boardroom discussion of company-wide policy and strategic direction.

Exercise price (strike price) The price at which an underlying will be bought (call) or sold (put) under an option contract.

Exit (1) The term used to describe the point at which a venture capitalist can recoup some or all of the investment made. (2) The closing of a position created by a transaction.

Exit barrier A factor preventing firms from stopping production in a particular industry.

Exotic A term used to describe an unusual financial transaction, e.g. exotic option, exotic currency (i.e. one with few trades).

Expansion capital Capital needed by companies at a fast-development phase to increase production capacity or to increase working capital and capital for the further development of the product or market. Venture capital is often used.

Expectations hypothesis of the term structure of interest rates (yield curve)
Long-term interest rates reflect the market consensus on the changes in short-term interest rates.

Expectations theory of foreign exchange The current forward exchange rate is an unbiased predictor of the spot rate at that point in the future.

Expected return The mean or average outcome calculated by weighting each of the possible outcomes by the probability of occurrence and then summing the result.

Experience curve The cost of performing a task reduces as experience is gained through repetition.

Expiry date of an option The time when the rights to buy or sell the option cease.

External finance Outside finance raised by a firm, i.e. finance that it did not generate internally, for example through profits retention.

External metrics Measures of corporate performance that are accessible to individuals outside the firm and concern the performance of the firm as a whole.

extraMARK A grouping or subset of investment companies and products on the Official List (q.v.) of the London Stock Exchange.

Extraordinary general meeting (EGM) A meeting of the company (shareholders and directors) other than the annual general meeting (q.v.). It may be convened when the directors think fit. However, shareholders holding more than 5 percent of the paid-up share capital carrying voting rights can requisition a meeting.

Extraordinary resources Those that give the firm a competitive edge. A resource that, when combined with other (ordinary) resources, enables the firm to outperform competitors and create new value-generating opportunities. Critical extraordinary resources determine what a firm can do successfully.

Face value *See* Par value.

Factor model A model that relates the returns on a security to that security's sensitivity to the movements of various factors (e.g. GDP growth, inflation) common to all shares.

Factor risk/non-factor risk A factor risk is a systematic risk in multifactor models describing the relationship between risk and return for fully diversified investors. Non-factor risk is unsystematic risk in multifactor models.

Factoring To borrow against the security of trade debtors. Factoring companies also provide additional services such as sales ledger administration and credit insurance.

Fair game In the context of a stock market, this is where some investors and fund raisers are not able to benefit at the expense of other participants. The market is regulated to avoid abuse, negligence and fraud. It is cheap to carry out transactions and the market provides high liquidity.

Fair value (fair market value) The amount an asset could be exchanged for in an arm's-length transaction between informed and willing parties.

Fallen angel Debt that used to rate as investment grade but that is now regarded as junk, mezzanine finance (q.v.) or high-yield finance.

FEER (Fundamental Equilibrium Exchange Rate) The exchange rate between two currencies that results in a sustainable current-account balance. The exchange rate is expected to move (in theory) so as to achieve current-account balance.

Filter approach to investment A technique for examining shares using historical price trends. The trader focuses on the long-term trends by filtering out short-term movements.

Final dividend The dividend announced with the annual accounts. The final dividend plus the interim dividend make the total dividend for the year for a company that reports results every six months.

Finance house A financial institution offering to supply finance in the form of hire purchase, leasing and other forms of instalment credit.

Finance lease (also called capital lease, financial lease or full payout lease) The lessor expects to recover the full cost (or almost the full cost) of the asset plus interest, over the period of the lease.

Financial assets (securities, instruments) or financial claim Contracts that state agreement about the exchange of money in the future, e.g. shares, bonds, bank loans, derivatives.

Financial distress Obligations to creditors are not met or are met with difficulty.

Financial gearing (leverage) *See* Gearing.

Financial Reporting Council (FRC) The UK's independent regulator responsible for ensuring high-quality corporate reporting, accounts and governance.

Financial risk The additional variability in a firm's returns to shareholders and the additional risk of insolvency that arises because the financial structure contains debt.

Financial Services and Markets Act The 2000 Act (and orders made under it) form the bedrock of financial regulations in the UK.

Financial Services Authority (FSA) The chief financial services regulator in the UK.

Financial slack Having cash (or near-cash) and/or spare debt capacity available to take up opportunities as they appear.

Financing gap The gap in the provision of finance for medium-sized, fast-growing firms. Often these firms are too large or fast-growing to ask the individual shareholders for more funds or to obtain sufficient bank finance. Also they are not ready to launch on the stock market.

Financing-type decision In an investment project the initial cash flow is positive.

Finished goods inventory period The number of days for which finished goods await delivery to customers. Equal to the average value of finished goods in stock divided by the average goods sold per day.

Fisher's equation The money rate of return m is related to the real rate of return h and the expected inflation rate i through the following equation: $(1 + m) = (1 + h)(1 + i)$.

Fixed assets Those held not for resale but for use in the business.

Fixed charge (e.g. fixed charged debenture or loan) Specific asset(s) assigned as collateral security for a debt.

Fixed cost A cost that does not vary according to the amount of goods or services that are produced. Those business costs that have to be paid, regardless of the firm's turnover and activity.

Fixed exchange rate The national authorities act to ensure that the rate of exchange between two currencies is constant.

Fixed interest (fixed rate) The Interest rate charged on a debt is constant over its life.

Fixed-interest securities Strictly, the term applies to securities, such as bonds, on which the holder receives a predetermined interest pattern on the par value (e.g. gilts, corporate bonds, eurobonds). However, the term is also used for debt securities even when there is no regular interest, e.g. zero-coupon bonds (q.v.), and when the interest varies, as with floating rate notes (q.v.), for example.

Flat rate The rate of interest quoted by a hire purchase company (or other lender) to a hiree that fails to reflect properly the true interest rate being charged as measured by the annual percentage rate (APR) (q.v.).

Flat yield *See* Yield.

Float (1) The difference between the cash balance shown on a firm's chequebook and the bank account. Caused by delays in the transfer of funds between bank accounts. (2) An exchange rate that is permitted to vary against other currencies. (3) An issuance of shares to the public by a company joining a stock market. (4) For insurance companies, the pool of money held in the firm in readiness to pay claims.

Floating charge The total assets of the company or an individual are used as collateral security for a debt. There is no specific asset assigned as collateral.

Floating exchange rate A rate of exchange that is not fixed by national authorities but fluctuates depending on demand and supply for the currency.

Floating-rate borrowing (floating interest) The rate of interest on a loan varies with a standard reference rate, e.g. LIBOR.

Floating-rate notes (FRNs) Notes issued in which the coupon fluctuates according to a benchmark interest rate charge (e.g. LIBOR – q.v.). Issued in the euromarkets generally with maturities of 7–15 years. Reverse floaters are those on which the interest rate declines as LIBOR rises.

Floor An agreement whereby, if interest rates fall below an agreed level, the seller (floor writer) makes compensatory payments to the floor buyer.

Flotation The issue of shares in a company for the first time on a stock exchange.

Focus strategy The selection of a segment in the industry to serve to the exclusion of others.

'Footsie' Nickname for FTSE 100 index. Trademarked.

Foreign banking Transactions in the home currency with non-residents.

Foreign bond A bond denominated in the currency of the country where it is issued when the issuer is a non-resident.

Foreign exchange control Limits are placed by a government on the purchase and sale of foreign currency.

Foreign exchange markets (Forex or FX) Markets that facilitate the exchange of one currency into another.

Forex A contraction of 'foreign exchange'.

Forfaiting A bank (or other lender) purchases a number of sales invoices or promissory notes from an exporting company; usually the importer's bank guarantees the invoices.

Forward A contract between two parties to undertake an exchange at an agreed future date at a price agreed now.

Forward agreement *See* Forward.

Forward-rate agreement (FRA) An agreement about the future level of interest rates. Compensation is paid by one party to the other to the extent that market interest rates deviate from the 'agreed' rate.

Founders' shares Dividends are paid only after all other categories of equity shares have received fixed rates of dividend. They usually carry a number of special voting rights over certain company matters.

Free cash flow Cash generated by a business not required for operations or for reinvestment. Profit before depreciation, amortization and provisions, but after interest, tax, capital expenditure on long-lived items and increases in working capital necessary to maintain the company's competitive position and accept all value-generating investments.

Free float (free capital) The proportion of a quoted company's shares not held by those closest (e.g. directors, founding families) to the company who may be unlikely to sell their shares.

Frequency function (probability or frequency distribution) The organization of data to show the probabilities of certain values occurring.

Friendly mergers The two companies agree to a merger.

Friendly society A mutual (co-operative) organization involved in saving and lending.

FRS 3 *See* Basic (FRS 3) earnings per share.

FTSE 100 share index An index representing the UK's 100 largest listed shares. An average weighted by market capitalization.

FTSE Actuaries All-Share Index (the 'All-Share') The most representative index of UK shares, reflecting about 620 companies' shares.

FTSE Eurofirst300 An index of European shares.

FTSE Global All Cap An index of share price movements around the world.

FTSE International (Financial Times and the London Stock Exchange) This organization calculates a range of share indices published on a regular (usually daily) basis.

Full-payout lease *See* Leasing.

Fund management Investment of and administering a quantity of money, e.g. pension fund, insurance fund, on behalf of the fund's owners.

Fund raising Companies can raise money through rights issues, etc.

Fundamental analysts Individuals that try to estimate a share's true value, based on future returns to the company. Data from many sources are used, e.g. company accounts, economic trends, social trends and technological changes.

Fundamental beta An adjustment to the risk premium on the average share, which amalgamates a number of operating and financial characteristics of the specific company being examined.

Fungible Interchangeable securities; can be exchanged for each other on identical terms.

Future A contract between two parties to undertake a transaction at an agreed price on a specified future date.

GAAP Generally accepted accounting principles. US accounting rules for reporting results. However, the term has come to mean any widely accepted set of accounting conventions.

GDP (nominal, real) Gross domestic product, the sum of all output of goods and services produced by a nation. Nominal means including inflation, and real means with inflation removed.

Gearing (financial gearing) The proportion of debt capital in the overall capital structure. Also called leverage. High gearing can lead to exaggeratedly high returns if things go well or exaggerated losses if things do not go well.

Gearing (operating) The extent to which the firm's total costs are fixed. This influences the break-even point and the sensitivity of profits to changes in sales level.

General inflation The process of steadily rising prices resulting in the diminishing purchasing power of a given nominal sum of money. Measured by an overall price index that follows the price changes of a 'basket' of goods and services through time.

General insurance Insurance against specific contingencies, e.g. fire, theft and accident.

Geometric mean The geometric mean of a set of n positive numbers is the nth root of their product, e.g. the geometric mean of 2 and 5 is $\sqrt{2 \times 5} = \sqrt{10} = 3.16$. The compound rate of return.

Gilts (gilt-edged securities) Fixed-interest UK government securities (bonds) traded on the London Stock Exchange. A means for the UK government to raise finance from savers. They usually offer regular interest and a redemption amount paid years in the future.

Globalisation The increasing internationalisation of trade, particularly financial product transactions. The integration of economic and capital markets throughout the world.

Goal congruence The aligning of the actions of senior management with the interests of shareholders.

Going concern A judgement as to whether a company has sufficient financial strength to continue for at least one year. Accounts are usually drawn up on the assumption that the business is a going concern.

Going long Buying a financial security (e.g. a share) in the hope that its price will rise.

Going public Market jargon used when a company becomes quoted on a stock exchange (the company may have been a public limited company, plc, for years before this).

Going short *See* Short selling.

Golden handcuffs Financial inducements to remain working for a firm.

Golden parachutes In a hostile merger situation, managers will receive large payoffs if the firm is acquired.

Golden shares Shares with extraordinary special powers over the company, e.g. power of veto over a merger.

Good growth When a firm grows by investment in positive-performance-spread activities.

Goodwill An accounting term for the difference between the amount that a company pays for another company and the sum of the market value of that company's individual assets (after deducting all liabilities). Goodwill is thus an intangible asset representing things such as the value of the company's brand names and the skills of its employees.

Grace period A lender grants the borrower a delay in the repayment of interest and/or principal at the outset of a lending agreement.

Greenbury Committee report Recommendations on corporate governance (1995).

Greenmail Key shareholders try to obtain a reward (e.g. the repurchase of their shares at a premium) from the company for not selling to a hostile bidder or becoming a bidder themselves.

Greenshoe An option that permits an issuing house, when assisting a corporation in a new issue (initial public offering), to sell more shares than originally planned. They may do this if demand is particularly strong.

Grey market A market in shares where the shares have not yet come into existence, e.g. in the period between investors being told they will receive shares in a new issue and the actual receipt they may sell on the expectation of obtaining them later.

Gross dividend yield $\dfrac{\text{Gross (before tax) dividend per share}}{\text{share price}} \times 100$

Gross domestic product *See* GDP.

Gross margin *See* Gross profit margin.

Gross present value The total present value of all the cash flows, excluding the initial investment.

Gross profit Turnover less cost of sales.

Gross profit margin (gross margin) Profit defined as sales minus cost of sales expressed as a percentage of sales.

Gross redemption yield (gross yield to redemption) A calculation of the redemption yield (*see* Yield) before tax.

Growth industries Those industries that grow almost regardless of the state of the economy.

Guaranteed loan stock (bond) An organisation other than the borrower guarantees to the lender the repayment of the principal plus the interest payment.

Hampel report A follow-up to the Cadbury (1992) and Greenbury (1995) reports on corporate governance. Chaired by Sir Ronald Hampel and published in 1998.

Hang Seng Index Main index for Hong Kong shares.

Hard capital rationing Agencies external to the firm will not supply unlimited amounts of investment capital, even though positive NPV projects are identified.

Hard currency A currency traded in a foreign exchange market for which demand is persistently high. It is unlikely to depreciate by large percentages. The major currencies (e.g. US dollar, euro and sterling) are considered hard currencies.

Headline (underlying, adjusted or normalized) earnings per share Directors produce these profit per share numbers by excluding one-off costs, exceptional items and goodwill amortiation to show underlying profit per share trend (or just to make the managerial performance look better).

Hedge or hedging Reducing or eliminating risk by undertaking a countervailing transaction.

Hedge fund A collective investment vehicle that operates relatively free from regulation allowing it to take steps in managing a portfolio that other fund managers are unable to take, e.g. borrowing to invest, shorting the market.

Her Majesty's Revenue and Customs (HMRC) The principal tax collecting authority in the UK.

Herstatt risk In 1974 the German bank Herstatt was closed by the Bundesbank. It had entered into forex transactions and received deutschmarks from counter-parties in European time but had not made the corresponding transfer of US dollars to its counterparties in New York time. It is the risk that arises when forex transactions are settled in different time zones.

Higgs Committee report Recommendations on corporate governance published in 2003.

High-yield debt *See* Mezzanine finance and Junk bonds.

High-yield shares (yield stocks, high yielder) Shares offering a high current dividend yield because the share price is low due to the expectation of low growth in profits and dividends or because of perceived high risk. Sometimes labelled value shares.

Hire-purchase (HP) The user (hiree) of goods pays regular instalments of interest and principal to the hire-purchase company over a period of months. Full ownership passes to the hiree at the end of the period (the hiree is able to use the goods from the outset).

Historical PER (P_0/E_0) Current share price divided by the most recent annual earnings per share.

Holding company *See* Parent company.

Holding period returns Total holding period returns on a financial asset consist of (1) income, e.g. dividend paid; and (2) capital gain – a rise in the value of the asset.

Homemade dividends Shareholders creating an income from shareholdings by selling a portion of their shareholding.

Horizontal merger The two companies merging are engaged in similar lines of activity.

Hostile merger The target (acquired) firm's management is opposed to the merger.

Hubris Overweaning self-confidence.

Hurdle rate The required rate of return. The opportunity cost of the finance provider's money. The minimum return required from a position, making an investment or undertaking a project.

Hybrid finance A debt issue or security that combines the features of two or more instruments, e.g. a convertible bond is a package of a bond with an option to convert. Also used to indicate that a form of finance has both debt risk/return features (e.g. regular interest and a right to receive principal at a fixed date) and equity risk/return features (e.g. the returns depend to a large extent on the profitability of the firm).

Idiosyncratic risk An alternative name for unsystematic risk.

Impact day The day during the launch of a new issue of shares when the price is announced, the prospectus published and offers to purchase solicited.

Imperfect hedge The hedge position will partly, but not exactly, mirror the change in price of the underlying.

In-the-money option An option with intrinsic value. For a call option (q.v.) the current underlying price is more than the option exercise price. For a put option (q.v.) the current price of the underlying is below the exercise price.

Income gearing The proportion of the annual income streams (i.e. pre-interest profits or cash flow) devoted to the prior claims of debt holders. The reciprocal of income gearing is the interest cover.

Income reinvested The performance of shares, other securities or portfolios is usually expressed as 'total return' including both capital gains or losses and the accumulated benefit of periodic reinvestment of income distributions in further shares or securities of the same kind as the original investment.

Income statement Alternative title for profit and loss account.

Income yield *See* Yield.

Incorporation The forming of a company (usually offering limited liability to the shareholders), including the necessary legal formalities.

Incremental cash flow The new cash flows that occur as a result of going ahead with a project.

Incremental effects Those cash flows indirectly associated with a project, e.g. the cash flows on an existing project are boosted if the new project under consideration goes ahead.

Incremental fixed capital investment Investment in fixed assets that adds to the stock of assets and does not merely replace worn-out assets.

Incubators Organizations established to assist fast-growing young firms. They may provide finance, accounting services, legal services, offices, etc.

Independent A venture capital organization that raises its capital from the financial markets – it is not owned by one institution.

Independent director A director that is not beholden to the dominant executive directors. Customers, suppliers and friends of the founding family are not usually regarded as independent.

Independent variables The two variables are completely unrelated; there is no co-movement.

Index *See* Market index.

Index funds (trackers) Collective investment funds (e.g. unit trusts) that try to replicate a stock market index rather than to pick winners in an actively managed fund.

Index-linked gilts (stocks) The redemption value and the coupons rise with inflation over the life of the UK government bond.

Index option An option on a share index, e.g. FTSE 100 or Standard & Poor's 500.

Indices *See* Market index.

Industry attractiveness The economics of the market for the product(s), part of which is determined by the industry structure.

Industry structure The combination of the degree of rivalry within the industry among existing firms; the bargaining strength of industry firms with suppliers and customers; and the potential for new firms to enter and for substitute products to take customers. The industry structure determines the long-run rate of return on capital employed within the industry.

Inevitables Companies that are likely to be dominating their field for many decades due to their competitive strength.

Inflation The process of prices rising resulting in the fall of the purchasing power of one currency unit.

Inflation risk The risk that the nominal returns on an investment will be insufficient to offset the decline in the value of money due to inflation.

Informal venture capitalist An alternative name for business angel (q.v.).

Information asymmetry One party to a transaction (e.g. loan agreement) has more information on risk and return relating to the transaction than the other party.

Information costs The cost of gathering and analyzing information, e.g. in the context of deciding whether to lend money to a firm.

Informed investors Investors that are highly knowledgeable about financial securities and the fundamental evaluation of their worth.

Initial margin An amount that a derivative contractor has to provide to the clearing house when first entering upon a derivative contract.

Initial public offering (IPO) (new issue) The offering of shares in the equity of a company to the public for the first time.

Insider trading (dealing) Trading shares, etc. on the basis of information not in the public domain.

Insolvent A company unable to pay debts as they become due.

Instalment credit A form of finance to pay for goods or services over a period through the payment of principal and interest in regular instalments.

Institutional neglect Share analysts, particularly at the major institutions, may fail to spend enough time studying small firms, preferring to concentrate on the larger 100 or so.

Institutionalisation The increasing tendency for organisational investing, as opposed to individuals investing money in securities (e.g. pension funds and investment trusts collect the savings of individuals to invest in shares).

Insurable risk Risk that can be transferred through the payment of premiums to insurance companies.

Intangible assets Those assets that you cannot touch – they are non-physical, e.g. goodwill.

Interbank brokers Brokers in the forex and other markets who act as intermediaries between buyers and sellers. They provide anonymity to each side.

Interbank market The wholesale market in short-term money and foreign exchange in which banks borrow and lend among themselves. It is now extended to include large companies and other organisations as lenders.

Interest-withholding tax *See* Withholding tax.

Interest cover The number of times the income (profit or cash flow) of a business exceeds the interest payments made to service its loan capital.

Interest rate cap *See* Cap.

Interest rate parity (IRP) of exchange rate determination The interest rate parity theory holds true when the difference between spot and forward exchange rates is equal to the differential between interest rates available in the two currencies.

Interest rate risk The risk that changes in interest rates will have an adverse impact.

Interest rate swap *See* Swap.

Interest yield *See* Yield.

Interim dividend A dividend related to the first half-year's (or quarter's) trading.

Interim profit reports A statement giving unaudited profit figures for the first half of the financial year, shortly after the end of the first half-year.

Intermediaries offer A method of selling shares in the new issue market. Shares are offered to financial institutions such as stockbrokers. Clients of these intermediaries can then apply to buy shares from them.

Intermediate debt *See* Mezzanine finance and Junk bonds.

Intermediate security To help solve the conflict of preferences between savers (investors) in society and the ultimate borrowers' intermediaries (e.g. banks) create intermediate securities (e.g. bank account) offering the characteristics attractive to investors, i.e. high liquidity, low risk and the ability to deal in small amounts.

Internal finance Funds generated by the firm's activities, and available for investment within the firm after meeting contractual obligations.

Internal metrics Measures of corporate performance available to those inside the company. They can be used at the corporate, SBU (q.v.) or product-line level.

Internal rate of return (IRR) The discount rate that makes the present value of a future stream of cash flows equal to the initial investment(s).

Internalisation of transactions By bringing together two firms at different stages of the production chain in a vertical merger, an acquirer may achieve more efficient co-ordination of the different levels.

International banking Banking transactions outside the jurisdiction of the authorities of the currency in which the transaction takes place – see euro markets and euro currency banking.

International bonds Some people use the term to mean the same as eurobonds, while others extend the definition to encompass foreign bonds as well.

International Capital Market Association (ICMA) A self-regulatory organization designed to promote orderly trading and the general development of the euromarkets.

International Petroleum Exchange (IPE) The energy futures and options exchange in London.

Interpolation Estimating intermediate data points on a set of data where observed points are at intervals.

Intrinsic value (company) The discounted value of the cash that can be taken out of a business during its remaining life.

Intrinsic value (options) The payoff that would be received if the underlying is at its current level when the option expires.

Introduction A company with shares already quoted on another stock exchange, or where there is already a wide spread of shareholders, may be introduced to the market. This allows a secondary market in the shares even though no new shares are issued.

Inventory *See* Stock.

Investing-type decision In an investment project the initial cash flow is negative.

Investment bank or merchant bank Bank that carries out a variety of financial services, usually excluding high street banking. Their services are usually fee-commission- or trading based, e.g. fees for merger advice to companies.

Investment-grade debt Debt with a sufficiently high credit rating (BBB– or Baa and above) to be regarded as safe enough for institutional investors that are restricted to holding only safe debt.

Investment trusts (investment companies) Collective investment vehicles set up as companies selling shares. The money raised is invested in assets such as shares, gilts, corporate bonds and property.

Invoice An itemised list of goods shipped, usually specifying the terms of sale and price.

Invoice discounting Invoices sent to trade debtors are pledged to a finance house in return for an immediate payment of up to 80 per cent of the face value.

Invoice finance A method of receiving finance secured by receivables (trade debtors). A finance house advances funds to a firm. When a customer pays on the invoice the company pays the finance house with interest. Also see factoring and invoice discounting.

IOU A colloquialism intended to mean 'I owe you'. The acknowledgment of a debt.

Irredeemable Financial securities with no fixed maturity date at which the principal is repaid.

Irrelevancy of the dividend proposition (by Modigliani and Miller) If a few assumptions can be made, then dividend policy is irrelevant to share value.

Issued share capital That part of a company's share capital that has been subscribed by shareholders, either paid up or partially paid up.

Issuing house *See* Sponsor.

Joint stock enterprise The ownership (share) capital is divided into small units, permitting a number of investors to contribute varying amounts to the total. Profits are divided between stockholders in proportion to the number of shares they own.

Joint venture A business operation (usually a separate company) is jointly owned by two or more parent firms. It also applies to strategic alliances between companies where they collaborate on, for example, research.

Junior debt (junior security) *See* Subordinated debt.

Junk bonds Low-quality, low-credit-rated company bonds. Rated below investment grade (less than BBB– or Baa). Risky and with a high yield.

Just-in-time stock holding Materials and work-in-progress are delivered just before they are needed and finished goods are produced just before being sent to customers.

Kicker *See* Equity kicker.

Lagging The postponement of a payment beyond the due date. A tactic used in international trade when the debtor expects the relative value of the currency in which the debt is expressed to fall.

Laissez-faire The principle of the non-intervention of government in economic affairs.

landMARK Groups of London Stock Exchanges Official List companies from particular UK regions.

LCH Clearnet (LCH) Settles mutual indebtedness between a number of organisations. It settles ('clears') trades for equity traders, derivative traders, bond traders and energy traders, and guarantees all contracts. It often acts as counterparty to all trades on an exchange.

Lead manager In a new issue of securities (e.g. shares, bonds, syndicated loans) the lead manager controls and organizes the issue. There may be joint lead managers, co-managers and regional lead managers.

Lead steer A term used to describe a dominant person with the power to induce others to follow.

Lead time The delay between placing an order with a supplier and the order being delivered.

Leading The bringing forward from the original due date of the payment of a debt.

Leasing The owner of an asset (lessor) grants the use of the asset to another party (lessee) for a specified period in return for regular rental payments. The asset does not become the property of the lessee at the end of the specified period. *See also* Finance lease and Operating lease.

Lender of last resort This is usually the central bank, which provides a group of financial institutions with funds if they cannot otherwise obtain them.

Lessee The user of an asset under a lease.

Lessor The provider of an asset under a lease.

Leverage *See* Gearing.

Leveraged buyout (LBO) The acquisition of a company, subsidiary or unit by another, financed mainly by borrowings.

Leveraged recapitalization The financial structure of the firm is altered in such a way that it becomes highly geared.

LIBOR (London Interbank Offered Rate) The rate of interest offered on loans to highly rated (low-risk) banks in the London interbank market for a specific period (e.g. three months). Used as a reference rate for other loans.

Lien A right is given to a lender to seize possession of the assets belonging to a borrower under the lien.

Life-cycle stage of value creation The longevity of competitive advantage and favourable industry economics can be represented in terms of a life cycle with four stages: development, growth, maturity and decline. In the early stages superior long-term value performance is expected because of a sustainable competitive advantage and favourable long-term industry economics.

Life insurance or life assurance Insurance under which the beneficiaries receive payment upon death of the policyholder or other person named in the policy. Endowment policies offer a savings vehicle as well as cover against death.

LIFFE (London International Financial Futures and Options Exchange) The main derivatives exchange in London – now owned by NYSE-Euronext (q.v.).

LIFFE CONNECT™ The computer system used by Euronext.liffe (q.v.) for trading derivatives (q.v.).

Limit bid In a book-building exercise, a potential institutional investor states that it will buy a given number of shares at a particular price.

Limit prices An order to a broker to buy a specified quantity of a security at or below a specified price, or to sell it at or above a specified price.

Limited companies (Ltd) 'Private' companies with no minimum amount of share capital, but with restrictions on the range of investors who can be offered shares. Limited liability for the debts of the firm is granted to the shareholders. They cannot be quoted on the London Stock Exchange.

Limited liability The owners of shares in a business have a limit on their loss, set as the amount they have committed to invest in shares.

Line of credit *See* Credit facility.

Line of least resistance Taking the path with the least hassle.

Liquidation value *See* Liquidation of a company.

Liquidation of a company The winding-up of the affairs of a company when it ceases business. This could be forced by an inability to make payment when due or it could be voluntary when shareholders choose to end the company. Assets are sold, liabilities paid (if sufficient funds) and the surplus (if any) is distributed to shareholders.

Liquidity The degree to which an asset can be sold quickly and easily without loss in value.

Liquidity-preference hypothesis of the term structure of interest rates The yield curve is predominately upward-sloping because investors require an extra return for lending on a long-term basis.

Liquidity risk The risk that an organization may not have, or may not be able to raise, cash funds when needed.

Listed companies Those on the Official List (q.v.) of the London Stock Exchange.

Listing agreement The UK Listing Authority (q.v.) insists that a company signs a listing agreement committing the directors to certain standards of behaviour and levels of reporting to shareholders.

Listing particulars *See* Prospectus.

Listing Rules The regulations concerning the initial flotation of a company on the London Stock Exchange and the continuing requirements the company must meet.

Lloyds Insurance Market An insurance business in London founded over two centuries ago. 'Names' supply the capital to back insurance policies. Names can now be limited liability companies rather than individuals with unlimited liability to pay up on an insurance policy.

LME London Metal Exchange.

Loan stock A fixed-interest debt financial security. May be unsecured.

Local authority bills/deposits Lending money to a UK local government authority.

London Metal Exchange (LME) Trades metals (e.g. lead, zinc, tin, aluminium, nickel) in spot, forward and option markets.

London Stock Exchange (LSE) The London market in which securities are bought and sold.

London Traded Option Market (LTOM) Options exchange that merged with LIFFE in 1992.

Long bond Often defined as bonds with a time to maturity greater than 15 years, but there is some flexibility in this, so a 10-year bond is often described as being long.

Long-form report A report by accountants for the sponsor of a company being prepared for flotation. The report is detailed and confidential. It helps to reassure the sponsors when putting their name to the issue and provides the basis for the short-form report included in the prospectus.

Long position A positive exposure to a quantity – if the market rises, the position improves. Owning a security or commodity; the opposite of a short position (selling).

Long-range structural analysis A process used to forecast the long-term rates of return of an industry.

Long-term incentive plan (LTIP) A scheme designed to motivate senior managers and directors of a company by paying bonuses if certain targets are surpassed (e.g. share price has risen relative to the market index).

Low-grade debt *See* Mezzanine finance and Junk bonds.

Low-yield shares (stocks) Shares offering a relatively low dividend yield expected to grow rapidly. Often labelled growth stocks.

Ltd Private limited company.

M & A Merger and acquisition.

Macroeconomics The study of the relationships between broad economic aggregates: national income, saving, investment, balance of payments, inflation, etc.

Main Market The Official List of the London Stock Exchange, as opposed to the Alternative Investment Market (q.v.).

Maintenance margin (futures) The level of margin that must be maintained on a futures account (usually at a clearing house). Daily marking to market of the position may reveal the need to put more money into the account to top up to the maintenance margin.

Making a book Market makers offering two prices: the price at which they are willing to buy (bid price) and the price they are willing to sell (offer price).

Management buy-in (MBI) A new team of managers makes an offer to a company to buy the whole company, a subsidiary or a section of the company, with the intention of taking over the running of it themselves. Venture capital often provides the major part of the finance.

Management buyout (MBO) A team of managers makes an offer to its employers to buy a whole business, a subsidiary or a section so that the managers own and run it themselves. Venture capital is often used to finance the majority of the purchase price.

Managementism/managerialism Management not acting in shareholders' best interests by pursuing objectives attractive to the management team. There are three levels: (1) dishonest managers; (2) honest but incompetent managers; (3) honest and competent managers but, as humans, subject to the influence of conflicts of interest.

Mandatory bid If 30 percent or more of the shares of a company are acquired the holder is required under the Takeover Panel rules to bid for all the company's shares.

Marché à Terme d'Instruments Financiers (MATIF) The French futures and options exchange.

Margin (futures) Money placed aside to back a futures purchase or sale. This is used to reassure the counterparty to the future that money will be available should the purchaser/seller renege on the deal.

Market capitalisation The total value at market prices of the shares in issue for a company (or a stock market, or a sector of the stock market).

Market entry Firms that previously did not supply goods or services to this industry now do so.

Market in managerial control Teams of managers compete for control of corporate assets, e.g. through merger activity.

Market index A sample of shares is used to represent a share (or other) market's level and movements.

Market makers Organizations that stand ready to buy and sell shares from investors on their own behalf (at the centre of the London Stock Exchange's quote-driven system of share trading).

Market portfolio A portfolio that contains all assets. Each asset is held in proportion to the asset's share of the total market value of all the assets. A proxy for this is often employed, e.g. the FTSE 100 index.

Market power The ability to exercise some control over the price of the product.

Market risk *See* Systematic risk.

Market segmentation hypothesis of the term structure of interest rates The yield curve is created (or at least influenced) by the supply and demand conditions in a number of submarkets defined by maturity range.

Market-to-book ratio (MBR) The market value of a firm divided by capital invested. ('Capital invested' is usually taken to be balance sheet net assets.)

Market value added The difference between the total amount of capital put into a business by finance providers (debt and equity) and the current market value of the company's shares and debts.

Marking to market The losses or gains on a derivative contract are assessed daily in reference to the value of the underlying price.

Matador A foreign bond issued in the Spanish domestic market.

Matched-bargain systems *See* Order-driven trading system.

Matching The company matches the inflows and outflows in different currencies covered by trade, etc., so that it is only necessary to deal on the currency markets for the unmatched portion of the total transactions.

Matching principle The maturity structure of debt matches the maturity of projects or assets held by the firm. Short-term assets are financed by short-term debt and long-term assets are financed by long-term debt.

Maturity, maturity date or final maturity (redemption date) The time when a financial security (e.g. a bond) is due to be redeemed and the par value is paid to the lender.

Maturity structure The profile of the length of time to the redemption and repayment of a company's various debts.

Maturity transformation Intermediaries offer securities with liquid characteristics to induce primary investors to purchase or deposit funds. The money raised is made available to the ultimate borrowers on a long-term, illiquid basis.

Maximization of long-term shareholder wealth The assumed objective of the firm in finance. It takes into account the time value of money and risk.

Mean (1) arithmetic mean: a set of numbers are summed, and the answer is divided by the number of numbers; (2) geometric mean: calculated as the nth root of the product of n number, e.g. the geometric mean of 2 and 5 is $\sqrt{2} \times 5 = 10 = 3.16$.

Mean reversion *See* Reversion to the mean.

Mean-variance rule If the expected return on two projects is the same but the second has a higher variance (or standard deviation) (q.v.), then the first will be preferred. Also, if the variance on the two projects is the same but the second has a higher expected return, the second will be preferred.

Medium-term note (MTN) A document setting out a promise from a borrower to pay the holders a specified sum on the maturity date and, in many cases, a coupon interest in the meantime. Maturity can range from 9 months to 30 years (usually 1–5 years). If denominated in a foreign currency they are called euro medium-term notes.

Memorandum of Association Lays down the rules that govern a company and its relations with the outside world, e.g. states the objective of the company.

Merchant bank *See* Investment bank.

Merger The combining of two business entities under common ownership.

Metric Method of measurement.

Mezzanine finance Unsecured debt or preference shares offering a high return with a high risk. Ranked behind secured debt but ahead of equity. It may carry an equity kicker (q.v.).

Minority shareholder A shareholder who owns less than 50 percent of a company's ordinary shares.

Mobilization of savings The flow of savings primarily from the household sector to the ultimate borrowers to invest in real assets. This process is encouraged by financial intermediaries.

Model Code for Directors' Dealings London Stock Exchange rules for directors dealing in shares of their own company.

Modified internal rate of return (MIRR) The rate of return that equates the initial investment with a project's terminal value, where the terminal value is the future value of the cash inflows compounded at the required rate of return (the opportunity cost of capital).

Momentum investing Buying shares that have recently risen and selling shares that have recently fallen.

Monetary policy The deliberate control of the money supply and/or rates of interest by the central bank.

Money cash flow All future cash flows are expressed in the prices expected to rule when the cash flow occurs.

Money markets Wholesale financial markets (i.e. those dealing with large amounts) in which lending and borrowing on a short-term basis takes place (<1 year). Examples of instruments include banker's acceptances, certificates of deposit, commercial paper and treasury bills.

Money rate of return The rate of return that includes a return to compensate for inflation.

Monopoly One producer in an industry. However, for Competition Commission purposes a monopoly is defined as a market share of 25 percent.

Moral hazard The presence of a safety net (e.g. an insurance policy) encourages adverse behaviour (e.g. carelessness). An incentive to take extraordinary risks

(risks that tend to fall on others) aimed at rectifying a desperate position. The risk that a party to a transaction is not acting in good faith by providing misleading or inadequate information.

Mortgage debentures Bonds secured using property as collateral.

Mortgage-style repayment schedule A regular monthly amount is paid to a lender that covers both interest and some capital repayment. At first most of the monthly payment goes towards interest. As the outstanding debt is reduced, the monthly payment pays off a larger and larger amount of the capital.

Mutual funds A collective investment vehicle the shares or units of which are sold to investors – a very important method of investing in shares in the USA.

Mutually owned organizations Organizations run for the benefit of the members (usually the same as the consumers of the organization's output) and not for shareholders. Examples include some insurance organizations, building societies and co-operative societies.

Naked (or uncovered) Long or short positioning in a derivative without an offsetting position in the underlying. *See also* Uncovered call option writing.

NASDAQ (National Association of Securities Dealers Automated Quotation system) A series of computer-based information services and an order execution system for the US over-the-counter securities (e.g. share) market.

National Savings Lending to the UK government through the purchase of bonds, and placing money into savings accounts.

Near-cash (near-money, quasi-money) Highly liquid financial assets but that generally are not usable for transactions and therefore cannot be fully regarded as cash, e.g. Treasury bills.

Negative covenants Loan agreement conditions that restrict the actions and rights of the borrower until the debt has been repaid in full.

Negotiability (1) Transferable to another – free to be traded in financial markets. (2) Capable of being settled by agreement between the parties involved in a transaction.

Net assets (net worth), net asset value (NAV) Total assets minus all the liabilities. Fixed assets, plus stocks, debtors, cash and other liquid assets, minus long-and short-term creditors.

Net current assets The difference between current assets and current liabilities (q.v.).

Net present value (NPV) The present value of the expected cash flows associated with a project after discounting at a rate that reflects the value of the alternative use of the funds.

Net profit (Net income) Profit after interest, tax and extraordinary charges and receipts.

Net realisable value What someone might reasonably be expected to pay less the costs of the sale.

Net worth Total assets minus total liabilities.

Netting When subsidiaries in different countries settle intra-organizational currency debts for the net amount owed in a currency rather than the gross amount.

Neuer Markt German stock exchange for smaller young companies. Now closed due to financial scandals and loss of confidence among investors.

New entrant A company entering a market area to compete with existing players.

New issue The sale of securities, e.g. debentures or shares, to raise additional finance or to float existing securities of a company on a stock exchange for the first time.

Newstrack A small company news service and a place where share prices for companies trading on PLUS market (q.v.) are posted.

Niche company A fast-growing small to medium-sized firm operating in a specialist business with high potential.

Nikkei index or Nikkei 225 Stock Average A share index based on the prices of 225 shares quoted on the Tokyo Stock Exchange.

Nil paid rights Shareholders may sell the rights to purchase shares in a rights issue without having paid anything for these rights.

Noise trading Uninformed investors buying and selling financial securities at irrational prices, thus creating noise (strange movements) in the price of securities.

Nominal return (or interest rate) The return on an investment including inflation. If the return necessary to compensate for the decline in the purchasing power of money (inflation) is deducted from the nominal return we have the real rate of return.

Nominal value *See* Par value.

Nominated adviser (Nomad) Each company on the AIM (q.v.) has to retain a nomad. They act as quality controllers, confirming to the London Stock Exchange that the company has complied with the rules. They also act as consultants to the company.

Nominated broker Each company on the AIM (q.v.) has to retain a nominated broker, who helps to bring buyers and sellers together and comments on the firm's prospects.

Nominee accounts An official holder of an asset is not the beneficial owner but merely holds the asset in a nominee account for the beneficiary. In the stock market, the most common use of nominee accounts is where execution-only brokers act as cominees for their clients. The shares are registered in the name of the broker, but the client has beneficial ownership of them.

Non-executive director (outside director) A director without day-to-day operational responsibility for the firm.

Non-recourse A lending arrangement, say in project finance, where the lenders have no right to insist that the parent company(s) pay the due interest and capital should the project company be unable to do so.

Non-voting shares A company may issue two or more classes of ordinary share, one of which may be of shares that do not carry any votes.

Normal rate of return A rate of return that is just sufficient to induce shareholders to put money into the firm and hold it there.

Normalized earnings per share *See* Headline earnings per share.

Note (promissory note) A financial security with the promise to pay a specific sum of money by a given date, e.g. commercial paper, floating rate notes. Usually unsecured.

Note issuance facility (note purchase facility) A medium-term arrangement allowing borrowers to issue a series of short-term promissory notes (usually 3–6 month maturity). A group of banks guarantees the availability of funds by agreeing to purchase any unsold notes at each issue date while the facility is in place.

NYSE The New York Stock Exchange.

NYSE-Euronext The organization that controls and integrates the stock exchanges in New York, Paris, Brussels, Amsterdam and Lisbon as well as owning Liffe.

Objective probability A probability that can be established theoretically or from historical data.

Off-balance-sheet finance Assets are acquired in such a way that liabilities do not appear on the balance sheet, e.g. some lease agreements permit the exclusion of the liability in the accounts.

Offer as unconditional *See* Unconditionality.

Offer document (1) A formal document sent by a company attempting to buy all the shares in a target firm to all the shareholders of the target setting out the offer. (2) The legal document for an offer for sale in a new issue.

Offer for sale A method of selling shares in a new issue. The company sponsor offers shares to the public by inviting subscriptions from investors. (1) Offer for sale by fixed price – the sponsor fixes the price prior to the offer. (2) Offer for sale by tender – investors state the price they are willing to pay. A strike price is established by the sponsors after receiving all the bids. All investors pay the strike price.

Offer for subscription A method of selling shares in a new issue. The issue is aborted if the offer does not raise sufficient interest from investors.

Offer price (1) The price at which a market maker in shares will sell a share, or a dealer in other markets will sell a security or asset. (2) The price of a new issue of securities, e.g. a new issue of shares.

Office of Fair Trading (OFT) The Director-General of Fair Trading has wide powers to monitor and investigate trading activities, and to take action against anti-competitive behaviour. He or she can also refer suspected monopoly situations to the Competition Commission (q.v.).

Official List (OL) The daily list of securities admitted for trading on highly regulated UK markets such as the London Stock Exchange. It does not include securities traded on the Alternative Investment Market (AIM) (q.v.).

Offshore investment Outside investors' home country jurisdiction and financial regulation, usually in tax havens.

Oligopoly A small number of producers in an industry.

Onshore fund A fund authorized and regulated by the regulator in the investor's home country.

Open-ended funds The size of the fund and the number of units depends on the amount investors wish to put into the fund, e.g. a unit trust. The manager adds to or liquidates part of the assets of the fund depending on the level of purchases or sales of the units in the fund.

Open-ended investment companies (OEIC) Collective investment vehicles with one price for investors. OEICs are able to issue more shares if demand increases from investors, unlike investment trusts. OEICs invest the finance raised in securities, primarily shares.

Open interest The sum of outstanding long and short positions in a given futures or option contract. Transactions have not been offset or closed out, thus there is still exposure to movements in the underlying (q.v.).

Open offer New shares are sold to a wide range of external investors (not existing shareholders). However, under clawback provisions, existing shareholders can buy the shares at the offer price if they wish.

Open outcry Where trading is through oral calling of buy and sell offers and hand signals by market members.

Operating gearing *See* Gearing.

Operating lease The lease period is significantly less than the expected useful life of the asset and the agreed lease payments do not amount to a present value of more than 90 percent of the value of the asset.

Operating margin *See* Operating profit margin.

Operating profit (operating income) The accounting income remaining after paying all costs other than interest.

Operating profit margin (operating margin, trading margin) Operating profit as a percentage of sales.

Operational efficiency of a market Relates to how the market minimizes the cost to buyers and sellers of transactions in securities on the exchange.

Operational risks The risks that come from the business activity itself rather than from, say, financial risks such as interest rates changing.

Opportunity cost The value forgone by opting for one course of action; the next best use of, say, financial resources.

Opportunity cost of capital The return that is sacrificed by investing finance in one way rather than investing in an alternative of the same risk class, e.g. a financial security.

Option A contract giving one party the right, but not the obligation, to buy or sell a financial instrument, commodity or some other underlying asset at a given price, at or before a specified date.

Option premium The amount paid by an option purchaser (holder) to obtain the rights under an option contract.

Order book system *See* Order-driven trading system.

Order-driven trading system Buy and sell orders for securities are entered on a central computer system, and investors are automatically matched according to the price and volume they entered (also called matched bargain systems) – SETS is an example (q.v.).

Ordinary resources Those resources that give the firm competitive parity. They provide a threshold competence.

Ordinary shares The equity capital of the firm. The holders of ordinary shares are the owners and are therefore entitled to all distributed profits after the holders of preference shares, debentures and other debt have had their claims met. They are also entitled to control the direction of the company through the power of their votes – usually one vote per share.

Organic growth Growth from within the firm rather than through mergers.

Out-of-the-money option An option with no intrinsic value. For a call option (q.v.) the current price of the underlying is less than the exercise price. For a put option (q.v.) the current price of the underlying (q.v.) is more than the exercise price.

Over-allotment issue Same as Greenshoe (q.v.).

Over-capacity An industry or company has significantly more capacity to supply a product than is being demanded.

Overdraft A permit to overdraw on an account (e.g. a bank account) up to a stated limit; to take more out of a bank account than it contains. This arrangement is usually offered for a period, say six months or one year, but most banks retain the right to call in the loan (demand repayment) at any time.

Overhang Blocks of securities or commodities that are known to be available for sale. This can lead to share (or commodity) price depression due to the anticipated sale of the large block of shares (or the commodity).

Overhead The business expenses not chargeable to a particular part of the work or product; a cost that is not directly associated with producing the merchandise.

Over-subscription In a new issue of securities investors offer to buy more securities (e.g. shares) than are made available.

Overtrading When a business has insufficient finance to sustain its level of trading (turnover). Too much cash is tied up in stocks and debtors, and too little is available to pay creditors and meet day-to-day expenses. A business is said to be overtrading when it tries to engage in more business than the investment in working capital will allow. This can happen even in profitable circumstances.

Over-the-counter (OTC) trade Securities trading carried on outside regulated exchanges. These bilateral deals allow tailor-made transactions.

Owner earnings Earnings plus depreciation, depletion, amortization and certain other non-cash charges less the amount of expenditure for plant and machinery and working capital, etc. that a business requires to fully maintain its long-term competitive position, its unit volume and to invest in value-generating opportunities.

PacMan defence or strategy In a hostile merger situation the target makes a counterbid for the bidder.

Paid-up capital The amount of the authorized share capital that has been paid for or subscribed for by shareholders.

Panel on Takeovers & Mergers *See* Takeover panel.

Paper A term for some securities, e.g. certificates of deposit, commercial paper.

Paper bid In a merger the acquirer offers shares in itself to buy shares in the target.

Par value (nominal, principal or face value) A stated nominal value of a share or bond. Not related to market value.

Parent company (holding company) The company that partially or wholly owns other companies.

Partnership An unincorporated business formed by the association of two or more people who share the risk and profits.

Pathfinder prospectus In a new issue of shares a detailed report on the company is prepared and made available to potential investors a few days before the issue price is announced.

Payables Trade credit received from suppliers.

Payback The period of time it takes to recover the initial cash put into a project.

Payment-in-kind (PIKs) notes and loans High-risk debt offering a very high rate of return (900 basis points over LIBOR or more). They do not pay out a coupon; they pay out in the form of more bonds or loans.

Payout ratio The percentage of after-tax profit paid to shareholders in dividends.

Pecking order theory of financial gearing Firms exhibit preferences in terms of sources of finance. The most acceptable source of finance is retained earnings, followed by borrowing and then by new equity issues.

Pension funds These manage money on behalf of members to provide a pension upon the members' retirement. Most funds invest heavily in shares.

Pension holiday When a pension fund does not need additional contributions for a time, it may grant the contributors, e.g. companies and/or members, a break from making payments.

PER *See* Price–earnings ratio.

Perfect competition (perfect market) Entry to the industry is free and the existing firms have no bargaining power over suppliers or customers. Rivalry between existing firms is fierce because products are identical. The following assumptions hold: (1) There is a large number of buyers. (2) There is a large number of sellers. (3) The quantity of goods bought by any individual transaction is so small relative to the total quantity traded that individual trades leave the market price unaffected. (4) The units of goods sold by different sellers are the same – the product is homogeneous. (5) There is perfect information – all buyers and all sellers have complete information on the prices being asked and offered in other parts of the market. (6) There is perfect freedom of exit from the market.

Perfect hedge Eliminates risk because the movements in the value of the hedge (q.v.) instrument are exactly contrary to the change in the value of the underlying (q.v.).

Perfect market *See* Perfect competition.

Perfect negative correlation When two variables (e.g. returns on two shares) always move in exactly opposite directions by the same proportional amount.

Perfect positive correlation When two variables (e.g. returns on two shares) always move in the same direction by the same proportional amount.

Performance spread The percentage difference between the actual rate of return on an investment and the required rate given its risk class.

Perpetuity A regular sum of money received at intervals forever.

Personal guarantee An individual associated with a company, e.g. director, personally guarantees that a debt will be repaid.

Personal pension A pension scheme set up for an individual by that individual. Contributions to the fund are subject to tax relief.

Physical delivery Settlement of a futures contract by delivery of the underlying (q.v.) rather than cash settlement based on price movement during the holding of the open position.

Placing, place or placement A method of selling shares and other financial securities in the primary market. Securities are offered to the sponsors' or brokers' private clients and/or a narrow group of institutions.

Plain vanilla A bond that lacks any special features such as a call or put provision.

Planning horizon The point in the future after which an investment will earn only the minimum acceptable rate of return.

Plc Public limited company.

PLUS-Markets Group plc This is a provider of primary and secondary equity market services independent of the London Stock Exchange. It operates and regulates the PLUS service.

Poison pills Actions taken, or that will be taken, that make a firm unpalatable to a hostile acquirer.

Political risk Changes in government or government policies impacting on returns and volatility of returns.

Pooled funds Organizations (e.g. unit trusts) that gather together numerous small quantities of money from investors and then invest in a wide range of financial securities.

Portfolio A collection of investments.

Portfolio approach to merger integration *See* Preservation approach to merger integration.

Portfolio investment (1) Investment in a variety of instruments; (2) (in national accounting) investment made by firms and individuals in bonds and shares issued in another country. An alternative form of foreign investment is direct investment, buying commercial assets such as factory premises and industrial plant.

Portfolio optimizer A computer program designed to select an optimal portfolio in terms of risk and return.

Portfolio planning Allocating resources within the company to those strategic business units (q.v.) and product/customer areas offering the greatest value creation, while withdrawing capital from those destroying value.

Portfolio theory Formal mathematical model for calculating risk–return trade-offs as securities are combined in a portfolio.

Post-completion audit The monitoring and evaluation of the progress of a capital investment project through a comparison of the actual cash flows and other benefits with those forecast at the time of authorization.

Precautionary motive for holding cash This arises out of the possibility of unforeseen needs for cash for expenditure in an unpredictable environment.

Pre-emption rights The strong right of shareholders of UK companies to have first refusal to subscribe for further issues of shares. *See* Rights issue.

Preference shares These normally entitle the holder to a fixed rate of dividend, but this is not guaranteed. Holders of preference shares precede the holders of ordinary shares, but follow bond holders and other lenders, in payment of dividends and return of principal. *Participating preference share*: share in residual profits. *Cumulative preference share*: share carries forward the right to preferential dividends. *Redeemable preference share*: a preference share with a finite life. *Convertible preference share*: may be converted into ordinary shares.

Preferred ordinary shares Rank higher than deferred ordinary shares for an agreed rate of dividend or share of profits. They carry votes. Not the same as preference shares.

Preliminary annual results (preliminary profit announcements, prelims) After the year-end and before the full reports and accounts are published, a statement on the profit for the year and other information is provided by companies quoted on the London Stock Exchange.

Premium (1) (On an option) the amount paid to an option writer to obtain the right to buy or sell the underlying. (2) (In foreign exchange) the forward rate of exchange stands at a higher level than the current spot rate. (3) (In investment trusts) by how much the share price exceeds the net asset value per share.

Present value The current worth of future cash flows when discounted.

Preservation approach to merger integration Little is changed in the acquired firm in terms of culture, systems or personnel. General management skills might be transferred from the parent, along with strict financial performance yardsticks and demanding incentive schemes.

Press Collective name for newspapers and periodicals.

Pre-tax margin *See* Pre-tax profit margin.

Pre-tax profit Profit on ordinary activities before deducting taxation.

Pre-tax profit margin (pre-tax margin) Profit after all expenses including interest expressed as a percentage of sales.

Price discovery The process of forming prices through the interaction of numerous buy and sell orders in an exchange.

Price–earnings ratio (PER, price–earnings multiple, PE multiple, PE ratio, P/E ratio) Share price divided by earnings per share over the latest twelve months. *Historical*: share price divided by most recently reported annual earnings per share. *Forward (prospective)*: share price divided by anticipated annual earnings per share.

Price–earnings ratio game (bootstrapping) Companies increase earnings per share by acquiring other companies with lower price–earnings ratios than themselves. The share price can rise despite the absence of an economic value gain.

Price formation The mechanisms leading to a price for an asset, e.g. many buyers and sellers in a company's shares through their buy or sell actions (e.g. via market makers or on a computerized system) arrive at a price to carry out transactions.

Price-sensitive information Information that may influence the share price or trading in the shares.

Price-to-book ratio (market to book) The price of a share as a multiple of per share book (balance sheet) value.

Pricing power An ability to raise prices even when product demand is flat, without the danger of losing significant volume or market share.

Primary investors The household sector contains the savers in society who are the main providers of funds used for investment in the business sector.

Primary market A market in which securities are initially issued to investors rather than a secondary market in which investors buy and sell to each other.

Principal (1) The capital amount of a debt, excluding any interest. (2) A person acting for their own purposes accepting risk in financial transactions, rather than someone acting as an agent for another. (3) The amount invested.

Principal–agent problem In which an agent, e.g. a manager, does not act in the best interests of the principal, e.g. the shareholder.

Private equity Share capital invested in companies not quoted on an exchange.

Private equity investment trusts (PEIT) Investment vehicles allowing investors to buy in to an established private equity fund run by an experienced management team which invests in a portfolio of unquoted companies. The PEIT shares are bought and sold on the stock market.

Private limited company (ltd) A company that is unable to offer its shares to the wider public.

Privatization The sale to private investors of government-owned equity (shares) in state-owned industries or other commercial enterprises.

Pro forma earnings Projected or forecast earnings. These are not audited and may be unreliable.

Profit and loss account Records whether a company's sales revenue was greater than its costs.

Profit margin Profits as a percentage of sales.

Profitability index A measure of present value per pound invested.

Project An investment within the business requiring medium- to long-term commitment of resources.

Project appraisal The assessment of the viability of proposed long-term investments in real assets within the firm.

Project finance Finance assembled for a specific project. The loan and equity returns are tied to the cash flows and fortunes of the project rather than being dependent on the parent company/companies.

Promissory note A debtor promises to pay on demand or at a fixed date or a date to be determined by circumstances. A note is created stating this obligation.

Proprietary transactions (proprietary trading) A financial institution, as well as acting as an agent for a client, may trade on the financial markets with a view to generating profits for itself, e.g. speculation on forex (q.v.).

Prospectus A document containing information about a company (or unit trust/OEIC – q.v.), to assist with a new issue (initial public offering) by supplying detail about the company and how it operates.

Provision (1) Sum set aside in accounts for anticipated loss or expenditure. (2) A clause or stipulation in a legal agreement giving one party a right.

Proxy votes Shareholders unable to attend a shareholders' meeting may authorize another person, e.g. a director or the chair, to vote on their behalf, either as instructed or as that person sees fit.

Public limited company (plc) A company that may have an unlimited number of shareholders and offer its shares to the wider public (unlike a limited company – q.v.). Must have a minimum share value of £50,000. Some plcs are listed on the London Stock Exchange.

Purchasing power parity (PPP) theory of exchange rate determination Exchange rates will be in equilibrium when their domestic purchasing powers at that rate of exchange are equivalent. Movements in exchange rates will be a function of the differential in the two currencies' inflation rates.

Put feature *See* Put option.

Put option Gives the purchaser the right, but not the obligation, to sell a financial instrument, commodity or some other underlying asset at a given price, at or before a specified date.

Qualitative analysis Relying on subjective elements to take a view, e.g. valuing shares by judging quality of management and strategic position.

Quant (quantum) analysis Quantitative analysis using complex mathematical models.

Quick asset value (net) Current assets minus stock minus current liabilities (q.v.).

Quick ratio (acid test) The ratio of current assets, less stock, to total current liabilities (q.v).

Quota Quantitative limits placed on the importation of specified goods.

Quote-driven trading system Market makers post bid and offer prices on a computerized system.

Quoted Those shares with a price quoted on a recognized investment exchange (RIE) or AIM, e.g. the Official List of the London Stock Exchange (q.v.).

Random walk theory The movements in (share) prices are independent of one another; one day's price change cannot be predicted by looking at the previous day's price change.

Ranking (debt) Order of precedence for payment of obligations. Senior debt receives annual interest and redemption payments ahead of junior (or subordinated) debt. So, if the company has insufficient resources to pay its obligations, the junior debt holders may receive little or nothing.

Rappaport's value drivers The seven key factors that determine value are: (1) sales growth rate, (2) operating profit margin, (3) tax rate, (4) incremental fixed capital investment, (5) incremental working capital investment, (6) planning horizon and (7) required rate of return.

Rating *See* Credit rating.

Raw materials stock period The average number of days raw materials remain unchanged and in stock. Equal to the average value of raw materials stock divided by the average purchase of raw materials per day.

Real assets Assets used to carry on a business. These assets can be tangible (e.g. buildings) or intangible (e.g. a brand) as opposed to financial assets.

Real cash flows Future cash flows are expressed in terms of constant purchasing power.

Real option An option to undertake different courses of action in the real asset market (strategic and operational options), as opposed to a tradeable option on financial securities or commodities.

Real rate of return The rate that would be required (obtained) in the absence of inflation. The nominal return minus inflation.

Recapitalization A change in the financial structure, e.g. in debt to equity ratio.

Receivable (accounts receivable) A sum due from a customer for goods delivered: trade credit.

Receiver Takes control of a business if a creditor successfully files a bankruptcy petition. The receiver may then sell the company's assets and distribute the proceeds among the creditors.

Recognised investment exchange (RIE) A body authorised to regulate securities trading in the UK, e.g. the London Stock Exchange.

Recourse If a financial asset is sold (such as a trade debt), the purchaser could return to the vendor for payment in the event of non-payment by the borrower.

Redemption The repayment of the principal amount, or the par value, of a security (e.g. bond) at the maturity date resulting in the retirement and cancellation of the bond.

Redemption yield *See* Yield.

Registrar An organization that maintains a record of share (and other securities) ownership for a company. It also communicates with shareholders on behalf of the company.

Regulated exchange market A market where there is a degree of supervision concerning market behaviour or other controls on the freedom of participants.

Regulatory News Service (RNS) A system for distributing important company announcements and other price-sensitive financial news run by the London Stock Exchange.

Reinvestment rate The rate of return on the periodic cash flows generated by a project when invested.

Relationship banking A long-term, intimate and relatively open relationship is established between a corporation and its banks. Banks often supply a range of tailor-made services rather than one-off services.

Rembrandt A foreign bond issued in the Netherlands.

Remuneration committee A group of directors of a company, all of which are independent of management, decide the remuneration of executive directors.

Repayment holiday *See* Grace period.

Reporting accountant A company planning to float on the London Stock Exchange employs a reporting accountant to prepare a detailed report on the firm's financial controls, track record, financing and forecasts.

Required return The minimum rate of return given the opportunity cost of capital.

Rescheduling Rearranging the payments made by a borrower to a lender – usually over a long period.

Rescue rights issue A company in dire trouble, in danger of failure, carries out a rights issue to raise capital.

Residual income An alternative term for economic profit.

Residual theory of dividends Dividends should be paid only when the firm has financed all its positive NPV projects.

Resistance line A line drawn on a price (e.g. share) chart showing the market participants' reluctance to push the price below (or above) the line over a period of time.

Resolution A proposal put to the vote at a shareholders' meeting.

Resolution of uncertainty theory of dividends The market places a greater value on shares offering higher near-term dividends because these are more certain than more distant dividends.

Restructuring costs The costs associated with a reorganization of the business, e.g. closing factories, redundancies.

Retail banking Banking for individual customers or small firms, normally for small amounts. High-volume, low-value banking.

Retail service providers (RSPs) Some market makers also offer automated computer dealing service to investors as RSPs.

Retained earnings That part of a company's profits not paid as dividends.

Retention ratio Retained profits for the year as a proportion of profits after tax attributable to ordinary shareholders for the year.

Return on capital employed (ROCE); return on investment (ROI) Traditional measures of profitability. Profit return divided by the volume of resources devoted to the activity. Resources usually include shareholders' funds, net debt and provisions. Cumulative goodwill, previously written off, may be added back to the resources total. *See also* Accounting rate of return.

Return on equity (ROE) Profit attributable to shareholders as a percentage of equity shareholders' funds.

Revaluation reserve A balance sheet entry that records accumulated revaluations of fixed assets.

Reverse floater *See* Floating-rate notes.

Reverse floating-rate notes *See* Floating-rate notes.

Reverse takeover The acquiring company is smaller than the target in terms of market capitalization and offers newly created shares in itself as consideration for the purchase of the shares in the acquirer. So many new shares are created that the former shareholders in the target become the dominant shareholders in the combined entity.

Reversing the trade *See* Closing out a futures position.

Reversion to the mean The behaviour of financial markets is often characterized as reverting to the mean, in which an otherwise random process of price changes or returns tends over the medium to long term to move towards the average.

Revolving credit An arrangement whereby a borrower can draw down short-term loans as the need arises, to a maximum over a period of years.

Revolving underwriting facility (RUF) A bank(s) underwrites the borrower's access to funds at a specified rate in the short-term financial markets (e.g. by issuing euronotes) throughout an agreed period. If the notes are not bought in the market, the underwriter(s) is obliged to purchase them.

Reward-to-variability ratio Alternative name for Sharpe ratio (q.v.).

Reward-to-volatility ratio Alternative name for Treynor's ratio (q.v.).

Rights issue An invitation to existing shareholders to purchase additional shares in the company in proportion to their existing holdings.

Risk A future return has a variety of possible values. Sometimes measured by standard deviation (q.v.).

Risk arbitrage Taking a position (purchase or sale) in a security, commodity, etc. because it is judged to be mispriced relative to other securities with similar characteristics. The comparator securities are not identical (e.g. shares in Unilever and in Procter & Gamble) and therefore there is an element of risk that the valuation gap will widen rather than contract. An extreme form of risk arbitrage is to take a position hoping to make a profit if an event occurs (e.g. a takeover). If the event does not occur, then there may be a loss. The word 'arbitrage' has been stretched beyond breaking point, as true arbitrage should be risk-free.

Risk averter Someone who prefers a more certain return to an alternative with an equal expected return but that is more risky.

Risk lover (seeker) Someone who prefers a more uncertain alternative to an alternative with an equal but less risky outcome.

Risk management The selection of those risks that a business should take and those that should be avoided or mitigated, followed by action to avoid or reduce risk.

Risk premium The extra return, above the risk-free rate for accepting risk.

Risk transformation Intermediaries offer low-risk securities to primary investors to attract funds, which are then used to purchase higher-risk securities issued by the ultimate borrowers.

Risk-free rate of return (RFR) The rate earned on riskless investment, denoted r_f. A reasonable proxy is short-term lending to a reputable government.

Risk–return line A line on a two-dimensional graph showing all the possible expected returns and standard deviation combinations, available from the construction of portfolios from two assets. This can also be called the two-asset opportunity set or feasibility set.

Roadshow Companies and their advisers make a series of presentations to potential investors, usually to entice them into buying a new issue of securities.

Rolled-over overdraft Short-term loan facilities are perpetuated into the medium and long term by the renewal of the overdraft facility.

Rolling settlement Following the purchase of shares the shares and cash are exchanged after a deal has been struck a fixed number of days later – usually after three days – rather than on a specific account day.

RPI (retail price index) The main UK measure of general inflation.

R-squared, R_2 *See* Coefficient of determination.

Running yield *See* Yield.

Safe haven Investing in a safe investment in time of trouble, such as major financial turmoil. UK and US government bonds and treasury bills, for example, are usually regarded as safe havens.

Sale and leaseback Assets (e.g. land and buildings) are sold to another firm (e.g. bank, insurance company) with a simultaneous agreement for the vendor to lease the asset back for a stated period under specific terms.

Sales ledger administration The management of trade debtors: recording credit sales, checking customer creditworthiness, sending invoices and chasing late payers.

Samurai A foreign bond, yen-denominated, issued by a non-Japanese entity in the domestic Japanese market.

S&P 500 Standard & Poor's index of 500 leading US shares.

Satisficed When a contributor to an organization is given just enough of a return to make their contribution, e.g. banks are given contracted interest and principal, and no more.

Scaledown In a new issue, when a company floats on a stock exchange, if demand is greater than supply at the offer price the applicants receive less than they applied for, according to a prearranged formula.

Scenario analysis An analysis of the change in NPV (q.v.) brought about by the simultaneous change in a number of key inputs to an NPV analysis. Typically a 'worst-case scenario', when all the changes in variables are worsening, and a 'best-case scenario', when all variable changes are positive, are calculated.

Scrip dividends Shareholders are offered the alternative of additional shares rather than a cash dividend.

Scrip issue The issue of more shares to existing shareholders according to their current holdings. Shareholders do not pay for these new shares. Company reserves are converted into issued capital.

SEAQ (Stock Exchange Automated Quotation System) A real-time computer-screen-based quotation system for securities where market makers on the London Stock Exchange report bid-offer prices and trading volumes, and brokers can observe prices and trades.

SEAQI (Stock Exchange Automated Quotation International) A real-time computer-screen-based quotation system for securities that allows market makers in international shares based on the London Stock Exchange to report prices, quotes and trading volumes.

Search costs The costs of finding another person or organization with which to transact business/investment.

Seasoned equity offerings (SEOs) Companies that have been on a stock exchange for some time selling new shares, e.g. via a rights issue.

Second lien loans Low-ranking loans paying high rates of return. The owners of the loans are in line behind senior secured creditors in a liquidation.

Secondary buy-out A company that has been backed by private equity finance is then sold to another private equity firm(s).

Secondary market Securities already issued are traded between investors.

Secondary market trading facility A system to allow current holders of shares or other securities to trade between themselves.

Second-tier markets Not those trading markets provided for the leading (biggest company) shares and other securities.

Securities and Exchange Commission (SEC) The US federal body responsible for the regulation of securities markets (exchanges, brokers, investment advisers, etc.).

Securities house This may mean simply an issuing house. However, the term is sometimes used more broadly for an institution concerned with buying and selling securities or acting as agent in the buying and selling of securities.

Securitization Financial payments (e.g. a claim to a number of mortgage payments) that are not tradable can be repackaged into other securities (e.g. bonds) and then sold. These are called asset-backed securities.

Security (1) A financial asset, e.g. a share or bond. (2) Asset pledged to be surrendered in the event of a loan default.

Security market line (SML) A linear (straight) line showing the relationship between systematic risk and expected rates of return for individual assets (securities). According to the capital asset pricing model (q.v.) the return above the risk-free rate of return (q.v.) for a risky asset is equal to the risk premium for the market portfolio multiplied by the beta coefficient.

SEDOL (Stock Exchange Daily Official List) A journal published daily giving prices and deals for shares on London's Official List. Companies are given SEDOL numbers to identify them.

Seedcorn capital or money (seed capital or money) The financing of the development of a business concept. High risk; usually provided by venture capitalists, entrepreneurs or business angels.

Self-amortizing A reduction in the amount outstanding on a loan by regular payments to the lender.

Self-regulation Much of the regulation of financial services in the UK is carried out by self-regulatory organizations (SROs), i.e. industry participants regulate themselves within a light-touch legislated framework.

Selling the rights nil paid In a rights issue those entitled to new shares (existing shareholders) are entitled to sell the rights to the new shares without the need to purchase the new shares.

Semi-annual Twice a year at regular intervals.

Semi-captive A venture capital organization that raises its capital from the financial markets but that is dominated by the participation of an organizing institution.

Semi-strong efficiency Share prices fully reflect all the relevant, publicly available information.

Senior debt *See* Subordinated debt.

Sensitivity analysis An analysis of the effect on project NPV of changes in the assumed values of key variables, e.g. sales level, labour costs. Variables are changed one at a time. It is a 'what-if?' analysis, e.g. what if raw material costs rise by 20 percent?

Separate legal person A company is a legal entity under the law. It is entitled to make contracts and be sued, for example, separately from the owners of the company.

Separation principle The decision on asset allocation can be split into (1) selecting the optimum market portfolio on the efficiency frontier and (2) allocating wealth between the optimum portfolio and the risk-free asset.

Serious Fraud Office (SFO) Investigates and prosecutes crimes of serious fraud in the UK.

SETS (Stock Exchange Electronic Trading System) An electronic order-book-based trading system for the London Stock Exchange. Brokers input buy and sell orders directly into the system. Buyers and sellers are matched and the trade executed automatically. The system is used for the largest UK shares.

SETSsq A share-trading system run by the London Stock Exchange with a focus on lightly traded shares (few trades per day).

Settlement The completion of a transaction, e.g. upon the sale of a share in the secondary market cash is transferred as payment; in return ownership is transferred.

Settlement price The price calculated by a derivatives exchange at the end of each trading session as the closing price that will be used in determining profits and losses for the marking-to-market process for margin accounts.

Share Companies divide the ownership of the company into ordinary shares. An owner of a share usually has the same rights to vote and receive dividends as another owner of a share. Also called equity (q.v.).

Share buy-back The company buys back a proportion of its shares from shareholders.

Share certificate A document showing ownership of part of the share capital of a company.

Share markets Institutions that facilitate the regulated sale and purchase of shares; includes the primary and secondary markets.

Share option scheme Employees are offered the right to buy shares in their company at a modest price some time in the future.

Share premium account A balance sheet entry represented by the difference between the price received by a company when it sells shares and the par value of those shares.

Share repurchase The company buys back its own shares.

Share split (stock split) Shareholders receive additional shares from the company without payment. The nominal (par) value of each share is reduced in proportion to the increase in the number of shares, so the total book value of shares remains the same.

Shareholder value analysis A technique developed by Rappaport (q.v.) for establishing value creation. It equals the present value of operating cash flows within the planning horizon *plus* the present value of operating cash flows after the planning horizon *plus* the current value of marketable securities and other non-operating investments *less* corporate debt.

Shareholder wealth-maximization The maximizing of shareholders' purchasing power. In a pricing efficient market, it is the maximization of the current share price.

Shareholders' funds (equity) The net assets of the business (after deduction of all short- and long-term liabilities and minority interests) shown in the balance sheet.

Sharpe ratio A measure relating risk and return. The extent to which a portfolio's (or share's) return has been greater than a risk-free asset divided by its standard deviation (q.v.).

Shell company A company with a stock market quotation but with very little in the way of real economic activity. It may have cash but no production.

Short position In a derivative contract, the counterparty in a short position is the one that has agreed to deliver the underlying (q.v.).

Short selling The selling of financial securities (e.g. shares) not yet owned, in the anticipation of being able to buy at a later date at a lower price.

Short-term sterling interest rate future (colloquially known as short sterling) The three-month sterling interest rate future contract traded on LIFFE (q.v.). Notional fixed-term deposits for three-month periods starting at a specified time in the future.

Short-termism A charge levelled at the financial institutions in their expectations of the companies to which they provide finance. It is argued that long-term benefits are lost because of pressure for short-term performance.

Shorting Same as Short selling.

Shorts UK government bonds (gilts) with less than five years to maturity.

Sight bank account (current account) A bank account where deposits can be withdrawn without notice.

Sigma A measure of dispersion of returns; standard deviation (q.v.).

Signalling Some financial decisions are taken to be signals from the managers to the financial markets, e.g. an increase in gearing, or a change in dividend policy.

Simple interest Interest is paid on the original principal; no interest is paid on the accumulated interest payments.

Sinking fund Money is accumulated in a fund through regular payments in order eventually to repay a debt.

SIS x-clear SIS x-clear AG is part of the corporate group Swiss Financial Market Services AG, the integrated Swiss financial market infrastructure provider. As Central Counterparty (CCP) Swiss x-clear offers clearing and risk management services for SWX Europe and SWX Swiss Exchange.

Small firm effect (size effect) The tendency of small firms to give abnormally high returns on the stock market.

Soft capital rationing Internal management-imposed limits on investment expenditure.

Solvency The ability to pay legal debts.

South Sea bubble A financial bubble (*see* Bubble) in which the price of shares in the South Sea Company were pushed to ridiculously high levels on a surge of over-optimism in the early eighteenth century.

Special dividend An exceptionally large dividend paid on a one-off basis.

Special drawing rights (SDRs) A composite currency designed by the International Monetary Fund (IMF). Each IMF member country is allocated SDRs in proportion to its quota.

Special-purpose vehicle or entity Companies set these up as separate organizations (companies) for a particular purpose. They are designed so that their accounts are not consolidated with those of the rest of the group.

Special resolution A company's shareholders vote at an AGM or EGM with a majority of 75 percent of those voting. Normally special resolutions are reserved for important changes in the constitution of the company. Other matters are dealt with by way of an ordinary resolution (50 percent or more of the votes required).

Specific inflation The price changes in an individual good or service.

Specific risk *See* Unsystematic risk.

Speculative grade Bonds with a credit rating below investment grade.

Speculative motive for holding cash This means that unexpected opportunities can be taken immediately.

Speculators Those that take a position in financial instruments and other assets with a view to obtaining a profit on changes in their value.

Sponsor Lends its reputation to a new issue of securities, advises the client company (along with the issuing broker) and co-ordinates the new issue process. Sponsors are usually merchant banks or stockbrokers. Also called an issuing house.

Spot market A market for immediate transactions (e.g. spot forex market, spot interest market), as opposed to an agreement to make a transaction some time in the future (e.g. forward, option, future).

Spot rate of interest *See* Spot market.

Spread The difference between the price to buy and the price to sell a financial security. Market makers quote a bid–offer spread for shares. The lower price (bid) is the price an investor receives if selling to the market maker. The higher (offer) price is the price if the investor wishes to buy from the market maker.

Stakeholder A party with an interest (financial or otherwise) in an organization, e.g. employees, customers, suppliers, the local community.

Standard and Poor's 500 An index of leading (largest) 500 US shares listed in the New York Stock Exchange. Companies are weighted by market capitalization of the NYSE.

Standard deviation A statistical measure of the dispersion around an average. A measure of volatility. The standard deviation is the square root of the variance. A fund or a share return can be expected to fall within one standard deviation of its average two-thirds of the time if the future is like the past.

Start-up capital Finance for young companies that have not yet sold their product commercially. High risk; usually provided by venture capitalists, entrepreneurs or business angels.

Statistically independent shares The movement of two variables is completely unrelated (e.g. the returns on two shares are unrelated).

Statutory Established, regulated or imposed by or in conformity with laws passed by a legislative body, e.g. Parliament.

Sterling bonds Corporate bonds that pay interest and principal in sterling.

Stock Another term for inventory of raw materials, work-in-progress and finished items.

Stock exchange A market in which securities are bought and sold. In continental Europe the term 'bourse' may be used.

Stock exchange automated quotations *See* SEAQ.

Stock market *See* Stock exchange.

Stock-out costs The cost associated with being unable to draw on a stock of raw material, work-in-progress or finished goods inventory (loss of sales, profits and goodwill, and also production dislocation).

Stocks and shares There is some lack of clarity in the distinction between stocks and shares. Shares are equities in companies. Stocks are financial instruments that pay interest, e.g. bonds. However, in the USA shares are also called 'common stocks' and the shareholders are sometimes referred to as the stockholders. So when some people use the term 'stocks' they could be referring to either bonds or shares.

Straight bond One with a regular fixed rate of interest and without the right of conversion (to, say, shares) or any other unusual rights.

Strategic analysis The analysis of industries served by the firm and the company's competitive position within the industry.

Strategic business unit (SBU) A business unit within the overall corporate entity that is distinguishable from other business units because it serves a defined external market where management can conduct strategic planning in relation to products and markets.

Strategic objectives Goals used as the criteria to guide the firm, e.g. market share targets. However, they may not always be good indicators of whether shareholder wealth is being maximized.

Strategic position A firm's competitive position within an industry and the attractiveness of the industry.

Strategy Selecting which product or market areas to enter/exit and how to ensure a good competitive position in those markets/products.

Strategy planes chart Maps a firm's, SBU's or product line's position in terms of industry attractiveness, competitive advantage and life-cycle stage of value potential.

Strike bid In a book-building exercise, a potential institutional investor states that it will buy a given number of shares within the initial price range.

Strike price (1) In the offer for sale by a tender, the price selected that will sell the required quantity of shares given the offers made. (2) The price paid by the holder of an option when/if the option is exercised – *see* Exercise price.

Strong form efficiency All relevant information, including that which is privately held, is reflected in the share price.

Subjective probability Probabilities are devised based on personal judgment of the range of outcomes along with the likelihood of their occurrence.

Subordinated debt A debt that ranks below another liability in order of priority for payment of interest or principal. Senior debt ranks above junior (subordinated) debt for payment.

Subscription rights A right to subscribe for some shares.

Subsidiary A company is a subsidiary of another company if the parent company holds the majority of the voting rights (more than 50 percent), or has a minority of the shares but has the right to appoint or remove directors holding a majority of the voting rights at meetings of the board on all, or substantially all, matters or it has the right to exercise a dominant influence.

Summary financial statement Companies often send small investors a summary of the financial statements rather than the full report and accounts. This suits many investors and saves the company some money. However, an investor is entitled to receive a full annual report and accounts. It may be necessary to make a request for this.

Sunk cost A cost that the firm has incurred or to which it is committed that cannot be altered. This cost does not influence subsequent decisions and can be ignored in, for example, project appraisal.

Super-normal return A rate of return above the normal rate.

Survivorship bias In empirical studies of share price performance, the results may be distorted by focusing only on companies that survived through to the end of the period of study. Particularly poor performers (i.e. liquidated firms) are removed from the sample, thus biasing the results in a positive direction.

Swap An exchange of cash payment obligations. An interest rate swap is where one company arranges with a counterparty to exchange interest-rate payments. In a currency swap the two parties exchange interest obligations (receipts) for an agreed period between two different currencies.

Swaption or swap-option An option to have a swap at a later date.

Symbiosis type of post-merger integration Large differences between acquired and parent firms in culture, systems, etc. are maintained. However, collaboration in communications and the cross-fertilization of ideas are encouraged.

Syndicated loan A loan made by one or more banks to one borrower.

Synergy A combined entity (e.g. two companies merging) will have a value greater than the sum of the parts.

Systematic (undiversifiable or market or residual) risk That element of return variability from an asset that cannot be eliminated through diversification (q.v.). Measured by beta (q.v.). It comprises the risk factors common to all firms.

Systemic risk The risk of failure within the financial system causing a domino-type effect bringing down large parts of the system.

Take-out Market expression of a bid made to a seller to 'take out' his or her position – e.g. venture-capital-backed companies are bought, allowing the venture capitalist to exit from the investment.

Takeover (acquisition) Many people use these terms interchangeably with merger. However, some differentiate takeover as meaning a purchase of one firm by another with the concomitant implication of financial and managerial domination. Usually applied to hostile (without target management approval) mergers.

Takeover Panel The committee responsible for supervising compliance with the (UK) City Code on Takeovers and Mergers (q.v.).

Tangible assets Assets that have a physical presence.

Tariff Taxes imposed on imports.

Tax allowance An amount of income or capital gain that is not taxed.

Tax avoidance Steps taken to reduce tax that are permitted under the law.

Tax evasion Deliberately giving a false statement or omitting a relevant fact.

Tax haven A country or place with low rates of tax.

Tax shield The benefit for a company that comes from having some of its capital in debt form, the interest on which is tax-deductible, resulting in a lower outflow from the company to the tax authorities.

Taxable profit That element of profit subject to taxation. This frequently differs from reported profit.

techMARK The London Stock Exchange launched techMARK in 1999. It is a subsection of the shares within the LSE's Official List (q.v.). It is a grouping of technology companies. It imposes different rules on companies seeking a flotation from those that apply to the other companies on the Official List (e.g. only one year's accounts are required).

Technical analysis Analysis of share price movements and trading volume to forecast future movements from past movements.

Tender offer A public offer to purchase securities.

Term assurance Life assurance taken out for less than the whole life – the insured sum is paid only in the event of the insured person dying within the term.

Term loan A loan of a fixed amount for an agreed time and on specified terms, usually with regular periodic payments. Most frequently provided by banks.

Term structure of interest rates The patterns of interest rates on bonds with differing lengths of time to maturity but with the same risk. Strictly it is the zero coupon implied interest rate for different lengths of time. *See also* Yield curve.

Terminal value The forecast future value of sums of money compounded to the end of a common time horizon.

Three-day rolling settlement (T+3) After a share transaction in the stock exchange, investors pay for shares three working days later.

Tick The minimum price movement of a security or derivative contract.

Tier one ratio of core capital That part of a bank's capital defined as shareholders' equity plus irredeemable and non-cumulative preference shares.

Tiger economies (or countries) The first four industrialized economies in Asia excluding Japan: Taiwan, South Korea, Singapore and Hong Kong (also referred to as 'dragon economies').

Time-adjusted measures of profitability The time value of money is taken into account.

Time value That part of an option's value that represents the value of the option expiring in the future rather than now. The longer the period to expiry, the greater the chance that the option will become in-the-money before the expiry date. The amount by which the option premium exceeds the intrinsic value.

Time value of money A pound received in the future is worth less than a pound received today – the present value of a sum of money depends on the date of its receipt.

Total (or market) capitalisation *See* Market capitalization.

Total shareholder return (TSR) or total return The total return earned on a share over a period of time: dividends per share plus capital gain divided by initial share price.

Touch prices *See* Yellow strip.

Tracker An investment fund that is intended to replicate the return of a market index. Also called an index fund or passive fund.

Trade acceptance *See* Acceptance credit.

Trade credit Where goods and services are delivered to a firm for use in its production and are not paid for immediately.

Trade debtor A customer of a firm who has not yet paid for goods and services delivered.

Trade sale A company buys another company in the same line of business.

Traded option An option tradeable on a market separate from the underlying (q.v.).

Trading floor A place where traders in a market (or their representatives) can meet to agree transactions face to face. However, investment banks often have 'trading floors' where they 'meet' counterparties on other trading floors to conduct transactions via the telephone or computer.

Trading margin *See* Operating profit margin.

Traditional option An option available on any security but with an exercise price fixed as the market price on the day the option is bought. Bilateral contracts between the option buyer and the option writer rather than exchange-traded instruments. All such options expire after three months and cannot be sold to a secondary investor.

Transaction risk The risk that transactions already entered into, or for which the firm is likely to have a commitment in a foreign currency, will have a variable value in the home currency because of exchange-rate movements.

Transactional banking Banks compete with each other to offer services at the lowest cost to corporations, on a service-by-service basis.

Transactional motive for holding cash Money is used as a means of exchange; receipts and payments are rarely perfectly synchronized and therefore an individual or business generally needs to hold a stock of money to meet expenditure.

Translation risk This risk arises because financial data denominated in one currency are then expressed in terms of another currency.

Treasury UK government department responsible for financial and economic policy.

Treasury bill A short-term money market instrument issued (sold) by a government, usually to supply the government's short-term financing needs.

Treasury management To plan, organize and control cash and borrowings so as to optimize interest and currency flows, and minimize the cost of funds. Also to plan and execute communications programmes to enhance investors' confidence in the firm.

Treynor's ratio or index A measure relating return to risk. It is the return on a portfolio (or share) minus the risk-free rate of return divided by beta.

TRRACK system A system to assist the analysis of a company's extraordinary resources under the headings Tangible, Relationships, Reputation, Attitude, Capabilities and Knowledge.

Trust deed A document specifying the regulation of the management of assets on behalf of beneficiaries of the trust.

Trustees Those that are charged with the responsibility for ensuring compliance with the trust deed.

Tulipmania A seventeenth-century Dutch bubble in which a mania for tulip bulbs pushed prices to those for a house (for one bulb!). *See* Bubble.

Turnover (revenue or sales) (1) Money received or to be received by the company from goods and services sold during the year. (2) In portfolio management, the amount of trading relative to the value of the portfolio.

Ultimate borrowers Firms investing in real assets need finance, which ultimately comes from the primary investors.

Uncertainty Strictly (in economists' terms), uncertainty is when there is more than one possible outcome to a course of action; the form of each possible outcome is known, but the probability of getting any one outcome is not known. However, the distinction between risk (the ability to assign probabilities) and uncertainty has largely been ignored for the purposes of this text.

Unconditionality In a merger (q.v.), once unconditionality is declared, the acquirer becomes obliged to buy. Target shareholders who accepted the offer are no longer able to withdraw their acceptance.

Unconventional cash flows A series of cash flows in which there is more than one change in sign.

Uncovered (naked) call option writing Writing a call option (q.v.) on an underlying (q.v.) when the writer does not own the underlying securities included in the option.

Underlying The asset (e.g. share, commodity) that is the subject of a derivative contract.

Underlying earnings per share *See* Headline earnings per share.

Underwriters These (usually large financial institutions) guarantee to buy the proportion of a new issue of securities (e.g. shares) not taken up by the market, in return for a fee.

Undifferentiated product A product that is much the same as that supplied by other companies.

Undiversifiable risk *See* Systematic risk.

Uninformed investors Those that have no or little knowledge about financial securities and the fundamental evaluation of their worth.

Unique risk *See* Unsystematic risk.

Unit trust An investment organization that attracts funds from individual investors by issuing units to invest in a range of securities, e.g. shares or bonds. It is open-ended, the number of units expanding to meet demand.

United Kingdom Listing Authority (UKLA) This organization is part of the Financial Services Authority (q.v.) and rigorously enforces a set of demanding rules on companies at the time when they join the stock market and in subsequent years.

Universal banks Financial institutions involved in many different aspects of finance, including retail banking and wholesale banking.

Unlisted Shares and other securities not on the Main Market of the London Stock Exchange (q.v.) are described as unlisted.

Unquoted firms Those shares with a price not quoted on a recognized investment exchange, RIE (e.g. the Official List or AIM of the London Stock Exchange – q.v.).

Unsecured A financial claim with no collateral or any charge over the assets of the borrower.

Unsystematic (unique or diversifiable or specific) risk That element of an asset's variability in returns that can be eliminated by holding a well-diversified portfolio.

Utility (1) The satisfaction, pleasure or fulfilment of needs derived from consuming some quantity of a good or service. (2) A business involved in basic goods and services, e.g. water, electricity.

Valuation risk (price risk) The possibility that, when a financial instrument matures or is sold in the market, the amount received is less than anticipated by the lender.

Value action pentagon This displays the five actions for creating value: (1) increase the return on existing capital; (2) raise investment in positive spread units; (3) divest assets from negative spread units to release capital for more productive use; (4) extend the planning horizon; (5) lower the required rate of return.

Value-based management A managerial approach in which the primary purpose is long-term shareholder wealth-maximization. The objective of the firm, its systems, strategy, processes, analytical techniques, performance measurements and culture have as their guiding objective long-term shareholder wealth-maximization.

Value chain The interlinking activities that take place within an organization or between organizations in the process of converting inputs into outputs. Identifying these activities and finding ways to perform them more efficiently is a way for companies to gain competitive advantage over their rivals.

Value creation The four key elements are: (1) amount of capital invested; (2) actual rate of return on capital; (3) required rate of return; (4) planning horizon (for performance-spread persistence).

Value-creation profile An analysis of the sources of value creation within the firm from its products and market segments, which maps value creation against the proportion of capital invested.

Value drivers Crucial organizational capabilities giving the firm competitive advantage. Different from Rappaport's value drivers (q.v.).

Value investing The identification and holding of shares that are fundamentally undervalued by the market, given the prospects of the firm.

Vanilla bond *See* Straight bond.

Variable costs Costs that rise or fall with product output and sales.

Variable rate bond (loan) The interest rate payable varies with short-term rates (e.g. LIBOR six months).

Variance A measure of volatility around an average value. It is the square of the standard deviation.

Variation margin The amount of money paid after the payment of the initial margin required to secure an option or futures position, after it has been revalued by the exchange or clearing house. Variation margin payments may be required daily to top the account up to the maintenance margin level.

Vendor placing Shares issued to a company to pay for assets, or issued to shareholders to pay for an entire company in a takeover are placed with investors keen on holding the shares in return for cash. The vendors can then receive the cash.

Venture and development capital investment trusts (VDCIT) Standard investment trusts (without tax breaks) with a focus on more risky developing companies.

Venture capital (VC) Finance provided to unquoted firms by specialized financial institutions. This may be backing for an entrepreneur, financing a start-up or developing business, or assisting a management buyout or buy-in. Usually it is provided by a mixture of equity, loans and mezzanine finance. It is used for medium-term to long-term investment in high-risk situations.

Venture capital trusts (VCTs) An investment vehicle introduced to the UK in 1995 to encourage investment in small and fast-growing companies. The VCT invests in a range of small businesses. The providers of finance to the VCT are given important tax breaks.

Vertical merger Where the two merging firms are from different stages of the production chain.

Virtual bid When a proper merger offer of one company for another has not been made, but the potential acquirer has raised the possibility of making a bid for the target firm.

Virt-x A share market operating electronically across borders. It mostly trades large Swiss company shares (it is part-owned by SWX Swiss Exchange). It is a recognized investment exchange supervised by the FSA in the UK.

Volatility The speed and magnitude of price movements over time, measured by standard deviation or variance (qq.v.).

Volume transformation Intermediaries gather small quantities of money from numerous savers and repackage these sums into larger bundles for investment in the business sector or elsewhere.

Warrant A financial instrument that gives the holder the right to subscribe for a specified number of shares or bonds at a fixed price at some time in the future.

Weak-form efficiency Share prices fully reflect all information contained in past price movements.

Wealth Added Index (WAI) A value metric devised and trademarked by Stern Stewart & Co. It measures the increase in shareholder's wealth through dividend and capital gains over a number of years after deducting the cost of equity capital, defined as the return required for shares of that risk class.

Weighted average cost of capital (WACC) (discount rate) This is calculated by weighting the cost of debt and equity in proportion to their contributions to the total capital of the firm.

White knight A friendly company that makes a bid for a company that is the subject of a hostile takeover bid. The white knight's bid is welcomed by the directors of the target company.

Whole-of-life policies Life assurance that pays out to beneficiaries when the insured dies (not limited to, say, the next 10 years).

Wholesale bank One that lends, arranges lending or supplies services on a large scale to corporations and within the interbank market. As opposed to retail banks dealing in relatively small sums for depositors and borrowers.

Wholesale financial markets Markets available only to those dealing in large quantities. Dominated by interbank transactions.

Winding-up The process of ending a company, selling its assets, paying its creditors and distributing the remaining cash among shareholders.

Winner's curse In winning a merger battle, the acquirer suffers a loss in value because it overpays.

Withholding tax Taxation deducted from income by the payer of that income (e.g. company paying interest or dividends) and then sent to tax authorities.

Work-in-progress period The number of days to convert raw materials into finished goods. Equal to the average value of work-in-progress divided by the average cost of goods sold per day.

Working capital The difference between current assets and current liabilities – net current assets or net current liabilities (q.v.).

Working capital cycle Typically, investment in raw materials, work-in-progress and finished goods is followed by sales for cash or on credit. Credit sales funds are usually collected at a later date. Investment is needed at each stage to finance current assets. The cycle may be expressed in terms of the length of time between the acquisition of raw materials and other inputs and the flow of cash from the sale of goods.

Write down (write off) Companies change the recorded value of assets when they are no longer worth the previously stated value.

Writer of an option The seller of an option contract, granting the right but not the obligation to the purchaser.

Writing-down allowance (WDA) (capital allowance) Reductions in taxable profit related to a firm's capital expenditure (e.g. plant, machinery, vehicles).

Yankees A foreign bond, US dollar-denominated, issued by a non-US entity in the domestic US market.

Yellow strip The yellow band on a SEAQ or SETS screen that displays the highest bid and the lowest offered prices that competing market makers are offering in a security. They are known colloquially as the 'touch' or 'yellow strip' prices.

Yield The income from a security as a proportion of its market price. The flat yield (interest yield, running yield and income yield) on a fixed interest security is the gross interest amount, divided by the current market price, expressed as a percentage. The redemption yield or yield to maturity of a bond is the discount rate such that the present value of all cash inflows from the bond (interest plus principal) is equal to the bond's current market price.

Yield curve A graph showing the relationship between the length of time to the maturity of a number of bonds and the interest rate offered on those bonds.

Yield stock *See* High yield shares.

Yield to maturity *See* Yield.

Z statistic A measure of the number of standard deviations away from the mean (average) value a point (say, an NPV outcome) is.

Zero-cost option A combination of option purchase and option writing. The price of the written option (premium) is the same as the price (premium) paid for the option that is purchased, so the net cost is zero.

Zero coupon bond (zero coupon preference share) A bond that does not pay regular interest (dividend) but instead is issued at a discount (i.e. below par value) and is redeemable at par, thus offering a capital gain.

The following websites provide definitions of financial terms:

http://financial-dictionary.thefreedictionary.com/
www.financial-terms.co.uk
www.global-investor.com
www.investopedia.com
www.investorwords.com
www.moneyterms.co.uk

FURTHER READING

Chapter 1

Arnold, G.C. (2000) 'Tracing the development of value-based management.' In Glen Arnold and Matt Davies (eds), *Value-based Management: Context and Application*. London: John Wiley & Sons.
A more detailed discussion of the objective of the firm is presented.

Donaldson, G. (1963) 'Financial goals: management vs. stockholders', *Harvard Business Review*, May–June, pp. 116–29.
Clear and concise discussion of the conflict of interest between managers and shareholders.

Doyle, P. (1994) 'Setting business objectives and measuring performance', *Journal of General Management*, Winter, pp. 1–19.
Western firms are over-focused on short-term financial goals (profit, ROI). Reconciling the interests of stakeholders should not be difficult as they are 'satisficers' rather than maximizers.

Financial Reporting Council (2010) The UK Corporate Goverance Code www.frc.org.uk
The current Combined Code is shown. There are likely to be minor changes in the Code over time.

Friedman, M. (1970) 'The social responsibility of business is to increase its profits', *New York Times Magazine*, 30 September.
A viewpoint on the objective of the firm.

Galbraith, J. (1967) 'The goals of an industrial system.' Reproduced in H.I. Ansoff, *Business Strategy*. London: Penguin, 1969.
Survival, sales and expansion of the 'technostructure' are emphasized as the goals in real-world corporations.

Ghoshal, S. (2005) 'Bad management theories are destroying good management practices', *Academy of Management's Learning and Education*, 4, 1, pp. 75–91.
Argues that the encouragement of shareholder wealth-maximization is wrong.

Hart, O.D. (1995a) *Firms, Contracts and Financial Structure*. Oxford: Clarendon Press.
A clear articulation of the principal–agent problem.

Hart, O.D. (1995b) 'Corporate governance: some theory and implications', *Economic Journal*, 105, pp. 678–9.
Principal–agent problem discussed.

Hayek, F.A. (1969) 'The corporation in a democratic society: in whose interests ought it and will it be run?'. Reprinted in H.I. Ansoff, *Business Strategy*. London: Penguin, 1969.
Objective should be long-run return on owners' capital subject to restraint by general legal and moral rules.

Jensen, M.C. (1986) 'Agency costs of free cash flow, corporate finance and takeovers', *American Economic Review*, 76, pp. 323–9.
Agency cost theory applied to the issue of the use to which managers put business cash inflows.

Jensen, M.C. (2001) 'Value maximisation, stakeholder theory, and the corporate objective function', *Journal of Applied Corporate Finance*, 14, 3, Fall.
Cogently argues against simple stakeholder balancing or a balance scorecard approach to directing a company because of the violation of the proposition that a single-valued objective is a prerequisite for purposeful or rational behaviour by any organization, thus politicizing the corporation and leaving managers empowered to exercise their own preferences.

Jensen, M.C. and Meckling, W.H. (1976) 'Theory of the firm: managerial behavior, agency costs and ownership structure', *Journal of Financial Economics*, pp. 305–60.
Seminal work on agency theory.

Kaplan, R. and Norton, D.P. (1996) *The Balanced Scorecard*. Boston, MA: Harvard Business School Press.
The managerial equivalent of stakeholder theory in which multiple measures are used to evaluate performance.

Kay, J. (2004) 'Forget how the crow flies', *Financial Times Magazine*, 17–18 January, pp. 17–21.
An imporant argument on obliquity is presented.

London, S. (2003) 'The long view: lunch with the FT, Milton Friedman', *Financial Times Magazine*, 7–8 June, pp. 12–13.

Smith, A. (1776) *The Wealth of Nations*. Reproduced in 1910 in two volumes by J.M. Dent, London.
An early viewpoint on the objective of the firm.

Smith, R. (2003) *Audit Committees Combined Code Guidance*. London: Financial Reporting Council, www.frc.org.uk.
One of the contributions to the Combined Code on Corporate Governance.

The Economist (2005) 'A survey of corporate social responsibility', 22 January.
A forcefully argued piece on the dangers of advocating corporate social responsibility if that means less attention to shareholder wealth.

Chapter 4

Alkaraan, F. and Northcott, D. (2006) 'Strategic capital investment decision-making: a role for emergent analysis tools? A study of practice in large UK manufacturing companies', *British Accounting Review*, 38, pp. 149–73.
As well as providing survey evidence on appraisal techniques used, this paper considers the issue of using alternative techniques for strategic investments.

Arnold, G.C. and Hatzopoulos, P.D. (2000) 'The theory–practice gap in capital budgeting: evidence from the United Kingdom', *Journal of Business Finance and Accounting*, 27(5) and (6), June/July, pp. 603–26.
Evidence of techniques used by UK firms, discussion of reasons for continued use of rule-of-thumb methods.

Bierman, H. and Smidt, S. (2006) *The Capital Budgeting Decision*, 9th edn. London: Routledge.
Beginner's guide.

Bierman, H. and Smidt, S. (2006) *Advanced Capital Budgeting*. London: Routledge.
For those who need more depth.

Graham, J.R. and Harvey, C.R. (2001) 'The theory and practice of corporate finance: evidence from the field', *Journal of Financial Economics*, 60(2–3), May, pp. 187–243.
Provides evidence of US corporate use of project appraisal techniques together with an easy-to-follow discussion.

Ho, S.M. and Pike, R.H. (1991) 'Risk analysis techniques in capital budgeting contexts', *Accounting and Business Research*, 21(83).
Survey of 146 UK firms' project risk analysis practices. Post-completion auditing evidence.

McIntyre, A.D. and Coulthurst, N.J. (1986) *Capital Budgeting Practices in Medium-Sized Businesses – A Survey*. London: Institute of Cost and Management Accountants.
Interesting survey of investment appraisal practices in UK medium-sized firms. More detailed than the later (1987) article.

McIntyre, A.D. and Coulthurst, N.J. (1987) 'Planning and control of capital investment in medium-sized UK companies', *Management Accounting*, March, pp. 39–40.
Interesting summary of empirical work explaining the capital budgeting processes in 141 medium-sized firms with turnovers in the range £1.4m–£5.75m.

Ross, S.A. (1995) 'Uses, abuses, and alternatives to the net present value rule', *Financial Management*, 24(3), Autumn, pp. 96 102.
Discussion of the value of NPV.

Steele, R. and Albright, C. (2004) 'Games managers play at budget time', *MIT Sloan Management Review*, Spring, p. 81
Executive game-play tactics revealed.

Chapter 5

Alkaraan, F. and Northcott, D. (2006) 'Strategic capital investment decision-making: a role for emergent analysis tools? A study of practice in large UK manufacturing companies', *British Accounting Review*, 38, pp. 149–73.

Arnold, G.C. and Hartzopoulos, P.D. (2000) 'The theory–practice gap in capital budgeting: evidence from the United Kingdom', *Journal of Business Finance and Accounting*, 27(5) and (6), June/July, pp. 603–26.
Discussion on the use of alternative risk adjustment methods is provided.

Amran, M. and Kulatilaka, N. (1999) *Real Options: Managing Strategic Investment in an Uncertain World*. Boston, MA: Harvard Business School Press.

Bierman, H. and Smidt, S. (2006) *The Capital Budgeting Decision*, 9th edn. London: Routledge.
An introduction to risk in project appraisal.

Bierman, H. and Smidt, S. (2006) *Advanced Capital Budgeting*. London: Routledge.

Brennan, M.J. and Trigeorgis, L. (eds) (2000) *Project Flexibility, Agency, and Competition: New Developments in the Theory and Application of Real Options.* Oxford, New York: Oxford University Press.
Contains a number of important papers on real options.

Chittenden, F. and Darregia, M. (2004) 'Capital investment decision making: some results from studying entrepreneurial businesses', www.icaew.co.uk.
Many entrepreneurial firms rely more on qualitative assessments than formal capital budgeting. Also they build in options through leasing, hiring and renting because they are cheap to get out of.

Copeland, T. and Tufano, P. (2004) 'A real-world way to manage real options', *Harvard Business Review*, March, pp. 1–11.
A simplified use of option analysis.

Dixit, A.K. and Pindyck, R.S. (1995) 'The options approach to capital investment', *Harvard Business Review*, May–June. (Also reproduced in J. Rutterford (ed.) *Financial Strategy.* New York: John Wiley & Sons, 1998.)
An easy-to-follow discussion of inadequacy of the traditional simple NPV approach and an introduction to the real options perspective.

Graham, J.R. and Harvey, C.R. (2001) 'The theory and practice of corporate finance: evidence from the field', *Journal of Financial Economics*, 60, 2–3, May, pp. 187–243.
Shows the use of risk techniques in US corporations.

Ho, S. and Pike, R.H. (1991) 'Risk analysis in capital budgeting contexts: simple or sophisticated', *Accounting and Business Research*, Summer, pp. 227–38.
Excellent survey of risk-handling techniques adopted in 146 large companies.

Moel, A. and Tufano, P. (2002) 'When are real options exercised? An empirical study of mine closings', *Review of Financial Studies*, Spring, 15, 1, pp. 35–64.
The usefulness of real option analysis is demonstrated.

Pike, R.H. (1988) 'An empirical study of the adoption of sophisticated capital budgeting practices and decision-making effectiveness', *Accounting and Business Research*, 18(72), pp. 341–51.
Interesting evidence on the practical use of risk analysis techniques.

Pike, R.H. (1996) 'A longitudinal survey of capital budgeting practices', *Journal of Business Finance and Accounting*, 23(1), January.
Clearly described evidence on the capital investment appraisal practices of major UK companies.

Schwartz, E.S. and Trigeorgis, L. (eds) (2001) *Real Options and Investment Under Uncertainty: Classical Readings and Recent Contributions.* London, Cambridge, MA: MIT Press.
The major articles in the field are included – dozens of them.

Van Putten, A.B. and MacMillan I.C. (2004) 'Making real options really work', *Harvard Business Review*, December, pp. 1–8.
Easy-to-read article explaining the complementary use of real option analysis and DCF analysis.

Chapter 6

Arnold, G.C. (2009) *The Financial Times Guide to Value Investing*, 2nd edn. London: FT Prentice Hall.

An investment book that considers corporate strategy and the potential for value creation.

Arnold, G.C. and Davies, M. (eds) (2000) *Value-Based Management*. London: John Wiley & Sons.

A collection of research monographs that focuses on this emerging field.

McKinsey & Co. (Koller, T., Goedhart, M. and Wessels, D.) (2005) *Valuation*, 4th edn. New York: John Wiley & Sons.

The management of value-based organizations and the principles behind the techniques are explained well.

McTaggart, J.M., Kontes, P.W. and Mankins, M.C. (1994) *The Value Imperative*. New York: Free Press.

A very good book showing the application of value-based techniques to strategy and other disciplines.

Pitman, B. (2003) 'Heading for value', *Harvard Business Review*, April, pp. 41–6.

The former CEO and chairman describes clearly and succinctly the evolution of Lloyds Bank from a company without a clear objective to a focus on shareholder value, using return on equity relative to cost of equity to evaluate company operations and reward managers. The logic of a value focus led to 'we had to accept that it was all right to get smaller, to stay close to home, to focus on unglamorous products . . . getting rid of unprofitable customers, getting out of unprofitable markets'.

Rappaport, A. (1998) *Creating Shareholder Value* (revised and updated version). New York: Free Press.

A landmark book. Presents an important value metric – shareholders' value analysis (SVA).

Reimann, B.C. (1989) *Managing for Value*. Oxford: Basil Blackwell.

Useful because it brings together strategy and value.

Stewart, G.B. (1991) *The Quest for Value*. New York: Harper Business.

Written by a founding partner in Stern Stewart and Co., the US consultancy that has so successfully promoted MVA and EVA. Some useful insights.

Stewart, G.B. (2001) 'Market myths', in *The New Corporate Finance*, 3rd edn. Edited by Donald H. Chew. New York: McGraw-Hill/Irwin.

An easy-to-read discussion of the difficulties with accounting metrics and the triumphing of value principles.

Chapter 7

Arnold, G. (2009) *The Financial Times Guide to Value Investing*, 2nd edn. London: FT Prentice Hall.

An integration of strategic analysis with equity market investment principles.

Arnold, G.C. (2010) *The Financial Times Guide to Investing*, 2nd edn. London: FT Prentice Hall.

Contains chapters on strategic evaluation of companies.

Arnold, G.C. and Davies, M. (eds) (2000) *Value-Based Management*. Chichester: John Wiley & Sons.
A collection of research monographs describing practical and theoretical issues in this field.

Buffett, W. (1984) *Berkshire Hathaway Annual Report*. Omaha, NE: Berkshire Hathaway.
As with all reports by Buffett, this one is full of profound and witty insight. www.berkshirehathaway.com.

Collis, D.J. and Montgomery, C.A. (2005) *Corporate Strategy: A resource-based approach*, 2nd edn. New York: McGraw-Hill.
A very important and easy-to-read book on the subject of resources of companies.

Davies, M. (2000) 'Lessons from practice: VBM at Lloyds TSB', in G.C. Arnold and M. Davies (eds) *Value-Based Management*. Chichester: John Wiley & Sons.
Insights into a company making use of VBM principles.

De Wit, B. and Meyer, R. (2004) *Strategy: Process, Content, Context*, 3rd edn. Cincinnati, OH: South-Western College Publishers.
Some interesting sections in a very long book.

Johnson, G. and Scholes, K. (2007) *Exploring Corporate Strategy*, 8th edn. Harlow: Pearson Education.
A well-regarded introductory textbook to the strategic management of firms.

Kay, J. (1993) *Foundations of Corporate Success*. New York: Oxford University Press.
A study of corporate strategy.

McKinsey & Co. (Koller, T., Goedhart, M. and Wessels, D.) (2005) *Valuation*, 4th edn. New York: John Wiley & Sons.
The management of value-based organizations and the principles behind the techniques are explained well.

McTaggart, J.M., Kontes, P.W. and Mankins, M.C. (1994) *The Value Imperative*. New York: Free Press.
A very good book showing the application of value-based techniques to strategy and other disciplines.

Porter, M.E. (1980) *Competitive Strategy*. New York: Free Press.
One of the most important books on strategy ever written.

Porter, M.E. (1985) *Competitive Advantage*. New York: Free Press.
More valuable insight into strategic analysis.

Prahalad, C.K. and Hamel, G. (1990) 'The core competence of the corporation', *Harvard Business Review*, 68, 3, May–June, pp. 79–91.
A paper that led to increased interest in seeing the corporation as a collection of resources, some of which are extraordinary.

Rappaport, A. (1998) *Creating Shareholder Value* (revised and updated edition). New York: Free Press.
A landmark book. Presents an important value metric – shareholder value analysis.

Reimann, B.C. (1989) *Managing for Value*. Oxford: Basil Blackwell.
Useful because it brings together strategy and value.

Stewart, G.B. (1991) *The Quest for Value*. New York: Harper Business.
Written by a founding partner in Stern Stewart & Co., the US consultancy that has so successfully promoted MVA and EVA. Some useful insights.

Chapter 8

Aggarwal, R. (2001) 'Using economic profit to assess performance: a metric for modern firms', *Business Horizons,* January/February, pp. 55–60.
A brief overview of the issues raised by implementing an EP-based programme.

Anderson, A.M., Bey, R.P. and Weaver, S.C. (2005) 'Economic Value Added® Adjustments: Much ado about nothing?', working paper. Bethlehem, PA: Lehigh University.
Casts doubt on the usefulness of moving away from EP. EVA's adjustments from accounting income and capital do not make much difference to residual income.

Arnold, G.C. and Davies, M. (eds) (2000) *Value-Based Management*. London: John Wiley & Sons.
A collection of research monographs.

Davies, M. (2000) 'Lessons from practice: VBM at Lloyds TSB', in Arnold, G.C. and Davies, M. (eds) *Value-Based Management*. London: John Wiley & Sons.
Insights into a company making use of VBM principles.

Martin, J.D. and Petty, J.W (2000) *Value Based Management: Corporate Response to the Shareholder Revolution*. Boston, MA: Harvard Business School Press.
There are good chapters on free cash flow and CFROI.

McKinsey & Co. (Koller, T, Goedhart, M. and Wessel, D.) (2005) *Valuation,* 4th edn. New York: John Wiley & Sons.
The management of value-based organizations and the principles behind the techniques are explained.

McTaggart, J.M., Kontes, P.W. and Mankins, M.C. (1994) *The Value Imperative*. New York: Free Press.
Showing the application of value-based techniques to strategy and other disciplines.

Rappaport, A. (1998) *Creating Shareholder Value* (revised and updated edition). New York: Free Press.
A landmark book. Presents an important value metric – shareholder value analysis.

Reimann, B.C. (1989) *Managing for Value*. Oxford: Basil Blackwell.
Useful because it brings together strategy and value.

Solomons, D. (1965) *Divisional Performance: Measurement and Control* (reproduced 1983). Connecticut: M. Weiner Publishing.
An early formulation of residual income (economic profit).

Stewart, G.B. (1991) *The Quest for Value*. New York: Harper Business.
Written by a founding partner in Stern Stewart & Co., the US consultancy that has so successfully promoted MVA and EVA. Some useful insights.

Stewart, G.B. (2001) 'Market myths', in Chew, D.H. (ed.), *The New Corporate Finance*. New York: McGraw-Hill/Irwin.
Advocating the value approach.

Tully, S. (1993) 'The real key to creating wealth', *Fortune*, 20 September, pp. 38–50.
The application of EVA to US corporations is described in an accessible style.

Wallace, J. S. (1997) 'Adopting residual income-based compensation plans: do you get what you pay for?', *Journal of Accounting and Economics*, 24, pp. 275–300.
Observes that firms that adapt economic profit for managerial incentive targets achieve a change in managerial actions (decreased new investment, sell-off of assets, raised share buy-backs and more intense asset utilization).

Weaver, S.C. (2001) 'Measuring Economic Value Added®: a survey of the practices of EVA® proponents', *Journal of Applied Finance*, Fall/Winter, pp. 7–17.
Evidence that EVA is implemented in a variety of ways (different 'adjustments', different WACC calculations).

Young, S.D. and O'Byrne, S.F. (2001) *EVA® and Value-based Management: A Practical Guide to Implementation.* New York: McGraw-Hill.
An easy-to-follow description of EVA with a critical edge.

Chapter 9

Stewart, G.B. (1991) *The Quest for Value*. New York: Harper Business.
Written by a founding partner in Stern Stewart and Co., the US consultancy that has so successfully promoted MVA and EVA®. Some useful insights.

Young, D.S. and O'Byrne, S.F. (2001) *EVA and Value-Based Management: A Practical Guide to Implementation.* New York: McGraw-Hill.
A useful overview of value-based management.

Chapter 10

Arnold, G.C. and Hatzopoulos, P.D. (2000) 'The theory practice gap in capital budgeting: evidence from the United Kingdom', *Journal of Business Finance and Accounting*, 27(5) and (6), June/July, pp. 603–26.

Barclays Capital *The Equity-Gilt Studies*. London: Barclays.
Annual source of data on historic returns.

Black, F. (1993) 'Beta and returns', *Journal of Portfolio Management*, 20, 8–18, Fall.
Estimating the relationship between beta and return on US shares 1926–91. Relationship is poor after 1965.

Blume, M. and Friend, I. (1973) 'A new look at the Capital Asset Pricing Model', *Journal of Finance*, March.
The evidence in this paper seems to require a rejection of the capital asset pricing theory as an explanation of the observed returns on all financial assets.

Blume, M.E. (1975) 'Betas and their regression tendencies', *Journal of Finance*, XXX, 3 June, pp. 785–95.
Betas tend to 1 over time.

Blume, M.E (1971) 'On the assessment of risk', *Journal of Finance*, XXVI March, 1, pp. 1–10.
Betas change over time.

Brealey, R.M., Myers, S.C. and Allen, F. (2010) *Principles of Corporate Finance*, 8th edn. New York: McGraw-Hill.
A textbook treatment with an emphasis on theory.

Chan, L.K.C. and Lakonishok, J. (1993) 'Are the reports of beta's death premature?', *Journal of Portfolio Management*, 19, Summer, pp. 51–62. Reproduced in S. Lofthouse (ed.) *Readings in Investment*, John Wiley & Sons, 1994.
Readable discussion of CAPM's validity in the light of some new evidence.

Corhay, A., Hawawini, G. and Michel, P. (1987) 'Seasonality in the risk-return relationship: some international evidence', *Journal of Finance*, 42, pp. 49–68.
Evidence on the validity of the CAPM in the UK, France, Belgium and USA. Not good news for CAPM.

Damodaran, A. (1999) *Applied Corporate Finance: A User's Manual*. New York: John Wiley & Sons.
An excellent book prepared to deal with the difficult practical issues of WACC calculation and employment.

Dimson, E., Marsh, P. and Staunton, M. (2002) *Triumph of the Optimists: 101 Years of Global Investment Returns*, Princeton, NJ: Princeton University Press.
Fascinating evidence on risk premiums.

Dimson, E., Marsh, P., Staunton, M. and Wilmot, J. (2009) *Credit Suisse Global Investment Yearbook*.
An annual publication providing statistics on security returns.

Fama, E.F. and French, K.R. (1992) 'The cross-section of expected stock returns', *Journal of Finance*, 47, pp. 427–65.
A study casting doubt on beta and showing size of company and book-to-market ratio affecting returns on shares.

Fama, E.F. and French, K.R. (2002) 'The equity premium', *Journal of Finance*, 57(2), April, pp. 637–59.
A discussion of the risk premium for shares over risk free investment.

Fama, E.F. and French, K.R. (2006) 'The value premium and the CAPM', *Journal of Finance*, LXI(5), October, pp. 2163–85.
A discussion of return on shares.

Fernandez, P and J del Campo (2010) Market Risk premium used in 2010 by Professors: a survey with 1,500 answers. IESE Business School. Available at http://ssrn.com/abstract=1606563
University professors tend to use between 5% and 6% for the equity risk premium.

Francis, G. and Minchington, C. (2000) 'Value-based metrics as divisional performance measures', in G.C. Arnold and M. Davies (eds) *Value-Based Management*. London: John Wiley & Sons.
Empirical evidence and discussion.

Friend, I. and Blume, M. (1970) 'Measurement of portfolio performance under uncertainty', *American Economic Review*, September, pp. 561–75.
A discussion of the usefulness of market-line theory and its ability to explain market behaviour.

Gordon, M.J. (1962) *The Investment, Financing and Valuation of the Corporation.* Homewood. IL: R.D. Irwin.
Dividend growth model.

Gordon, M.J. and Shapiro, E. (1956) 'Capital equipment analysis: the required rate of profit', *Management Science*, III, pp. 102–10.
Dividend growth model.

Gregory, A. and Rutterford, J. (1999) 'The cost of capital in the UK: a comparison of industry and the city', *CIMA Monograph*, May.
Evidence on UK practice.

Levy, R.A. (1971) 'On the short-term stationarity of beta coefficients', *Financial Analysts Journal*, Nov–Dec. pp. 55–62.
Betas change over time.

Lockett, M. (2001) *Calculating the Cost of Capital for the Regulated Electricity Distribution Companies*, Aston University MBA project.
A through analysis of the theoretical and practical issues.

Lockett, M. (2002) 'Calculating the cost of capital for the regulated electricity distribution companies', *Power Engineering Journal*, October, pp. 251–63.
An excellent summary of this issue with particular emphasis on regulated companies.

Pike, R.H. (1983) 'A review of recent trends in formal capital budgeting processes', *Accounting and Business Research*, Summer, pp. 201–8.
Evidence of practitioner approaches.

Rosenberg, B. and Rudd, A. (1986) 'The corporate uses of beta', in J.M. Stern and D.H. Chew (eds), *The Revolution in Corporate Finance*. Oxford: Basil Blackwell.
Using CAPM to find discount rate for projects. Incorporates other risk factors: growth, earnings variability, leverage and size. Easy to read article aimed at the novice.

Rutterford, J. (2000) 'The cost of capital and shareholder value', in G.C. Arnold and M. Davies (eds) *Value-Based Management*. London: John Wiley & Sons.
Some fascinating evidence of UK practice.

Shiller, R.J. (2000) *Irrational Exuberance*. Princeton, NJ: Princeton University Press.

Solomon, E. (1963) *The Theory of Financial Management*. New York: Columbia University Press.
WACC presented for the first time.

Solomons, D. (1985) *Divisional Performance, Measurement and Control*, 2nd edn. Connecticut: Weiner Publishing.
An early use of the concept of economic profit.

Strong, N. and Xu, X.G. (1997) 'Explaining the cross-section of UK expected stock returns', *British Accounting Review*.
More evidence of the poor relationship between beta and returns.

Chapters 11 and 12

Ambrose, B.W. and Megginson, W.L. (1992) 'The role of asset structure, ownership structure, and takeover defences in determining acquisition likelihood', *Journal of Financial and Quantitative Analysis*, 27(4), pp. 575–89.

Bhide, A. (1993) 'The causes and consequences of hostile takeovers', in Chew, Jr, D.H. (ed.), *The New Finance: Where Theory Meets Practice*. New York: McGraw-Hill.
Target firms are poor performers.

Buffett, W. (1982) Letter to shareholders accompanying the Berkshire Hathaway Annual Report. Omaha, NE. www.berkshirehathaway.com.
Words of wit and wisdom forged by business experience.

Buffett, W. (1995) Letter to shareholders accompanying the Berkshire Hathaway Annual Report. Omaha, NE. www.berkshirehathaway.com.
Words of wit and wisdom forged by business experience.

Buono, A. and Bowditch, J. (2003) *The Human Side of Mergers and Acquisitions*. Beard Books.
Explains the importance of the management of people during and after merger.

Cartwright, S. and Cooper, C. (1992) *Mergers and Acquisitions: The Human Factor*. Oxford: Butterworth Heinemann.
Cultural and other 'soft' issues of mergers are discussed.

Conyon, M.J. and Clegg, P. (1994) 'Pay at the top: a study of the sensitivity of top director remuneration to specific shocks', *National Institute of Economic and Social Research Review*, August.
Growth of the firm (sales) is positively related to directors' pay.

Coopers & Lybrand and OC & C (1993) *A Review of the Acquisition Experience of Major UK companies*. London: Coopers & Lybrand.
An interesting survey of the top 100 firms' reasons for difficulties and triumphs in post-merger management.

Conn, R.L., Cosh, A., Guest, P.M. and Hughes, A. (2005) 'The impact on UK acquirers of domestic, cross-border, public and private acquisitions', *Journal of Business Finance and Accounting*, 32(5) and (6), June/July.
UK-quoted companies acquiring UK companies results in relatively poor returns around the announcement date and over the subsequent three years on average (–22 per cent). UK acquirers in cross-border mergers of quoted companies are also poor performers. However, private UK (not on stock market) acquirers tend to produce zero post-acquisition returns on average.

Cosh, A., Guest, P.M. and Hughes, A. (2006) 'Board share-ownership and takeover performance', *Journal of Business Finance and Accounting*, 33(3/4), April/May pp. 459–510.
UK study. The larger the holding of shares in the company by the chief executive, the better the post-merger long-term share returns.

Cowling, K., Stoneman, P. and Cubbin, J., *et al.* (1980) *Mergers and Economic Performance*. Cambridge: Cambridge University Press.
Discusses the societal costs and benefits of mergers.

Devine, M. (2004) *Successful Mergers: Getting the People Issues Right*. London: The Economist/Profile Books.
An accessible introduction to the 'soft' managerial issues.

The Economist (2000) 'Merger briefs' (two-page post-merger analysis of successes and failures) in the following editions: DaimlerChrysler, 29 July 2000; HypoVereinsbank, 5 August 2000; Boeing, 12 August 2000; Compaq, 22 July 2000; AOL Time Warner, 19 August 2000; Citicorp, 26 August 2000.

Epstein, M.J. (2005) 'The determinants and evaluation of merger success', *Business Horizons*, 48, pp. 37–46.
Offers six key factors needed for merger success; US case study incorporated.

Fee, C.E. and Thomas, S. (2004) 'Sources of gains in horizontal mergers: evidence from customer, supplier, and rival firms', *Journal of Financial Economics*, 74(3), December, pp. 423–60.
Improved productivity and buying power as a result of merger.

Firth, M. (1980) 'Takeovers, shareholders' returns and the theory of the firm', *Quarterly Journal of Economics*, 94, March, pp. 235–60.
UK study. Results: **a** the target shareholders benefit; **b** the acquiring shareholders lose; **c** the acquiring firm's management increases utility; **d** the economic gains to society are, at best, zero.

Firth, M. (1991) 'Corporate takeovers, stockholder returns and executive rewards', *Managerial and Decision Economics*, 12, pp. 421–8.
Mergers leading to increased size of firm result in higher managerial remuneration.

Franks, J. and Harris, R. (1989) 'Shareholder wealth effects of corporate takeovers: the UK experience 1955–85', *Journal of Financial Economics*, 23, pp. 225–49.
Study of 1,800 UK takeovers. Gains of 25–30 percent for targets. Zero or modest gains for acquirers. Overall there is value created for shareholders.

Franks, J. and Mayer, C. (1996) 'Hostile takeovers and correction of managerial failure', *Journal of Financial Economics*, 40, pp. 163–81.

Ghosh, A. (2004) 'Increasing market share as a rationale for corporate acquisitions', *Journal of Business Finance and Accounting*, 31(1) & (2), January/March, pp. 209–47.
US study of 2,000 acquisitions. Increasing market share following merger is correlated with positive acquirer abnormal returns and operating performance.

Goergen, M. and Renneboog, L. (2004) 'Shareholder wealth effects of European domestic and cross-border takeover bids', *European Financial Management*, 10(1), pp. 9–45.
Europe-wide study. On average, bidder performance is roughly the same as the market during the four months around the merger announcement date. Bids financed by equity produce better announcement period returns than those financed by cash.

Gregory, A. (1997) 'An examination of the long-run performance of UK acquiring firms', *Journal of Business Finance and Accounting*, 24(7–8), September, pp. 971–1002.
More evidence on the poor performance of acquirers.

Gregory, A. (2005) 'The long run abnormal performance of UK acquirers and the free cash flow hypothesis', *Journal of Business Finance and Accounting*, 32(5) and (6), June/July, pp. 777–814.
UK acquirers underperform the market by 19.9 percent over 60 months, 1984–92. Acquirers with a high level of free cash flow perform better than acquirers with low free cash flow in the five years following merger as measured by total return.

Harding, D., Rovit, S. and Corbett, A. (2005) 'Three steps to avoiding merger meltdown', *Harvard Management Update*, March, pp. 1–5.
A short article offering post-merger integration advice.

Hasbrouck, J. (1985) 'The characteristics of takeover targets: q and other measures', *Journal of Banking and Finance*, 9, pp. 351–62.

Haspeslagh, P. and Jemison, D. (1991) *Managing Acquisitions*. New York: Free Press.
A thorough and well-written guide to the management of firms that engage in mergers.

Higson, C. and Elliot, J. (1993) 'The returns to takeovers – the UK evidence', IFA Working Paper. London: London Business School.
More evidence on the poor performance of the shares of acquiring firms.

Hunt, J.W., Lees, S., Grumber, J. and Vivian, P. (1987) *Acquisitions: The Human Factor*. London: London Business School and Egan Zehnder International.
Forty UK companies investigated. Merger motives, success or failure rates and success factors (particularly people factors) are explored.

Jensen, M.C. (1986) 'Agency costs of free cashflow, corporate finance and takeovers', *American Economic Review*, May, p. 323.
Dividend payouts reduce managers' resources and lead to greater monitoring if they go to the capital markets for funds. Internal funding is thus preferred and surplus cash flow leads to value-destroying mergers. Easy to read.

Jensen, M.C. and Meckling, W.H. (1976) 'Theory of the firm: managerial behavior, agency cost and ownership structure', *Journal of Financial Economics*, October, pp. 305–60.
An important paper on agency theory.

Kuehn, D. (1975) *Takeovers and the Theory of the Firm: An Empirical Analysis for the United Kingdom 1957–1969*. Basingstoke: Macmillan.
Acquiring firms that engage in multiple acquisitions display profitability, growth rates, etc., that are no different from those of firms which engage in few takeovers.

Lev, B. (1992) 'Observations on the merger phenomenon and a review of the evidence.' Reprinted in J.M. Stern and D. Chew (eds), *The Revolution in Corporate Finance*, 2nd edn. Oxford: Blackwell.
Merger motives, and who wins from mergers, are discussed in an introductory style.

Levine, P. and Aaronovitch, S. (1981) 'The financial characteristics of firms and theories of merger activity', *Journal of Industrial Economics*, 30, pp. 149–72.
An early paper on mergers.

Limmack, R. (1991) 'Corporate mergers and shareholder wealth effect, 1977–86', *Accounting and Business Research*, 21(83), pp. 239–51.
'Although there is no net wealth decrease to shareholders in total as a result of takeover activity, shareholders of bidder firms do suffer wealth decreases.'

Loughran, J. and Vijh, A.M. (1997) 'Do long term shareholders benefit from corporate acquisitions?', *Journal of Finance*, 52(5), pp. 1765–90.
Empirical evidence on post-merger performance.

Louis, H. (2004a) 'Earnings management and the market performance of acquiring firms', *Journal of Financial Economics*, 74(1), October, pp. 121–48.
Evidence suggesting that acquiring firms overstate earnings in quarter before acquiring – linked to poor post-merger performance.

Louis, H. (2004b) 'The cost of using bank mergers as defensive mechanisms against takeover threats', *Journal of Business*, 77(2) pt.1, pp. 295–310.
Evidence to show that by acquiring other banks managers can avoid being taken over.

Lynch, P. (1990) *One Up on Wall Street*. New York: Penguin.
One of the greatest investors comments on companies and managers in a witty fashion.

Manson, S., Stark, A. and Thomas, H.M. (1994) 'A cash flow analysis of the operational gains from takeovers', *Research Report 35*. London: Chartered Association of Certified Accountants.

Post-merger and pre-merger consolidated operating performance measures are compared. Operational gains are produced on average. A study of 38 companies.

McKinsey and Co. (Koller, T., Goedhart, and Wessels, D.) (2005) *Valuation*, 4th edn. New York: John Wiley & Sons Ltd.
Provides some useful and easy-to-follow guidance on merger management.

Meeks, G. (1977) *Disappointing Marriage: A Study of the Gains from Mergers*. Cambridge: Cambridge University Press.
Evidence on merger failure from the acquiring shareholders' point of view.

Meeks, G. and Whittington, G. (1975) 'Director's pay, growth and profitability', *Journal of Industrial Economics*, 24(1), pp. 1–14.
Empirical evidence that directors' pay and firm sales (size of firm) are positively correlated.

Mitchell, M.L. and Lehn, K. (1990) 'Do bad bidders become good targets?', *Journal of Political Economy*, 98(2), pp. 372–98.
'Hostile bust-up takeovers often promote economic efficiency by reallocating the targets' assets to higher valued uses . . . In aggregate, we find that the returns to acquiring firms are approximately zero; the aggregate data obscure the fact that the market discriminates between "bad" bidders which are more likely to become takeover targets, and "good" bidders, which are less likely to become targets.'

Moeller, S.B., Schlingemann, F.P. and Stulz, R.M. (2004) 'Firm size and the gains from acquisitions', *Journal of Financial Economics*, 73, pp. 201–228.
US study. Acquiring firm announcement period abnormal return is on average slightly positive for small firms but negative for large firms. Given that larger firms offer larger acquisition premiums and enter acquisitions with negative dollar synergy gains, 'the evidence is consistent with managerial hubris playing more of a role in the decisions of large firms'.

Moeller, S.B., Schlingemann, F.P. and Stulz, R.M. (2005) 'Wealth destruction on a massive scale? A study of acquiring-firm returns in the recent merger wave', *Journal of Finance*, LX(2), April, pp. 757–82.
US study. On average acquirer shareholders experience a poor return in the few days around acquisition announcement – particularly so in the period 1998–2001 (hi-tech boom period).

Morosini, P. and Steger, U. (eds) (2004) *Managing Complex Mergers: Real World Lessons in Implementing Successful Cross-Cultural M&As*. Harlow: Financial Times Prentice Hall.
Provides an accessible overview of thinking on the issue of merger failure and merger management.

Palepu, K.G. (1986) 'Predicting takeover targets: a methodological and empirical analysis', *Journal of Accounting and Finance*, 8, pp. 3–35.

Panel on Takeovers and Mergers, The City Code. www.thetakeoverpanel.org.uk
The complex set of rules are laid out in reasonably easy-to-follow fashion. Updated regularly.

Powell, R.G. and Stark, A.W. (2005) 'Does operating performance increase post-takeover for UK takeovers? A comparison of performance measures and benchmarks', *Journal of Corporate Finance*, 11(1 and 2), March, p. 293–317.

Powell, R.G. and Thomas, H.M. (1994) 'Corporate control and takeover prediction', working paper 94/07, Department of Accounting and Financial Management, University of Essex.

Rappaport, A. (1998) *Creating Shareholder Value*. New York: Free Press.

Revised and updated. Chapter 8 provides a shareholder value perspective on mergers.

Rau, P.R. and Vermaelen, T. (1998) 'Glamour, value and the post-acquisition performance of acquiring firms', *Journal of Financial Economics*, 49(2), pp. 223–53.

Ravenscraft, D. and Scherer, F. (1987) *Mergers, Sell-Offs and Economic Efficiency*. Washington, DC: Brookings Institution.
An overview of mergers: rationale, activity, profitability, economics. US-based.

Roll, R. (1986) 'The hubris hypothesis of corporate takeovers', *Journal of Business*, 59(2), pt. 1, April, pp. 197–216. Also reproduced in R. Thaler (ed.) (1993) *Advances in Behavioral Finance*. New York: Russell Sage Foundation.
'Bidding firms infected by hubris simply pay too much for their targets.'

Schweiger, D. (2002) *M&A Integration: A Framework for Executives and Managers*. Oxford: McGraw-Hill Education.
Deals with post-merger management.

Singh, A. (1971) *Takeovers*. Cambridge: Cambridge University Press.
Provides evidence on the type of firms which become targets.

Sirower, M.L. (1997) *The Synergy Trap: How Companies Lose the Acquisition Game*. New York: Free Press.
A practical, easy-to-read guide to mergers and the reasons for the failure to create value.

Stahl, G. and Mendenhall, M. (2005) *Mergers and Acquisitions: Managing Culture and Human Resources*. Stanford, CA: Stanford University Press.
The human aspect of mergers.

Sudarsanam, S. (2003) *Creating Value from Mergers and Acquisitions: The Challenge*. Harlow: FT Prentice Hall.
An easy-to-read comprehensive guide to all aspects of mergers – well worth reading.

Sudarsanam, S. and Mahate, A. (2003) 'Glamour acquirers, methods of payment and post-acquisition performance: The UK evidence', *Journal of Business Finance and Accounting*, 30(1 and 2), pp. 299–341.

Sudarsanam, S., Holl, P. and Salami, A. (1996) 'Shareholder wealth gains in mergers: effect of synergy and ownership structure', *Journal of Business Finance and Accounting*, July, pp. 673–98.
A study of 429 UK mergers, 1980–90. Financial synergy dominates operational synergy. A marriage between companies with a complementary fit in terms of liquidity slack and surplus investment opportunities is value creating for both groups of shareholders. But high-rated acquirers taking over low-rated firms lose value.

Van de Vliet, A. (1997) 'When mergers misfire', *Management Today*, June.
An excellent, easy-to-read overview of merger problems with plenty of examples.

Chapter 13

Arnold, G. (2009) *The Financial Times Guide to Value Investing*, 2nd edition. Harlow: FT Prentice Hall.
An integration of strategic analysis with equity market investment principles.

Arnold, G. (2010) *The Financial Times Guide to Investing* 2nd edition. London: FT Prentice Hall.
An introduction to share valuation including guidance on industry and competitive position analysis.

Blake, D. (2000) *Financial Market Analysis,* 2nd edn. New York: John Wiley & Sons.
Chapter 6 contains a valuable discussion on share valuation.

Bodie, Z., Kane, A. and Marcus, A.J. (2005) *Investments,* 6th edn. New York: McGraw-Hill.
Contains a well-written chapter (18) on valuation models – easy to follow.

Damodaran, A. (2002) *Investment Valuation,* 2nd edn. New York: John Wiley & Sons.
Covers many aspects of share and company valuation at introductory and intermediate level.

Damodaran, A. (2005) *Applied Corporate Finance: A User's Manual,* 2nd edn. New York: John Wiley & Sons.
A good chapter on share valuation.

Gordon, M.J. (1962) *The Investment, Financing and Valuation of the Corporation.* Homewood, IL: Irwin.
An early statement of a dividend growth model.

Gordon, M.J. and Shapiro, E. (1956) 'Capital equipment analysis: the required rate of profit', *Management Science,* III, pp. 102-10.
Dividend growth model presented.

Lofthouse, S. (2001) *Investment Management,* 2nd edn. Chichester: John Wiley & Sons.
A practitioner assesses the theoretical models and empirical evidence on investment issues, including valuation. Very easy to follow.

Lowe, J. (1997) *Warren Buffett Speaks.* New York: John Wiley & Sons.
A knowledgeable, witty and wise financier's comments are collected and presented. An excellent antidote to theoretical purism.

McKinsey and Co. (Koller, T., Goedhart, M. and Wessels, D.) (2005). *Valuation,* 4th edn. New York: John Wiley & Sons.
Some valuation issues are presented in an accessible style.

Outram, R. (1997) 'For what it's worth', *Management Today,* May, pp. 70–71.

Rappaport, A. (1999) *Creating Shareholder Value.* New York: Free Press. Revised and updated.
Describes cash flow valuation models clearly.

Sharpe, W.F., Alexander, G.J. and Bailey, J.V. (1999) *Investments,* 6th edn. Upper Saddle River, NJ: Prentice-Hall.
A wider range of valuation issues is discussed in an accessible introductory style.

Solomon, E. (1963) *The Theory of Financial Management.* New York: Columbia University Press.
An early discussion of the Gordon and Shapiro dividend growth model.

Stephens, G. and Funnell, J. (1995) 'Take your partners ...', *Corporate Finance,* London: Euromoney monthly journal, July.
Discusses the difficult issue of valuation of telemedia companies.

Chapter 14

Baker, H.K., Powell, G.E. and Veit E.T. (2002) 'Revisiting managerial perspectives on dividend policy', *Journal of Economics and Finance,* 26(3), pp. 267–83.
Evidence for avoidance of dividend cuts and the maintenance of dividend continuity.

Baker, M. and Wurgler, J. (2004) 'A catering theory of dividends', *Journal of Finance,* 59(3), June, pp. 1125–65.
'Managers give investors what they currently want.'

Brav, A., Graham, J.R., Harvey, C.R. and Michaely, R. (2005) 'Payout policy in the 21st century', *Journal of Financial Economics,* 77, pp. 483–527.
A survey of US executives. Confirms Lintner's (1956) observation that perceived stability of future earnings affects dividend policy. Signalling is asymmetric, therefore firms are reluctant to cut dividend.

Brealey, R.H. (1986) 'Does dividend policy matter?', in Stern, J.M. and Chew, D.H. (eds), *The Revolution in Corporate Finance.* Oxford: Basil Blackwell.
Argues that dividend policy is irrelevant to wealth except that this is affected by taxes. Also acknowledges the information effect.

Brennan, M. (1971) 'A note on dividend irrelevance and the Gordon valuation model', *Journal of Finance,* December, pp. 1115–21.
A technical discussion of the opposing theories of MM and Gordon.

Damodaran, A. (1999) *Applied Corporate Finance.* New York: John Wiley & Sons.
Chapters 10 and 11 consider dividend policy in a practical exposition.

Dhanani, A. (2005) 'Corporate dividend policy: the views of British financial managers', *Journal of Business Finance and Accounting,* 32 (7) and (8), September/October, pp. 1625–72.
A survey of UK managers. Signalling and clienteles (with the influence of tax) are apparent.

Easterbrook, F.H. (1984) 'Two *agency-cost* explanations of dividends', *American Economic Review,* 74(4), September, pp. 650–60.
Managers may act in their own self-interest. Agency cost explanation of dividends.

Elton, E.J. and Gruber, M.J. (1970) 'Marginal stockholder tax rates and the clientele effect', *Review of Economics and Statistics,* February, pp. 68–74.
Evidence is found which supports the clientele effect – shareholders in higher tax brackets prefer capital gains to dividend income.

Fama, E.F. and French, K.R. (2001) 'Disappearing dividends: changing firm characteristics or lower propensity to pay?', *Journal of Financial Economics,* 60(1), April, pp. 3–43.
Only 20.8 percent of US quoted firms paid cash dividends in late 1990s.

Gordon, M.J. (1959) 'Dividends, earnings and stock prices', *Review of Economics and Statistics,* 41, May, pp. 99–105.
Discusses the relationship between dividends, earnings and share prices.

Gordon, M.J. (1963) 'Optimal investment and financing policy', *Journal of Finance,* May.
A refutation of the MM dividend irrelevancy theory based on the early resolution of uncertainty idea.

Graham, J.R. and Kumar, A. (2006) 'Do dividend clienteles exist? Evidence on dividend preferences of retail investors', *Journal of Finance* 61(3), June, pp. 1305–36.
Evidence for clienteles (e.g. older investors prefer high dividend yields). Also tax influences preferences of clienteles.

Grullon, G. and Michaely, R. (2002) 'Dividends, share repurchases, and the substitution hypothesis', *Journal of Finance,* 57(4), pp. 1649–84.
US companies have increasingly substituted share repurchases for dividends – tax considerations were a major reason.

Gustavo, G. and Roni, M. (2004) 'The information content of share repurchase programs', *Journal of Finance*, April, 59 (2), pp. 651–80.
Finds evidence consistent with free cash flow hypothesis of dividend policy.

Jagannathan, M., Stephens, C.P. and Weisbach, M.S. (2000) 'Financial flexibility and the choice between dividends and stock repurchases', *Journal of Financial Economics*, 57(3), September, pp. 355–84.
US study. Repurchases are pro-cyclical, dividends are steady. Repurchases used to distribute high temporary cash flows.

Jensen, M.C. (1986) 'Agency costs of free cash flow, corporate finance and takeovers', *American Economic Review*, 76, pp. 323–9.
Managers act in their own interests therefore increased dividends increase value of mature cash-generating companies.

Julio, B. and Ikenberry, D.L. (2004) 'Reappearing dividends', *Journal of Applied Corporate Finance*, 16(4), Fall, pp. 89–100.
A discussion of dividend policy of US firms.

Keane, S. (1974) 'Dividends and the resolution of uncertainty', *Journal of Business Finance and Accountancy*, Autumn.
Discusses the 'bird-in-the-hand' theory of dividend policy.

Koch, A.S. and Sun, A.X. (2004) 'Dividend changes and the persistence of past earnings changes', *Journal of Finance*, 59 (5), October, pp. 2093–116.
'Results confirm the hypothesis that changes in dividends cause investors to revise their expectations about the persistence of past earnings changes', thus dividend changes act as a signalling device.

Lewellen, W.G., Stanley, K.L., Lease, R.C. and Schlarbaum, G.G. (1978) 'Some direct evidence of the dividend clientele phenomenon', *Journal of Finance*, December, pp. 1385–99.
An investigation of the clientele effect.

Lintner, J. (1956) 'Distribution of income of corporations among dividends, retained earnings and taxes', *American Economic Review*, 46, May, pp. 97–113.
An empirical study and theoretical model of dividend policy practices.

Litzenberger, R. and Ramaswamy, K. (1982) 'The effects of dividends on common stock prices: tax effects or information effects?', *Journal of Finance*, May, pp. 429–43.
A technical paper that presents 'evidence consistent with the Tax–Clientele CAPM'.

Miller, M.H. and Modigliani, F. (1961) 'Dividend policy, growth and the valuation of shares', *Journal of Business*, 34, October, pp. 411–33.
In an ideal economy, dividend policy is irrelevant – algebraic proofs.

Mougoué, M. and Rao, R.P. (2003) 'The information signalling hypothesis of dividends: evidence from cointegration and causality tests', *Journal of Business Finance and Accounting*, 30(3) and (4), April/May, pp. 441–78.
Evidence consistent with the information-signalling hypothesis.

Nissim, D. and Ziv, A. (2001) 'Dividend changes and future profitability', *Journal of Finance*, 56(6), pp. 2111–33.
Strong support for the information content of dividends hypothesis.

Pettit, R.R. (1977) 'Taxes, transaction costs and clientele effects of dividends', *Journal of Financial Economics*, December.
Discusses the clientele effect.

Rozeff, M. (1986) 'How companies set their dividend payout ratios'. Reprinted in J.M. Stern and D.H. Chew (eds), *The Revolution in Corporate Finance*. Oxford: Basil Blackwell.

A discussion of the information effect of dividends, the agency problems, industry rules of thumb. Easy-to-follow arguments.

Shefrin, H.M. and Statman, M. (1984) 'Explaining investor preference for cash dividends', *Journal of Financial Economics*, 13, pp. 253–82.

Individuals impose a rule that prevents spending from capital: only dividends may be used for consumption, which cannot be boosted by selling shares. This is to impose discipline and reduce the need for willpower. Some of these individuals form a clientele for companies pursuing a high-dividend payout policy – particularly older people. Other investors prefer low payouts.

Solomon, E. (1963) *The Theory of Financial Management*. New York: Columbia University Press.

Chapter 11 contains an interesting early discussion of the dividend policy debate.

Tse, C.B. (2005) 'Use dividends to signal or not: an examination of the UK dividend payout patterns', *Managerial Finance*, 31(4), pp. 12–33.

'Some firms need to use dividends to signal but some do not need to. For example, a firm that has built up reputational capital can communicate directly with shareholders.'

3i (1993) 'Dividend policy.' Reported in *Bank of England Quarterly Review* (1993), August, p. 367.

The most important factor influencing dividend policy is long-term profit growth. Cuts in dividends send adverse signals.

Chapter 15

Arnold, G. (2011) *Modern Financial Markets and Instruments*. Harlow: FT Prentice Hall.
A university textbook describing the financial markets and instruments.

Arnold, G. (2011) *Financial Times Guide to Financial Markets*. Harlow: FT Prentice Hall.
An easy-to-follow introduction to the modern financial markets and instruments.

Bank of England, www.bankofengland.co.uk.
Numerous useful publications on sources of finance for businesses.

Better Payment Practice Group (1998) 'Better payment practice', www.payontime.co.uk.
Some practical advice for those granting trade credit and those accepting trade credit.

Buckley, A. (2004) *Multinational Finance*, 5th edn. Harlow: FT Prentice Hall.
Contains some easy-to-follow descriptions of types of finance available to firms.

Clark, T.M. (1978) *Leasing*. Maidenhead: McGraw-Hill.
Old but still useful – easy to read.

Credit Management Research Centre, Leeds University Business School (2005) *Credit Policy in the UK Economy*. Prepared for the Small Business Service, www.payontime.co.uk.
Full of facts and figures on trade credit.

Finance and Leasing Association. *Finance and Leasing Association (FLA) Annual Report*. London: FLA.
Gives some insight into HP and leasing in the UK, www.fla.org.uk.

Chapter 16

To keep up to date and reinforce the knowledge gained by reading this chapter I can recommend the following publications: *Financial Times, The Economist, Corporate Finance Magazine* (London: Euromoney) *Bank of England Quarterly Bulletin, Bank for International Settlements Quarterly Review* (www.bis.org), *The Treasurer* (a monthly journal), *The Treasurer's Handbook* (by the Association of Corporate Treasurers) and *Finance and Leasing Association (FLA) Annual Report* (www.fla.org.uk.)

Arnold, G. (2011) *Modern Financial Markets and Instruments*. Harlow: FT Prentice Hall.
A university textbook describing the financial markets and instruments.

Arnold, G. (2011) *Financial Times Guide to Financial Markets*. Harlow: FT Prentice Hall.
An easy-to-follow introduction to the modern financial markets and instruments.

Arnold, G. and Smith, M. (1999) *The European High Yield Bond Market: Drivers and Impediments*. London: Financial Times Finance Management Report.
A comprehensive exploration of the potential of the junk bond market in Europe – a history of the US market is also given.

Blake, D. (2000) *Financial Market Analysis*, 2nd edn. Chichester: John Wiley & Sons.
A technical and detailed examination of long-term debt markets.

Brealey, R.A., Cooper, I.A. and Habib, M.A. (2001) 'Using project finance to fund infrastructure investments', in D.H. Chew (ed.) *The New Corporate Finance*, 3rd edn. New York: McGraw-Hill Irwin.
A more detailed treatment of project finance.

Brigham, E.F. (1966) 'An analysis of convertible debentures: theory and some empirical evidence', *Journal of Finance*, March, pp. 35–54.
Valuation of convertibles and the major factors influencing price. Evidence that most firms issue convertibles to raise equity finance.

Buckle, M. and Thompson, J. (2004) *The UK Financial System*, 4th edn. Manchester: Manchester University Press.
The eurosecurities markets are discussed clearly and concisely. There are useful sections on the domestic bond market and the term structure of interest rates.

Buckley, A. (2004) *Multinational Finance*, 5th edn. Harlow: FT Prentice Hall.
Some additional detail on some of the issues discussed in this chapter – easy to read.

Chew, D.H. (ed.) (2001) *The New Corporate Finance*, 3rd edn. New York: McGraw-Hill Irwin.
A collection of articles, written in an easy-to-read style, describing US debt markets.

City of London/London Stock Exchange/Oxera (2006) *The Cost of Capital: An International Comparison* (available from www.londonstockexchange.com).
Contains an excellent easy-to-read description of the trading of bonds and costs of listings.

Eiteman, D.K., Stonehill, A.I. and Moffett, M.H. (2003) *Multinational Business Finance*, 10th edn. Reading, MA: Addison Wesley.
Some useful, easy-to-follow material on international debt markets.

Fabozzi, F.J. (2003) *Bond Markets, Analysis and Strategies*, 5th edn. Harlow: FT Prentice Hall.
A detailed yet accessible description of bonds with a US bond market focus.

Graham, J.R. and Harvey, C.R. (2001) 'The theory and practice of corporate finance: evidence from the field', *Journal of Financial Economics*, 60, 2–3, May, pp. 187–243.
US survey of corporate use of debt.

Hickman, B.G. (1958) 'Corporate bond quality and investor experience', *National Bureau of Economic Research,* 14, Princeton.
Early research into the returns and default rates on bonds.

Valdez, S. (2010) *An Introduction to Global Financial Markets,* 6th edn. London: Palgrave Macmillan.
Easy-to-read background on international bond markets and banking.

Chapter 17

Arnold, G. (2010) *The Financial Times Guide to Investing*, 2nd edn. Harlow: FT Prentice Hall.
An introduction to financial markets, including the new issue market.

Arnold, G. (2011) *Modern Financial Markets and Instruments*. Harlow: FT Prentice Hall.
A university textbook describing the financial markets and instruments.

Arnold, G. (2011) *Financial Times Guide to Financial Markets*. Harlow: FT Prentice Hall.
An easy-to-follow introduction to the modern financial markets and instruments.

British Private Equity and Venture Capital Association, London, www.bvca.co.uk.
Variety of paper publications and online material that give an insight into a variety of aspects of venture capital.

Campbell, K. (2003) *Smarter Ventures: A Survivor's Guide to Venture Capital Through the New Cycle*. Harlow: FT Prentice Hall.
Practical advice for entrepreneurs and venture capitalists.

City of London/London Stock Exchange/Oxera (2006) 'The cost of capital: an international comparison', available at www.londonstockexchange.com.
Compares various costs associated with raising capital on stock markets.

European Private Equity and Venture Capital Association, www.evca.com.
Displays various useful publications.

London Stock Exchange (2004) *A Practical Guide to Listing on the London Stock Exchange*, available at www.londonstockexchange.com.
A clear and succinct guide to the essential issues.

Mason, C. and Harrison, R. (1997) 'Business angels – heaven-sent or the devil to deal with?', in Birley, S. and Muzyka, D.F. (eds) *Mastering Enterprise*, London: Pitman Publishing/Financial Times.
Easy-to-read summary of business angel activity in the UK.

Ritter, J.R. (2003) 'Differences in European and American IPO markets', *European Financial Management*, 9, pp. 421–34.
IPO discounting evidence in 38 countries.

Zider, B. (1998) 'How venture capital works', *Harvard Business Review*, November–December, pp. 131–9.
An easy-to-read account of the mechanisms of venture capital funding.

Chapter 18

Alti, A. (2006) 'How persistent is the impact of market timing on capital structure?',
   Journal of Finance, 61(4), August, pp. 1681–710.
Evidence from the US that 'market timing' of equity issues does affect gearing (because if
shares are easy to sell in large volume firms take advantage of that fact – the firms studied are 'hot' IPO stocks). However, the effect is short-lived – 'at the end of the second
year following the IPO, the impact of market timing on leverage completely vanishes'.

Anderson, R.C., Mansi, S.A. and Reeb, D.M. (2003) 'Founding family ownership and the
   agency cost of debt', *Journal of Financial Economics*, 68, pp. 263–85.
Evidence is presented that suggests that debt holders' agency worries are less in companies with family ownership of shares. Interest rates are less because the founding family
better protects debt holders' interests, it is posited.

Baker, A. and Wurgler, J. (2002) 'Market timing and capital structure', *Journal of
   Finance*, 62(1), February, pp. 1–32.
Firms tend to issue equity when market values are high, and repurchase shares when
market values are low. These actions influence the debt to equity ratio in the short, and,
more surprisingly, over the long run. Thus 'capital structure is largely the cumulative outcome of past attempts to time the equity market. In this theory, there is no optimum
capital structure, so market timing decisions just accumulate over time into the capital
structure outcome.'

Ball, M., Brady, S. and Olivier, C. (1995) 'Getting the best from your banks', *Corporate
   Finance*, July, pp. 26–47.
Fascinating insight into the world of high finance.

Bevan, A.A. and Danbolt, J. (2004) 'Testing for inconsistencies in the estimation of UK
   capital structure determinants', *Applied Financial Economics*, 14, pp. 55–66.
UK empirical evidence showing debt (relative to asset base) rises with company size, perhaps because larger firms have less financial distress and agency cost risk. Also more
profitable companies have lower debt levels (pecking order theory support?). And companies with more tangible assets carry more debt (adverse selection and moral hazard
lead lenders to demand collateral).

Booth, L., Aivazian, V., Demirgue-Kunt, A. and Maksimovic, V. (2001) 'Capital structures
   in developing countries', *Journal of Finance*, 61(1), February, pp. 87–130.
The same decision variables influence capital structure in developing and developed
countries. This is especially true of pecking order factors, e.g. the more profitable the
firm the lower the debt.

Brealey, R.H., Myers, S.C. and Allen, F. (2010) *Principles of Corporate Finance*, 10th
   edn. New York: McGraw-Hill.
A more detailed treatment of the theoretical material is provided.

Brierley, P. and Bunn, P. (2005) 'The determination of UK corporate capital gearing',
   Bank of England Quarterly Bulletin, Autumn, pp. 356–66.
Empirical evidence that UK companies' gearing is positively related to company size and
negatively correlated with growth opportunities and the importance of intangible assets.
Until 1995 highly profitable firms had low gearing, but this changed after 1995.

Bunn, R. and Young, G. (2004) 'Corporate capital structure in the United Kingdom: determinants and adjustment.' Bank of England working paper 226 www.bankofengland.co.uk/
   wp/index.html.

Evidence that UK companies comply with the trade-off model by borrowing to take advantage of the tax benefits of debt, which they set against possible costs of over-indebtedness. Also companies adjust gearing through dividend payments, new equity issues and to a lesser extent lowering or raising capital investment.

Damodaran, A. (1999) *Applied Corporate Finance*. New York: John Wiley & Sons.
An accessible introduction to the practical estimation of optimum capital structure.

Donaldson, G. (1961) *Corporate Debt Policy and the Determination of Corporate Debt Capacity*. Boston, MA: Harvard Graduate School of Business Administration.
A study of the financing practices of large corporations: discussion of pecking order theory. Proposes a measure of debt capacity based on distressed cashflow.

Fama, E.F. and French, K.R. (2005) 'Financing decisions: who issues stocks?', *Journal of Financial Economics*, 76, pp. 549–82.
Evidence against the pecking order theory prediction that firms rarely issue equity.

Flannery, M.J. and Rangan, K.P. (2006) 'Partial adjustment toward target capital structures', *Journal of Financial Economics*, 79, pp. 469–506.
Provides evidence that US companies have target ratios of debt/equity and try to (fairly rapidly) move towards them – thus supporting the trade-off theory. The evidence provides only weak support for the pecking order theory or the idea that firms decrease gearing when their share price is high by issuing more shares (the 'market-timing theory').

Frank, M.Z. and Goyal, V.K. (2003) 'Testing the pecking order theory of capital structure', *Journal of Financial Economics*, 67, pp. 217–48.
Evidence contradictory to the pecking order model.

Graham, J.R. and Harvey, C.R. (2001) 'The theory and practice of corporate finance: evidence from the field', *Journal of Financial Economics*, 60(2–3), pp. 187–243.
Empirical evidence on capital structure decisions.

Hart, O. (1995) *Firms, Contracts and Financial Structure*. Oxford: Oxford University Press.
High debt helps to align the interests of owners and managers.

Harvey, C.R., Lins, K.V. and Roper, A.H. (2004) 'The effect of capital structure when expected agency costs are extreme', *Journal of Financial Economics*, 74, pp. 3–30.
Evidence that the issuance of debt (e.g. syndicated term loans, international bonds and Yankee bonds) that come with restrictive operational covenants and monitoring of firms reduces agency costs and information problems. In particular, overinvestment is reduced. The more intensive monitoring and the constraints serve shareholders well.

Jensen, M.C. (1986) 'Agency costs of free cashflow, corporate finance and takeovers', *American Economic Review*, 26 May, p. 323.
Discusses the problem of encouraging managers to pay to shareholders cash above that needed for all positive NPV projects.

Jensen, M.C. (1989) 'Eclipse of the public corporation', *Harvard Business Review*, September–October, pp. 61–74.
High debt levels impose a discipline on managers. In particular they are forced to distribute cash, reducing the potential waste of free cash flow investment. Also in LBOs managers are incentivized by becoming owners.

Journal of Economic Perspectives (1988) Fall.
A collection of review articles on MM propositions.

Kisgen, D.J. (2006) 'Credit ratings and capital structure', *Journal of Finance*, 61(3), June, pp. 1035–72.

US firms' capital struture decisions are influenced by credit ratings.

Korajczyk, R.A. and Levy, A. (2003) 'Capital structure choice: macroeconomic conditions and financial constraints', *Journal of Financial Economics*, 68, pp. 75–109.

Macroeconomic conditions affect capital structure.

Leary, M.T. and Roberts, M.R. (2005) 'Do firms rebalance their capital structures?', *Journal of Finance*, 60(6), December, pp. 2575–619.

Findings: 'We find that firms activity rebalance their leverage to stay within an optimal range. Our evidence suggests that the persistent effect of shocks on leverage observed in previous studies is more likely due to adjustment costs than indifference toward capital structure.'

Lowenstein, L. (1991) *Sense and Nonsense in Corporate Finance*. Reading, MA: Addison-Wesley.

A sceptical approach to the over-elaborate algebraic examination of financial structure.

Marsh, P. (1982) 'The choice between equity and debt: an empirical study', *Journal of Finance*, 37, March, pp. 121–44.

Evidence that companies appear to have target debt levels. These targets are a function of company size, bankruptcy risk and asset composition.

Merton, R.C. (2005) 'You have more caital than you think', *Harvard Business Review*, November, pp. 1–10.

Argues that modern large firms can use derivatives to lower risk thus allowing a reduction in equity capital.

Miller, M.H. (1977) 'Debt and taxes', *Journal of Finance*, 32, May, pp. 261–75.

A further contribution to the theoretical debate – technical and US-focused.

Miller, M.H. (1988) 'The Modigliani–Miller propositions after thirty years', *Journal of Economic Perspectives* (Fall). Also reproduced in Chew, D.H. (ed.) (2001) *The New Corporate Finance*. New York: McGraw-Hill, 3rd edn.

Miller muses on the original propositions and the debate over 30 years. He acknowledges the departure of real-world practice from the artificial world constructed for the models.

Miller, M.H. (1991) 'Leverage', *Journal of Finance*, 46, pp. 479–88.

An interesting article by a leader in the field.

Modigliani, F. and Miller, M.H. (1958) 'The cost of capital, corporation finance and the theory of investment', *American Economic Review*, 48, June, pp. 261–97.

The classic original economic modelling approach to this subject.

Modigliani, F. and Miller, M.H. (1963) 'Corporate income taxes and the cost of capital: A correction', *American Economic Review*, 53, June, pp. 433–43.

A technical account of the important correction to the 1958 article – allows for taxes.

Modigliani, F. and Miller, M.H. (1969) 'Reply to Heins and Sprenkle', *American Economic Review*, 59, September, pp. 592–5.

More on the economic model approach.

Myers, S.C. (1974) 'Interaction of corporate financing and investment decisions – implications for capital budgeting', *Journal of Finance*, 29 (March), pp. 1–25.

The adjusted present value method is developed in this article.

Myers, S.C. (1984) 'The capital structure puzzle', *Journal of Finance*, 39, July, pp. 575–82.

Easy-to-read consideration of capital structure theory – particularly of pecking order theory.

Myers, S. and Majluf, N. (1984). 'Corporate financing and investment decisions when firms have information investors do not have', *Journal of Financial Economics*, June, pp. 187–221.

Pecking order theory is advanced as an explanation for capital structure in practice.

Passov, R. (2003) 'How much cash does your company need?', *Harvard Business Review*, November, pp. 1–8.

Knowledge-based companies need low debt or net cash to allow ongoing investment without resort to the financial market where finance can be exorbitantly expensive or simply unavailable.

Ross, S. (1977) 'The determination of financial structure: the incentive-signalling approach', *Bell Journal of Economics*, 8, pp. 23–40.

The signalling hypothesis of debt increases is advanced.

Ross, S.A., Westerfield, R.W. and Jaffe, J. (2002) *Corporate Finance*, 6th edn. New York: McGraw-Hill.

More on the theoretical elements than in this chapter.

Shyam-Sunder, L. and Myers, S.C. (1999) 'Testing static trade off against pecking order models of capital structure', *Journal of Financial Economics*, 51, pp. 219–44.

Supporting evidence for the pecking order model.

Stern, J. (1998) 'The capital structure puzzle', *Journal of Applied Corporate Finance*, II(I), Spring, pp. 8–23.

A round-table discussion between Joel Stern, Stewart Myers and other capital structure specialists. It focuses particularly on managerial performance and incentives. There is also a discussion of financial slack by the Treasurer of Sears – very interesting.

Stewart, G.B. (1990) *The Quest for Value*. New York: Harper Business.

Chapter 13 is written in praise of capital structures with high debt levels.

Tirole, J. (2006) *The Theory of Corporate Finance*. Princeton, NJ: Princeton University Press.

An algebraic/theoretical approach to the borrowing question.

Watson, R. and Wilson, N. (2002) 'Small and medium size enterprise financing: a note of some empirical implications of a pecking order', *Journal of Business Finance and Accounting*, 29(3) and (4) April/May, pp. 557–78.

A testing of the pecking order model in UK shares. Evidence found in support.

Welch, I. (2004) 'Capital structure and stock returns', *Journal of Political Economy*, 112(1), pp. 106–31.

A major influence on the gearing level is fluctuations in the equity market capitalization raising or lowering the equity figure in the debt/equity ratio. Firms are slow to raise or pay off finance to counteract market capitalization fluctuations. This is an 'inertia' explanation of capital structure.

Corporate Finance. Monthly journal. London: Euromoney.

Provides insight into high-level corporate finance issues of a practical nature. Includes a useful chapter introducing money market instruments.

The Treasurer (a monthly journal). London: Euromoney.
Up-to-date consideration of treasurers' matters.

The Treasurer's Handbook. London: Association of Corporate Treasurers.
An annual publication. A useful reference work with articles from practitioners.

Chapters 19 and 20

Andersen, T.J. (2006) *Global Derivatives: A Strategic Management Perspective*.
    Harlow: FT Prentice Hall.
Describes the use of derivatives from a corporate perspective. Easy to read and takes the
reader from an introductory level to an intermediate level.

Arnold, G. (2010) *The Financial Times Guide to Investing*, 2nd edn. Harlow: FT
    Prentice Hall.
A wider range of derivative instruments is discussed.

Arnold, G. (2011) *Modern Financial Markets and Instruments*. Harlow: FT Prentice
    Hall.
A university textbook describing the financial markets and instruments.

Arnold, G. (2011) *Financial Times Guide to Financial Markets*. Harlow: FT Prentice
    Hall.
An easy-to-follow introduction to the modern financial markets and instruments.

Bank of England Quarterly Bulletins.
An important and easily digestible source of up-to-date information.

Blake, D. (2000) *Financial Market Analysis*, 2nd edn. Chichester: John Wiley & Sons.
Some very useful material – but your maths has to be up to scratch!

Buckley, A. (2003) *Multinational Finance*, 5th edn. London: FT Prentice Hall.
Contains some easy-to-follow chapters on derivatives.

The Economist.
Valuable reading for anyone interested in finance (and world affairs, politics, economics,
science, etc.)

Financial Times.
An important source for understanding the latest developments in this dynamic market.

Galitz, L. (1998) *Financial Engineering*, 2nd edn. London: FT Prentice Hall.
A clearly written and sophisticated book on use of derivatives. Aimed at a professional
readership but some sections are excellent for the novice.

Headley, J.S. and Tufano, P. (2001) 'Why manage risk?', Harvard Business School note.
    Available from Harvard Business Online.
A short easy-to-read description of why companies hedge risk.

McDonald, R.L. (2006) *Derivatives Markets*, 2nd edn. Harlow: Pearson/Addison Wesley.
A more technical/theoretical approach. US-focused.

Miller, M.H. (1997) *Merton Miller on Derivatives*. New York: John Wiley & Sons.
An accessible (no maths) account of the advantages and disadvantages of derivatives to
companies, society and the financial system.

Pilbeam, K. (2010) *Finance and Financial Markets*, 3rd edn. Basingstoke: Palgrave
    Macmillan.
Contains a few introductory chapter on derivatives.

Taylor, F. (2007) *Mastering Derivatives Markets*, 3rd edn. London: FT Prentice Hall.
A good introduction to derivative instruments and markets.

Vaitilingam, R. (2005) *The Financial Times Guide to Using the Financial Pages*, 6th edn. London: FT Prentice Hall.
Explains the tables displayed by the *Financial Times* and provides some background about the instruments – for the beginner.

Valdez, S. (2010) *An Introduction to Global Financial Markets*, 6th edn. Basingstoke: Macmillan.
A good introductory description of instruments, with a description of markets around the world.

Chapter 21

Arnold, G. (2011) *Modern Financial Markets and Instruments*. Harlow: FT Prentice Hall.
A university textbook describing the financial markets and instruments.

Arnold, G. (2011) *Financial Times Guide to Financial Markets*. Harlow: FT Prentice Hall.
An easy-to-follow introduction to the modern financial markets and instruments.

Buckley, A. (2003) *Multinational Finance*, 5th edn. London: FT Prentice Hall.
There is much more in this book than in this chapter on FX risk and other aspects of companies dealing overseas.

Desai, M.A. (2004) 'Foreign exchange markets and transactions', Harvard Business School note. Available at Harvard Business School website.
A very easy-to-follow introduction to the basics of forex markets.

Eiteman, D.K, Stonehill, A.I and Moffett, M.H. (2007) *Multinational Business Finance*, 11th edn. Reading, MA: Pearson/Addison Wesley.
A good introduction to many financial aspects of running a multinational business. Easy to read. Useful case studies.

Hallwood, C.P. and MacDonald, R. (2000) *International Money and Finance*, 3rd edn. Boston, MA and Oxford: Blackwell.
Detailed discussion of economic aspects of forex.

Levi, M.D. (2005) *International Finance*, 4th edn. New York: Routledge.
Covers the international markets and the international aspects of finance decisions for corporations in an accessible style. US-based.

Madura, J. and Fox, R. (2007) *International Financial Management*. London: Thomson.
A good introductory book that goes into much more depth than this chapter.

Taylor, F. (2003) *Mastering Foreign Exchange and Currency Options*, 2nd edn. London: FT Prentice Hall.
A good introduction to the technicalities of the forex markets and their derivatives. Plenty of practical examples.

Taylor, F. (2007) *Mastering Derivatives Markets*, 3rd edn. London: FT Prentice Hall.
Contains some easy-to-read sections on currency derivatives.

Vaitilingam, R. (2005) *The Financial Times Guide to Using the Financial Pages*, 6th edn. London: FT Prentice Hall.
A helpful guide to the way in which the *Financial Times* reports on the forex markets, among others.

Valdez, S. (2010) *An Introduction to Global Financial Markets*, 6th edn. Basingstoke: Palgrave Macmillan.
A clear and concise introduction to the international financial scene.

INDEX

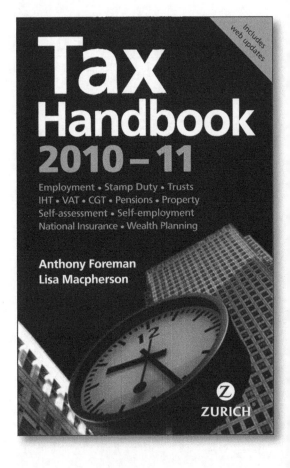